SOCIAL STUDIES

MACMILLAN

Macmillan Social Studies

NATIONS OF THE WORLD

SENIOR AUTHOR
John Jarolimek

Walter Lefferts
Israel Soifer

GEOGRAPHY CONSULTANT
Loyal Durand, Jr.

Macmillan Publishing Company
New York
Collier Macmillan Publishers
London

Parts of this work were published in earlier editions of Macmillan Social Studies.

Macmillan Publishing Company
866 Third Avenue, New York, New York 10022
Collier Macmillan Canada, Inc.

Printed in the United States of America
ISBN 0-02-147400-1
9 8 7 6 5 4 3 2

Acknowledgments

The publishers gratefully acknowledge permission to reprint the following copyrighted material:

Excerpt from *The Works of Anne Frank* by Anne Frank. Copyright © 1952, 1959 by Otto H. Frank. Reprinted by permission of Doubleday & Company, Inc. and World's Work, Ltd.

Chart from *Jambo Means Hello:* Swahili Alphabet Book by Muriel Feelings. Copyright © 1974 by Muriel Feelings. Reprinted by permission of the publisher, Dial Books for Young Readers, a Division of E. P. Dutton.

CONTENTS

Maps

Diagrams, Charts, and Graphs

ATLAS

THE WORLD
POLITICAL

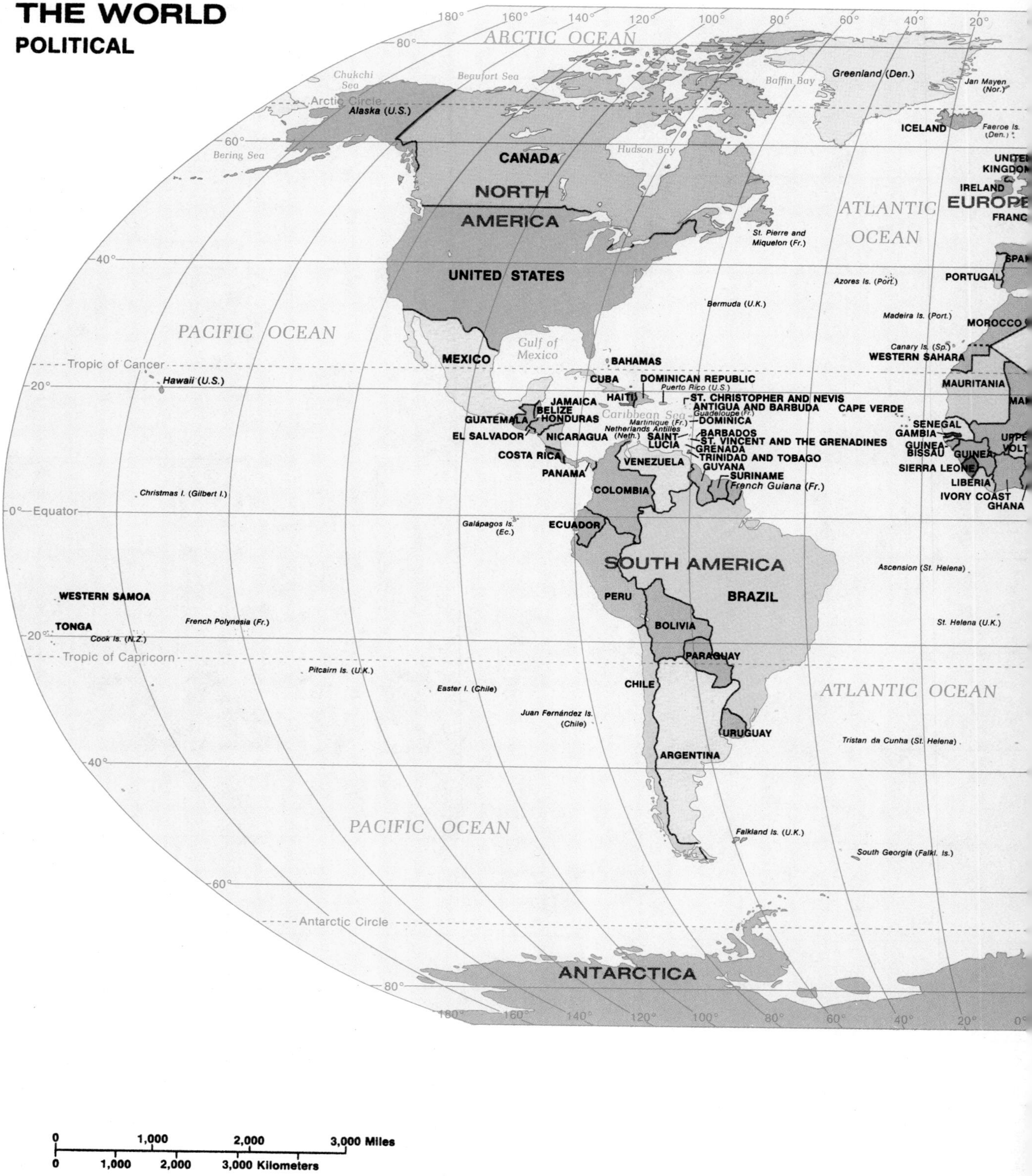

ARCTIC OCEAN
Chukchi Sea
Beaufort Sea
Baffin Bay
Greenland (Den.)
Jan Mayen (Nor.)
Arctic Circle
Alaska (U.S.)
ICELAND
Faeroe Is. (Den.)
Bering Sea
Hudson Bay
CANADA
NORTH AMERICA
IRELAND
EUROPE
ATLANTIC OCEAN
St. Pierre and Miquelon (Fr.)
UNITED STATES
Azores Is. (Port.)
PORTUGAL
Bermuda (U.K.)
Madeira Is. (Port.)
MOROCCO
PACIFIC OCEAN
Gulf of Mexico
Canary Is. (Sp.)
WESTERN SAHARA
MEXICO
BAHAMAS
Tropic of Cancer
Hawaii (U.S.)
CUBA
DOMINICAN REPUBLIC
Puerto Rico (U.S.)
MAURITANIA
JAMAICA
HAITI
ST. CHRISTOPHER AND NEVIS
ANTIGUA AND BARBUDA
CAPE VERDE
BELIZE
GUATEMALA
HONDURAS
Caribbean Sea
Guadeloupe (Fr.)
Martinique (Fr.)
DOMINICA
SENEGAL
EL SALVADOR
NICARAGUA
Netherlands Antilles (Neth.)
SAINT LUCIA
BARBADOS
ST. VINCENT AND THE GRENADINES
GRENADA
GAMBIA
GUINEA-BISSAU
GUINEA
COSTA RICA
TRINIDAD AND TOBAGO
VENEZUELA
GUYANA
SIERRA LEONE
PANAMA
SURINAME
LIBERIA
COLOMBIA
French Guiana (Fr.)
Christmas I. (Gilbert I.)
IVORY COAST
GHANA
Equator
Galápagos Is. (Ec.)
ECUADOR
SOUTH AMERICA
Ascension (St. Helena)
WESTERN SAMOA
PERU
BRAZIL
TONGA
French Polynesia (Fr.)
BOLIVIA
St. Helena (U.K.)
Cook Is. (N.Z.)
Tropic of Capricorn
PARAGUAY
Pitcairn Is. (U.K.)
CHILE
ATLANTIC OCEAN
Easter I. (Chile)
Juan Fernández Is. (Chile)
URUGUAY
Tristan da Cunha (St. Helena)
ARGENTINA
PACIFIC OCEAN
Falkland Is. (U.K.)
South Georgia (Falkl. Is.)
Antarctic Circle
ANTARCTICA
180° 160° 140° 120° 100° 80° 60° 40° 20° 0°
80° 60° 40° 20° 0° 20° 40° 60° 80°
0 1,000 2,000 3,000 Miles
0 1,000 2,000 3,000 Kilometers

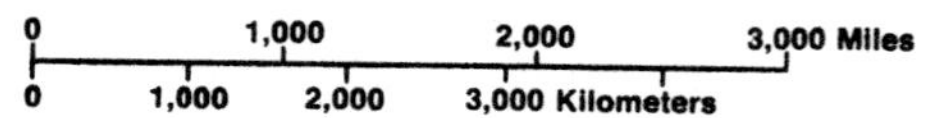

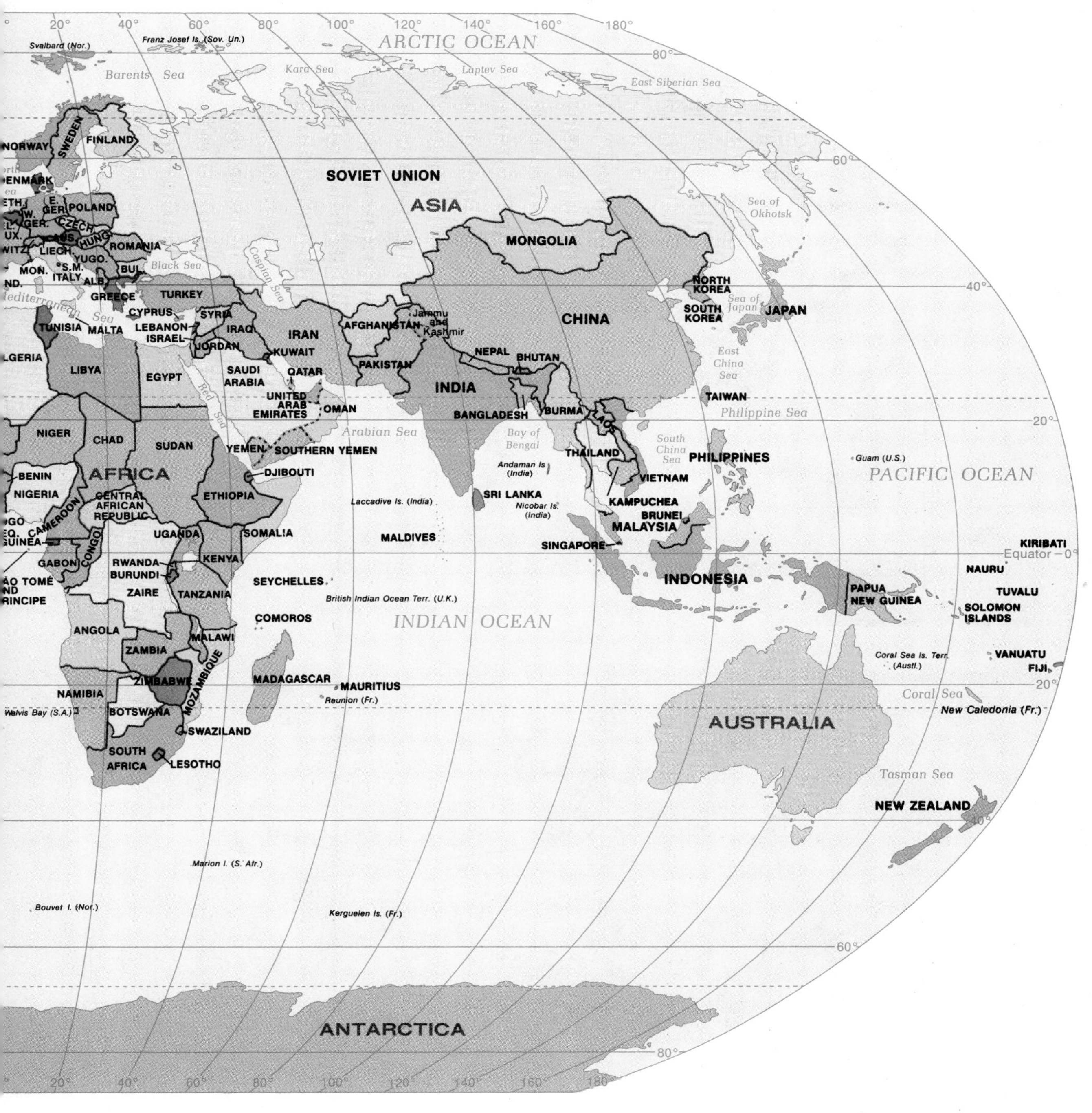

ALB. = ALBANIA
AND. = ANDORRA
AUS. = AUSTRIA
BEL. = BELGIUM
BUL. = BULGARIA
CZECH. = CZECHOSLOVAKIA
E.GER. = EAST GERMANY
HUNG. = HUNGARY
LIECH. = LIECHTENSTEIN
LUX. = LUXEMBOURG
MON. = MONACO
NETH. = NETHERLANDS
S.M. = SAN MARINO
SWITZ. = SWITZERLAND
W.GER. = WEST GERMANY
YUGO. = YUGOSLAVIA

World Climate

180°
120°
60°
0°
60°
120°
180°
Arctic Circle
60°
60°
30°
30°
Tropic of Cancer
Equator
0°
Tropic of Capricorn
30°
60°
Antarctic Circle
120°
60°
0°
60°
120°
180°
Icecap
Mountain
Subpolar
Subarctic
Oceanic
Continental wet
Subtropical wet
Mediterranean
Desert
Continental dry
Tropical wet and dry
Tropical wet

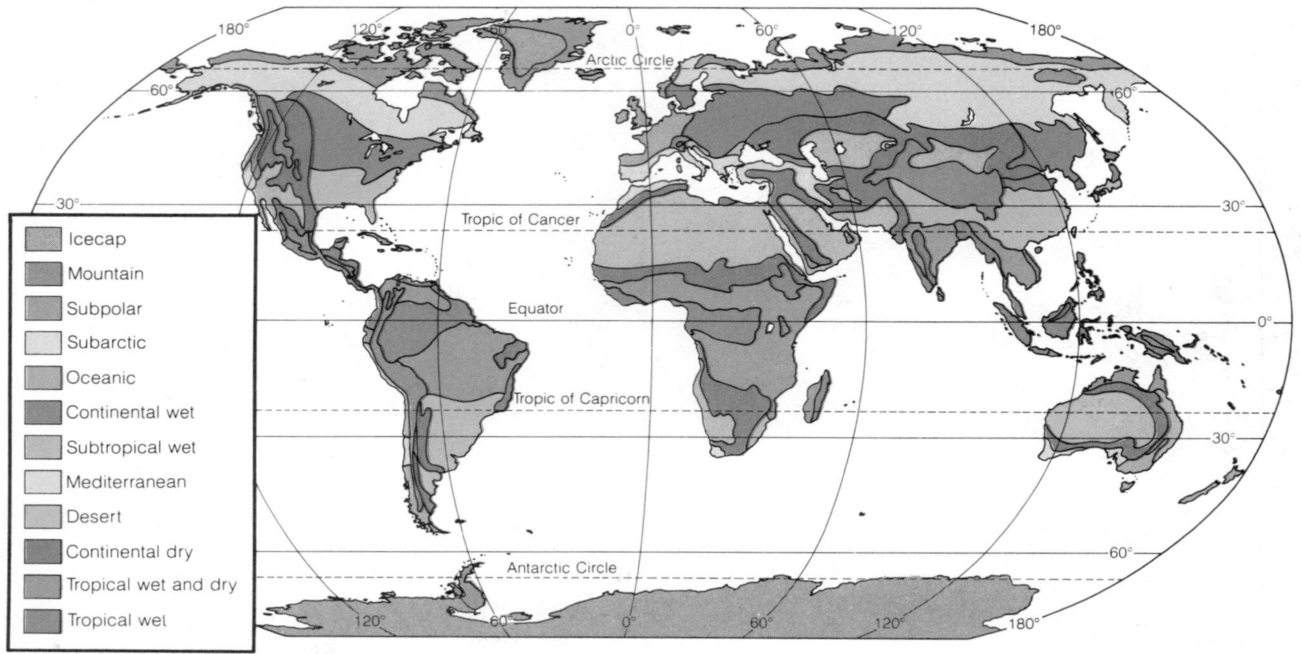

World Annual Precipitation

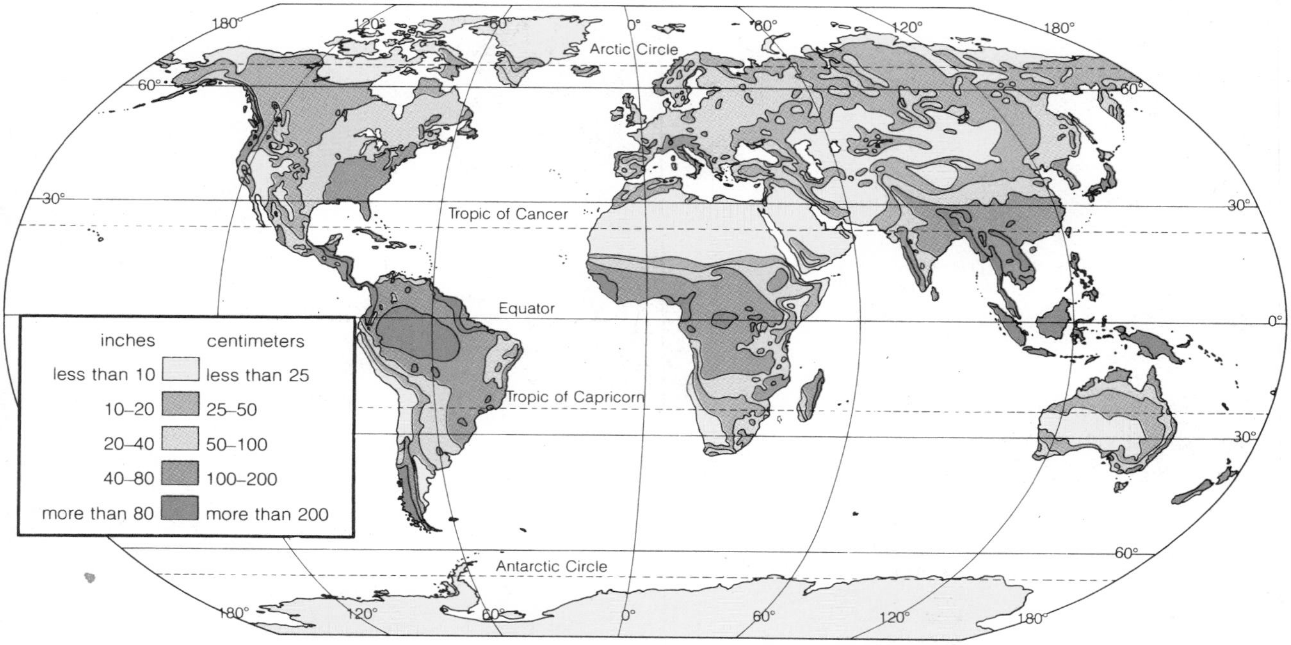

180°
120°
60°
0°
60°
120°
180°
Arctic Circle
60°
60°
30°
30°
Tropic of Cancer
Equator
0°
Tropic of Capricorn
30°
60°
Antarctic Circle
180°
120°
60°
0°
60°
120°
180°
inches
centimeters
less than 10
less than 25
10–20
25–50
20–40
50–100
40–80
100–200
more than 80
more than 200

World Vegetation

180°
120°
60°
0°
60°
120°
180°
Arctic Circle
60°
30°
Tropic of Cancer
Equator
0°
Tropic of Capricorn
30°
60°
Antarctic Circle
Needleleaf forest
Broadleaf evergreen forest
Broadleaf deciduous forest
Mixed deciduous and evergreen forest
Mediterranean vegetation
Grassland
Desert vegetation
Tundra vegetation
Mountain vegetation
Little or no vegetation

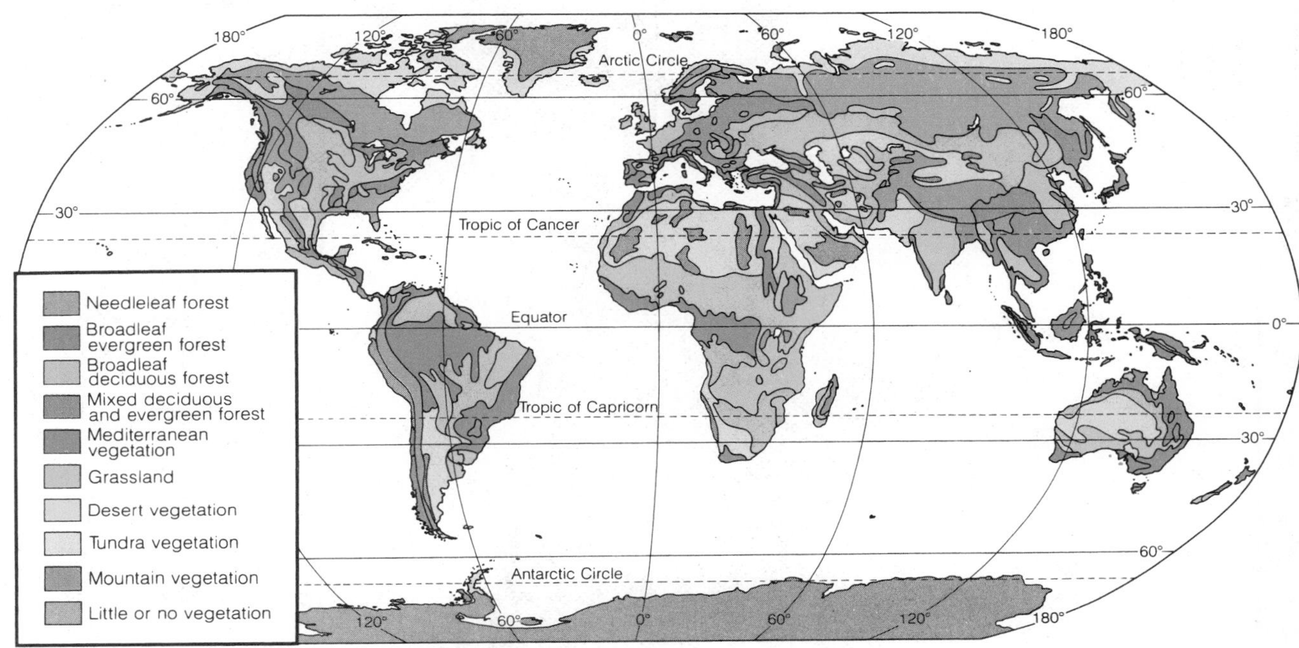

World Population

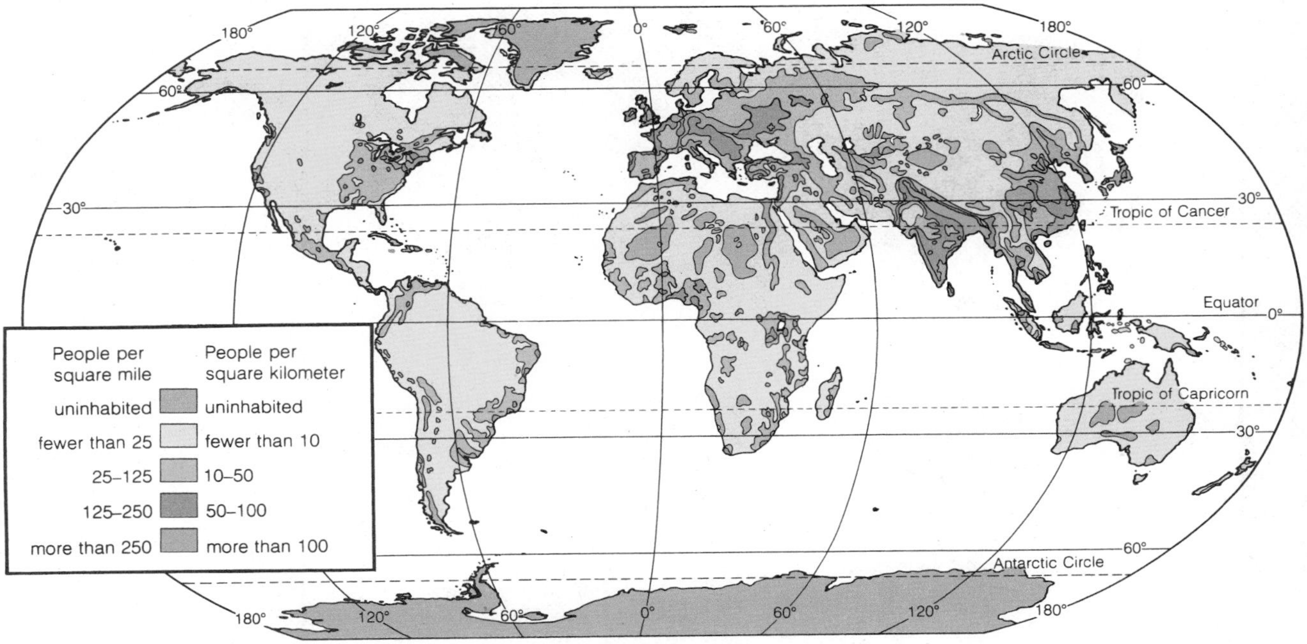

180°
120°
60°
0°
60°
120°
180°
Arctic Circle
60°
30°
Tropic of Cancer
Equator
0°
Tropic of Capricorn
30°
60°
Antarctic Circle
People per square mile
People per square kilometer
uninhabited
uninhabited
fewer than 25
fewer than 10
25–125
10–50
125–250
50–100
more than 250
more than 100

ASIA
POLITICAL
National boundary
Boundaries: Indefinite, disputed or under treaty
National capital
Other city
500
1,000 Miles
500
1,000 Kilometers
EUROPE
AFRICA
AUSTRALIA
ATLANTIC OCEAN
ARCTIC OCEAN
PACIFIC OCEAN
INDIAN OCEAN
North Pole
SOVIET UNION
SIBERIA
CHINA
MONGOLIA
TIBET
INDIA
PAKISTAN
AFGHANISTAN
IRAN
IRAQ
TURKEY
SYRIA
LEBANON
ISRAEL
JORDAN
CYPRUS
SAUDI ARABIA
KUWAIT
BAHRAIN
QATAR
UNITED ARAB EMIRATES
OMAN
YEMEN
SOUTHERN YEMEN
NEPAL
BHUTAN
BANGLADESH
SRI LANKA
MALDIVES
BURMA
THAILAND
LAOS
KAMPUCHEA
VIETNAM
MALAYSIA
SINGAPORE
BRUNEI
INDONESIA
PHILIPPINES
TAIWAN
NORTH KOREA
SOUTH KOREA
JAPAN
PAPUA NEW GUINEA
Murmansk
Tallinn
Leningrad
Arkhangelsk
Vilnius
Minsk
Moscow
Kiev
Kishinev
Odessa
Kharkov
Saratov
Volgograd
Astrakan
Ankara
Nicosia
Tbilisi
Yerevan
Baku
Tabriz
Beirut
Damascus
Jerusalem
Amman
Baghdad
Tehran
Basra
Abadan
Kuwait
Medina
Mecca
Riyadh
Doha
Abū Dhabi
Muscat
San'a
Aden
Socotra (S. Yemen)
Arabian Peninsula
Kabul
Islamabad
Lahore
Jammu and Kashmir
Karachi
Delhi
New Delhi
Kathmandu
Thimphu
Dacca
Calcutta
Ahmadabad
Bombay
Hyderabad
Madras
Columbo
Male
Laccadive Is. (India)
Andaman Is. (India)
Nicobar Is. (India)
Tashkent
Alma-Ata
Frunze
Karaganda
Omsk
Novosibirsk
Tomsk
Irkutsk
Yakutsk
Okhotsk
Anadyr
Wrangel I.
Ulan Bator
Lhasa
Chongqing (Chungking)
Wuhan
Shanghai
Canton
Victoria
Hong Kong (U.K.)
Macao (Port.)
Hainan
Beijing (Peking)
Tianjin (Tientsin)
Shenyang (Mukden)
Qiqihar (Tsitsihar)
Luda (Darien)
Pyongyang
Seoul
Vladivostok
Sapporo
Tokyo
Yokohama
Osaka
Nagasaki
Honshū I.
Shikoku I.
Kyūshū I.
Hokkaidō I.
Kuril Islands
Sakhalin Island
Kamchatka Pen.
Komandorski Is.
Ryukyu Is. (Japan)
Okinawa I.
Taipei
Mandalay
Rangoon
Bangkok
Vientiane
Hanoi
Phnom Penh
Ho Chi Minh City (Saigon)
Manila
Quezon City
Luzon
Mindanao
Kuala Lampur
Singapore
Jakarta
Sumatra
Java
Borneo
Celebes
Ujung Pandang (Makasar)
Bali I.
Flores I.
Timor Island
Seram I.
Halmahera I.
Jayapura
New Guinea
Port Moresby
New Britain
New Ireland
Mariana Islands (U.S.)
Guam (U.S.)
Caroline Islands
North Sea
Baltic Sea
Barents Sea
Black Sea
Mediterranean Sea
Caspian Sea
Aral Sea
Lake Balkhash
Lake Baikal
Red Sea
Persian Gulf
Str. of Hormuz
Gulf of Aden
Arabian Sea
Bay of Bengal
Gulf of Siam
South China Sea
East China Sea
Yellow Sea
Sea of Japan
Sea of Okhotsk
Bering Sea
Bering Str.
Philippine Sea
Celebes Sea
Java Sea
Banda Sea
Gulf of Papua
Formosa Str.
Luzon Strait
Franz Josef Is.
Novaya Zemlya
Severnaya Zemlya
New Siberian Is.
Volga River
Ural R.
Ob River
Irtysh R.
Yenisey River
Lena River
Amur R.
Huang (Hwang) River
Chang (Yangtze) R.
Brahmaputra River
Irrawady R.
Indus R.
Euphrates R.
Arctic Circle
Tropic of Cancer
Equator
A-6

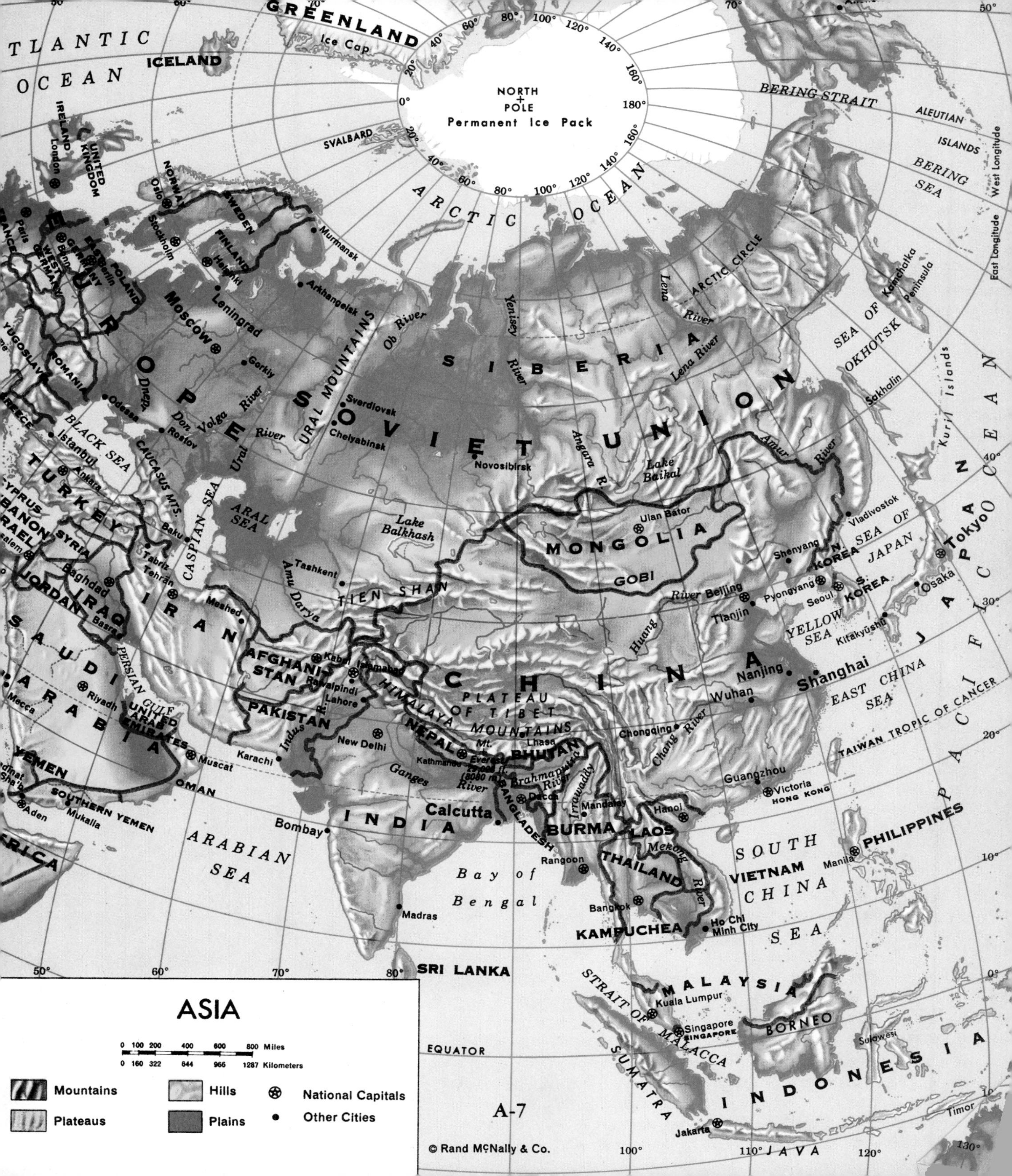

ASIA
0 100 200 400 600 800 Miles
0 160 322 644 966 1287 Kilometers
Mountains
Hills
National Capitals
Plateaus
Plains
Other Cities
GREENLAND
Ice Cap
ICELAND
ATLANTIC OCEAN
NORTH POLE
Permanent Ice Pack
SVALBARD
ARCTIC OCEAN
BERING STRAIT
ALEUTIAN ISLANDS
BERING SEA
West Longitude
East Longitude
IRELAND
London
UNITED KINGDOM
NORWAY
Oslo
SWEDEN
Stockholm
FINLAND
Helsinki
Murmansk
Paris
FRANCE
WEST GERMANY
Bonn
EAST GERMANY
Berlin
POLAND
YUGOSLAVIA
ROMANIA
GREECE
EUROPE
Moscow
Leningrad
Arkhangelsk
Gorkiy
Odessa
Dnepr
Don
Volga River
Rostov
BLACK SEA
Istanbul
Ankara
TURKEY
CYPRUS
LEBANON
ISRAEL
Jerusalem
SYRIA
JORDAN
IRAQ
Baghdad
Basra
CAUCASUS MTS.
Baku
Tabriz
Tehran
IRAN
Meshed
CASPIAN SEA
ARAL SEA
Ural River
URAL MOUNTAINS
Sverdlovsk
Chelyabinsk
Ob River
Yenisey River
SIBERIA
SOVIET UNION
Novosibirsk
Angara R.
Lena River
ARCTIC CIRCLE
Lake Baikal
Lake Balkhash
Tashkent
Amu Darya
TIEN SHAN
Ulan Bator
MONGOLIA
GOBI
Amur River
Vladivostok
SEA OF OKHOTSK
Kamchatka Peninsula
Sakhalin
Kuril Islands
PACIFIC OCEAN
SEA OF JAPAN
Shenyang
N. KOREA
Pyongyang
Seoul
S. KOREA
JAPAN
Tokyo
Osaka
Kitakyushu
Beijing
Tianjin
Huang River
YELLOW SEA
CHINA
Nanjing
Shanghai
Wuhan
EAST CHINA SEA
TROPIC OF CANCER
TAIWAN
Chongqing
Chang River
Guangzhou
Victoria
HONG KONG
PLATEAU OF TIBET
Lhasa
HIMALAYA MOUNTAINS
Mt. Everest
NEPAL
Kathmandu
BHUTAN
Brahmaputra River
AFGHANISTAN
Kabul
Islamabad
Rawalpindi
Lahore
PAKISTAN
Indus R.
Karachi
New Delhi
Ganges River
INDIA
Calcutta
BANGLADESH
Dacca
Bombay
Madras
SRI LANKA
ARABIAN SEA
Bay of Bengal
Irrawaddy River
Mandalay
BURMA
Rangoon
Hanoi
LAOS
Mekong River
THAILAND
Bangkok
VIETNAM
Ho Chi Minh City
KAMPUCHEA
SOUTH CHINA SEA
PHILIPPINES
Manila
SAUDI ARABIA
Riyadh
Mecca
PERSIAN GULF
UNITED ARAB EMIRATES
Muscat
OMAN
YEMEN
SOUTHERN YEMEN
Aden
Mukalla
AFRICA
MALAYSIA
Kuala Lumpur
Singapore
SINGAPORE
STRAIT OF MALACCA
SUMATRA
BORNEO
Sulawesi
INDONESIA
Jakarta
JAVA
Timor
EQUATOR
© Rand McNally & Co.

EUROPE
POLITICAL
National boundary
National capital
Other city
0
150
300 Miles
0
150
300 Kilometers
AFRICA
A-8
Arctic Circle
Barents Sea
White Sea
Norwegian Sea
ATLANTIC OCEAN
North Sea
Baltic Sea
Gulf of Bothnia
Gulf of Finland
Irish Sea
English Channel
Bay of Biscay
Str. of Gibraltar
Mediterranean Sea
Adriatic Sea
Ionian Sea
Aegean Sea
Black Sea
Bosporos
ICELAND
Reykjavik
Faeroe Is. (Den.)
Shetland Is. (U.K.)
Orkney Is.
Outer Hebrides Is.
NORWAY
Hammerfest
Narvik
Trondheim
Bergen
Oslo
Stavanger
Kristiansand
SWEDEN
Kiruna
Stockholm
Göteborg
Malmö
L. Vänern
L. Vättern
Gotland I.
FINLAND
L. Inari
Oulu
Vaasa
L. Saimaa
Tampere
Helsinki
U.S.S.R.
DENMARK
Copenhagen
UNITED KINGDOM
Glasgow
Edinburgh
Belfast
Birmingham
Bristol
London
IRELAND
Dublin
Cork
NETHERLANDS
Amsterdam
Antwerp
Brussels
BELGIUM
LUXEMBOURG
Luxembourg
Guernsey (U.K.)
Jersey (U.K.)
Hamburg
Bremen
Dortmund
Bonn
Frankfurt
WEST GERMANY
Stuttgart
Munich
Strasbourg
Elbe R.
Rhine R.
EAST GERMANY
Berlin
Leipzig
Dresden
POLAND
Gdánsk
Vistula R.
Warsaw
Lódź
Wroclaw
Cracow
Prague
CZECHOSLOVAKIA
Bratislava
Vienna
AUSTRIA
Graz
Vaduz
LIECHTENSTEIN
SWITZERLAND
Bern
L. Geneva
HUNGARY
Debrecen
Budapest
ROMANIA
Cluj
Timiscora
Bucharest
Danube R.
BULGARIA
Sofia
Plovdiv
Istanbul
FRANCE
Brest
Paris
Seine R.
Nantes
Loire R.
Lyon
Rhône R.
Bordeaux
Toulouse
Marseille
Nice
Monaco
MONACO
Andorra
ANDORRA
SPAIN
Bilbao
Ebro R.
Madrid
Barcelona
Valencia
Sevilla
Málaga
Cartagena
Gibraltar (U.K.)
Tagus R.
Balearic Is. (Sp.)
PORTUGAL
Porto
Lisbon
ITALY
Milan
Turin
Po R.
Genoa
Venice
SAN MARINO
San Marino
Rome
Naples
Bari
Corsica (Fr.)
Sardinia (It.)
Cagliari
Palermo
Sicily (It.)
Catania
MALTA
Valleta
YUGOSLAVIA
Zagreb
Belgrade
Sarajevo
Skopje
ALBANIA
Tiranë
GREECE
Thessaloniki
Athens
Crete (Gr.)
30°
20°
10°
0°
70°
60°
50°
40°

EUROPE
100 200 300 400 Miles
161 322 483 644 Kilometers
National Capitals
Other Cities
Mountains
Plateaus
Hills
Plains
ARCTIC CIRCLE
Reykjavík
ICELAND
NORWEGIAN SEA
Lofoten Islands
Murmansk
WHITE SEA
NORWAY
SWEDEN
FINLAND
GULF OF BOTHNIA
Faeroe Islands
Shetland Islands
60°
Bergen
Oslo
Stockholm
Helsinki
Leningrad
GULF OF FINLAND
BALTIC SEA
Glasgow
Edinburgh
Belfast
Dublin
IRELAND
UNITED KINGDOM
NORTH SEA
DENMARK
Göteborg
Copenhagen
Riga
Liverpool
SOVIET UNION
Minsk
Hamburg
Elbe
NETHERLANDS
Amsterdam
Rhine
FED. REP. OF GER.
Berlin
GER. DEM. REP.
Oder River
Vistula River
POLAND
Warsaw
London
Antwerp
Essen
Cologne
BELGIUM
Brussels
Bonn
LUX.
ATLANTIC OCEAN
ENGLISH CHANNEL
Le Havre
Seine River
Paris
Prague
Kiev
50°
Nantes
Loire
CZECHOSLOVAKIA
CARPATHIANS
Dnestr River
Bay of Biscay
Danube
Munich
Vienna
FRANCE
JURA
Bern
SWITZERLAND
Budapest
AUSTRIA
HUNGARY
ROMANIA
Bordeaux
Lyon
ALPS
Drava
Odessa
Garonne River
Rhône River
Milan
Venice
YUGOSLAVIA
Bilbao
PYRENEES
Po River
Belgrade
Bucharest
Oporto
PORTUGAL
SPAIN
Genoa
Marseille
Nice
Florence
APENNINES
ADRIATIC SEA
Morava River
Danube River
Lisbon
Madrid
CORSICA
Barcelona
ITALY
BULGARIA
Sofia
Rome
Istanbul
Balearic Islands
Córdoba
Seville
SARDINIA
Naples
Tiranë
ALBANIA
Mt. Olympus
40°
STRAIT OF GIBRALTAR
Tanger
Gibraltar
Cartagena
MEDITERRANEAN SEA
AEGEAN SEA
Rabat
Algiers
SICILY
IONIAN SEA
GREECE
Izmir
Athens
Tunis
Rhodes
ATLAS MOUNTAINS
MALTA
AFRICA
Crete
A-9
0°
10°
20°

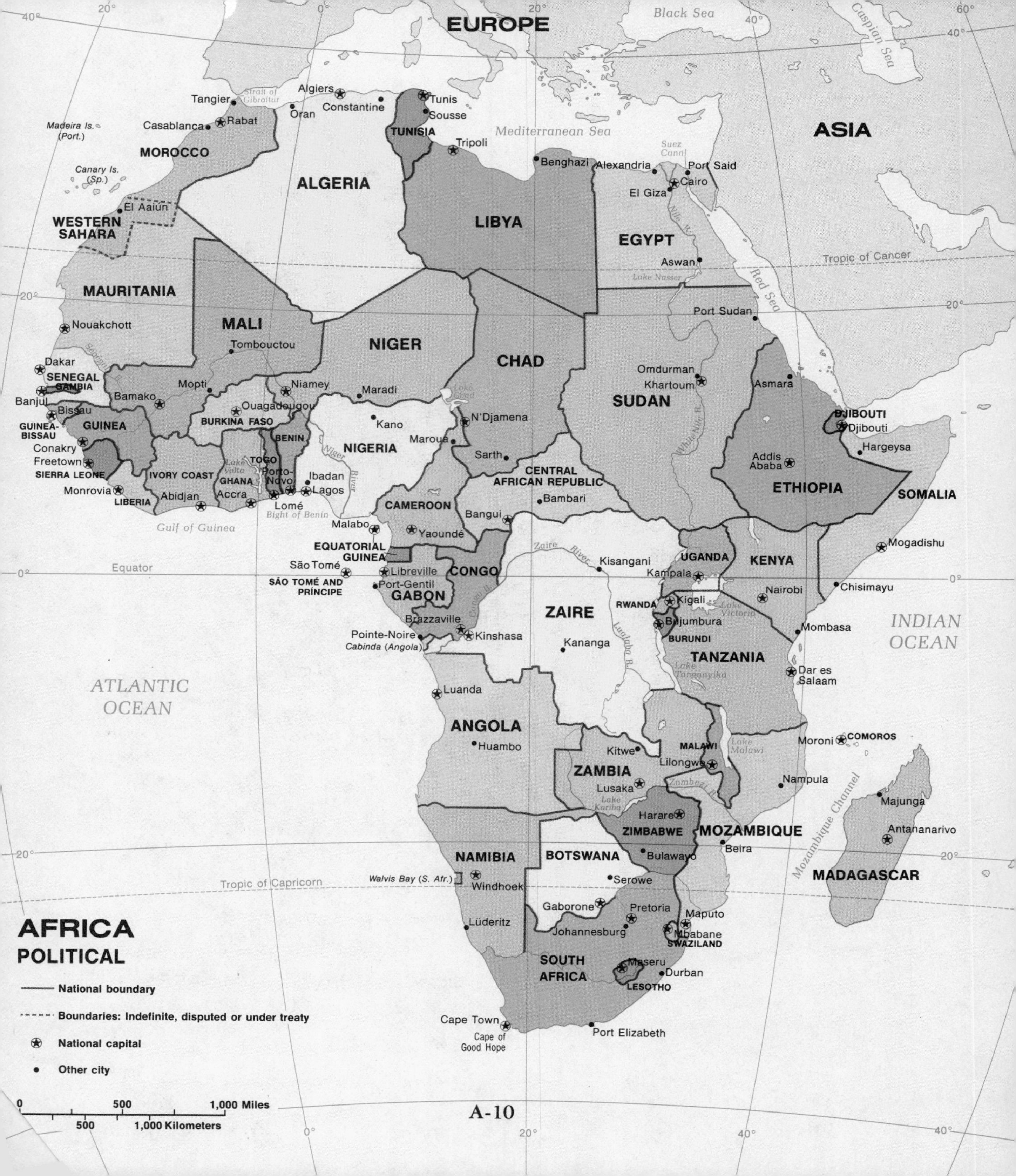

AFRICA
POLITICAL
National boundary
Boundaries: Indefinite, disputed or under treaty
National capital
Other city
0
500
1,000 Miles
500
1,000 Kilometers
EUROPE
ASIA
Black Sea
Caspian Sea
Mediterranean Sea
Red Sea
Strait of Gibraltar
Suez Canal
ATLANTIC OCEAN
INDIAN OCEAN
Gulf of Guinea
Bight of Benin
Mozambique Channel
Tropic of Cancer
Tropic of Capricorn
Equator
Madeira Is. (Port.)
Canary Is. (Sp.)
MOROCCO
ALGERIA
TUNISIA
LIBYA
EGYPT
WESTERN SAHARA
MAURITANIA
MALI
NIGER
CHAD
SUDAN
SENEGAL
GAMBIA
GUINEA-BISSAU
GUINEA
SIERRA LEONE
LIBERIA
IVORY COAST
BURKINA FASO
GHANA
TOGO
BENIN
NIGERIA
CAMEROON
CENTRAL AFRICAN REPUBLIC
ETHIOPIA
DJIBOUTI
SOMALIA
EQUATORIAL GUINEA
SÃO TOMÉ AND PRÍNCIPE
GABON
CONGO
ZAIRE
UGANDA
KENYA
RWANDA
BURUNDI
TANZANIA
ANGOLA
ZAMBIA
MALAWI
MOZAMBIQUE
ZIMBABWE
NAMIBIA
BOTSWANA
SOUTH AFRICA
SWAZILAND
LESOTHO
MADAGASCAR
COMOROS
Tangier
Rabat
Casablanca
Algiers
Oran
Constantine
Tunis
Sousse
Tripoli
Benghazi
Alexandria
Port Said
Cairo
El Giza
Aswan
Lake Nasser
Nile R.
El Aaiún
Nouakchott
Tombouctou
Dakar
Banjul
Bissau
Conakry
Freetown
Monrovia
Abidjan
Accra
Lomé
Porto-Novo
Lagos
Ibadan
Bamako
Mopti
Ouagadougou
Niamey
Maradi
Kano
Lake Volta
Niger River
Lake Chad
N'Djamena
Maroua
Sarh
Bambari
Bangui
Port Sudan
Omdurman
Khartoum
White Nile R.
Asmara
Djibouti
Hargeysa
Addis Ababa
Mogadishu
Chisimayu
Malabo
Yaoundé
São Tomé
Libreville
Port-Gentil
Brazzaville
Kinshasa
Pointe-Noire
Cabinda (Angola)
Congo R.
Zaire River
Kisangani
Kananga
Lualaba R.
Kampala
Kigali
Bujumbura
Nairobi
Lake Victoria
Mombasa
Lake Tanganyika
Dar es Salaam
Luanda
Huambo
Kitwe
Lusaka
Lake Kariba
Zambezi R.
Lilongwe
Lake Malawi
Moroni
Nampula
Majunga
Antananarivo
Harare
Bulawayo
Beira
Walvis Bay (S. Afr.)
Windhoek
Serowe
Gaborone
Pretoria
Johannesburg
Maputo
Mbabane
Lüderitz
Maseru
Durban
Cape Town
Cape of Good Hope
Port Elizabeth

AFRICA
0 100 200 400 600 800 Miles
0 161 322 644 966 1287 Kilometers
National Capitals
Other Capitals
Other Cities
Mountains
Hills
Plateaus
Plains
ATLANTIC OCEAN
Azores Islands
Madeira Islands
Canary Islands
Madrid
Lisbon
Strait of Gibraltar
Tanger
Fès
Rabat
Casablanca
Marrakech
Mt. Toubkal
MOROCCO
ATLAS MOUNTAINS
Sidi Ifni
El Aaiún
WESTERN SAHARA
Algiers
Tunis
TUNISIA
Touggourt
Tripoli
ALGERIA
LIBYA
AHAGGAR MOUNTAINS
SAHARA
TIBESTI MOUNTAINS
MEDITERRANEAN SEA
Rome
Athens
Istanbul
Ankara
BLACK SEA
CASPIAN SEA
ARAL SEA
ASIA
Baghdad
Alexandria
Bengasi
Cairo
Suez Canal
EGYPT
PERSIAN GULF
Riyadh
TROPIC OF CANCER
Lake Nasser
Nile River
RED SEA
Mecca
Port Sudan
MAURITANIA
Nouakchott
Timbuktu
Gao
MALI
AIR
NIGER
CHAD
Niamey
Sénégal River
Dakar
SENEGAL
GAMBIA
Gambia River
Banjul
Bissau
GUINEA-BISSAU
Ouagadougou
BURKINA FASO
Bamako
Niger River
Kano
NIGERIA
Lake Chad
Ndjamena
Khartoum
White Nile
Blue Nile
SUDAN
Asmara
Aden
GULF OF ADEN
Djibouti
DJIBOUTI
Addis Ababa
ETHIOPIA
GUINEA
Conakry
Freetown
SIERRA LEONE
LIBERIA
Monrovia
IVORY COAST
Abidjan
GHANA
Lake Volta
Accra
TOGO
Lomé
BENIN
Porto Novo
Ibadan
Lagos
River Benue
CENTRAL AFRICAN REPUBLIC
Bangui
CAMEROON
Yaoundé
Malabo
Bioko
EQUATORIAL GUINEA
GULF OF GUINEA
SÃO TOMÉ AND PRÍNCIPE
EQUATOR
Libreville
GABON
CONGO
CONGO BASIN
(Zaïre) River
Kisangani (Stanleyville)
ZAIRE
Kasai
Brazzaville
Pointe-Noire
CABINDA
Kinshasa (Léopoldville)
RUWENZORI
Lake Albert
Lake Rudolf
UGANDA
Kampala
KENYA
Kirinyaga
Nairobi
SOMALIA
Mogadishu
RWANDA
Bujumbura
BURUNDI
Kigali
Lake Victoria
Mt. Kilimanjaro 19,340 ft. (5895 m)
Lake Tanganyika
TANZANIA
Mombasa
Zanzibar
Dar es Salaam
INDIAN OCEAN
SEYCHELLES
Luanda
Ascension Island
KATANGA
Lubumbashi (Élisabethville)
ANGOLA
ZAMBIA
Lusaka
Lilongwe
MALAWI
Lake Nyasa
Moroni
COMOROS
Zambezi River
Victoria Falls
Kariba Lake
Harare
ZIMBABWE
MOZAMBIQUE
MOZAMBIQUE CHANNEL
MADAGASCAR
Antananarivo
Port Louis
MAURITIUS
St. Helena Island
NAMIB DESERT
NAMIBIA
Windhoek
WALVIS BAY (S.A.)
BOTSWANA
Gaborone
Limpopo River
Pretoria
KALAHARI DESERT
Johannesburg
Maputo
Mbabane
SWAZILAND
Orange River
SOUTH AFRICA
Maseru
LESOTHO
Durban
Bloemfontein
Cape Town
Cape of Good Hope
Port Elizabeth
West Longitude
East Longitude

AUSTRALIA AND NEW ZEALAND
POLITICAL
National boundary
State boundary
National capital
State / Territory capital
Other city
0 200 400 Miles
0 200 400 Kilometers
ASIA
INDIAN OCEAN
Arafura Sea
Timor Sea
Torres Strait
Solomon Sea
Coral Sea
PACIFIC OCEAN
Tasman Sea
Fiji Sea
Tropic of Capricorn
Great Australian Bight
Gulf of Carpentaria
Great Barrier Reef
Bass Strait
WESTERN AUSTRALIA
NORTHERN TERRITORY
SOUTH AUSTRALIA
QUEENSLAND
NEW SOUTH WALES
VICTORIA
AUSTRALIAN CAPITAL TERRITORY
TASMANIA
NEW ZEALAND
SOLOMON ISLANDS
VANUATU
Melville I.
Darwin
Larrimah
Broome
Fitzroy R.
Victoria R.
Alice Springs
Carnarvon
Kalgoorlie
Perth
Albany
Lake Eyre
L. Torrens
L. Gairdner
Port Augusta
Whyalla
Adelaide
Kangaroo I.
Mt. Gambier
Cairns
Townsville
Cloncurry
Flinders R.
Mackay
Rockhampton
Charleville
Fraser I.
Brisbane
Darling River
Lachlan R.
Murray River
Dubbo
Port Macquarie
Newcastle
Sydney
Canberra
Ballarat
Melbourne
King I.
Flinders I.
Hobart
Choiseul I.
Sta. Isabel I.
Malaita I.
Guadalcanal I.
San Cristobal I.
Espiritu Santo I.
Malekula I.
Efate I.
New Caledonia (Fr.)
Loyalty Is. (Fr.)
Norfolk Island (Austl.)
North Island
South Island
Auckland
Wellington
Christchurch
Dunedin
Stewart I.
120° 130° 140° 150° 160° 170° 180° 110°
10° 20° 30° 40°

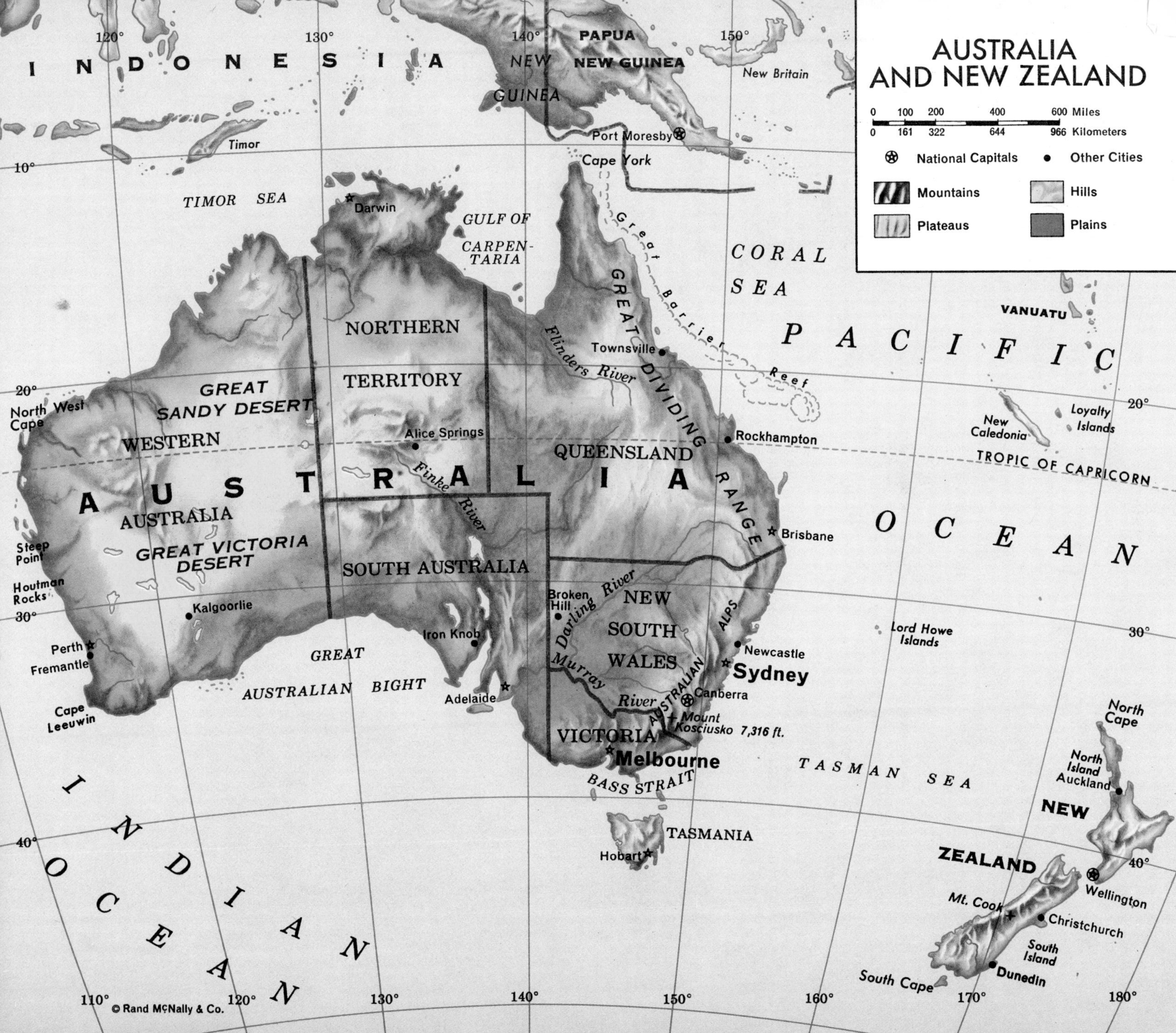
AUSTRALIA
AND NEW ZEALAND
0 100 200 400 600 Miles
0 161 322 644 966 Kilometers
National Capitals
Other Cities
Mountains
Hills
Plateaus
Plains
INDONESIA
Timor
TIMOR SEA
PAPUA
NEW GUINEA
NEW
GUINEA
New Britain
Port Moresby
Cape York
Darwin
GULF OF
CARPEN-
TARIA
CORAL
SEA
Great Barrier Reef
VANUATU
PACIFIC
OCEAN
NORTHERN
TERRITORY
GREAT
SANDY DESERT
WESTERN
AUSTRALIA
GREAT VICTORIA
DESERT
AUSTRALIA
North West
Cape
Steep
Point
Houtman
Rocks
Perth
Fremantle
Cape
Leeuwin
Kalgoorlie
Alice Springs
Finke River
Flinders River
Townsville
GREAT DIVIDING RANGE
Rockhampton
QUEENSLAND
Brisbane
New
Caledonia
Loyalty
Islands
TROPIC OF CAPRICORN
SOUTH AUSTRALIA
Iron Knob
GREAT
AUSTRALIAN BIGHT
Adelaide
Broken
Hill
Darling River
NEW
SOUTH
WALES
Murray
River
AUSTRALIAN
ALPS
Newcastle
Sydney
Canberra
Mount
Kosciusko 7,316 ft.
VICTORIA
Melbourne
BASS STRAIT
TASMANIA
Hobart
Lord Howe
Islands
TASMAN SEA
INDIAN
OCEAN
NEW
ZEALAND
North
Cape
North
Island
Auckland
Wellington
Mt. Cook
Christchurch
South
Island
Dunedin
South Cape
10°
20°
30°
40°
110°
120°
130°
140°
150°
160°
170°
180°
© Rand McNally & Co.

Dictionary of Geographical Terms

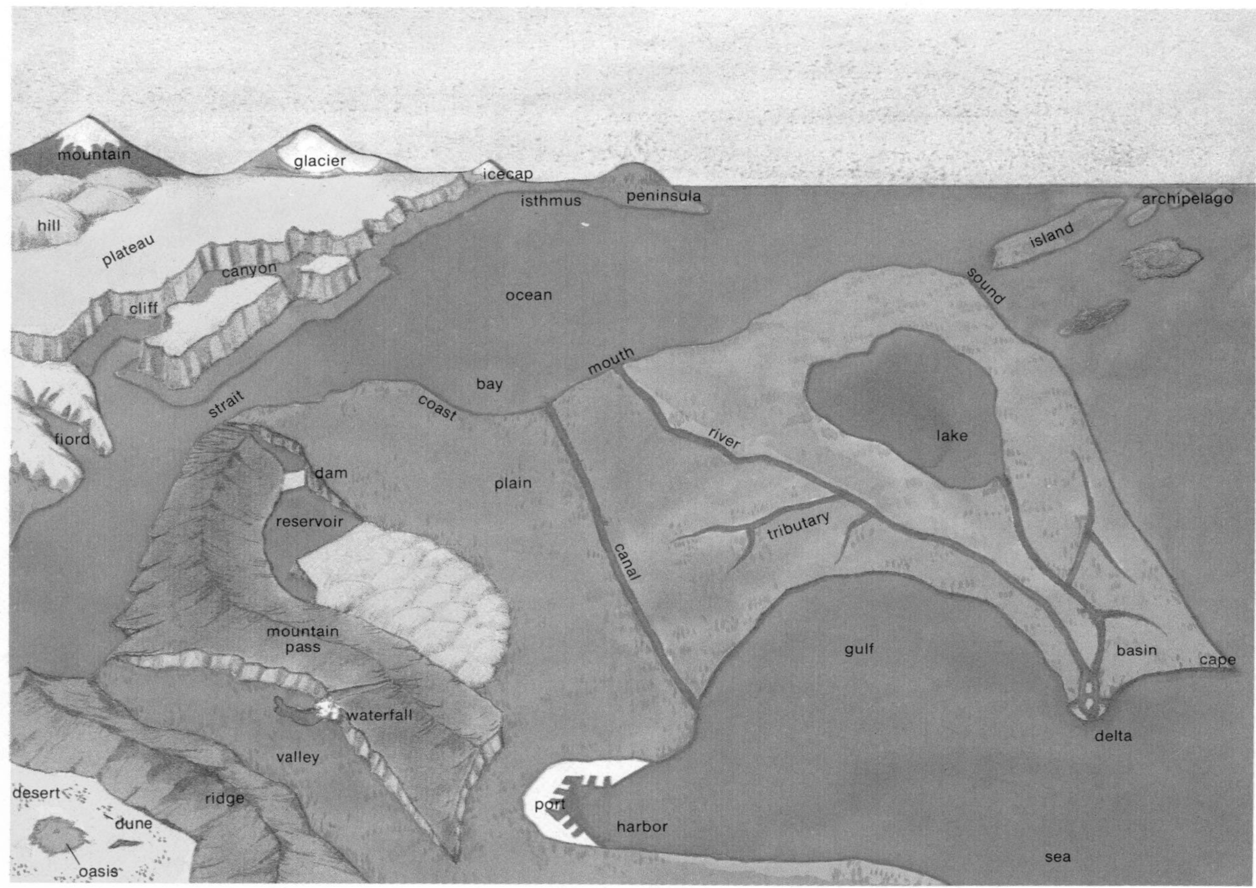

archipelago (är′kə pel′ ə gō′): a large group of islands

basin (bā′sin): all the land drained by a river and its tributaries

bay (bā): an arm of a sea or lake, extending into the land, usually smaller than a gulf

canal (kə nal′): a waterway built to connect two other bodies of water

canyon (kan′yən): a deep valley that has steep sides

cape (kāp): a point of land extending from the coastline into the sea or a lake

cliff (klif): a high, steep face of rock or earth

coast (kōst): land along a sea or ocean

dam (dam): a wall built across a river to hold back the water

delta (del′tə): land at the mouth of a river, made of sand and silt, usually shaped like a triangle

desert (dez′ərt): a very dry area where few plants grow

dune (dōōn): a hill, mound, or ridge of sand formed by the wind

fiord (fyôrd): a deep, narrow inlet of the sea between high cliffs or banks carved by a glacier

glacier (glā′shər): a large body of ice that moves very slowly over the land

gulf (gulf): an arm of a sea or lake extending into the land, usually larger than a bay

harbor (har′bər): a protected place on an ocean, sea, lake, or river where ships can shelter

hill (hil): a rounded and raised landform, not as high as a mountain

icecap (īs′kap′): a dome-shaped glacier covering a land area and moving out from the center in all directions

island (ī′lənd): a body of land surrounded by water, smaller than a continent

isthmus (is′məs): a strip of land bordered by water that connects two larger bodies of land

lake (lāk): a body of water surrounded by land

mountain (mount′ən): a high rounded or pointed landform with steep sides, higher than a hill

mountain pass (mount′ən pas′): a narrow gap in the mountains

mouth (mouth): the place where a river flows into the ocean or into another body of water

oasis (ō ā′sis): a place in the desert that is fertile because it has a water supply

ocean (ō′shən): the body of salt water covering nearly three fourths of the earth's surface

peninsula (pə nin′sə lə): land extending from a larger body of land, nearly surrounded by water

plain (plān): an area of flat or almost flat land

plateau (pla tō′): flat land with steep sides, raised above the surrounding land

port (pôrt): a place where ships load and unload goods

reservoir (rez′ər vwär′): a body of water formed behind a dam

ridge (rij): a long and narrow chain of hills or mountains

river (**riv**′ər): a large stream of water that flows across the land and usually empties into a lake, ocean, or another river

sea (sē): a large body of water partly or entirely enclosed by land; another term for the ocean

sound (sound): a long inlet or arm of the sea

strait (strāt): a narrow channel that joins two larger bodies of water

tributary (trib′yə ter′ē): a river or stream that flows into a larger river or stream

valley (val′ē): an area of low land between hills or mountains

waterfall (wô′tər fôl′): a flow of water falling from a high place

Map Symbols

Map symbols vary from map to map. Some maps use the same or similar symbols. Other maps use different symbols. You will see some of the commonly used symbols shown below on the maps in this book.

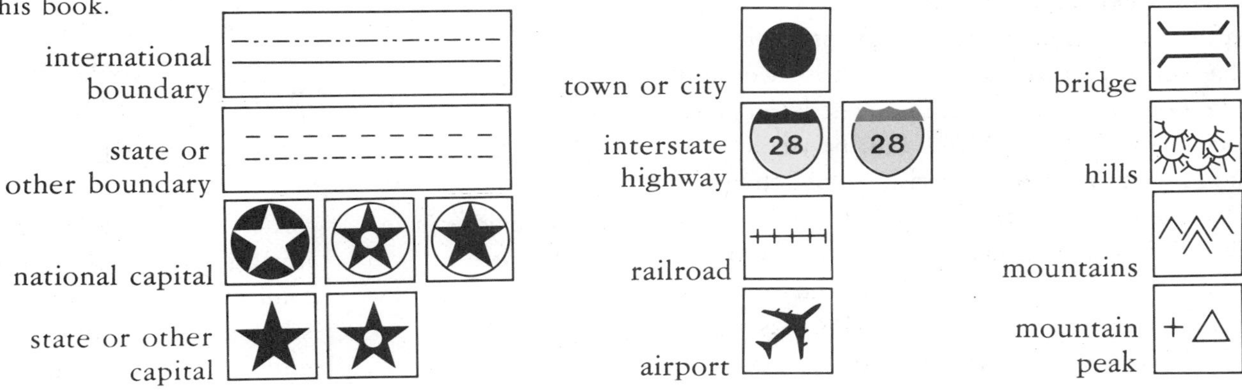

1 The Earth

Unit Preview

Today most of the earth has been explored. Now people are beginning to venture forth into the space that surrounds the earth. But long ago people knew little about the earth. First they had to learn to survive. They needed food, water, clothing, and shelter. Later they needed to learn about government and law.

Through centuries of study, people have learned much about the earth. They have learned that the earth rotates on its axis and travels around the sun. We know why seasons change and what climate is.

Maps can help us describe what we know about the earth. Maps can show the size of continents and oceans and the location of cities and rivers. Maps also may be used to show the rainfall or population of an area or the goods produced in a country.

Time lines help us to describe when events in history took place. Events on a time line are divided between those that occurred before or after the birth of Christ. For events that happened before the birth of Christ, we place the letters B.C. after the date. The letters B.C. stand for "Before Christ." For the years following the birth of Christ, we use the letters A.D., an abbreviation for the Latin phrase *Anno Domini,* which means "In the Year of Our Lord." No one can be certain of the exact date of some events in history. For this reason, historians use *c.* before the dates of some events. The *c.* stands for *circa* which means "about." You will see B.C., A.D., and *c.* used on time lines in this book.

Things to Discover

If you look carefully at the picture, map, and time line on these pages, you can answer these questions.

1. Why would the site shown in the picture be a good place to build a community? How have people changed the environment in the area? How are they using the resources of the region?
2. There are 7 continents, or large bodies of land, on the earth. Six of them are shown on the map. What are they?
3. Who was the leader of the first voyage around the world? When did it take place?

Words to Learn

You will meet these words in this unit. As you read, you will learn what they mean and how to pronounce them. The Word List will help you.

altitude	equator	law
axis	flint	longitude
circumference	glacier	meridian
climate	government	plateau
continent	hemisphere	produce
culture	isthmus	rotation
custom	latitude	satellite

People learn to use fire
c. 400,000
People learn to farm and to tame animals
c. 6400
People learn to use the wheel
c. 3300
B.C.
A.D.
Magellan sails around the world
1522
Copernicus states the earth moves around the sun
1543
U.S. astronauts land on moon
1969
"Voyager" sends back photos of Jupiter
1979

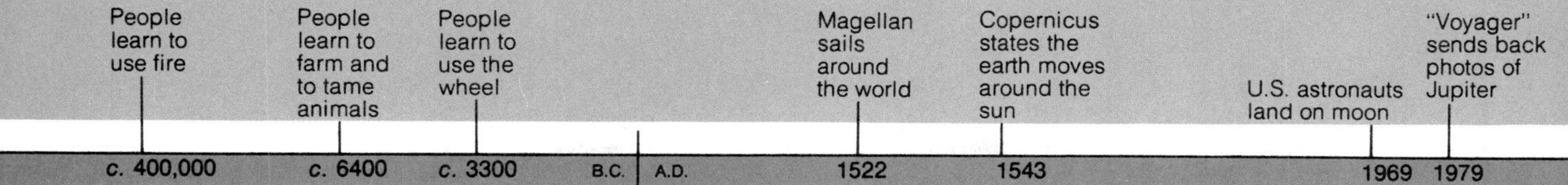

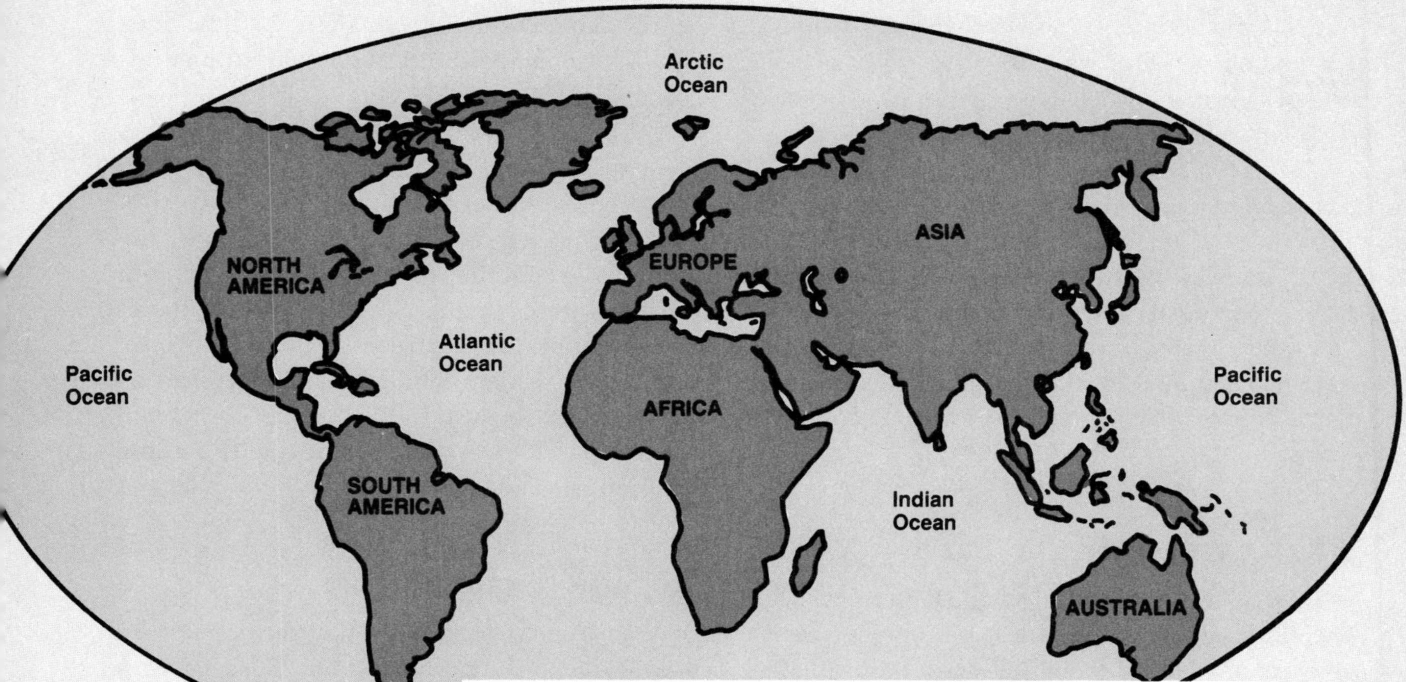

Arctic Ocean
NORTH AMERICA
EUROPE
ASIA
Atlantic Ocean
Pacific Ocean
Pacific Ocean
AFRICA
SOUTH AMERICA
Indian Ocean
AUSTRALIA

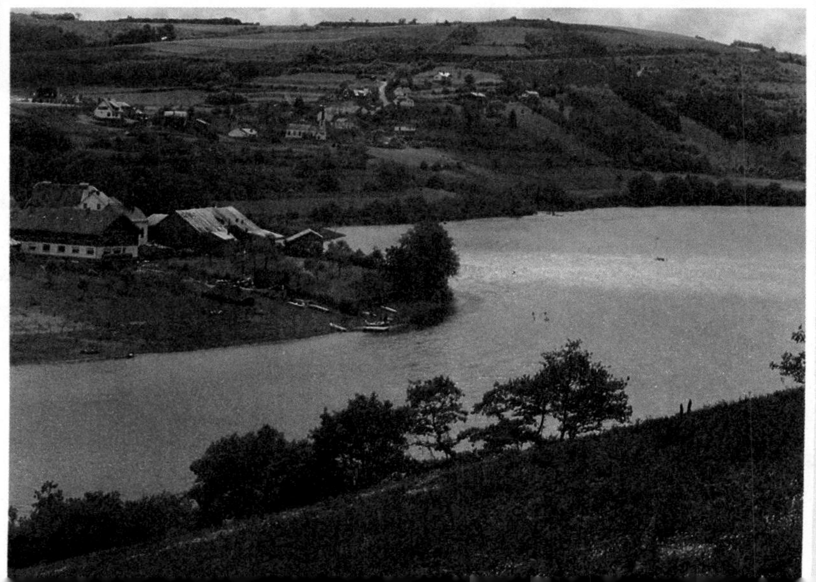

1
What the Earth is Like

What do we know about this earth we all live on? Your school globe shows that the earth has a round shape. This was proved in 1522, when one of Ferdinand Magellan's five ships returned to Spain after sailing around the world.

The earth, however, is not perfectly round. It has a slight bulge near the *equator* (i kwā′tər). This is the imaginary line that circles the globe midway between the North and South Poles. Scientists measuring the *circumference* (ser kum′fər əns) of the earth in 1743 found this out. The distance around the globe was greater at the equator than around the North and South Poles.

The Divisions of the Earth

On the globe we see only half of the earth at one time. *Hemisphere* (hem′is fĕr′) is the name given to any half of the globe. Each hemisphere has large bodies of land called *continents* (kont′ən ənts). There are seven continents.

The Western Hemisphere has two continents: North America and South America. These two continents are joined by a narrow strip of land called an *isthmus* (is′məs). This is the Isthmus of Panama. The Panama Canal has been dug across the isthmus.

The Eastern Hemisphere has four continents: Europe, Asia, Africa, and Australia. Although usually referred to as two continents, Europe and Asia are actually one large land mass called Eurasia (yoo rā′zhə).

Africa and Asia are joined by an isthmus. Today they are separated by a canal called the Suez (so͞o ez′) Canal which has been dug through this isthmus.

Southeast of Asia lies Australia. Australia is the earth's smallest continent.

Antarctica (ant′ärk′ti kə) is the seventh continent. This continent, which surrounds the South Pole, is almost entirely covered with thick ice. It is in the Southern Hemisphere. Find the Southern Hemisphere on the globe on page 13. Although Antarctica is larger than either Europe or Australia, it has no permanent inhabitants. The only humans who set foot on it are scientists and explorers.

Motions of the Earth

Once many people thought that the sun moved around the earth. But in 1543 a Polish scientist named Nikolaus Copernicus (kə pur′ni kəs) claimed that the earth was actually traveling around the sun. Today we know that Copernicus was right.

The earth really has two main motions. It travels in a wide circle around the sun, and it spins like a top at the same time. That is, it turns around its own center as if an imaginary rod passed through the center from end to end. We call the imaginary rod on which the earth turns its *axis* (ak′sis). At one end of the axis is the North Pole. At the other end is the South Pole.

The Western Hemisphere

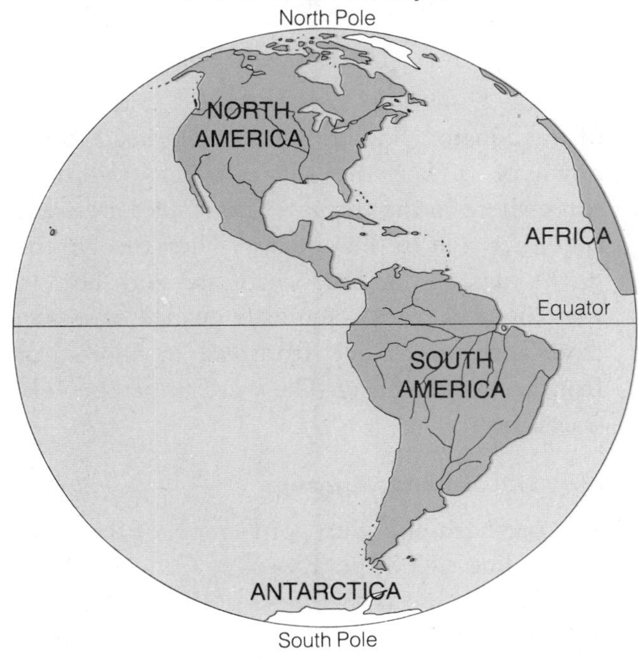

The Eastern Hemisphere

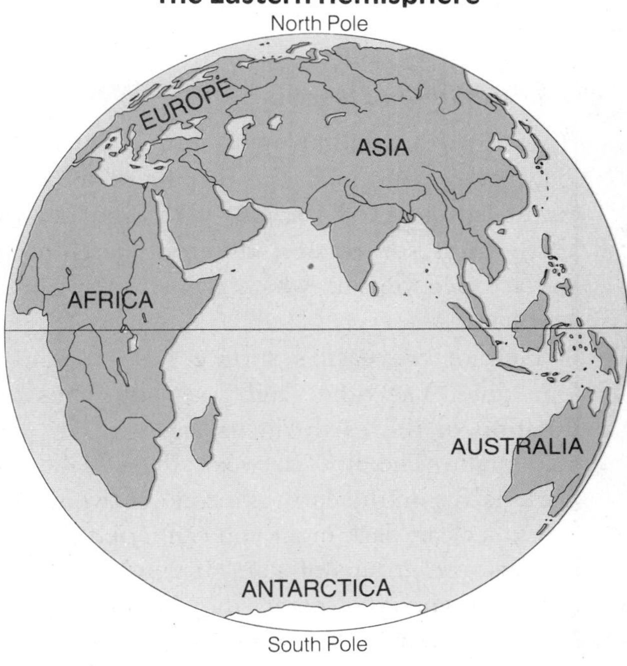

The Northern Hemisphere

The Southern Hemisphere

The Earth On Its Axis

The earth turns completely around on its axis once every 24 hours. The turning of the earth on its axis is called *rotation* (rō tā′shən). As the earth turns, or rotates, different parts of its surface face the sun, which gives the earth light and heat.

Half of the earth's surface has sunlight at one time. The other half does not. Thus the rotation of the earth on its axis gives us day and night. The line between these light and dark halves on the earth is a zone of twilight.

On a clear, dark night you can look up at the sky and see groups of stars. If you look at star groups night after night, they seem to swing around a northern center. That center is a fairly bright star which does not seem to move. It always keeps its place in the north. This is the North Star.

It is the rotation of the earth that makes the stars seem to swing around in a circle. The North Star does not seem to move because one pole of the earth's axis is always pointed toward the star. The North Pole points almost exactly to the North Star.

While rotating on its axis, the earth also tilts to one side as it goes around the sun. If it did not tilt, day and night would always be equal in length. The earth tilts only slightly, but it is enough to vary the length of the days and nights. The half that tilts toward the sun has longer days and shorter nights than the half tilted away from the sun.

The sun is usually directly overhead at the equator. But because the earth tilts a little, the sun is not always directly overhead even at the equator. Sometimes it is overhead to the south of the equator. Sometimes it is overhead to the north of it. But the sun is always overhead somewhere in the tropics. The tropics are areas on either side of the equator. They receive the direct rays of the sun, which are very hot. In the tropics there is often little change of season from summer to fall, from fall to winter, or from winter to spring. The weather can be very warm there.

Why the Seasons Change

The northern boundary, or border, of the tropics is a line called the Tropic of Cancer. Along this line the sun is overhead on June 21 or 22. This is the longest day of the year in the Northern Hemisphere.

The southern boundary of the tropics is a line called the Tropic of Capricorn. There the sun is overhead on December 21 or 22. This is the longest day of the year in the Southern Hemisphere.

From this you can see that the seasons in the Northern Hemisphere are exactly opposite to the seasons in the Southern Hemisphere. When it is summer in the Northern Hemisphere, it is winter in the Southern Hemisphere. The United States, for example, has summer weather at the time when it is winter in Argentina.

In late December, as the earth turns on its axis, an area around the North Pole is in darkness all 24 hours. In late June, this area has light throughout the 24 hours. We call the boundary between this region and the rest of the earth the Arctic Circle.

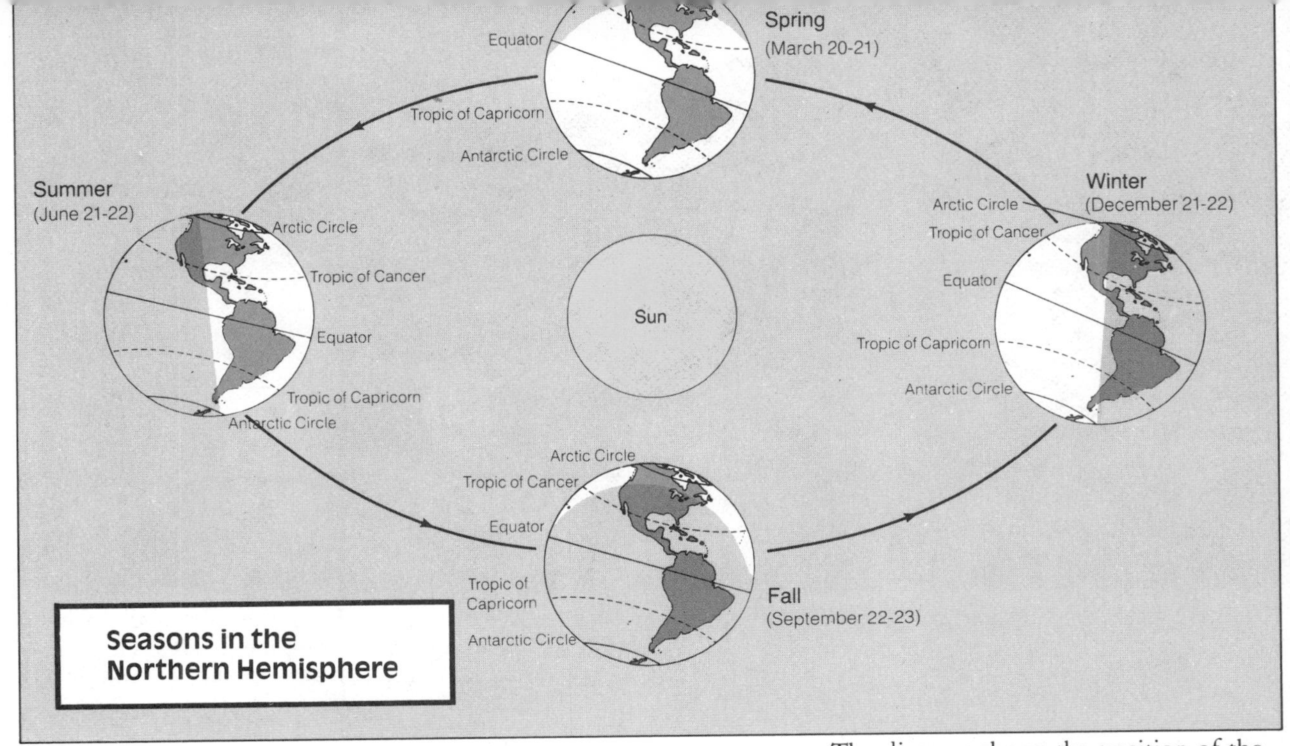

The diagram shows the position of the earth at the beginning of each season. In summer, the Northern *Hemisphere* faces toward the sun. In winter, what *hemisphere* faces the sun?

While the region near the North Pole is in darkness during December, the South Pole is receiving sunlight. The area near the South Pole receives some light all 24 hours. The time of darkness around the South Pole is in June. We call the boundary between this region and the rest of the earth the Antarctic Circle.

The area within the Arctic Circle and the area within the Antarctic Circle are known as the polar regions. These areas never receive the sun's direct rays. At certain times, as we have seen, the sun does not shine there at all.

While turning on its axis, the earth moves around the sun once each year. The movement of the earth around the sun gives us our change of seasons. In winter the northern half of the earth is tilted away from the sun. So it receives less sunlight than it does in summer, when it is tilted toward the sun. In summer the northern half is tilted toward the sun, and it receives more sunlight than in winter.

Thus we see that changes of temperature and changes in the lengths of the days and nights divide the year into periods. We call these periods seasons. Most of the United States has four seasons. But the tropics in general have just two seasons, a wet season and a dry season. The polar regions also have only two seasons, a season of light and a season of darkness. These regions are cold during both seasons. But the season of darkness is much the colder of the two.

The diagram above shows the path of the earth as it travels around the sun. It also shows the position of the earth on the path at the beginning of each of the four seasons.

We learn more about the earth and space by using special equipment. This is a model of the Voyager spacecraft used on a picture-taking mission to Jupiter.

Learning More About the Earth

We are still learning about the earth. On October 4, 1957, the first *satellite* (sat′əl īt′), or artificial moon, was launched into orbit. Since 1957, a great many satellites have been launched. Some of them have carried humans into space. Satellites send back information about the earth and its resources. Satellites provide information to help us predict the weather more accurately.

We have continued to explore space. In 1969 two U.S. astronauts were the first humans to walk on the moon. In 1979 two Voyager spacecrafts flew by the planet Jupiter and sent back to earth photos of the surface of Jupiter.

We are also exploring the unknown depths of the sea. Experiments that began in 1965 are taking us to parts of the sea floor deeper than we have ever been before. Under the sea and in space, there is much to be discovered about the earth and its surroundings.

What Climate Is

The weather that a place has over many years is its *climate* (klī′mit). This means how hot or cold the place is, how long or short its summers and winters are, and the average amount of rain it receives.

Climate and the Equator

Climates may be warm or cold, wet or dry. In general, the lands near the equator have the warmest climates because the sun shines on them most directly. As we go away from the equator, either to the north or to the south, the climate becomes cooler.

Effect of Oceans on Climate

Other conditions affect climate too. For example, oceans and other large bodies of water help change the climate of neighboring lands. Water heats up more slowly than land, and cools off more slowly. Winds blowing over an ocean or another large body of water cause nearby lands to have warmer winters and cooler summers.

Winds over an ocean often bring water to the land. Warm air can take up and hold more water than cool air. As the warm ocean winds pass over land, they grow cool and some of their moisture falls as rain or snow.

Effect of Altitude on Climate

The climate of a place is also affected by its *altitude* (al′tə tood′), or height above sea level. The higher we go, the cooler the air becomes. Some high mountains are covered with snow all year even though the land at the foot of the mountains is very hot. Most *plateaus* (pla tōz′), or flat stretches of high land, are also cooler than low areas.

Mountains have another important effect on climate. Air that blows against mountains is forced to rise higher up the slope. There it cools off and drops its moisture on the mountainside. As the air passes over the mountains, it comes down as a dry wind on the other side. Then the dry wind grows warm and absorbs moisture instead of losing it.

Latitude and Longitude

Suppose that you visit a strange city and you wish to find a certain house. If you know that the house is on Seventh Street near where Seventh Street crosses Oakland Street, you can find the house. In somewhat the same way we can locate places on the earth.

Underwater laboratories are places where we can explore unknown parts of the sea. Scientists live weeks at a time on the sea floor in labs like this one.

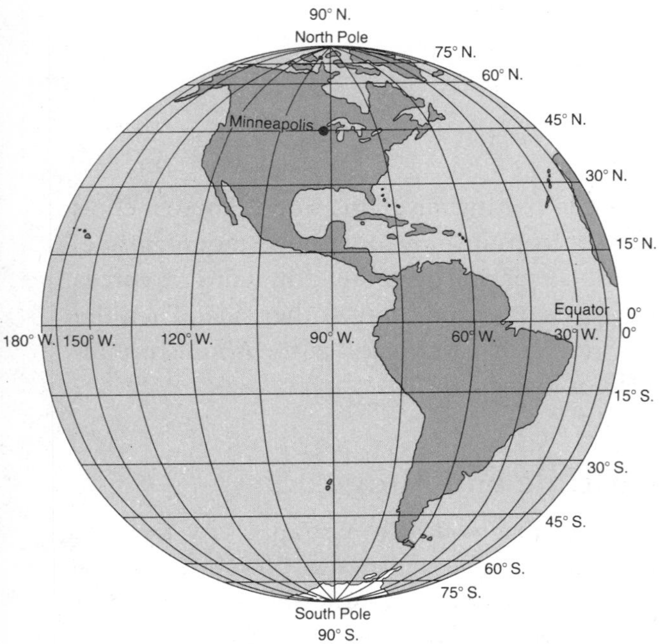

Lines of *latitude* and lines of *longitude* are used on maps and globes to locate places on the earth. Starting at the North Pole, trace your finger along 90° W. Stop at 45° N. What city is located there?

Imaginary Lines

To help us locate places on the surface of the earth, we use imaginary lines on globes and maps. Like the streets of a city, these guide lines cross each other. They are called lines of *latitude* (lat′ə to͞od) and lines of *longitude* (lon′jə to͞od). Lines of latitude run east and west. Lines of longitude run north and south.

There must be starting places for these lines. Let us start with latitude, which helps us measure distance north and south. All places north of the equator are said to be in north latitude. All places south of it are in south latitude. Other imaginary circles run parallel to—or at equal distances from—the equator. These circles are called parallels of latitude. The map above has such parallels.

How Latitude Is Measured

Latitude is measured by degrees. The equator is numbered 0. Moving north from the equator, we can tell how many degrees north latitude a certain place is located. Going south from the equator, we can measure how many degrees south latitude a place is. The points farthest from the equator are the poles. The North Pole is at 90 degrees north latitude, and the South Pole at 90 degrees south latitude.

To show degrees, we use a small circle to the right and slightly above the number. Thus the North Pole is at 90° north latitude, and the South Pole is at 90° south latitude. Minneapolis, in Minnesota, is 45° north latitude, or 45° N. In other words, Minneapolis is exactly halfway between the equator and the North Pole.

As you can see from the map on this page, the longest parallels of latitude are near the equator. The shortest parallels of latitude are near the poles.

How Longitude Is Measured

To measure distance east and west, we use longitude. Longitude is also measured by degrees. To show longitude, we use imaginary lines on the earth's surface extending from one pole to the other. These lines are called *meridians* (mə rid′ē ənz). Meridians of longitude are not parallel, but they are all of equal length, and they come together at the poles.

One of the meridians must be the starting point of measuring east and west around the earth. The meridian used for this purpose is

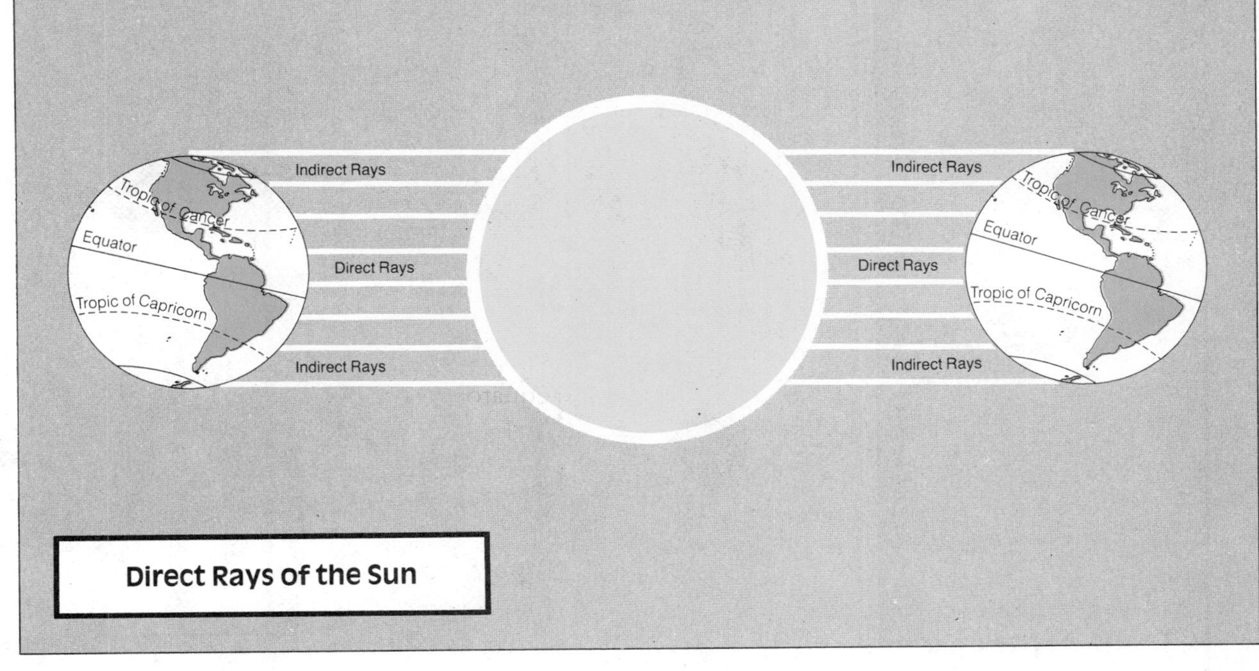

This diagram shows where direct rays of the sun fall on the earth in summer and in winter. In summer direct rays fall on the Tropic of Cancer. In winter they fall on the Tropic of Capricorn.

the 0° meridian, which runs through Greenwich, a town near London, in England. The 0° meridian is called the prime meridian. The word "prime" means "first."

Longitude is measured east or west from the prime meridian. Points east of the prime meridian are said to be at a certain number of degrees east longitude. Points west of it are said to be at so many degrees west longitude. For example, Philadelphia is about 75 degrees (75°) west longitude. Melbourne, in Australia, is about 145 degrees (145°) east longitude.

Temperature Regions

Many people think that in summer the sun is exactly over their heads at noon. That is not true anywhere in the United States except in Hawaii. But it is true in the tropics. As the earth turns towards the sun or away from it, the place where the sun's direct rays fall at noon changes. The reason for this is that the direct rays can fall on only one point at a time. If you aim the beam of a small but bright flashlight on a slowly turning globe, you will understand this better.

Late in March the direct rays of the sun at noon fall upon the equator. As spring advances, these direct noon rays creep farther northward each day. Late in June, when the Northern Hemisphere has its longest day in the year, the direct rays are as far north as they ever get. At that time they fall on a line 23½° north of the equator. This line is the Tropic of Cancer. Find the Tropic of Cancer on the map on page 21.

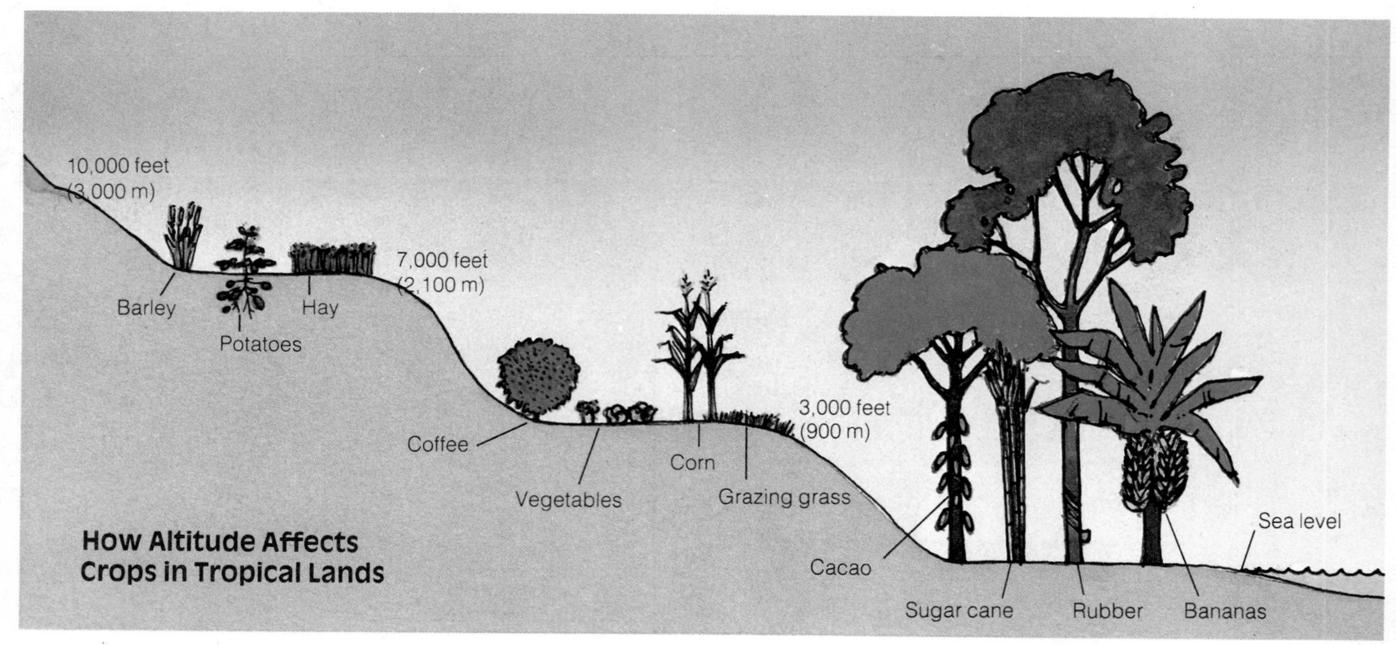

On page 17 you read about how *altitude* affects *climate.* This diagram shows how *altitude* and *climate* affect vegetation. Study the diagram and tell what crops grow at different levels in tropical lands.

When the direct noon rays have moved as far north as they can, they start to return south. Day by day they move southward. Although the weather may still be hot, the days steadily grow shorter. Late in September the direct noon rays have come back to the equator. Days and nights are of equal length all over the earth.

The direct noon rays continue to move southward. Late in December they reach a line 23½° south of the equator. This line is the Tropic of Capricorn. Find it on the map of the world on pages 22 and 23, and see through what continents it passes.

The Southern Hemisphere has its summer while we are having our winter. Would you prefer to visit Melbourne, Australia, in December or in June? What kind of weather would you find there at each time?

What the Low Latitudes Are Like

The belt around the earth between the Tropic of Cancer and the Tropic of Capricorn is called the low latitudes. Places in this region are near the equator, which is numbered zero. Thus these areas have parallels of latitude with low numbers.

The low latitudes are also called the tropics. The direct rays of the sun never go outside the tropics. The countries near the equator, therefore, receive a great deal of heat all through the year. Many people in the tropics live on plateaus or mountain slopes where it is cooler.

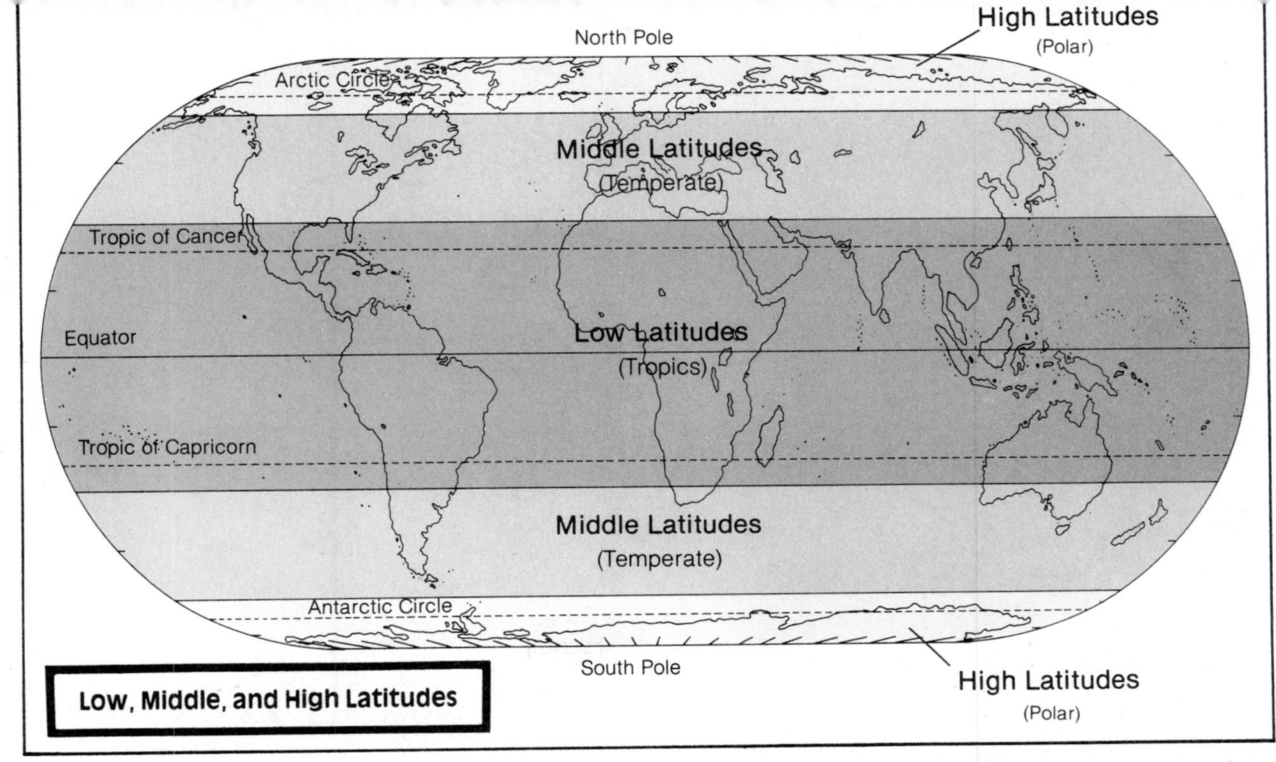

Low, Middle, and High Latitudes

Find North America on the map. In what *latitude* is most of the *continent?* What other *continents* have land in that *latitude?* Find the low *latitudes.* What kind of *climate* do lands have there?

What the Middle Latitudes Are Like

North and south of the low latitudes are the middle latitudes. The middle latitudes have parallels with larger numbers than the parallels within the tropics.

The middle latitudes are also called the temperate regions. "Temperate," a word which means "mild," should apply to places having a climate that is neither very hot nor very cold. However, regions called temperate can be extremely hot in summer and very cold in winter. By "temperate" we mean that in these regions the weather average for the year—halfway between the coldest days and the hottest days—is mild. Find the temperate regions, or middle latitudes, on the map above.

The parts of the middle latitudes which border on the tropics are called the subtropics. The subtropics sometimes have frost, but not often. Except for places high above sea level, the tropics never have frost. It is summer there all the time.

What the High Latitudes Are Like

North and south of the middle latitudes are the areas with parallels of latitude that have high numbers. These high latitudes are located within the Arctic Circle and within the Antarctic Circle. The high latitudes, or polar regions, are so cold that few people live in them. Find the high latitudes on the global map above.

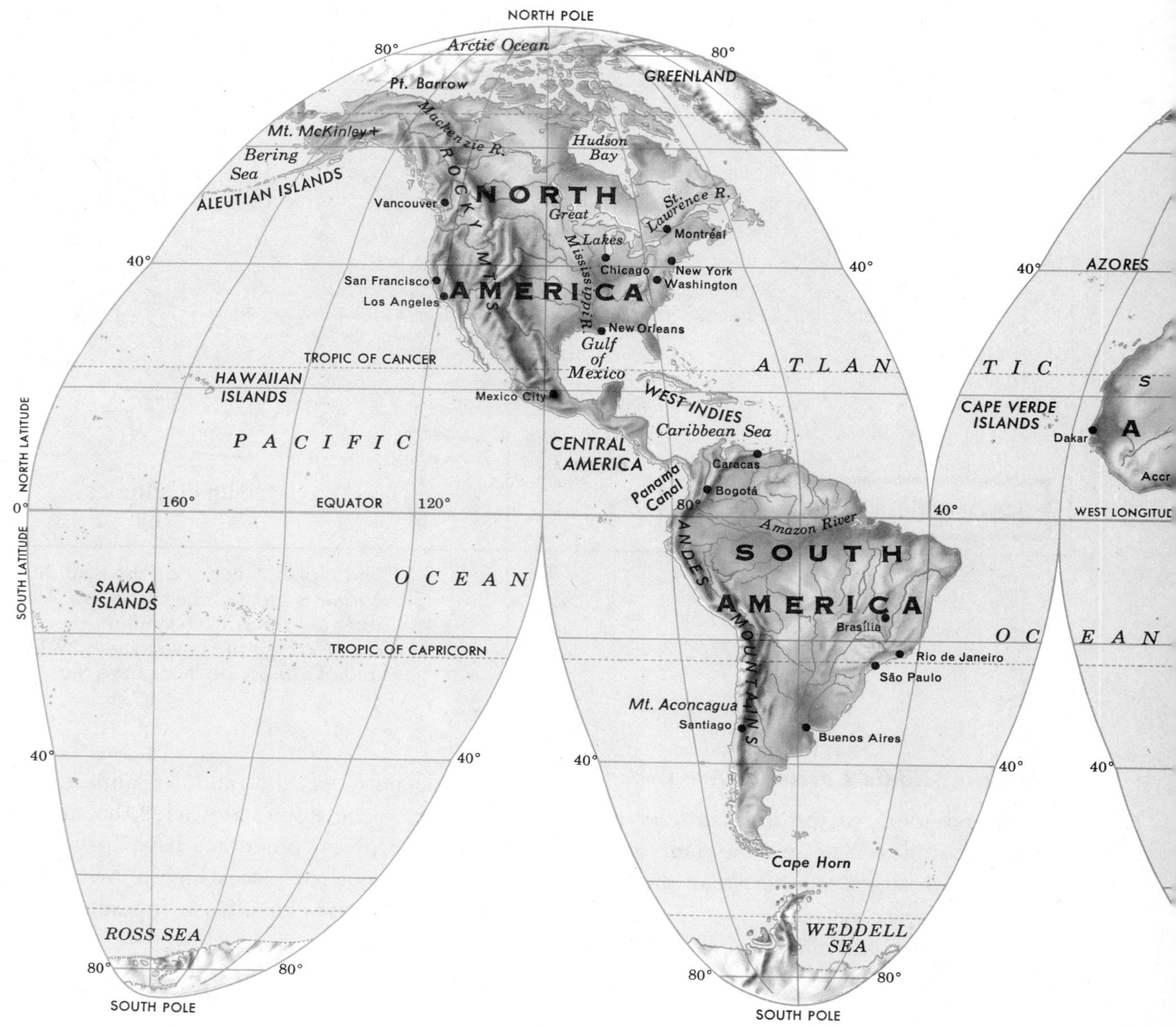

Kinds of Maps

Maps are like pictures of the world. There are many kinds of maps, each picturing all or part of our world in a different way. Some maps show natural features such as hills, lakes, and rivers. Others show boundaries, cities, parallels, and so on. Some maps show both natural and other features. Others portray facts about such matters as population, vegetation, and rainfall.

Physical Maps

A physical map shows the natural features of the earth—its mountains, oceans, lakes, rivers,

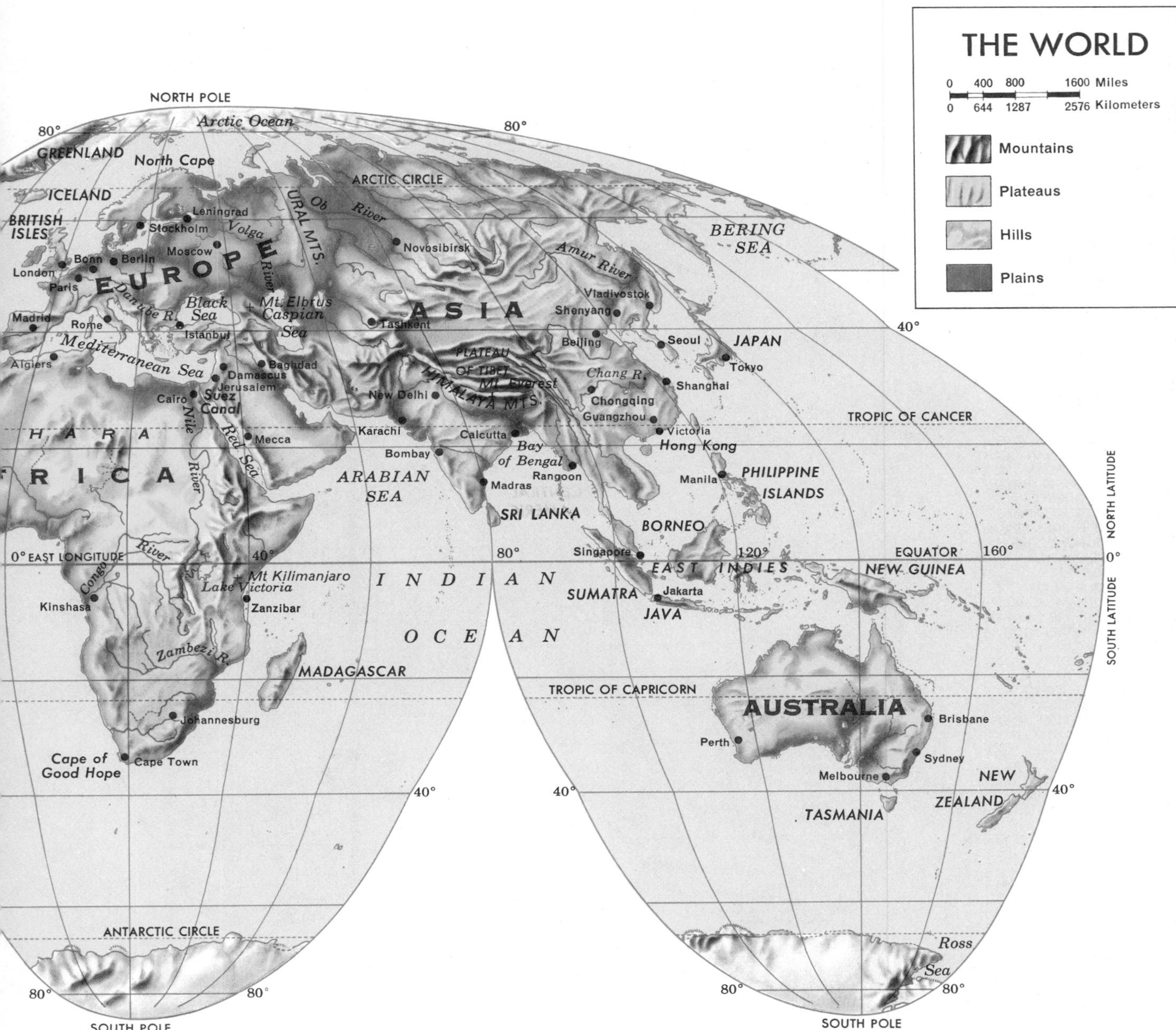

deserts, and plains. On a physical map the different kinds of land are often shown in different colors. In this book one color is used to represent the plains. Another is used for plateaus. Hills and mountains are also shown in different colors. The physical map above shows how these colors have been used.

Each physical map in this book has a key which shows what kinds of land the colors represent. Use the key at the side of the map above to answer the following questions. Where are mountains found in North America? About how much of South America is plains? What large continent is mostly hills and plateaus?

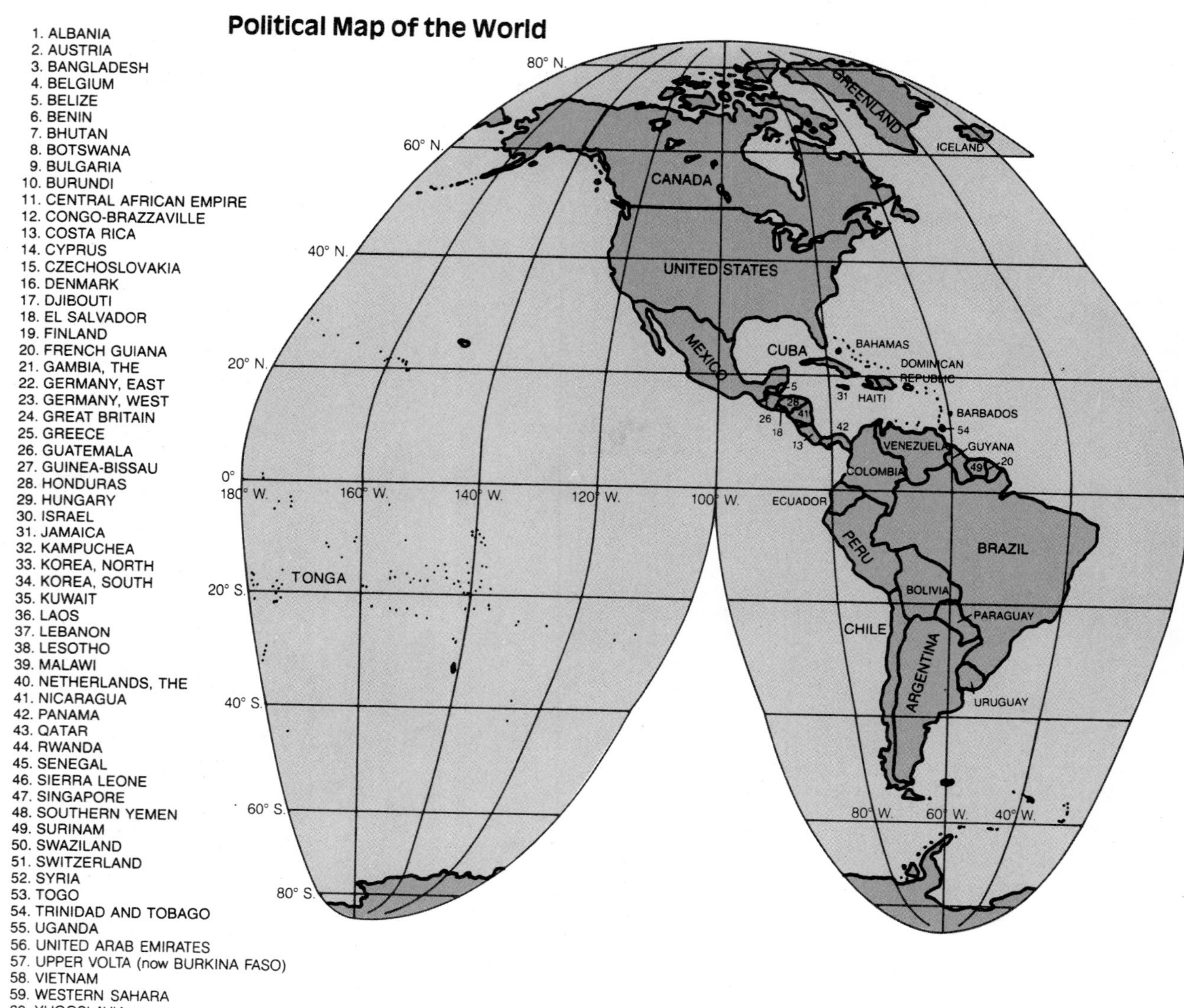

Political Maps

A political map shows features such as national and state boundaries or borders, and cities. On this page and page 25 is a political map showing all the countries of the world. The boundary lines help us see the sizes and shapes of the countries.

Other Kinds of Maps

Some maps show special kinds of information.

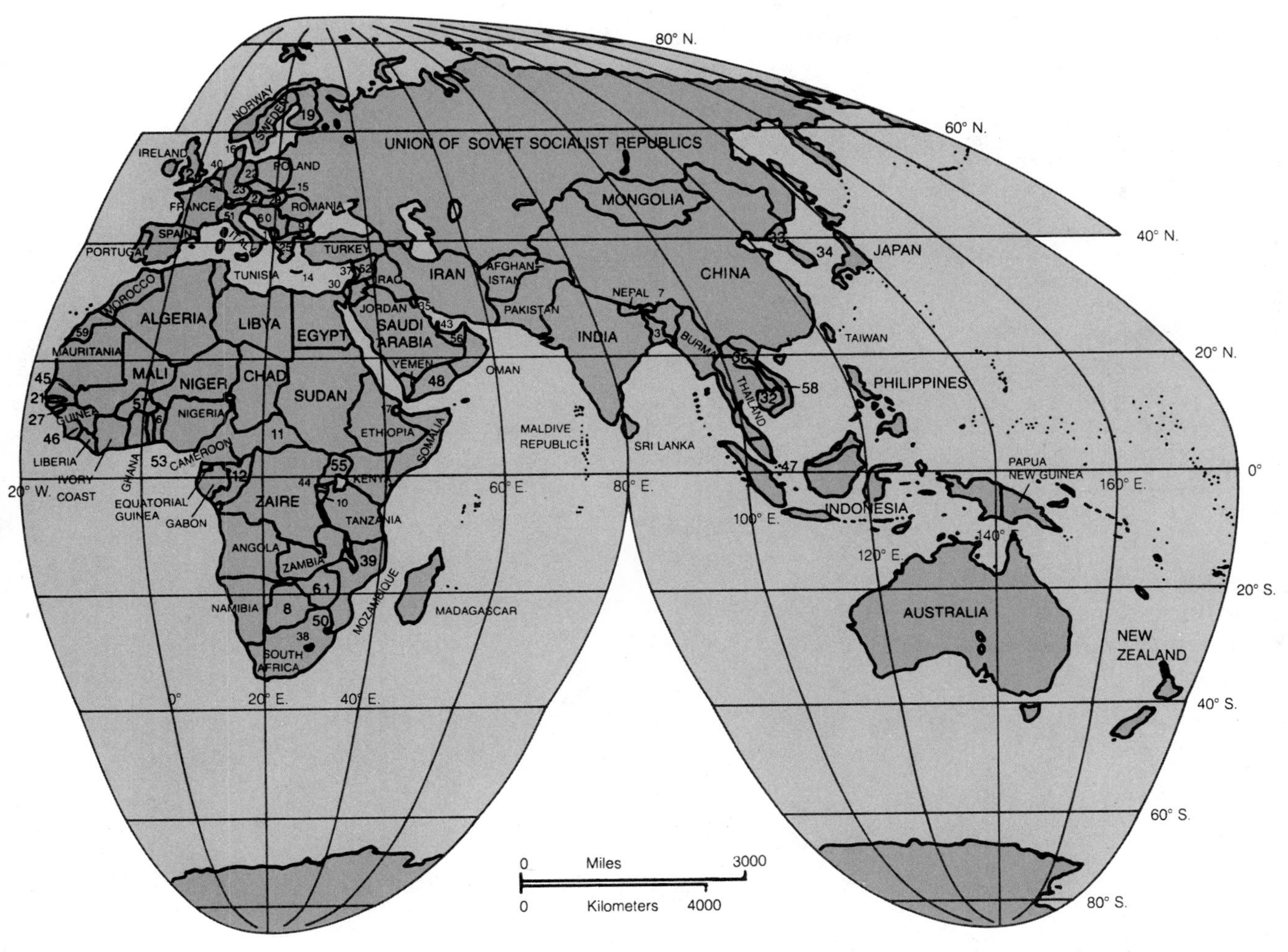

For example, a map telling how many people live in certain countries or regions of the world is called a population map. You will find a population map of the world on page 26. By referring to the key, you can find out which parts of the world have many people and which parts have few. How many people per square mile live in the part of Australia that is shown in yellow? What colors are used to show the areas of heaviest population?

World Population

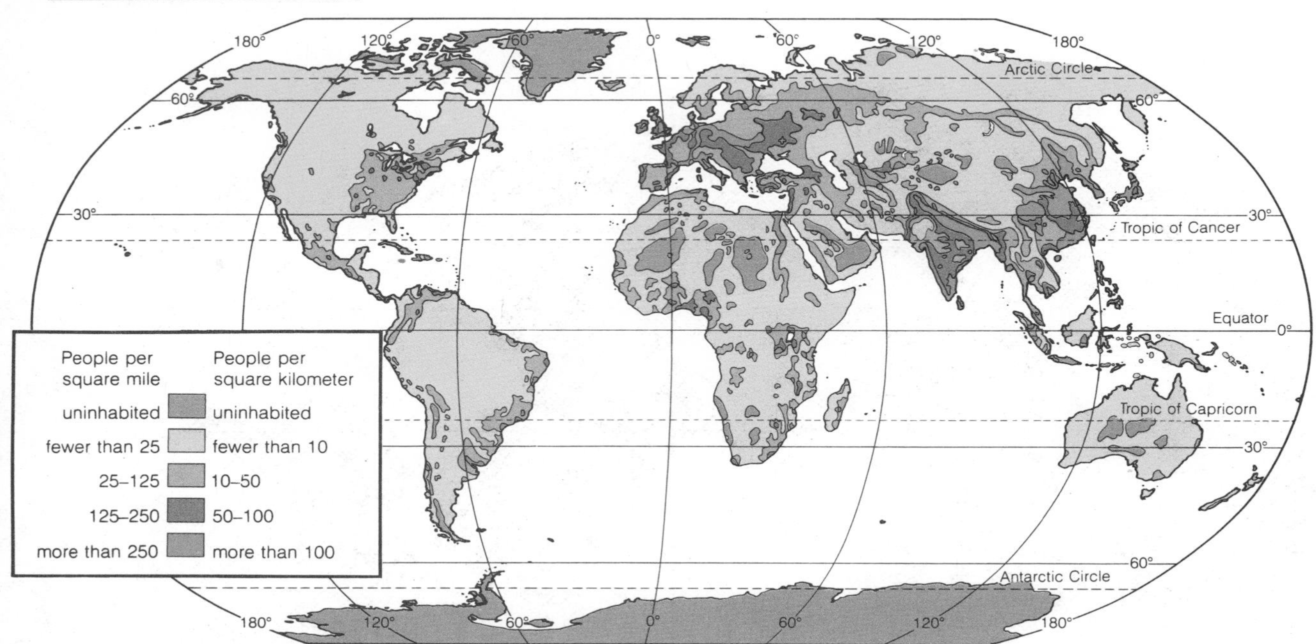

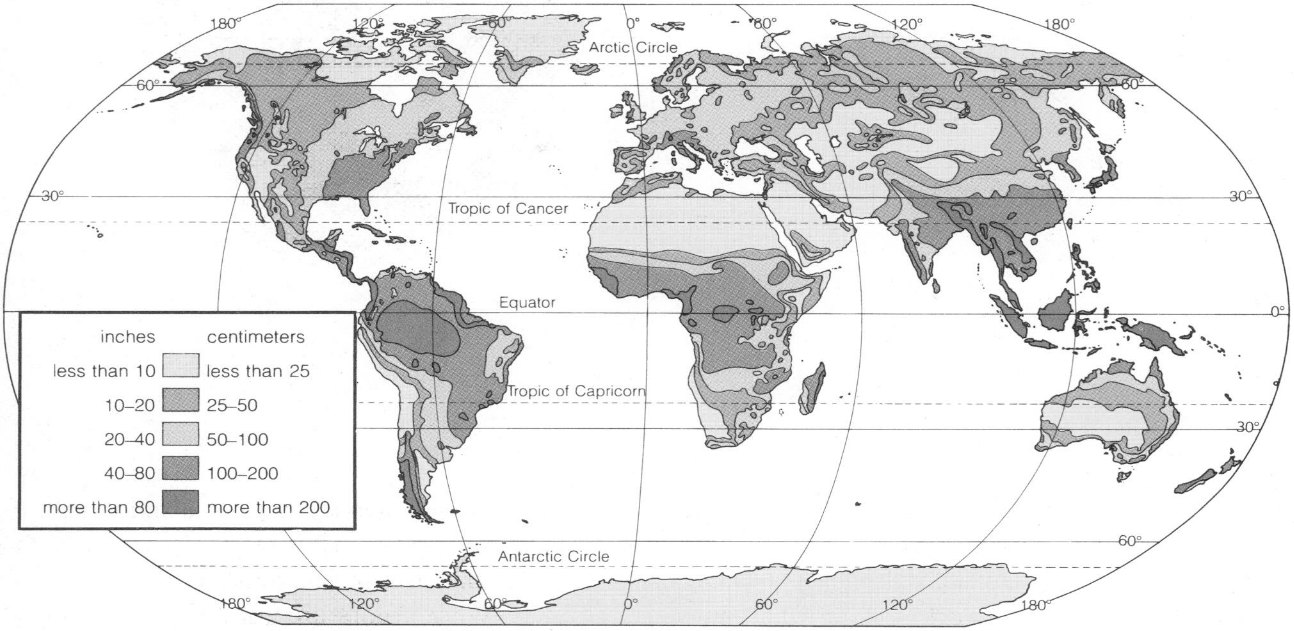

180°
120°
60°
0°
60°
120°
180°
Arctic Circle
60°
30°
Tropic of Cancer
Equator
0°
Tropic of Capricorn
30°
60°
Antarctic Circle
People per square mile
People per square kilometer
uninhabited
uninhabited
fewer than 25
fewer than 10
25–125
10–50
125–250
50–100
more than 250
more than 100

World Annual Precipitation

180°
120°
60°
0°
Arctic Circle
60°
120°
180°
60°
30°
Tropic of Cancer
Equator
0°
Tropic of Capricorn
30°
60°
Antarctic Circle
inches
centimeters
less than 10
less than 25
10–20
25–50
20–40
50–100
40–80
100–200
more than 80
more than 200

World Vegetation

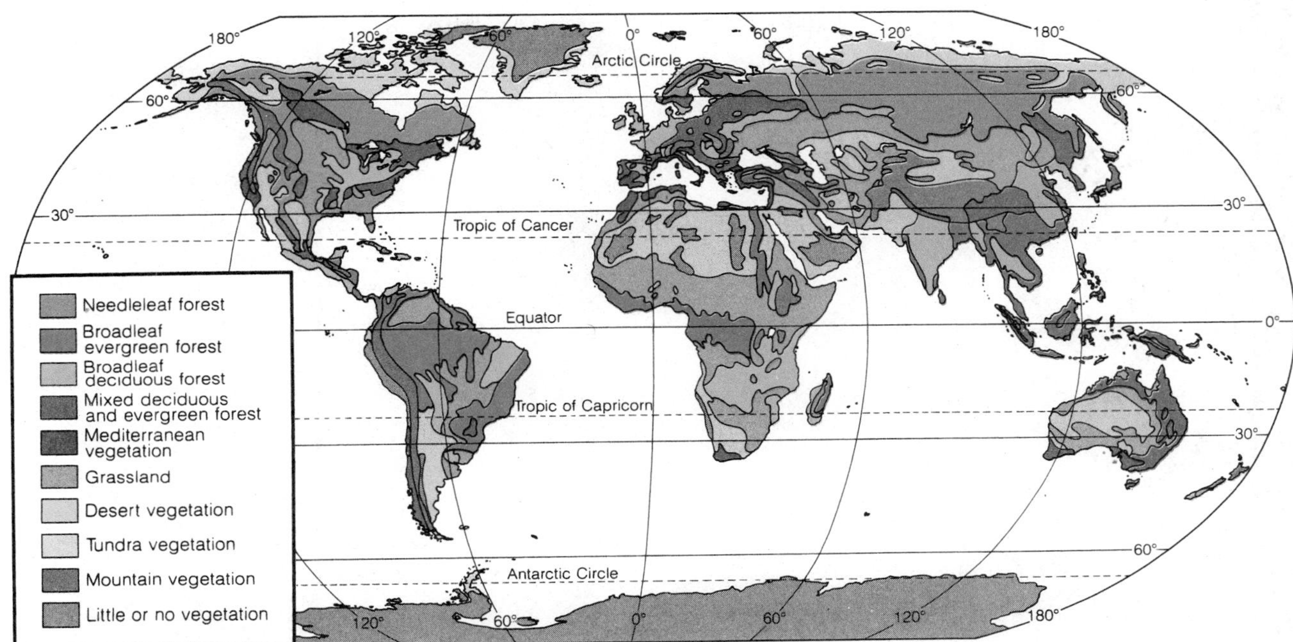

The map on the bottom of page 26 uses different colors to show the different amounts of rainfall. For what period of time was the rainfall measured in making this map? What color is used to represent the lightest rainfall? What color is used to represent the heaviest rainfall?

Maps that show plant life in a region are called vegetation maps. Look at the vegetation map on this page. What kinds of vegetation grow along the equator? What kinds grow in the far north?

Map Scales

Maps must represent large areas of the world in a small space. For example, on the map on page 49, each inch (2.5 cm) stands for 259 miles (414 km). But on the map on page 79 each inch (2.5 cm) stands for 496 miles (794 km). The number of miles or kilometers represented by an inch or centimeter is called the scale of a map.

Do You Know?

1. How many continents are there on the earth? Where is each located?
2. What two kinds of motion does the earth have? What kind of motion causes day and night?
3. What three conditions cause the climate of a place to be warm or cold?
4. Which line of latitude is numbered 0°? Which line of longitude, or meridian, is numbered 0°?
5. What kinds of maps are found in this unit?

Before You Go On

Using New Words

altitude	climate
circumference	rotation
continent	axis
longitude	hemisphere
equator	satellite
meridian	plateau
latitude	isthmus

Number your paper from 1 through 14. After each number write the word or term that matches the definition.

1. The weather of a certain place over many years
2. An imaginary line circling the earth midway between the North and South poles
3. The turning of the earth on its axis
4. Distance north or south of the equator
5. Half of the globe
6. The imaginary rod on which the earth seems to turn
7. An imaginary line on the earth's surface reaching from pole to pole
8. A narrow strip of land connecting two larger bodies of land
9. An artificial moon
10. A flat stretch of high land
11. The height of a place above sea level
12. The distance around the globe
13. A large body of land
14. Measurement of distance east and west on the earth's surface

Finding the Facts

1. What is the name of the scientist who claimed that the earth was actually traveling around the sun?
2. Which two continents make up a large land mass called Eurasia?
3. Why are day and night not equal in length all over the world?
4. Where do the sun's direct rays fall when they are as far north as they ever get? Where do they fall when they are as far south as they ever get?
5. How is latitude measured? Where are the high latitudes? The low latitudes? The middle latitudes?
6. What is longitude? Where is the prime meridian?
7. What do physical maps show? What do political maps show?
8. Look at the map on page 26. Which continent has the largest number of people?
9. Why does Antarctica have no permanent population?

2
How Early People Lived

Early humans did not write history because they did not have a system of writing. But they left things behind that help us to know something about them. We know what weapons and tools they used and the kind of food they ate. We know about the places in which they lived, the villages they built, and the way they buried their dead. From these things we can form a good idea of the kind of life they lived.

Ways of Living

Since many groups of early people lived in warm climates, they needed few clothes. These people roamed about searching for food, such as birds' eggs, fruits, roots, seeds, and fish, which they ate raw.

The early people were not as strong nor as quick as some of their animal enemies. But they had two great advantages. They had hands with thumbs which could close up against the fingers. With their hands people could use sticks and stones to kill animals. And it was the ability to think that made humans skillful in the use of weapons and powerful over wild beasts.

The Ice Age

As time passed, a great change came over parts of the earth. The climate became very cold. Cold temperatures caused *glaciers* (glā′shərz), or great sheets of ice, to form. The glaciers moved

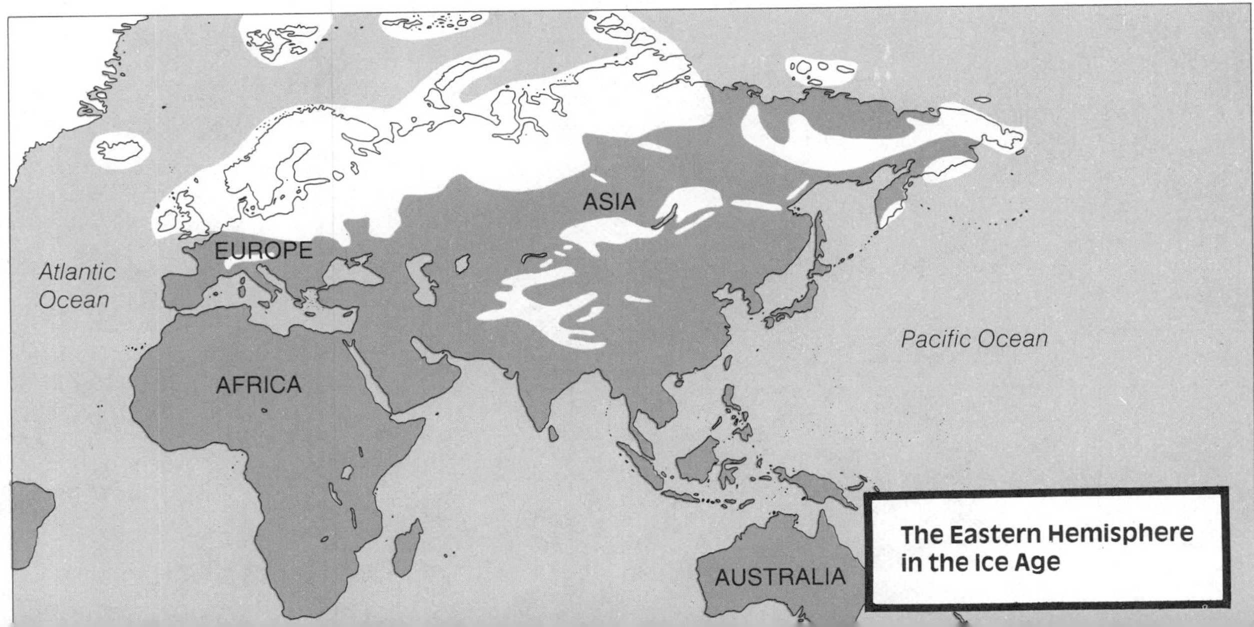

During the Ice Age, great sheets of ice called *glaciers* covered much of Europe and parts of Asia.

from the Arctic regions southward until they covered northern parts of Europe and North America.

This period of time when the glaciers were moving southward is now known as the Ice Age. Such animals as the reindeer and the mammoth moved far south. The mammoth was a great beast with long, curved tusks.

The Ice Age lasted for many thousands of years. As the sheets of ice grew thicker and covered more and more land, humans had to adapt themselves to the cold. They wore the furs of animals to keep themselves warm. And they looked for caves to shelter themselves against biting winds.

In time the climate became mild again, and the ice sheets melted. Grass and trees grew again. People increased in numbers.

The Importance of Fire

Humans were using fire about 400,000 years ago. Fire frightened away wild beasts and kept caves warm and dry. Within these snug shelters people could store extra food and wood.

The Discovery of Fire

We do not know how humans learned to use fire. Perhaps someone saw a stroke of lightning set trees or grass on fire. Perhaps a mass of melted rock came rolling out of a volcano and set a forest on fire. Somehow people learned to keep fire alive for weeks or even months. To keep a fire burning for a long time was a hard task, even in the shelter of caves.

Early humans found shelter in caves. Fires provided warmth and protection from animals. Meat was preserved by drying over fire. The man is making a flint spearhead here, like the one shown at the left.

Early hunters banded together. With better tools they could fell game from a distance. Can you explain how a spear-thrower was used?

When fire came into use, it made a great difference to humans. With fire people could cook food. They could smoke and dry meat so that it would keep for a longer time.

Making pottery was another important use of fire. Clay pots could be used for cooking. Also, people stored food and articles in bowls and pots.

Early People as Hunters

Early people found it easy to kill small animals with a stone or club. To kill large animals, however, people needed to be brave and clever. Sometimes they rolled rocks down from cliffs as the beasts passed underneath. Sometimes they led or chased animals into pits or marshes from which they could not escape. Often they lay in wait for young animals that strayed from their herds.

Improved Weapons

After a time, humans began tying a stone to the end of a club and using it as a weapon. To fasten the head of the club tightly to the handle, they cut notches into the end of the handle. Then they used thin strips of animal skin, or rawhide, to fit into the notches and to bind the stone fast. Rawhide shrinks and becomes very hard as it dries. It held the club head tighter to the handle than hands alone could tie it.

Humans learned that they could fight beasts and kill them without always being close to them. When they used a club, they could stay the distance of the club handle away from the animal. The spear helped people fight from a still greater distance because it could be thrown.

The bow and arrow also allowed people to stay far away from their prey. When a person

These fine-edged tools were made by people who lived during the New Stone Age. Shown clockwise are an arrowhead, a bone needle, a spearhead, and an axe head.

shot an arrow from a bow, it sped swiftly to its distant mark. Reindeer, bison, bear, tiger, and even mammoth fell before this weapon. The bodies of the animals gave humans useful materials. They got meat to eat and furs to wear. They also got skins of animals with which to make covers and containers. When cut into strings, the skins could be used as rope. When tanned into leather, the skin of some animals made good clothing. Bone, horn, and ivory were valuable materials for weapons and tools.

The Use of Flint

Long before knives were used, people found that the sharp edges of broken stones were good to cut with. They probably tried many kinds of rock before they found that *flint* (flint) would cut the best.

Flint is a stone which is very hard but breaks easily, leaving sharp edges. From flint humans made arrowheads, knives, scrapers, awls to pierce with, and daggers. Pieces of flint, when struck together, threw off sparks and thus gave people a way to start fires. People often made their homes near a place where much flint was found in the ground.

The Stone Age

Although humans had wooden tools and weapons, the use of stone was a great help to them. Stone was hard and could be sharpened. We call the time before people began to shape tools well the Old Stone Age.

Finally, people began to grind and polish their stone tools and weapons. For heavy work they used the stone ax, chisel, and hammer. These tools were polished, smoothed, and had a fine edge. Because bone was easier to grind down than stone, it too was a valuable material. Bone needles were used in cave homes. Outside, pickaxes made from deerhorns were used. The age of polished stone and bone is called the New Stone Age.

The Taming of Animals

Sometime during the New Stone Age people began to tame animals. When hunters killed a mother animal, her young were sometimes brought back as pets. As the young animals grew up, they became tame.

One of the first animals to become the servant of humans was the dog. Sheep, goats, cattle, and pigs were other animals that were tamed.

When animals became tame, they furnished humans with a sure supply of food. People did not have to do so much hunting. They took

By building rafts and canoes, early people were able to travel on rivers and across lakes. Can you describe how people carried things when walking?

care of animals, and the tame beasts grew in number. When the mother animals produced milk, this too was used as food.

Herders and Shepherds

Certain groups lived entirely by tending and raising sheep, goats, and cattle. They lived on great, grassy plains where their flocks and herds could be driven from one good pasture to another. Because these herders and shepherds often changed their camps, they made shelters that were easily moved, such as tents. Some groups of people in Africa and Asia still follow this wandering life, moving their animals from pasture to pasture.

When humans began to raise animals, they increased the amount of food which they could get from a certain area. Because of the milk and meat which the herds gave, many more people could live by herding than by hunting.

The Importance of Crops

While people developed their skills of hunting and herding, they also began to use planting as a way of increasing their food supply. People began to plant seeds in fields about 8,400 years ago. They planted grains such as wheat and barley. These seeds, which we call cereals, could be used for bread. They also planted the seeds of vegetables such as cabbages, beans, and squash. People learned that by planting and raising crops, much food could be produced in a small amount of space. By farming and by raising cattle, many more people could make a living than by hunting animals.

The Beginning of Village Life

When people farm, they must remain in one place during the growing season. Hunters and herders can move about, but farmers cannot shift their growing crops from place to place.

Plant fibers or animal hair can be spun into thread. Threads are woven into cloth on looms. Farming and domestic animals were dependable sources for clothing.

Farmers must stay by their crops. By farming, a fairly large number of people can live in one neighborhood; so villages grew up near the fields.

Making Clothing

To clothe themselves, people in warm climates wrapped up in leaves or bark, woven or pressed together. In cold climates they dressed in furs. After a time people began to make leather from animal skins.

The Use of Leather

To make leather, people scraped the fat and hair from the skins of animals. Then the skins were rubbed with fat to make them soft. Changing raw skins into leather is called tanning. Raw skins decay easily, but leather does not.

Because leather is flexible, or easily bent, it could be pieced or sewn together to make clothing.

Sewing needles were made from long, sharp thorns or from pieces of wood or bone. Many polished Stone Age needles made of bone have been found. For thread the tendons of animals were often used. Tendons are tough white cords which join muscle to bone.

The Use of Flax

While some people hunted, others looked for plants with strong, threadlike parts, or fibers. Plants such as the blue-flowered flax and the tall, feathery hemp had very long and slender fibers. These fibers could be woven together into cloth.

Cloth made from flax is called linen. Cloth is much softer than leather, fits more closely to

Early farmers had to live in one place to care for their crops. Pottery became very important to store and cook grain. Clay pots were shaped and fired for strength.

the body, and does not get hard after being wet. Cloth is better in some climates. Leather and fur are better in other climates.

The Use of Wool

The long hair of animals could also be made into cloth. People twisted the hair of goats and camels and the wool of sheep into threads. Several threads could then be twisted into one long string of yarn. Making threads this way is called spinning.

The yarn was stretched from top to bottom over a simple frame called a loom. Then other threads or yarns were passed in and out, across these strands. This is called weaving. As the weavers worked, they pushed the threads closer together to make the cloth firm. If you examine the wire in a window screen, you will see how strands of material are criss-crossed in weaving. By spinning and weaving, people could make clothing, cloth coverings for beds, and woven coverings to spread on the ground.

Transporting Goods

In early times, just as today, people had to transport goods from one place to another. One way was to carry goods and *produce* (prō′do͞os), such as fruits and vegetables, on their heads. A second way of transporting goods was to make a rough sled for carrying them. Dogs and oxen were used to drag the sleds. After the wheel was invented, about 3300 B.C., carts and wagons were used.

Travel by Water

When it was necessary to travel by water, people used a floating log. To get a large, flat

Early people liked to decorate the walls of their caves with paintings. Cave artists made bright colors by mixing earth of different colors with oil. These pictures show a herd of bison and a deer hunt.

surface for carrying a bigger burden, they tied several logs together and made a raft. A raft could carry a number of people or a heavy load of goods. To make the kind of canoe we call a dugout, people hollowed out a log. Such a boat was faster and lighter than a raft. After the invention of the canoe, people could cross rivers and lakes. They could travel by water to places which once had been shut off to them.

The Beginning of Art

We know there were artists in early times because examples of their work have been found. People then liked to decorate their weapons, tools, and the walls of their caves.

Ancient caves have proved to be good places in which to find the drawings and carvings of early artists. The caves protected the people who lived in them. Long after the people vanished, articles and drawings left by them were preserved in the caves.

Early Paintings

In both Spain and France there are many caves that have been the scenes of exciting art discoveries. The pictures in these caves show us the animals that early people knew, such as deer and bison. The artists painted with different kinds of red and brown earth mixed with oil.

Pictures of early people also were drawn on the cave walls. One cave picture shows a battle with bows and arrows.

Pictures of animals may have been used as charms to bring good luck in hunting. For example, a hunter might draw a picture of a bison before going out to hunt. The picture may have meant that the artist hoped to kill such an animal that day.

Early Statues

Early artists also used clay to make little statues of men, women, and animals. One clay statue shows a bear with arrowheads thrust into it. The statue may have been made to celebrate the killing of a bear. Or it may have been a charm which the artist hoped would bring good hunting.

Art had an important place in the life of that long-ago, far-off time. By their drawings and carvings people in early times showed that they loved beauty.

Do You Know?

1. How do we know about how early people lived?
2. What was the Ice Age? How did people manage to live in the Ice Age?
3. What weapons did early people have? How did they improve these weapons?
4. Why did raising crops bring great changes to people's lives?

3 People on the Earth Today

There are more than 4 billion people on the planet earth. They live on six of the seven continents and on many islands as well. No two people on earth are exactly alike.

Culture

People all over the world have the same basic needs—for water, food, shelter, clothing. These needs are filled in hundreds of different ways. All people also need to learn how to live and act in their world. The ways people fill these needs are determined by the *culture* (kul′chər) of the group of people they live with. Culture is the learned behavior of a group of people. It is the way a group of people live, think, and act.

Many things make up a people's culture. *Customs* (kus′təmz) are social habits or ways of living of a group. People who live together for a long time come to do things in the same way. Giving presents to friends on their birthdays is a custom for most of us.

Some ways of behaving become so fixed that they become *laws* (lôz). Laws are rules of social conduct made by the leaders of a group. Important leaders of a group or elected officials may make laws. People who do not do as the law

People around the world do the same things, but they may do them differently. Shown are three ways of greeting people, used in American, Japanese, and Nigerian *cultures*.

tells them to may be punished. When people live together in an orderly way, obeying laws, they are said to live under a *government* (guv′ərn mənt).

Everything you do in the course of a day is affected by the culture you live in—the kind of food you eat and the way it is prepared, the kind of clothes you wear, the kind of school you go to, the language you speak, the way you greet others. Things that seem natural to you may not be natural for people in other cultures. For example, when you talk to people, do you look them straight in the eye? In our culture this is a common thing to do. But in some cultures, looking a person straight in the eye is considered rude.

Culture is so basic that most of the time we take it for granted. Our beliefs, the way we live, and what we eat are not things that we think about every day. Usually it is only when we see how people of other cultures do these things that we pay much attention to them.

Western Culture

Most Americans can trace their beginnings back to many different lands. But American culture today is part of a larger culture that is shared by the countries of Western Europe and the countries of North and South America. Because it spread out from Western Europe, this culture is often called "Western culture."

As you will read later, scientists and historians trace the beginnings of Western culture back to ancient times, to the Near East and to ancient Greece and Rome. Then it spread to other parts of Europe. Europeans brought it to America. And Americans and others have brought it to other parts of the world.

Non-Western Cultures

Where do people who do not share Western culture live? For one thing, wherever there are people there are cultures—ways of doing things. People with non-Western cultures live in many parts of the world, including parts of the United States. Here some American Indian tribes still follow their own ways of living. They have adopted some Western ways of living, but still have their own cultures.

In Africa, Asia, and in parts of South America, there are many other cultures. Some of these go back thousands of years.

In some parts of the world there are groups of people who follow simple ways of life that have not changed for many years. These tribes or small groups have had little contact with modern ways of living until very recently.

Values

Highly prized ideas called values are an important part of every culture. Values are ideas about what is right and wrong, about what is important in people's lives. Western culture values the individual. Individual rights are protected. Many of our laws and customs are designed to help people become the kind of individuals they want to be.

Some cultures are not so concerned with the individual. To them the group is more important. Their laws and customs protect the group, not the individual.

Family

The family is the most important group in almost every culture. Every family is, of course, different. But there are many similarities. Americans tend to live in nuclear families. That means that one or both parents and their children live together in one dwelling.

Some Americans, though, may live in extended families. That means grandparents, aunts, uncles, and cousins may live as a family unit. The extended family is the usual family unit in some cultures. In these societies, elderly people are treated with great respect. In American society, elderly people are respected too.

Learning

In most cultures, children are first taught by their parents. But the Western world is very complicated. There are many things to learn. You will also go to school for many years. In order for you to live in your world, you will have to learn about many different things.

You will study the history of your country and the world. You will study mathematics and science. You will read stories and write essays.

Learning how to read and write is not important in all cultures. In some cultures, children don't learn to read or write. But they do not grow up ignorant. They may learn to fish or hunt or to weave cloth. They learn what they need to know to live in their world.

Two Kinds of Knowledge

You need to know how to count and how to read and write. If you couldn't write, count, or read signs, you would have a difficult time.

A young member of the Arunta tribe can do none of those things. But an Arunta can do many things you probably do not know how to do. Aruntas live in the desert of central Australia. The young Aruntas learn how to track wild animals. They learn how to find water in the desert. These things are important for the Arunta child to know.

Who is smarter, you or the Arunta child? The answer, of course, is neither of you. Both of you know what is important for your world. Neither kind of knowledge is better than the other. They are just different. Each kind of knowledge is essential for the culture in which the person lives.

Homes

People of every culture build their living places according to where they live. In big cities, people work and live in skyscrapers. In more open areas, many Americans live in one-story ranch houses.

Climate also is important in home building. In warm areas, people build open, airy houses. In areas of heavy snow, people may build houses with steep roofs so that the snow can slide off.

How people make their living is also important. The Bedouins (bed'o͞o inz) are Arab tribes who live in North Africa and the Middle East. Some Bedouins move their herds of camels or sheep all year long from one pasture to another. When they are on the move they live in tents. These are made of wooden or cane frames covered with cloth. The tents are easily taken down, moved, and set up again.

Other Bedouins live in one place all year long. They build more permanent houses out of stone or brick. In both cases, their houses fit the ways they live.

Art

Every culture in the world has some kind of art. Art is one way people express their feelings about life. Art takes many forms. It may be painting, music, dancing, sculpture, stories, or poems. Art is an important way humans express themselves. Art is a celebration of life. It is part of being human.

The Unknown

Human cultures deal with more than the practical world. They also deal with things that are not explained. In western culture, science explains many things about our world. Scientists study life, matter, time. Scientists study weather. They study and cure some diseases. Practical scientists, called engineers, invent machines that make our lives easier.

Science can explain many things that are difficult to understand. But there are other things science cannot explain. For example, science cannot tell us the meaning of life or the

Culture is reflected in art. The Chinese painting on the right and the French painting on the left both portray a mountain scene, but they are strikingly different from each other.

best way to live it.

Almost every culture relies on religion to live in the world. Religion is the way people deal with that which cannot be explained. Religion comforts people and gives meaning to their lives.

There are many different religions. The religions of Western cultures worship one god. Some religions in other parts of the world worship God in several forms.

In earlier times, many people felt that their particular religion was the only one that was right. Some people still feel that way. Wars have been fought over religious beliefs.

The Human Family

The story of humanity is like a rich mixture of many colors. There is great variety among the peoples of the world. No one culture is better than another. They are simply different.

Today, more than ever, it is important for all people to understand one another. The world has grown smaller. Modern communication and inventions have left few people anywhere who do not have contact with other people.

Western science has helped solve many problems. But it has created some problems too. Preventing pollution and war are most important problems. How to feed the world's growing population is another problem. These problems involve all life on earth. Their solution needs the help of everybody.

Today, more than ever, it is important for all people in all nations of the world to recognize their membership in the human family to which we all belong.

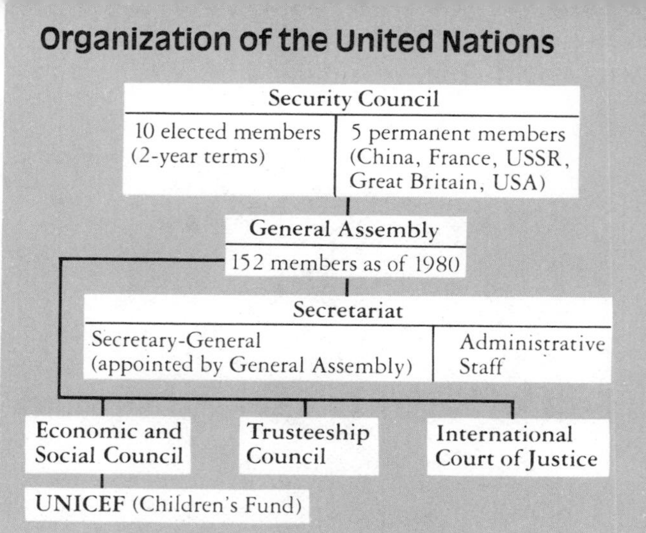

The United Nations building is in New York City. It is the large, rectangular building in the left foreground. The chart shows how the United Nations is organized.

The United Nations

Several different groups have been formed to work together for peace and cooperation among nations. One of these is the United Nations. It was organized in 1945, the year that World War II ended. Membership is open to all peace-loving nations. The United Nations gives member nations a chance to discuss their problems and work them out peacefully. Its headquarters is in New York City. All the member nations send representatives to meetings there.

The largest body in the United Nations is the General Assembly. In 1980 it was made up of representatives of 152 nations. The General Assembly studies and discusses the problems brought before it. The Assembly also watches over the work of many smaller committees (see the diagram on this page).

The most important body of the UN is the Security Council. It is made up of the representatives of 15 nations. Ten countries are elected by the General Assembly for two-year terms. Five other countries are permanent members of the Security Council. They are the United States, Great Britain, the Soviet Union, France, and China. These five nations were world leaders at the end of World War II when the UN was first formed. The five permanent members have the right to overrule a proposal in the Council.

The United Nations has a special council that works to improve the ways people live. It encourages higher standards of living, educational cooperation among nations, and protection of human rights.

Do You Know ?

1. What is culture? How do you get it?
2. Do children all over the world learn the same things? Why not?
3. What is the United Nations? What is its purpose? How many nations belong to it?

To Help You Learn

Using New Words

culture	government
custom	hemisphere
flint	equator
glacier	climate
law	produce

Number a paper from 1 through 10. After each number write the word or term that matches the definition.

1. A rule for social conduct made by the leaders of a group
2. A hard stone with sharp edges used to make weapons and to strike fire
3. A plan under which people live together in an orderly way, obeying laws
4. A social habit that people living together have followed for a long time
5. A great sheet of ice
6. Learned behavior of a group of people
7. The weather of a certain place over many years
8. Half of the globe
9. An imaginary line circling the earth midway between the North and South Poles
10. Farm products, such as fruits and vegetables

Finding the Facts

1. In what ways did the discovery of fire help humans?
2. In early times many animals were larger, stronger, or could run faster than humans could. What ability did humans have that enabled them to outwit the animals?
3. Name three animals that early humans hunted. Name three that were tamed.
4. How do we know there were artists among the early people who lived before the days of written records?
5. Name three things that people do in everyday life that reflect their culture.

Learning from Maps

1. Maps use signs or symbols to show the earth's natural features, such as mountains, hills, and rivers. The drawing below shows pictures of these natural features. Turn to the map of the world on pages 22–23 and find these natural features. The drawing below also shows some artificial or constructed features. Name these. Which would not be shown on the physical world map?

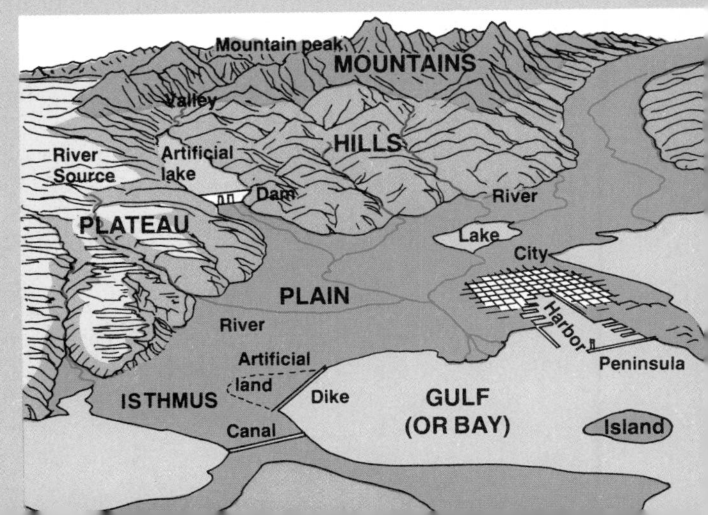

2. Turn to the map showing world population on page 26. What continents have areas where there are more than 250 people per square mile? What continents have areas of fewer than 25 people per square mile?
3. Turn to the map showing world rainfall on page 26. Name three regions that have 40 or more inches of rain a year. Name three that have less than 10 inches a year.
4. Turn to the map showing world vegetation on page 27. Name three regions where tropical forests grow. On what continents do you find deserts? Tundra?
5. Look at the map of the Eastern Hemisphere in the Ice Age on page 29. Which continents had large areas of ice covering them? Which continents did not?
6. As they moved southward, the glaciers wore down the tops of mountains, carrying rocks and soil with them. When the ice and snow melted, water filled the hollow places. These became lakes. Find some of these in North America on the map on page 22 – 23. What are these lakes called today?

Using Study Skills

1. **Time Line:** A time line helps us to understand history. It is a device on which events are arranged in the order in which they happened. Place the following events in the proper order of time: Accurate measurement of the circumference of the earth; exploration of the sea floor; first satellite sent into orbit; founding of the United Nations.

   Copy down the time line on page 11. Add these new events to your time line. Study the completed time line and answer the following questions: How many years did it take between sailing around the world and measuring the circumference of the earth? Between using the wheel and landing on the moon?
2. **Chart:** Look at the chart of the United Nations on page 42. Who appoints the Secretary General? Which nations are always represented on the Security Council? What council oversees the work of UNICEF?
3. **Diagram:** Look at the diagram of how altitude affects crops in tropical lands on page 20. At what altitude range would you find coffee? Which of the following crops would you find between 7,000 and 10,000 feet: rubber, sugar, hay, coffee, bananas, potatoes, barley?

Thinking It Through

1. Why are some areas of the world less populated than others? What part does climate play in influencing where people live?
2. In this unit you learned how early humans lived. What would people today have to learn to survive under such conditions?
3. Lightning may have helped early people discover fire. Lightning also helped an American, Benjamin Franklin, make a discovery about electricity. How has human life changed since electricity has been put to use?

4. In this unit you learned how early people solved problems such as making weapons, using fire, and transporting goods. What kinds of problems are people trying to solve today? Name several.

Projects

1. Perhaps you would find it interesting to form a social studies club. If so, have a meeting of your class. At the meeting choose a leader, or president. Choose a secretary to keep the minutes—that is, to write down what is done at the meetings.

   Every club must have committees to do its work. A committee is made up of several members who do one kind of work. Each committee has a leader, called a chairperson.

   Each committee should meet with its chairperson to plan its work. It should decide what each member is to find out and when meetings are to be held to check up on progress. When they have finished their work, the committees should report to the whole class and be prepared to answer questions.

   One group of pupils might like to belong to an Explorers' Committee to find out more about little-known parts of the world. This committee might learn how different explorers made a race to the South Pole, in Antarctica. They might also trace the explorers' routes on a map.

   Some pupils might like to belong to a Research Committee to learn more about history. History is the story of people and events of the past. The Research Committee might like to find information about scientists such as Ruth Benedict who study other cultures.

   Still other pupils might form a Reading Committee. Its members would find interesting books to read and share with the class. The books may be stories about people who lived long ago or about people who live now.

2. Take a sheet of construction paper. Cut down the long way of the paper, making 8 strips, each one inch (2.5 cm) wide, but stop cutting one inch (2.5 cm) before you reach the end of the paper. Now take a second sheet of paper and cut all the way down its length, making 8 strips, each one-inch wide. Arrange the cut strips over the strips still attached to the paper. Take care that if the first strip began *over,* the second strip should begin *under*. You have just made a weaving. How can the woven paper be made into a basket? (You may have to cut free the ends still attached to the paper.) The class may wish to discuss how baskets and woven cloth are alike. Does this suggest early people may have learned to make one from the other?

2 The Countries of the Middle East

Unit Preview

The Middle East is where much of European and Western civilization began. Most of the region is hot and dry, but there is fertile land in the river valleys. People built the first cities in these valleys. Later, explorers set forth by ship from the cities of the Middle East, sailing to distant lands.

Humankind's great adventures with the wheel, with law, and with writing also began in the Middle East. Early people in this region observed the stars and the movement of the sun, moon, and planets. They developed an alphabet and number system. They learned how to work with metals.

The people of the Middle East, especially the ancient Egyptians, learned to build with stone and clay. The pyramids of Egypt, one of which is as tall as a 40-story building, were built as tombs for Egypt's rulers. Paintings and objects inside the pyramids reveal much about early ways of living in Egypt.

The Middle East is the region where the Jewish, Christian, and Muslim faiths had their beginnings. The ideas and arts of Middle Eastern civilizations were spread far and wide by explorers, traders, and warriors.

Today, the petroleum resources of the Middle East are in great demand. Refining and transporting oil are important industries. Pipelines carry the oil to coastal cities. From there it is shipped to other countries.

Things to Discover

If you look carefully at the picture, map, and time line on these pages, you can answer these questions.

1. On which continent is most of the Middle East located? Part of this region is on what other continent?
2. Which ocean borders the area?
3. When the Great Pyramid was built, which people were able to write about it?
4. How many years passed between the founding of the ancient Hebrew Kingdom of Israel and the new nation of Israel?
5. How does the picture show that the modern and the traditional exist side by side in the Middle East?

Words to Learn

You will meet these words in this unit. As you read, you will learn what they mean and how to pronounce them. The Word List will help you.

aqueduct	mandate
bazaar	Mediterranean climate
caravan	minaret
census	mosque
city-state	nomad
civilization	oasis
cuneiform	prophet
delta	refugee
empire	regent
Holocaust	republic

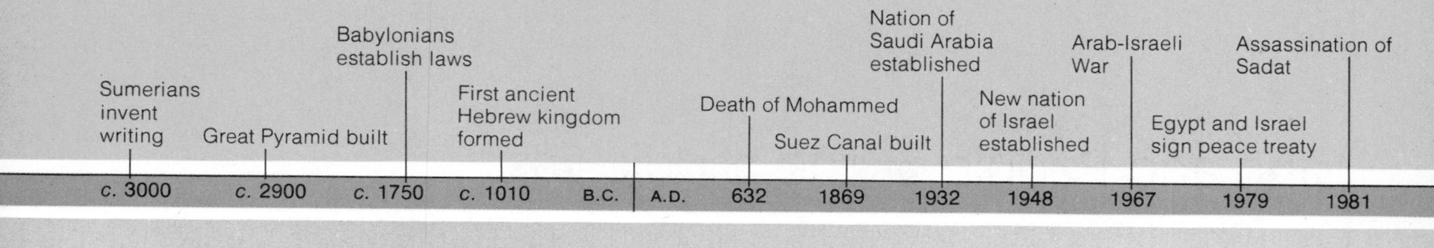

Arctic Ocean
Atlantic Ocean
EUROPE
ASIA
AFRICA
Pacific Ocean
Indian Ocean
AUSTRALIA

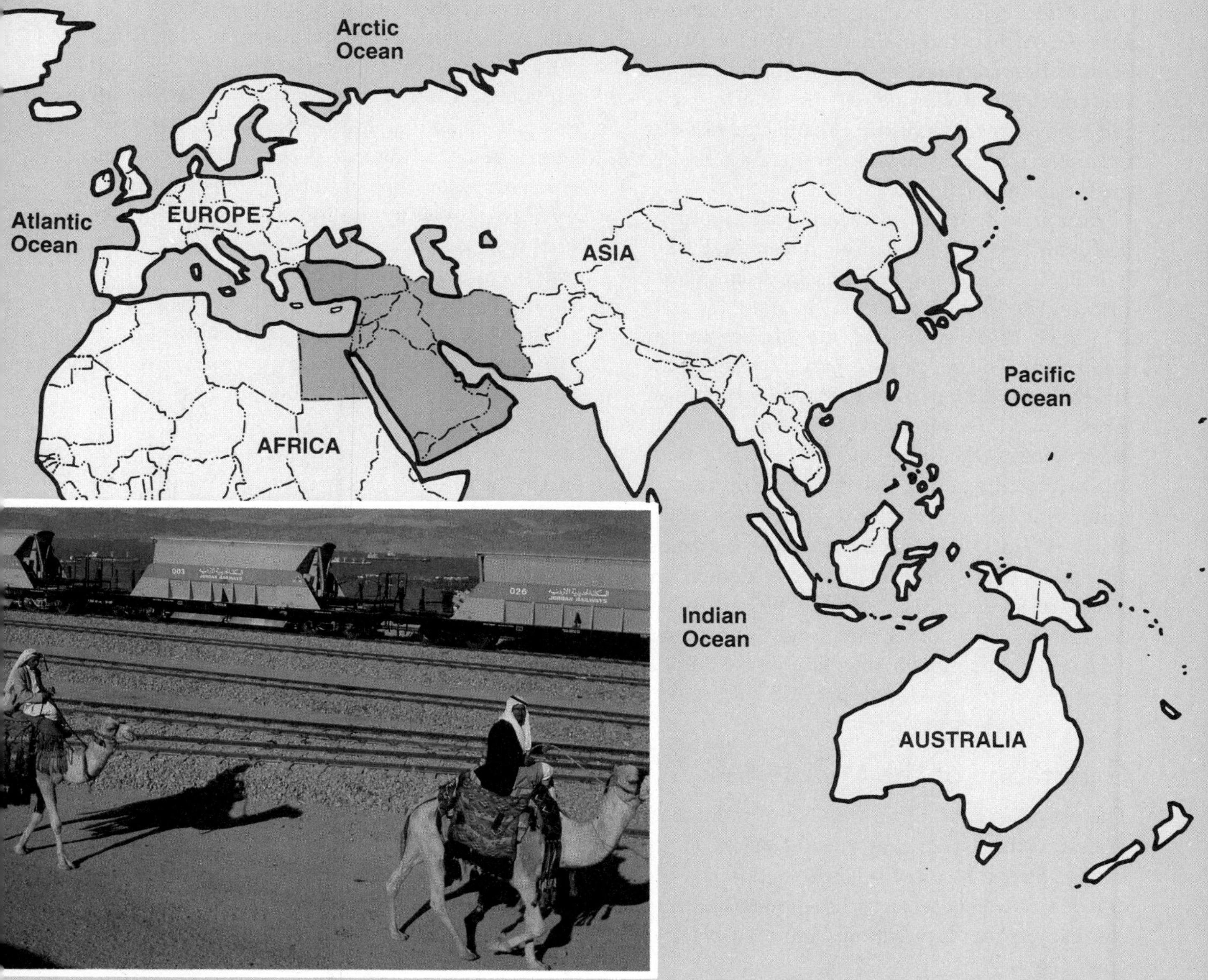

1

Land and People of the Middle East

The Middle East lies on three continents—Europe, Africa, and Asia. See the map of the Middle East on page 49. To the northwest are the countries of Europe. To the southwest lie the sands and rocks of the Sahara, the vast desert in North Africa. Beyond, to the East, are the great cultures of Asia.

Although Egypt is on the African continent, it is a Middle Eastern nation. A part of Turkey is in Europe and the rest lies in Asia. All the rest of the Middle East is in Asia. Stretching down the east side of the Mediterranean (med′ə tə rā′ nē ən) Sea are Syria, Lebanon, and Israel. Behind them to the east are Jordan, Iraq (i rak′), and Iran. Most of the Arabian Peninsula is occupied by Saudi Arabia (sä o͞o′dē ə rā′bē ə), but on its edge along the Persian Gulf are the nations of Kuwait (kə wāt′), Bahrain (bä rān′), Qatar (kä′tər), United Arab Emirates (ə mēr′ əts), and Oman. On the south are Yemen and Southern Yemen. The island of Cyprus, the African country of Sudan, and Afghanistan (af gan′ə stan), though they adjoin the Middle East, are not considered part of this region.

Geography of the Middle East

The Middle East covers an area more than three-fourths as large as the 50 states of the United States. Most of this vast region is a hot, dry desert which receives little rain. The traveler can go for days without seeing a blade of grass.

Here and there are a few well-watered river valleys. One fertile valley is along the Nile River in Egypt. Another is along the Tigris (tī′gris) and Euphrates (yo͞o frā′tēz) rivers in Iraq. Mountains and plateaus cover much of Turkey and Iran. There are also mountains on the southern and western coasts of the Arabian Peninsula.

A belt of well-watered lowland curves northward from the head of the Persian Gulf to the eastern end of the Mediterranean Sea. This curved, or crescent-shaped, belt of fertile land is called the Fertile Crescent (furt′əl kres′ənt). Trace the Fertile Crescent on the map on page 70.

The Fertile Crescent is like a broad road between the desert on one side and the mountains on the other. Its soil is rich and well watered. Far back in history cities grew up along it. Armies marched over it. Camels carrying goods traveled its length. The world has profited by the exchange of both ideas and goods at this meeting place in times past.

Resources of the Middle East

The natural resource most needed by the Middle East is water. One abundant resource in some parts of the Middle East is petroleum, or oil. Iran, Iraq, and the lands of the Arabian Peninsula have rich deposits of petroleum. Scientists estimate that about half of the world's petroleum is located in this region. The pumping, refining, and transporting of oil make up the most important industry.

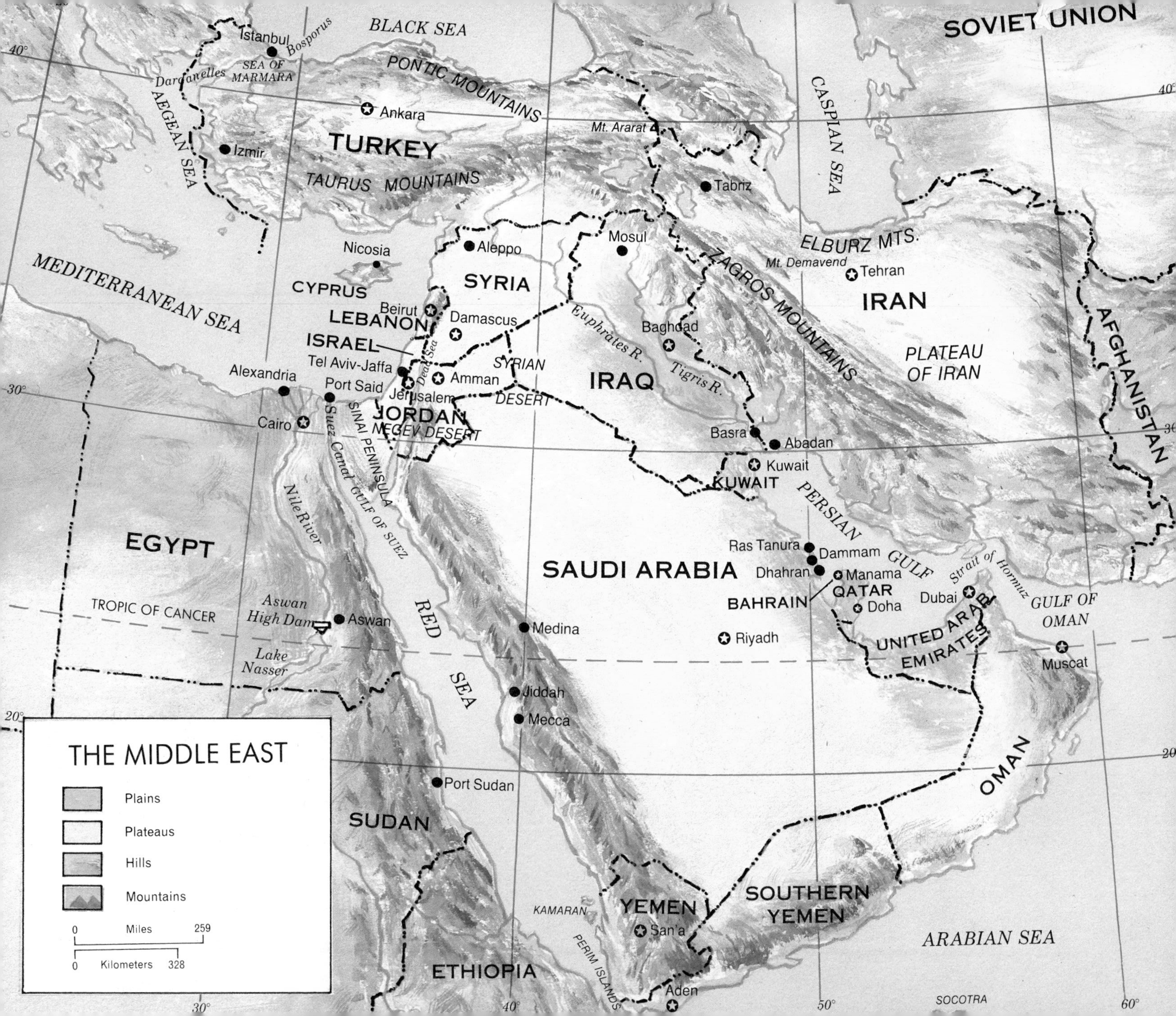
THE MIDDLE EAST
Plains
Plateaus
Hills
Mountains
0 Miles 259
0 Kilometers 328
SOVIET UNION
BLACK SEA
Istanbul
Bosporus
SEA OF MARMARA
Dardanelles
AEGEAN SEA
PONTIC MOUNTAINS
Ankara
TURKEY
Izmir
TAURUS MOUNTAINS
Mt. Ararat
CASPIAN SEA
Tabriz
ELBURZ MTS.
Mt. Demavend
Tehran
IRAN
ZAGROS MOUNTAINS
PLATEAU OF IRAN
AFGHANISTAN
MEDITERRANEAN SEA
Nicosia
CYPRUS
Aleppo
SYRIA
Mosul
Beirut
LEBANON
Damascus
ISRAEL
Tel Aviv-Jaffa
Dead Sea
Amman
Jerusalem
JORDAN
NEGEV DESERT
SYRIAN DESERT
Euphrates R.
Baghdad
Tigris R.
IRAQ
Alexandria
Port Said
Cairo
Suez Canal
SINAI PENINSULA
GULF OF SUEZ
Nile River
Basra
Abadan
Kuwait
KUWAIT
PERSIAN GULF
EGYPT
Ras Tanura
Dammam
Dhahran
Manama
SAUDI ARABIA
BAHRAIN
QATAR
Doha
Strait of Hormuz
Dubai
GULF OF OMAN
TROPIC OF CANCER
Aswan High Dam
Aswan
Lake Nasser
Medina
RED SEA
Riyadh
UNITED ARAB EMIRATES
Muscat
Jiddah
Mecca
OMAN
Port Sudan
SUDAN
SOUTHERN YEMEN
YEMEN
KAMARAN
San'a
PERIM ISLANDS
ARABIAN SEA
ETHIOPIA
Aden
SOCOTRA
40°
30°
20°
50°
60°

The Mediterranean Climate

Although most of the land in the Middle East has a subtropical climate, the areas along the Mediterranean Sea have rainy winters, cool but not cold. Summers are hot and almost rainless. This is called the *Mediterranean climate* (med′ə tə rā′ nē ən klī′ mit). If you think of the climate in southern California, you will know what grows well in these areas. Oranges, lemons, olives, figs, and prunes are plentiful.

In spring these Mediterranean regions have many colorful flowers. In summer the hills are bare and brown, with dusty soil. These are lands where there are more sheep and goats than cattle. The lowlands are fine pasture lands in winter and spring, but the animals must go up into the mountains in summer to find grass.

People of the Middle East

The countries of the Middle East have more than 170 million people. Because so much of the land is too dry to be farmed, large areas have few inhabitants. The population is densest in river valleys, in cities, and near oil fields.

Followers of Mohammed

Most of the people of the Middle East are Arabs. The Arabic language is spoken in most of the countries. The people of these countries share many of the same ways of living.

In their religious beliefs nearly all of the people are Muslims. Muslims are followers of a leader named Mohammed (mō ham′ id). Their sacred book is the Koran (kô ran′). The Koran says, "There is only one God, Allah, and Mohammed is his *prophet*" (prof′ it). A prophet is one who speaks for God.

Mohammed was born about the year 570, in Arabia. Find Arabia on the map of the Middle East on page 49. To Arabs, who then worshipped idols, he preached the religion of one God. Many believed that Mohammed was a true prophet and accepted his teachings. Mohammed died in 632. Two years later his followers began a "holy war." They set out to win the peoples of the world for the Muslim faith, spreading their religion by using the sword. The Arabs conquered many lands before they gave up this effort.

The religious beliefs of Christians, Jews, and Muslims all had their beginnings in this region. Today the only countries in the Middle East where most of the people are not Muslims are Lebanon and Israel. About half of the people of Lebanon are Christians. Most people of Israel are Jews.

Importance of the Middle East

The Middle East is important to the world because it is on the crossroads where Europe, Africa, and Asia meet. The shortest sea route between most places in Europe and the Far East passes through the Suez Canal. Find this canal on the map of the Middle East on page 49. Without the Suez Canal ships would have to sail around Africa when traveling between western Europe and the Far East. Even so, some tankers are too large for the canal. Land and air routes also pass through the area.

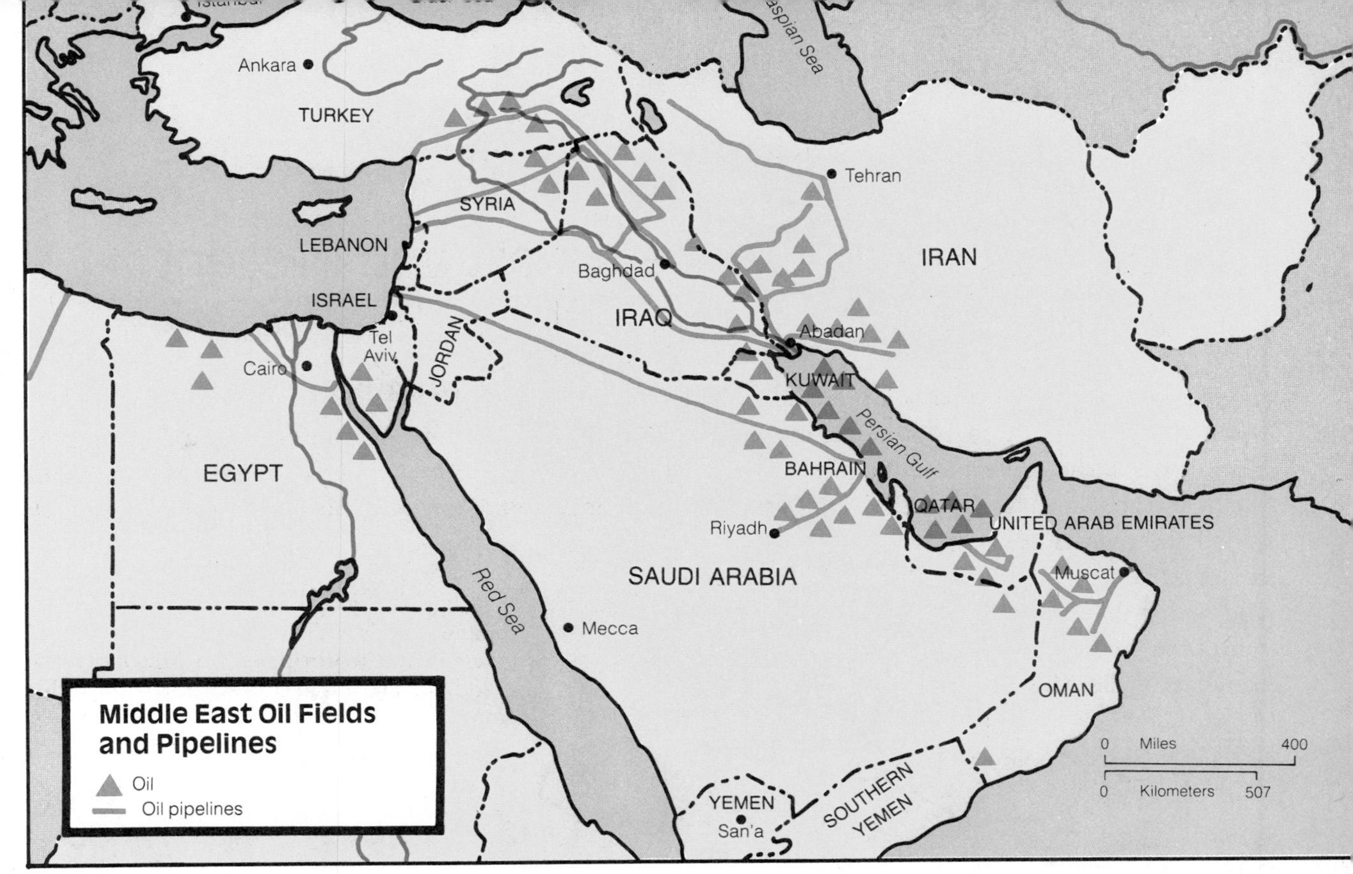

Countries of the Middle East supply much of the world with oil. This valuable fuel is carried from oil fields to ports in pipelines that extend across the desert. Which country has the most oil fields?

The Middle East is important also because it furnishes much of the oil that the world needs. Western Europe and the United States get most of their oil from this region. Without the oil from the Arabian Peninsula, the world would have a hard time meeting its needs.

We are also interested in the Middle East because of its long and interesting history. The Middle East was the home of early *civilizations* (siv′ə li zā′shənz). Civilizations are large groups of people that form an orderly society. Civilizations have laws, government, and usually writing. For all of these reasons it is important that we learn about the Middle East.

Do You Know?

1. Where is the Middle East?
2. What natural resource does this region lack? Which resource is abundant?
3. How many people live in the Middle East? What are their religions?
4. Why is this region of interest to us?
5. Why did Muslims fight a "holy war"?

2

The Land of the Twin Rivers, Past and Present

To the west of the Caspian Sea is a land of high mountains. From these mountains two rivers flow toward the Persian Gulf. They flow so much in the same direction that they are often called the twin rivers. One river is the Euphrates. The other river is the Tigris. It is shorter and wider than the Euphrates. Find the mountains, the two rivers, and the Persian Gulf on the map of the Middle East on page 49.

Ancient Mesopotamia

In ancient times the country through which the two rivers flowed was called Mesopotamia (mes′ə pə tā′ mē ə). This name means "the land between the rivers."

Some people believe that the first *civilizations* in the world began in Mesopotamia. Find the Tigris and Euphrates rivers on this map.

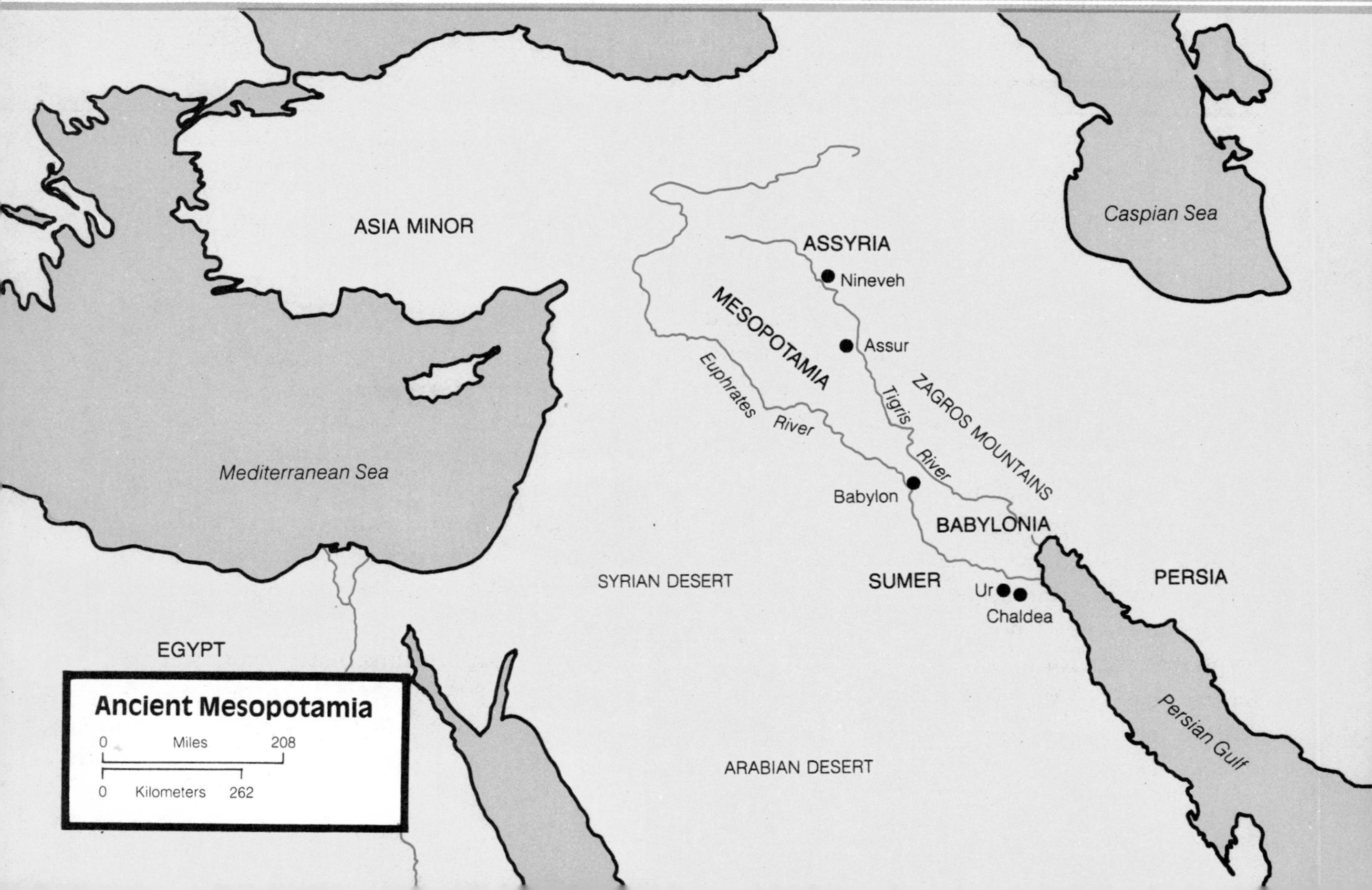

At one time the twin rivers flowed into the Persian Gulf some distance apart. Now they have united about 100 miles (160 km) from the gulf to form one stream. They bring down so much mud that the gulf is filling in at the rate of one mile (1.6 km) every 50 or 60 years.

The Sumerians in Mesopotamia

The earliest people of Mesopotamia lived in villages on the low ground near the mouths of the twin rivers. They were known as the Sumerians (sōō mer′ē ənz).

How the Sumerians Farmed

The Sumerians found that the new land could grow enough food to support them if they learned to work with nature. They dug many canals along the river to carry water to dry areas. The canals also drained marshy land near the river. The Sumerians then drained and farmed the land.

Cities and Government

As their population grew, the Sumerians built more settlements farther north along the Euphrates. Around Sumerian cities were high brick walls made of dried clay.

Over each city ruled a chief, who was both priest and ruler. Some of these chiefs grew so strong that they extended their rule over the land which surrounded their cities. We call a city of this kind a *city-state* (sit′ē stāt′).

The leading city-state was Ur. The most famous king of Ur was Ur-Nammu. He is chiefly remembered for the good laws and law courts that he gave his people.

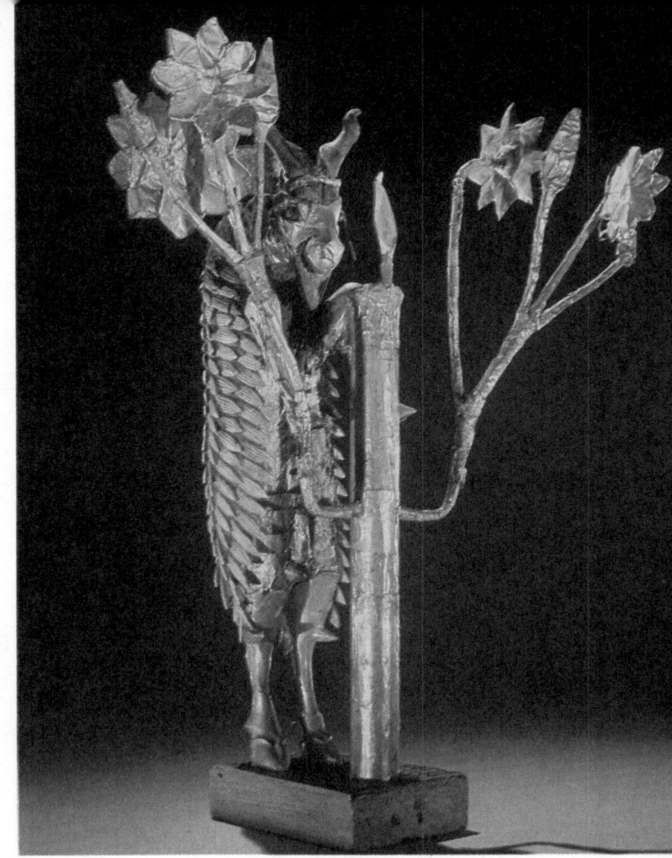

This golden goat, found in a grave at Ur, and the flowering tree he leans upon is made of wood overlaid with gold.

How the Sumerians Used Metals

Not all the people were needed to farm the land and raise food. So some of the Sumerians became skilled in the use of metals. They learned to work with copper and to mix copper and tin to make bronze. They also made many beautiful figures of gold and silver.

Sumerian troops wore armor made of bronze and carried spears with bronze tips. Their metal armor and spears helped them win battles. They locked their shields together and pushed forward, with their spears forming a bristling mass.

One of the Sumerians' greatest achievements was the invention of *cuneiform* writing. Wedge-shaped symbols were pressed into wet clay.

How the Sumerians Used Clay

Southern Mesopotamia had little stone, but clay was plentiful. The Sumerians built their houses of clay bricks which had been dried in the sun. They also used clay to make pottery. They shaped their pottery on a wheel and baked it in an oven. Even their writing tablets were made of clay.

Sumerian Ways of Writing

By 3000 B.C. the Sumerians had invented a system of writing. The people who wrote were called scribes. They wrote with short wooden sticks or with strong plant stems. The writing stick, or stylus (stī′ləs), had a sharp edge. A scribe pressed the stylus into a tablet of wet clay, making wedge-shaped symbols. Such writing is called *cuneiform* (kyo͞o nē′ə fôrm′).

The clay tablet was then baked. In the baking, the tablet hardened. If a message was long, several tablets were used. The clay tablets were heavy to carry. But paper had not yet been invented. These tablets lasted a long time, though. Many may be seen today.

The Sumerians never made an alphabet. The cuneiform symbols stood for syllables, which were combined to make words. There were several hundred of these syllables. Learning to read and write was difficult for Sumerians.

Sumerian Ways of Counting

The Sumerians counted by 60s. In some ways this is a convenient way to count. As you may prove for yourself, 60 can be divided evenly by a good many numbers. When we count 60 minutes to an hour, we are following the example of the Sumerians.

The Trading Babylonians

One of the city-states on the Euphrates River was the city of Babylon (bab′ə lən). Babylon was about 150 miles (240 km) north of Ur.

A Famous King

The kingdom of Babylonia had a number of powerful rulers. Hammurabi (hä′moo rä′bē), its greatest king, came to the throne in about 1750 B.C. Hammurabi brought most of the city-states to the south under his rule. Southern Mesopotamia became known as Babylonia. See the map of Ancient Mesopotamia on page 52.

Hammurabi was a fighter and a conqueror. But he was proud of the ways in which he made life better for his people. "With pasturage and water I provided them and settled them in peaceful dwellings," he said.

The Laws of Hammurabi

Hammurabi was the first ruler to give his people a complete set of written laws. Some of the punishments for crime were severe. But even today most of the laws seem just.

In the dry region of Babylonia, the life of the people depended on getting enough water for crops and pasture for animals. Many laws of Hammurabi had to do with the use of land and irrigation. Hammurabi had his laws engraved on pillars of hard black stone. The pillars were set up in different parts of the kingdom. One of the pillars has been found. It contains almost 300 laws. Everyone who could read knew the law and could tell others about it.

Business in Babylonia

The Babylonians spent most of their time at such tasks as farming and building. But Babylon, the capital of the kingdom, grew to be a great trading city. It had tall buildings and palm-shaded gardens.

The Babylonians produced so much grain and wool, and so many dates and leather goods that they began trading with neighboring peoples. Donkeys carried the goods to the West. They brought back products from far places. Boats loaded with cargo moved along the many irrigation canals.

The Babylonians carried on business in some of the ways we use today. Merchants drew up agreements which were stamped with government seals. Seals were also used on letters and on bales of goods. The seals could not be broken without it being known that the messages and packages had been opened unlawfully. Businesspeople sent bills to those people who owed them money. Some merchants lent money and borrowers paid fees to use it.

Hammurabi was the first ruler to give his people written laws. They were written in *cuneiform* on stone pillars. Only one pillar has been found. It shows Hammurabi standing before a sun-god.

Married women had the right to own property and to engage in business. Thus Babylonian women enjoyed many rights that women in some countries do not have today.

The Assyrians

While Babylonians were busily trading, another nation grew up a few hundred miles to the north. From the town of Assur (ä′soor), their capital, the people came to be called Assyrians (ə sir′ē ənz). The Assyrians took on many ways of the Babylonians.

The War Methods of Assyria

Unfortunately for their neighbors the Assyrians decided they would become the masters of their world. As a help in making this come about, they used iron, a metal little known up to this time. The Sumerians had used bronze. Bronze is easy to form, but it is not as hard as iron. The Assyrians built war chariots of iron and used horses to pull them. Their troops were armed with iron-headed spears and iron swords. They won victory after victory.

When their foes shut themselves up in walled cities, the Assyrians used a tower on wheels with soldiers shooting arrows from the top. The tower was pushed up to the walls of the city. While soldiers shot arrows at the defenders of the wall, others inside the tower worked a battering ram. The battering ram hit the wall with such force that it made an opening in the wall. Through this opening the attackers rushed in and captured the city.

The Assyrians warred against many neighboring lands and brought them together into an *empire* (em′ pīr). An empire is a government that holds power over many countries.

Finally, the Assyrians conquered Babylon and destroyed it. They built a new capital, called Nineveh (nin′ ə və), on the Tigris River. Here they brought the riches they had seized. Nineveh became prosperous.

To supply Nineveh with water, one king built a broad stone *aqueduct* (ak′ wə dukt′) across a valley which was 1,000 feet (300 m) wide. An aqueduct is a pipe or channel used to carry water long distances. This is the oldest city aqueduct known.

To keep in touch with the different parts of his land, one Assyrian ruler built roads. Over the roads, he sent messengers to the different parts of his empire. This was an early kind of postal service.

The Fall of Assyria

But the Assyrians overlooked an important fact. They were using too many resources to arm their troops for battle. Too many workers were

Flanked by archers, a king of Assyria uses a battering ram to attack a walled city. Notice how some of the bricks are beginning to fall. How did action like this help to build an *empire*?

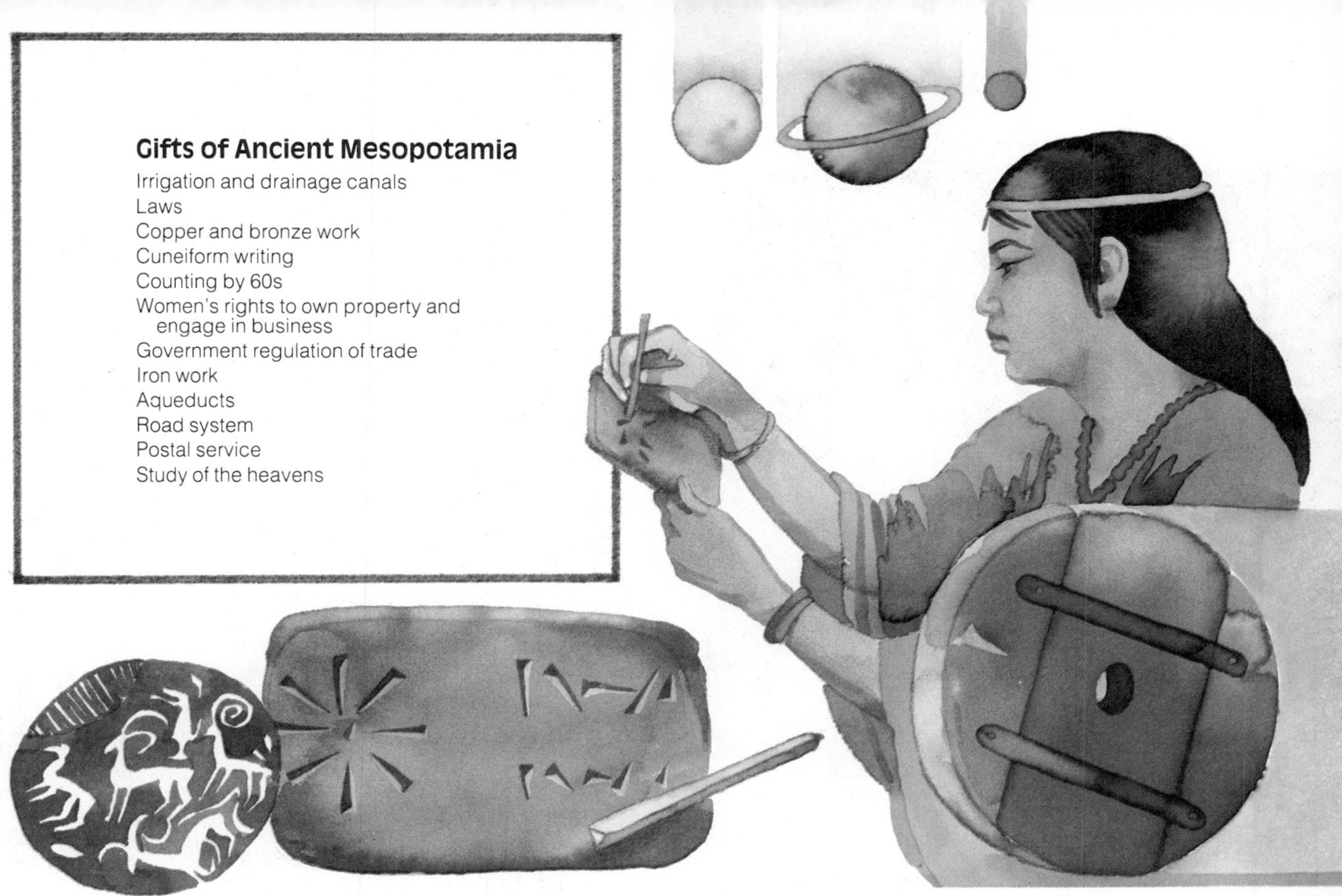

Gifts of Ancient Mesopotamia

Irrigation and drainage canals
Laws
Copper and bronze work
Cuneiform writing
Counting by 60s
Women's rights to own property and engage in business
Government regulation of trade
Iron work
Aqueducts
Road system
Postal service
Study of the heavens

fighting instead of working. Busy with war, the people neglected farming and trade. Assyria lost so many people in battle that it grew weak.

After a time other countries joined together to attack Assyria. Nineveh was destroyed and the Assyrians defeated.

The Empire of the Chaldeans

Later on the city of Babylon, destroyed by the Assyrians, rose again. The city was rebuilt by the Chaldeans (kal dē′ ənz), a new people who settled in the area. The Chaldeans came from lands to the south. Their king, Nebuchadnezzar (neb′ ə kəd nez′ ər), decided that Babylon should outshine every other city.

The Babylon which rose again by the Euphrates measured 40 miles (64 km) around. Its walls were so thick that on top two chariots could easily pass each other. Babylon became the capital of the Chaldean Empire.

Nebuchadnezzar married a woman from the mountains. In the flat land of Chaldea she grew homesick. The king decided to build a roof garden for her. He had a number of platforms added to the roof of the palace. On the platforms, or terraces, were layers of earth in which flowers and trees were planted. Slaves pumped up the water which kept the gardens green. These high terraces looked like hanging gardens, and that is what they came to be called, the Hanging Gardens of Babylon.

The Chaldeans also were early observers of the heavens. They figured out the paths of the

Iraqi children must attend school from ages six to twelve. This Iraqi boy is learning arithmetic in a school near Basra.

sun, the moon, and the planets as they moved through the sky. They also recorded eclipses, or darkenings of the sun and moon.

The End of Chaldea

The kings who followed Nebuchadnezzar were not as strong as he had been. Chaldea was conquered, and the city of Babylon fell as Nineveh had fallen before it. The canals that had supplied water to the land of Chaldea had been neglected.

Iraq, a Desert Land

The country through which the twin rivers flow is now called Iraq. Iraq is somewhat larger than our state of New Mexico. As you can see by the map of the Middle East on page 49, much of Iraq lies outside the valleys of the Euphrates and Tigris rivers.

West of those rivers the desert stretches for 500 miles (800 km). Few people can live in that region. Even along the rivers there is little rain. The air is dry, and the heat is great. Wherever water does not actually touch the soil, the ground is baked hard and dry by the hot sun.

The soil of the Tigris-Euphrates Valley has been brought down by these two streams. It is very rich and needs only water to produce fine harvests.

Basra, Iraq's Seaport

Iraq's main seaport is Basra (bus′rə). If you know the story of Sinbad the Sailor, told in the *Arabian Nights,* you may recall that he sailed from Basra. Today Sinbad would be surprised to see that Basra is much farther from the Persian Gulf than it was in his day. Can you tell how this change came about?

Basra lies at the point where the two rivers meet. Ships must sail 75 miles (120 km) upstream to reach the city. Most of the goods that Iraq imports and exports pass through Basra.

Products of Iraq

Millions of date palms, watered by irrigation, surround Basra. Their clusters of yellow fruit hang heavily from the branches. Most of the imported dates eaten in the United States come from this region. In the Middle East, dates are an important food.

A date grove can produce much more food for human use than the same area planted in wheat. However, the people often raise wheat,

Mosques are a common sight in Iraq, where most of the people are Muslims. This gleaming *mosque* with its golden domes and *minarets* is in the city of Baghdad.

too, on the ground around the palm trees. The wheat grows and ripens during the mild, sunny winters.

Along the Tigris-Euphrates river, fields are supplied with water. Wheat, barley, rice, and cotton are grown on these irrigated lands.

The People of Iraq

Iraq has more than 12 million people. Large numbers of people live in cities. Almost all of the people of Iraq are Muslims. The buildings where Muslims pray and worship are *mosques* (mosks). All mosques have tall towers called *minarets* (min′ə rets′). From these minarets the people are called to worship. They pray in the mosques, or wherever they happen to be, five times a day.

In Iraq, the parents and their sons' families usually live together. The oldest man is expected to make the important decisions for the rest of the family. Girls and boys are brought up in different ways. Girls are taught household work. When they move outside their homes they usually cover their heads and sometimes their faces with scarves. Boys can expect to farm or work at a trade when they are older. Throughout Iraq groups of Bedouin (bed′o͞o in) Arabs pitch their tents near rivers. Bedouins are a desert people. They depend for their living on camels, donkeys, and goats. Their

Camels are well suited to travel across desert lands. Their padded feet move easily over rock and sand. Donkeys are sometimes used for short trips.

chief foods are dates, grain, and milk.

Many Bedouins do not stay long in one place but move about with their herds from winter pastures to summer pastures. Such people are called *nomads* (nō′madz). There are Bedouins in Israel, Jordan, and other countries of the Middle East.

The summer heat in most parts of Iraq reaches 100° F (38° C) or more day after day. People often build their mud-brick houses with thick walls which keep out much of the heat. At night, when the earth cools off, it is pleasant to sit on the flat roof under the stars.

Two Inland Cities

Iraq has two ancient inland cities that are still important. One is Baghdad (bag′dad), the capital. The other is Mosul (mō sōōl′), a city located near oil wells.

Baghdad, the Capital of Iraq

In the days of the Sumerians, a city stood near the place where Baghdad is today. Baghdad can trace its history back to those ancient times. Located in the Fertile Crescent, the city grew because of trade. In Baghdad travelers and merchants from the East met those from the West. There was lively bargaining in silks, furs, pearls, and other goods.

To make Baghdad a modern city, its rulers have opened some wide streets. But in Baghdad the sun is hot most of the year. So the people prefer narrow streets, which are cooler because they are shady.

As in most Middle East cities, there are also *bazaars* (bə zärz′). Bazaars are marketplaces or streets lined with shops with many kinds of goods for sale. There are separate streets for shoemakers, tailors, metal workers, dealers in vegetables and fruits, and so on. On these streets, covered with awnings, the shops are small, open stalls. In their shops the owners sit cross-legged on the floor with their goods displayed around them.

We might also see a *caravan* (kar′ ə van′) moving in from the desert. A caravan is a group of merchants or travelers who cross the desert together, using camels or trucks to carry them and their goods. One sound heard all day long in Baghdad is the tinkle of camel bells. Up and down the streets go lines of camels, pushing through the crowd. The camel is well suited to desert travel. Its big, padded feet move easily over hard rock and do not sink into deep sand. Its thick lips and mouth have no trouble with the thorny bushes of the desert on which it often has to feed. The camel stores fat in its hump, and thus can go without food for days at a time. No wonder the Arabs call the camel the "ship of the desert."

Mosul, a Rich Oil City

More than 200 miles (320 km) up the Tigris River from Baghdad is the city of Mosul. Here Nineveh once stood in all its glory. It was in Mosul that the weavers first made a kind of fine cotton cloth, called muslin.

Today the city of Mosul is important because rich oil fields are nearby. Oil is the life of modern transportation. Cars, airplanes, railroads, and most ships would come to a halt if there were no oil.

Oil makes up all but a small part of Iraq's exports. Iraq is a member of the Organization of Petroleum Exporting Countries (OPEC). OPEC nations supply nearly half of the world's oil.

Iraq in Modern Times

Iraq has seen the rise and fall of ancient civilizations. In modern times Iraq was for many years a part of the Turkish Empire.

In 1914 a great struggle involving many nations broke out. In this war, known as World War I, the land of Iraq became one of the important battlegrounds. On one side were Germany, Austria, and several other countries of Central Europe. On the other side, the chief nations were Great Britain, France, Russia, Italy, Japan, and, in 1917, the United States. This group of nations was called the Allies.

When the war reached Iraq, Basra was captured by British soldiers. Later, the British sent an army into the area north of the Persian Gulf. The purpose of this expedition was to capture Baghdad, an important point on a new railway connecting Asia and Europe. The British finally took much land, including Iraq, from the Turks.

Iraq, an Independent Nation

After World War I, Iraq was placed under the control of the British. But the people of Iraq wished to be free. They established a national government and elected a king. In 1932, when Great Britain recognized the independence of Iraq, the two countries signed an agreement. Under the agreement each was to help the other if war came.

In 1939 Germany began a new war. This war was called World War II. True to its agreement, Iraq allowed the British to land troops at Basra. Later Iraq sent soldiers to help the Allies. World War II lasted until 1945, when the Allies won the victory.

Iraq Today

Iraq had a king until 1958. In that year a revolution broke out in Iraq and the king was killed. Army officers took control of the government. Iraq became a *republic* (ri pub′lik) with a president instead of a king as the head of its government. A republic is a nation that elects its leaders.

In 1961 a group of people who live in northern Iraq, called the Kurds, demanded self-government. Fighting between the Kurds and Iraqi troops continued on and off for years. In 1975, when the Kurds had been largely defeated by government forces, a cease-fire was declared.

Iran, Land of Mountains

East of the Tigris River rises range after range of mountains. They mark the boundary between Iraq and a country once called Persia, but now known as Iran. Iran stretches from the Caspian Sea to the Persian Gulf.

Persia's Past

Persia was the center of a great empire in the ancient world. The boundaries of this empire extended far beyond the territory now occupied by Iran. The power of Persia rose and fell as its rulers won and lost wars. But Persia was an important nation until about the time that our own country became independent.

Persia's Gifts to the World

The ancient Persians developed the peach and the apricot as well as the lilacs that delight us in the spring. The pistachio nut also was first grown in Persia.

The Persians were skillful weavers. They were famous for their brocade. Brocade is a kind of cloth with raised designs.

The Persians kept great flocks of sheep, so they had plenty of wool for weaving shawls and rugs. Sometimes a weaver would work at a loom for many months weaving a fine carpet. On the Persian hills grew plants that were used for dyeing the wool.

The Geography and Resources of Iran

Iran is separated from its neighbors to the west and north by mountains. The thin strip of land along the shores of the Caspian Sea has much rain. The climate is warm enough to raise tea and cotton. But mountains on the south block off rain-bearing winds and leave most of Iran a desert.

The mountains shut off rain, but they do furnish water in the form of streams. These streams, fed by melting snow, flow down the mountainsides and are soon lost in the desert. Near every stream are towns and villages that use its water for irrigation.

Iran has been one of the world's largest producers of oil. Like Iraq, it is a member of OPEC. Iran is also a leading producer of natural gas. On a smaller scale, it produces coal, iron, sulphur, and turquoise.

The People of Iran

The traveler may journey for many miles in Iran and not see a human being. Yet Iran has more people than we might expect from its great amount of desert. In area, it is larger than our four states of Washington, Oregon, California, and Texas together. Its population is about 35 million people.

About half of the people in Iran live in small farm villages and make their living from raising crops or livestock. Most others work in the oil fields and refineries. Some work in factories that produce cotton and woolen textiles, tobacco products, cement, brick, refined copper, soap, silk, and other products.

Works of art from Persia's past range from great stone sculptures to carefully detailed pottery. Portrayed in stone is a Persian prince. The plate is decorated with the figures of a man and a lion.

Formerly, the farmers who worked the land did not own their farms. Farms were owned by wealthy landlords, who usually lived in cities. In 1962 the government started a plan to help farmers buy their land.

In the mountains of Iran live people called Kurds. Many Kurds also live in northern Iraq, as you read earlier. Most Kurds make their living raising sheep. The wool from the sheep is dyed and used to make beautiful rugs.

The city people, like most of those in the Middle East, are handicraft workers. Iranian shoemakers, weavers, carpenters, and bakers have their own little shops where they make the things they sell.

An Independent Iran

During the 1800s and the 1900s other countries controlled parts of Iran. But the Iranians insisted on being free. They were successful when first Russia and then Great Britain gave up claims to Iranian territory. In 1925 Iran became fully independent once more. An army officer, Reza Kahn Pahlavi (rē′zə kän pə lä′vē) became shah, a ruler much like a king. He was succeeded by his son, Mohammed Reza Pahlavi (mō häm′id rē′za pə lä′vē), in 1941.

After World War II, Iran's ruler began to bring about changes in the country. He freed the women from the need to wear veils over

This beautiful tiled *mosque* in Tehran is one example of the fine Persian architecture in that city. Tehran is Iran's capital.

their faces when appearing in public. In 1963 women voted for the first time in Iran's history. With money from the sale of Iran's oil, the shah encouraged the development of industry. The country's transportation system was expanded and new schools were built. Many foreigners, especially Americans and British, came to the country.

But these developments did not please all Iranians. Many felt that the shah had become a dictator. His secret police used brutal force against those who disagreed with him.

The nation's poor remained poor. Further, many of the people, almost all of whom were Muslims, felt that the new ways of doing things were against their religion. They resented the presence of so many foreigners.

In 1979 the shah was overthrown and fled the country. A religious leader, the Ayatollah Khomeini (ī yə tō′lä hō mān′ē), became a powerful figure in the nation. Feelings against the United States ran high for its earlier support of the shah. Late in 1979 a group of Iranian students seized the American embassy in Tehran (te′hə rän′). Some 53 Americans were held hostage. The students demanded that the shah be returned to their country to stand trial for his treatment of the people.

No nation would return the shah. He stayed out of Iran and died in Egypt in 1980. Even after this, the Iranians continued to hold the 53 American hostages. President Jimmy Carter worked for 14 months to free the Americans. The hostages were released on January 20, 1981, just minutes after Ronald Reagan was inaugurated as the 40th President of the United States.

Do You Know?

1. Who were the Sumerians? What were the special features of their civilization?
2. Which new metal did the Assyrians use? How did they use it?
3. What are Iraq's most important cities? Its most important resources?
4. Why was Iran's shah overthrown?

Before You Go On

Using New Words

mosque	civilization
empire	Mediterranean climate
prophet	nomad
minaret	aqueduct
caravan	city-state
bazaar	cuneiform
republic	

Number a paper from 1 through 13. After each number write the word or term that matches the definition.

1. A city that rules a large area of surrounding land
2. Writing on clay with wedge-shaped symbols
3. One who speaks for God
4. A pipe or channel used to carry water long distances
5. A group of merchants or travelers who cross the desert together
6. A tower on a mosque
7. A building where Muslims worship
8. A government that holds power over many countries
9. A marketplace or street lined with shops
10. A large group of people that forms an orderly society
11. A member of a group that moves about with their herds from winter pastures to summer pastures
12. A climate with rainy, cool winters and hot, almost rainless summers
13. A nation that elects its leaders

Finding the Facts

1. What are the two important river valleys in the Middle East?
2. How is bronze made? How was it used by the Sumerians?
3. Who was the first ruler to give his people a complete set of written laws? When did he come to power?
4. Why are camels useful animals in the desert?
5. What material did the Sumerians use to build their houses? What else did they make from this material?
6. Why are the Assyrians said to have had the first postal service?
7. Why do some Bedouin Arabs move about from place to place?
8. What rights did women of ancient Babylonia have that many women do not have today?
9. What fruits and nuts first grew in Persia?

3
Turkey, Old and New

On the map of the Middle East, Turkey stands out as the northernmost country of the region. It is also the only Middle Eastern land with a small part of its territory in Europe. The rest of Turkey is in Asia. An air traveler leaving Tehran, in Iran, flies mostly west to reach Turkey. See the map of the Middle East on page 49.

Turkey's Geography

A large part of Turkey is too hilly to be farmed. Much of the land is barren and dry. Most farms are located in the coastal area where there is a Mediterranean climate.

Ankara (än′kə rə) is the capital of Turkey. It stands almost in the center of the big peninsula that was once called Asia Minor, or "lesser Asia." The peninsula is now called by the Turkish name of Anatolia.

Separating the European and Asian parts of Turkey is a narrow stretch of water called the Bosporus (bos′pər əs) Strait. It is an important location because the Bosporus is part of the waterway that connects the Mediterranean Sea and the Black Sea. (See the map of the Middle East on page 49.) Today a bridge connects the parts of the city built on both sides of the strait. The city is now called Istanbul (is′tan bo͞ol). It is a thriving modern city of almost two and a half million people. In the past it has also been known as Constantinople (kon′stan tə nō′pəl) and as Byzantium (bi zan′shē əm). It is one of the oldest and most famous cities in the world, known both as a trading and a cultural center.

Turkey's History

The city of Istanbul can control both land and sea routes between Europe and Asia. For this reason people from many different places have always wanted to live there. In the 8th century B.C., Greek colonies were built there. In 330 A.D., Constantine I, who was the first Roman emperor to become a Christian, made it the capital of his Eastern Empire. It then became known as Constantinople, the city of Constantine. For more than 1,000 years it was the most important city in eastern Europe. During this time it was a trading point of Europe with cities of Asia. The early Turks were a warlike people who came from east of the Caspian Sea. The region from which they came is known as Turkestan. The Turks were tough, hard fighters. They took Arab lands and adopted the Muslin faith. Their leaders dreamed of conquering Europe.

The Ottoman Empire

Later a second group of Turks appeared. They were called the Ottoman Turks after their leader, Othman.

The Ottoman Turks conquered large areas of Asia and Africa. In 1453, not long before the discovery of America, they took the city of Constantinople. They made this city the capital

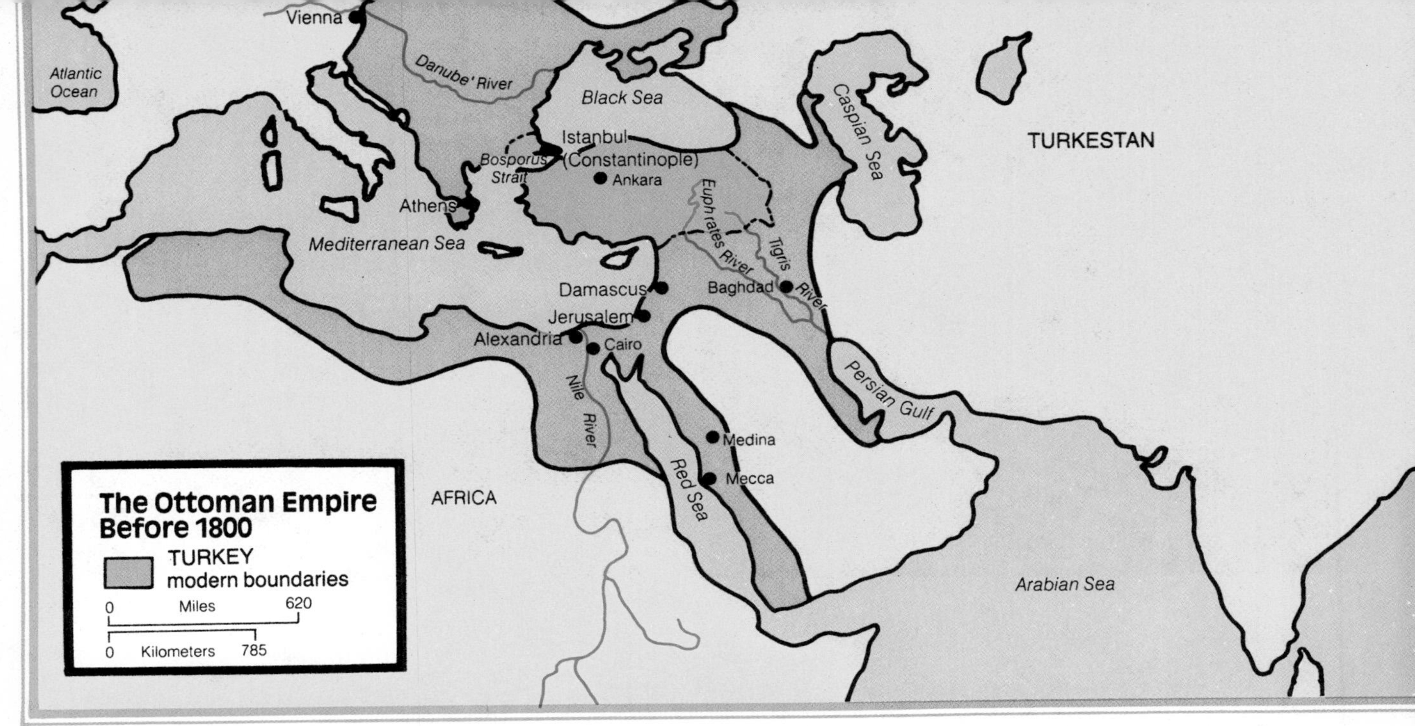

The Ottoman Turks built a powerful *empire* that included large parts of southeastern Europe, the Middle East, and North Africa. The *empire* reached its peak during the late 1600s.

of the Ottoman Empire. See the map of the Ottoman Empire Before 1800 on this page. For more than 200 years their armies continued to advance and to add new land to the empire. They finally reached Vienna, in the center of Europe. But the city of Vienna was successfully defended.

During the siege of Vienna, Turkish power was at its peak. After that, the Turkish empire began to crumble. One part and then another of the European lands taken by the Turks became independent. In Constantinople the Turkish rulers, called sultans, saw their empire become smaller and weaker.

By 1914, when World War I began, the Turks had no European lands except a small area that included Constantinople. They also held the Bosporus Strait, the water passage on which the city stands. Even today Istanbul, as Constantinople is now called, guards the passage.

Modern Turkey

In World War I, Turkey was a partner of Germany. Germany was defeated, and Turkey lost much land. Then a strong leader, Mustafa Kemal (moos tä′fə kə mäl′), arose in Turkey. The sultan left the country, and Kemal became the head of the new republic.

A New Government

Kemal wished to see his country strong and powerful. To carry out his plan, he moved the capital to Ankara, in Asia, in the center of Turkey. He built new government buildings in Ankara.

The Galata Bridge in Istanbul connects the Asian part of the city with the European part. People traveling to and from work cross the bridge daily. In the distance are seen *minarets* and a *mosque.*

At Ankara, Kemal and his helpers made laws to change Turkey. They realized that the old ways of living had kept the nation from becoming modern.

New Ways of Living

The new leaders did away with the Arabic way of writing. They adopted the alphabet used by the people of western Europe and the United States. It then became much easier for Europeans to learn to read and write Turkish. It also became easier for Turks to learn European languages.

They decided that every person should take a last name, or surname. This made it easier to keep track of the thousands of people who had only first names, many of which were the same. Kemal himself was given the surname of Atatürk (at′ə tərk′), which means "chief Turk."

According to Muslim custom, all Muslim women had to wear black veils to hide their faces when they went out. Kemal understood that Turkey could not make progress unless women were given their proper rights. He ruled that Turkish women need no longer wear veils. Taking away their veils was like tearing down a wall that kept women from being free. This was an important change.

Better Farming Methods

In recent times the government of Turkey has continued the work begun by Kemal. Most of the people in Turkey are farmers. For that reason the government teaches better ways of farming. Much of the land is dry. The government agents show the people how to make the best use of the rain that falls. The farmers learn to raise crops suited to dry soil.

Why Izmir Is Important

Southwest of Istanbul, on the shore of the Mediterranean Sea, is one of Turkey's chief seaports. It was formerly known as Smyrna (smur′nə). The Turks now call it Izmir (iz′mēr). Izmir is in a region with a Mediterranean climate.

A visitor to Izmir finds rugs and carpets for sale in the shops. They are made from the wool of the sheep raised in Anatolia. Bales of cotton are piled on wharves along the sea. Here also are bundles of licorice root, used for flavoring candy, and tobacco from the region around the Black Sea. Smyrna figs, noted for their fine flavor, are exported to many countries all over the world.

Do You Know?

1. Where is Turkey located? What is its capital today?
2. What important Turkish city is located in Europe?
3. Who was Mustafa Kemal? What changes did he bring to Turkey?
4. What is the religion of most Turks?

Countries of the Eastern Mediterranean

An airplane flying south and east from Istanbul will reach the eastern end of the Mediterranean Sea. The four small countries of Syria, Lebanon, Jordan, and Israel are located in this region. Find them on the map of the Middle East on page 49.

For thousands of years, many civilizations have developed in this area. Before Hammurabi's time the region was ruled by Babylon. The Assyrians took control after they defeated Babylon. With the rise of the Chaldeans the region again was ruled from Babylon. In these early times this area along the Mediterranean was called Syria. It was inhabited by mixed groups of people. The most important of these were the Phoenicians (fə nish′ənz).

The Phoenicians, Early Sea Traders

The Phoenicians lived on a fertile strip of coast land between the Lebanon Mountains and the Mediterranean Sea. The Phoenicians built city-states similar to those along the Euphrates River. See the map of the Fertile Crescent on page 70.

Living near the Mediterranean, the Phoenicians became a seafaring people. From the great

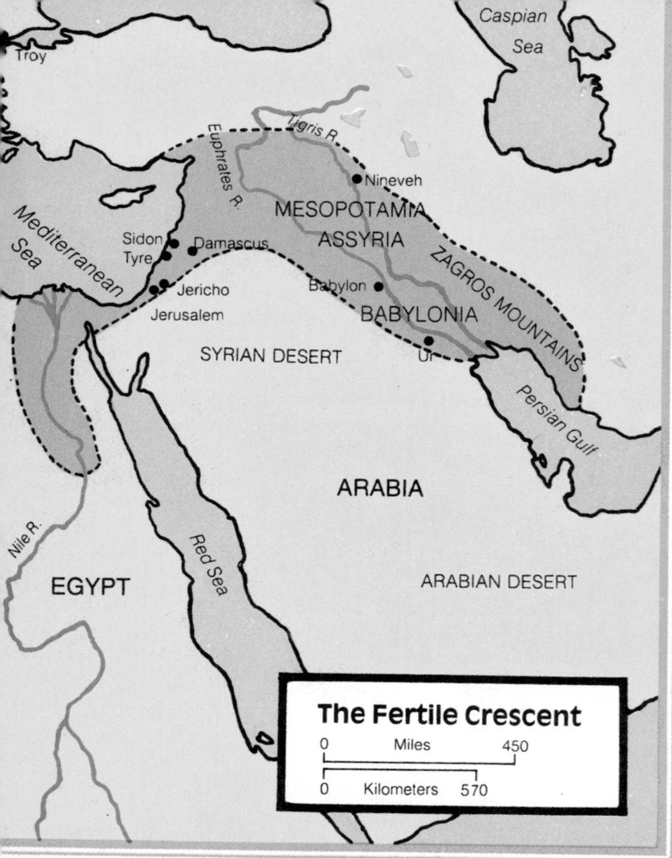

The Fertile Crescent is an area where an early *civilization* began. Because of the climate, rich farmland, and water supply, agriculture became important there.

cedar trees that grew on the Lebanon Mountains they built strong ships that could stand rough weather. The ships had two rows of oars as well as sails. Thus equipped, the vessels could journey to faraway places.

The bold Phoenicians became the great sailors and traders of their day. They went to the island of Cyprus, just west of the coast, and came back with copper ore. Beyond Cyprus to the west is another island, Crete (krēt). The civilization of Crete was highly developed in many ways. The Phoenicians carried on a lively trade with them.

Phoenician ships went as far as Spain, where the Phoenicians had copper mines and trading posts. Then they went through the Strait of Gibraltar and sailed on the Atlantic Ocean as far north as Britain. From Britain they brought back tin. The tin, as you know, was mixed with copper to make bronze.

The people of Phoenicia made beautiful glass. They carved ivory and worked in metal. They wove linen cloth and dyed it.

Three Great Phoenician Cities

The oldest Phoenician city was Byblos (bib′lōs). Byblos was located near the spot where Beirut (bā ro͞ot′), a city in Lebanon, now stands. The sailors of Byblos brought back with them from Egypt sheets of paper made from a plant called papyrus (pə pī′rəs). Papyrus sheets were used for writing letters and to make books. Byblos became so important in the trade of papyrus sheets that rolls of papyrus sheets were called "biblia." You can see how the word Bible came into use.

South of Byblos stood Sidon (sīd′ən), another large Phoenician city. On an island near Sidon was Tyre (tīr), the greatest and proudest Phoenician city. The people of Tyre discovered how to make a fine purple dye from the bodies of sea snails.

Hiram, who was king of Tyre about 3,000 years ago, had many expert workers at his call. When Solomon, king of the Hebrews, began to build a fine temple at Jerusalem, he turned to Hiram for help. Hiram's men cut many great cedars and hauled them to Jerusalem. They did most of the work of building the temple. They also made the gold dishes for the religious services.

For hundreds of years after the time of King Hiram, Tyre and Sidon were important cities. Rival armies marched through the region, but the Phoenicians went on trading. Tyre's position on an island protected it from attack for years. In time, European armies destroyed both cities.

The Gifts of the Phoenicians

The Phoenicians were the greatest builders of their time. They were also the greatest seafaring and trading people of the ancient world.

In their travels the Phoenicians met the Seirites (sē′ər īts), who lived north of the Red Sea. See the map of the Middle East on page 49. The Seirites used a simple form of picture symbols, or letters, which they had learned from the Egyptians. The Phoenicians adopted this method of writing in keeping their business accounts. In trading with other peoples, the Phoenicians shared with them this valuable tool, the alphabet.

Through the Phoenicians, the alphabet spread. With some changes it became the basis of our alphabet today. In helping to develop the alphabet, the Phoenicians made their greatest gift to the world.

The Land of Syria

Syria today is a little larger than Missouri and has a population of more than 8 million. The Lebanon Mountains extend along the Mediterranean coast of Syria. A narrow strip of fertile land lies between two mountain ranges. Between the mountains and the sea lies another fertile strip. The rest is desert. One-sixth of the people are Bedouins, who move about the desert taking their herds from one pasture to another.

Syria Today

For centuries Syria was ruled by Turks. After World War I Syria was given as a *mandate* (man′dāt) to France. A mandate is the responsibility given to a powerful nation to control and protect a weaker one.

The people of Syria wanted to be entirely free from foreign rule. Their opportunity to manage their own affairs came during World War II. Syria proclaimed its independence, and foreign troops left its soil at the end of the war.

In 1958 Syria and Egypt decided to form a new nation called the United Arab Republic. Soon Syria became unhappy with this union with Egypt. In 1961 it withdrew from the United Arab Republic and declared itself independent again. The government announced that its new name would be the Syrian Arab Republic.

Damascus, the World's Oldest City

On its way to the sea, a railroad passes through Damascus, a center of caravan trade in Syria. Damascus is the oldest inhabited city in the world. While other famous cities have been destroyed or deserted, Damascus has remained. It is the largest city in Syria. Damascus lies on an *oasis* (ō ā′ sis), in the Fertile Crescent. An oasis is a green and fertile spot in a desert. See the map of the Fertile Crescent on page 70.

The main street of Damascus, a mile (1.6 km) long, is named Straight. Iron arches extend across the street from one house to another. Awnings placed over the arches protect people from the hot sun. This street has existed without much change for almost 2,000 years.

The bazaars of Damascus sell many kinds of woven cloth. When the light shines on them in a certain way, one can see a pattern woven into them. Cloth woven in this way is known as damask.

The Republic of Lebanon

Bordering Syria and facing the sea is Lebanon. Lebanon has one city of more than 150,000 people, the seaport of Beirut. Beirut is almost directly west of Damascus. It is the capital of Lebanon.

In the busy city of Beirut is a university supported by the United States. Here the young people of Lebanon, Syria, and other nearby countries study. Lebanon is an Arab country, but about half the people are Christians.

Lebanon is an independent nation. Its people elect their officials and are free to direct their own progress.

In 1975 civil war broke out in Lebanon. Most of the Muslims were on one side of the war. Most of the Christians were on the other. The Palestine Arabs and Syria supported the Muslims. Israel, fearing that Lebanon would be used as an Arab base to attack it, supported the Christians. In 1982 Israeli forces invaded Lebanon. The civil war has continued to cost Lebanon much in lives and property.

The Kingdom of Jordan

South of Syria is the Arab kingdom of Jordan. Its area is slightly larger than Indiana. Its population is just under 3 million.

Jordan is named for the Jordan River that flows through the land. The river divides the land into the east bank and the west bank. The east bank is large, mostly desert area. Amman, the capital and largest city, is there. The west bank is a small, hilly area. Since the 1967 war, Israel has controlled the west bank. The people who live there are Palestinians. Many are *refugees* (ref′yo͞o jēz′) from Israel. Refugees are people who flee their homes because of some danger or misfortune.

Most of the people in Jordan are Muslims. The rest are Christians. About half live in villages and farm the land nearby. Those who live in cities work in trade and manufacturing.

Israel, Past and Present

South of Syria, on the Mediterranean Sea, lies the country of Israel. See the maps of ancient Palestine and modern Israel on pages 73 and 77. Its territory was carved out of Palestine, often called the Holy Land. The Jewish people of Israel are descendants of the Hebrews, whose history goes back to Biblical times.

The History of the Hebrews

About 5,000 years ago Palestine was inhabited by the Canaanites (kā′nə nīts′). They lived in walled cities and led much the same kind of life as the Babylonians. Then in about 1900 B.C. a tribe of shepherds led by a man called Abraham settled there. His descendents are called Hebrews.

When a famine came to Canaan, some of the Hebrews went to Egypt in search of food. There they were forced to do hard labor by the Egyptians. They rebelled, and under their leader Moses, returned to Canaan.

The journey across the desert took a long time. Because the Hebrews had been slaves in Egypt for many years they did not know how to act as free people. Moses taught them the rules to live by. The laws which he gave to his people are still observed by many people. Among these laws were the Ten Commandments.

In Canaan the Hebrews gradually gave up the wandering life of shepherds. Many began to live in cities as did the Canaanites.

Jerusalem, the Hebrew Capital

In about 1010 B.C. the Hebrew tribes formed a monarchy under King Saul. A monarchy means a rule by a king or queen, which passes on to their children. A period of fierce warfare between the Hebrews and the invading Philistines (fil′is tēnz′) came to an end when David became king. He captured the hill town of Jerusalem and made it the new capital of the Hebrews. David was a skillful ruler, a brave warrior, and a poet and musician.

The next king was Solomon, David's son. Solomon was said to be the wisest of kings. His reign was the most splendid age of Hebrew history. He had a great fleet of ships that sailed to many places to trade. Solomon built the famous temple at Jerusalem.

The Divided Kingdom

Solomon built great palaces and spent money freely. To pay for this, he taxed the people heavily. On his death, the kingdom split in two. Ten of the twelve Hebrew tribes formed the northern kingdom of the Israelites. The two other tribes became known as the Judeans. They kept Jerusalem as their capital.

As the years passed, the land was conquered in turn by the Assyrians, the Chaldeans, and the Persians. The temple of Solomon was destroyed, and later rebuilt. For many centuries, the Jews, as the descendants of the Hebrews came to be called, were not a free people. At the time that Jesus was living in Nazareth, the area was a part of the powerful Roman empire. In A.D. 66 the Jews rebelled against the Roman government. This rebellion was not successful. It led to the destruction of Jerusalem. Nearly all the Jews were driven from Palestine. Since then the Jews have lived in many countries.

What the Hebrews Gave the World

The Hebrews believed in one God. Although some neighboring nations worshiped idols, or images, the Jews were forbidden to do so.

The idea of one God, the Ten Commandments, and the teachings of the Hebrew prophets gave the world a new religion. The sacred books of the Hebrews are called the Torah (tôr′ ə). They contain stories and beliefs shared by many religions practised today throughout the world. Jews, Christians, and Muslims are sometimes called the "people of the book," because they all respect the same early Hebrew prophets.

The Return to Palestine

Although they were widely scattered, many Jews never gave up hope of again claiming Palestine as their homeland. At last, there was a plan to make this dream come true. This plan was called Zionism after Zion, an ancient name for Jerusalem. Jews from many different countries went to settle in Palestine.

The Arabs, who had lived in Palestine for hundreds of years, were not pleased when Jews came in such large numbers. Many of the new settlers worked on the land, irrigating dry areas and raising good crops. But many Arabs did not favor the ways of the newcomers and were fearful of losing Palestine to them.

The New Nation of Israel

During World War II Adolph Hitler led Germany in one of the most terrible schemes the world has ever known. Hitler's plan was to kill all the Jews living in Germany and its conquered lands. By the time the war ended 6 million Jews had been killed. They were not killed in warfare, but in camps built for that purpose. Many of those killed were children. This terrible crime is called the *Holocaust* (hol′ ə kôst′). A holocaust is a great destruction.

When World War II came to an end the nations of the world felt great sorrow about what had happened to the Jews in Europe. They wanted the Jews to have the homeland they had waited for so long. In 1947 the United Nations voted to end British control of Palestine and divide the country into a Jewish state and an Arab state. Jerusalem was to remain an international city. The day the British mandate ended, May 14, 1948, the new nation of Israel came into existence.

Arab Opposition

The Arabs did not accept the division of Palestine. Israel was at once attacked by five Arab nations. Finally a truce was arranged, but border battles continued. In 1967 the fighting became a full-scale war that Israel won. Israel took possession of various lands, including the west bank of the Jordan River and Jerusalem. In 1973 war broke out again, but a settlement was reached. Then in 1979, Israel and Egypt signed a peace treaty which promised the end of 30 years of conflict between the two nations.

The Israeli-Egyptian treaty, however, did not bring peace to the region. Relations remained tense between Israel and its other Arab neighbors. Disagreements existed among the Arab nations themselves. Also unresolved was the problem of the Palestinian Arabs, who have long demanded their own independent nation.

Jerusalem

At first the headquarters of Israel's government was in Tel Aviv. But in 1950 the capital was moved to Jerusalem.

After Israel's war for independence, Jerusalem was divided into two parts. The western part was controlled by Israel, and the eastern part by Jordan. But in the 1967 war, Israel took the eastern part of Jerusalem from the Jordanians and the city was united again.

Jerusalem is a holy city to the people of three different religions. To the Jew it is the city of the great temple. To the Christian it is the city where many happenings in the life of Jesus occurred. To the Muslim it is the place from which the prophet Mohammed ascended into heaven on the back of a winged horse.

Jews pray at the Western Wall in Jerusalem. The *mosque,* called "Dome of the Rock," is sacred to Muslims.

Tel Aviv-Jaffa, the largest city in Israel, lies on the Mediterranean coast. It consists of the modern city of Tel Aviv and the ancient seaport of Jaffa.

Golda Meir: Prime Minister of Israel

The Zionists who founded the new nation of Israel came from all over the world. One, who rose to become prime minister of that country, spent her early years in Wisconsin.

Golda Meir was born in Russia, but came to the United States with her parents when she was 8 years old. She was raised in Milwaukee, and was a schoolteacher there until 1921. Then she and her husband moved to Palestine.

Golda Meir was prime minister for 5 years, from 1969 to 1974. She continued to work for a peaceful Israel until her death in 1979.

The Geography of Israel

East of Jerusalem the land falls away to a deep valley which runs through parts of Israel and Jordan. In this valley are the Dead Sea and the Sea of Galilee. From the fishermen on the Sea of Galilee Jesus chose some of the 12 men who became his disciples.

From the Sea of Galilee, south through the deep valley, runs the Jordan River. Many cattle and sheep find pasture along its banks. Fruit orchards border its course. Some of the orchards have olive trees that have borne fruit for a hundred years.

The Jordan River flows into the Dead Sea. It forms part of the border between Israel and Jordan. See the map of modern Israel on page 77. This sea is the lowest spot on any continent. It is nearly 1,300 feet (390 m) below sea level. Neither fish nor water plants can survive in the sea. Only small desert plants grow on the shores of the Dead Sea.

The reason for the lack of life is that the Dead Sea has no outlet. Most water contains salt. Water is constantly drawn up by the heat of the atmosphere. The salt remains behind. When a body of water has no outlet to carry away the salt, the water becomes very salty indeed. That is why the oceans, the Great Salt Lake, and the Dead Sea are salty.

The Dead Sea is five times as salty as the ocean. Bathers cannot sink in it. Some people think that bathing in the waters is a good treatment for certain diseases.

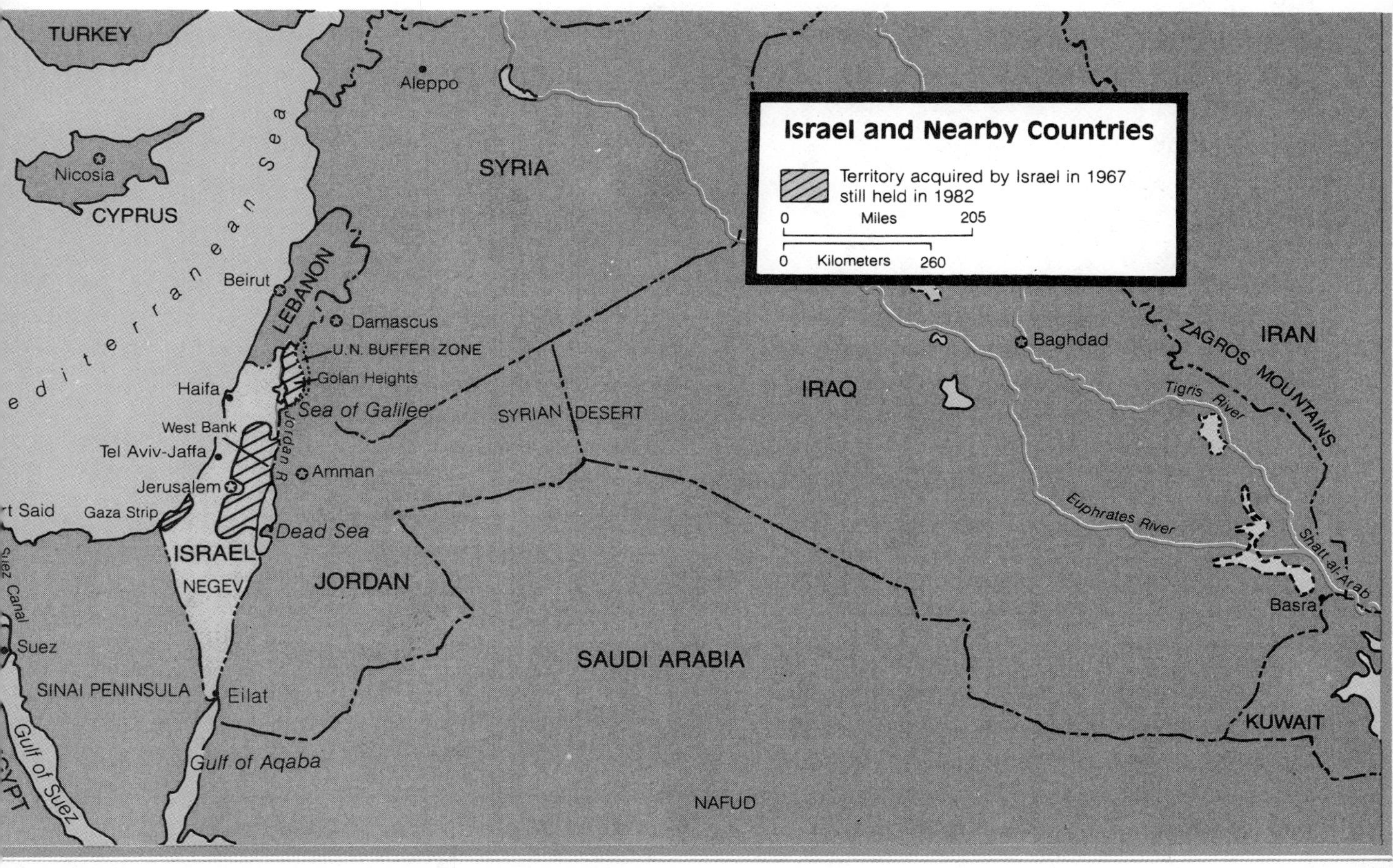

Israel's Seaports

In the northern part of Israel is the seacoast town of Haifa (hī′fə). Haifa is the port of Israel which is nearest Syria. Much of Israel's trade with other countries passes through the port of Haifa.

Northwest of Jerusalem is the ancient seaport of Jaffa. Ships leaving Jaffa carry fine oranges raised on irrigated land. The ships also carry olive oil and wine. Like many old cities of this area, Jaffa has narrow streets crowded with many little shops where Israeli crafts are sold.

The modern city of Tel Aviv was built close to Jaffa. It has wide streets, up-to-date stores, hotels, and many factories. These two cities were combined into one called Tel Aviv-Jaffa, the largest city in the nation of Israel.

Israel has a large fleet of ocean-going ships. In 1966, the seaport of Ashdod was built. It is about 20 miles south of Tel Aviv-Jaffa. Eilat, on the Gulf of Aqaba (ä′kä bä′), was built in ancient times and modernized in 1956. Eilat gives Israel a trade outlet to the Indian Ocean by way of the Red Sea.

This Israeli works at an oil refinery in Israel. Why is oil important to a modern industrial nation such as Israel?

Modern Israel

Israel is about the size of Massachusetts. It has a population of about 4 million people. There are some Muslims and some people of other religions. But most are Jews, more than a million of whom immigrated from other countries. Eilat and Ashdod have grown because of the immigrants.

Many of Israel's people have found jobs in the country's new factories. They produce processed foods, textiles, chemicals, building materials, and electrical goods.

Other people are busy turning Israel's desert into productive farm land. They have built many dams, aqueducts, wells, pipelines, and canals to bring water to dry land. In this way Israel has more than doubled the amount of land that can be farmed. Some foods have become plentiful enough for Israel to export them. The chief exports are fruits and grain.

Many farm communities called kibbutzim (ki boot′sēm) have been built near the newly irrigated land. Many of the workers are new immigrants to Israel. Until their communities are well established, they must do without many things. Israel also has many old and well established kibbutzim, which played an important role in the development of the nation.

Do You Know?

1. Who were the Phoenicians? With what faraway lands did they trade?
2. In which Arab country is about half the population Christian?
3. Where is Israel? What has Israel done to double the amount of land that can be farmed?
4. Where is the Dead Sea? Why cannot fish and plants live in it?

5

Arabia, Riches of the Desert

The Arabs once ruled an area which stretched from central Asia into Spain. The Arabian Peninsula made up part of this empire. The peninsula is almost twice as large as our state of Alaska. The country of Saudi Arabia fills about two-thirds of the peninsula.

The Nation of Saudi Arabia

The Arabs held control of their lands for a long time, but at last many territories slipped from their grasp. As the Arabs grew weaker, Turkey gained control over much of the Arabian Peninsula. The Turks kept the region until the early years of the twentieth century. Then a leader named Ibn-Saud (ib′ən sä o͞od′) united the Arabs in most of the peninsula. He did this by winning lands back from the Turks. He formed the kingdom of Saudi Arabia and became its first king. See the map of Arabia on this page.

The peninsula is a barren land, for most of it has little or no rain and no real rivers. None of its streams is more than a few feet wide.

Back from the sea the land rises high enough so that from time to time the winds bring some rain. The people in these favored places raise date palms, vegetables, alfalfa, coffee and grain.

Medina and Mecca, Holy Cities

Many pilgrims visit the holy city of Medina. Some of the pilgrims are from Saudi Arabia itself. Others come on long journeys from distant lands. In Medina the pilgrims worship at the grave of the religious leader, Mohammed. Mohammed spent the latter part of his life in Medina. A still holier city than Medina is Mecca (mek′ə), where Mohammed was born. Mecca lies south of Medina.

No unbeliever, or non-Muslim, is allowed to set foot inside either Mecca or Medina. It is possible, however, to fly over Mecca and look down into a great courtyard where a stone

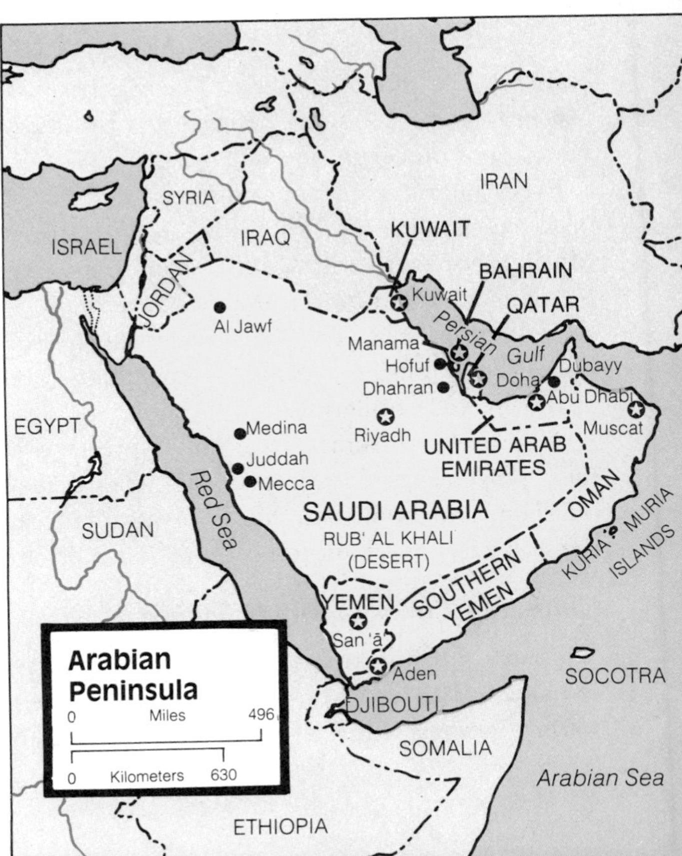

Mecca draws millions of Muslim pilgrims who come to visit the shrine called the Kaaba. After walking around the shrine, the pilgrims kiss the sacred stone.

building, the Kaaba, stands. The Kaaba is a Muslim shrine. Muslims believe it is the most sacred spot on earth.

Every pilgrim to Mecca must kiss the sacred black stone set in the wall of the Kaaba. Every Muslim hopes to visit Mecca sometime. All Muslims who visit Mecca are considered holy.

Neither Mecca nor Medina has much real trade. Their business comes from taking care of the crowds of pilgrims.

Wherever Muslims live, they spread out their prayer rugs five times a day. They kneel on them and bow their heads toward Mecca, the holy city they want to visit.

Changing Times in Saudi Arabia

Ibn-Saud of Saudi Arabia, who gave the country its name in 1932, was a strong ruler. He stopped warfare among tribes of the region by taking away their rifles. Thus he made the country more peaceful. By having many new wells dug, he provided more water. He built roads. He started health centers with free medical care. Many of the changes that he began were continued by his heirs. A son, Faisal, was killed in 1975. Faisal was followed by King Khalid. The king also holds the post of prime minister.

Money to improve life in Saudi Arabia came from oil. In 1935 vast oil fields were discovered. Since then oil wells have been dug and refineries and pipelines have been built. This nation is one of the richest oil producing countries. See the map of Middle East Oil Fields and Pipelines on page 51. For years, Saudi Arabia shared its oil profits with American and other foreign companies that pumped the oil. But in 1974 Saudi Arabia began to acquire total rights to its oil. Like Iraq and Iran, it is a member of OPEC.

Kuwait, Another Oil-Rich Land

Find the tiny land of Kuwait (kə wāt′) on the map of Middle East Oil Fields and Pipelines on page 51. Until 1961, Kuwait was under the protection of Great Britain. Since then it has become one of the leading oil producing countries and one of the richest. It lies on a waterless and almost rainless desert, but scientists have developed drinking water from sea water and discovered an underground lake.

Other Small Arab Countries

Two countries, Yemen (yem′ən) and Southern Yemen, lie at the southwestern corner of the Arabian Peninsula. Yemen borders the Red Sea. It is about the size of South Dakota. It has many mountains, and enough rain to grow fruits, vegetables, grain and good quality coffee, called mocha (mō′kə). It was once part of the Ottoman Empire and for a while had close ties with Egypt. In 1974, army leaders took control of the government.

Southern Yemen is officially named the People's Democratic Republic of Yemen. It is at the southern end of the Arabian Peninsula, below the entrance to the Red Sea. It borders on the Gulf of Aden and on the Indian Ocean. The islands of Socotra (sə cō′trə), Kamaran, and Perim (pər im′) are part of Southern Yemen. Most of the country is hot and dry. Aden, its capital, is an ancient city. It is now an important port with an oil refinery. In ancient times, the whole region was crossed by trade routes leading to Europe, Asia, and Africa.

A third nation in this area is Oman, lying along the southeastern coast. Oman is ruled by a sultan. It receives just enough rain to permit the growing of fruits and grains. Muscat is its capital city, a port from which dates are exported.

North of Oman, bordering the Persian Gulf, are the little lands of Bahrain, an island, Qatar, and the United Arab Emirates.

Bahrain, an island nation, gained its independence from Great Britain in 1971 and is ruled by an emir. Emir is the title given to the chief or ruling prince in some Arab countries. Oil refining is important, but springs of water along the northern coast permit farming.

Qatar also gained its independence from Great Britain in 1971. Oil refining is also important. It is a forward-moving nation of only about 100,000 people ruled by an emir.

The United Arab Emirates is a group of seven states. This group was formed in 1971. It is located between Qatar and Oman. The port of Dubai is a center of oil activity.

Do You Know?

1. What is Saudi Arabia's chief resource? What resource does it lack?
2. Why do Muslim pilgrims travel to Mecca and Medina?
3. What resource makes Kuwait important?
4. Why is Aden an important city?

6
Egypt, a Child of the Nile

Egypt resembles its neighbors in the Middle East in many ways. It has a desert climate. Its people are united with the peoples of nearby lands in following the teachings of Mohammed. Like its neighbors, Egypt has many poor people who yearn for a better life. But today, as it has for thousands of years, life in Egypt centers around the Nile River.

The Great Nile River

The Nile is the greatest river in Africa. It begins south of Lake Victoria and flows northward more than 4,000 miles (6,400 km) into the Mediterranean. Trace the river on the map of the Middle East on page 49.

The Delta of the Nile

The Nile has a very large *delta* (del′tə). A delta is a stretch of land built up at a river's mouth by the mud and sand brought down by the river. Like most deltas, the delta of the Nile is in the shape of a triangle. It now measures about 150 miles (240 km) from north to south. It is as large as our state of Maryland.

A Trip Along the Nile

On the western edge of the Nile Delta is Alexandria, the great trading port of Egypt. South of Alexandria the miles of fertile delta are green with crops of rice, cotton, corn, and sugarcane.

At the place where the delta begins stands the city of Cairo (kī′rō), the capital of Egypt. Cairo is a city with fine hotels, many bazaars, and shining white mosques.

Leaving Cairo and going southward up the Nile, the traveler sees the river as a busy waterway with many boats. On either side of the river is the narrow Nile Valley. This valley is never more than 10 miles (16 km) wide, and at some places it is only 2 miles (3.2 km) across. Beyond the valley on each side is the scorching desert. The desert is almost without plant life. The narrow strip of green valley supports Egypt's people.

Hundreds of miles up the Nile from Cairo stands a great dam. The Aswan High Dam was completed in 1970. This dam and others hold back the water until it is needed for use in irrigation. When the waters rise high, the lake back of the dam is 200 miles (320 km) long. The Aswan High Dam irrigates 2 million acres (800,000 ha) otherwise too dry to grow crops.

Life in Ancient Egypt

Civilization developed along the Nile River because it was a good place for people to settle down and tend crops. The climate, the soil, and water from the river helped early farmers produce good harvests.

How Civilization Began

People were living along the lower Nile River early in the Stone Age. Here was a land whose

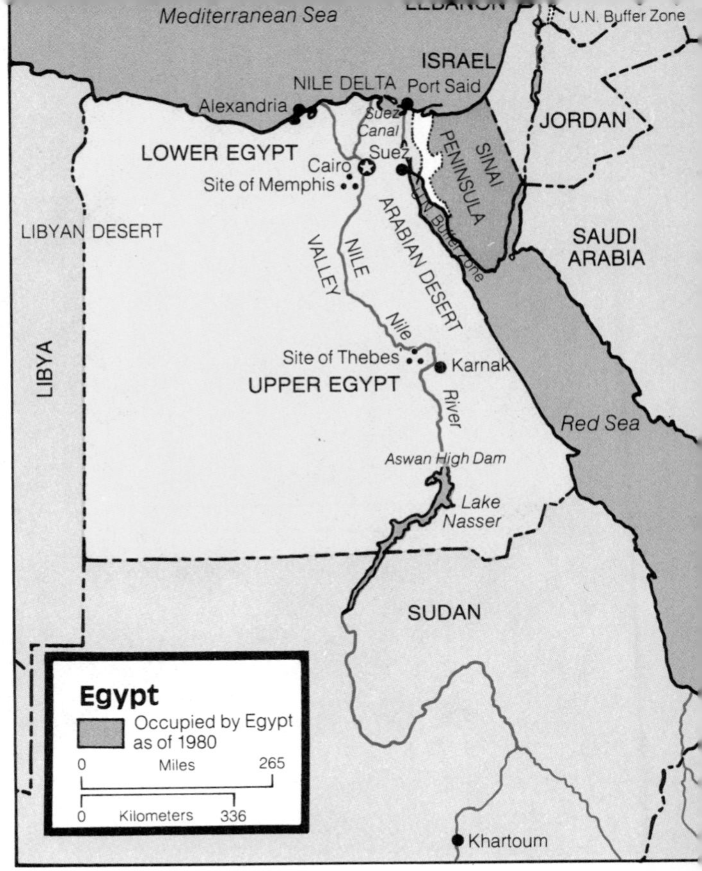

rich soil was capable of producing a plentiful supply of food. The air was hot in the daytime, but during the early morning and at night it was pleasantly cool.

Egypt was almost hidden from the rest of the world. On the north and the east sides it bordered the Mediterranean and Red Seas. On the other sides the desert helped to keep unwelcome visitors away. Early Egyptians lived peacefully in their pleasant climate. They had a chance to improve their skills in growing food, in weaving, and in building. Thus people in Egypt developed civilized ways faster than did early people in most other parts of the world.

The Importance of the Nile

The melting snows on the highlands of central Africa, together with the spring rains, cause the Nile waters to rise every spring. The higher the river rises, the more water there will be for irrigating crops.

Today, as in the past, the Nile begins to rise in May. But its waters are now turned into lakes. Dams have been built along the river to hold back the flood waters. The water is used for irrigation and for hydroelectric power.

The Nile overflowed its banks once each year and flooded the land on either side. When the water drained away, a layer of mud was left. The mud made the land fertile.

For thousands of years people farmed the fertile land. The early Egyptians scattered seeds on the soil. Sometimes they used herds of sheep to trample the seeds into the soil. The hot sunshine made the grain grow quickly and produce an abundant harvest.

Irrigation in Egypt

After 100 days of Nile floods the sun's rays would bake the land dry again. As in Mesopotamia, the land had to be irrigated. Dams, dikes, reservoirs, and canals were needed for irrigation. To plan, build, and use them required skill and cooperation.

Through irrigation the Egyptians extended their farm land far beyond the area covered by the Nile floods. Two or three crops could be raised on the same land in one year.

Writing, an Egyptian Skill

The people of Mesopotamia had one style of writing. The ancient Egyptians had a different form of writing. They used pictures of the objects. For example, an ox was represented by a simple drawing of the head of an ox. In the

The ancient Egyptians developed a system of writing based on pictures called hieroglyphs. The hieroglyphs shown here decorate the tomb of an Egyptian king.

same way pictures stood for a hawk, a lion, a snake, a house, a man, a woman, the sun, the moon, and so on. Such pictures were called hieroglyphs (hī′ ər ə glifs′). This word came from "hiero," meaning "sacred," and "glyph," meaning "writing." In the beginning, only priests and a few other persons could read and write the hieroglyphs.

At first each picture stood for a word. Then the Egyptians worked out a plan of having each picture represent a syllable. Words were written by putting syllables together. There were about 600 syllable signs.

The Egyptians knew that syllable writing was hard. So they worked out a way of writing in which each sound had its own sign, or letter. However, the Egyptians never made full use of their alphabet. They used hieroglyphics, syllable signs, and letters all at the same time.

The Egyptians also developed the material on which scribes wrote. Along the Egyptian waterways grew a tall plant with a feathery top, called papyrus. The Egyptians cut papyrus stems into thin strips and laid them side by side. Across these they placed another layer of papyrus strips. By beating, pressing, and rolling the two layers together, they made a smooth, yellowish-white sheet. From papyrus we get our word "paper."

The scribes wrote with pens made of reeds spread out at their end into tiny brushes. They dipped the brush into ink. The ink was made of vegetable gum, water, and black soot. The papyrus sheets were pasted together into a strip which might be 100 feet or more long. The sheets could be rolled up and tied.

Egyptian Ways of Measurement

The Egyptians were good at measuring. There were surveyors, or people trained to measure land. Each year, after the Nile waters had gone down, the surveyors laid out the boundary lines that had been swept away by the flood. Skillful measuring was also needed in building.

In harvesting crops and in storing grain, the Egyptians needed to use numbers. They had to find the amount of grain the storehouses would hold. In trading, they had to be able to figure and to keep accounts.

The Egyptians were also interested in measuring time. As early as 4000 B.C. the Egyptians had worked out a calendar. Their calendar had 12 months of 30 days each. This left 5 days over at the end of the year. These extra days were grouped together as feast days or holidays.

The Egyptian Religion

The ancient Egyptians were a religious people. They carried their religious ideas into every part of life. They believed in many gods, but their most important gods were those connected with raising food.

The Egyptians believed there was a life after death. The life of each person would continue through his "ka," or spirit. But the ka could do nothing unless the dead body was preserved as a home to which the ka could return. So the Egyptians developed a method of embalming, or preserving bodies after death.

An embalmed body was called a mummy. Thousands of these Egyptian mummies have been found. Many museums in the United States have Egyptian mummies in their collections.

The Egyptian rulers believed they could take their property with them into the next world. They built fine tombs for themselves. In their grave rooms were piled such things as food, furniture, musical instruments, and jewelry. Careful study of the objects found in the tombs of these rulers has provided us with much information about the early Egyptians and the things they considered important.

Gifts of Ancient Egypt

- System of writing
- Calendar
- Pyramids and obelisks
- Surveying and measuring land
- Large-scale irrigation
- Sailing vessels
- Well-run government and accounting

The Sphinx and the Pyramids of Giza show the great skill of ancient Egyptian stone carvers. The Sphinx has the body of a crouching lion and the face of the Egyptian king Khafre.

The Egyptians as Builders

Egypt had many stony cliffs. The Egyptians learned to cut big blocks of limestone and granite from the cliffs. They also learned to form these stone blocks into great buildings.

Egyptian Pyramids

Some Egyptian rulers built stone pyramids where their mummies would be safe and surrounded by the things they would need in the next world. A pyramid has a square base and four three-sided faces which meet at a point at the top. The Great Pyramid, near Cairo, is the largest. It was built around 2900 B.C. as the tomb of the ruler Cheops (kē′ops). Almost 500 feet (150 km) high, it covers an area as large as 12 football fields.

To build such great monuments required a great amount of time and toil on the part of many people. The builders did their work so perfectly that it is difficult, even today, to find the joints where the stones meet.

The Egyptian Sphinx

Near the Great Pyramid is a famous piece of sculpture known as the Sphinx. In a large limestone rock on the desert, one of the Egyptian kings saw the likeness of a crouching lion. He ordered his workers to make the likeness better. In front, they carved out long legs and paws. The head was made to look like the king himself.

Tutankhamen, the Boy-King

In 1922, an Englishman named Howard Carter entered a tomb that had not been opened since ancient times. "Can you see anything?" a companion asked Carter. "Yes," he replied, "wonderful things."

This was the tomb of the king Tutankhamen (too'tängk ä'mən). Its four rooms were filled with furniture, jewelry, games, weapons, and other things a king might need in his life after death. The tomb also contained Tutankhamen's mummy, preserved in an inner coffin of solid gold.

Tutankhamen's treasures are stored in the Egyptian museum in Cairo. Recently objects from the tomb have been exhibited in the United States. Everywhere they were shown they drew record crowds.

The reign of Tutankhamen lasted only 9 years, from about 1334 B.C. to about 1325 B.C. He was just a child, about 9 years old, when he became king, and a *regent* (rē'jənt) ruled with him. A regent is someone who rules in place of a king who is either sick, away, or too young. Tutankhamen was married when he was still a child, and he and his young queen are pictured on many of the objects found in his tomb. He died when he was 18 or 19. No one knows just how.

The golden throne of Tutankhamen was richly decorated with pieces of glass and stone. The king and his queen are pictured on the back of the chair.

Egyptian Obelisks

A few miles from the present city of Cairo the old capital of Egypt once stood. It was called Memphis. Find the site of Memphis on the map of Egypt on page 83. Here, as in other places, were put up slender, pointed shafts of stone called obelisks (ob'ə lisks'). The obelisks were covered with hieroglyphics praising the ruler.

Each obelisk was formed of a single piece of rock. Some of the obelisks were about 100 feet (30 m) tall. Many obelisks still remain in Egypt, but some have been removed to foreign lands. Rome, London, Paris, and New York each has an Egyptian obelisk. The Washington Monument in our capital has the shape of an obelisk.

The World's Greatest Temple

Far up the Nile River was the city of Thebes (thēbz). It became the capital city when Lower Egypt and Upper Egypt were united about 3100 B.C. Lower Egypt was the delta country. Upper Egypt was the land between the delta and the first waterfall on the Nile.

The kings, who were priests as well as rulers, built great temples at Thebes. One of these places of worship, the Temple at Karnak, was the largest temple the world has ever known. Leading up to the temple is a broad avenue from the Nile. The avenue is bordered with ramheaded sphinxes. Much of the Temple of Karnak is now in ruins, but in its time it was a wonderful building.

Burial Places of the Theban Kings

Across the Nile, on the west side, rise the wild cliffs that mark the beginning of the Libyan Desert. Into these cliffs the Egyptian rulers cut many deep tombs to be used as their burial places. Nearby the wealthy nobles of Thebes were buried.

The walls of the tombs are covered with paintings. From them we have learned much about life in this ancient land. Here are pictures of the ancient Egyptians at work and at play. The paintings show that women had an

This model shows how the Temple of Karnak once looked. Beautifully decorated columns supported the roof of the building. Silver and gold once shone from every part of the temple.

honored and important part in Egyptian life. They also show that the Egyptians believed in a life after death.

The Government of Ancient Egypt

From early times Egypt was ruled by a king, called a pharaoh (fer′ō). "Pharaoh" is an Egyptian title from a word meaning great house.

The Power of the Pharaoh

The pharaohs were so powerful that the people believed they were sons of the sun god. The god ruled in the sky, and the pharaoh ruled on earth.

The pharaoh came to have complete power over his people. Since he was thought to be descended from the gods, Egyptians believed it sinful to disobey him.

Several women were co-rulers of ancient Egypt. The most famous was Queen Nefertiti. She and her husband, King Akhenaton, were responsible for many reforms.

Life Under the Pharaohs

Because the Nile supplied water and because the water was skillfully used in irrigation, food was plentiful in Egypt. So Egypt came to be a well-populated country. Great cities arose.

The nobles lived in comfort in large houses built of sun-dried brick and wood. They employed many skillful workers—builders, sculptors, painters, furniture makers, and jewelers.

The farmers lived in smaller houses. They paid taxes. They did not pay in money, for Egypt did not have money. They paid in grain, meat, dates, wine, or anything else the pharaoh wanted.

This limestone sculpture shows the Egyptian queen Nefertiti. She was the wife of King Akhenaton, who ruled in 1370 B.C. As co-ruler of Egypt, she supported her husband's reforms.

Every few years the pharaoh had the people of his kingdom counted. This counting is called a *census* (sen′səs). The census was taken to learn how many people were to be taxed and how much each should pay.

Under the pharaohs, skilled workers made many things. The tables of rich people shone with dishes of silver, gold, and rock crystal made by craftspeople. The guests drank from shining glass and dressed in linen so finely woven that it was as soft as silk. Some of this beautiful linen has been found, in good condition, wrapped around mummies.

Wealthy people wore valuable jewelry. The

In some parts of Egypt, the people still depend on ancient methods of irrigation. For example, oxen are used to turn a wheel that draws water from a well.

music of harps and flutes was heard through the houses. Outside, the children bounced balls and played with marbles and tops.

For those who were rich and powerful, life was pleasant in Egypt thousands of years ago. The rest of the people lived in poor conditions.

Modern Egypt

Egypt today is about as large as Texas and New Mexico combined. It has more than 39 million inhabitants. Nearly all of them live in the fertile Nile Valley.

Some Egyptians work in the recently discovered oil fields. Others find jobs in Egypt's cities. But most Egyptians earn a living from farming.

Farming in Egypt Today

As in ancient times, the farmers bring water from the Nile to irrigate their small fields. They use tools much like those used in the time of the pharaohs.

Egypt does not produce enough food to meet its people's needs, so hunger is a threat. To make matters worse, the population is growing rapidly while the food supply stays about the same.

The largest crop in Egypt is not food, but cotton. One-third of all the farm land is planted in cotton. Egyptian cotton is of high quality. Its fibers are longer than those of cotton grown in the United States. It makes very strong thread. Egyptian cotton is sought by customers in many parts of the world.

The Aswan High Dam has helped control the floodwaters of the Nile River. The dam provides water to irrigate larger areas of farmland in Egypt.

The Suez Canal

Long ago, people saw that a canal through the Isthmus of Suez, which united Africa and Asia, would greatly shorten voyages between Europe and the Far East. By using such a canal, ships could sail from European ports through the Red Sea and reach the Indian Ocean. They could sail to the Far East without having to go around Africa.

A little more than 100 years ago a French engineer, Ferdinand de Lesseps, undertook to build the canal. Many persons doubted that De Lesseps would be successful. But after 10 years the Suez Canal, 100 miles (160 km) long, was finished.

Through this canal ships sailed from Port Said (sä ēd′), on the Mediterranean, to Suez, on the Red Sea. Each ship that went through paid a toll, or fee. The profits from running the canal went to the owners of the canal. Most of the shares were owned by French stockholders and Great Britain. Since the canal opened in 1869, thousands of ships have used the canal to move between Europe and the countries of Asia. The building of giant oil tankers that are too large to use the canal has made it less useful.

The British in Egypt

After the opening of the Suez Canal, the British had a great interest in Egypt. For many years they ruled the country. The British directed the building of many irrigation dams, hospitals, and schools.

Cairo
Where the Old Meets the New

Cairo was once known as the city of a thousand minarets. Today these tall, slender towers still rise above the rooftops of the city's new skyscrapers. From the balconies of the minarets, criers call faithful Muslims to prayer five times a day. The call is heard by shoppers who haggle over prices in Cairo's old bazaars. The crier's call is also heard by Muslims on their way to modern movie theaters. From the windows of the tall office and apartment buildings the people can see the ancient pyramids in the distance beyond Cairo.

Cairo was built by a Muslim general in 969. Later it became an important center of Muslim culture and learning. Conquering nations have controlled the city: the Ottoman Turks, European nations, and Great Britain. Many people in the city speak English. But today Cairo is the capital city of an independent Egypt. With nearly 6 million people, it is the largest city in the Middle East and Africa. Old ways of living have been combined successfully with new. ■

Independence

But the Egyptians wanted to be free. The British gave up most of their power in 1922, though they kept their soldiers in the Canal Zone. This was important in World War II. The British were able to stop German and Italian forces moving eastward toward Egypt and the canal. After the war, the British kept troops in the Canal Zone despite the wishes of the Egyptians.

In 1952, the corrupt Egyptian king was forced to leave. Egypt became a republic in 1953. Gamal Abdel Nasser, an army officer, rose to power and became president.

Six years later, the British removed their troops. Soon after this President Nasser seized the canal. He said the tolls would be used to help build the badly needed Aswan High Dam. Shortly afterward, Israel, Great Britain, and France attacked Egypt. The United Nations restored peace in the area, and the Suez Canal was reopened in March 1957 under Egyptian management.

Egypt as a Republic

Seizing the canal was just one of the steps that President Nasser took to increase Egypt's importance. He made Egypt leader of the Arab League. He dreamed of Egypt as the center of power in the Middle East. In 1958, Egypt joined Syria to form the United Arab Republic, but the union lasted only 3 years.

In June of 1967, war broke out again between Egypt and Israel. Egypt was backed by most of the Arab countries, but in a few days Israel had occupied the Sinai Peninsula east of the canal. The Soviet Union began to step up military and economic aid to Egypt, and sent Soviet troops to operate a complex missile system. An undeclared war with Israel flared off and on.

President Nasser died in 1970 and was replaced by Anwar Sadat. Two years later, Egypt rejected a very short-lived treaty of friendship with the Soviet Union. Soviet troops and military advisors, or experts, were asked to leave.

In 1975 an agreement was reached with Israel. Israel agreed to remove its troops from a part of the Sinai that it had held since the 1967 war. In return, Egypt reopened the Suez Canal, closed since 1967. In 1979 Egypt and Israel signed a peace treaty. Egypt thus became the first Arab country to recognize Israel's right to exist as a nation. For this, Egypt was suspended from membership in the Arab League. Then, in 1981, President Sadat was killed by assassins.

Do You Know?

1. What made Egypt a favorable place for the development of civilization?
2. How did the Nile River control the farming of the people in Egypt?
3. What is Egypt's most important crop? Why is it used all over the world?
4. Who manages the Suez Canal?

To Help You Learn

Using New Words

nomad	delta
civilization	Holocaust
mandate	census
oasis	regent
Mediterranean climate	republic
refugee	mosque

Number a paper from 1 through 12. After each number write the word or term that matches the definition.

1. A climate with cool, rainy winters and hot, almost rainless summers
2. A member of a group that moves about with their herds from winter pastures to summer pastures
3. The responsibility given a powerful country to control and protect a weaker one
4. A stretch of land built up at a river's mouth by the mud and sand brought down by the river
5. The counting of people in an area
6. A large group of people that form an orderly society
7. A green and fertile spot in a desert
8. A person who flees his or her home because of danger or misfortune
9. Someone who rules in place of a king
10. A great destruction, especially referring to the killing of many Jews during World War II
11. A building where Muslims worship
12. A nation that elects its leaders

Finding the Facts

1. Tell two ways business in Babylon was conducted like business today.
2. How is papyrus made? How did the ancient Egyptians use it?
3. What are two other names for Istanbul? Name two empires that have controlled the city during its long history.
4. What are the Phoenicians best known for?
5. Name three contributions ancient Egypt made to the world.
6. Why are mountains important to Iran's farming?

Learning from Maps

1. Look at the map of the Middle East on page 49 and answer these questions: On what rivers are the cities of Iraq built? Why are they located there? What countries border on the Mediterranean Sea?
2. Compare the map of Arabia on page 79 with the map of Egypt on page 83 and answer these questions: How do Egypt and Saudi Arabia compare in size? Use the map scales.
3. On the map of the Middle East on page 49, locate the nations of the Middle East and their capitals.

Using Study Skills

1. **Graph:** Graphs are used at times to give information in convenient form. The graph shown below is a line graph. A line graph is useful to show the amount of production of a farm crop, or of shoes in a factory, or of other products over a period of time. The line rises or falls on the graph as the amount of the product increases or decreases.

Use this graph to answer these questions: What product is measured on this graph? What period of time does it cover? In what year did oil production first reach 50 million metric tons? When did oil production reach 100 million metric tons? In what 10-year period did oil production increase most rapidly?

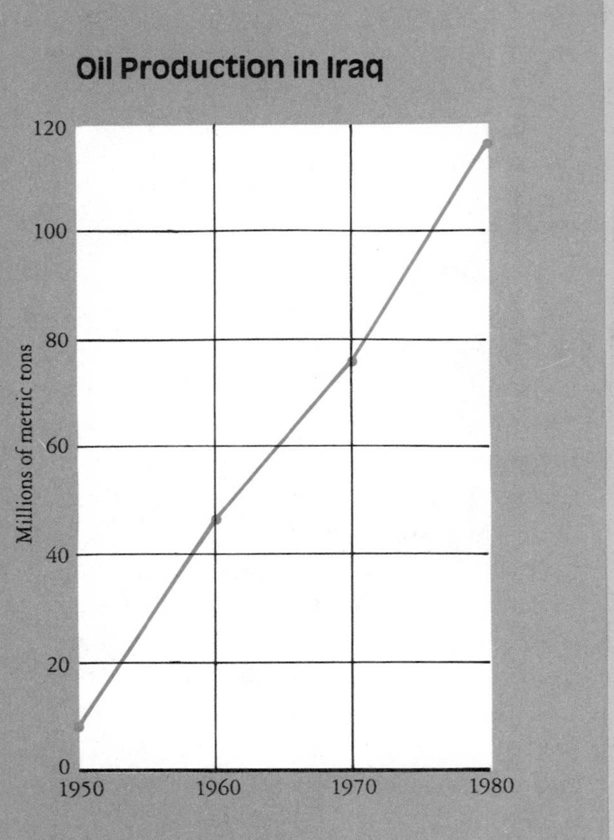

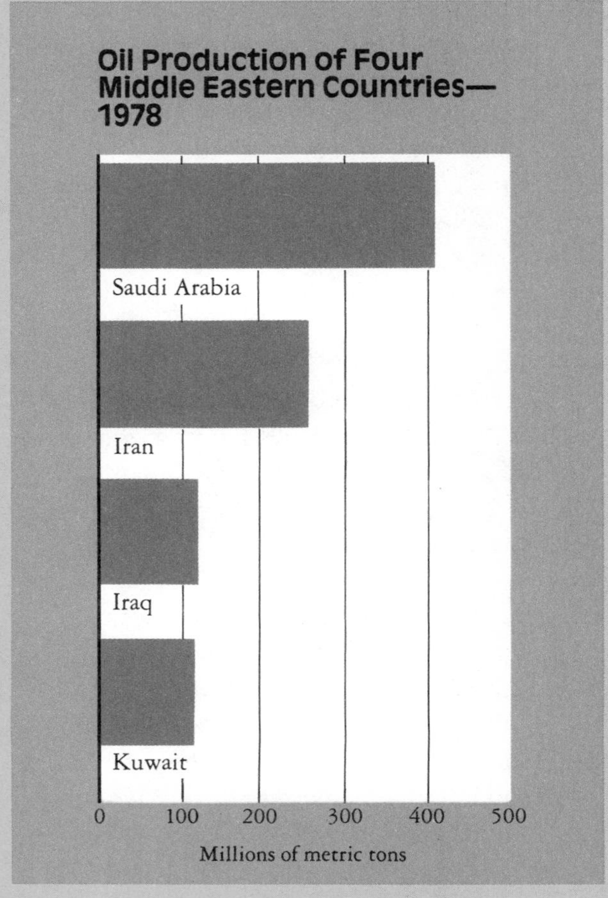

2. **Graph:** Now look at the other graph. This is a bar graph. A bar graph is useful to compare the amount of production of a crop or of a commodity in different places during a certain period.

What product is shown in this graph? Which four countries are compared? Which country produced more than 300 million metric tons? Which country produced the most oil?

Thinking It Through

1. One of Hammurabi's laws reads: "If a builder made a house but did not make his work strong, and the house fell down and caused the death of the owner, the builder shall be put to death." What does the law tell you about Babylonian society?
2. Most early civilizations developed along river valleys. Why do you think this was so?
3. The invention of writing and of the alphabet changed people's lives greatly. Name six means of communication based on the written word. Which ones do you use? Do radio and television have as great an effect on us as the written word?

Projects

1. Using old magazines, see how many photographs you can find of different forms of transportation used in the Middle East today. Arrange these in a display for your classroom.
2. Invent a kind of picture-writing. Divide into two teams. Write a letter to the other team using pictures cut out of old magazines. Exchange letters, and see how well you communicated.
3. The Explorers' Committee might like to follow the adventures of a scientist digging in the ruins of Babylon, Nineveh, or Ur. Tell the class about the discoveries made and point out the places on a map.
4. The Research Committee might like to do research on the Israeli kibbutz, or farm community. How do the lives of boys and girls on the kibbutz differ from your own? Make a report to your class.
5. Hummurabi carved the laws of Babylonia on stone pillars for all to read. Our country has so many laws that we cannot read all of them. But we have one set of laws that every American should know. It is the Constitution of the United States. The king made the laws in Babylonia and was all-powerful. Who has the final power in the United States? The Research Committee might like to look up the first sentence of the Constitution, called the Preamble. It can then report to the class the answer to the question.

3 India and Southeast Asia

Unit Preview

Five thousand years ago, a number of small settlements of people were scattered throughout the Indus River Valley. This valley runs through present-day Pakistan. From the settlements, the first civilized communities of India and Southeast Asia developed. Here also, a new religion began. It was based on the teachings of Buddha.

The mountain ranges in the north only partially separated India from the Middle East. Several times in India's history foreigners swept through the mountain passes in attempts at conquest. The Aryan tribes came from Central Asia, Alexander the Great led his army from the northwest, and the Muslims also came from Central Asia.

In modern times the British controlled much of the country. But many Indians wanted freedom through self-government. The movement for independence was led by a peace-loving man named Gandhi. He was dedicated to achieving freedom without war. Gandhi's dream of a free India was finally realized in 1947.

The lowlands of southeastern Asia have been occupied many times by foreigners. Malaysia was once a group of British colonies. The British wanted to control the rubber plantations and tin mines there. Vietnam was part of French-held Indochina. The United States fought its longest war in this area.

Things to Discover

If you look carefully at the picture, map, and time line on these pages, you can answer these questions.

1. What ocean is east of the area highlighted on the map? What other ocean borders the area?
2. How long did the British rule India?
3. The picture shows workers harvesting tea, an important crop in Southeast Asia and India. What kind of land is used for growing tea?
4. Buddha was an important religious leader. When was he born?
5. What ancient military leader invaded India in 326 B.C.?
6. The Indus River flows through Pakistan. How many years after a civilization developed there did Pakistan gain its independence?

Words to Learn

You will meet these words in this unit. As you read, you will learn what they mean and how to pronounce them. The Word List will help you.

Buddhism	maharaja
caste system	monsoon
Hinduism	pagoda
jade	partition
jute	teak
landlocked	truce
latex	untouchable

Indus River civilizations established
c. 2500
Aryans invade India
c. 1500
Birth of Buddha
c. 563
Alexander the Great invades India
326
Asoka becomes ruler of India
272
B.C.
A.D.
Taj Mahal built
1653
British control India
1757
India and Pakistan become independent
1947
Federation of Malaysia formed
1963
Vietnam war ends
1975

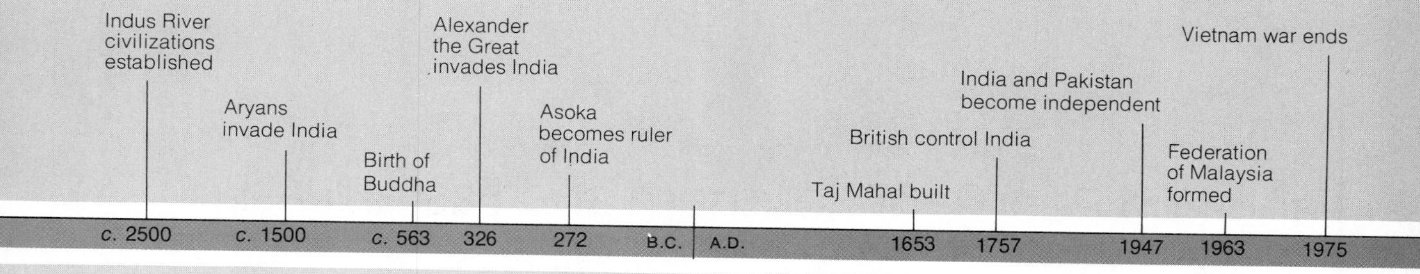

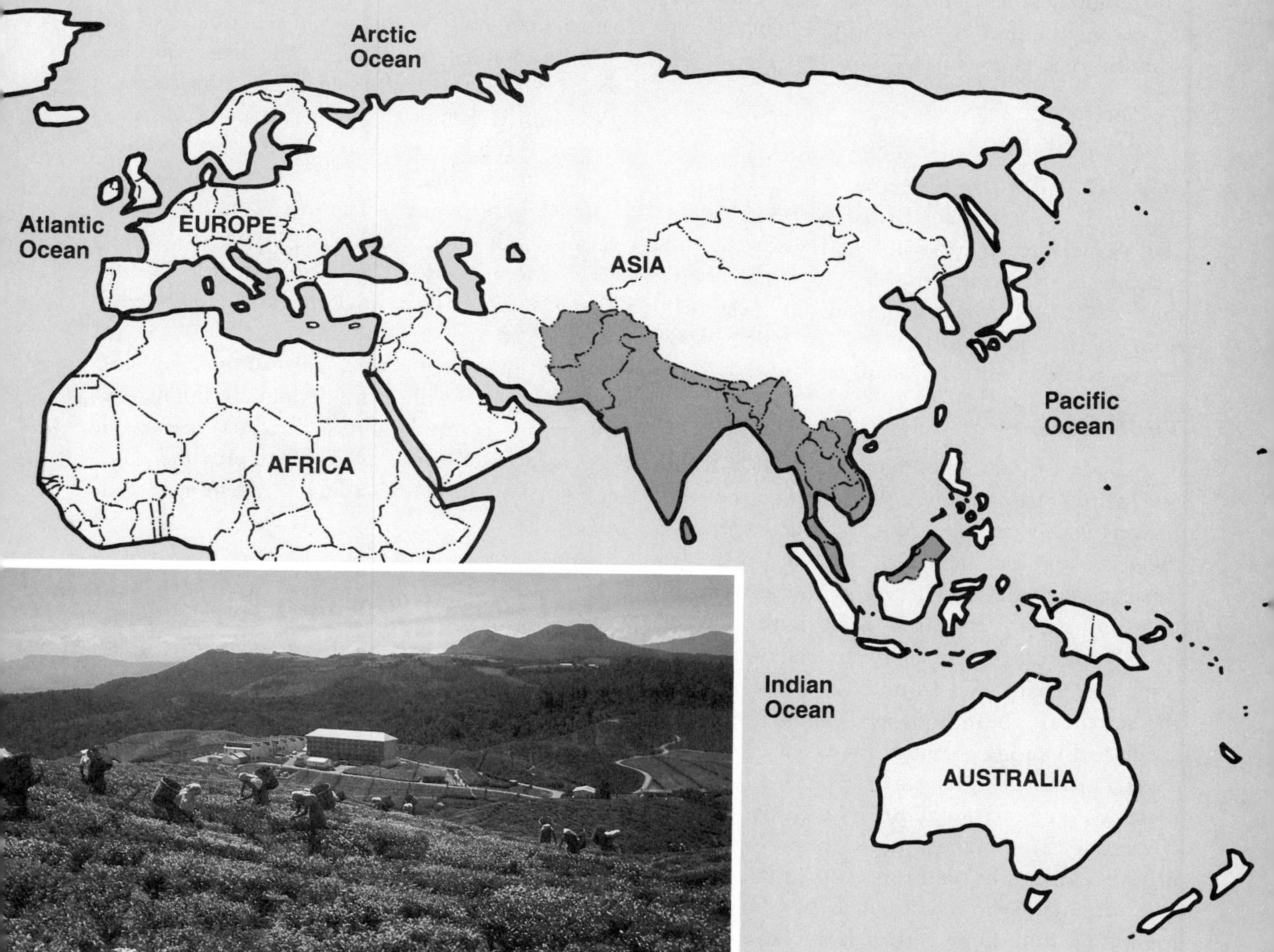

Arctic Ocean
Atlantic Ocean
EUROPE
ASIA
AFRICA
Pacific Ocean
Indian Ocean
AUSTRALIA

1
Land and People of Southern and Eastern Asia

The countries of Southern and Eastern Asia occupy a large part of the continent. Let us first examine Asia as a whole.

The Continent of Asia

Asia is the giant among the world's continents. Its area is greater than that of North America and South America combined. Africa, the second largest continent, is only about two-thirds as large as Asia. So huge is Asia that some of its lands north of the Arctic Circle freeze, while other regions are very hot.

The Geography of Asia

The lands of Asia face many different oceans and seas. The continent is bounded by the Indian Ocean on the south, by the Pacific on the east, and by the Arctic on the north. Its western boundaries are the Mediterranean, Caspian, Black, and Red seas, with Europe lying to the northwest. Only the narrow Bering Strait separates Asia from North America on the northeast. Hundreds of islands, large and small, form a long chain off the coast of Asia.

Asia has the greatest plains, the largest plateaus, and the highest mountains of any continent. The highest peak in the world is Mount Everest, in the Himalayas (him'ə lā'əz). The mountains of Asia formed barriers which for a long time kept people from crossing the continent. Even today few people live in the mountains and the desert regions.

The People of Asia

More than half of the world's people live in Asia. And most of these people live near the coasts where the land is level and the rainfall plentiful. This means that some parts of Asia are more thickly populated than are any other parts of the world.

There are many differences among these people. But they are also alike in important ways. Most of them are farmers, for raising food for the large population is their greatest need. Few are factory workers. Many Asian nations have been slow in building up industries. Nearly all of the people are poor, too. In every country some persons are well educated and enjoy a comfortable life. But most Asians lead lives touched by hunger and illness.

The Lands of Southern Asia

Our study begins in southern Asia with India, Pakistan, and Bangladesh (bang'glə desh'). We will go east through Burma, Thailand (tī'land'), Laos (lä'ōs), Kampuchea (käm pōō chē'ə), Vietnam (vē'et näm'), Malaysia (mə lā'zhə), and Singapore.

This broad stretch of Asia is sometimes called the Far East, or the Orient (ôr'ē ənt). China and Korea, as well as the island countries of Japan, Indonesia, the Philippines, and other islands of the Pacific Ocean are also included in the Orient. We shall read about these countries later.

ASIA
0 100 200 400 600 800 Miles
0 160 322 644 966 1287 Kilometers
Mountains
Hills
National Capitals
Plateaus
Plains
Other Cities
© Rand McNally & Co.
NORTH POLE
Permanent Ice Pack
GREENLAND
Ice Cap
ICELAND
ATLANTIC OCEAN
ARCTIC OCEAN
BERING STRAIT
ALEUTIAN ISLANDS
BERING SEA
Anchorage
West Longitude
East Longitude
SVALBARD
IRELAND
UNITED KINGDOM
London
NORWAY
Oslo
SWEDEN
Stockholm
FINLAND
Helsinki
Murmansk
FRANCE
Paris
WEST GERMANY
EAST GERMANY
Bonn
Berlin
POLAND
Arkhangelsk
Leningrad
Moscow
EUROPE
YUGOSLAVIA
ROMANIA
GREECE
Gorkiy
Odessa
Dnepr
Don
Volga River
Rostov
Ural River
BLACK SEA
Istanbul
Ankara
TURKEY
CYPRUS
LEBANON
ISRAEL
SYRIA
JORDAN
IRAQ
Baghdad
Basra
CAUCASUS MTS.
CASPIAN SEA
Baku
Tabriz
Tehran
IRAN
Meshed
ARAL SEA
URAL MOUNTAINS
Sverdlovsk
Chelyabinsk
Ob River
SOVIET UNION
SIBERIA
Yenisey River
Lena River
ARCTIC CIRCLE
Novosibirsk
Angara R.
Lake Baikal
Amur River
SEA OF OKHOTSK
Kamchatka Peninsula
Sakhalin
Kuril Islands
PACIFIC OCEAN
Lake Balkhash
Tashkent
Amu Darya
TIEN SHAN
Ulan Bator
MONGOLIA
GOBI
Vladivostok
Shenyang
N. KOREA
S. KOREA
Pyongyang
Seoul
SEA OF JAPAN
JAPAN
Tokyo
Osaka
Kitakyushu
Beijing
Tianjin
Huang River
YELLOW SEA
CHINA
Nanjing
Shanghai
Wuhan
EAST CHINA SEA
TROPIC OF CANCER
TAIWAN
Chongqing
Chang River
Guangzhou
Victoria
HONG KONG
SAUDI ARABIA
Riyadh
Mecca
PERSIAN GULF
UNITED ARAB EMIRATES
Muscat
OMAN
YEMEN
SOUTHERN YEMEN
Aden
Mukalla
AFRICA
AFGHANISTAN
Kabul
Islamabad
Rawalpindi
Lahore
PAKISTAN
Indus R.
Karachi
HIMALAYA MOUNTAINS
PLATEAU OF TIBET
Lhasa
NEPAL
Kathmandu
Mt. Everest 29,028 ft. (8080 m)
BHUTAN
Brahmaputra River
Ganges River
New Delhi
INDIA
Calcutta
Dacca
BANGLADESH
Bombay
ARABIAN SEA
Bay of Bengal
Madras
SRI LANKA
Irrawaddy
Mandalay
BURMA
Rangoon
LAOS
Vientiane
Hanoi
Mekong River
THAILAND
Bangkok
Phnom Penh
KAMPUCHEA
Ho Chi Minh City
VIETNAM
SOUTH CHINA SEA
PHILIPPINES
Manila
MALAYSIA
Kuala Lumpur
Singapore
SINGAPORE
STRAIT OF MALACCA
BORNEO
Sulawesi
SUMATRA
INDONESIA
Jakarta
JAVA
Timor
EQUATOR

The Past of These Countries

The cultures of South and Southeast Asia are thousands of years old. Two centers of very early civilizations were in river valleys in India and China. Mountains and deserts shut off these valleys to a large extent from the Middle East and from each other.

India and China developed civilizations in early times. When Europeans met the Indians and the Chinese, they found that there was much to be learned from them.

These Countries Today

Many of the countries in Asia were ruled by foreigners for long periods of time. Most of the countries did not gain independence until after World War II, which ended in 1945.

Do You Know?

1. How large is Asia? What oceans border it? What different land surfaces are found on this continent?
2. Where do most people in Asia live?

2 The Indian Peninsula

Extending southward from the continent of Asia is the peninsula of India. This peninsula is half as large as the mainland of the United States. The peninsula today is divided into three nations. They are India, Pakistan, and Bangladesh.

The Geography of the Peninsula

The map of India and Nearby Lands shows that the peninsula on which the republics of India, Pakistan, and Bangladesh are located is shaped like a triangle. It is a large land mass that in early times was almost shut off from the rest of Asia.

On the north the Himalayas, the highest mountains in the world, rise like a great wall. Mountains and wide desert lands form the western boundaries of the peninsula. Southward, the peninsula grows narrower. The Bay of Bengal on the east and the Arabian Sea on the west wash India's coasts. To the southeast, in the Indian Ocean, lies the island of Sri Lanka (srē län′kə).

Two great rivers which arise in the mountains pour down upon the plains of

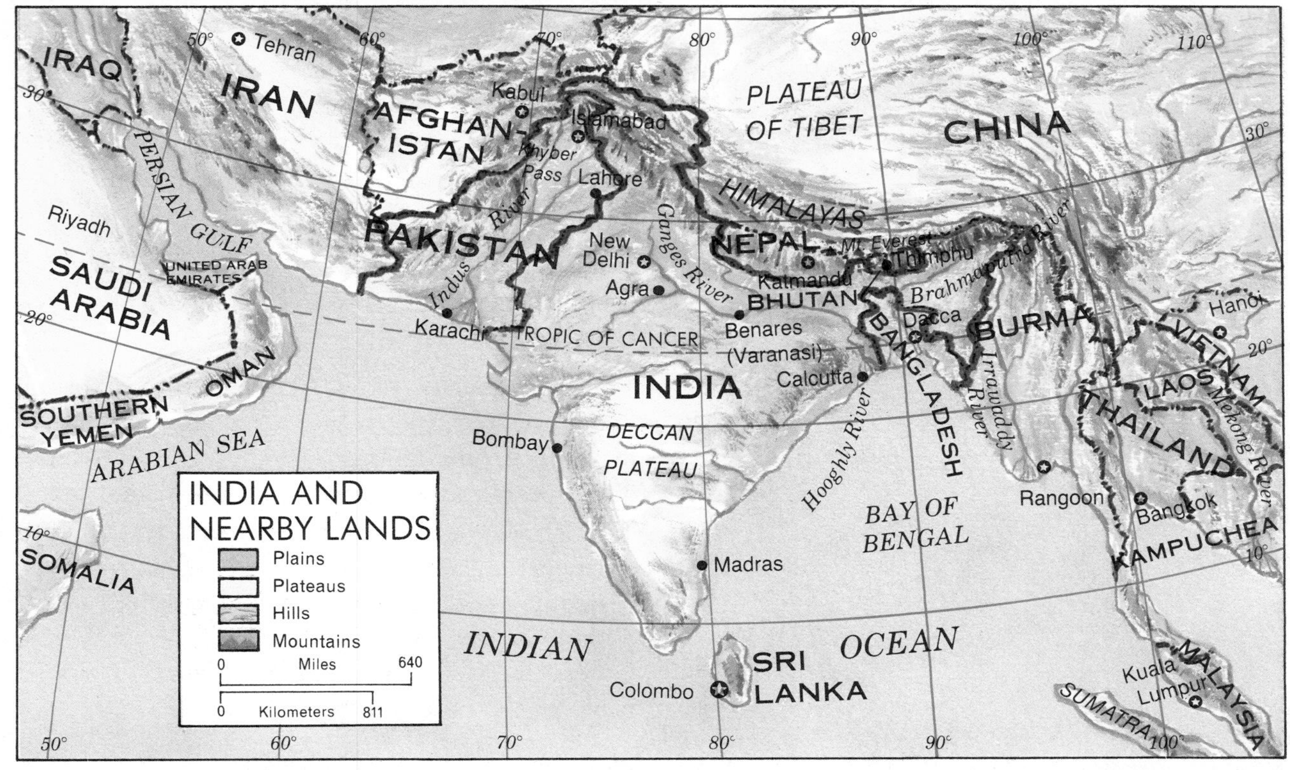

northern India. The Ganges (gan′jēz), over 1,500 miles (2,400 km) long, moves across India into the Bay of Bengal. The Indus (in′dəs), longer still, flows across Pakistan into the Arabian Sea. These large rivers flow through fertile plains. Most of Pakistan's people live in the valley of the Indus River.

The Monsoon Seasons

Anyone who has ever lived in India or who has read about the region has heard of the *monsoons* (mon so͞onz′). A monsoon is a wind which blows across southern Asia. There is a summer monsoon and a winter monsoon.

When summer comes to that part of Asia, the land grows hot. During this time, a wind blows for several months from the southwest, from the sea to the land. This is the summer monsoon.

The summer monsoon generally meets hills or mountains as it reaches the shore. The wind travels up the slopes, grows cool, and drops its water as rain. Summer, in most of southern Asia, is the wet season.

In winter the open stretches of land cool off. The wind now blows from the northeast, from the land toward the sea. This wind lasts for about 6 months. It is the winter monsoon.

Since the winter monsoon blows from the interior of Asia, the winter is a dry season through most of South Asia.

In winter in these regions the trees lose their leaves, the grass turns brown, pasture is scarce, and crops dry up. There is little water in the smaller streams, and the roads are deep with dust. As the month of May comes on, the weather grows hotter and hotter. Fresh winds blow at times. But when these die away, both people and animals swelter in the heat.

Finally, the rain arrives. It pours for weeks or months. The rivers overflow their banks, and the dust turns into mud. Soon grass covers

The summer *monsoon* in India begins in June and ends in September. It brings most of India's rain. People in India look forward to the coming of the *monsoon*.

the earth. The farmers then plant their crops.

Sometimes the summer monsoon is late in coming, or it does not bring enough rain. With too little moisture no crops are raised, and millions of people in the region go hungry. To them the coming of the summer monsoon is the most important event in the year.

The Early History of the Peninsula

The peninsula of India, like Egypt and Mesopotamia, was the scene of an ancient civilization. Communities grew up more than 4,000 years ago, in what is now Pakistan. They flourished there for many years and then disappeared.

People were building, manufacturing, and trading in the Indus Valley 5,000 years ago. Others were doing much the same on the banks of the Nile and the Euphrates.

The Coming of the Aryans

About 1500 B.C. a major wave of tribes of herders from Central Asia came down through the mountain passes into India. These people were fair-skinned, had tamed the horse, and drove chariots far superior to any yet known. They called themselves Aryans (er′ē ənz).

Everywhere the Aryans went they conquered the local people and then lived with them. Some tribes went southwest from their homeland into India. Others moved east or south and are the ancestors of many present-day Europeans. The language of the Aryans was Sanskrit (sans′krit). Sanskrit words are found in many modern languages, including English. The Sanskrit word "mata" became "mother" in English.

The Aryans conquered only the people of northern India, but gradually their influence spread through most of the country. Much of the Indian culture can be traced back to the Aryans.

The Caste System

The Aryans were divided into two groups, nobles and ordinary tribe members. When they settled down in India, they placed the people of that country into new social groups. Over many centuries the *caste system* (kast sis′təm) developed. A caste system is a way of life that keeps each person in a certain class or group for life.

Indian society was made up of four classes: priests, warriors, merchants, and laborers. Some people were completely outside the caste system. They became known as outcastes. Because they were given the most lowly work to do they were not supposed to touch members of higher castes. For this reason they were also called *untouchables* (un tuch′ ə bəlz).

Each class was further divided into many subgroups. As time went on the customs, habits, and ways of making a living of each caste differed from one another. People had no choice about their caste. They were born into it. No person could eat with a member of another caste. A person could only marry someone from the same caste, and work at only certain kinds of work. Those who disobeyed these rules could be severely punished.

The caste system is still a part of Indian life. But many changes have taken place. In 1950 the new government outlawed people's being treated as untouchable.

Annual festivals are an important part of worship for Hindus in India. One festival honors Vishnu, the god of preservation. Shown below is a statue of Shiva, the god of destruction and rebirth.

This stone sculpture shows a scene from the life of Gautama, known to Indians as the Buddha. The sculpture shows him seated at the foot of a tree, preaching. His followers surround him.

The caste system was a part of a way of life called *Hinduism* (hin′ do͞o iz′əm). Its followers are known as Hindus. Though most of the people of India are Hindus, not everyone worships in the same way. They all accept differences in one another's beliefs and respect all forms of life.

Birthplace of a New Religion

Near the foot of the Himalayas about 2,500 years ago there lived a young prince named Gautama (gô′tə mə). He had a splendid palace which he seldom left, and great riches. But when he was still a young man he became troubled by the misery, illness, and death that he saw about him.

Gautama's Search for Truth

"How can we break out of the misery?" the young prince asked. No one could tell him. "I must go away and find the answer," he decided.

For 7 years the prince lived like other Indian holy men. Wearing beggar's rags, he listened to what others had to teach. He learned to control his hunger and his emotions. Still, he did not find an answer to his question.

As he sat one day under the cool shadow of a large tree, the truth seemed to come to him.

"To end suffering," he thought, "we must learn to be unselfish, and we must love one another. We must overcome anger by kindness, and evil by good."

The Spread of Buddhism

Gautama died in about 483 B.C., but the people of India continued to follow his teachings. They called him the Buddha. Buddha means Enlightened One, or the Teacher of Truth. The religion based on the Buddha's teaching is called *Buddhism* (bood′iz′əm). Buddhism spread into China and later into Japan.

Today Buddhism has more followers in other Asian countries than in India. All over the Far East there are many Buddhist temples.

Rulers of India

Not long after the death of the Buddha a general named Alexander the Great invaded the peninsula from the northwest. Alexander the Great led an army from southern Europe across the mountains and conquered the Indus Valley in 326 B.C. Alexander did not remain in India. But his conquest put India in touch with lands to the west.

One of India's greatest rulers was Asoka (ə shō′kə). He reigned about 272–232 B.C. Asoka's empire extended throughout most of

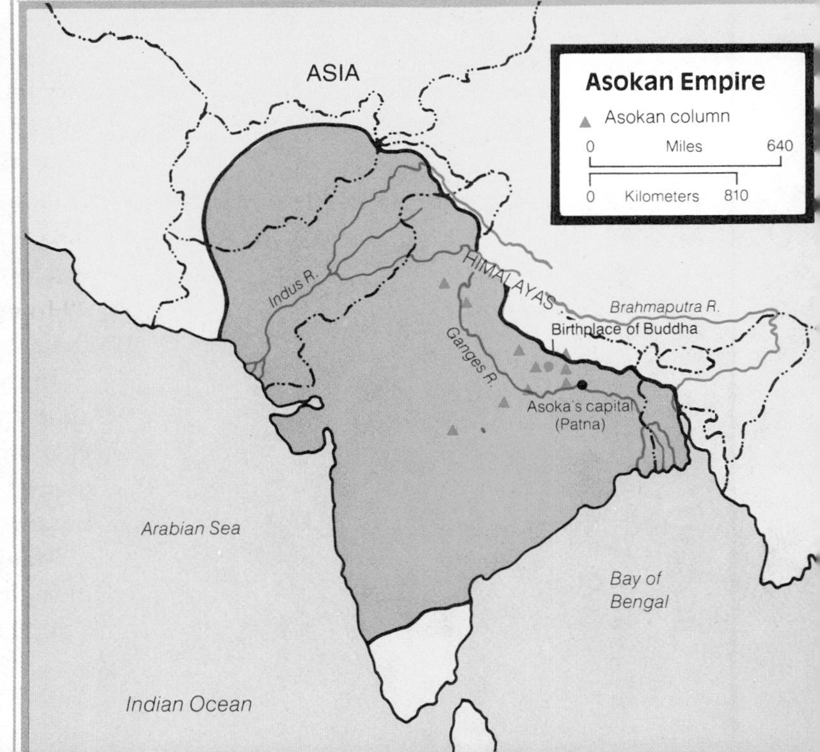

Until 232 B.C., Asoka ruled most of the Indian peninsula. A devout Buddhist, Asoka placed throughout his kingdom columns inscribed with Buddhist principles.

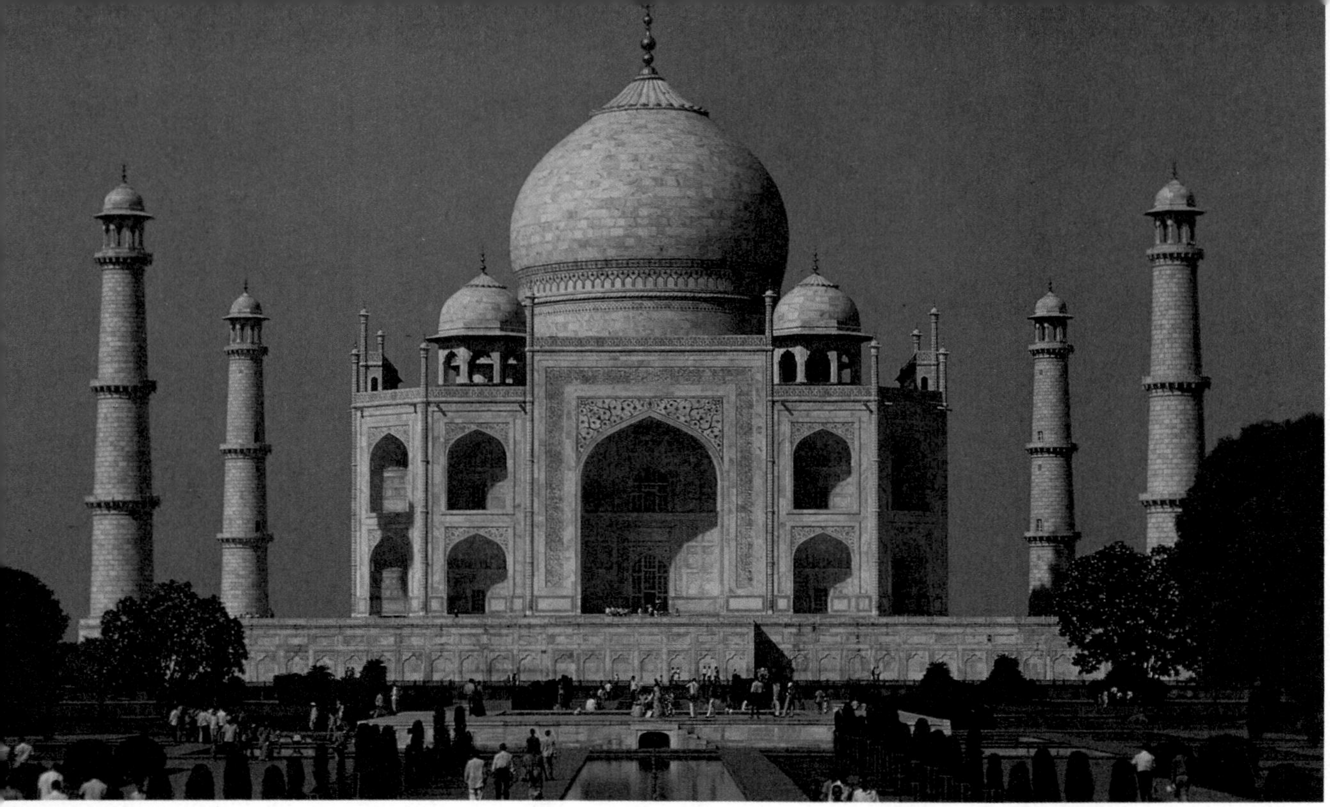

One of India's and the world's most beautiful buildings is the splendid Taj Mahal in the city of Agra. Find Agra on the map on page 103. Other important Indian contributions are shown below.

Gifts of Ancient India

Our system of numbers
The zero
Medicines from plants
Cotton cloth
Buddhism

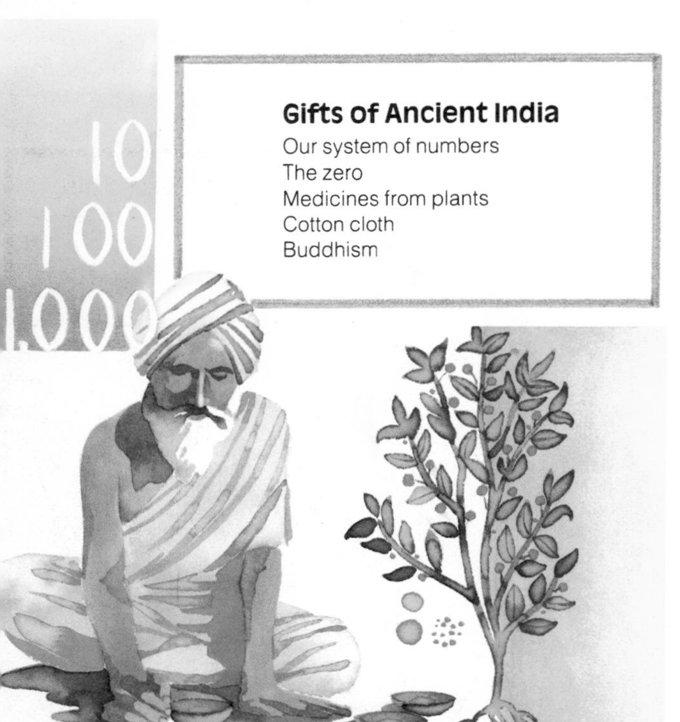

the Indian peninsula. For the first time India was united as a nation.

Asoka wished to spread the message of the Buddha. Throughout his kingdom he set up huge stone columns. On these were his instructions. The instructions told people to live peacefully, obey their parents, and respect their teachers.

In the centuries following Asoka, India again split up into smaller kingdoms. Then the Moguls, who were Muslims from Central Asia, conquered most of northern India. Many Indians became followers of Mohammed.

Many splendid palaces and tombs were built in India by the Muslims. Some people think the Taj Mahal (täzh′ mə häl′) is the world's most beautiful building. It was built by Shah Jahan (shä jə hän′) as a tomb for his wife. About 20,000 workers labored for over 20 years to build the magnificent white tomb. It was completed in 1653.

India Under British Rule

The next foreign power to rule India was Great Britain. About the time that the British began to found colonies in North America, they also became interested in India. English businesses organized the East India Company to handle trade with India. Aided by the British army, the company controlled most of India after 1757.

In 1858 the British government took over the lands of the East India Company. British India was then governed by a British official. The rest of India was divided into about 600 states, under Indian rulers.

Most of the rulers of these states bore the title of *maharaja* (mä′hə rä′ jə). Maharaja means "great chief." Most of the maharajas lived like kings in fine palaces with many servants. Some of them governed well. But some spent more time thinking of their own comforts than of the needs of their people.

The British made many contributions to India. They brought peace to troubled areas. They provided safe drinking water. Hospitals and schools were built in many cities. British engineers built irrigation systems for farms in dry areas. They also constructed thousands of miles of railroads and highways so that food and other goods could be shipped where they were needed.

The Movement for Independence

Under British rule, the people of India had little voice in the government of their country. Like the early Americans, they wanted to be free.

In World War I, India fought on the side of the British. Soon after this, a movement for independence swept through India. The Indian National Congress party was organized to carry on the work of making India free. The leader of this movement was Mohandas Gandhi (mō′han däs′ gän′dē).

Gandhi, Father of Modern India

Gandhi taught the Indians to struggle against British rule by refusing to work for the British and by refusing to obey British laws. This kind of peaceful resistance without fighting proved to be a powerful weapon.

Britain had imposed a tax on salt. The people of India felt this was unjust. They felt that because the salt came from Indian oceans it should be free to all the people. Gandhi led his followers in a march toward the sea to make their own tax-free salt. The British jailed Gandhi and some 60,000 others. But the local jails could not hold so many people and the British soon released them.

Gandhi worked all his life to help women get better jobs and education, to reform the caste system, and to improve the life of untouchables. Gandhi was called Mahatma (mə hät′mə) by his people. It means "Great Soul." Gandhi was shot to death in 1948 by a Hindu who objected to the leader's reforms.

Mohandas Gandhi used nonviolence to free the people of India from British rule. The mild, peace-loving Gandhi was considered by his followers to be a saint.

Two New Nations

When World War II was over, Britain promised the Indian leaders their country's freedom if they could agree among themselves. But there were many differences between the chief religious groups. The Hindu and Muslim leaders could not agree on the part each group should play in the new government.

Finally they all reluctantly decided to divide the country into a Muslim nation, called Pakistan, and the largely Hindu nation of India. In 1947 the division was made, and the British left India. But the *partition* (pär tish′ən), or division of the country, caused great hardships. Twelve million people were uprooted and moved from one country to another. Thousands were killed in fierce rioting between the two groups before peace was restored.

The Republic of India

The peninsula of India is so large that it is almost a continent in itself. With so much land and so many people, this region plays an important part in the world today.

The Government of India

New Delhi is the capital of India. Here the elected officials from every part of India meet. New Delhi was built next to the old city of Delhi, which had been a capital during Muslim rule. The two Delhis are a blend of old and new, and of people from various parts of India.

Hindi is the national language of India. For many years English was also a national language.

The first prime minister of India was Jawaharlal Nehru (jə wä′hər läl′ nā′ro͞o). Like Gandhi, he was a leader in the independence movement. Nehru's daughter, Indira Gandhi (in dēr′a gän′dē), became prime minister in 1966. After her party lost the leadership of the country, she was out of office for a brief time. Then she was re-elected. She was murdered in 1984.

Farming and Manufacturing in India

India is about half the size of Europe, yet it has nearly as many people. Its population is growing at a rapid rate. Three out of four Indians are farmers. About two-thirds of them

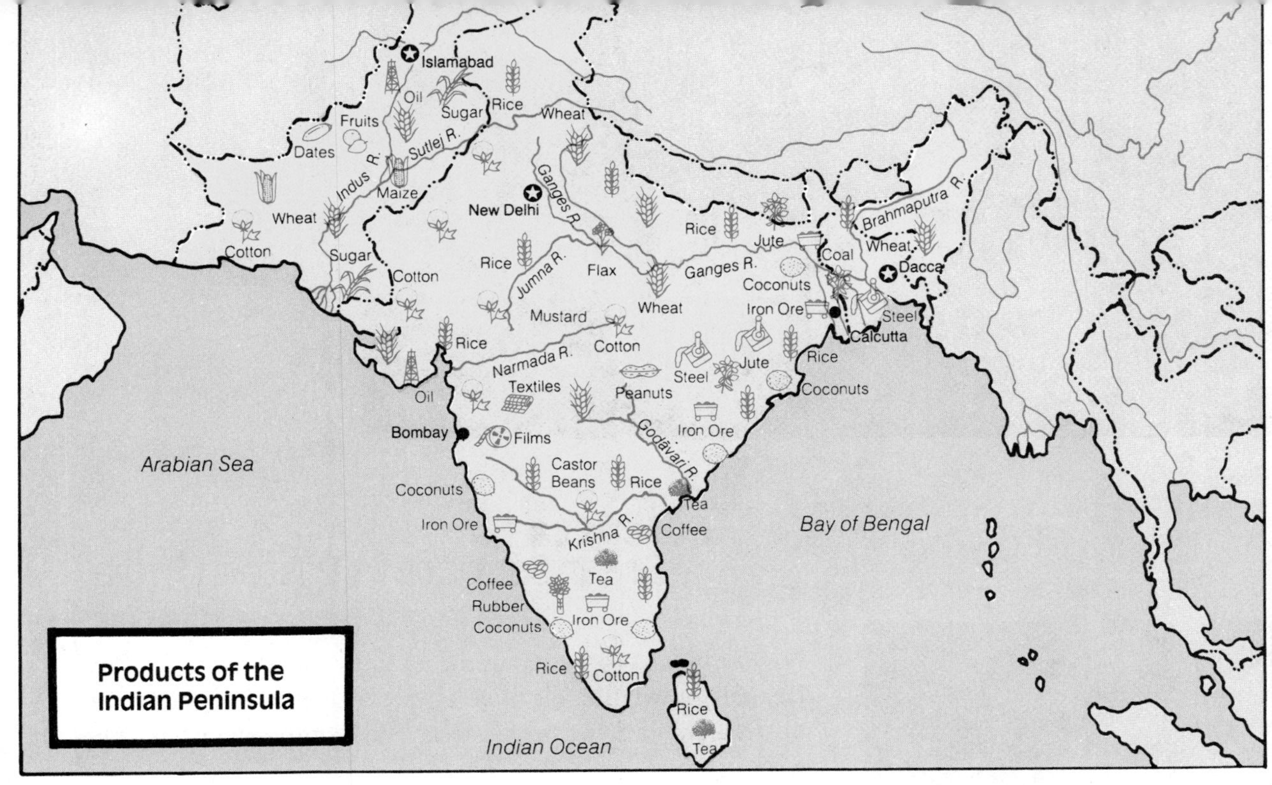

own their own land. India's main problem is to produce enough food for its rapidly growing population. When the crops are not good, the people must depend on shipments of food from countries like the United States to keep from starving.

Since becoming independent, the country has greatly increased the amount of irrigated farmland. Farmers are learning better methods of producing crops. The government gives them improved seed and teaches modern ways of farming.

India produces great quantities of coconuts, flaxseed, cottonseed, peanuts, mustard seed, and castor beans. These are pressed into oil used in making soap, paint, and medicine. Some are made into lubricating, or smoothing, oil. Others are used in cooking and in salad dressings. Some of these oils are pressed out in India's own factories. But large amounts are shipped in the form of raw materials to Europe, where the oil is manufactured nearer the places where it will be used.

Besides oils, India also produces rice, wheat, coffee, tea, cotton, and sugarcane.

Since 1947 India's steel production has increased many times. Textile manufacturing, begun under the British, continues to be important. Building irrigation and electric plants also provides jobs. New projects in education are teaching people the skills needed to earn a living.

Calcutta
A Great Seaport in Eastern India

Ninety miles (144 km) up the Hoogly River from the Bay of Bengal sprawls India's huge city of Calcutta. For miles both upstream and downstream from the city the river banks bulge with wharves.

Calcutta is a major port because of its location. It is the gateway of the great Ganges river valley to the northwest. It is in a rich delta area. Produce grown in the delta is processed in the city's factories then shipped out from the port. And in this northeast corner of India are the country's main coal fields, iron mines, and steel-making centers.

The people who have crowded into the city to find jobs are Calcutta's most serious problem. Sleeping space, water, transportation, are all in short supply. The government of India is working hard to solve these problems.

The city of Benares plays an important part in the Hindu religion. It is built on the banks of a river sacred to Hindus. Each year Hindus come to Benares to cleanse and purify themselves in the water.

Bombay, a Cotton City

Bombay is a busy city on the western coast of India. The buildings are in European style, but the people in the streets do not dress like Europeans. They wear white cotton robes and turbans, which are cool in the hot moist climate.

India is second only to the United States as a cotton-growing country. It produces about one-half as much as the United States. Hundreds of textile mills in Bombay turn cotton into cloth.

Bombay is also a film capital of the world. Movies made in India are popular throughout Asia and the Middle East.

A City on the Ganges

Far different is the city of Benares (bənär′is), also called Varanasi (vərä′nəsē). Benares is an ancient city built on the banks of the Ganges. Beautiful temples and palaces stand along the river bank. Every year millions of people come to bathe in the river. To the Hindus, the Ganges River is a sacred river. It is worshipped as the giver of life.

In Benares cattle wander through narrow streets and monkeys scamper along rooftops. Hindus respect all forms of life. Most of all, they show respect for the cow. Because cows provide milk, they are like mothers to all. No Hindu will eat beef out of respect for the cow.

One of the largest cities in Pakistan is Lahore. Many beautiful buildings, such as this mosque, can be found there. The city is a center for industry and education.

Two Islamic Nations

In 1947, Pakistan became independent. It was divided into two parts, West Pakistan and East Pakistan. The two divisions were almost 1,000 miles (1,600 km) apart. The people of the two land areas spoke different languages and were different in many other ways. The distance and the differences made it hard for them to work together as one nation. In 1971, there was a civil war between the two divisions. After 9 months of fighting, East Pakistan gained its independence. It became the Republic of Bangladesh.

The Republic of Pakistan

West Pakistan is now the Republic of Pakistan. It is a little larger in area than the states of Texas and Oklahoma combined. Most of the people are farmers or herders. They live in a fertile plain called the Punjab. The capital, Islamabad (is läm′ä bäd), lies in this area of northeast Pakistan. Much of western Pakistan is dry, so fields must be irrigated with water from the Indus River and its tributaries. Pakistan shares these waters with India. Pakistan's main crops are wheat, cotton, corn, sugarcane, and rice.

The Republic of Bangladesh

Bangladesh is small and very crowded. It has a hot, rainy climate that is good for farming. Farming is carried on near the banks of the Ganges and Brahmaputra (brä′mə po͞o′trə) rivers. Farmers grow rice, sugarcane, cotton, tea, tobacco, and jute (jo͞ot). Jute is a plant with strong fibers that is used to make rope and burlap. There is not enough food produced to feed all the people.

When Bangladesh became a republic in 1971, after its war with Pakistan, millions of people were without homes. There were many floods and there was little food. In 1978 the population swelled further when about 150,000 Muslim refugees from Burma fled to Bangladesh.

Mountain Lands

North of India, Pakistan, and Bangladesh are Afghanistan (af gan′ə stan′), Nepal (nə pol′), and Bhutan (bo͞o tän′). These lands are almost completely shut off from the outside world by towering mountains. As you can see from the map of India and Nearby Lands on page 103, all three are *landlocked* (land′lokt′) countries. That is, they have no seacoast. How does being landlocked affect trade with other countries?

Afghanistan and the Khyber Pass

Afghanistan is about the size of Texas. Most of it is covered with mountains and desert. In fertile valleys farmers raise grain, fruits, vegetables, and cotton. Most of them earn a living by herding sheep and cattle. Besides milk and meat, the animals furnish wool and skins, which are two of Afghanistan's exports. Other exports are cotton, rugs, and dried fruits.

Afghanistan is largely shut off from its neighbors by the deserts and mountains. Entering and leaving the country is made possible by mountain passes. The most famous of these is Khyber Pass, which leads into Pakistan.

Inside Afghanistan the traveler can journey by either camel caravan or airplane. There are no railroads, and few roads are good enough for automobile travel in Afghanistan.

In 1980 the Soviet Union invaded Afghanistan in support of the communist government. The government had been losing its control. Many people in Afghanistan fought bravely against the invasion, despite their lack of good weapons. To protest the invasion, the United States, along with many other nations, refused to participate in the 1980 Summer Olympic Games that were held in the Soviet Union.

Nepal, Land of Mount Everest

Nepal is a small country between India and Tibet. Mount Everest, in the Himalayas, is the world's highest mountain peak. It stands on Nepal's border with Tibet.

Before 1953 many teams of climbers had tried to climb Mount Everest, but all failed. The two who finally made the ascent to the top were Edmund Hillary, of New Zealand, and Tenzing Norgay, his Nepali guide. The expeditions to Everest and other Himalayan peaks have helped to make Nepal better known to the world.

Nepal is an independent country which is a little larger than our state of Arkansas. It has plains and low hills along its border with the Republic of India. From the plains the land rises sharply to the Himalayas along the border with Tibet.

Most of the people of Nepal live in fertile valleys around Kathmandu (kät'män d$\overline{oo}$'), the capital. Many of them work as farmers, growing rice, other foods, and jute. In the mountains sheepherders tend flocks of sheep and yaks, and woodcutters cut timber for export to India.

Do You Know?

1. What three nations are on the peninsula of India today?
2. What are the monsoons? Why are they important to India?
3. Who was Gautama Buddha? To what lands did his teachings spread?
4. How did Gandhi help India?
5. What differences are there between Pakistan and Bangladesh?

Before You Go On

Using New Words

caste system
Hinduism
monsoon
maharaja
landlocked
partition
untouchable
Buddhism
jute

Number a paper from 1 through 9. After each number write the word or term that matches the definition.

1. A word describing a country that has no seacoast
2. A religion and a way of life in India
3. The title of a ruler
4. A way of life that keeps each person in a certain class or group for life
5. A religion that began in India and spread to China and Japan
6. A wind of southern Asia that blows from the southwest in summer and from the northeast in winter
7. A person outside the caste system in India, who at one time was given the most lowly work
8. A plant with strong fibers used to make rope and burlap
9. Division of a country

Finding the Facts

1. How does the continent of Asia compare in size to other continents?
2. What important river flows into the Arabian Sea from Pakistan?
3. What is the climate of India in the winter? In the summer?
4. Who were the Aryans?
5. Who was Asoka?
6. What are three of India's chief cities? Why are they important?
7. Which country on the peninsula of India was once divided into two parts? What country did West Pakistan become? What country did East Pakistan become?
8. What is the Taj Mahal? When was it completed?
9. Where is Mt. Everest located? What mountain range is it part of?
10. How did the caste system develop in India?

3
The Countries of Southeast Asia

Seven countries are located in Southeast Asia. They are Burma, Thailand, Vietnam, Laos, Kampuchea (formerly Cambodia), the Federation of Malaysia, and Singapore.

Land and People

This area is densely populated. The population for all seven countries is more than 150 million. In many ways—in climate and in the ways of living of the people—the countries of Southeast Asia are alike. But we shall also learn about their differences.

The map of Southeast Asia on this page shows that large rivers flow toward the south through these countries. Burma has the Irrawaddy (ir′ə wod′ē), Thailand has the Menam (me näm′), and Vietnam has the Mekong

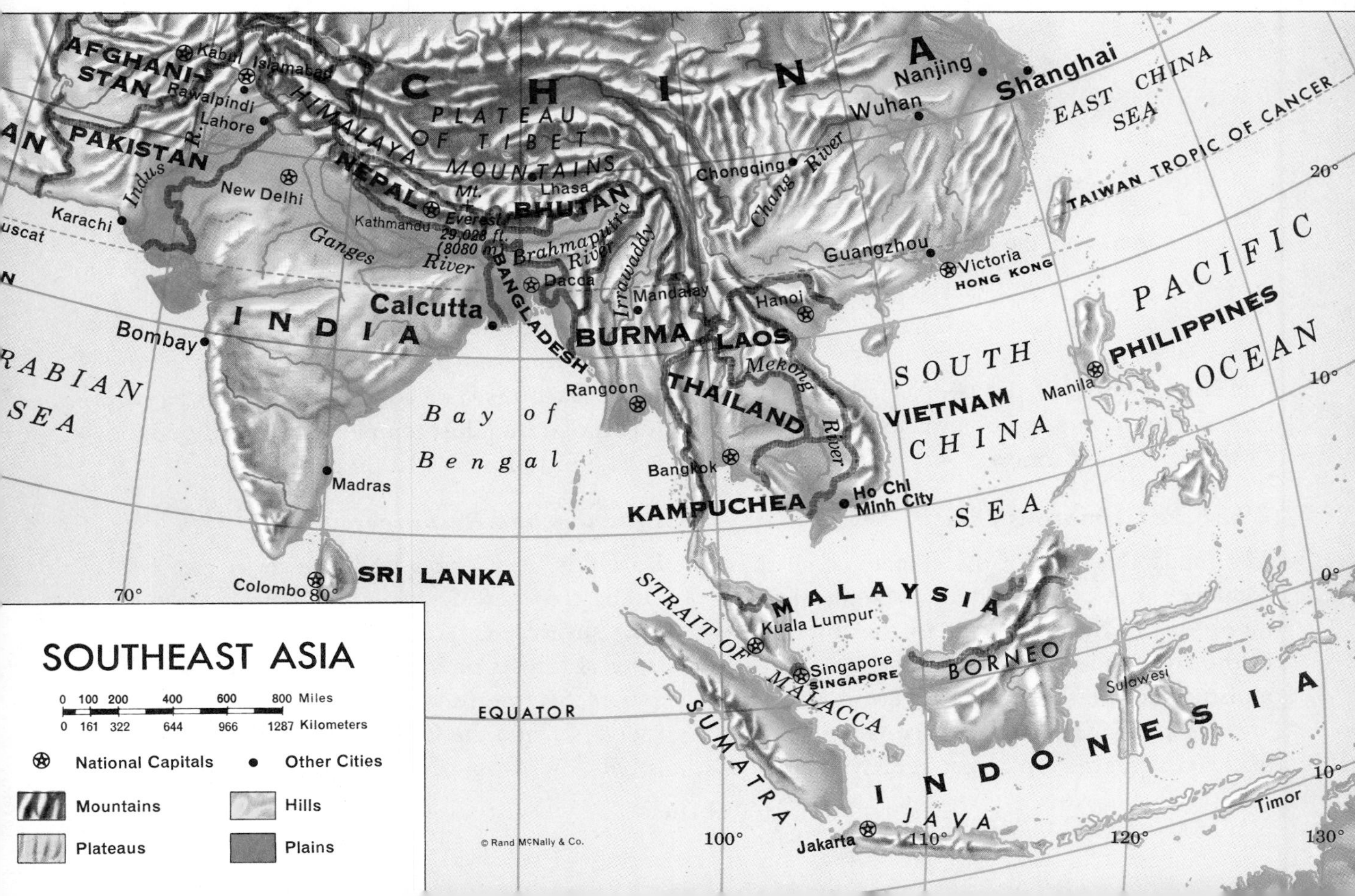

In front of the golden Shwe Dagon *pagoda*, a Buddhist monk walks along a street in Rangoon. The *pagoda* is thought to be the holiest in Burma.

(mā kong′). Most of the people live in the valleys of these rivers and of streams joining them. Most people are farmers.

What the Climate is Like

The monsoons control the climate of all these countries just as in the Indian Peninsula. The monsoons bring much rain to the lower parts of the river valleys. But they lose most of their moisture before they reach the northern areas.

Burma and Thailand are rice-growing countries, yet there are great grassy plains in the north. On the mountain slopes and near the rivers are thick forests and jungles. The cities of Rangoon (rang gōōn′) and Bangkok (bang′kok) are in the tropics. For this reason, their climate is hot.

Modern Burma

Burma was once a part of India. But in 1937 the British made Burma into a colony with the right to govern itself in most matters. In 1948 Burma was given complete independence. It became a republic. Burma lies east of India. The capital of Burma is Rangoon.

A "Golden Land"

The Burmese call their country the "Golden Land" because the rice crop turns the land gold-colored. Also, all throughout Burma are gold-covered *pagodas* (pə gō′dəz) and yellow-robed priests. A pagoda is a high temple with a series of roofs.

As a plane approaches Rangoon, the passengers first see the tall, golden spire of the Shwe Dagon (shā dä gôn′) pagoda. This pagoda is part of a Buddhist temple. It is considered the holiest of Rangoon's 1,000 pagodas.

Products and Resources

Burma is the world's leading exporter of rice. Other crops are beans, corn, cotton, peanuts, tea, sugarcane, and tobacco. Burma's rich tropical forests provide timber and bamboo for export. See the product map of Southeast Asia, Indonesia, and the Philippines on page 505.

Oil flows from central Burma by pipeline to

Rangoon. But Burma produces only enough oil for its own use.

Burma has mines where rubies are dug out of the ground. It also has mines that produce jade (jād), a white or green stone prized for carving into jewelry, vases, and other art objects.

Factories in Rangoon manufacture pottery and silk and cotton cloth.

A Voyage on the Irrawaddy

From Rangoon ships can go upstream nearly 1,000 miles (1,600 km) on the Irrawaddy River. From a ship the traveler sees elephants dragging and pushing big, heavy logs of hard *teak* (tēk) wood along the banks. Teak is a valuable wood for shipbuilding because worms do not like it. It is often used for fine furniture.

The Kingdom of Thailand

Next to Burma, on the east, is Thailand, whose capital is Bangkok. Thailand is the only land in Southeast Asia that has never been ruled by a European nation. See the map of Southeast Asia on page 117.

Siamese Cats and Elephants

Thailand was long known as Siam (sī am′). Then it changed its name to Thailand, which means "land of the free." It is the home of many tropical plants and animals. It became famous around the world for its cats. Siamese cats make fine pets.

Elephants do most of the heavy work moving logs in the teak forests. In fact, Thailand was once known as "the land of white elephants." There are no really white elephants, but a few are a light shade of gray. These elephants were prized and were kept for the king's use.

In Burma elephants often work in the lumber industry. The animals are caught in the jungle, tamed, and trained to carry logs between their tusks and trunks.

Sometimes the king would give a friend one of his white elephants. The person who received the elephant had to keep it and care for it. Otherwise, the king would be offended. But a white elephant was not put to work like other elephants. It was so expensive to keep a white elephant that owning one was a burden. Today we often speak of something useless as a "white elephant."

Bangkok, City of Canals

Bangkok is larger than Rangoon. It is a city almost as large as Detroit. The city is famous for its network of canals. In the past, thousands

Canal villages can still be seen in Thailand. People travel along the "streets" in boats. Life in these villages is a contrast between old and new. What contrasts can you find in this picture?

of Bangkok families spent their whole lives on boats, which were their homes. Others lived in houses perched on stilts over the water. Now most of the people who once had floating homes live on land.

Nearly all Thailand's trade passes through Bangkok. The city is a railway center as well as a seaport. Life in Bangkok in some ways is like life in any large city.

The Indochina Region

Indochina is a tropical region in Southeast Asia, with high temperatures and heavy rainfall. It includes the countries of Kampuchea, Laos, and Vietnam. The rains make it possible to grow two crops a year.

The Mekong is the longest river. On it and the other waterways, the people travel and carry freight by boat. Hanoi (ha noi′), in the north, and Ho Chi Minh City (hō′ chē′ min′) in the south, are the leading cities and ports of Vietnam. Until 1975, Ho Chi Minh City was called Saigon (sī gon′).

Temple Ruins in the Jungle

In Kampuchea are the ruins of a very old temple in the ancient city of Angkor (an′kôr′). The people who built this and other places of worship, perhaps 800 years ago, were rich and powerful. Later they lost their power when attacked by the Siamese. No one knows what happened to the people. The jungle swallowed up their fields and hid their temples.

For hundreds of years Angkor remained unknown to the rest of the world. Then the French cleared out the jungle. The clearing laid bare the ruins of the temple and other signs of a great city. Around the city were irrigation canals.

Other cities like Angkor may be awaiting discovery, but it is hard to explore the jungles. Crocodiles lie in the rivers. Tigers, leopards, and panthers prowl on land.

World War II

Before World War II Vietnam was ruled by the French, and during the war by the Japanese. After the Japanese were defeated, the French again controlled Indochina. But Communist-supported forces fought the French to free Indochina. The war ended in 1954 with a *truce* (trōōs), or agreement, to stop fighting. Indochina was carved into four nations—Cambodia (now called Kampuchea), Laos, North Vietnam, and South Vietnam. North Vietnam became a communist nation, with Hanoi as the capital. South Vietnam became a republic, with Saigon as its capital.

After 1954, the Communists who remained in South Vietnam and the Communists in North Vietnam tried to overthrow the South Vietnamese government. The United States sent economic and military aid to South Vietnam. The fighting became increasingly fierce and the United States began to bomb North Vietnam. By 1968 more than 500,000 Americans were fighting alongside the South Vietnamese to keep South Vietnam free of the Communists.

American forces were withdrawn from South Vietnam in 1973. Two years later South Vietnam surrendered and came under the rule of North Vietnam. As a result there is now one nation, ruled by Communists.

The Malay Peninsula

South of Thailand is a long, narrow strip of land called the Malay Peninsula. The peninsula is shaped like the head and neck of a snake. At one place it is only 45 miles (72 km) wide.

Burma and Thailand occupy the northern part of the peninsula. In the southern half is East Malaysia. East Malaysia is part of a new country formed in 1963 called the Federation of Malaysia, or just Malaysia. Its capital is Kuala Lumpur (kwä′lə loompoor′).

Malaysia

Malaysia reaches almost to the equator. Its hot, moist climate creates a jungle in which are found tigers, wild elephants, and poisonous snakes. Large areas have been cleared for rice fields and rubber plantations. Other products raised are oil palms, pineapples, tea, tapioca, sugarcane, pepper, and coconuts.

Rubber, an Important Product

Until 1910 most of the world's rubber came from wild trees in the jungles of South America. Then seeds from those trees were taken first to England and then to Malaysia. With its hot and humid climate, Malaysia was very well suited to growing rubber trees. Soon it was producing a large part of the world's natural rubber.

Rubber is made from milky white juice, called *latex* (lā′teks), of the rubber tree. On the rubber plantations of Malaysia thousands of laborers cut small gashes in the bark of the trees to let the latex flow out. The latex is then caught in cups tied to the trees. The latex goes through machines from which it comes out as slabs or sheets of pure rubber. To make greater profit from the plantations the Malay farmers sometimes grow pineapples between the young rubber trees.

During World War II the Japanese captured Malaysia and its rubber supply. Scientists had to work out ways of making artificial rubber. Now most nations find they need both natural rubber and artificial rubber. Each has qualities that make it useful.

Tin, an Important Metal

Tin has also made Malaysia important. Tin is one of the rarest of well-known metals. Everyone knows how useful the tin can is in preserving food. Today the tin can is not made entirely of tin, but of thin sheets of steel covered with a coating of tin.

A belt of tin-bearing rocks runs from southern China south into Malaysia. Tin is so plentiful in Malaysia that none of it needs to be taken from deep mines. It is washed out of the sand and gravel brought down by streams, just as was gold in the early days of California.

The Founding of Singapore

Singapore was created as a British colony in 1819 by Sir Stamford Raffles, an Englishman. The city overlooks the Strait of Malacca (mə lak′ə). This strait forms a passageway between the Malay Peninsula and the island of Sumatra (soo mä′trə). Many trading ships pass through the strait.

Singapore became a free port, where goods could be landed by different nations and then shipped out again free of tax. Singapore has grown into a large and profitable city. Almost half the world's tin and more than half the world's rubber passes through its docks.

Modern Singapore and Malaysia

During World War II the Japanese conquered Singapore. They wanted control of the rubber and tin of Malaysia. At the end of the war the British regained the country and in 1957 Malaysia became independent. In 1963 Malaysia joined together with Singapore and the North Borneo states of Sabah (sä′bə) and Sarawak (sə rä′wäk) to form the Federation of Malaysia.

Singapore has a population that is 75 percent Chinese. This created tension in the Federation, and in 1965 Singapore withdrew and became an independent country.

Do You Know?

1. What are the countries of Southeast Asia?
2. Why is Burma called a "Golden Land"?
3. What are Malaysia's chief products?
4. For what is Thailand famous?

To Help You Learn

Using New Words

truce	partition
pagoda	monsoon
Buddhism	latex
teak	jade

Number a paper from 1 through 8. After each number write the word or term that matches the definition.

1. The milky white juice of the rubber tree
2. A high temple with a series of roofs
3. An agreement to stop fighting
4. A white or green stone used for jewelry and art objects
5. A hard wood used in building ships and furniture
6. A religion that began in India and spread to China and Japan
7. A wind of southern Asia that blows from the southwest in summer and from the northeast in winter
8. Division of a country

Finding the Facts

1. Name three gifts ancient India gave the world.
2. What countries are in Indochina?
3. When and how did Burma get its independence?
4. Name two ways in which the countries of Southeast Asia are alike.
5. How is natural rubber made?
6. Why do summer monsoons bring rain?

Learning from Maps

1. Study the map of Europe and Asia on page 101 and answer the following questions:

   What ocean borders Asia on the north? On the south? On the east?

   What parallel of latitude runs through the peninsula of India? About what latitude is the southern tip of the peninsula? What does this tell you about the climate of the peninsula?

   What meridian runs just west of Afghanistan? What meridian runs near the coast of Vietnam? How many degrees of longitude are there between these meridians? What does this tell you about South and Southeast Asia from east to west?
2. Turn to the maps of Europe and Asia on page 101 and of India and nearby lands on page 103 to help you answer the following questions:

   Name and locate the countries of South and Southeast Asia. The capitals of the independent nations are shown by a star within a circle. Locate the capital of each and name it.

   What country is west of India? What country is between India and Burma? Where is the highest mountain found?

Using Study Skills

1. **Time Line:** A time line helps us to understand history. It is a device on which events are arranged in the order in which they happened. Study the time line of India and Southeast Asia on page 99. Copy it, and add to it other events mentioned in the text. Include the death of the Buddha and the founding of Singapore. Also include the independence of Indochina and Bangladesh.

2. **Diagram:** A diagram can show us how something is done. The diagram below shows us, step by step, how rubber is made. Try to draw a diagram which shows why the summer monsoons bring rain. Read page 103 again to review the steps you should include.

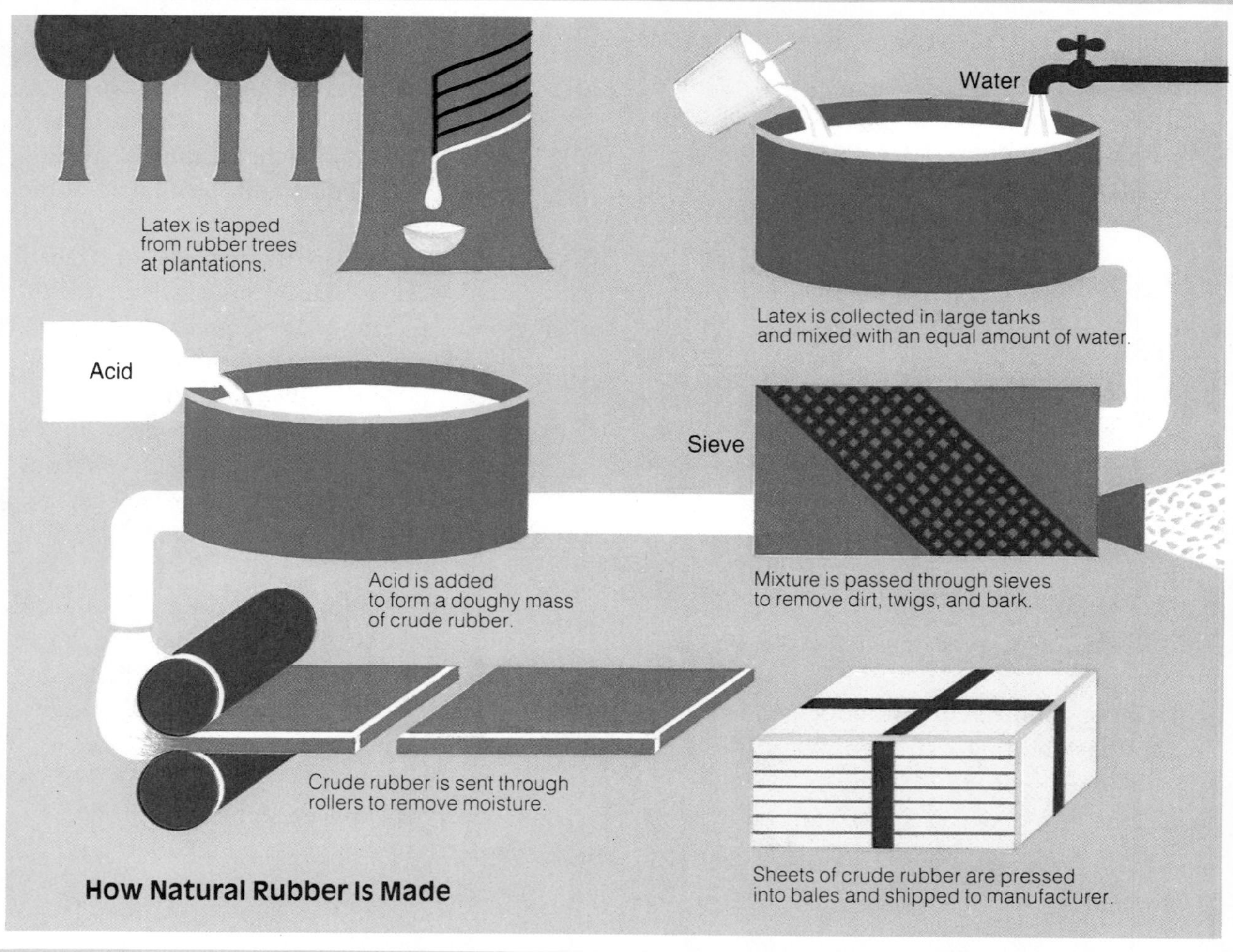

How Natural Rubber Is Made

Thinking it Through

1. During World War II artificial rubber and silk were used instead of the natural materials. Name some artificial materials. Can all natural materials be replaced by artificial ones? Are artificial materials ever as good as natural ones?
2. In 1955 Martin Luther King and his followers refused to ride Montgomery, Alabama, buses. This was because blacks were forced to ride in the backs of the buses. The plan was a success. The United States Supreme Court ruled against the practice of the Montgomery bus line. How was Martin Luther King's action like those used by Mohandas Gandhi in India? Why do you think they were so effective?

Projects

1. Bring in products grown or made in South and Southeast Asia. Group them together in a bazaar. Arrange by use, with food, clothing, jewelry, art objects, household objects, and industrial materials in separate locations. Label each object with the country it came from.
2. In 1961 the United States set up an organization called the Peace Corps. The purpose of this organization is to help people in other parts of the world. Many Americans joined the corps and went to nations where their help was requested. Soon Americans were busy in India, Pakistan, Thailand, and other Asian countries. They were teaching school, training farmers to raise better crops, building bridges, and working in health clinics. The Research Committee can find out about the work of the Peace Corps in Southern and Eastern Asia.
3. Watch the newspapers, magazines, and television for news about South and Southeast Asia. Share your findings with the class by presenting short reports or displaying pictures and articles on a bulletin board.
4. Make a time line to cover important historical events from a number of units. To do this hang a clothesline across your classroom. When you read of an important event, note it on a small card. Attach the card in its proper place on your own time line.

4 China, Korea, Japan

Unit Preview

The civilizations of China, Korea, and Japan developed independently of other civilizations. Broad deserts, the highest mountain ranges in the world, and vast oceans separated these areas from the rest of the world.

Chinese culture, like other great ancient civilizations, started along a river valley. In time, traders and explorers carried Chinese ideas and ways of doing things to neighboring areas. Chinese customs and beliefs influenced the cultures of Korea and Japan.

For centuries, these countries tried to protect themselves from foreign conquest. China built a Great Wall between itself and the Mongols and Manchus, tribes of northern and central Asia. After the first visits of European ships, Japan closed its ports to the outside world.

Many changes have taken place in these countries during the past 50 years. Today, the nations of China, Korea, and Japan combine in their own ways ancient traditions and modern methods of doing things.

On January 1, 1979, the People's Republic of China adopted a new system of spelling Chinese proper names. This system is known as Pinyin (pin′yin). Pinyin spelling is used by the United Nations, the United States government, and American newspapers and magazines. It is used in this unit. The traditional spellings of Pinyin names are included in the Index at the back of the book.

Things to Discover

If you look carefully at the picture, map, and time line on these pages, you can answer these questions.

1. The picture shows a Buddhist shrine in Japan. How do the Japanese visitors show that modern and traditional ways exist side by side in their country?
2. How many years passed between the bombing of Pearl Harbor and the end of World War II?
3. How many years passed between the time the People's Republic of China was set up and the United States established diplomatic relations with that country?
4. China, Korea, and Japan are highlighted on the map. What continent are they part of?
5. What ocean borders these countries?

Words to Learn

You will meet these words in this unit. As you read, you will learn what they mean and how to pronounce them. The Word List will help you.

bamboo	porcelain
commune	puppet government
communism	samurai
Japan Current	Shinto
junk	sorghum
lacquer	textile
millet	tung oil
open-door policy	warlord

Chinese civilization established
c. 1500
Great Wall of China begun
c. 200
B.C.
A.D.
First Europeans visit Japan
1543
Japan closed to outside world
1639
U.S. Commodore Perry arrives in Japan
1853
Japan attacks Pearl Harbor
1941
World War II ends
1945
Chinese Communists set up People's Republic of China
1949
North and South Korea sign truce
1953
U.S. and China establish diplomatic relations
1979

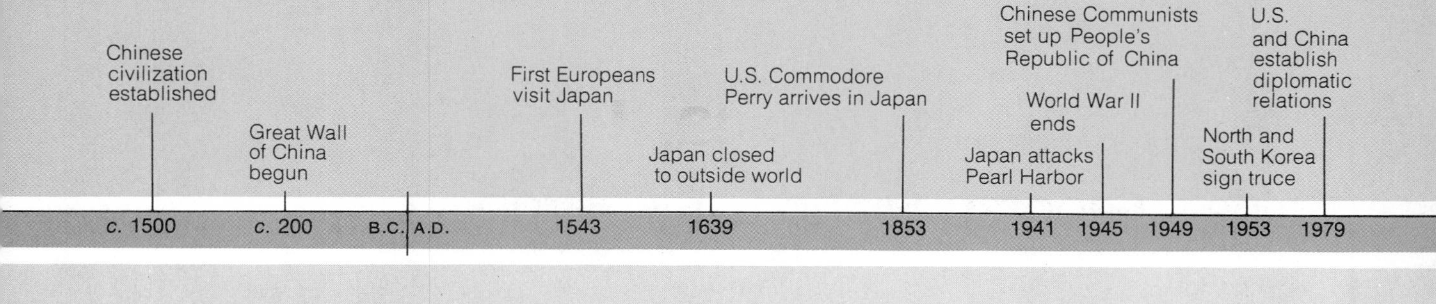

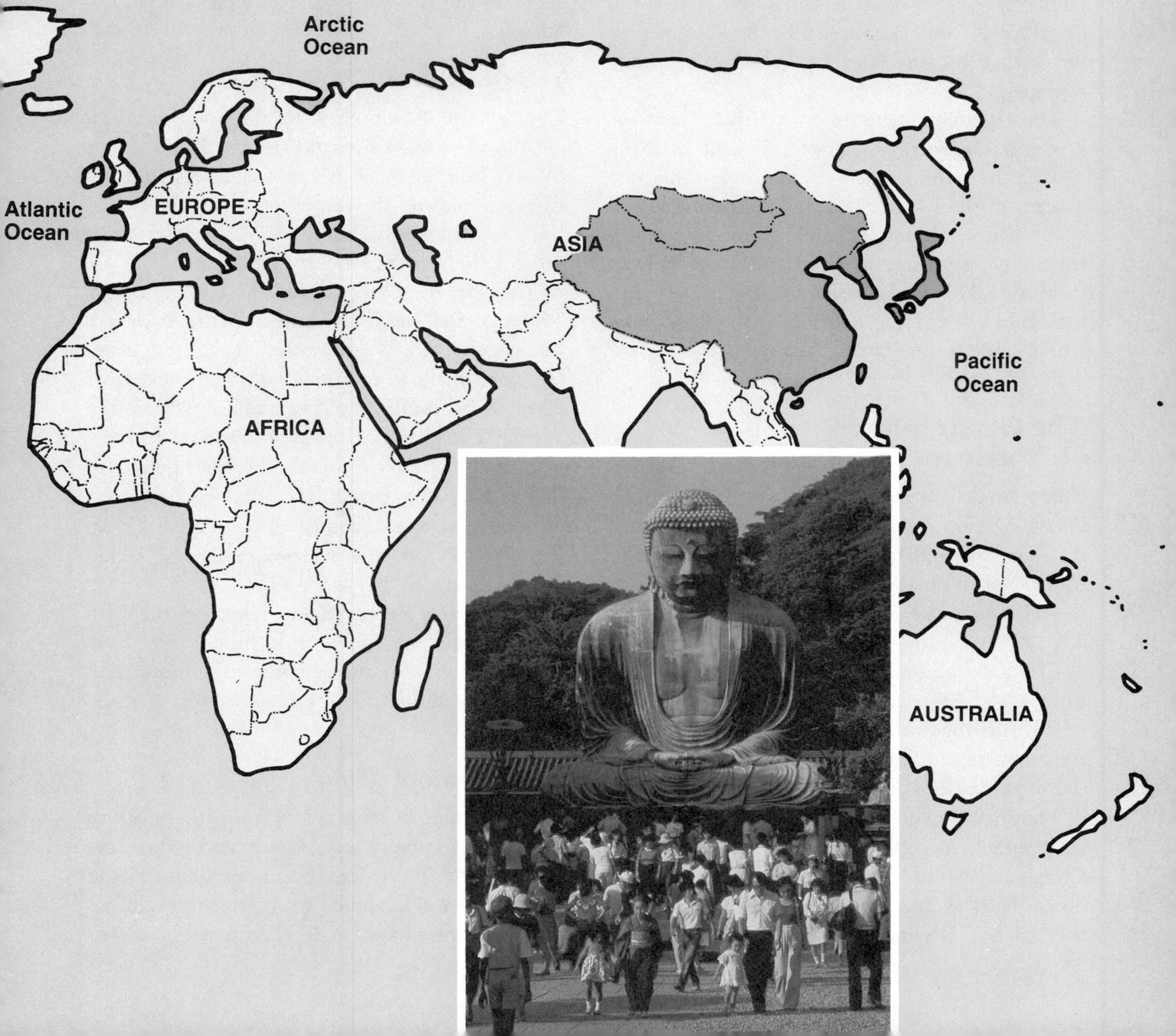

Arctic Ocean
Atlantic Ocean
EUROPE
ASIA
AFRICA
Pacific Ocean
AUSTRALIA

1
China's Geography and Early History

China is a very old country. A civilization developed there about 1500 B.C. In recent years this ancient land has undergone many changes.

The People's Republic of China extends across a huge area of the continent of Asia. This is the nation that we call China. Nearly a quarter of the world's people live there.

A second, much smaller Chinese country called the Republic of China occupies Taiwan (tī wän′). This is an island off the Chinese mainland. We shall learn a little later how China came to be divided into two nations.

The Geography of North and South China

China covers more than one-fifth of Asia. The Pacific Ocean is east of China. The Himalayas, the world's highest mountains, rise on the south. Great plateaus and deserts lie along the west. See the map of China and Korea on page 129.

China is watered by two great rivers, the Huang (hwäng) in the north and the Chang (chäng) in the south. The area through which these rivers and their branches flow is one of the most densely populated regions on earth.

These two rivers divide China into two large geographic regions. They are called North China and South China. The dividing line is about halfway between the Huang River and the Chang River. Mountains and low hills separate the two river valleys. Near the sea the land is flat.

Two Great Rivers

The Huang River rises in the mountains of Tibet, west of China. It flows 2,500 miles (4,000 km) into the Yellow Sea. As it flows through the north and west plains it carries away much yellow soil. For this reason it is often called the Yellow River.

The Huang River is full of mud and silt. Much of the silt is deposited in the riverbed. So much silt is deposited that the river becomes shallow. It overflows when the waters formed by melting snows rush down in the spring. The ancient Chinese built dikes to keep the river within its banks. When the river broke through the dikes, the country was flooded and thousands of people were killed. Because of this, the river came to be called "China's sorrow."

The Chang River, to the south, is the fifth longest river in the world. Ships can come inland as far as Wuhan (woo hän′), more than 600 miles (960 km) from the sea. Near the sea, the Chang River is 3 miles (4.8 km) wide.

The Climate of China

North China receives less rain than South China, its summers are shorter, and its winters colder. But floods can occur suddenly if the Huang River happens to break through its dikes. This has happened many times.

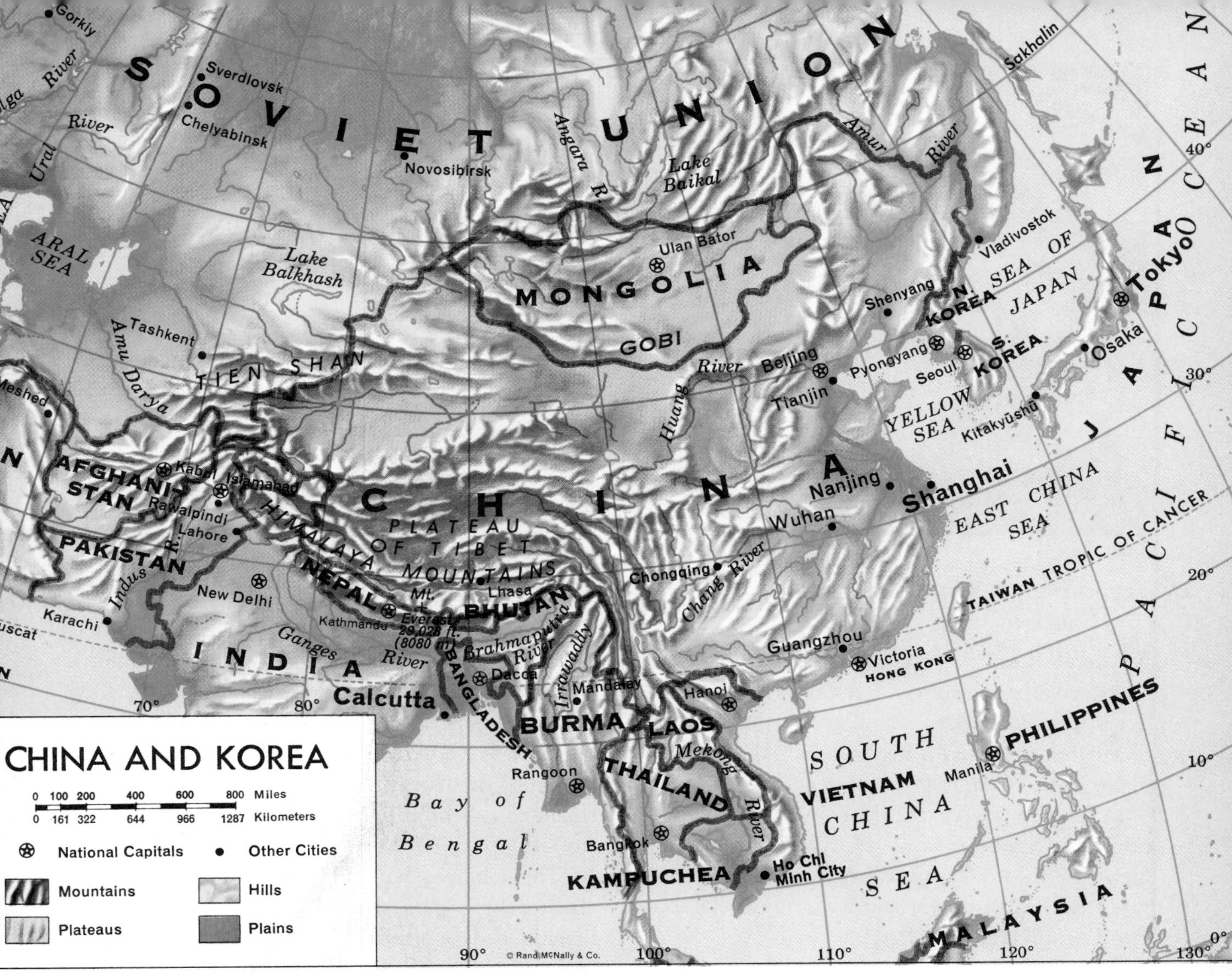

Because of the long spells of dry weather, the soil of the North China region is generally yellow or brown in color. Dust usually lies deep in the roads or flies about in clouds. In winter the winds are strong and cold.

South China is called "green China" because its climate is warm and rainy. The Chang is its greatest river. South China also receives monsoons, which bring plentiful rain.

China's Early History

We know little about China's early history for two reasons. First, scientists have not studied China as much as the other ancient civilizations. Second, the early records of the Chinese were made on wooden tablets, most of which have rotted away. What we do know about China tells us that a civilization had grown up there in very early times.

Chinese writing is a form of art that requires great patience and skill. It is done with a brush and pen. The characters are read in columns from right to left.

Beginning of Chinese Civilization

We have seen that several early civilizations began in river valleys. Civilization in China developed in the river valley of the Huang. From there the civilization spread south to the plains of the Chang River.

In the flat valleys or plains of their two great rivers the Chinese were left free for hundreds of years to work out their own ideas. They preferred peace to war and became excellent at farming and crafts.

China's System of Canals

The Chinese made great use of irrigation. For this purpose they dug both canals and ditches. Some are still in use today.

The Chinese were the first people to use their canals for carrying freight and passengers. The Grand Canal of China, 700 miles (1,120 km) long, runs north from the Chang River to the mouth of the Huang River. It is probably the world's longest constructed, or artificial, waterway. China has thousands of miles of canals.

The Chinese Education

The Chinese developed a language that has no alphabet. It is a language based on syllables. Instead of learning 26 letters, as we do, the Chinese must learn more than 2,000 characters, or symbols. Chinese books are written in columns of single characters. Columns are read from top to bottom. Pages are read from right to left.

The Chinese have always valued education. In early times the Chinese government established a free school system, with an official in charge of instruction. This is the plan of education used in the United States today.

The Chinese thought that all public officials should be highly educated. The educated person knew the best Chinese writings and could pass an examination in them. Only those who passed the examinations could hold public office.

Confucius, a Great Teacher

In 551 B.C. a boy named Kung was born. When Kung was 3 years old, his father died. His mother gave him a good education.

At that time China was in great disorder. There was no strong central government, and crimes were seldom punished. Kung wanted to do something for his country.

Kung thought that government could not be good unless it was carried on by wise rulers. He spent much time traveling about the country, with a group of followers, studying and learning. By the time he was 30 years old, Kung was known as a learned man and a great teacher. People called him Kung Fuzi, or Kung, the Master. This name became known in the West as Confucius (kən fyo͞o′shəs).

Master Kung felt that the old ways were good ways. He collected the poems and laws of China and the sayings of the wise people who had passed away. He taught that people always should use special forms of politeness and should be calm under all conditions. Kung also taught that people should have special respect for their parents.

Confucius was even more honored after his death. Finally one of the emperors ordered that the books of Confucius should be the foundation of China's religion. For about 2,000 years his writings were the school textbooks and were memorized. Although he was not worshiped as a god, the teachings of Confucius became sacred.

Master Kung taught that each person should honor his or her parents, grandparents, and other ancestors as far back as they could be traced. This developed into a kind of religion called ancestor worship.

Ancestor worship made people think about the past. The Chinese believed that their

The Great Wall of China was built in ancient times to protect China from enemy invaders. Warriors on horseback rode along the top of the wall and watched for attackers.

ancestors possessed all wisdom and that old customs should not be changed. For this reason, new ideas were not very welcome. Changes did come about, but only very slowly.

The Great Wall of China

North of Beijing (bā jing′), from east to west, stretches a long wall known as the Great Wall of China. The wall was built by the first emperor, or ruler, of China, about 200 B.C. Its purpose was to keep out the Mongols (mong′gəlz) and other wild, wandering tribes of the north. Later rulers of China extended the wall until it was more than 2,000 miles (3,200 km) long. This is the longest defensive

In 1974, more than 7,000 life-size clay figures were found buried in China. The first emperor of China had warriors and horses made as a guard for his grave.

wall in the world. To imagine how long it is, think of a wall between the United States and Canada stretching from Maine to the eastern border of Montana.

The high, thick wall with its many lookout towers served its purpose more than 1,000 years. But in the thirteenth century A.D., the Mongols finally succeeded in sweeping down into China from the north. The eastern half of the Great Wall is the stronger part. It was built not long before Columbus sailed across the Atlantic.

It was during the time of the Mongols that an Italian explorer visited China. His name was Marco Polo. He traveled in China for 17 years, from 1275 to 1292. He carried back to Europe exciting reports of life in China.

In the fourteenth century the Chinese drove out the Mongols and ruled themselves for 300 years. The next invaders were the Manchus man′cho͞oz). They came from the land called Manchuria (man choor′ē ə) to the northeast. The Manchus seized control of the government in 1644 and held it for more than 250 years, until 1911.

Ancient China's Gifts to the World

The ancient Chinese were skillful carvers of stone and jade. They used clay to make a fine pottery called *porcelain* (pôr′sə lin). Porcelain is so thin that it is often called "eggshell" china.

The Chinese developed special styles in art and architecture. The Chinese pagoda is like a tower, with many stories. Each of the stories has a decorated roof which hangs over the roof below.

Builders used the giant, treelike grass known as *bamboo* (bam bo͞o′). They made houses, furniture, and many smaller things from its strong, hollow stem. Books were made of bamboo until a way of making paper from rags and rope was discovered.

In China a small tree called the varnish tree grows. Its sticky juice makes a good coating for wood, called *lacquer* (lak′ər). Today, as long ago, Chinese workers use a brush to put several coats of lacquer on wood. The layers of lacquer form a hard, smooth surface which can be painted or carved.

The Chinese were also the first to use gunpowder, to print books with wooden blocks, and to make paper money.

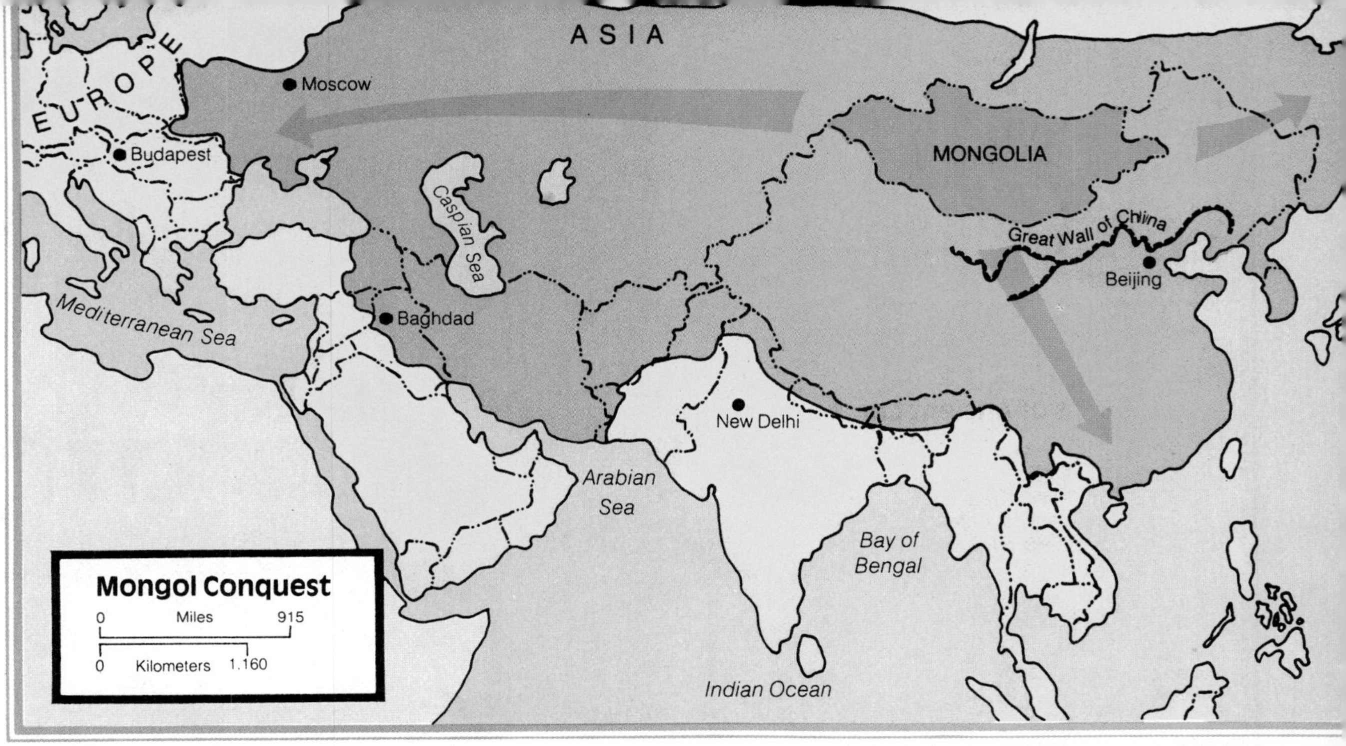

In the thirteenth century Mongols from the north invaded China and ruled it for the next 100 years. What did the invaders have to cross to take over China?

The tea plant was first grown by the Chinese. Tea made from its leaves has since become the drink of people all over the world.

The Chinese also were the first people to use silk. They learned how to unwind the threads of the cocoon, or wrapping of silk which the silkworm spins for itself. They then used the threads from the cocoon to weave cloth. The silk was colored with brilliant dyes and made into beautiful robes. Artists painted on silk wall hangings.

Silk trade and silk making began to spread to other countries as early as the second century B.C. Some travelers to China who

Ancient Chinese *porcelain* combined beauty with strength. Dragons were often considered symbolic guardians of royalty.

knew the beauty and value of silk secretly took silkworm eggs back to Europe. After this, people in Europe began to raise silkworms and to make silk cloth.

Influence on Neighboring Lands

The ways of living of the Chinese were much admired by neighboring peoples. Among these were the Koreans, the Japanese, and some of the peoples who lived in Southeast Asia.

In early times the Chinese learned that there were islands to the east. A Chinese emperor sent out a group of explorers. They came back with the news that the people of these islands were friendly.

After a time the Japanese began to visit China and to invite Chinese to Japan. In a few hundred years the Japanese had copied many skills and customs from China. The early Koreans, too, adopted some of their ways of living from the Chinese.

South of China lie the countries of Southeast Asia. Chinese travelers found their way into these lands and introduced Chinese customs. West of China is Tibet. In this region many Chinese ways of living were adopted. Even the wandering herders of Mongolia on the north learned Chinese customs.

Today we can still find Chinese ways of living in these neighboring countries.

Do You Know?

1. What two large rivers flow through China?
2. Who was Confucius?
3. Why was the long wall known as the Great Wall of China built?
4. How long is China's Grand Canal?

2
China in Modern Times

For centuries China was largely shut off from the rest of the world. The coming of foreign ships to China marked the beginning of a new chapter in Chinese history. The Chinese were to have many changes in their lives.

China Opened to Trade

About the time of the first settlements in North America trading ships from European nations visited China. They were given the right to use the port of Guangzhou (gwäng zhō′) and to engage in trade with southern China.

As time went on, European nations wanted to increase their trade with China. But the Chinese did not welcome foreigners. They fought to keep them out. In 1844 China was forced to open its ports to European merchants. The island of Hong Kong, off the China coast, became a British possession. The United States was also given the right to trade in certain ports.

In 1899 the United States persuaded China to adopt an *open-door policy* (ō′pən dôr′ pol′ə sē). This means a country opens its ports to trade with all nations.

At this time the Chinese leaders decided that China should be made into a modern nation. They wanted China to take its place among the other nations of the world. But some Chinese still wanted to cling to old ways and drive out the foreigners.

China Becomes a Republic

In 1912 China changed from being ruled by an emperor to electing its own government. Dr. Sun Yat-sen (so͞on′ yät′sen′) became president. With the change to a republic China did not become a united nation. Many generals, or *warlords* (wôr′lôrdz′), raised armies that lived off the land in the parts of the country where they were stationed. A warlord is a general who controls an area by force. These warlords often fought each other. Torn by the conflicts, China was an unstable nation.

Two political parties in China at this time wanted to lead the government.

Sun Yat-sen was leader of the political party in power, the Nationalists. When he died the leadership passed over to Chiang Kai-shek (chäng′ kī′shek′). Another political party was made up of Communists led by Mao Tse-tung (mou′tsə toong′). *Communism* (kom′yə niz′əm) is a system of government in which property and goods are controlled by the government. Everyone works for the government. The Nationalists and the Communists fought for control of China for many years.

At one point the Nationalist armies forced the Communists to move far back into the countryside. In 1934 the Communists walked on foot 6,000 miles (9,600 km). This is called "The Long March." Of 100,000 who began the year-long march, only a few thousand survived. This became a famous event in Chinese Communist history.

The Republic of China is a thriving but densely populated nation off the coast of the Chinese mainland. The nation came under control of the Nationalists at the end of World War II.

The Japanese Invasion of China

Starting in the 1890s, the Japanese, with many people crowded onto their small islands, tried to spread out on the mainland of Asia. First they took over Korea. Next, in 1931, they invaded Manchuria, a part of North China. Then they began to try to get control of the part of China just south of Manchuria and along the Huang River.

Japanese power was too great for the Chinese. All the important seaports—Shanghai (shang hī′), Guangzhou, and the island of Hong Kong—fell into Japanese hands. They seized most of the railroads. At Beijing and at Nanjing the Japanese set up *puppet governments* (pup′it guv′ərn məntz). A puppet government is one in which the officials are controlled, or told what to do, by another government's leaders. That is, they behave like puppets.

Chongqing, a Wartime Capital

The Japanese captured many cities. But the great China that lay back of the seacoast was still free. Chiang Kai-shek set up a temporary capital at Chongqing (chun king′), far in the interior. Find Chongqing on the map of China and Korea on page 129.

Many Chinese chose to leave their homes in eastern China and go west rather than live under Japanese rule. Teachers and students carried away the books of their universities and set up their schools again in places which had never before seen books or teachers. The Chinese took the machinery of their mills. They tore up railroads. Fifty or sixty million people made this great move.

To resist the Japanese, the people of China united more fully than they ever had in the past. Great Britain and the United States sent help to the Chinese, but the lack of roads and railroads made it difficult to reach the new capital. Some supplies were flown in by air. Japanese planes bombed Chongqing many times, but their armies did not reach the city.

China—A Divided Nation

The spirit of unity did not last long. As World War II ended, disagreements again arose.

The Defeat of the Nationalist Armies

In 1946 war broke out again. The Nationalists, who controlled the Chinese government, fought against the Chinese Communists.

Nationalist armies were weakened by the long struggle with the Japanese. In that time, the Chinese Communists had had a chance to win the support of farmers in North China. The Communists promised to break up large areas of land belonging to warlords and divide it among the farmers. The Communists had also gained support in other regions of China.

After a time the Communist armies gained more and more victories. The Nationalist armies were forced to withdraw to the island of Taiwan, off the Chinese mainland. The Taiwan government is called the Republic of China. In area Taiwan is somewhat larger than the state of Maryland. Its population is about 17 million, or four times Maryland's.

The Chinese Communists

In 1949 the Chinese mainland came under Communist rule. Under the leadership of Mao Tse-tung, the Communists set up the People's

Government-controlled newspapers are available in Chinese cities, but in both cities and rural areas wall posters are another way of communicating.

Republic of China, with its capital in Beijing.

Under a Communist system, the people, through the government, own all property—land, factories, mines. They do not believe in private property. People may own clothes or furniture but not land or businesses. The government assigns people to work where they are needed. The government also decides how much workers are paid.

Under the Chinese Communists, new industries and modern factories were built. New mines were opened. Turning China into an industrial power was a chief Communist goal.

The many villages of China are grouped into *communes* (kom′yo͞onz). In a commune, property is owned in common and work and living quarters are shared. Each commune includes a number of villages. The commune produces what the government orders.

Communes were established in modern China to create a society in which all people were equal and worked together for a common good. What does the picture suggest about *commune* living?

To help increase agricultural production, farmers in communes are given small private plots of land. These are in addition to the much larger plots shared by everyone. On their private plots farmers can plant whatever they wish. They can either eat their crops or sell them at local markets or fairs.

For many years the United States refused to recognize the People's Republic of China. Finally in 1971, the United States voted to admit the People's Republic of China to the United Nations. In the years since then relations between the two nations have continued to improve. But tensions increased between China and the Soviet Union. This caused China to look to Western nations for help in modernizing the country.

To establish better relations between the two countries, President Richard Nixon visited China in 1972. In 1979 the United States and the People's Republic of China established diplomatic relations. That means China sent representatives to Washington, D.C., to represent their country in the United States. In exchange the United States sent people to China.

Making a Living in China Today

Three out of four workers in China are farmers. The Communists have introduced land reforms and more use of farm machinery. But most farming is still done by hand or with the help of animals.

The winter winds of North China are strong and cold. In each house is a k'ang (käng), or brick table, sometimes large enough to fill nearly half the living room. Inside is a fireplace from which openings lead through the k'ang. The k'ang is both a stove and a bed. On winter nights the family lie down on it. It is not a soft bed, but it is a warm bed for at least a part of the night.

The people of North China must raise crops which grow quickly during the spring rains and which can stand long weeks of dry weather. Such crops are wheat, beans, *sorghum* (sôr′gəm), and *millet* (mil′it). Sorghum and millet are grasslike plants that can be eaten as food. In the North the usual food of the Chinese workers is a bowl of noodles made from wheat or millet. Workers in the South have a bowl of rice for their meals.

Rice produces more food to the acre than wheat, but it needs much more hand labor. Rice plants are raised in a seed bed, where they grow as thickly as blades of grass. The young plants are carefully uprooted and taken to the rice fields, where they are set out by hand in the mud and water.

China also produces grain, corn, peas, and jute. Its production of coal ranks third in the world.

Many Chinese people make a living from farming. They often work without the aid of machinery.

South China's Waterways

The Chinese make great use of their rivers and canals, especially in the south. China is said to have more small boats carrying freight and passengers than all the rest of the world.

On the ocean and its bays, as well as on the broad Chang River, move the big sailing vessels known as *junks* (jungks), with their bamboo sails. A junk can hold a great amount of goods. Many junks are also strong and swift enough to make long sea voyages.

On the smaller streams and canals of China, other kinds of boats can be seen. Some carry freight for long distances. Some are fishing boats, from which fishers cast their nets. Some Chinese fishers have trained large, black birds, called cormorants (kôr′mər ənts), to catch fish for them. The cormorants sit on the edge of the boat waiting their turn to dive. Each bird knows its name or number. When its turn comes, it swoops down and seizes a fish from the water below. It wears a ring around its neck to prevent it from swallowing the fish. It keeps the fish in its mouth until its owner takes it away and tosses it into a basket. When enough fish have been caught, the birds are given their share as a reward for their work.

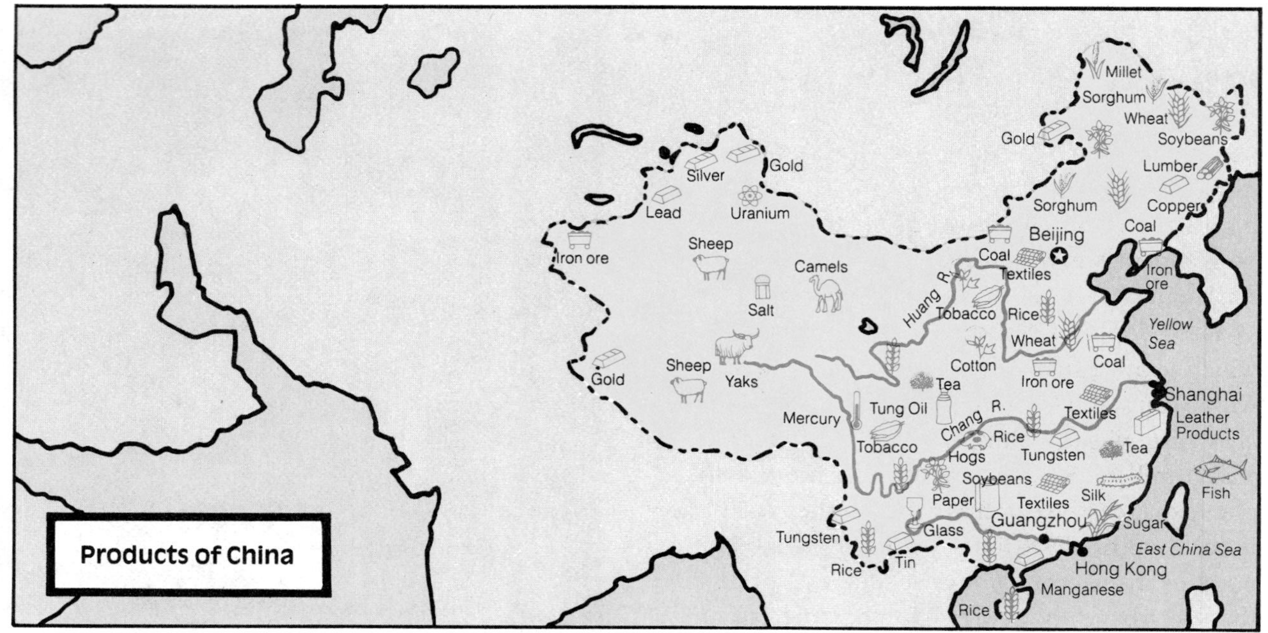

Special Products of China

China is well known for certain special products. Among these are *tung oil* (tung oil), silk, tea, and soybeans.

Tung oil is made from the nuts of the tung tree. Paint or varnish mixed with tung oil dries quickly. Paint made with this oil also has a tough surface which is waterproof and will not crack under heat. Even acid will not eat through a good coat of this oil. From the dark-colored particles which settle to the bottom of the oil, a very black ink can be made.

The Importance of Tea

For many years almost the only product that China exported to Europe and America was tea. The tea plant is really a tree, but the Chinese keep it cut low like a bush so that its leaves can be picked easily. The tree needs the heat and sun of South China, but it grows best on hillsides or mountain slopes, not on the rice lowlands.

China probably produces more tea than any other country, but most of it is used at home. Most Chinese tea is green tea, stronger than the black tea from Sri Lanka and India. Tea becomes green or black according to the method that is used when it is processed.

The Valuable Soybean

Soybeans are one of China's greatest crops. Soybeans are especially valuable because they furnish the same body-building material that is obtained from meat and milk. With too little room for herds of cattle, the Chinese do not have much meat and milk. But they do grow large crops of soybeans. Soybeans grow well in both the dry lands of North China and the damp climate of South China.

Besides its value as a food the soybean has many other uses. The bean contains much oil. The Chinese press out this oil and use it to light lamps in their homes. Paper or cloth soaked in soybean oil lets light come through.

The Chinese learned to use such paper or cloth instead of glass in the windows of their homes. The Chinese also use soybean oil in cooking, and they flavor foods with a soybean sauce.

The Production of Silk

Along the slopes of the hills above the rice fields, mulberry trees grow. Mulberry leaves are the silkworm's favorite food.

In many Chinese homes silkworms are grown. The worms, lying on large trays, eat almost all the time, day and night. People pick the leaves and care for the trays. The worms then spin cocoons.

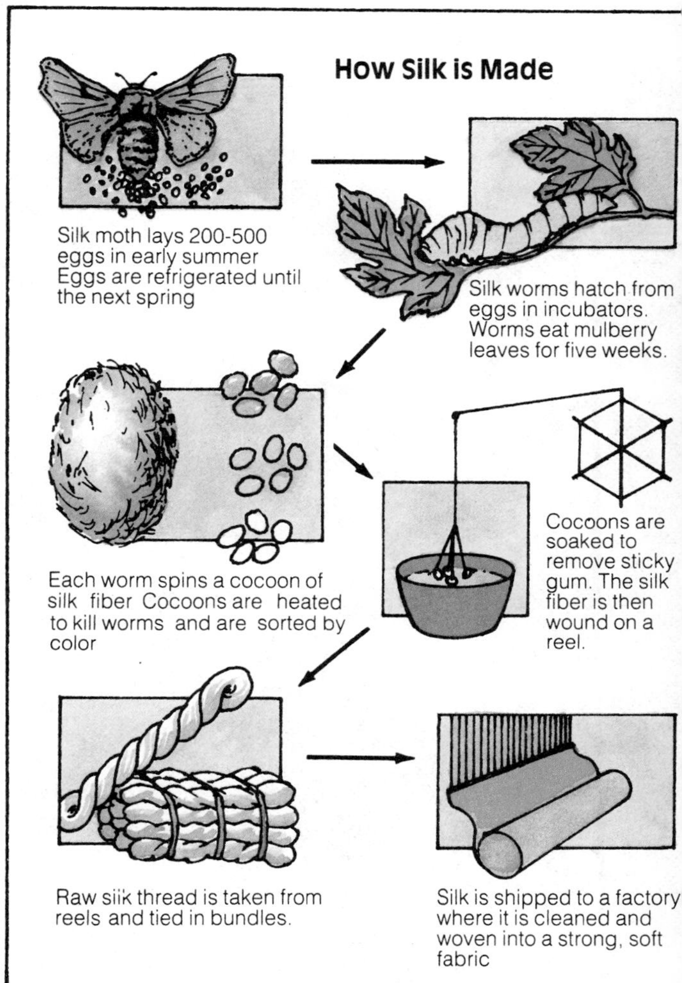

For more than 2,000 years the Chinese were the only people in the world who knew how to make silk. With its fine strength and smoothness, silk is a very valuable fabric.

Cities of China

China has many cities that have been famous for centuries. Most are still important today.

Beijing, a North China City

For more than 700 years Beijing has been the capital city of China. Sometimes the capital has been moved for short periods to another city. But since 1949 the Communists again have made this popular city the capital of the nation.

Beijing is a blend of old and new. The old "Forbidden City" is sealed off by walls and by a moat, which is a deep ditch filled with water. Here are the old Imperial Palaces of former emperors who would forbid outsiders to enter the palaces. The Great Hall of the People serves the same purpose as the capitol building in Washington. In it is a banquet hall that can seat 5,000 people. Beijing is a showplace of modern China.

Tianjin, on the Grand Canal

Southeast of Beijing, at the northern end of the Grand Canal, stands Tianjin (tan jin′). Tianjin, China's third largest city, is about the same size as Chicago. Tianjin is located on a river. Using the river, ships can sail from the ocean to the heart of the city. Through this seaport most of the trade of Beijing and the surrounding area is carried on.

Many goods are moved through Shanghai, which is China's center of trade. Why do the buildings in the picture look so European?

Shanghai, China's Greatest Port

Shanghai is one of the world's largest seaports. With over 10 million people it is also China's largest city. Because of its location Shanghai is the trading center of central China. The city lies along the bank of a small river that empties into the Chang River near the sea. Constant dredging keeps the harbor deep enough for ocean-going ships. Dredging means scooping from the bottom of the harbor the loose mud and sand brought down by the river.

In 1842 when China was still a weak nation, it was forced to give away sections of the city to the British, American, French, and later the Japanese. The foreigners lived in a separate section and also helped govern the city. After World War II the Chinese regained control of Shanghai and again used it as a center of trade.

The Island of Hong Kong

Hong Kong is a British colony. It lies at the mouth of the Xi (zhē) River , on the coast of South China. Besides the island, Hong Kong includes a small district on the mainland.

The beautiful city on the island is called Victoria. It has one of the finest natural harbors in the world.

The British obtained possession of Hong Kong in 1842. They have kept it ever since, except during World War II, when the Japanese held it.

Before the Communists gained control in China, Hong Kong was an important trade city. In recent years it has had to look for other ways to do business. The garment industry now supplies almost half of Hong Kong's exports.

The River Port of Guangzhou

Nearly 100 miles (160 km) inland from Hong Kong, on the Xi River, is Guangzhou. Guangzhou is a city of canals, crowded with more than 100,000 boats.

The city lies at a meeting point of the inland waterways and the sea. It is a major trade city of southern China, and has been an important city for foreign contact. The first Europeans who visited China came through its port.

Mongolia

Mongolia (mon gō′lē ə) is a Communist country that lies between China and the Soviet Union. It is more than twice the size of Texas but has only about 1,500,000 people. High mountains and plateaus cover most of this rugged land. Except in the summer, it has little rainfall. Temperatures are usually very hot or cold.

Mongolia was once a land of nomads, or traveling herders. Today more than half work on cooperative livestock farms set up by the government. They raise sheep, cattle, goats, horses, and camels. A cooperative farm is owned and operated by its members. The members share in the farm's work and profits or benefits.

Mongolia is the home of the Mongols. In the thirteenth century under Genghis Kahn (jen′gis kän′) and Kublai Khan (ko͞o′blī kän′), the Mongols conquered all of China, Korea, and parts of Europe. See the map of the Mongol Conquest on page 133. From the 1680s to 1911, China controlled Mongolia. With Russian help, it became independent in 1921. It remains largely under Russian influence.

North Korea and South Korea

For a long time North Korea and South Korea were under the domination of China. The country was called Korea. Then, from 1905 until the end of World War II, the area was occupied by Japan. After the war the peninsula was divided along the 38th parallel into two nations. North Korea became a Communist country, and South Korea became a free republic.

In 1950 the North Koreans invaded South Korea, hoping to make that country Communist, too. The United States and other members of the United Nations helped South Korea. China helped North Korea. When a truce was signed in 1953, South Korea was still free.

At the time Korea was divided, most of the industry was in North Korea. South Korea was mainly a farming nation. In addition, the war in 1950–1953 destroyed many of South Korea's cities. But since then, with the help of the United States, South Korea has rebuilt its cities and developed many new industries. These include electronics, shipbuilding, rubber, glass, chemicals, oil products, and steel. New dams provide hydroelectric power for these industries. South Korea became prosperous.

Do You Know?

1. Who was Sun Yat-sen? Who became leader of the Nationalists when he died?
2. Who was Mao Tse-tung?
3. What is the capital of China? What is in the "Forbidden City" section?
4. Why did North Korea invade South Korea?
5. What other nations took sides when North Korea fought with South Korea?

Before You Go On

Using New Words

tung oil	junk
communism	open-door policy
porcelain	lacquer
warlord	sorghum
bamboo	millet
commune	puppet government

Number a paper from 1 through 11. After each number write the word or term that matches the definition.

1. A general who controls an area by force
2. A government whose officials are controlled by another government's leaders
3. A kind of varnish that gives wood a smooth hard surface that can be carved
4. A system of government in which all property and goods are controlled by the government
5. Oil made from nuts and used in paint or varnish
6. A fine, thin kind of pottery
7. Opening ports for trade to all nations
8. A giant, treelike grass
9. A group of people who live, work, and own property together
10. Two kinds of grasslike plants that people can use as food
11. A large Chinese sailing vessel

Finding the Facts

1. Why is Huang called the Yellow River? Why is it also sometimes called "China's sorrow"?
2. Name four contributions of ancient China to the world.
3. In what river valley did civilization first develop in China?
4. Who was Marco Polo?
5. Name two countries that adopted Chinese ways of living?
6. When did European trading ships first visit China?
7. What was "The Long March"?
8. Where did the Nationalists go when they lost control of China to the Communists?
9. Name three ways soybeans can be used for food. Name two non-food uses for soybeans.
10. How is a harbor dredged? Why?
11. Where is Hong Kong? Which country controls it?
12. Where is Mongolia?
13. How do most Chinese make a living?
14. Name two ways North Korea differed from South Korea at the start of the Korean War.
15. What country close to China has many cooperative farms? How are these farms run?

3
Japan, from Early to Modern Times

Japan is an island nation. The sea has thus played an important part in the lives of the Japanese.

The Geography of Japan

As the map of Japan on this page shows, Japan has four main islands. Together they occupy an area about as large as Montana.

The islands were formed mostly by the action of volcanoes. The principal mountain, Mount Fuji (fo͞o′ jē), which is snow-capped for part of the year, is a dead volcano. Japan has several active volcanoes. Earthquakes sometimes shake the islands, bringing great damage.

Much of the soil of Japan is rich, but the islands have so many mountains that not more than one-sixth of the land can be farmed. Still, the Japanese depend greatly on farming. Over 115 million people live in Japan. This is about

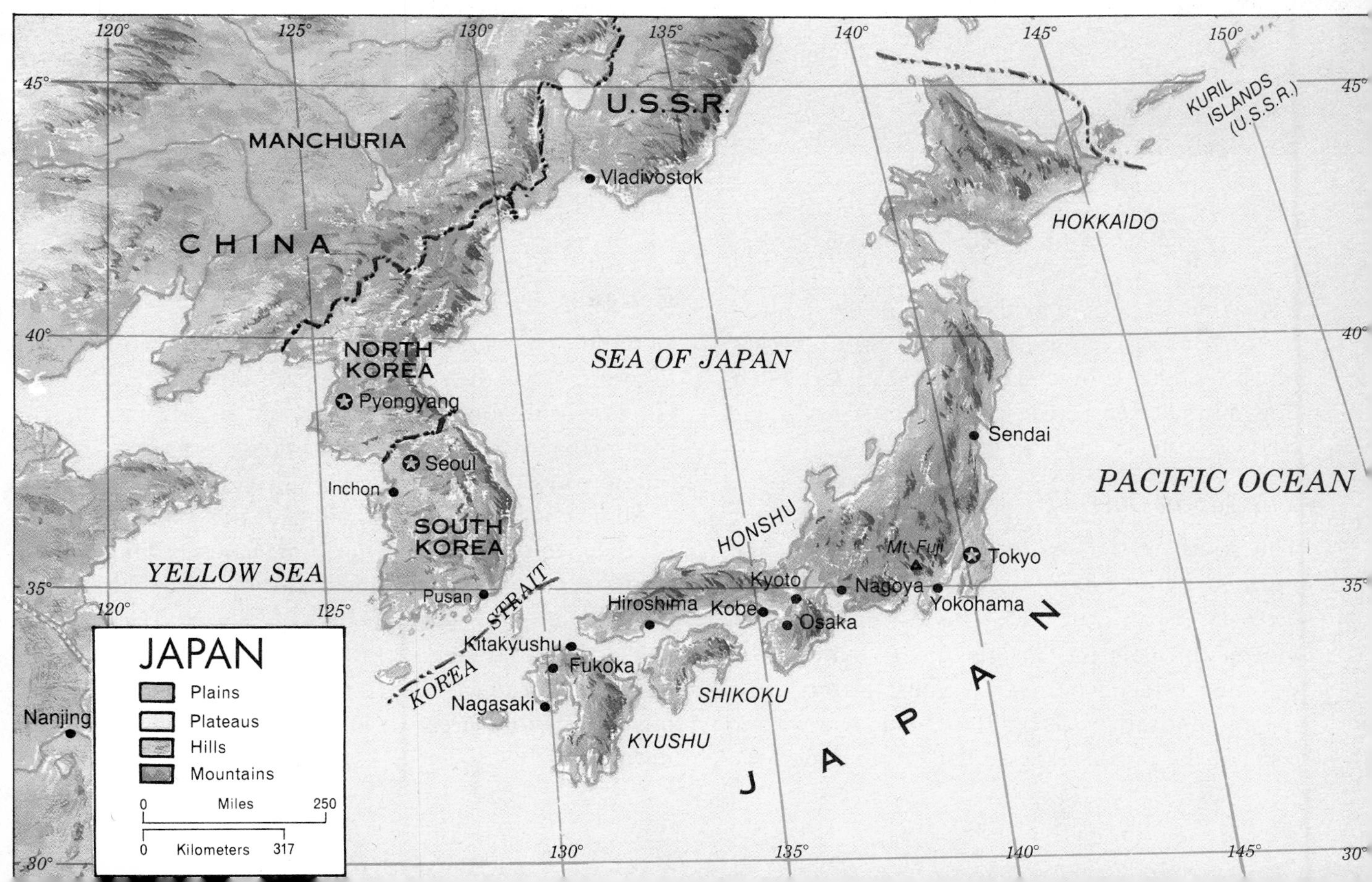

Shintos believe that spiritual forces are found in nature. Besides the shrine, what in the picture would harbor such forces?

half as many people as there are in the United States. But the United States has fifty times as much land to cultivate as Japan has. Crowded into a small space, the people must use their land carefully.

The Japan Current

The southern and eastern coasts of Japan are warmed by an ocean current called the *Japan Current* (jə pan′ kur′ənt). This current of water moves through the Pacific Ocean and has a warming effect wherever it goes. From Japan the current moves across the Pacific and warms parts of the northwest coast of North America.

The Early History of Japan

Little is known about the early history of Japan. The Japanese call their country Nippon (ni pon′), which means rising sun. Early histories combined myths, or stories, with facts. One story told that Japan was founded by the Sun Goddess. Her grandson became the first emperor of Japan. All later emperors claimed they were descended from the Sun.

Chinese Influence on Japan

Buddhist ideas reached Japan from Korea and China in about the sixth century. Buddhists also taught the Japanese the Chinese system of writing, ways of building, and many other Chinese ways of doing things.

The Japanese first used Chinese characters to write down their own language. As in Chinese, each character represented a word. Later on simpler writing systems were used in which each character represents a sound.

Religion

The oldest religion in Japan is *Shinto* (shin′tō). Shinto means "the way of the gods." Even after Chinese missionaries introduced Buddhism, many Japanese Buddhists continued to observe Shinto ways.

Shinto began in early times with the worship of the sacred power found in nature. This power, or sacred force, might be within a rock, a mountain, or another object. Shintos believed the same kind of power was also held by the spirits of dead heroes and by ancestors. In this way Shinto grew to include the worship of ancestors.

Like Chinese writing, Japanese writing is considered to be a highly developed art. Students of Japanese writing practice brush strokes in a Tokyo class.

We shall see later on how military leaders used Shinto beliefs to turn Japan into a warlike nation.

The Arts of Japan

Japan's fondness for nature was also expressed in its arts. Though Japan took over many Chinese ideas, it did things in its own way. Its centuries of isolation from its neighbors and from the West helped Japan develop its own art style. A part of this was based on harmony with nature. The Japanese admired the materials and form of a clay pot as much as they did the decoration. In their poems as well as their paintings they tried to express themselves simply, and in a few words or strokes of the brush.

Early European Visitors to Japan

Europeans had long known about the Japanese islands. But it was not until 1543 that Portuguese (pôr′chə gēz′) sailors found their way to Japan. When they returned to Portugal and told about what they had seen, traders and Christian missionaries were eager to visit Japan.

Japanese gladly received the Portuguese. They were eager to trade. They also listened to the teachings of the Christian missionaries. A little later the Dutch came also. After a time, urged by the Buddhists, the Japanese began to fear that the foreigners from Europe might take over the government. They decided to take steps to make sure this would not happen.

Japan's Closed Door

In 1639 the Christian missionaries were driven out, and Christianity was forbidden. The Portuguese were sent away and the Japanese themselves were made to stay at home. The government refused to allow Japanese ships to leave Japanese waters. All foreign traders were kept out except the Dutch, who were allowed to send a trading ship once a year to Japan. The Chinese were also permitted to trade.

This period of Japan's history is sometimes compared to the Middle Ages in Europe a century or two earlier. In both parts of the world it was a time when changes occurred very slowly. In Japan, lords who had pledged support of the emperor each controlled small sections. The lords lived in castles with high stone walls. Each lord had warriors, called *samurai* (sam′oo rī′). The samurai pledged to assist their lords in battle.

Japan's Open Door

After 200 years the United States assigned Commodore Matthew Perry to open trade relations with Japan. In 1853, and again in 1854, Commodore Perry sailed American warships into Tokyo Bay. At first Japan opened only two ports to trade. Not long afterward, trading ships from other nations visited Japan. Before long, representatives from the United States government and from other nations were sent to Japan. Japan as a nation was no longer closed to the world.

The Japanese quickly recognized that they were weaker than the Western peoples. Their leaders decided that the nation must become more modern in order to become great and powerful. The old system of lords and walled castles was swept away. A modern army and navy were built up. A modern school system was established. Many young people of Japan were sent to Europe and to the United States to learn about Western ways.

The Empire of Japan

As Japan learned new ways, it began to grow in strength. With its added power, it set out to build an empire. Shinto was made the state religion and the emperor became the head of state. Japanese children were taught to worship the emperor as a descendant of the Sun God.

Japan's Wars Against China and Russia

Japan and China are near neighbors. They became rivals. In 1895 the two countries fought each other and Japan won. As a result, China was forced to give the island of Formosa, now Taiwan, to Japan.

Not long after the war with China, war broke out between Japan and its large neighbor, Russia. Both wanted certain parts of Chinese territory. One of these areas was Korea, which had long been ruled by China. Japan won the war against Russia. Korea became a part of the Japanese empire.

Russia was also interested in Manchuria. Russia had obtained from China certain rights in this area and had built a railroad across it. After losing the war, Russia had to give to Japan the important railway across south Manchuria.

Japan's Gains in World War I

Four years after Japan took Korea, World War I began. Japan joined the Allied nations against Germany. After the war, the Allies gave Japan the right to look after most of the Pacific islands that had belonged to Germany. The Japanese began putting weapons on the islands.

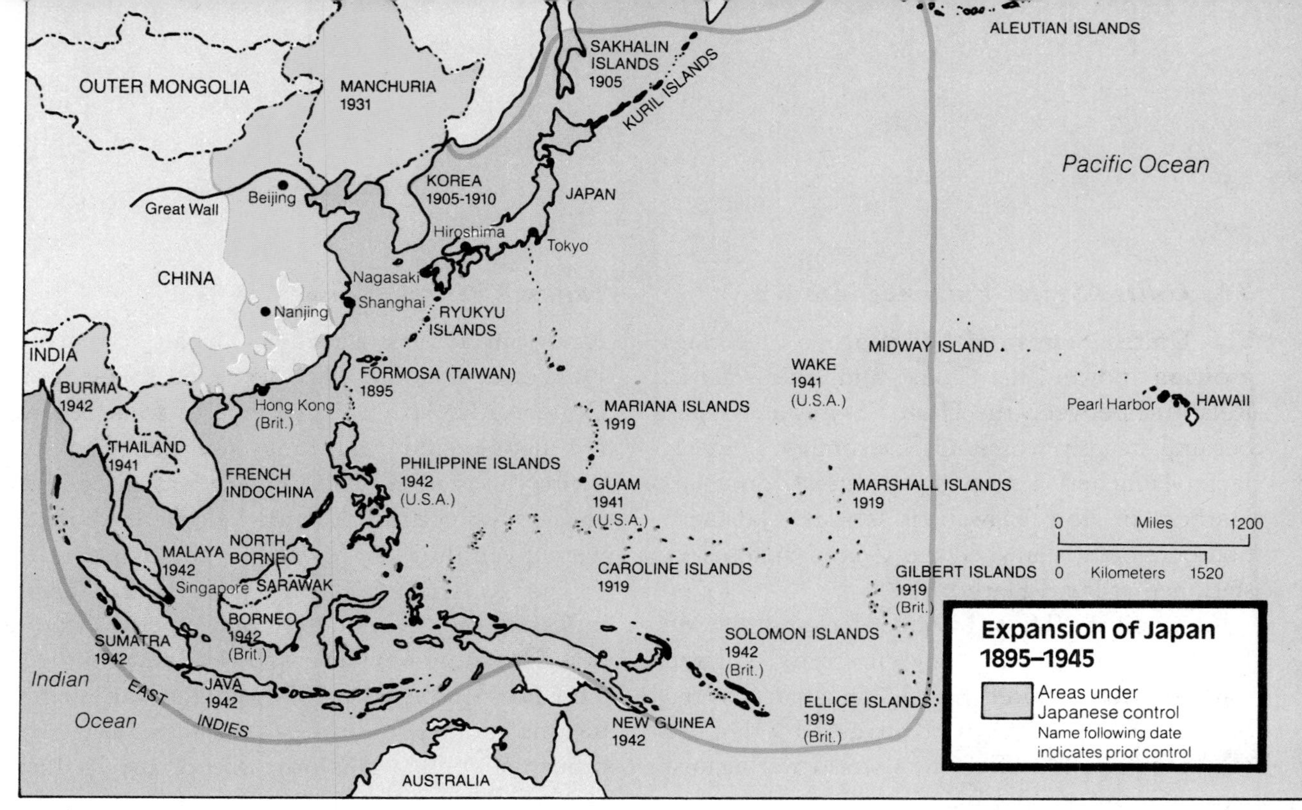

Japan's expansion reached its maximum just prior to World War II. After each place name is the year of its capture by Japanese forces.

They tried to keep foreigners away. These fortified islands were a threat to the Philippines, the East Indies, and Australia.

The Seizing of Manchuria

Japan, overcrowded with people, had kept its eyes on Manchuria for years. Most of Manchuria is a great plain with few trees and rich soil. It also has rich deposits of coal and iron. The area was claimed by China but because it was beyond the Great Wall, it was not thickly settled.

In 1931 Japan invaded Manchuria. Their soldiers occupied the country. The next year, the Japanese set up a supposedly independent nation. This country had a puppet ruler who followed Japanese orders.

The Attack on China

Japan wanted to extend its influence in China. Since Manchuria was already under Japanese control, the invasion forces could enter China from the north. In 1937 Japanese troops were sent through Manchuria, over the Great Wall, and into China. They captured Beijing, Shanghai, and Nanjing.

Eastern China was overrun by the invaders, with almost every seaport in the hands of the Japanese. China was nearly cut off from the rest of the world, but supplies were brought in from India by road and by air. General Chiang Kai-shek was an important leader of the Chinese forces. China kept on fighting and later became an ally of the United States in World War II.

The United States Entrance into War

The United States did not approve of Japan's growing power in China and the Pacific. Relations between the United States and Japan became steadily worse. On December 7, 1941, Japan launched a surprise air attack on Pearl Harbor in the Hawaiian Islands. Japanese bombers badly damaged the United States fleet stationed at Pearl Harbor.

At once the United States declared war on Japan. Germany and Italy, in turn, declared war upon the United States. Thus the United States joined with Great Britain and a number of other nations to fight in a world war against Japan, Germany, and Italy.

World War II in the Pacific

Japan was ready for war, but the United States was not. The bombing of Pearl Harbor had crippled the United States fleet. Island after island in the Pacific fell to Japan. At the height of their success, Japan controlled the Philippines, Hong Kong, Singapore, New Guinea (nōō gin′ē), and the Solomon Islands at the very door of Australia.

The battle of Midway marked the turning point in the war. The United States and their allies gradually took back islands taken by Japan.

The United States began to attack the Japanese mainland. Airplanes bombed Japan's chief cities. In August, 1945, Nagasaki (nä gə sä′kē) and Hiroshima (hēr′ō shē′mə) were almost wiped out by atomic bombs. The atomic bomb was a powerful and terrible new weapon. The Japanese surrendered, and United States forces took control of the country.

Japan After the War

American troops stayed in Japan for many years after the war. They were led by General Douglas MacArthur. The emperor went before the people and told them the belief in his divinity was false. The military was disbanded and a new constitution was adopted. Women were given the right to vote for the first time.

The Americans' stay in Japan had a great influence on that country. Many people combined Japanese ways and American ways in their daily lives. In the years following the war Japan's income and new industries grew faster than any other nation. Japan is now one of the leading industrial nations of the world.

The Principal Cities of Japan

Three-quarters of the population of Japan live in cities. Tokyo (tō′kē ō′) is its largest city. Next to it, and forming a single large urban area with it, is Yokohama (yō′kə hä′mə). Together they have a population of almost 12 million. Yokohama has a fine port and handles most of the nation's foreign trade. It is an important railway center. It also has many shipyards and factories.

Other Japanese Cities

Southwest of Yokohama is Kyoto (kyō′tō), Japan's fourth largest city. For more than a thousand years it was the capital of Japan. Later, the capital was moved to Tokyo. Many travelers go to Kyoto each year to see its beautiful Buddhist temples and gardens. Students go to classes at Kyoto University.

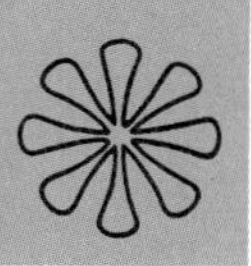

Tokyo
Japan's Largest City

Great contrasts are found in every large city, but perhaps only in giant Tokyo are there such strong contrasts. Tokyo has a fascinating combination of Oriental and Western ways of living.

More than 8 million people live in Tokyo and crowding creates problems. High-speed trains and subways are jammed full. Traffic clogs the streets. There is a severe housing shortage, though new large apartment projects have been built recently.

City dwellers in Tokyo may have television sets, washing machines, and refrigerators. They may shop in supermarkets. But traditional Japanese ways of living are not forgotten. The office workers in a modern skyscraper may come home and change into Japanese robes to relax. Leisure time may be used to study the ancient arts of flower arranging and tea serving.

Every night thousands of people surge along Tokyo's brightly lit main street, the Ginza (ginz'ə). They are on their way to theaters, movie houses, and bowling alleys. But the contrast between the West and the East can be seen here too. One theater shows a Broadway musical while the theater next door presents a 400-year-old Japanese play. ■

As in most Asian countries, rice is a major crop in Japan. Because rice needs a great amount of water to grow, it is planted in flooded fields.

South of Kyoto is Osaka (ō sä′ kə), a city of more than 3 million. There are over 800 bridges criss-crossing the canals and rivers that cut through the city. It is a great industrial center where steel, electronics equipment, automobiles, and other products are produced. Much of Osaka's output is exported to other countries.

West of Osaka, on the Inland Sea, is the busy port of Kobe (kō′ bē). It has more than a million inhabitants. When Japan was opened to foreign trade, Kobe was only a small fishing village. Today it has shipyards, steel mills, and a large foreign trade.

Japanese Ways of Living

Japan today is busy and prosperous. Its people work hard on small farms, in modern factories, on fishing boats, and in many kinds of business.

What Japanese Homes Are Like

Traditional Japanese homes are very simple. There are almost no pictures on the walls, and there is little furniture. Sliding screens separate the rooms. People sit on the floor, which is covered with soft straw mats. They eat at tables just a few inches from the floor. Members of the family sleep on quilts laid over the floor mats. Shoes are never worn in the house.

Now many homes combine Western and Eastern ways. One room may have Western-style furniture and a carpet on the floor. A family may have many modern electrical appliances. Most city families have television sets.

Japanese Gardens

The Japanese countryside is beautiful. Many Japanese carry this beauty into the cities by making gardens. Even in small spaces, flowering shrubs and dwarf trees can be planted. Many gardens have goldfish ponds surrounded by smooth colored pebbles raked into patterns.

The Japanese love flowers. Each year they watch for the blossoming of plum trees and cherry trees. The national flower of Japan is the chrysanthemum (krə san′thə məm).

Sports in Japan

Baseball is Japan's most popular sport. In fact, a first baseman for the Yomiuri Giants in 1977 broke Hank Aaron's world record for home runs. His name is Sadaharu Oh (sä dä′hä ro͞o ō′). Other popular sports are sumo, a kind of Japanese wrestling, and judo, a type of self-defense.

Farming in Japan

Japan has little level land, and the farms are small. However, the farmers know how to make their soil produce good crops. To obtain more land, the Japanese have built terraces for growing rice along the lower slopes of hills. The terraces reach a height of several hundred feet, giving farmers more land on which to grow rice.

The small fields also require special small farm machines. These are built in Japanese factories. Better seeds and more fertilizer have also helped to increase rice production. Before World War II Japan had to import rice to feed its people. Now fewer people work on the farms but the fields produce enough to feed the nation with a little to spare. Many Japanese farmers work part-time in the fields and part-time in nearby factories.

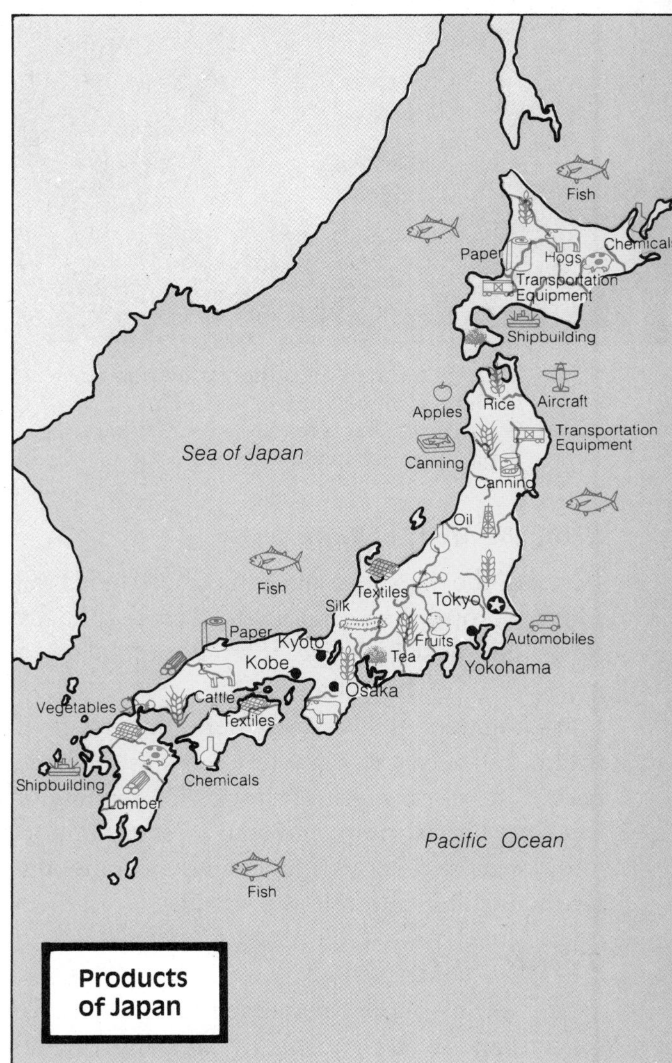

Along with rice, wheat is an important crop. Other crops are sweet potatoes, beans, vegetables, seeds for cooking oil, fruit, tobacco, and tea. It is warm enough in the south to grow two crops a year. More cattle and hogs are being raised every year.

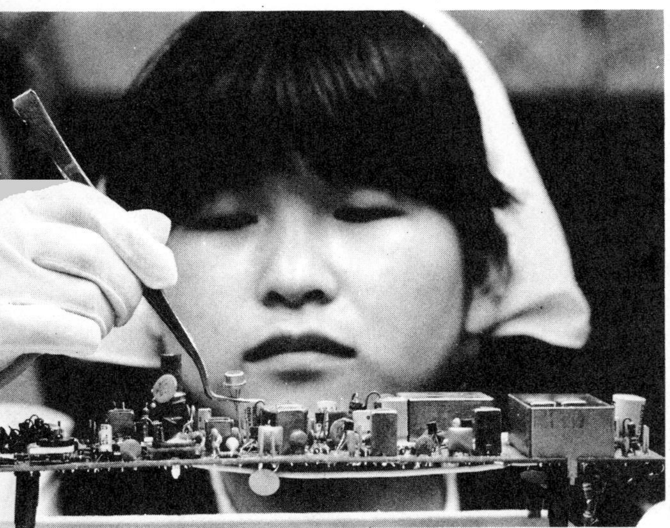

Japan today is a leading industrial nation. Here a young woman assembles transistors for a television set. What other products are made in Japan?

Fish, the Meat of Japan

Because the Japanese need most of their land to grow crops, they cannot afford to keep many cattle. For most Japanese, fish takes the place of meat.

As islanders, the Japanese send thousands of fishing boats out to sea every fair day. A large part of the catch goes to factories for canning or freezing. Fish, shrimp, and crab meat are important Japanese exports. Japan has become the leading fishing nation in the world.

Textiles in Japan

Japan is a major manufacturer of *textiles* (teks′tīlz), or cloth made by weaving threads together. Silk was once an important textile product. Today other textiles are much more important. Cotton, wool, rayon, and synthetic materials are made into textiles in modern factories. Much is exported to many parts of the world.

A Leading Industrial Nation

Japan has made greater progress in industry than any other Asian nation. Although Japan imports four-fifths of all materials its factories need, it leads in manufacturing. Its many steep rivers provide plenty of hydroelectric power. The people make up for their lack of natural resources by working hard and developing skills.

Before World War II the Japanese produced many inexpensive articles such as toys. Today Japan is one of the top three industrial nations in the world. It is the world's leading producer of ships, buses, trucks, computers, sewing machines, stereo equipment, radios, cameras, and television sets. It is second only to the United States in the production of automobiles. It is also one of the largest exporters of electronic equipment, textile machinery, cement, ceramics, and household appliances.

Japan sells many of its factory products to its own people. To keep its factories busy, Japan also carries on much trade with other countries. It exports many manufactured articles. In return, it imports food and raw materials.

Do You Know?

1. In what ways was Japan influenced by China in early times?
2. Why do many visitors go to the Japanese city of Kyoto each year?
3. How did the United States establish trade relations with Japan?

To Help You Learn

Using New Words

textile	puppet government
commune	open-door policy
communism	Japan Current
Shinto	samurai

Number a paper from 1 through 8. After each number write the word or term that matches the definition.

1. The Japanese religion, in which nature, heroes who died in battle, and ancestors are worshipped
2. Opening ports for trade to all nations
3. In Japan's Middle Ages, a member of the warrior class
4. A cloth made by weaving threads together
5. Government officials who are told what to do by another government's leaders
6. A stream of water in the Pacific Ocean which has a warming effect on Japan and many other Pacific lands
7. A system of government in which property and goods are controlled by the government
8. A group of people who live, work, and own property together

Finding the Facts

1. Why do we know so little about China's early history?
2. Who was Genghis Khan?
3. Name four chief products of China.
4. What city is located at the northern end of the Grand Canal?
5. What happened to South Korea after the Korean war?
6. How were the islands of Japan formed?
7. Why is fishing important to Japan?
8. What is unusual about Japanese farming?
9. What did Japan gain by joining the Allies in World War I?
10. Why did Japan invade Manchuria?
11. Where did Japan attack the United States? When did this happen?
12. What two Japanese cities join to form a continuously settled area?
13. What is an important source of power for Japanese industries?

Learning from Maps

1. Turn to the map of China and Korea on page 129. Which port city is farther from the sea: Shanghai or Guangzhou? Which city is farther from Japan: Beijing or Chongqing?
2. Turn to the map of the Expansion of Japan on page 149. In what year did Japan get Taiwan? What islands did it control in 1919? What was the year the empire was largest? How far west did it reach?

Using Study Skills

1. **Graph:** Below is a graph showing the number of passenger automobiles in Japan and the number of television sets. Study the graph and then answer the following questions: What years are covered in the study? Did more Japanese own cars or TVs? In the last year covered, about how many people owned cars? About how many people owned TVs?

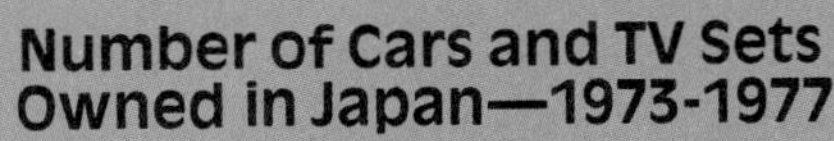

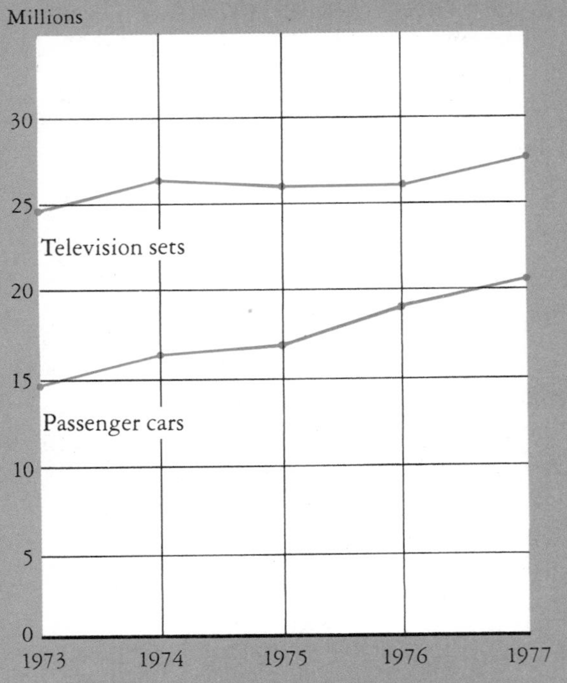

2. **Time Line:** Place the following events in the proper order of time: Japan invades Manchuria, Marco Polo visits China, Buddhism reaches Japan, birth of Confucius, Manchus seize control of China, China adopts open-door policy.

   Copy the time line from page 127. Add these events to your time line.

   Study the completed time line and answer the following questions. Which happened first, the birth of Confucius or the introduction of Buddhism in Japan? How many years went by between the Manchus seizing control of China and the Japanese invasion of Manchuria? Between the Japanese invasion of Manchuria and the Japanese attack on the United States?

3. **Time Line:** Make a time line of ancient civilizations. Using the time line on page 127, write in the date of the earliest Chinese civilization. Refer back to the time line for Unit 2 on page 47. Copy from it the dates for ancient Sumerians, Babylonians, Egyptians, and Hebrews. Add these to your time line. From page 99 in Unit 3 add the date for the Indus River civilization and the Aryan invasion of India.

   Study the completed time line and answer the following questions: What is the earliest civilization on your time line? What two events in Asia happened about the same time?

4. **Diagram:** Look at the diagram of the production of silk thread from silkworms, page 141. What does the silkworm feed on? How does it produce the silk? How is the silk taken from the cocoon?

Thinking It Through

1. The Chinese developed gunpowder long before it was known in Europe. They also made paper, printed books, and used paper money before these things were done in other parts of the world. Why do you suppose it took so long for these skills to become known in Europe?
2. China, Korea, and Japan paid great respect to their ancestors. In fact, ancestor worship became a part of their religion. What did ancestor worship teach? In China, what effect did ancestor worship have on the idea of progress? What effect did it have as Japan set out to build an empire?
3. Before World War II Japan had a growing population it could not feed at home. This caused it to want to build an empire beyond its own borders. How was Japan's way of solving these problems different after World War II?

Projects

1. Find pictures of Chinese or Japanese art in magazines or books. Show them in class.
2. The Research Committee might find out more about how one of these is made into products: silk, porcelain, jade, teakwood, tea. Pictures or samples of the products will help to make your reports more interesting.
3. The Explorers' Committee might like to read more about Marco Polo and trace his route on a map.
4. The Reading Committee might like to read about lives of boys and girls in China, Korea, and Japan today. Find out more about their games and sports, festivals, and family life. Report to the class on a book you read.
5. In China wall posters are an important way people communicate with one another. Start a "People's Wall" in a corner of your classroom. Put on it pictures, cartoons, newspaper clippings, handwritten comments, or your own drawings about what you are studying in class. Put a date on everything that goes on the wall. Appoint a committee to keep things neat and to take things off the wall after they have been up five days.
6. Begin a picture booklet showing building styles of past civilizations. Arrange them according to the date they were built. You may use either drawings you make yourself or photos cut from old magazines or travel leaflets. You may wish to keep the booklet and add other buildings to it when studying other civilizations.

5 Greece and the Balkans

Unit Preview

Each time the Olympic games take place, the world remembers ancient Greece. But the ancient Greeks have given much more to the world than the idea of Olympic games. Many of their ideas about government, about science, and about human life have come down to us and enriched our lives. The ancient Greeks also created wonderful plays and poems, and built beautiful buildings. Their statues of bronze and marble are still greatly admired today. Their myths and fables continue to be read and told.

The city-states of ancient Greece, including Athens and Sparta, were at the southern tip of the shaded area on the map, where it almost touches the continent of Asia. As you can see, the civilizations of the Middle East, including ancient Persia, were not far away. Even ancient Egypt, in northern Africa, was not far off and could be reached by ships.

For all its glory, Greece has not been without conflicts. Greece was conquered in ancient times by Alexander the Great, and later by the Romans and the Turks. It regained its freedom from Turkey in 1829.

The other Balkan countries are Albania, Yugoslavia, Romania, and Bulgaria. Cyprus is an island in the eastern part of the Mediterranean Sea. There is a great variety of different languages and customs in these countries. Farming is important, but more factories are being built.

Things to Discover

If you look carefully at the picture, map, and time line on these pages, you can answer these questions.

1. On what continent are Greece and the Balkans located?
2. What Middle Eastern country conquered Bulgaria in 1396?
3. The picture shows the ruins of an ancient theater in Greece. Why would the site shown in the picture be a good place to build a theater?
4. Many plays were written while Pericles ruled Greece. When did he become the Greek ruler?
5. How long was it from the beginning of the Age of Pericles to Philip's conquest of Greece?

Words to Learn

You will meet these words in this unit. As you read, you will learn what they mean and how to pronounce them. The Word List will help you.

bauxite	guerrilla
capital	javelin
comedy	jury
democracy	league
discus	open city
epic	tragedy
fable	tyrant
frieze	

Knossos falls
c. 1400
Olympic games begin in Greece
776
The Age of Pericles begins
461
Philip of Macedonia conquers Greece
338
Romans conquer Greece
146
B.C.
A.D.
Turks conquer Bulgaria
1396
Greeks regain freedom from Turks
1829
Communists take over Balkans, except Greece
1945–1947
Greek army sets up military government
1967
Greece adopts a new constitution
1975

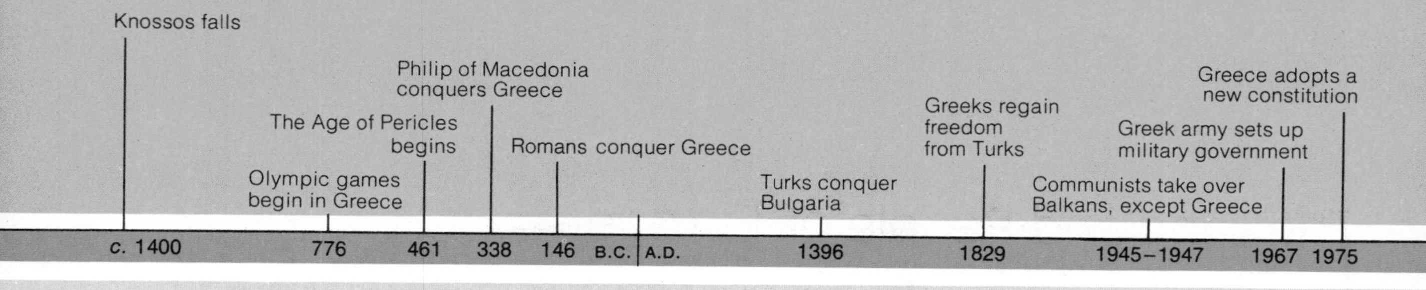

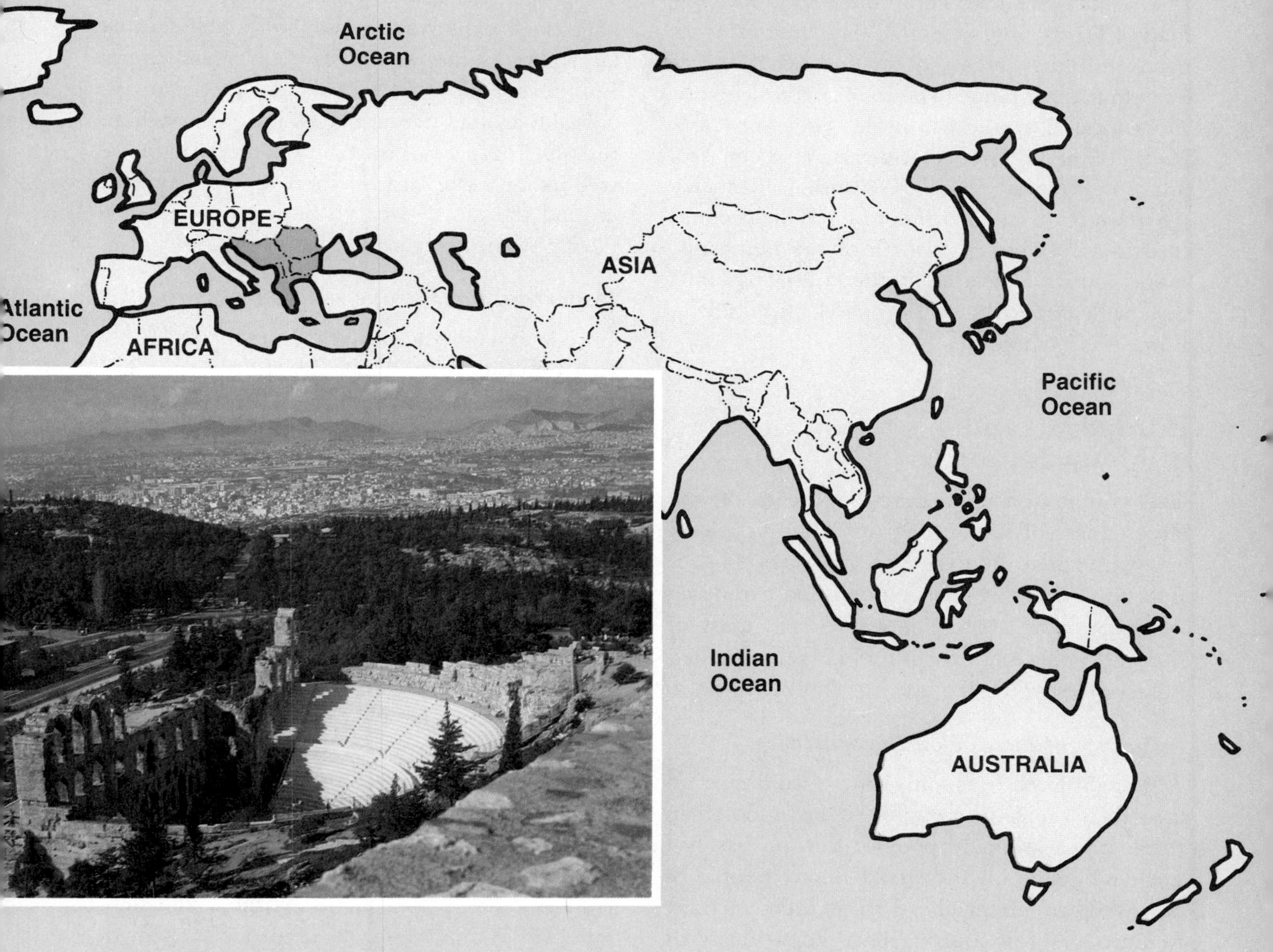

Arctic Ocean
EUROPE
ASIA
Atlantic Ocean
AFRICA
Pacific Ocean
Indian Ocean
AUSTRALIA

1 The Land and People of Europe

The Balkan (bôl′kən) Peninsula is shown on the map of Europe on page 161. The area gains its name from the Balkan Mountains, which are its most important range. The Balkan countries are those located on the peninsula. They are Albania (al bā′nē ə), Greece, Bulgaria (bul ger′ē ə), and Yugoslavia (yo͞o′gō slä′vē ə). Romania (rō mā′nē ə) is also considered a Balkan country, though it lies just north of the peninsula. Since this and several of the following units deal with countries of Europe, let us look at Europe as a whole.

Europe, a Land of Many Nations

The continent called Europe is part of the largest mass of land on earth. When you look at a world map like the one on pages 24–25, Europe appears as a large peninsula extending westward from Asia. The entire land mass of Europe and Asia together is often called Eurasia. Can you tell why?

Influence of Europe on the World

Although Europe is only one-third larger in area than the United States, it has more than three times as many people. Europe has had great influence on the world. Many people of the Western Hemisphere trace their ancestry to Europe. From Europe have come many of our ideas about freedom, law, government, and art.

For the past 500 years the people of Europe have been exploring, trading with, and settling large parts of the world. For many years several European nations like England and Spain had colonies around the globe. Today most of these regions in Asia, South America, and Africa are free nations. But almost wherever we may look around the globe, we can find traces of European ways of living.

Importance of Europe's Resources

Europe is favored with many resources. It has rich deposits of minerals and fertile soil. The sandy beaches of the Mediterranean, the lofty Alps Mountains, the pleasant countryside, and the river valleys attract tourists from all over the world.

In early times Europe's closeness to the sea was a constant invitation to its people to explore what lay beyond the horizon. Its long, winding coastline provided harbors in which trading cities grew up.

Because of its location Europe has a favorable climate in which people may live and work. The southern coast is washed by the warm waters of the Mediterranean Sea. On the west and northwest Europe faces the Atlantic Ocean and the North Sea. Since it is close to these water bodies, western Europe has a climate that is not as cold as other places in the world at the same latitude. Winds from the ocean also provide much of Europe with plenty of rainfall to produce abundant crops.

EUROPE
100 200 300 400 Miles
161 322 483 644 Kilometers
National Capitals
Other Cities
Mountains
Plateaus
Hills
Plains
ARCTIC CIRCLE
ICELAND
Reykjavík
NORWEGIAN SEA
Faeroe Islands
Shetland Islands
NORWAY
SWEDEN
FINLAND
Murmansk
WHITE SEA
GULF OF BOTHNIA
Bergen
Oslo
Stockholm
Helsinki
Leningrad
BALTIC SEA
Göteborg
Riga
Glasgow
Edinburgh
Belfast
IRELAND
Dublin
UNITED KINGDOM
NORTH SEA
DENMARK
Copenhagen
Liverpool
SOVIET UNION
Minsk
Hamburg
Elbe
NETHERLANDS
Amsterdam
FED. REP. OF GER.
Berlin
GER. DEM. REP.
ATLANTIC OCEAN
London
Antwerp
Essen
Cologne
Rhine
Oder
Vistula River
Warsaw
POLAND
ENGLISH CHANNEL
BELGIUM
Brussels
Bonn
LUX.
Prague
Kiev
Seine River
Paris
Nantes
Loire
CZECHOSLOVAKIA
CARPATHIANS
Dnestr River
Bay of Biscay
FRANCE
Danube River
Munich
Vienna
Bern
SWITZERLAND
AUSTRIA
Budapest
Bordeaux
Lyon
ALPS
Drava
HUNGARY
ROMANIA
Odessa
Garonne River
Rhône River
Milan
Venice
Bilbao
PYRENEES
Po River
Genoa
Belgrade
Bucharest
Danube River
PORTUGAL
SPAIN
Marseille
Florence
ADRIATIC SEA
YUGOSLAVIA
Morava River
BALKANS
BULGARIA
Lisbon
Madrid
CORSICA
APENNINES
ITALY
Barcelona
Rome
Sofia
Istanbul
Balearic Islands
Córdoba
Seville
SARDINIA
Naples
Tirane
ALBANIA
STRAIT OF GIBRALTAR
Tanger
Cartagena
MEDITERRANEAN SEA
Mt. Olympus
AEGEAN SEA
Rabat
Algiers
SICILY
IONIAN SEA
GREECE
Izmir
Athens
Tunis
Rhodes
ATLAS MOUNTAINS
MALTA
AFRICA
Crete
60°
50°
40°
0°
10°
20°
© Rand McNally & Co.

The people of Europe live in many countries and speak different languages. They have had a hard time getting along together and have suffered from many wars.

Since World War II, the people of Western Europe have been working together in various ways. They are trying to solve their problems through trade agreements and conferences.

Do You Know?

1. How has Europe influenced the world? Name three ways.
2. What are Europe's chief resources?
3. What are some of Europe's problems?

2
The Greeks and Their Land

The land of Greece has helped to shape Greek life. The map of Greece and the Balkans on page 163 shows Greece's many bays and its ragged coastline. No spot in Greece is more than 40 miles (64 km) from the sea. It is easy to see why the Greeks became a seafaring people.

The Geography of Greece

The mountains from the north extend into every part of the peninsula. Only one-fifth of the land can be farmed. Small areas are walled off from each other by mountains. Do you think this would help to unite the Greeks or keep them apart?

Greece has little fertile land. The land in the plains produces grain. But the woods that once covered the upper slopes of the mountains have been cut away, and only bare rock remains. On the lower slopes sheep and goats graze. On the hillsides grow olive trees that yield a rich oil.

As you study Greece, keep in mind its rocky coast, the mountain walls dividing the land, and the lack of fertile soil. This will help you understand the life of the Greeks in the past and at present.

Early Times in Aegean Lands

More than 3,000 years ago large groups of fair-skinned people moved from the north into what is now Greece. They were armed with iron weapons which helped them to conquer the local people.

The newcomers gained much from the civilizations they conquered. Among other skills, they learned how to sail ships. They visited many small islands in the Aegean

GREECE AND THE BALKANS
Plains
Plateaus
Hills
Mountains
Miles
0
80
Kilometers
0
101
AUSTRIA
Vienna
HUNGARY
Budapest
U.S.S.R.
CARPATHIAN MTS.
ROMANIA
Trieste
Zagreb
Belgrade
Bucharest
Constanta
YUGOSLAVIA
Sarajevo
Split
ADRIATIC SEA
Danube River
BALKAN MTS.
BLACK SEA
Sofia
BULGARIA
RHODOPE MTS.
ITALY
ALBANIA
Tirane
Naples
Istanbul
Bosporus Strait
SEA OF MARMARA
MACEDONIA
Salonika
Dardanelles
Site of Troy
ASIA MINOR
Mt. Olympus
GREECE
TURKEY
IONIAN ISLANDS
IONIAN SEA
AEGEAN SEA
Izmir
Piraeus
Marathon
Corinth
Athens
Site of Olympia
Bay of Salamis
Sparta
Site of Knossos
CRETE
MEDITERRANEAN SEA
14°
18°
22°
26°
30°
46°
42°
38°

(i jē′ ən) Sea. They probably sailed as far south as the island of Crete (krēt). Find Crete on the map of Europe on page 161.

The people of Crete had a fine civilization in early times. They were good sailors, traders, and skilled workers. Scientists have uncovered the ruins of Knossos (nos′ əs), the capital city in northern Crete. The king's palace had handsome columns, a grand staircase, and running water. The art of the people of Crete was of a very high quality. The king of Knossos held power over the other cities of the island. Paved roads connected these cities with Knossos.

The Fall of Knossos

About the year 1400 B.C. misfortune fell upon Knossos. The palace and many of the houses were burned by an enemy from another land. Scientists think these raiders came from Greece. Their skill in using ships enabled them to sail to Crete. Their iron weapons helped them conquer the city of Knossos.

The Coming of the Greeks

By the year 1000 B.C. the whole Greek peninsula and the islands of the Aegean Sea, including Crete, had been settled by the new people. We call them Greeks, but they spoke of themselves as Hellenes (hel′ ēnz), after Hellas, an area of Greece.

The Hellenes learned much from the people among whom they settled. As time went on they developed a fine civilization.

As we read about the Hellenes, we find much to admire in their government, art, and science.

The Greek City-States

As the years passed Greece developed into a land of a hundred or more little city-states. The city-states were separated by mountains. Each had its own government.

The Greeks loved their own cities. Travel was difficult. People in one city-state did not often visit people of other states. Because the cities were so separated, the people were likely to be suspicious of one another. Ancient Greece was not a nation under one government, such as Greece is today.

Although not united, all the people were proud to be Hellenes. Their language differed a little from city to city, but they could understand one another.

The Religion of the Greeks

All Greeks believed in the same gods and goddesses. The Greeks thought that their gods and goddesses lived on top of Mount Olympus (ō lim′ pəs), in the northern part of Greece.

Zeus (zo͞os) was the father-god of this group. Among his family were his wife Hera (hēr′ ə), goddess of children and the home; Ares (er′ ēz), god of battle; Apollo (ə pol′ ō), god of sunlight and music; and Athena (ə thē′ nə), goddess of wisdom. Poseidon, the god of the sea, and Hades, the god of the underworld, were the brothers of Zeus.

The Greeks thought of their gods and goddesses as supermen and superwomen. The gods protected those they liked and did harm to those they disliked. Greeks who wanted to keep on good terms with the gods offered gifts and held festivals in their honor.

Remains of Grecian–style buildings can still be seen in many of the lands the Greeks settled. This Greek temple, now in ruins, is in Sicily.

Greek Settlements in Other Lands

The Greeks learned to build ships like those of the Phoenicians. They set out during the summer, going from one port to another. As the years went by, the Greeks reached all the islands in the Aegean. They settled on these islands and on land across the Aegean in Asia Minor, in what is now Turkey. Near the Black Sea they founded Byzantium (bi zan′shē əm), now known as Istanbul.

The Greeks also sailed to Mediterranean lands. To the west of Greece is Italy, shaped like a boot with the island of Sicily (sis′ə lē) at the toe. The Greeks explored this land. They founded the towns of Naples (nā′pəlz) in Italy, Syracuse (sir′ə kyo͞os′) in Sicily, and Marseille (mär sā′) in France.

The Olympic Games

The Greeks held many sacred festivals. These were holidays for the people.

Some of the festivals became so popular that visitors from many parts of Greece took part in them. The greatest of these festivals was held every 4 years at Olympia, in western Greece.

The tradition of the Olympic games held in ancient Greece continues today. Shown here are the opening ceremonies of the 1980 Winter Olympic games in Lake Placid, New York.

It honored the god Zeus. This festival became known as the Olympic games. The first Olympic games were held in 776 B.C.

How the Games Were Held

Only men took part in the ancient Olympic games. First a young man had to prove his ability in contests in his own district. If he passed these, he received special training for ten months before the games.

The Olympic games lasted five days. There were long and short races. Two-horse and four-horse chariot races were an exciting part of the program.

In order that the young men might display all-round strength and skill, the managers of the games arranged a five-part contest. Each athlete in this contest had to take part in the broad jump, 200-yard dash, and the wrestling match. They also had to show their skill in throwing a kind of spear, called a *javelin* (jav′lin). Another object they had to throw was a circular plate of stone or metal, called a *discus* (dis′kəs). When a young man had won three out of these five contests, he was declared the over-all champion.

At the end of five days the winners received prizes. Their chief reward was a wreath of leaves from a sacred olive tree which grew behind the temple of Zeus. When the athlete reached home, banquets were held to celebrate his victory. Statues of him were made. Poems were written about him.

During the month of the Olympic games the priests commanded that there be peace. Nothing should stop the festival. Thus people from different cities could meet in a friendly way. The games helped draw the Greeks together.

These games were the beginning of our modern Olympic games.

Greek Ways of Living

Among the city-states of ancient Greece were two of great importance, Sparta and Athens. Sparta was in the south. Athens was northeast of Sparta.

Each city-state developed its own customs. Athens and Sparta had very different ways of living.

Life in Ancient Sparta

In Sparta soldiers ruled. People who farmed and carried on various trades took orders from soldiers. Spartan warriors could spend all their time on military matters.

Spartans had little interest in reading, writing, or in art. Their thoughts were on keeping themselves fit for warfare. A Spartan boy grew up learning to endure hardship and pain without complaint. In winter as in summer, he wore only a single garment. He did not wear shoes. He slept on a bed of reeds. From childhood, he took part in games to prepare for battle.

Sparta conquered a number of its neighbor city-states. "Other states admired Sparta for her power," one Athenian wrote. "But none wished to be like her."

Life in Ancient Athens

The customs of Athens differed greatly from those of Sparta. Athenians took part in games to develop their bodies and enjoy sports. They did, however, learn to be good soldiers who could defend Athens in time of need. Athenian children learned to read, write, and sing songs. An Athenian had a free and happy life. Even Athenian slaves were well treated.

Boys and girls had different training. When about 6 years old boys went to school. Girls were taught at home. They learned how to run the household, to weave and sew cloth, and to cook. Most things a family needed had to be made at home.

The Government of Athens

Athens, like almost every city-state of Greece, had a government whose officials were elected by its citizens. Such a government is called a *democracy* (di mok′rə sē). Democracy means "rule by the people."

In Athens male citizens over 18 years of age met several times a year on a hillside in Athens to discuss the running of their city. There they discussed their problems freely. They elected their leaders. Women did not vote.

Sometimes, when war came or the people quarreled among themselves, a strong leader took control of the government. The Greeks called such a ruler a *tyrant* (tī′rənt). Some of the tyrants governed well. But the sons who followed them often ruled cruelly. Thus, the word "tyrant" has come to mean a harsh and cruel person.

Solon's Wise Rule

The Greek leader who gave Athens its real beginning in democratic government was an army hero named Solon (sō′lən). Solon was elected head of the government when there was much unrest. One class of people, the nobles, owned much of the farm land. Many small farmers had gone so deeply into debt to the nobles that they had become slaves.

Solon drafted new laws that freed all debt-slaves. He passed a law which said that people should never again be made slaves just because they could not pay their debts. He also made it possible for the poor men as well as the rich to sit in the Athenian assembly.

Trial by Jury

Solon provided that anyone who had lost a lawsuit could have the case tried by a *jury* (joor′ē). A jury is a group of persons who listen to both sides of a case and give their decision about it.

We who live in the United States have the right of trial by jury. The idea of the jury trial comes from Athens. But the Greek juries were different from our juries. In our jury trials jurors (joor′ərz) sit in a courtroom, listen to what is said, and judge whether the accused person is guilty or innocent. In trials in Athens a large number of jurors sat on stone benches under the blue sky. If the case was an important one, there might be a hundred or more jurors listening at the same time. When the arguments on both sides of the case had been heard, the jurors voted. Athenians thus had an important part to play in seeing that justice was done.

The Persian Wars

The Athenians came into conflict with the Persians. The Persians had built up a great empire in western Asia and North Africa. They took over the Greek city-states on the coast of Asia Minor. But the people living there did not forget they were Greeks. They kept on trading with Greece and were eager for news from Greece.

Then the cities of Asia Minor rebelled against Persia. Athens sent ships to help them. So Darius (də rī′ əs), the Persian king, decided the Athenians must be punished for their part in the rebellion.

The Defeat at Marathon

In 490 B.C. a Persian army landed at Marathon (mar′ə thon′) near Athens. Ten thousand Greeks, mostly Athenians, met the Persians. The Persians were skilled in the use of bows and arrows. They had twice as many soldiers as the Greeks. But the Greeks were fine warriors. They rushed with their sharp spears against the Persians, and the Persians fled to their ships. This victory cheered the Greeks.

The news of the victory at Marathon was carried to Athens, about 25 miles (40 km) away, by an Athenian soldier. The soldier ran the entire distance. He delivered his message, then died. The word "marathon" now means any long-distance race. It helps us remember the Athenians and a soldier who brought honor to his city.

The Final Defeat of the Persians

Ten years later another Persian king, Xerxes (zurk′sēz), tried to defeat the Greeks. He moved his large army into Europe over a bridge formed by lashing boats together across the narrow waterway near Byzantium. After a fierce struggle Athens and Sparta were

Athenians developed a high level of excellence in painting and sculpture during the Age of Pericles. They often painted scenes on vases, such as this picture of women weaving.

captured. But the Greek fleet, made up chiefly of Athenian vessels, sailed away to a nearby bay between the island of Salamis (sal′ə məs) and the mainland.

The Greek and Persian fleets met in a great battle in the Bay of Salamis. The Persians were caught by surprise and were soundly defeated. From his golden throne overlooking the bay, Xerxes watched as the Persian ships were sunk.

The next year the Athenians and Spartans met the Persians in one last great battle. In the year 479 B.C. the Persians were driven from Greece forever.

The Age of Pericles

After the war with Persia, Athens had peace for about 30 years. A young noble named Pericles (per′ə klēz) became head of the government. Athens reached its greatest glory under Pericles. The period from 461 to 431 B.C. is called the Age of Pericles.

The Athenian League

Athens became the leader of the Greek city-states. With Athens at their head about 200 cities formed a *league* (lēg), or union, to protect themselves. The Athenian League assembled a

The beauty of the human form was a favorite subject of the sculptors of ancient Greece. They admired the body's strength and grace. Sculptors preserved this nobility in a form we still enjoy.

powerful fleet of ships. Athens took yearly payments from the cities and built the ships.

The Rebuilding of Athens

In the Age of Pericles, Athens, which had been burned by the Persians, was rebuilt. The peace which followed the war gave Greeks a chance to build a new life. The Athenians set about making their city beautiful.

In the center of Athens, rising hundreds of feet above the narrow streets that surrounded it, was a steep hill. The top of this hill was called the Acropolis (ə krop′ə lis). On the Acropolis, under the direction of the artists and builders employed by Pericles, many fine temples were built.

Greatest and finest of the public buildings on the Acropolis was the Parthenon (pär′thə non′). The Parthenon was a white marble temple built for the worship of the goddess Athena. Graceful columns surrounded it. The *capitals* (kap′it əlz), or tops, of the columns were in the style called Doric. Doric columns were simpler in design than the other frequently used styles. (See the diagram of the column capitals below.)

On the outside walls of the temple was a *frieze* (frēz), or band of carved marble, all around the building. The pictures in the frieze showed Athenians moving in a procession to worship the goddess of Athens. So lovely was the frieze that the world still treasures the fragments which remain.

Greek sculptors created statues of people in graceful poses. Most of the statues made by the

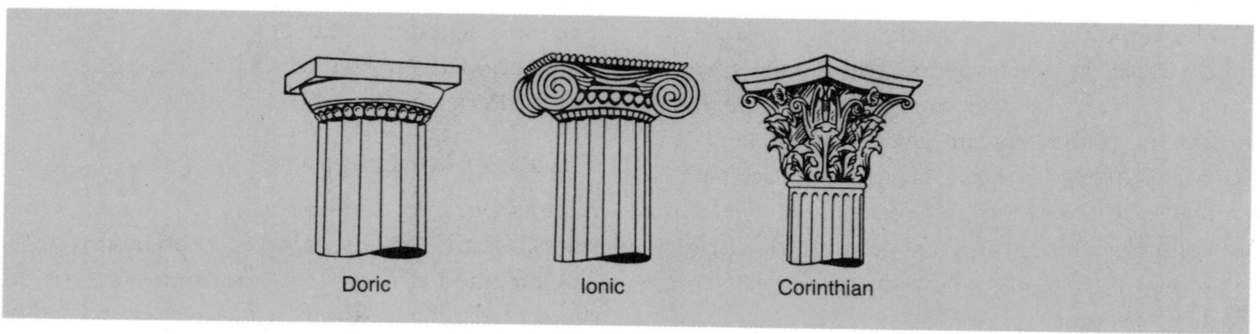

The outdoor theater at Delphi was once the stage for *comedies* and *tragedies*. Greeks enjoyed watching human drama against a large natural background. Dramas were not played at night. Can you tell why?

Greeks have been lost to the world. Those which remain are the most beautiful of their kind ever made.

Athens, the Birthplace of Drama

The Athenians enjoyed plays. Their theater was outdoors on a hillside which had curved rows of stone seats facing the stage. In the morning they would see a *tragedy* (traj′ ə dē), or serious play. A tragedy is a play in which the hero or heroine comes to a sad end because he or she has done wrong or has made a bad mistake. In the afternoon the people would see a *comedy* (kom′ ə dē). A comedy is a play that is amusing or has a happy ending. The Athenians liked both kinds. Some of their plays are still performed today.

The Fall of Greece

Many fine Greek city-states such as Abydos (ə bid′ əs) and Rhodes grew up on the islands and shores of Asia Minor. The people of these city-states traded with Athens and with other city-states on the mainland. They looked to Athens to protect them. Athens did so for a time, but the later leaders of Athens were not always wise or fair.

Instead of treating the other Greek city-states justly, Athens forced them to pay heavy taxes. Finally, some of the Greek city-states rebelled against Athens and its allies. Athens was defeated in 404 B.C. After this, the city-states went on fighting among themselves. This weakened the country, and outsiders saw their chance to invade.

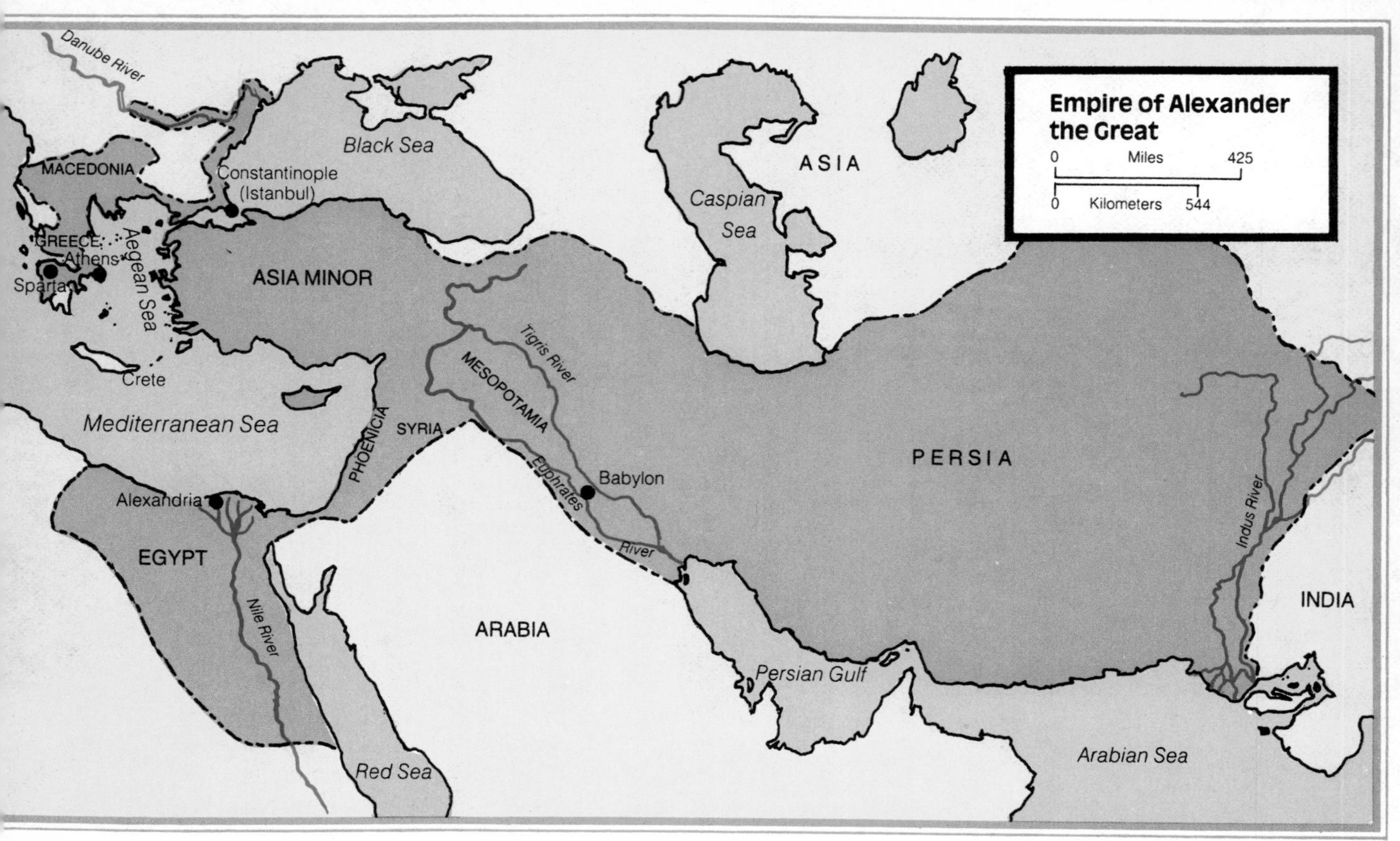

Alexander the Great built a large empire that reached to India. He wanted to make Europe and Asia one country. After his death his empire was divided, but the Greek customs he brought remained.

Conquest by Macedonia

About 100 years after the death of Pericles, Greece was invaded by soldiers from Macedonia (mas′ə dō′ nē ə), a land to the north. Philip, ruler of Macedonia, with his well-trained army conquered Greece in 338 B.C. When Philip died in 336 B.C., his son, who became known as Alexander the Great, became king of Macedonia.

With the strong army his father had trained, Alexander kept Greece under his control. He marched eastward as far as northeast India, conquering as he went.

Alexander's boyhood teacher was a wise Greek named Aristotle (ar′ is tot′ əl). Taught by Aristotle, Alexander learned to admire the Greeks and their ways of living. He introduced the Greek customs into all the lands that he conquered.

Conquest by Rome

Alexander's empire did not hold together after his death. Soon a new conqueror appeared on the Mediterranean. In 146 B.C. the armies of Rome, from the nearby peninsula of Italy, ran over Greece. Greece lost its freedom and became a part of the Roman Empire. It was during the Roman rule of Greece that Christianity spread among the people.

Conquest by the Turks

When the Turks, about whom you have already read in Unit 2, moved into Europe, they conquered Greece. The Turks were Muslims. But the Greeks did not accept the religion of their Muslim conquerors. Instead, they kept the Christianity they had adopted.

The Greeks were very unhappy under Turkish rule. They never ceased to dream of freedom and to work for it. In 1829, after nearly 2,000 years, the Greeks regained their freedom. They united and set up a nation under their own king.

Do You Know?

1. Why were the ancient Greeks a seafaring people?
2. What were the Olympic games?
3. How was Athens governed?

3 Greece's Gifts to the World

We remember ancient Greece because its people had strong bodies, skillful hands, inquiring minds, and a love of beauty. All these things helped them create one of the world's finest civilizations.

Some Famous Greeks

Some of the most famous people of all time lived in ancient Greece. These people were writers and teachers. One was a well-known doctor.

Homer, the Blind Poet

Homer, who was blind, recited his poetry to music. His long story-poems, the *Iliad* (il′ē əd) and the *Odyssey* (od′ə sē), tell us much about the ancient Greeks, their gods, their history, and their customs. A long poem that tells the story of a heroic person or persons is called an *epic* (ep′ik). Homer's epics have delighted people ever since.

Sappho, a Woman Poet

Sappho (saf′ō′) was another famous Greek poet. Only one of her poems has come down to us complete. We know her chiefly from the writings of other Greeks who admired her so much that they quoted from her works. Homer's poems were long and told a story. But Sappho's poems were brief songs of love and nature. Sappho spent most of her life on

While Athenians traded in the market-place, the Greek teacher Socrates talked to students. Socrates taught people to seek the truth.

one of the Greek islands, as head of a school for girls.

Sophocles, a Writer of Plays

As you read earlier, the Greeks liked to go to plays. The greatest of their play writers was Sophocles (sof′ə klēz′). His plays dealt with serious subjects. He was the first writer of plays to show that a person's troubles were often caused by mistakes that he or she made.

Before the time of Sophocles, men and women in Greek plays had been at the mercy of luck or fate. Because of his understanding of people, Sophocles' plays seem natural and real today.

Aesop and His Fables

Aesop (ē′səp) is remembered for the *fables* (fā′belz) he told. A fable is a short tale in which animals are the main characters. These animals usually have the power to talk. The fables teach lessons.

In one of Aesop's fables a mouse persuades a lion not to kill him. Later, the lion is captured and tied up by hunters. The mouse frees the lion by chewing the ropes that bind him. This fable's lesson is: "Sometimes the weakest can help the strongest."

Socrates, a Great Teacher

One of the greatest teachers the world has ever known was a Greek named Socrates (sok′rə tēz′). He taught people to seek truth as the most important thing in life. Socrates thought that no person is really bad. He believed that goodness is based on knowledge and that wickedness is due to ignorance.

Some people in Athens felt that Socrates' teachings might encourage young people to disobey the laws. They brought charges against him. He was tried and condemned to death. The great teacher spent his last hours talking with his friends. Then, when night came, he drank a cup of poison, as the law required.

Socrates was a seeker after truth. His beliefs did not die with him but were passed on through his pupils to the world.

Hippocrates, a Famous Doctor

About 400 years before Christ there lived a man who became one of the world's most famous doctors. He was a Greek, and his name was Hippocrates (hi pok′rə tēz). Before Hippocrates' time the only doctors were the priests. The hospitals were in the temples of the god of medicine. The priests in these hospitals often used charms to try to make people well. Sometimes they used drugs which did more harm than good.

Hippocrates studied the effect of drugs on certain diseases. He kept a record of what happened to the people who took the drugs. In this way he and the doctors who worked with him knew what to do when others had the same disease. His students took a vow, called the Oath of Hippocrates. In the oath they made a solemn promise to do all they could for the sick. For hundreds of years, medical students took this oath. In some schools they still do.

Love of Freedom and Beauty

It is obvious, then, that we owe a lot to the ancient Greeks. Many modern governments are based upon the Greek model of democracy. Freedoms that we take for granted were begun by the ancient Greeks. The Greeks also gave us much fine poetry, art, and music. Their love of freedom and beauty has made the world a better place.

Do You Know?

1. Who was Homer? Who was Sappho?
2. Why was Hippocrates famous?
3. What is a fable? Which Greek is remembered for his fables?
4. What form of government did the Greeks give the world?

Before You Go On

Using New Words

frieze	jury
comedy	tragedy
epic	capital
javelin	tyrant
democracy	discus
fable	league

Number a paper from 1 through 12. After each number write the word or term that matches the definition.

1. A union of governments which agree to work together
2. In Greece, a strong ruler who seized power
3. A group of persons who listen to both sides of a case and give their decision about it
4. A circular plate made of stone or metal, thrown by athletes
5. A kind of spear
6. A serious play with an unhappy ending
7. An amusing play
8. A band of carved marble on a building
9. Rule by the people
10. A short tale about animals that teaches a lesson
11. A long poem about a great hero
12. The top of a column or pillar

Finding the Facts

1. What is Eurasia?
2. What was Knossos? What happened to it?
3. Who were the Hellenes? Why are we interested in them?
4. Name three cities in other lands that were first settled by Greeks.
5. Who was Zeus? Where did he live? Name two other Greek gods or goddesses and tell who they were.
6. How were the winners of Olympic games rewarded?
7. Who elected the leaders of ancient Athens?
8. Who was Solon? Why is he remembered?
9. Name three styles of columns.
10. Describe the theaters in which the people of Athens saw plays.
11. Why did the Greek cities in Asia Minor finally revolt against Athens?
12. Who was Philip?
13. Name two countries that conquered Greece.
14. Who was Socrates?

4

The Balkan Countries Today

For thousands of years the mountainous part of Europe now called the Balkans has been the borderland between Eastern and Western peoples. Armies of conquering nations have marched back and forth. Each conqueror has left a mark on the dwellers in the Balkans until now there is a great variety of peoples, languages, and customs.

Bulgaria, in 1396, was the first Balkan nation to be conquered by the Turks. In time, all of the Balkan nations were controlled by Turkey. They were part of the Ottoman Empire. (See the map of the Ottoman Empire on page 67.)

When the Balkan countries fought for their freedom from Turkey, Russia and other European countries helped them. In 1913, after nearly a hundred years of war, Turkey lost all the Balkans, except for a small area near Istanbul. The Balkan countries had finally won their independence.

The Balkans Since Independence

Even free from Turkish rule, the Balkan countries did not prosper. They had few factories and little to sell to the rest of the world.

During World War II Germany and Italy reached out toward the Balkans. The German army conquered the whole area. But Greece and Yugoslavia never stopped struggling against them. Strong bands of *guerrillas* (gə ril′ əz), or civilian fighters, in both countries continued to attack the invaders throughout the war. After World War II all the countries but Greece fell under Communist rule.

Modern cities have been built along the coast of the Adriatic Sea. The sea is like a highway over which cities ship their goods. The land extends into the sea and forms good harbors.

Fishing is a major industry in Greece, which has a long coastline along the Aegean, Mediterranean, and Ionian seas. The fishermen in this Greek port are repairing their nets.

Greece Today

The present-day nation of Greece is the size of Alabama. Its population is about equal to Michigan's. Most of its people work on the soil or fish in waters along the coast. Greek farmers raise grain, figs, currants, olives, lemons, and oranges, and have large vineyards. They also grow cotton and tobacco.

Athens

Athens is in southern Greece. It was the leading city of ancient Greece. It is also the capital of modern Greece. The first place most visitors want to see is the Parthenon.

The Parthenon is a grand building that sits on top of a steep hill high above the city. But much of that ancient building is now in ruins. The destruction took place a long time ago. Athens was captured by the Turks when they overran eastern Europe. Later, in 1687, the city-state of Venice, in Italy, fought the Turks. During the war the Turks used the Parthenon as a storehouse for gunpowder. Then Venice attacked Athens and shelled the city from its fleet in the harbor. A shell exploded the powder kept in the Parthenon and ruined the wonderful building.

The temple stood in ruins for a hundred years. Then Great Britain bought some of the pieces. Many of the sculptures were taken away to England where they can be seen in a museum.

Piraeus and Salonika

Athens lies on a plain about 5 miles (8 km) from the Aegean Sea. To carry on its ocean trade, Athens uses the port of Piraeus (pi rē′ əs), a few miles to the southwest. Most of the ships that come and go from Piraeus are owned and run by Greeks. Ships carry barrels of olive oil, bags of currants, and boxes of raisins from Greece all around the world.

In the harbor can be seen small boats that carry sponge fishers. Sponges are not caught on a hook like fish. Instead, divers have to go down into the water after them. At one time the waters around Piraeus were the best sponge fisheries in the world. When larger sponge fisheries were found in Florida, these fisheries lost their importance. Today plastic sponges are widely used.

Salonika (sə lon′ i kə) is a seaport in northern Greece. For a long time it was a Turkish city. Slender minarets on the many mosques rise above the city. Salonika is a leading industrial center. Its industries include shipyards and flour and textile mills. It makes tobacco products, soap, and leather goods.

Favorite Greek Foods

Mavros and Zoe are two Greek children. One day they asked an American friend, Alice, to stop at their home. They served her grapevine leaves folded around a stuffing. These were called dolmades (dōl mä′ des). "I think you will like these dolmades," Zoe said. "They are stuffed with ground lamb, rice, and raisins. Lamb and kid, which is young goat, are favorite meats in Greece."

"Thank you," said Alice, as she took a bite, "and could I please have a glass of milk?"

"Yes, if you like goat's milk," Zoe said.

"I'll be glad to try it," Alice answered.

"Goat's milk is used in almost every home along the Mediterranean," Mavros remarked. "Shepherds use goat's milk to make feta (fet′ ə) cheese. It is soft and white. We do not have the cool, moist climate necessary for thick grass. Goats can eat dry, thorny bushes that cows cannot live on."

Greece in Wartime and After

During World War II, the Greeks feared that damage would be done to both the old and the new buildings of Athens. To protect their capital, they declared that it was an *open city* (ō′ pən sit′ ē). By declaring it an open city, they meant that they would not fight to defend it or make it the scene of war activities. Although some parts of Athens were damaged in the war, many famous buildings escaped harm.

The Germans held Greece and its capital for about 3 years in World War II. Then British troops, aided by the Greeks, drove out the German forces. After the war the United States helped the Greeks rebuild their country.

Greece had a king as head of state. In 1952, Greece adopted a constitution. The king remained, but had no power. The people elected officials to govern their country.

In 1967, a group of army officers took control. The king left the country. In 1973 Greece became a republic. In 1974, a civilian government took over. A new constitution was adopted in 1975.

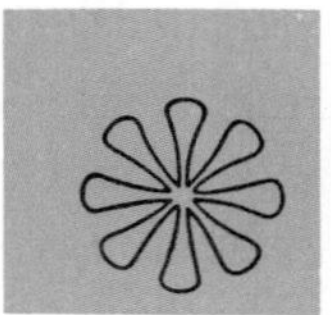

Athens
Where the New Encircles the Old

The Acropolis, topped by the ruins of the Parthenon, dominates Athens as in ancient times. But the Parthenon now looks down upon a modern Athens. The new city spreads out in a great half circle around the old one. It is located on a plain between the mountains and the sea, about 5 miles (8 km) from the harbor of Piraeus. Modern Athens and Piraeus together have more than 2 million people, and they are growing rapidly.

Athens today is different from ancient Athens in many ways. It is the main industrial center of Greece. Within sight of the Parthenon, factory workers enter textile mills and chemical plants. Many people rush in and out of the hotels, theaters, apartment houses, and shops in downtown Athens. The streets are jammed with buses and cars.

But many things in Athens have not changed. Grain and olive oil were important products in ancient Greece, and still are today. Ancient Greeks sailed throughout the Mediterranean. Today one of the largest merchant fleets in the world sails from Piraeus. ■

In many Romanian farming villages, work is still done by hand. These farmers use a team of oxen to plow a field. In the distance are the Carpathian Mountains.

Romania

Romania is the northernmost Balkan country. It extends along the Black Sea south of the mouth of the Danube (dan′yo͞ob) River.

The Geography of Romania

Romania is nearly as large as Oregon. Part of the country is covered with mountains. But it has fertile plains also. The plains are important farm lands.

The Danube is the greatest river of Central Europe. But the Romanians say, "The Danube flows the wrong way." They mean that ships on the river move toward the parts of Europe which have fewer people. Smaller ships can carry freight and passengers as far up the Danube as the German border. Still there is not enough trade to support a great seaport at the mouth of the river in the Black Sea.

The Products of Romania

Romania produces much grain. The fields are a beautiful sight when the wheat, oats, and barley are ripe. The weather is warm and moist enough for corn. On the mountain pastures many sheep graze.

Romania has valuable oil fields. The Romanians are also building more factories. Each year thousands of people move from the country to the cities. In 1980, for the first time, more Romanians lived in the cities than in the country.

The Government of Romania

Before World War II, Romania was a kingdom. It is now a Communist nation. Bucharest (bo͞o′kə rest), its capital and largest city, was once called "Little Paris."

After the war, Communists took over the government. The king was forced to give up his throne. In 1965 a constitution was adopted. Though the leaders of Romania are Communist, the country tries to be independent of the Soviet Union.

Bulgaria and Yugoslavia

South of Romania is Bulgaria. To the west of Bulgaria lies Yugoslavia.

The Geography of Bulgaria

The Balkan Mountains extend east and west, dividing Bulgaria into halves. Sofia (sō fē′ə), the capital, is midway between the northern and southern parts.

In northern Bulgaria, where the winters are very cold and the summers dry, people raise wheat and sugar beets. The southern part of Bulgaria, which is sheltered by mountains, has a mild climate. Here are the famous rose fields, where workers pick the scented flowers. It takes thousands of rose petals to make a few drops of the precious liquid called attar of roses. Attar of roses is used in making perfume. Bulgaria's factories produce chemicals, machinery, metals, and textiles.

The Government of Bulgaria

Bulgaria came under the Communists after World War II. Much of the farm land is owned and run by the Communist government. Bulgaria has only a few factories, also owned by the government.

The Geography of Yugoslavia

After World War I, the Allies created a new country from a part of the Balkans, called Yugoslavia. It is the largest Balkan country. The name "Yugoslavia" means "land of the southern Slavs." Slavs are a group of people who live in many countries of Eastern Europe. They speak similar languages.

Belgrade, on the Danube River, is the capital of Yugoslavia. From Belgrade a natural road through two river valleys goes from Central Europe to the Greek port of Salonika, giving that area an outlet to the sea.

Yugoslavia contains some of the fertile and level Danube Valley in the north. Its long coastline on the Adriatic (ā′drē at′ik) Sea is a popular resort area. But most of the country is mountainous. Shut in by steep ridges, each valley community provides for most of its own needs.

The Products of Yugoslavia

Most of Yugoslavia's people are farm workers. The chief crops are corn, tobacco, and sugar beets. Many sheep, cattle, goats, and pigs are raised. The nation leads Europe in mining lead and *bauxite* (bôk′sīt). Bauxite is the mineral from which aluminum is made. More factories are built every year. These factories produce steel, chemicals, wood products, cement, and textiles.

The Government of Yugoslavia

In the early years of World War II, Yugoslavia found itself almost entirely surrounded by lands conquered by the German armies. Early in April, 1941, the German armies conquered the country. The young king, Peter II, fled to England.

The Yugoslavs did not give up easily. The people banded together secretly and continued to fight the enemy undercover. But these groups quarreled among themselves. War broke out between the groups. After a time, a Communist leader named Tito (tē′tō) gained control.

When the war was over, Tito set up a Communist government. Tito made himself the head of the new government. For a while under Tito's rule the new nation had close ties with the Soviet Union. But when the Soviet Union wanted to control Yugoslavia, Tito objected. Even after Tito's death in 1980, Yugoslavia remained a Communist nation, but not under the control of the Soviet Union.

Albania

Albania is the smallest of the Balkan countries. It is located on the west coast of the Balkan Peninsula.

More factories and roads are being built in Yugoslavia every year. Most factory towns, like this one, are found in the northwest part of the country.

The Geography of Albania

This small mountainous country lies between Yugoslavia and Greece. It is just a little larger than Maryland. Albania is not a modern country. Oxcarts, horses, and donkeys carry people and freight over the rough mountain roads. Many of the rivers have no bridges. People must cross the rivers in small canoes. Railroads are still rare in Albania, for the mountains make it hard to build roads. But air service has been developed between Albania and some other nations of Europe.

The Products of Albania

Less than one-tenth of the land in Albania can be cultivated. Cattle, sheep, and goats are

Both traditional and modern forms of transportation can be found in Yugoslavia. Horse–drawn carts are often used in farming villages. Modern forms of transportation can be found in the cities.

raised. Tobacco, grain, cotton, sugar beets, and corn are the main crops. Lack of roads makes it difficult to use the coal, oil, and copper which are found in the mountains. This is part of the reason why Albania has been slow to develop industry. Its major industrial products are chemical fertilizers and textiles.

The Government of Albania

Like other Balkan nations Albania was once under the rule of Turkey. But as Turkey's power in Europe grew weak, the people of Albania began to work for freedom. Soon after World War I, a republic was set up in Albania. In 1928 the president made himself king.

At the outbreak of World War II, Italian armies invaded Albania. The king of Albania fled. After the war Albania was taken over by the Communists. Today it is still under the control of a Communist government.

Cyprus

Cyprus is an island in the eastern Mediterranean. Although it is the third largest island in the Mediterranean Sea, it is smaller than Connecticut.

Four-fifths of its people are Greek. The rest are Turkish. The people do not live together peacefully. In 1974 Turkey invaded Cyprus and took over large areas of land.

Do You Know?

1. Why do the Greeks raise many goats?
2. What is the name of the great building that stands above Athens?
3. What are two seaports in modern Greece?
4. Which Balkan countries are under Communist rule?

To Help You Learn

Using New Words

comedy	guerrilla
epic	fable
open city	democracy
frieze	bauxite

Number a paper from 1 through 8. After each number write the word or term that matches the definition.

1. Rule by the people
2. An amusing play with a happy ending
3. A long poem about a great hero
4. The mineral from which aluminum is made
5. A band of carved marble around a building
6. A short tale about animals that teaches a lesson
7. In wartime, a city that is not to be made a scene of fighting
8. A civilian fighter

Finding the Facts

1. Which area has more people, Europe or America?
2. Why was ancient Greece made up of many city-states?
3. Why is a long-distance race called a marathon?
4. What did Pericles do to help Athens?
5. In what ways were Spartans and Athenians alike? In what ways did they differ?
6. What is the Parthenon? Why is it in ruins?
7. How did the Balkans win independence?
8. What are Yugoslavia's chief products?
9. Why do Romanians say, "The Danube flows the wrong way"?
10. What change took place in Romania in 1980?
11. What Balkan countries continued to fight even after they had been conquered by the Germans in World War II?

Learning from Maps

1. Turn to the map of Greece and the Balkans on page 163. Locate the Balkan Peninsula. What mountains cross it? What meridian crosses the Balkan Peninsula? What parallel of latitude crosses Greece?
2. From the map of Europe on page 161, name four European countries that border the Mediterranean sea. Which seven countries border Yugoslavia?

Using Study Skills

1. **Time Line:** Place the following events in the proper order of time: Destruction of the Parthenon, Battle of Marathon, Germany's conquest of Yugoslavia.

   Copy the time line from page 159. Add these events to your time line.

   Study the completed time line and answer the following questions: How many years passed between the beginning of the Age of Pericles and the Roman conquest of Greece? Between the Turks' conquest of Bulgaria and Greece's regaining its freedom from the Turks? Between the first Communist takeover of the Balkans and Greece's new constitution?

2. **Time Line:** Make a time line of ancient civilizations. Put on it the Fall of Knossos, the beginning of the Age of Pericles, Philip's conquest of Greece, and the Roman conquest of Greece. The time line on page 159 of this unit will help you. Add to your time line the following events from units you have already studied: The building of the Great Wall of China, *c.* 200 B.C.; First Chinese civilization, *c.* 1500 B.C.; Beginning of Asoka's rule in India, 272 B.C.; Aryan invasion of India, *c.* 1500 B.C.

   Study the completed time line and answer the following questions: What two events were happening in Asia at about the same time? Which happened first, the Roman conquest of Greece or the building of the Great Wall of China? The Age of Pericles or Asoka's rule?

3. **Graph:** With the help of the line graph below answer these questions. What is the highest average temperature in Athens? When does it get that hot? What is the lowest average temperature in Athens? When does it get that cold? Water freezes at 32° F (0° C). When does Athens have freezing weather?

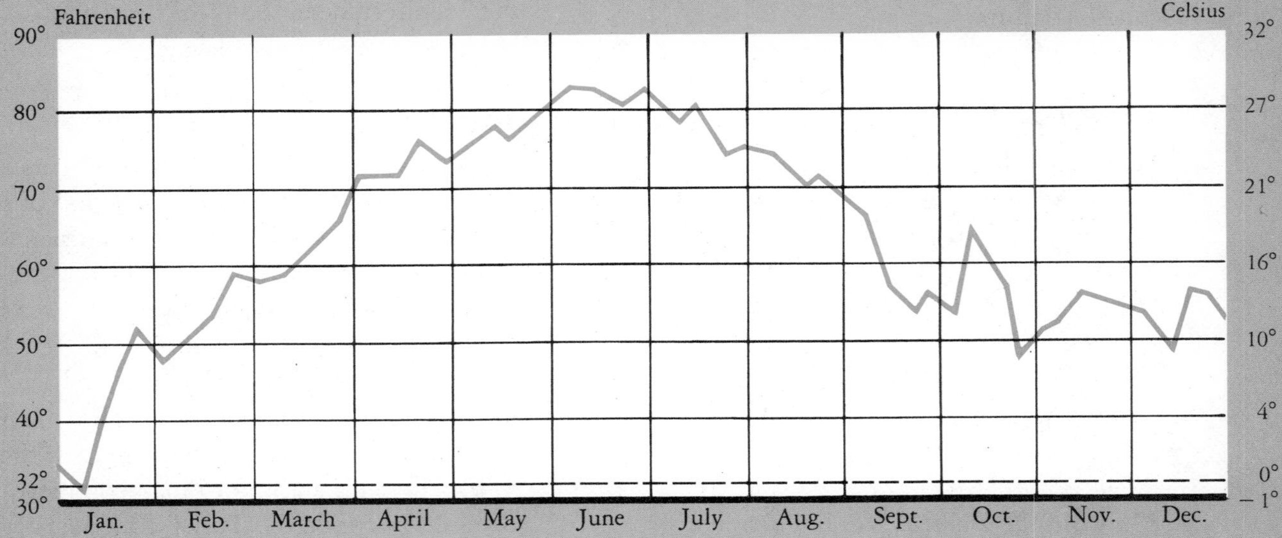

Thinking It Through

1. The government of the ancient Greeks was called a democracy. Today we also call the United States a democracy. How is our democracy like that of the ancient Greeks? How is it different?
2. The Parthenon was destroyed in fighting between armies of Venice and Turkey. One hundred years later an Englishman, Lord Elgin, saw the ruins. He feared the beautiful sculpture would be lost to the world forever. He asked the Turkish government for permission to take some sculptures to England. Today they can be seen in the British Museum.

   Art lovers in England and Greece argue about who should take care of these sculptures. What reasons can you give for their staying in England? For their being sent back to Greece?
3. Look at the list of ancient Greece's contributions to civilization on page 175. Choose one. How might our lives have been different without it?
4. Romania's population is moving from the country to the cities. What do you think causes people to make such a move? What changes do you think it might bring in their lives?

Projects

1. The ancient Greeks developed three types of columns which are still used. See the diagram on page 170. See what types are used on buildings in your community or state capital. Report back to the class.
2. Divide your class into two groups—one will pretend to be a group of Spartans and the other a group of Athenians. Let each side discuss the advantages and disadvantages of its city. You may wish to do some more reading to help your side prepare its case.
3. In this unit you read about the origin of the Olympic games. The Research Committee might find out about the most recent Olympic games and report on them to the class. What events have been added since the first Olympic games? What awards are given to the winners in modern Olympic contests? When and where will the next Olympic games be?
4. Tell or read your favorite Aesop fable to the class. Draw a picture to illustrate the story or dramatize it.
5. The Reading Committee might like to read about the ancient Greek gods or the stories told by the poet Homer. Retell, draw, or dramatize an incident from one of these books.

6 Ancient Rome and Modern Italy

Unit Preview

The boot-shaped piece of land reaching down from southern Europe is the Italian Peninsula. Halfway up the western coast is the city of Rome. At one time, Rome was the center of the greatest empire the world has ever known.

Ancient Rome was once a republic. The people who ran the government were elected. It was during this time that Rome conquered most of the ancient world. The Roman Republic first conquered all of the Italian Peninsula. The Roman armies then conquered parts of Asia, Europe, and Africa.

The ancient Romans' interest in government and law also helped them to build and to hold on to their empire. Because the Romans had developed a good system of justice for themselves, they ruled with justice. Many legal systems in the world today are based on the laws of Rome.

A fine system of roads linked distant parts of the empire to Rome. In the days when the Roman Empire was most powerful, some people said, "All roads lead to Rome."

The city of Rome, which became the center of the Christian religion after the fall of Rome in A.D. 476, remains today the capital of modern Italy. Great churches and cathedrals, as well as ancient Roman ruins, still can be seen there.

Modern Italy is becoming an important manufacturing country. More people work in factories than on farms.

Things to Discover

If you look carefully at the picture, map, and time line on these pages, you can answer these questions.

1. Italy is highlighted on the map. What is this country's shape similar to?
2. What continent is Italy part of?
3. Did Rome rule the rest of Italy before or after it became an empire?
4. When was the country called Italy united?
5. What form of government did modern Italy have when it joined the Common Market?
6. The picture shows the city of Venice in northern Italy. The main streets are canals because the city is built on many islands. Bridges connect some islands. How would people reach other islands?

Words to Learn

You will meet these words in this unit. As you read, you will learn what they mean and how to pronounce them. The Word List will help you.

amphitheater	forum
arena	gladiator
barbarian	gondola
breakwater	legion
Common Market	patrician
consul	plebeian
dictator	tribune
Fascist	veto

Rome becomes a republic
c. 509
Rome rules all of Italian Peninsula
265
Rome becomes an empire
27
B.C.
A.D.
Roman Empire ends
476
St. Peter's Church completed
1626
Italian states united under a king
1870
Italy becomes a modern republic
1946
Italy joins Common Market
1957

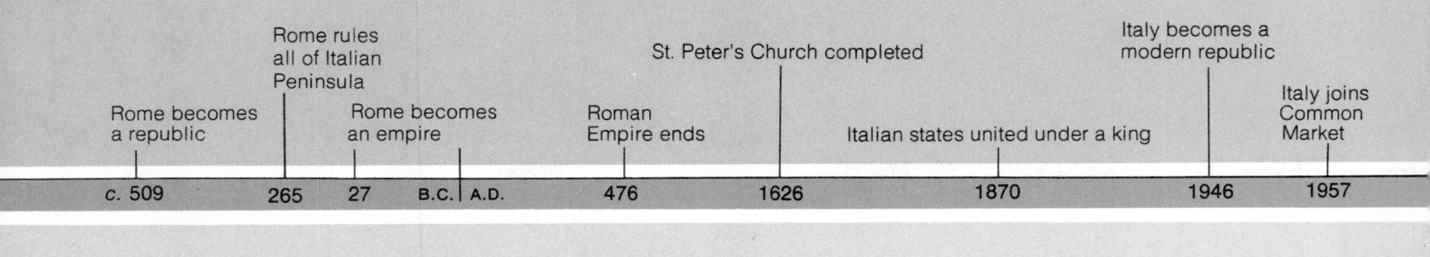

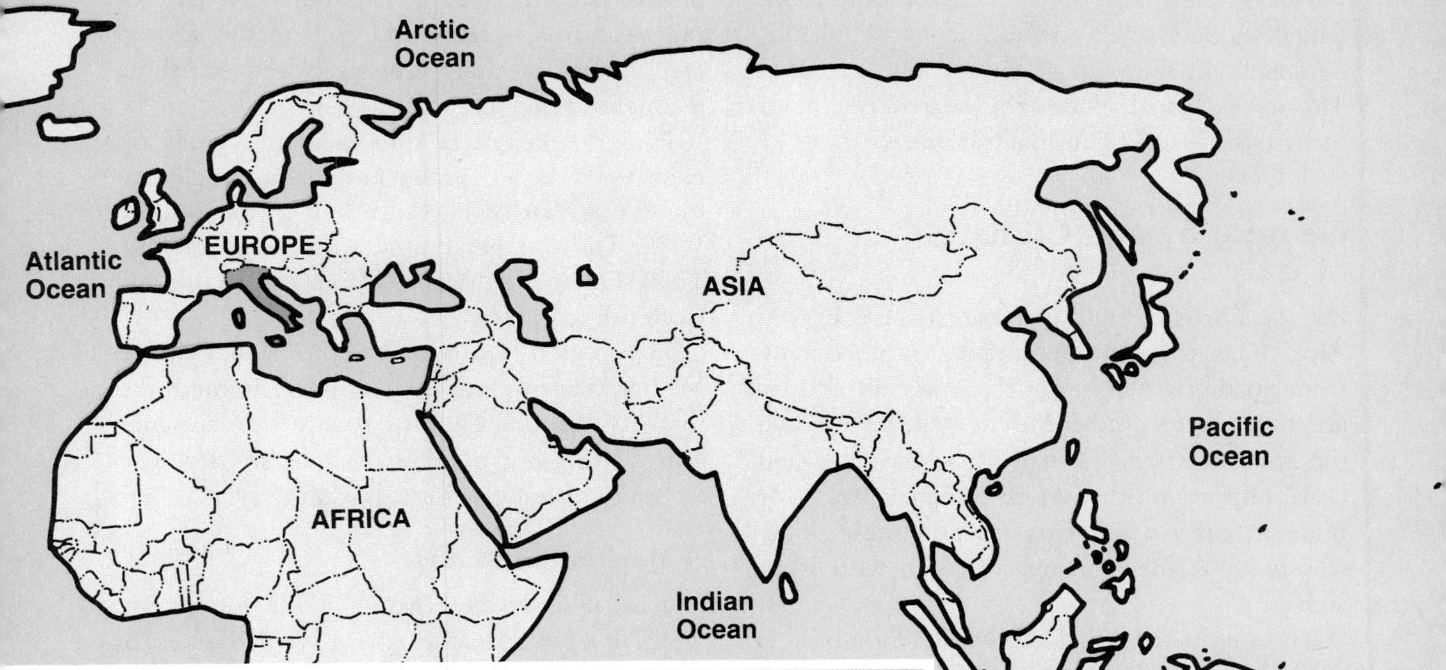

Arctic Ocean
EUROPE
Atlantic Ocean
ASIA
AFRICA
Pacific Ocean
Indian Ocean
AUSTRALIA

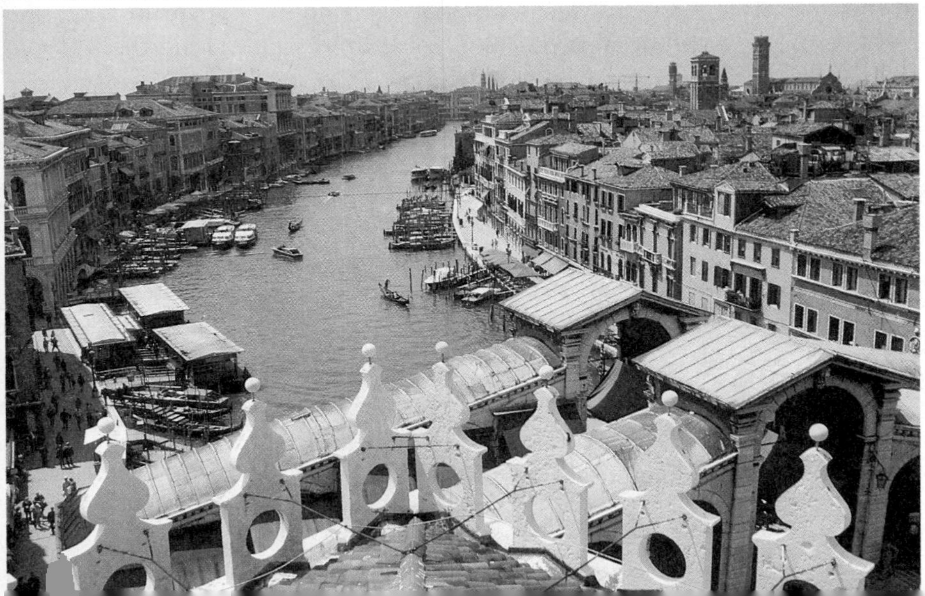

1
The Peninsula of Italy

Italy occupies one of three great peninsulas which extend south from Europe. Find this peninsula on the map of Europe on page 161. The nation also includes the nearby islands of Sicily (sis′ə lē) and Sardinia (sär din′ē ə).

Geography and Climate of Italy

On the north of Italy is a wall formed by the Alps. The towering mountains protect Italy from northerly winds. On the other three sides are the waters of the Mediterranean Sea and the small seas that join it. You have learned how important the Mediterranean was for trade in early days. This sea still serves Italy well today in the exchange of goods with other lands.

The map shows that the Italian Peninsula is shaped like a boot. At the toe is the island of Sicily. North and west of Sicily is Sardinia, another island that is a part of Italy.

Climate of the Peninsula

Italy has a sunny, warm climate although it does not lie far to the south. Rome, in central Italy, is in about the same latitude as Boston, which we think of as a northern city. Yet travelers often go to Italy in the winter to enjoy the sunshine and the mild climate. Why is this true?

Besides having the protection of the Alps on the north, Italy benefits from the warm waters of the Mediterranean. The northern part of the peninsula is rainy and cold in the winter. But much of Italy enjoys warm sunshine throughout the year.

Find the Po River on the map of Italy on page 191. The Po Valley has a summer climate much like that of our corn belt in the Middle West. The weather is hot, with plenty of rain. There are sudden changes from wet to dry and from hot to cooler.

The region south of the Po Valley has a Mediterranean climate. Its climate is mild like that of southern California with little summer rain. During hot weather the hills are dry. The far south of Italy is also sunny and dry.

A Mountainous Land

Much of Italy is covered with mountains. The Alps tower in the north. Near the city of Genoa (jen′ō ə), the Apennine (ap′ə nīn′) Mountains begin. They extend south along the length of the peninsula. Both the Apennines and the Alps receive snow that melts and sends water into streams below during the spring.

The water is used for irrigation. In some places, where there are waterfalls, the power of the falling water is used to make electricity. Italy needs electric power because it lacks the coal and petroleum needed to run factories. The country has few minerals of any kind. Probably the most important resources taken from the hills and mountains of Italy are fine marble and other stones useful for building.

Italy has a rugged surface, but most of its coastline is straight and smooth. As a result, Italy has few good harbors. Its leading seaports are Naples, Genoa, and Venice (ven′is).

What Sicily Is Like

Sicily's location made it important to the people who lived long ago in the lands surrounding the Mediterranean Sea. Today it is valuable to Italy because its fine climate attracts tourists in winter, and it produces many valuable crops.

Along the coasts of Sicily are lemon and orange groves like those in southern California. Sicily supplies most of the lemons for European markets. On the upper slopes of the Sicilian hills and mountains are olive trees. Below the

Mount Etna, an active volcano in Sicily, has caused great damage. In 1971, lava from a major eruption flowed into nearby towns, wrecking roads and bridges.

mountains is a vast plateau, mostly covered with wheat fields.

At the seaport of Messina (mə sē′nə), Sicily almost touches the mainland of Italy. South of Messina rises the great volcano of Etna. Mount Etna is the highest active volcano in Europe. Snow lies on its great crater, or opening, most of the year. Wherever there are active volcanoes we may look for earthquakes. Messina twice has been destroyed by earthquakes and rebuilt.

Active volcanoes deposit sulfur inside their craters. From this yellow mineral sulfuric acid is made, which is used in certain kinds of manufacturing. At one time much sulfur was mined at Mount Etna. Today fewer people work in the mines because the world gets much of its sulfur from other places.

But Sicily also has oil. The oil is piped to refineries near the port of Augusta (ô gus′tə), just north of Syracuse (sir′ə kyo͞os′). This area has many industries based on oil.

What Sardinia Is Like

Sardinia, Italy's other large island, is slightly smaller than Sicily. Mountains cover so much of Sardinia that there is little good farming land. Sheep, goats, and cattle feed on the hilly pastures. A little wheat, some olives and oranges, and many vegetables are grown.

Besides farmers Sardinia has fishers and miners. The miners dig iron, zinc, lead, copper, and silver. Some coal has also been found on the island.

Do You Know?

1. Where is the Italian Peninsula located? Why is this a good location?
2. What is the climate of Italy like?
3. What are the chief products of Sicily? Of Sardinia?

2
The Rise of Rome

The Greeks built many cities in southern Italy and Sicily. But it was Rome, a small village on the banks of the Tiber River, which grew until it became the center of the Roman Empire.

The Founding of Rome

If you could have visited Italy about the year 1000 B.C., you would have seen a group of tribes living on the central plains. These people were the first Romans.

The Legend of Rome's Founding

In Rome there is a bronze statue of a she-wolf and two baby boys named Romulus and Remus. The old Romans told the story that the boys, who were twins, had been abandoned by their cruel granduncle. They were found by a wolf, so the legend goes, and the wolf mothered them. After a time shepherds found the two boys and raised them.

When Romulus and Remus grew up, each gathered a band of followers and decided to build a settlement. As Romulus and his helpers were putting up a wall, Remus jumped over it to show how poor a defense it was. In a rage Romulus killed him. Remus's followers then joined Romulus and his group. They built a village and called it Rome, after their leader.

The Real Beginning of Rome

According to the legend, Rome was founded in 753 B.C. We know this was not a true story. But we are not sure exactly when Rome began. However, we know that when Greece already had a fine civilization, the people of Italy were working small farms. They called the district where they lived Latium. The language they spoke was Latin. This small tribe and its Latin language were to become famous.

The Tiber River separated Latium from the land of the Etruscans. (See the map of Italy on page 191.) The Etruscans (i trus′kənz) were a prosperous people who had developed their own civilization.

The people of Latium set up a marketplace on the Tiber River where they could trade with the Etruscans. This was the beginning of Rome, a city built on seven hills. After a time the city and the people of Latium were conquered by the Etruscans.

In the south of Italy were many prosperous Greek settlements. One of these was Naples. On the island of Sicily was the fine Greek city of Syracuse.

After 200 years the Etruscan kings were driven out of Rome. Rome was then free to develop its own ideas.

Rome as a Republic

The Romans thought that government should not be controlled by one person, so they set up a republic in about 509 B.C. In a republic the officers who make and carry out the laws are elected.

During times of peace Rome was ruled by two *consuls* (kon′səlz), who were the highest officials of the government. The consuls were elected by the Assembly, a citizens' group made up mostly of farmers and working people. The Romans realized that disagreements between the consuls would be dangerous to the republic in time of war. So they provided that during a war there would be only one ruler. This ruler would have complete power. He was called a *dictator* (dik′tā′tər). The dictator was chosen by the people, and his power could last for only 6 months.

Rome also had a Senate, chosen from the nobles and rich landowners. All the laws and anyone to be elected to office had to be approved by the Senate.

The Growth of Rome

The neighboring groups of people who quarreled with the Romans found that the Romans were brave soldiers. One after another these peoples were conquered by the Romans. However, the conquered peoples were treated fairly, and many were given the rights of citizens.

The Romans then had disputes with the Greek cities in Italy and Sicily. The cities were soon conquered. Thus the whole peninsula of Italy came under Roman government. The Romans could be cruel in war, but they did not govern cruelly. The conquered people became allies of Rome.

The Good Roman Roads

We have learned that the Romans built many roads to connect the various parts of Italy with Rome. They built such fine roads that some parts of them are still in good condition. Best known of these ancient highways is the Appian (ap′ē ən) Way.

Easy travel made trade increase. In carrying on their business, the people of Italy came to depend on Roman power and to admire Roman ways. They used Roman coins and spoke the Latin language. They thought it was a great honor to be a Roman citizen.

The Roman People

The stories that Roman parents told their children show the good qualities of the Romans. The Romans felt that good Romans could be depended upon to do their duty in war and peace. One of their favorite stories was about Cincinnatus, who was a good farmer as well as a great general.

Cincinnatus was called from his plowing to command the army in time of great danger. After he had won the victory, Cincinnatus went back to his plow. He did not choose to become a dictator. By returning to the farm, he helped maintain the strength of the republic. Our city of Cincinnati, Ohio, preserves the name of this ancient Roman.

Another story that Roman children liked was about Horatius (hə ra′shəs). In the war with the Etruscans the Etruscan army had almost reached Rome before the Romans realized the danger. To reach Rome, the enemy had to cross the bridge over the Tiber. There was just one thing to do—destroy the bridge. Horatius and two others held the enemy off at the river gate, while the consul and his helpers used axes to

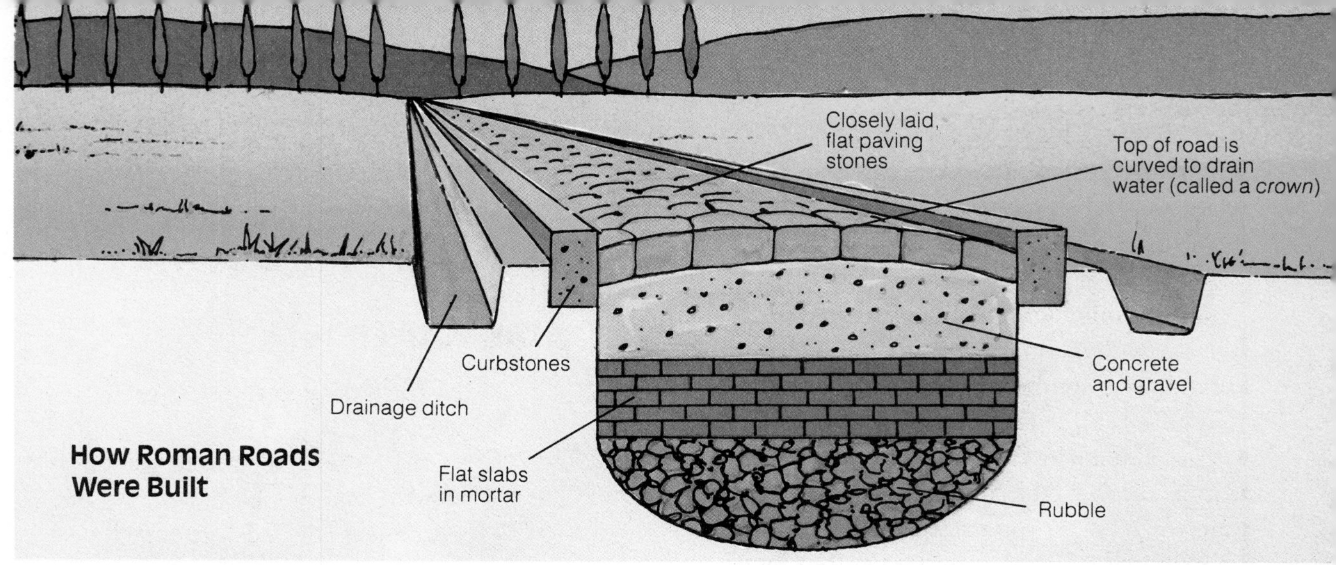

The Romans built solid, long-lasting roads. Some ancient Roman roads are still in use today.

destroy the bridge. After the bridge went down, Horatius, though wounded, swam back across the rushing rivers of the Tiber to safety. In Rome he was welcomed as a hero.

Loyalty to one's city, one's friends, and one's parents was a respected value in Rome. Under such conditions, Rome became a united and powerful nation.

Patricians and Plebeians

The nobles, or *patricians* (pə trish′ənz), of Rome had a long struggle with the common people, or *plebeians* (pli bē′ənz). In the early days of the republic the patricians owned most of the property. They also held many more rights and privileges than the plebeians did. At first, the two consuls were always chosen from among the patricians, as were members of the Senate. All citizens took part in the Assembly, but the patricians had more power than the plebeians.

The plebeians threatened to set up a government of their own. In this way they gained the right to elect officers, called *tribunes* (trib′yo͞onz), from among their own numbers.

It was the duty of the tribunes to protect the rights of the plebeians. By shouting "Veto!"—which means "I forbid!"—the tribunes could prevent decisions which they thought were unjust. The *veto* (vē′tō) power is still used in our government today. The plebeians also demanded that the laws should be written down and made public.

The power of the plebeians grew. It was a glad day for them when the first plebeian consul was elected. It then became a regular practice that one consul should be plebeian. Later, a few plebeians were elected to the Senate each year. After many years plebeians and patricians learned to cooperate with each other. The extending of rights brought true union.

The Armies of Ancient Rome

The ancient Roman army was made up of men who were strong, well paid, and well equipped. The soldiers received strict training. Disobedience or cowardly conduct could be punished by death.

Each soldier was proud of his *legion* (lē′ jən), the large division of troops to which he belonged. The symbol of the legion was the eagle.

Wherever a legion halted in its march, it built a camp and a fort. Thus the soldiers were secure from sudden attack and could choose their own time to fight. As long as the legions were made up of patriotic Roman citizens, they were able to go from victory to victory.

Do You Know?

1. What form of government did early Rome have?
2. Who were the patricians?
3. Who were the plebeians?
4. How did the tribunes protect the rights of the plebeians?

3
Building the Roman Empire

By the year 265 B.C. Rome ruled the whole peninsula of Italy. The Romans then became interested in trading by sea.

Conquest of the Mediterranean

In sea trading Rome had a powerful and dangerous rival. This was Carthage (kär′ thij).

Carthage's Rise to Power

Many years before Rome was founded, the Phoenicians planted a colony on the African coast, not far from Sicily. It was an excellent spot for trading both to the west and to the east. There, near the present city of Tunis (to͞o′ nis), grew up the great city of Carthage. (Find Tunis on the map of Italy on page 191.)

Carthage was a city-state, surrounded by fertile fields where grain and olives were grown. Its stout walls protected an area three times as large as Rome. The ships of Carthage traveled everywhere through the Mediterranean.

Through trade Carthage became wealthy and powerful. It grew until it had settlements on many islands in the Mediterranean and in southern Spain.

The War Against Carthage

Carthage held the western part of Sicily. If it could gain control of the whole island, Carthage could keep Roman ships from sailing between the eastern and western ports of Italy. Wars broke out between Rome and Carthage for the control of Sicily.

The wars lasted more than 100 years, from

Hannibal, a famous general, led the army of Carthage in some wars against Rome. Hannibal brought elephants from Africa to help his troops. Most of the elephants died crossing the Alps.

264 B.C. to 146 B.C. Rome conquered and destroyed Carthage. Northern Africa, with its rich grain fields and olive trees, became Roman territory. So did Spain, with its useful silver and copper mines. No nation could now dispute Rome's power in the western Mediterranean. Rome gained the trade that had once belonged to Carthage.

While the wars with Carthage were going on, Rome had quarrels in Greece and Asia Minor. When each of these disputes was over, the Romans usually gained more territory. Gradually Rome came to rule over the land and peoples of the eastern Mediterranean also. (See the map of the Roman Empire on page 199.)

Rome as an Empire

One of the greatest Roman leaders was a general named Julius Caesar (jo͞ol′yəs sē′zər). He was governor of Gaul (gôl), a Roman territory in northwestern Europe. The fierce people of Gaul did not want the Romans to rule them. But in 8 years of war Julius Caesar conquered them. What is now France was once a part of ancient Gaul.

The Rule of Julius Caesar

Julius Caesar led his legions into Rome and made himself the head of the Roman government. He had been a consul before he went to Gaul. Now the Senate made him dictator for

Julius Caesar, a brilliant general, was one of Rome's greatest rulers.

life. The old Roman republic was dead. Caesar did not call himself king, but he had a king's power.

Caesar's reign brought many contributions to Roman life. He had many fine roads built. He improved the government of the cities and made business safe throughout Italy. He introduced a new calendar. He founded colonies in Italy, in Greece, and on the spot where Carthage stood. He gave rights as citizens to the conquered people who lived under Roman law. However, in 44 B.C., in the midst of his work, he was murdered by a band of jealous Romans.

Under Julius Caesar, Rome conquered many lands. Its possessions extended from the Mediterranean east into Asia Minor and Syria. To the north it included what is today France, a large part of Germany, Belgium, and the Netherlands. Julius Caesar went to Britain and brought part of the island under Roman rule. Caesar's armies later withdrew from Britain.

The Rule of Octavian

Before Julius Caesar died, he made his nephew and adopted son, Octavian (ok tāv′ē ən), his heir. Octavian was 18 years of age at the time of Julius Caesar's death. Octavian took the name of Caesar and had himself appointed a general. Then, just as Julius Caesar had done, he led his army into Rome and forced the Senate and Assembly to make him consul. He was little more than 30 years of age when Rome became an empire in 27 B.C. and he was made its first emperor.

The Senate gave Octavian the title of Augustus (ô gus′təs), meaning "grand." Augustus, as he was now called, conquered new lands. This gave the empire more easily guarded borders, such as oceans and large rivers. Like Julius Caesar, Augustus was a strong ruler. He put honest and capable men into office. He wanted the conquered peoples to respect and honor Rome for its government in all parts of the empire.

Under Augustus, Rome was strong but not warlike. During this time Rome built many fine buildings. Writers produced great works, especially in poetry. This period, the Augustan Age, is sometimes called Rome's "Golden Age."

It was during the reign of Augustus that Jesus was born in the part of the Roman empire which was then called Palestine. His followers,

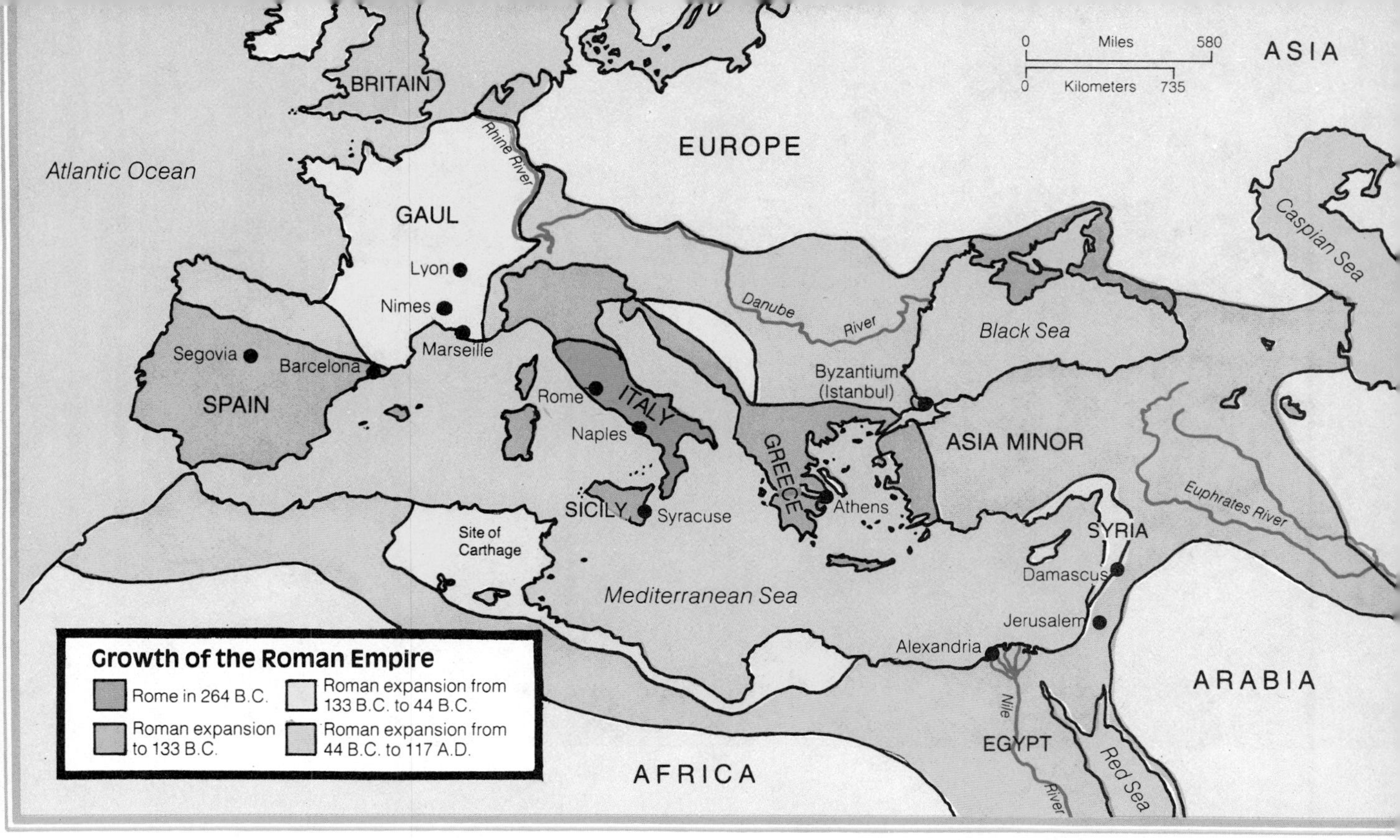

Four stages of Roman expansion are shown on this map. You can see that the Roman Empire once included land all around the Mediterranean Sea. From what city did the empire grow?

the first Christians, were peaceful. They worshiped in small groups and did not try to spread their religious beliefs by force. The new faith spread slowly. When some early Christians came to Rome, they were treated cruelly because their teachings did not agree with the Roman belief in gods and goddesses. But Christianity grew in strength. Under the emperor Constantine (kon′stən tīn′), who ruled about 300 years after Augustus, Rome became a Christian nation.

Roman Government and Law

The Romans were always ready to fight, if necessary, to defend their empire. But the early emperors thought that peace was better than war. Conquered peoples were treated fairly. If they paid taxes, their free men could become Roman citizens. And the Roman soldiers would protect their land. For almost 200 years the "peace of Rome" rested on the world. This is the longest peace among civilized people in the recorded history of the world.

The citizens of the Roman Empire respected the law. When people learn to obey laws instead of armies, they have taken a great step forward. The long period of peace gave the arts a chance to develop. Rome learned from other countries, and they in turn learned from Rome.

An arched bridge leads across the Tiber River to Castel Sant' Angelo, which was originally built as a tomb for the emperor Hadrian. The building later became a fort.

Roman Ways of Living

The Romans are remembered today for their good roads, their fine public buildings, and for their sports and amusements.

Roman Roads and Buildings

Roman engineers built arched bridges, sewers, and aqueducts which brought water from far away. Some of these old aqueducts still supply water to Rome's many fountains. The Romans built long walls, or *breakwaters* (brāk′wô′tərz), out to the sea. These breakwaters made the harbors safer and provided shelter for ships by breaking the force of the waves.

But the real triumph of Roman architects and engineers was in their public buildings. They constructed wonderful temples, outdoor theaters, and public bathhouses. They built arches to celebrate Roman victories.

The *forum* (fôr′əm) in a Roman city was the open space where markets and public festivals were held. The forum in Rome was surrounded by fine public buildings. As the city grew, five more forums were built in Rome. Every important city in the Roman Empire was likely to have at least one forum.

The Romans learned how to make a kind of building material called concrete. To make concrete, they ground up volcanic rock and made it into cement. Then they mixed the cement with small stones. The mixture, after being poured into molds, hardened into artificial rock, or concrete. Large quantities of concrete could be made quickly and cheaply.

Gladiator fights and contests between men and large animals took place in the Colosseum. At times the *arena* was flooded so boat battles could be staged.

Roman Sports and Amusements

Many Roman sports and spectacles were held in large buildings open to the sky, called *amphitheaters* (am′fə thē′ə tərz). An amphitheater was built in a circle, with rows of seats around it. Its central space, where the events took place, was the *arena* (ə rē′nə). The Roman amphitheater was called the Colosseum (kol′ə sē′əm) because of its great, or colossal, size.

Chariot races were held in a long race course surrounded on three sides by rows of seats and divided lengthwise by a wall through the middle. Such a building was called a circus. One, the Circus Maximus, or Great Circus, of Rome held more than 300,000 people. Here the greatest chariot races took place.

In the later days of the Roman Empire there was little work for many of the people to do. Amusements were held in the amphitheaters to entertain the idle citizens. The emperor's purpose was to keep the citizens quiet. This also encouraged them to vote for the leaders who provided the entertainment.

Grain was given free to the people. Roman holidays were celebrated by parades, plays in the theater, and contests in the Colosseum. In the arena armed men or *gladiators* (glad′ē ā′tərz), fought in pairs or in groups to amuse the people. The gladiators struggled with fierce animals and were sometimes killed. The empire was searched to find the fiercest beasts and the most powerful men. Such fearful shows proved that Rome was on the downward path. The free food and entertainment came to be called "bread and circuses." The once sturdy and independent Romans accepted this, showing that as a people they had undergone a great change from the early days.

Public bathhouses or baths were very popular at the height of the Roman Empire. Here an emperor discusses plans with his builder to make the baths even bigger.

The Roman Baths

As Rome grew rich, its well-to-do people built fine homes. Many homes had special rooms for bathing. Those who could not afford such rooms in their homes paid for baths in public buildings.

In these great buildings there were hot and cold showers and pools in which to bathe. Halls, gymnasiums, and rooms for eating, drinking, or lounging could be used either before or after bathing.

Romans set the fashion of using public bathhouses. Other cities throughout the empire built such houses.

When the Roman Empire grew weak, most of the aqueducts were not kept repaired. Water became harder to get. In the later days of the empire, bathtubs in houses could rarely be found, and public bathhouses were few.

Family Life

A Roman family consisted of a husband and wife, their children, their married sons, and their families. If the family was wealthy, they had slaves. The father was the absolute head of the family. He made the decisions for everyone else.

Women were respected but had few rights of their own. They managed the households. Before a woman married she obeyed the commands of her father. After her marriage she obeyed her husband.

Rome's Debt to Greece

The Romans did not admire the Greeks either as fighters or as rulers. But the Romans did think highly of the Greeks as thinkers and as artists.

The Greeks and Romans had many of the same gods and goddesses. The names of these beings were different, but the people believed they had the same powers.

Greece's Influence on Rome

After they had conquered Greece, Roman generals brought many beautiful Greek statues back to Italy. Thousands of educated Greeks were taken to Rome as slaves. The sons of rich Romans were often taught by Greek slaves.

Well-to-do Romans began to adopt Greek ways of living. Educated Romans read Greek.

What Roman Art Was Like

The Romans copied Grecian art. They built fine temples to the gods, with statues and columns copied from the Greeks. Their chief gods and goddesses were the same as those the Greeks worshiped except that they had different names.

What Roman Literature Was Like

Before they met the Greeks, the Romans had no poetry and no plays. Then they began to translate, which means to change into another language, the Greek books they admired. They built a theater to present Greek plays. After a time they gave plays by Roman authors.

The *Iliad* (il′ē əd), an epic by the Greek poet Homer, was greatly admired in Rome. Later, the Roman poet Virgil wrote an epic about the wanderings and adventures of the hero Aeneas (i nē′ əs). This long story-poem was called the *Aeneid* (i nē′ id).

The Fall of Rome

After conquering and holding a great empire for hundreds of years, Rome's government began to weaken. At first Rome took great riches from the countries it conquered. But most of the wealth went to a few citizens, who purchased large pieces of land. To work these estates, they bought slaves captured in war. The farmers on small farms could not raise crops as cheaply as could the owners of the big estates with their slaves. The poorer farmers were often forced out of business.

Weakening of the Empire

During the time when the empire was at peace and no prisoners of war were taken, there were fewer slaves. Then the rich landowners did not have enough workers on their estates. They agreed to give people land to farm in exchange for rent. But after the workers had settled on the estates, the landlords had laws passed forbidding them to leave the land. Each estate became a little community in itself, raising and making most of the things it needed. This hurt the trade of the cities.

In some ways it was hard for the Romans to govern their large empire properly. Though the empire had good roads, the only way to travel rapidly was to use horses. Even by using fresh horses every few miles messengers could ride only 100 miles (160 km) a day.

Farmers who could once be counted on to enlist in time of war were no longer to be found. Many soldiers of the regular army were not patriotic. The emperors were forced to hire soldiers from distant lands to fight. Rome was losing power.

Division of the Empire

At last Constantine, who became emperor in A.D. 324, thought so little of the city of Rome as a capital that he built another one. This new capital was Constantinople (kon′stan tə nō′pəl), formerly called Byzantium, on the Bosporus (bos′pə rəs). Now the Roman Empire was divided into two empires. The Eastern Empire had its capital at Constantinople. The Western Empire had its capital at Rome.

The Roman emperors became weaker. *Barbarians* (bär ber′ē ənz) from the north came down. The barbarians were foreign tribes who were not part of the Greek and Roman civilizations. Thus the word has come to mean "uncivilized." These tribes eventually overran much of the Roman Empire. By A.D. 476, there was no longer a Roman Empire. Though the Eastern Empire continued for another 1,000 years, the old Roman Empire broke up in disorder.

Everyday Gifts of the Romans

Rome made such wide conquests that most of today's European nations were once governed by it. The customs and languages of many nations have been influenced by Rome.

In our own everyday living, we are reminded of our debt to the ancient Romans. The capital letters of our alphabet were given their final form by the Romans. Roman numerals are still used today. (See the chart on page 218.) We sometimes see these numbers on clock faces or as dates on public buildings.

The names of our months come from Rome. At one time Rome used a calendar which had 10 months. Julius Caesar decided that Rome should use the Egyptian calendar, which had 12 months. The month of July was named for

Julius Caesar. August was named for Augustus Caesar. After that September (from the Latin "septem" or "seventh") was no longer the seventh month of the year but the ninth.

The Importance of Latin

In many of the western countries that Rome governed, Latin became a part of the language. The people mixed their own speech with Latin, and so new languages resulted. The French, Italian, Spanish, Portuguese, and Romanian languages developed in this way. They are so much like Latin that we call them the Romance (or Roman) languages. Learning any one of the Romance languages is a help to us in learning another. The English language also has many words that have come from Latin.

Do You Know?

1. Why did Rome and Carthage go to war? How long did the wars last?
2. What did Julius Caesar do for Rome?
3. How did the Romans amuse themselves?

Before You Go On

Using New Words

gladiator	plebeian	patrician
dictator	breakwater	consul
legion	amphitheater	forum
arena	tribune	barbarian
veto		

Number a paper from 1 through 13. After each number write the word from the above list that matches the definition.

1. A large, round building with rows of seats around a central space, used for sports and spectacles
2. A wall built to protect a harbor from the force of waves
3. An open space where markets and public festivals were held
4. The central space of an amphitheater where the events took place
5. In ancient Rome, an armed man who fought to amuse the people
6. In ancient Rome, a leader given absolute power in time of war
7. One of the common people of ancient Rome
8. A Roman officer elected to protect the rights of the common people
9. One of the two highest officials of the ancient Roman republic
10. A noble of ancient Rome
11. In ancient times, a foreigner who was not part of Greek or Roman civilization
12. A large division of Roman troops
13. The power of elected officials to prevent decisions that they think are unjust

Finding the Facts

1. What are the Italian Peninsula's most important resources? How are they used?
2. What are Italy's chief sea ports?
3. What changes took place during the rule of Augustus Caesar?
4. Name three Romance languages. What do they have in common?
5. In ancient Rome, what was a circus?
6. Who had more rights in the early days of the Roman republic, patricians or plebeians?
7. How did Rome treat its conquered lands?
8. What kind of position did women have in ancient Rome?
9. What was the Senate? What did it do?
10. What was the Appian Way?
11. How long did the "peace of Rome" last? Why is this a record?
12. Why did the Romans build breakwaters?
13. How were Roman holidays celebrated?
14. Who wrote the *Aeneid?* What is it about?
15. What is concrete? How did the Romans make concrete?
16. What was the capital of the Eastern Roman Empire? The Western Roman Empire?
17. Who were Horatius and Cincinnatus?

4
Modern Italy

The ancient city of Rome is today the capital of Italy. This modern nation is a crowded land. In an area about twice as large as Florida live more than one-fourth as many people as there are in the whole United States.

The Farms of Italy

The best farming area in Italy is in the north, in the level valley of the Po River. The Po Valley receives enough rainfall to make the grass and other feed crops grow well. Many cattle are raised in this region, providing milk to make Italian cheese. Wheat and corn also grow well in northern Italy. Rice is raised in irrigated fields. Grapes are another important product of the region.

The region south of the Po Valley receives little summer rain. So there is not enough moisture to produce grass for dairy cows. Sheep and goats are the chief grazing animals. The fields are planted largely in crops that can grow in dry weather. Familiar sights in this region are olive trees, grapevines, and orange trees.

Until very recent times far more Italian people worked on farms than in factories. Today, factories provide more jobs than farms do. But farming continues to be important.

The Cities of Italy

Italy has many important and famous cities. Most of them have been important since the days of the Romans.

The Po Valley has the best farmland in Italy. The farmers in this northern region grow wheat, corn, rice, and a variety of other crops.

Naples, a Great Seaport

On the southwest coast of Italy is Naples, a city of more than 1 million people. Naples has a beautiful bay. Artists often sit beside the blue water to paint the fort which protected the city in Roman times. The city is full of historical interest. The University of Naples was built in 1224. Tourists come from all over the world.

Naples is also well known for its spaghetti, macaroni, and noodles made from hard wheat. The United States used to ship much wheat to Italy. But in recent years the Italian government decided that Italy should raise all of the wheat it uses. It has built factories to make fertilizer for enriching the soil. It has taught farmers better farming methods.

Naples is also an important shipping and manufacturing center. Ship building, automobiles, chemical products, and textiles are some important industries.

Not far from Naples is Mount Vesuvius (vi so͞o′vē əs), a famous volcano. Vesuvius always shows some signs of the heat that is within it. A red glow hangs over the crater by night. By day a tiny cloud of smoke rises.

Vesuvius, which seldom erupts, came to life with a roar in the early days of the Roman Empire. Vesuvius has been active since then on several occasions. One town was destroyed three times but was rebuilt each time. The people remain because the region around Vesuvius is one of the most fertile sections of Italy. Lava, the hot liquid rock which comes from a volcano, helps to make rich soil. The ashes from the volcano, left on the ground for many years, make good fertilizer.

A Buried City

In this part of Italy is Pompeii (pom pā′). Here in the year A.D. 79 was a town of 20,000 people. Then the hot ashes and lava from Vesuvius covered the town. For 1,500 years Pompeii was forgotten.

Then scientists began to dig away the layers of lava, cinder, and ashes which had protected the ruins of Pompeii. More than half of the buried city has now been uncovered. A visitor may see the ruins of the old public square with many of the surrounding buildings as they stood almost 2,000 years ago.

The discoveries at Pompeii add much to our knowledge of ancient Roman ways. We know that the Romans liked games, for the amphitheater of Pompeii was large enough to hold all the people of the town. The wall paintings show the kind of art these people enjoyed. The stone pathways are the same streets they used.

Vatican City, the Home of the Pope

Within Rome is a tiny independent state, about the size of an average city park. This is Vatican City, where the Pope, who is the head of the Roman Catholic Church, lives. The Pope is the ruler of Vatican City.

In Vatican City is Saint Peter's, the largest church in the world. It was completed in 1626. It is the special church of the Pope. People from every country visit St. Peter's.

The great dome of the church was designed by the famous painter, sculptor, and architect, Michelangelo (mī′kəl an′jə lō′).

Next to Saint Peter's is the Vatican, the home and office of the Pope. The Vatican is the world's largest palace. In it are famous art treasures and a great library.

The Vatican Palace houses one of the most extensive libraries and art collections in the world. Michelangelo painted the ceiling of the Sistine Chapel, which is in the Vatican.

Florence, a Great Art Center

North of Rome lies Florence, a city probably better known for art than any other city in Italy. It is a treasure house of famous paintings and statues.

Many of these treasures were ruined, however, in a flood that took place in 1966. The rain-swollen Arno River sent torrents of mud and oily water into the famous galleries and churches. Afterward volunteers from all over the world came to Florence. Working through the winter, they dug the city out of the mud and restored its beauty.

Genoa, Italy's Busiest Port

South of Milan on the coast is Genoa, a city with a population of about 800,000. Genoa is the largest and busiest Italian port. Ships bring in coal, oil, iron, and cotton for Italy's industries. Shipped out of Genoa are Italian textiles, machinery, and chemicals. Christopher Columbus was born in Genoa. The lighthouse that signaled to ships in his time still overlooks the harbor.

Venice, City on the Adriatic

The port of Venice lies across the Italian Peninsula from Genoa. The Venetians built their city on low islands in the Adriatic Sea.

People travel in *gondolas* and other boats along the Grand Canal in Venice. Many beautiful palaces and other old buildings line the banks of the canal.

They drove thousands of tree trunks into the mud and built their city over them.

Today many of the islands have been joined together, but canals still separate some of them. The Grand Canal is so wide and deep that ocean-going ships can use it to reach the main part of the city.

In Venice, people can take long flat-bottomed boats, called *gondolas* (gon′də ləz), to move about the city. People called gondoliers row the boats. Boats of many other kinds also use the canals of Venice. Hundreds of bridges connect the islands, so most places can also be reached on foot. But the narrow streets and bridges make it impossible to use horses or automobiles.

Rome
The "Eternal City"

Rome is called the "Eternal City" because it has been one of the world's great cities for more than 2,500 years. During that time it has had its periods of glory and its years of decline. But it has always returned as a center of art, learning, religion, and government.

The modern capital city of Italy is about as large as the city of Los Angeles. Its streets are jammed with automobiles. Their exhaust fumes eat away at the stone of its many beautiful monuments from the past.

Modern Rome spreads on either side of the Tiber River, beyond the original seven hills of ancient Rome. The vast crumbling ruins of those classical days still stand. Chief among them is the Colosseum, that huge amphitheater that once echoed to the cries of gladiators.

Rome is a city of views, an open-air museum. Walk down a narrow crooked street, turn a corner, and you suddenly find yourself in the middle of a plaza, or open space. In front of you is a sculptured fountain. Nearby are palaces and churches which house wonderful sculptures and paintings by Michelangelo, Raphael, and other great artists. ■

Milan
Italy's Business Center

In the year 1200 a knight who needed a new suit of armor might have gotten it from Milan. A silk merchant who needed a new supply of cloth might have placed an order in Milan. Many other businesses developed there too. As the city became rich, bankers in Italy began to make it their headquarters.

Milan has not supplied armor for a long time. Yet merchants from all over the world still order silk cloth from Milan. More important, bankers in Italy have continued to make the city their headquarters. Over the centuries Milan has become the business capital of Italy.

Look at the map of Italy on page 191. You will see that Milan, the factory city of Turin, and the port of Genoa form a triangle. This is Italy's great "industrial triangle." Here are most of the country's factories.

Milan is also famous as a center of culture. Rich merchants of the past paid for its beautiful buildings and works of art. Today the city's businesses still contribute money to the arts. Milan was and still is a city where great wealth has brought great beauty.

Michelangelo's greatest works include the Bible scenes he painted on the ceiling of the Sistine Chapel. This painting shows God creating the stars and planets.

The Arts of Italy

For centuries Italy has been a leader in the arts. Its people love music. Many great operas, which are plays sung rather than spoken, were written by musicians of Italy. Its artists have created many beautiful churches and palaces. Then they have made these buildings even more beautiful by the paintings and sculptures placed inside them.

Michelangelo, Creator of Beauty

One of the greatest artists of Italy and of all the world was Michelangelo. He was born in a small mountain village in 1508. When he was 13 years old he began his art studies with a famous painter in Florence. But he was attracted even more to sculpture. As a young man he became famous for his sculptures, which were lifelike and full of strong feelings.

His paintings on the ceiling of the Sistine Chapel in Rome show Hebrew prophets and stories from the Bible. For 4 long years he lay on his back on a scaffold, 70 feet (21 m) above the ground, to make the paintings.

Michelangelo was an old man when he was asked to design the dome of St. Peter's church. The dome was completed after his death. It has been copied in churches and public buildings all over the world.

The great power of Michelangelo's sculpture can be seen in the large, lifelike hands and the muscular body of the *Moses*.

Uniting the Peninsula

For hundreds of years after the fall of the Roman Empire, the Italian Peninsula was divided into many small states. Some were city-states, such as Florence, Venice, and Genoa. These areas were frequently conquered by foreign peoples. As the church grew stronger, the popes led the attempts to defend Italy. The popes came to rule an area in Central Italy called the Papal States. But unrest and invasion by foreign countries continued.

The feeling of the Italian people for a united nation grew very strong. In 1870 all of Italy finally became a kingdom. Rome was made the capital of the new nation. But the Vatican City, within Rome, remained the property of the Roman Catholic Church.

Italy Under the Fascists

After World War I, many Italians thought that Italy needed a more powerful government. They organized a party called the Fascisti, or *Fascists* (fash′ists). They hoped to see their country become as powerful as it had been under the Caesars. They planned ways to improve Italian industry and agriculture. Their leader was Benito Mussolini.

In 1935, Mussolini's power was reaching its climax. He is addressing his troops here, just before invading Ethiopia.

The Fascists became very powerful, and the king gave up the throne. By 1927 Mussolini became Italy's dictator, or all-powerful leader. All political parties except the Fascists were outlawed. No one was allowed to speak against the new regime. Italy made some progress during these years. Swamps were drained and the new land was farmed. Electric power plants were built to run new factories.

Mussolini was not satisfied to make Italy prosperous by peaceful methods. He wished to conquer much of Africa.

Seeking an Empire

The Fascists came into power in 1922. Ten years earlier, Italy had taken from the Turks the province of Libya, in Africa. Italy had other possessions in Africa, Eritrea (er′ə trē′ə) along the Red Sea and Somalia (sə mä′lē ə) below the Gulf of Aden.

Also in this region is the Empire of Ethiopia (ē′thē ō′pē′ə), a country larger than Texas and California combined. Much of Ethiopia is high plateau with good land for grazing and farming. Mussolini decided to make Ethiopia an Italian possession.

In 1935 the Italian army landed in Africa and attacked Ethiopia. The Ethiopians were brave, but they were poorly armed. With modern weapons, the Italians easily defeated the Ethiopians.

Italy in World War II

Italy and Germany formed a league called the Axis (ak′sis). Great Britain and France, later called the Allies, were pledged to defend each other and many nations in eastern Europe against any attack. When Germany attacked Poland in 1939, war broke out between the Axis and the Allies. World War II had begun. The United States entered the war in 1941.

British troops defeated the Italians in Ethiopia in 1941. Two years later the Germans and Italians were driven back through the Libyan desert. After losing Libya, the Axis troops retreated into Tunisia (too͞ nē′zhə) and then to Sicily.

The Allied armies conquered Sicily and pursued the Axis troops northward through Italy, capturing Naples, Rome, Florence, and Genoa. Weary of war, the Italian people turned against Mussolini and executed him.

Mussolini's empire was lost. Ethiopia had regained its freedom. Libya was ruled by the Allies. Italy also gave up Eritrea, which became a part of Ethiopia.

The manufacture of automobiles has become one of the major industries in Italy. Many Italians work in this car factory in Turin.

A New Italy

After World War II, which ended in 1945, the Allies controlled Italy. They sent food to its people and helped them rebuild their country. The Allies made it possible for free elections to be held so that the Italians could choose the form of government they wanted. The people remembered that the king had worked with Mussolini, so in 1946 they voted to make Italy a republic.

Building Factories

For many years Italy had been a farming nation. It had some factories but they did not supply nearly as many jobs as farms did. Yet the farms did not provide a good living for all of the people who depended on them. Year after year, more and more farmers moved to the cities in search of work.

But there were too few opportunities in the cities. Factory owners did not have jobs for all the people who came to look for work. To end this job shortage, the government of Italy began helping the people build factories. Italy came to produce over twice as many goods as it did before the war.

Although Italy still has farms, it has also become an important manufacturing and industrial nation. Today many more Italians earn their living in industry than on farms.

Thousands of other Italians have gone to work in factories in other European countries like West Germany and the Netherlands. However, in recent years there have been fewer jobs available abroad. Many Italians have returned home and found jobs in Italian factories.

Italian factories, old and new, make a variety of products including machinery, machine tools,

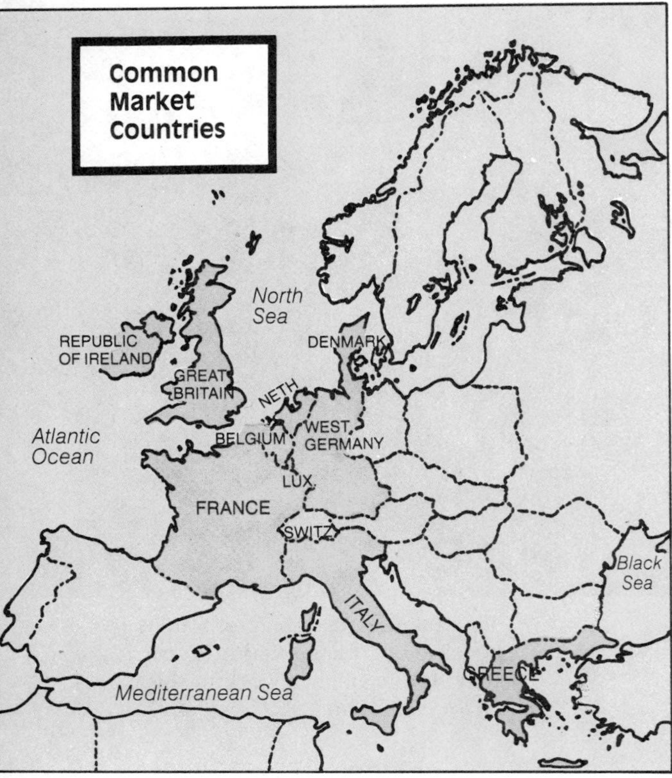

The ten European nations that make up the *Common Market* are shown above. These nations cooperate in maintaining low import taxes on one another's products. Low taxes encourage trade.

steel, processed foods, chemicals, textiles, and cars. Italy exports these products to other nations, including the United States.

To supply power for its factories, Italy imports coal and oil. It also operates electric power stations alongside rushing mountain streams. And it has been building nuclear power plants. As Italy gains more of these plants, it can depend less and less on imported fuels.

A Partner with Its Neighbors

Italy today cooperates with its world neighbors in many ways. It belongs to several groups of nations that are working for peace and prosperity.

One of these groups is made up of ten European countries: Italy, Belgium, the Netherlands, Luxembourg, France, West Germany, Great Britain, Ireland, Greece, and Denmark. It is called the *Common Market* (kom′ən mär′kit). The Common Market is also known as the European Economic Community. The members of this organization banded together in 1957 for the purpose of buying and selling more goods among themselves. They do this by lowering the taxes which each nation charges on goods imported from other member nations. When such taxes are low, the imported goods are cheaper and people can buy them more easily. Thus, Italy can sell more of its products to the other member nations. These nations in turn can buy more from Italy as well as from each other.

Italy is an important member of the Common Market. Later we shall study the other countries of the Common Market.

Do You Know?

1. What city was buried by lava from Mount Vesuvius in ancient times?
2. Who lives in Vatican City? Where is it?
3. Who was Mussolini?

To Help You Learn

Using New Words

consul	Fascist
plebeian	Common Market
veto	gondola

Number a paper from 1 through 6. After each number write the word or term from the above list that matches the definition.

1. One of the common people of ancient Rome
2. A long, flat-bottomed boat used on the canals of Venice
3. Member of the party formed after World War I which wanted to make Italy a powerful country
4. One of the two highest officials of the ancient Roman republic
5. The power of elected officials to prevent decisions that they think are unjust
6. An organization of European nations formed for the purpose of buying and selling goods among themselves.

Finding the Facts

1. What two large islands in the Mediterranean belong to Italy?
2. Why did the Romans establish a republic?
3. Who were the consuls? How could they be replaced by a dictator?
4. How did Rome become an empire?
5. Who was the ruler of Rome during its Golden Age? Why is his reign given this name?
6. Name three ways in which Rome was influenced by Greece.
7. Name three things we owe to the ancient Romans.
8. Why do many people from different parts of the world like to visit Italy?
9. Why are olive trees grown in the region south of the Po Valley?
10. Why can many different crops be grown in the region of the Po Valley?
11. Why is Rome called the "Eternal City"?
12. What is Vatican City? How large is it?
13. Who was Mussolini? What did he seek to do for Italy?
14. What kind of government does Italy have today?
15. What makes up Italy's industrial triangle?
16. What happened to Pompeii? What did we learn from its discovery?

Learning from Maps

1. Look at the map of Italy on page 191. By what bodies of water is the peninsula almost surrounded? What are the chief rivers of Italy? In which part of the country would you expect to find more people engaged in farming: in the north along the Po River, or in the southwestern tip of the peninsula? Why?
2. Look at the world map on pages 24–25 and the world rainfall map on page 26. In what ways is Sicily like California? Compare the

latitude, mountains, and amount of rainfall of the two regions.

3. Look at the map of Italy on page 191. What Italian city is an important port on the northern Adriatic? On the southern Adriatic? About how far apart are these two cities? Use the scale of miles or kilometers on the map to measure the distance.

Using Study Skills

1. **Chart:** Look at the chart of Roman and Greek gods and goddesses on page 203. Who was the chief Roman god? Chief Greek goddess? What were the Roman and Greek names for the god of the sea? What was the Roman name for Athena? What was the Greek name for Diana?
2. **Diagram:** Look at the diagram of the construction of a Roman road on page 195. What was used to make the bottom layer of the road? The top layer?
3. **Chart:** Look at the chart of Roman numerals below. Then write these numbers using Roman numbers: 54, 129, 1980. Read these dates: MDCXXVI, CDLXXVI. What happened on these dates? (The time line on page 189 will help you with this.)
4. **Outline:** An outline is a list of the different parts, or headings, of a subject. It helps you see the plan of a book or of a part of a book. It also helps you remember material. Below is an outline of part of Unit 6. Copy it, reread the text, and complete the outline.

I. The peninsula of Italy
- **A.**
  - **1. Climate of the peninsula**
  - **2.**
- **B. What Sicily is like**
- **C. What Sardinia is like**

II. The rise of Rome
- **A. The founding of Rome**
  - **1. The legend of Rome's founding**
  - **2.**
- **B. Rome as a republic**
  - **1. The growth of Rome**
  - **2. The good Roman roads**
  - **3.**
  - **4.**
  - **5.**

Roman Numerals

I (1)	VIII (8)
II (2)	IX (9)
III (3)	X (10)
IV (4)	L (50)
V (5)	C (100)
VI (6)	D (500)
VII (7)	M (1,000)

2,674	=	2,000	+	600	+	70	+	4
MMDCLXXIV	=	MM	+	DC	+	LXX	+	IV

Thinking It Through

1. The Romans had no automobiles, but they were able to travel about on their highways more easily than could many of your great-grandparents when they were young. Why was this true? Why are good roads important to the community where you live?
2. Curius Dentatus was an important Roman senator but very poor. He had no slaves and lived simply. One day some foreigners offered him a large amount of gold to support a treaty favorable to them. He refused, saying "Which is more honorable, to possess gold, or to give orders to those who possess it?"

   What does this story tell us about Roman values?

Projects

1. Find out and tell the class the origin of the names of the months of the year.
2. Italian foods are popular in many parts of our country. Collect recipes of typical Italian dishes or menus from Italian restaurants. You might plan a class party featuring a typical Italian meal.
3. In recent years the number and variety of products manufactured in Italy and imported to this country have increased. This is particularly true of clothing and machines for home and office (sewing machines, typewriters, calculators). If you see advertisements for such products, show them to the class.
4. In studying the early history of America, we learn about three famous Italians: Christopher Columbus, Amerigo Vespucci, and John Cabot. The Explorers' Committee might show on a map the voyages of these early explorers.
5. Americans of Italian birth or ancestry have contributed greatly to life in our country. A few who achieved success in their chosen fields were: Enrico Fermi, atomic scientist; Arturo Toscanini, musical conductor; Gian-Carlo Menotti, composer; Ella Grasso, governor of Connecticut, and Maria Montessori, educator. The Research Committee might find out about these or other people of Italian ancestry who have contributed to life in America.
6. A great many of our English words are related to Latin. Some English words have kept the same spelling and meaning they had in Latin. This is true of the following: index, error, axis, exit, labor. What does each of these words mean?

   Some Latin words which are related to English are spelled a little differently. Examples of these are: familia, senatus, theatrum, templum, lanterna. What English word came from each?

7 The Continent of Africa

Unit Preview

Africa is a vast continent with tropical rain forests, snow-capped mountains, steep waterfalls, and the largest desert in the world.

The people of Africa developed different ways of living in this land of contrasts. The nomads of the desert herd their flocks from place to place in search of water and grass. South of the desert there are farms. In the rain forests, hunting and gathering supply basic needs.

From an earlier unit, you may remember that an ancient civilization developed along the Nile River. Egypt was not the only great empire of Africa. Other powerful kingdoms grew up south of Egypt and in western and central Africa. Trade in gold and ivory, copper and salt made the rulers wealthy.

Africa knew the glory of empire, but it also knew conquest. In 1500 the first Europeans came to the continent. Several European countries claimed land after that. These countries also began to take Africans away from their homes to work as slaves in other parts of the world.

Slavery finally came to an end, but it was many years before the Europeans gave up control of their African colonies.

Africa became a continent of independent nations only after much strife. These nations are creating new forms of government and learning how to develop their resources.

Things to Discover

If you look carefully at the picture, map, and time line on these pages, you can answer these questions.

1. What continent is north of Africa?
2. What oceans border Africa?
3. The picture shows a scene in Nigeria. There are more than 200 different groups of Nigerians. What do you see in the picture that indicates the variety of customs and traditions in this African nation?
4. How many years was it between the colonization of most of Africa and independence of all nations?
5. Ethiopia is on the east coast of Africa. When did an ancient kingdom begin there?
6. What country became independent in 1957?
7. What land areas that you have studied lie closest to Africa?

Words to Learn

You will meet these words in this unit. As you read, you will learn what they mean and how to pronounce them. The Word List will help you.

acacia	hydroelectricity
alloy	manioc
apartheid	oral tradition
baobab	reserve
clan	Sahel
dialect	savanna
dromedary	vassal
endangered species	veldt

300	Axum kingdom in Ethiopia formed
1324	Mansa Musa travels to Mecca
1468	Songhai destroys Mali empire
c. 1500	Slave trade begins
1591	Timbuktu destroyed
1798	Dutch establish colony at Cape Town
1804	Denmark passes anti-slavery law
1914	Most of Africa colonized
1957	Ghana gains independence
1977	Most African nations independent
1980	Rhodesia becomes Zimbabwe

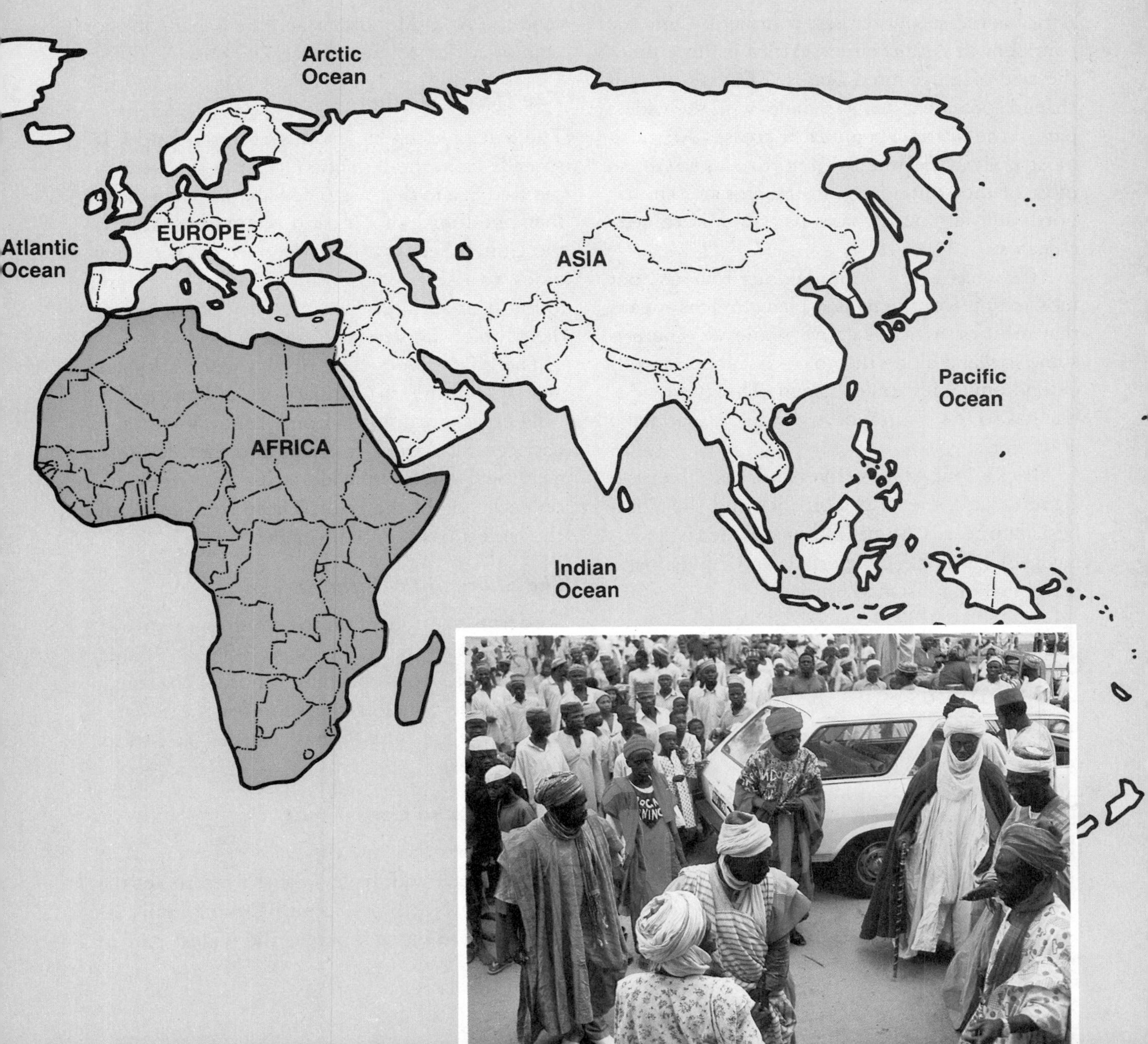

1
The Geography of Africa

Africa is the second largest continent. Only the continent of Asia is larger. Africa is three times the size of the United States. The continent is shaped somewhat like a triangle, with the widest part in the north. The equator crosses Africa almost midway between the north and south, so most of the continent is in the tropics. The far north and far south coasts have Mediterranean climates.

Africa has a few mountainous regions, but most of the continent is a plateau. This means that most of Africa is above sea level. There is some lowland along the coast, but the lowlands extend only a few miles inland. That is why Africa has so few natural bays and inlets that make good ports.

Africa's four longest rivers are the Nile, the Zaire (zä ir′), the Niger (nī′ jər), and the Zambesi (zam bē′ zē). Some sections of the rivers are navigable. But steep waterfalls and rapids make travel for long distances difficult.

Contrasting Lands and Climates

Because Africa is so vast, many different kinds of land are found there. The Atlas Mountains are in the northwest. Some peaks of this mountain range reach 11,000 feet (3,300 m) above the sea. These high peaks are covered with snow almost all year round.

South of the Atlas Mountains is the Sahara (se har′ ə). Sahara means "desert" in Arabic. Find the Atlas Mountains and the Sahara on the map of Africa on page 223.

The Desert Region

The Sahara is the largest desert in the world. It spreads from the Atlantic Ocean in the west to the Red Sea in the east. The Sahara covers more than one-fourth of Africa. It is almost as large as the United States. It is dry land except for a few oases (ō ā′ sēs). These small fertile areas are found near springs. They are very important to the people who live in the desert.

The Nile River, one of the world's longest rivers, is in the eastern part of the Sahara. The Nile flows northward from Lake Victoria in east central Africa. It drains into the Mediterranean Sea. There are wide strips of fertile land on each side of the river. These lands make up the largest oases in the Sahara.

The Shore of the Sahara

Bordering the Sahara on the south is a semiarid grassland known as the *Sahel* (sä hel′). Sahel is an Arabic word meaning "shore." You may think of the Sahel as the shore of the Sahara. Here there are tufts of grass, shrubs, and short thorny trees.

The Savanna Grasslands

The Sahel merges into the *savanna* (sə van′ ə). A savanna is a broad, grassy plain. It resembles the prairies of North and South Dakota. This savanna region extends across the widest part of

AFRICA
National Capitals
Other Capitals
Other Cities
Mountains
Hills
Plateaus
Plains
Miles
Kilometers
ATLANTIC OCEAN
MEDITERRANEAN SEA
BLACK SEA
CASPIAN SEA
ARAL SEA
EUROPE
ASIA
PERSIAN GULF
RED SEA
GULF OF ADEN
GULF OF GUINEA
INDIAN OCEAN
MOZAMBIQUE CHANNEL
TROPIC OF CANCER
EQUATOR
West Longitude
East Longitude
SAHARA
ALGERIA
LIBYA
EGYPT
MOROCCO
TUNISIA
WESTERN SAHARA
MAURITANIA
MALI
NIGER
CHAD
SUDAN
ETHIOPIA
SOMALIA
DJIBOUTI
KENYA
UGANDA
RWANDA
BURUNDI
TANZANIA
ZAIRE
CONGO
GABON
CAMEROON
CENTRAL AFRICAN REPUBLIC
NIGERIA
BENIN
TOGO
GHANA
IVORY COAST
BURKINA FASO
LIBERIA
SIERRA LEONE
GUINEA
GUINEA-BISSAU
GAMBIA
SENEGAL
EQUATORIAL GUINEA
SÃO TOMÉ AND PRÍNCIPE
CABINDA
ANGOLA
ZAMBIA
MALAWI
MOZAMBIQUE
ZIMBABWE
BOTSWANA
NAMIBIA
SOUTH AFRICA
LESOTHO
SWAZILAND
MADAGASCAR
COMOROS
SEYCHELLES
MAURITIUS
WALVIS BAY (S.A.)
Azores Islands
Madeira Islands
Canary Islands
Ascension Island
St. Helena Island
Lisbon
Madrid
Rome
Istanbul
Ankara
Athens
Algiers
Tunis
Tripoli
Bengasi
Alexandria
Cairo
Baghdad
Riyadh
Mecca
Port Sudan
Asmara
Khartoum
Aden
Djibouti
Addis Ababa
Mogadishu
Nairobi
Kampala
Kigali
Bujumbura
Mombasa
Zanzibar
Dar es Salaam
Tanger
Fès
Rabat
Casablanca
Marrakech
Sidi Ifni
El Aaiún
Touggourt
Nouakchott
Timbuktu
Gao
Dakar
Banjul
Bissau
Bamako
Ouagadougou
Niamey
Kano
Ndjamena
Conakry
Freetown
Monrovia
Abidjan
Accra
Lomé
Porto Novo
Lagos
Ibadan
Malabo
Bioko
Yaoundé
Bangui
Libreville
Brazzaville
Kinshasa (Léopoldville)
Pointe-Noire
Kisangani (Stanleyville)
Luanda
Lubumbashi (Élisabethville)
Lusaka
Lilongwe
Harare
Windhoek
Gaborone
Pretoria
Johannesburg
Maputo
Mbabane
Maseru
Bloemfontein
Durban
Cape Town
Port Elizabeth
Cape of Good Hope
Antananarivo
Moroni
Victoria
Port Louis
Strait of Gibraltar
ATLAS MOUNTAINS
Mt. Toubkal
AHAGGAR MOUNTAINS
TIBESTI MOUNTAINS
AÏR
Lake Nasser
Nile River
White Nile
Blue Nile
Suez Canal
Sénégal River
Gambia River
Niger River
Benue River
Lake Volta
Lake Chad
CONGO BASIN
Congo (Zaïre) River
Kasai River
RUWENZORI
Lake Albert
Lake Edward
Lake Victoria
Lake Rudolf
Lake Tanganyika
Mt. Kilimanjaro 19,340 ft. (5895 m)
Kirinyaga
KATANGA
Lake Nyasa
Zambezi River
Victoria Falls
Kariba Lake
Limpopo River
Orange River
NAMIB DESERT
KALAHARI DESERT
© Rand McNally & Co.

Many different kinds of land are found in Africa. Its biggest desert, the Sahara, is the largest in the world. Its grassland, or savanna, supports much wildlife. Its tropical rain forest, in the middle of the continent, has lush vegetation.

Africa. It ranges from the Atlantic coast in the west to Ethiopia (ē′thē ō′pē ə) in the east, and from the Sahel in the north to the wet lands near the equator in the south. (See the map of Africa on page 225.)

The savanna receives most of its rainfall in the summer. Winters are hot and dry. This is a good climate for certain trees.

The trees of the savanna are larger and more numerous than the trees of the Sahel. Groves of trees are scattered through lands covered by very tall grass. Two common trees are the *baobab* (bā′ō bab′) and the *acacia* (ə kā′shə). The baobab has a thick trunk that stores water, and a gourdlike fruit that is used for food. The acacia is shaped like an open umbrella. It is a source of gum arabic, which is used to make adhesive.

The Tropical Rain Forest

Farther south, in the middle of the continent, are the tall trees of the hot, wetlands near the equator. These tropical forests are located mainly in the Zaire River valley. They reach westward to the Atlantic Ocean, along the northern coast of the Gulf of Guinea (gin′ē).

The thick forests near the equator receive much rainfall. Plants grow rapidly. The tops of gigantic trees form a ceiling overhead and block the sunlight from the ground. Most of the wildlife, such as monkeys and birds, live in the trees.

South of the Equator

The climatic zones are repeated south of the equator. Just south of the Zambezi River there are savannas that end at the large Kalahari (kal′ə här′ē) Desert. Most of southern Africa is a plateau region. Here in the Republic of South Africa and Zimbabwe (zim bäb′wē) is the area of open grassland with scattered bushes and trees known as the *veldt* (velt).

The Great Rift Valley

One major landform in East Africa is the Great Rift Valley. It is a series of deep valleys that cut from north to south. This split in the earth's crust is so large that it could be seen by the astronauts as they walked on the moon. The valley is the site of several large lakes. On the borders of the Great Rift Valley are mountains and volcanoes. The Ruwenzori (ro͞o′wan zōr′ē) Range, often called the Mountains of the Moon, stretch above the valley. Near the valley to the east are Mount Kilimanjaro (kil′ə mən jär′ō) and Mount Kenya (ken′yə). Mount Kilimanjaro peaks at

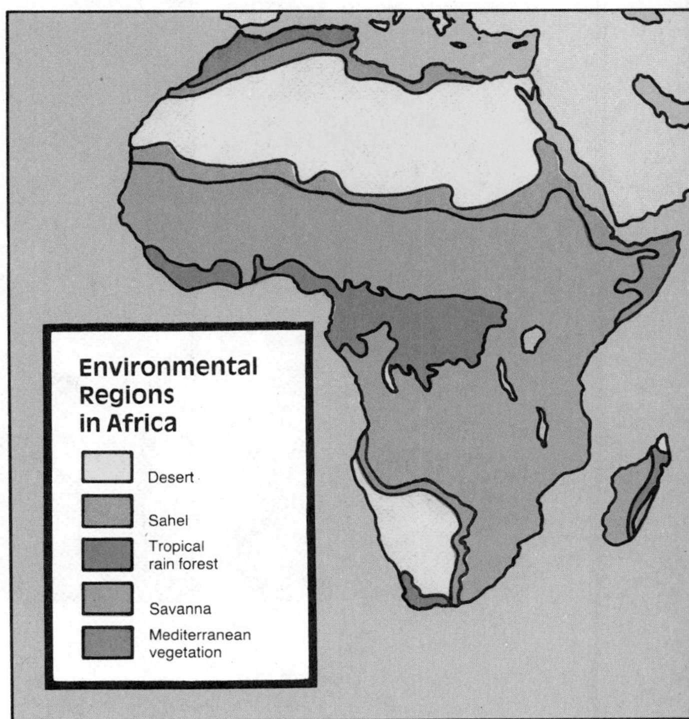

Rainfall in Africa

Land Region	Average Yearly Rainfall	
	inches	centimeters
Desert	less than 10	less than 25
Savanna	30-50	75-125
Rain Forest	more than 80	more than 200

The map shows the environmental regions of Africa. The chart shows the average yearly rainfall for some of these regions.

Whether scarce or abundant, water is an important resource in Africa. A woman in East Africa carries precious water from a spring; Victoria Falls in Zimbabwe may be used for *hydroelectric* power.

about 20,000 feet (6,000 m). It is Africa's tallest mountain and is almost the height of Mount McKinley in Alaska.

Natural Resources

Africa has a rich variety of minerals. In southern Africa are found two-thirds of the world's gold, three-fourths of the world's cobalt (kō′bôlt), and one-half of its antimony (an′ti mō′nē). Cobalt and antimony are used to make *alloys* (al′oiz). An alloy is a metal formed by combining two or more metals. Africa also has large supplies of aluminum, chromium, copper, iron, and lead. The Republic of South Africa has the world's largest diamond mines.

Several African countries have large amounts of monazite (män′ə zīt) sands. Monazite sands contain phosphate (fos′fāt), which is made into fertilizers used by farmers around the world. Countries with monazite deposits include Zaire, South Africa, Gabon (gä bōn′), the Central African Republic, Niger, Senegal (sen′ə gôl′) and Madagascar (mad′ə gas′kər).

Water Reserves

Many parts of southern and northern Africa suffer from a shortage of rainfall. But there is much rainfall in the forest lands and in the savannas during some seasons. The heavy rains fill the rivers and provide nearby regions with major water power resources. The waterfalls and rapids may be used to turn generators that create electricity. Energy made this way is called *hydroelectricity* (hī′drō i lek tris′ə tē), or electricity produced by water. The forest lands of Africa have so much water they could produce one-fifth of the world's hydroelectricity. The Zaire

Basin is very important to Africa because it supplies almost half of Africa's water.

Energy Reserves

Africa also has very large amounts of energy resources in its northern regions. For a long time the Sahara was thought to be only wasteland. Then oil was found beneath its sands. Today there are many oil wells in that desert. In Libya (lib′ē ə) and Algeria (al jēr′ē ə) there are large amounts of high-grade natural gas and oil. To the south, Nigeria (nī jēr′ē ə) has large oil deposits. Today Nigeria is a leading oil producer.

Africa has only small amounts of coal. Most of it is mined in the Republic of South Africa.

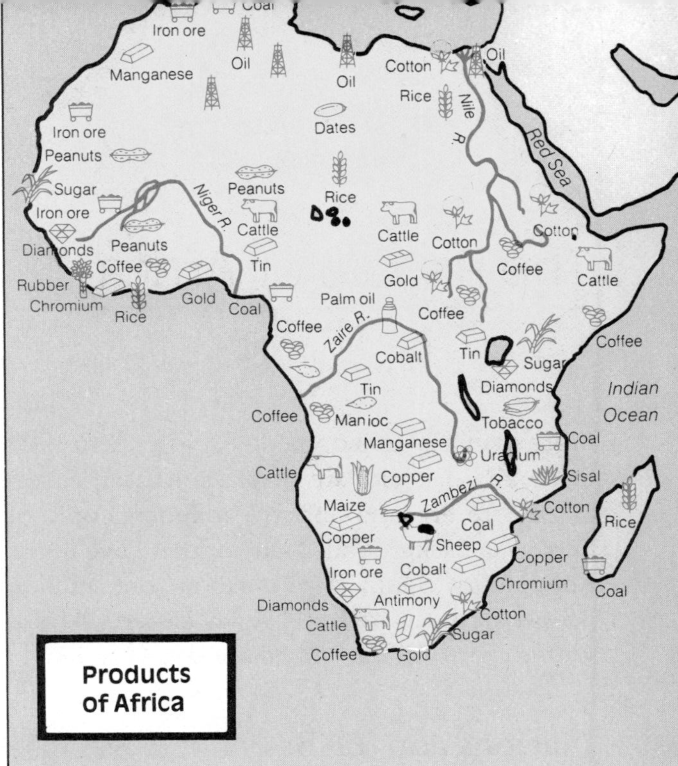

Products of Africa

Animal Reserves

Because Africa has such a wide variety of environments it also has many kinds of animals. The *dromedary* (drom′ə der′ē) is a camel with one hump that lives in the Sahara. Dromedaries can travel for several days across the desert with little food or water. Herds of elephants roam the savannas. Lions, antelope, zebra, and rhinoceros (rī nos′ər əs) are found in the grasslands. In the rain forest are monkeys, chimpanzees, and huge gorillas. Hippopotamuses (hip′ə pot′ə mə səz) and crocodiles thrive in the rivers of the tropical forest.

Many of the animals have been killed for their fur or, in the case of elephants, their ivory. Farmers have extended fields into the animals' natural grazing and hunting lands. As a consequence many of the animals are now *endangered species* (en dān′jərd spē′shēz). This means types of animals or plants that are in danger of dying out. In order to protect the remaining animals, Uganda (yo͞o gan′də), Kenya, Tanzania (tan′zə nē′ə), and a few other countries have set aside lands for wild animals. Something set aside for a special purpose, such as land, is called a *reserve* (ri zurv′). Animals roam free in reserves. No hunting is permitted. Each year tourists come to Africa to see animals in reserves.

Do You Know?

1. Why does Africa have few natural ports?
2. What river waters the Sahara?
3. Name three African countries with large oil reserves.
4. Give two reasons why some animals in Africa are in danger of dying out.

2
The People of Africa

More than 450 million people live in Africa. Of these, the majority are of black African ancestry. There are also about 5 million people of European background. Many of them live in the Republic of South Africa. About one million people of Asian origin live in eastern Africa, southeastern Africa, and on Madagascar.

Nations and Tribes

If you look at the political map of Africa on page 232 you will note there are more than 45 nations in Africa. Yet nearly all the boundaries shown did not exist before the nineteenth century. It was then that large numbers of European settlers came to Africa and divided it up among themselves. Sometimes the European governments simply drew boundary lines on pieces of paper and then put them into effect. Most of the time they ignored the boundaries African peoples had set for themselves.

The map on this page shows how the Africans divided their land. The divisions set up by the Europeans did not follow the tribal boundaries.

A tribe is a group of people who share the same traditions and way of life. Within a tribe there are *clans* (klanz). A clan is a group of families who claim descent from the same ancestor. Grandparents, their sons or daughters, and their sons' or daughters' children usually live together, as an extended family. Most African people are very loyal to their clans and tribes.

African Languages

Between 800 and 1,000 languages are spoken in Africa. An African language often varies from one village to another. A form of a language spoken by a particular group of people is called a *dialect* (dī′ə lekt′). Often the history of a group of people or their relationships with neighbor-

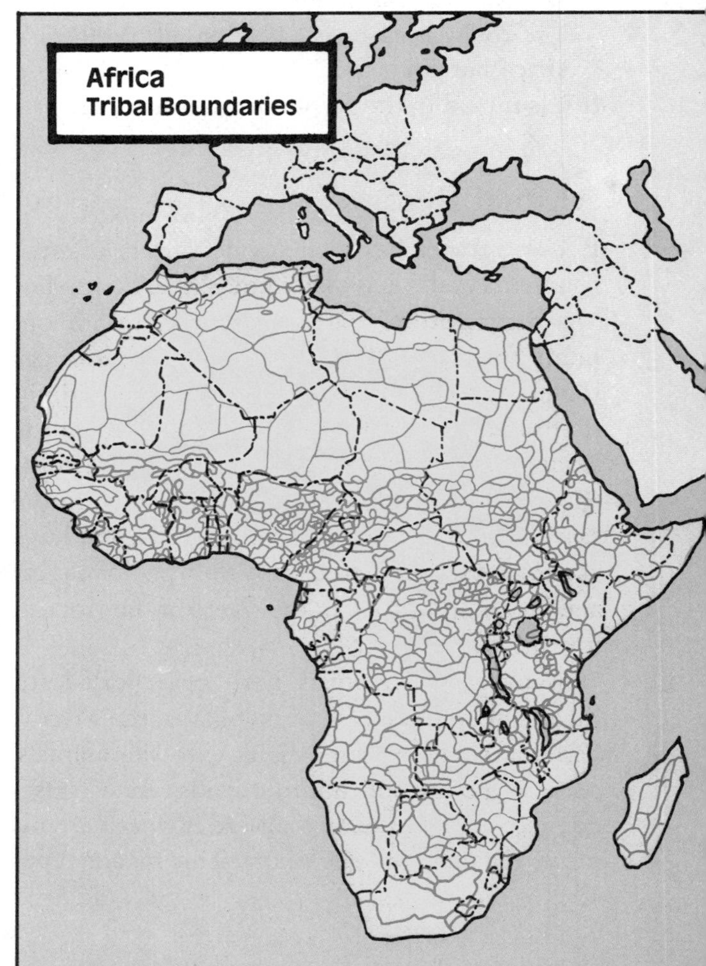

ing groups have influenced the language they speak.

The largest language group of Africa is Bantu (ban′ to͞o). This group of languages is spoken in an area that extends from north of the equator into southern Africa. Some 60 million Africans speak a form of the Bantu language. Swahili (swä hē′lē) is a Bantu language spoken by 20 million Africans who live on the east coast in Somalia (sə mä′lē), Tanzania, and Mozambique (mō zəm bēk′).

In the dry lands of southern Africa, languages of the Khoisan (koi sän′) group are spoken. African peoples called Bushmen and Hottentots (hot′ən totz′) speak these tongues. These languages are known for some letters which are spoken with a clicking sound. This sound is hard to imitate.

European Languages

Europeans left another mark on Africa besides political boundaries. They also left behind their languages. The most common ones spoken are English, French, and Portuguese. Many black Africans speak one of these languages in addition to their own language and a dialect. In some African nations a European language is the official language because there may be many tribal languages.

In the Republic of South Africa, Afrikaans (af′ri käns′) is spoken. This language is Dutch with the addition of some African words. When Dutch settlers came to this area in the 1600s, they learned words from the Africans living there and began to use them.

In much of Africa, art is useful as well as beautiful. These pots, for sale at an Ivory Coast market, will be used every day, yet they are finely crafted.

The Arts of Africa

Africa has a variety of interesting art forms. Culture, environment, and use all play a part in shaping the arts of a region. In North Africa, for example, much of the architecture is like that of neighboring Muslims in the Middle East. For Africans south of the Sahara, art must be useful as well as beautiful. Baskets and pottery are finely crafted, but they are used every day. One art form often develops along with another. In many parts of Africa music, dance, sculpture, and costume all come together in exciting dance-dramas.

Dance is an important part of the arts in Africa. It often combines African sculpture, as seen in the dance mask shown here, and African music.

The Oral Tradition

History and literature that is spoken, rather than written, and passed down from person to person is called *oral tradition* (ôr′əl trad dish′ən). Early African stories and poems were not written down. Instead a storyteller told them to the rest of the villagers. The storyteller also taught the stories to younger villagers. In this way stories and poems were kept alive for hundreds of years. Much of Africa's history is preserved in its oral tradition.

The Mandingo (män din′gō) and other West African peoples give one person the task of learning the history of the local villagers. That person is called a griot (grē′ō). The griot memorizes the names of family members for several generations, and events that happened to them. The griot recites or sings family histories while playing a harplike musical instrument.

Most African people are very fond of proverbs and riddles. The Ibo (ē′bō) in West Africa say: "Proverbs are the palm oil with which words are eaten." Proverbs express some commonly agreed on truth or social rule. Riddles are like proverbs except that they are meant to amuse as much as to teach.

The lifelike bronze portraits made by the ancient people of southwestern Nigeria are treasured for their quality. This figure depicts a sixteenth- century king.

Music and Dance

In Africa the people who are skillful dancers and musicians are highly respected. The main African instrument, the drum, has many variations throughout the continent. In some areas there are large orchestras made up only of drums. In Ghana (gä′nə), in West Africa, the "talking drum" can imitate speech. This is done through changing the rhythm and the pitch of the drum while it is being played. Sometimes the talking drum is used to send messages long distances.

Dances are used to celebrate personal and community events. A successful hunt, a bountiful harvest, a wedding, a birth, or a death may be the occasion for a dance. To keep dance tradition alive in times of change, some countries now stage annual dance competitions. Local contests are held and the best dance teams then travel to the capital for the finals. Villagers may practice for many months in preparation for these events.

Sculpture

Most African sculpture is made of wood, but metal, clay, and ivory are also used. Nigerian sculptors were making detailed bronze figures as early as A.D. 1000. Among the finest African sculptures are their dance masks. Some masks are used by dancers who belong to secret societies. The artists carve the masks far from the villages and hide them away. At the right time the masked dancers suddenly appear in the middle of the village. Often this happens late at night when the dancers are seen only by firelight and starlight. This adds to the excitement.

Religions of Africa

Africans practice a variety of religions. In North Africa most people are Muslims. They follow the religion of Islam. Ethiopia converted to Christianity in A.D. 300, making it one of the oldest Christian nations in the world. Elsewhere Africans are Christians because of the work of missionaries.

Many Africans continue to practice their traditional religions. These religions celebrate nature, ancestors, and tribal customs.

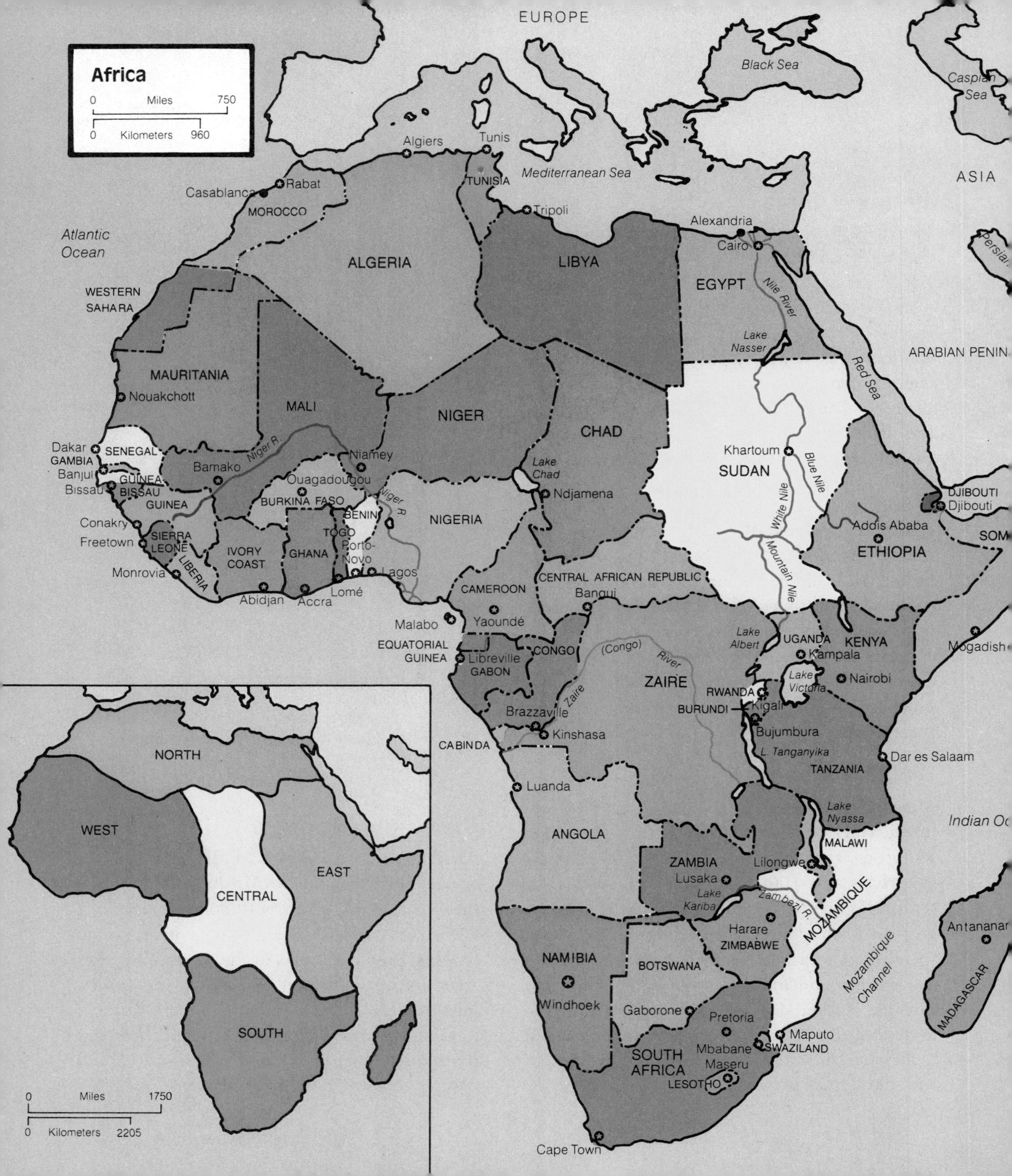

Africa
0 Miles 750
0 Kilometers 960
EUROPE
Black Sea
Caspian Sea
ASIA
Mediterranean Sea
Atlantic Ocean
Algiers
Tunis
Rabat
Casablanca
MOROCCO
TUNISIA
Tripoli
Alexandria
Cairo
ALGERIA
LIBYA
EGYPT
Nile River
WESTERN SAHARA
Lake Nasser
Red Sea
ARABIAN PENIN
MAURITANIA
Nouakchott
MALI
NIGER
CHAD
SUDAN
Khartoum
Blue Nile
White Nile
Dakar
GAMBIA
SENEGAL
Banjul
Bissau
GUINEA-BISSAU
GUINEA
Bamako
Niger R.
Niamey
Ouagadougou
BURKINA FASO
Lake Chad
Ndjamena
DJIBOUTI
Djibouti
Conakry
Freetown
SIERRA LEONE
LIBERIA
Monrovia
IVORY COAST
GHANA
TOGO
BENIN
Porto-Novo
Lagos
NIGERIA
Addis Ababa
ETHIOPIA
SOM
Abidjan
Accra
Lomé
CAMEROON
CENTRAL AFRICAN REPUBLIC
Bangui
Mountain Nile
Malabo
Yaoundé
EQUATORIAL GUINEA
Libreville
GABON
CONGO
(Congo) River
Lake Albert
UGANDA
Kampala
KENYA
Mogadish
ZAIRE
Lake Victoria
Nairobi
RWANDA
Kigali
BURUNDI
Bujumbura
Zaire
Brazzaville
Kinshasa
CABINDA
L. Tanganyika
TANZANIA
Dar es Salaam
Luanda
ANGOLA
Lake Nyassa
Indian Oc
MALAWI
ZAMBIA
Lusaka
Lilongwe
Lake Kariba
Zambezi R.
MOZAMBIQUE
Harare
ZIMBABWE
NAMIBIA
BOTSWANA
Windhoek
Gaborone
Pretoria
Mozambique Channel
Antananar
MADAGASCAR
Maputo
Mbabane
SWAZILAND
Maseru
LESOTHO
SOUTH AFRICA
Cape Town
Persian
NORTH
WEST
CENTRAL
EAST
SOUTH
0 Miles 1750
0 Kilometers 2205

The North Africa Region

Climate, land, and tradition influence how Africans live. We will now explore the major land areas of Africa and talk about one or more groups who live there. The first region is North Africa. This includes the modern nations that border the Mediterranean Sea. These are Morocco (mə rok′ō), Algeria, Tunisia (to͞o nē′zhə), and Libya. Egypt is also in North Africa. We read about Egypt earlier, in Unit 2. Sudan too is often grouped with North African nations. Find these places on the map of Africa on page 232.

Cities of the Coast

North Africa is the most urbanized region of Africa. This means that here more Africans live in cities than in any other part of Africa.

The cities of the coast—Alexandria, Egypt; Tripoli (trip′ə lē), Libya; and Tangier (tan jēr′), Morocco—are Africa's fastest growing cities. As we read in Unit 2, Cairo, Egypt, is the largest city in all of Africa.

Part of the reason for the growth of these cities is oil. There are large deposits of oil in Libya and Algeria. Oil brings a great deal of money to these nations. The cities offer a wide variety of jobs.

The Desert Dwellers

The Sahara is the home of farmers and animal herders. The people known as Berbers work small plots of land in oases. Here they live in mud-brick houses and raise crops of dates, citrus fruits, and grain.

At one time the Berbers stayed at the edge of the Sahara. They feared the extreme heat and lack of water. But in 642 Arabs came into the valley of the Nile. They brought with them camels and date palms. Berbers use camels to go into the desert and plant date palms on the oases. They use the dates for food for themselves and their camels.

Also in the Sahara live the Tuaregs (twä′regz′). Most Tuaregs are nomads. They move through the desert from one pasture to another with their herds of goats, sheep, or camels. Their homes are tents made of cloth woven from camel's hair or wool. In recent

These Berber children are near the village of mud houses where they live. Their village is in the High Atlas Mountains. Find these mountains on the map of Africa on page 223.

Desert dwellers in Libya wear white robes to reflect the light and heat of the desert. Their veils protect them from the sun and from blowing sand.

times some Tuaregs have begun to use trucks to move food and water to their herds, instead of moving their herds to water. Like the Berbers, Tuaregs are Muslims.

The West Africa Region

The term West Africa refers to the area that stretches from the Sahara on the north to the Gulf of Guinea on the south. It includes those modern nations that border the Atlantic Ocean, from Senegal in the north to Cameroon in the south. The inland nations of Burkina Faso, Mali (mä′lē), and Niger are also considered West African nations, at least in part. Find these nations on the political map of Africa, page 232.

The Farmers on the Savanna

Farming is possible on the savanna south of the Sahara. Nearly all of the people who live there raise crops. The main crops are cacao, coffee, cotton, palm oil, and peanuts.

Most people live in small villages. They farm community plots. Land is considered sacred and

Many of the Hausa in Nigeria are Muslims. They live in the northern part of the country. The largest city in that area is Kano. It is the religious center for Nigerian Muslims.

is seldom sold. Usually the men clear the land and prepare it for planting. Women then plant and tend the crops. The harvesting is done by everyone, young and old.

The People of Nigeria

Nigeria is the most heavily populated area of Africa. About 250 different groups of Nigerians speak over 400 languages and dialects. This makes the country hard to unite. To help unify the country the government has made English the official language. Most Nigerians speak English and one or more African languages.

The largest group in Nigeria is called the Hausa (hou′sə). About 12 million Hausa live in Nigeria. Most are Muslims and live in the northern part of the country. The largest city in the area is Kano (kän′ō). This ancient walled city is the religious center for Nigeria's Muslims. There are many beautiful mosques. The Kano market serves as a trading center for goods from Tuareg caravans coming south from the Sahara.

Ibadan, Nigeria, is one of central Africa's largest cities. Here, Yoruba women manage the market, following a tradition that is many generations old.

The Yoruba (yôr′ə bə) make up the next largest group of Nigerians. The Yoruba live in the southwest part of the country. The Yoruba have lived in cities for centuries. Ibadan (ē bä′ dän) is one of the largest completely non-European cities in Africa.

Trade and handicrafts are well developed among the Yoruba. Marketplaces are everywhere. Men do the hunting and the heavy farm work, and women run the marketplaces.

The Ibo make up the third largest group of Nigerians. Many are Christians. The Ibo are active in Nigeria's government and business.

As in most parts of Africa, the family unit is extremely important to Nigerians. Many Nigerian families live in small farming villages. They live in settlements called compounds. Members of an extended family live near one another in a group of huts which surround a central area. Cooking for the whole family is done in this area. Sometimes a single compound may be home for several hundred people.

The Central Africa Region

Central Africa begins at the southern edge of the Sahara and extends south to the Zambesi River. It includes the modern nations of the

The Zaire River is like a major highway. People living in villages along its banks depend on the river for food, water, and transportation. It is also an important river for traders.

Central African Republic, Congo, Gabon, Chad, and Zaire.

Much of Central Africa is covered by tropical rain forests. Here the people live in small farming villages. They grow root crops such as sweet potatoes, yams, and *manioc* (man′ē ok′). Manioc is a plant grown for its starchy roots, which are used for food. The roots are pounded into powder and cooked with water, then eaten with a fish or meat sauce.

The People of Zaire

The largest nation in the area is Zaire. Most of the nation lies in the giant river basin of the Zaire River (formerly called the Congo). About 17 million people belonging to about 200 different tribes make their home here. Nearly all speak at least one Bantu language. The official government language is French, but few people outside the cities speak it.

The Forest People

The Mbuti (em boo′ tē) live in the rain forests of eastern Zaire. The Mbuti are a small people. They never grow to be very tall. Because of this, Europeans called them Pygmies (pig′ mēz), which is a word meaning any small things or people.

The Mbuti live by hunting animals and gathering nuts and berries. During the course of the year, small groups of 3 or 4 families move from place to place in search of food. The men hunt with bows and arrows and with spears. They sometimes form larger groups of up to 20 families, and hunt game with nets. No one is the chief of the group. Everyone, both men and women, are free to have a say on where the group should go the next day.

The hunting groups are abandoned during the months of June and July. This is the honey season. Then everyone looks for a tree in which the bees have hidden the honey. It is a time of great merriment, with feasting, singing, and dancing.

The Mbuti live in simple huts made by sticking branches in a circle in the ground, bending them over, and tying them together in the center. The sticks are covered with leaves. When the group moves on the huts are abandoned.

In recent years forests have become smaller as farmers cleared land for planting. New roads restrict the movement of game. Some Mbuti have begun to leave the forests.

The Mbuti have always traded with nearby villages. Products of the forest, such as meat and nuts, are traded for bananas and rice of the villages.

Sometimes a group of Mbuti will settle down near one village for a time. They will enter into a kind of cooperative agreement with the village to exchange goods and services. The arrangement does not last for too long. The Mbuti usually return to the forest, which they love above all other places.

The East Africa Region

East Africa is made up of those countries in the central part of Africa that border on the Indian Ocean. They are Somalia, Kenya, and Tanzania. The region also includes the inland nations of Uganda, Burundi (bə run′dē), and Rwanda (ro͞o än′də). Just to the north are the nations of Ethiopia and Djibouti (jə boot′ē). Find these nations on the map of Africa on page 232.

The region of East Africa is among the most beautiful areas of Africa. This is the area of the Great Rift Valley, the volcanic region of deep blue lakes. Elephants, lions, zebra, and giraffes roam freely on the highlands and grasslands.

Most of the people who live in East Africa are descendants of early Africans. Most people who live in East Africa speak a Bantu or Hamitic language.

The Masai

One interesting East African tribal group is the Masai (mä sī′). They are a people who take fierce pride in their work as herders. Masai live mainly on a strip of elevated land that extends from Kenya south to Tanzania. The Masai live in mud-covered huts arranged in a circle. The cattle are penned inside the circle of huts.

The Masai consider their cattle symbols of wealth. Lions and leopards are common in the areas where the Masai live. The young men of the tribe band together to kill any animal that threatens the cattle. The young men are called "protectors of the cattle. "Before they can take on adult responsibilities in the tribe they must show their ability to hunt fierce animals. Only then are they allowed to marry.

When their livestock have eaten the grass, the Masai break camp and move on. When they find another pasture, they build another village.

The Kikuyu

The Kikuyu (ki kū′yoo) are the largest tribe of Kenya. They are mainly farmers. They feel as strongly about the land as Masai do about their cattle. The Kikuyu work the land in the cool highlands near Mount Kenya and the city of Nairobi (nī rō′bē). Their main crops are coffee, corn, wheat, and vegetables. These crops are sometimes sold at roadside markets.

Each member of a Kikuyu farming family has special chores. The workday begins at daybreak. Breakfast is usually cold porridge with leftovers from the night before. The men and women go to the fields to do the planting, weeding, and harvesting. Younger children gather firewood and bring water from the nearest waterhole. Older children help with herding and care for younger brothers and sisters. After sunset the family gathers for supper.

The Southern Africa Region

The region of Southern Africa covers the lower one-third of the continent. It stretches from the mouth of the Zaire River on the Atlantic Ocean across to the Indian Ocean and all the way south to the Cape of Good Hope. The region includes the modern nations of Angola (ang gō′lə), Zambia (zam′bē ə), Malawi (mə lä′wē), Zimbabwe, Mozambique, Namibia (nə mib′ē ə), Botswana (bot swä′ nə), Swaziland (swä′ zē land′), Lesotho (lə sō′tō), and the Republic of South Africa. It also includes the island country of Madagascar and some smaller islands. Find these countries on the political map of Africa, page 232.

One of the largest cities in the Republic of South Africa is Johannesburg. Its many tall buildings are similar in style to those of European and American cities.

In this region live the largest group of people with European origins. The world's largest gold and diamond mines are here, as well as many modern industries.

Here too is a barren desert and a people who live in it much the way their ancestors did hundreds of years before. We begin our exploration of this region at its southernmost point.

The Republic of South Africa

The 24 million people who live in the Republic of South Africa can be divided into four main groups. About three-fourths of the people are black Africans. Most belong to groups called the Zulu (zoo′loo) and the Hottentot.

The whites, who are mainly people of Dutch and English backgrounds, make up about one-fifth of the total. A smaller group, called the "colored," is of mixed background. The smallest group are Asians, who are mainly descendants of people who came to South Africa from India.

Apartheid

The people of European background hold the greatest power in South Africa. They control the government and have set up a policy of *apartheid* (ə pär′ tīd). This means segregating, or keeping apart, different races. Apartheid comes from an Afrikaans word meaning "apartness."

Black Africans who live in rural areas must live separately on reserves. They are not permitted to use land outside the reserves. Blacks who work in cities must live in special suburbs outside the cities. They cannot enter the city without a special pass.

Most people of European background live in the larger cities of Cape Town, Johannesburg (jō han′is burg′), and Pretoria (pri tôr′ē ə), and work in the offices of the large industries of the nation. Such industries manufacture steel, cars, and chemicals.

Black Africans often work in coal, gold, and diamond mines. About three-fourths of South Africa's young black males work in the mines.

There are rich farmlands to the north in an area called the Transvaal (trans väl′), which means "across the Vaal River." Here the European owners grow corn and raise livestock. On the coast, the Mediterranean climate permits warm-weather crops such as sugarcane, pineapples, and grapes.

The Kalahari Bushmen

To the east, in the Kalahari, live the Bushmen. The Bushmen have adapted well to life in this desert land. They are expert at hunting and at locating water. But now many are leaving the desert to work on the livestock ranches to the south and west.

Asians in Southern Africa

A small number of people of Asian descent also live in this region. Most live on the island of Madagascar off the east coast of Africa in the Indian Ocean.

Most people who live here are descendants of Malaysians and Indians who were brought in to work on the sugar plantations. Others came to build ports and railroads in South Africa. Now some own small businesses or work as skilled workers.

Do You Know?

1. What is the largest African language group?
2. Name the five major regions of Africa.
3. How did the political boundaries set up by the Europeans in Africa differ from the original divisions established by the tribes?
4. Under the apartheid system, what are the four classes of people in the Republic of South Africa?
5. Why do farmers on the savanna south of the Sahara rarely sell their land?

Before You Go On

Words to Learn

veldt	baobab	hydroelectricity
Sahel	dialect	endangered species
manioc	apartheid	oral tradition
acacia	reserve	dromedary
clan	savanna	alloy

Number a paper from 1 through 15. After each number write the word or term that matches the definition.

1. A camel with one hump
2. A group of families who claim descent from the same ancestor
3. A metal formed by combining two or more metals
4. Energy produced by water
5. A broad, grassy plain
6. A policy in South Africa of segregating or keeping apart different races
7. Semiarid grassland bordering the desert
8. History and literature spoken rather than written and passed down from person to person
9. An umbrella-shaped tree that is a source of gum arabic
10. In South Africa and Zimbabwe, an open grassland with scattered bushes and trees
11. Something set aside for a special purpose, such as land
12. An African tree with a thick trunk that stores water and a gourdlike fruit used for food
13. Types of animals and plants that are in danger of dying out
14. A form of a language spoken by a particular group of people
15. A plant grown for its starchy roots, which are used for food

Finding the Facts

1. Most of the land in Africa is of what type?
2. Name four important rivers of Africa.
3. What is Afrikaans?
4. What land regions lie on either side of the northern Sahel?
5. What is the Great Rift Valley? Where is it located?
6. What does a griot do?
7. What is a talking drum?
8. Name three events that might be celebrated by dancing.
9. What two things brought by the Arabs made it possible for the Berbers to move farther into the desert?
10. Why is Kano's location important?
11. Describe the housing of the Mbuti.
12. What do the Masai young men do before they can be considered adults?
13. Name four main crops grown by the Kikuyu.
14. What is the Transvaal?
15. What are compounds in Nigeria? How are they set up?

3

Age of Empires

The histories of Africa's people are among the longest of any people in the world. They are also among the most varied. Some ancient African nations owe their origin to the discovery of gold. The gold was traded for other goods which brought wealth and prosperity. The wealth brought these kingdoms fame that spread across Europe and Asia.

Other African nations developed as a result of movements of peoples into Africa from nearby lands. The Arabs, especially, influenced the history of the peoples in the northern part of Africa.

Some of these nations disappeared after a short period of time. Others survived for many centuries and exist today in a different form.

Africa's early history comes to us from stories and legends passed down from person to person. In addition to this oral tradition, we have the reports of visitors and explorers, especially Arabs and Portuguese. Monuments and art left behind provide still more information about the early kingdoms of Africa.

Ethiopia, an Ancient Christian Kingdom

The modern nation of Ethiopia has roots that go back more than 2,000 years. In about 600 B.C., there were a number of settlements on the southwest coast of Arabia. Look at the map of Africa on page 232 to see how close this part of Arabia is to Africa. The Arabs and Jews who lived on the southwest coast of Arabia were trading peoples. They came into contact with other traders from Phoenicia, Greece, Africa, and India. They built up a trade of incense and spices.

As the Arabian settlements grew, the Arab traders sailed the short distance to the African coast to look for more land to settle. There they met an African people called the Cushites (koosh′ītz). These people were also traders, who met travelers from the Far East and from the north.

The Kingdom of Axum

The Arabs and Cushites mixed easily and began to form an empire based on trade. By A.D. 300 they had formed a kingdom called Axum (äk soom′). About this time Christianity became the official religion of the Roman Empire. The Empire influenced the king of Axum to convert to Christianity in 330. This made Axum one of the world's first Christian nations.

As Axum's trade of spices and incense increased, its people began pushing farther inland. There the people began farming the rich lands of the highlands. Axum's wealth enabled the king to raid and bring down the once powerful empires to the north.

Beginning in 642 the Arabs, who were Muslims, began their conquest of North Africa. Though they easily conquered Egypt, they left Axum alone. The king was friendly with the Arabs and they agreed to leave Axum in peace.

But this arrangement did not last. Axum lost power and territory as the Muslims expanded their empire along the Red Sea.

The Arabs soon controlled all trading on the African coast. As their own wealth from trade fell off, the people of Axum pushed farther and farther into the interior. Here they conquered many black African peoples. The Arab influences mixed with black African cultures. From this beginning the modern state of Ethiopia developed. Although about one-third of the Ethiopians became Muslims, most remained Christians.

Lalibela's Rock-Cut Churches

One famous king of Ethiopia was Lalibela (lä′lē bā′lä). In 1150 he ordered churches built to unite the Ethiopian people. These were not ordinary buildings. They were carved out of the solid volcanic rock of the mountains near Roha. Ten chapels and churches were carved directly out of the rock. The styles used in building the churches came from Rome, Greece, and Africa. King Lalibela's wish to be remembered in future centuries came true. Today these remarkable churches remain and King Lalibela is considered a saint by Ethiopia's Christian Church.

Kingdoms of West Africa

Arab explorers provided information to the rest of the world about the early kingdoms of Africa. When the Arabs made their first trips across the Sahara to West Africa, they found several black African kingdoms. Three of the most powerful were Ghana, Mali, and Songhai (sawng′hī).

The Church of St. George is one of ten such churches carved from volcanic rock in Lalibela, Ethiopia. This church was made more than 800 years ago.

Ancient Ghana

The ancient kingdom of Ghana has no connection with the modern nation of Ghana on the Atlantic Ocean. Look at the map of West African Kingdoms on page 244. Ancient Ghana was an inland nation, north of the Senegal and Niger rivers.

Ghana expanded in size. As it did, its resources and opportunities for trade also grew. The years between 800 and 1000 were peak years for Ghana. The kingdom exported gold, ivory, and honey north across the Sahara and received salt and other products in return. Salt was rare south of the Sahara, and an important item of trade.

The trade in gold and salt made the kings of Ghana very wealthy. One Arab writer described the ruler of Ghana as wearing beautiful clothes made of fine silks and a cap of gold. When this king appeared in public he was accompanied by

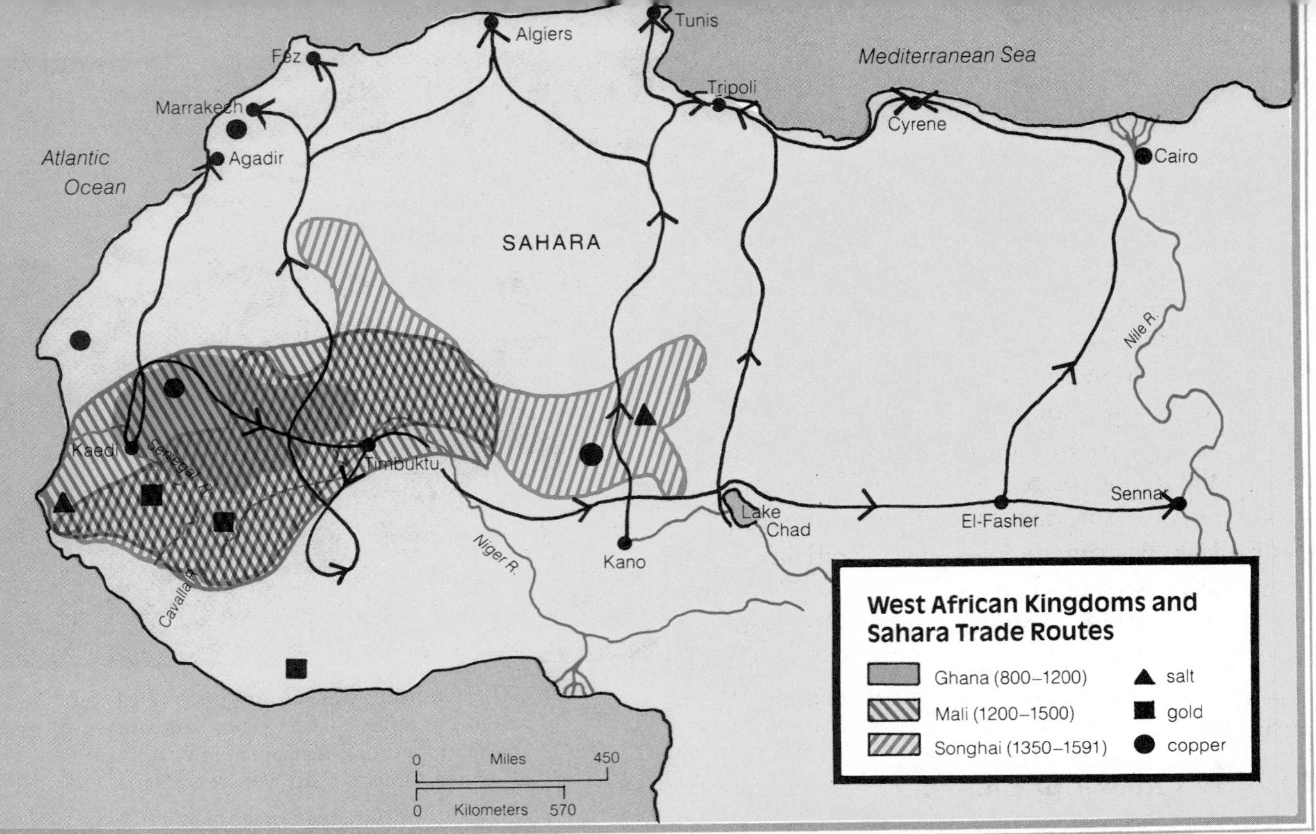

The kingdoms of Ghana, Mali, and Songhai flourished during different periods of time in West Africa. Some of their major trade routes are shown on this map.

servants who carried gold swords. He gave banquets at which thousands of guests were fed at one time. When the king sat in court, he was surrounded by watchdogs, armed guards, town ministers, and sons of neighboring kings.

These neighboring kingdoms were called *vassal* (vas′əl) states. A vassal is a person or state that owes allegiance to another.

A Muslim group called the Almoravids (al′mə rä′vidz) lived northwest of Ghana. The Almoravids were very religious. They wished to spread their Muslim faith throughout the empire. They invaded the capital of Ghana in about 1076 and controlled it for 20 years. About this time many West African kingdoms became Muslim.

The people of Ghana recovered their capital, but it was too late. The empire was not united. The vassal states no longer obeyed the weak Ghana government. Merchants began to move away. Trade slowed down. Finally Ghana was conquered by a vassal state and a new West African empire began.

The Kingdom of Mali

Northeast of Ghana was the ancient kingdom of Mali. Mali came to power under the leadership of King Sundiata (soon′dē ä′tə). His armies defeated the last king of Ghana in 1235. Sundiata extended Mali's territories and developed a rich trade across the Sahara in salt, gold, copper, and food products.

This map of West Africa, drawn in 1375, uses stone walls to represent the Atlas Mountains. The king crowned in gold and holding a gold nugget is Mansa Musa, known as the richest king in Africa at the time.

The Splendor of Mansa Musa

The years between 1307 and 1332 were rich years for Mali. Sundiata's grandson, Mansa Musa (män′sə mü′sə), was now king. He was very religious. Like most Muslims, Mansa Musa wished to visit the holy shrine of Mecca in Arabia before he died. He made a pilgrimage there in 1324. His caravan included 500 slaves, each carrying gold staffs and 100 pounds (45 kg) of gold. On the way, Mansa Musa stopped in Cairo. While there the generous king gave away so much gold that the value of gold dropped in Cairo.

News of such splendor and generosity spread quickly throughout the Middle East and Europe. Mali and its king became famous.

In Mecca Mansa Musa met a well-known poet and architect, as-Saheli (as sa hē′lē). As-Saheli agreed to return to Mali with the king. In Mali he designed and built Arabian-style buildings.

A mosque constructed of sun-baked mud soars above the streets of a Mali town. Like many structures in this area, the mosque resembles a giant piece of pottery.

He is said to be the first architect to use fired red brick in that part of Africa.

Mali's period of success ended after Mansa Musa's death in 1332. Poor leadership and the rival Songhai people weakened Mali. In 1468 Mali met defeat. In a famous battle the Songhai leader Sonni Ali (son′ē ä lē′) captured the Mali city of Timbuktu (tim′buk too′).

The Songhai Empire

Sonni Ali's capture of Timbuktu marked the beginning of the Songhai Empire. But Sonni Ali did not have the respect of his people. The taxes he made them pay were not fair. Not until his successor, Askia Mohammad (äs kē′yə mō ham′id), took over in 1493 did Songhai begin to flourish.

Askia Mohammad made many changes in the government. He imposed fairer taxes. And he set up a better system of communication with all parts of the kingdom. Then he travelled to Mecca. There he took the advice of Muslim scholars, ministers, and government workers.

When he returned to Songhai, Askia Mohammad put their ideas into practice. But he paid attention to the advice of his own chiefs as well as to the outsiders. This made him a highly respected leader.

Timbuktu, the major city in Songhai, became a center of learning and trade. Its library and university were famous all over Europe and the Middle East. Many people were envious of this fame. When in 1591 Muslims from North Africa captured Timbuktu, they destroyed the library. Gradually the empire at Songhai lost its importance. There is still a city in Africa called Timbuktu. But it is only a shadow of that once great city ruled by Askia Mohammad.

Zimbabwe, a Southern Kingdom

Few large kingdoms grew up in Southern Africa. Zimbabwe was an exception.

The ruins of Zimbabwe lay hidden until about 100 years ago. Then, in 1868, a European hunter came upon an amazing sight. Spread out over a 60-acre (24 ha) site not far from Harare were the ruins of many granite buildings. Surrounding these ruins was a great wall measuring some 10 feet (3 m) thick and 30 feet (9 m) high. The buildings and wall had been built without mortar. Instead, the rectangular granite stones had been carved to fit exactly next to one another. Who had built this great monument?

It is now believed that the ironworkers of Zimbabwe were a Bantu-speaking people who moved into the area. They were farmers, but they also knew iron. From this metal they made tools and weapons. They discovered the rich gold deposits in the area and began mining it. They carried the precious metal the short distance to the Indian Ocean coast where they traded it for other products. Traders from Arabia, China, Persia, and India came to the coastal cities to bargain for gold and ivory in exchange for fine textiles, porcelains, and other products.

By the fifteenth century the Zimbabwe empire was very wealthy. It was ruled by a king who was considered sacred by his people. They believed that the welfare of the kingdom depended on the health of the king. If he were to fall ill, the empire would be in danger. One of the large stone buildings at Zimbabwe may have been the king's palace. It may also have been a place of worship.

Portuguese traders came to know about Zimbabwe in the 1500s when they began to land on the east coast of Africa. Like the Arabs in the north, the Portuguese soon began to control trading on the coast. This upset the old trading patterns of the Zimbabwe and other African peoples. By the 1600s the Portuguese controlled nearly all trade, which speeded up the decline of Zimbabwe.

The Zimbabwe empire survived in a weakened state into the 1830s. Then it was attacked by the Zulu, who were looking for new land to settle on. The Zulu had been pushed north from their homes in South Africa by English and Dutch settlers. Today the Zimbabwe ruins are all that remain of a once great empire.

Do You Know?

1. How do we know about the early history of Africa?
2. Name three ancient kingdoms of West Africa.
3. What goods did the Kingdom of Ghana export across the Sahara? What did it receive back in trade?
4. How did the Portuguese help bring about the decline of Zimbabwe?

4
The Age of European Colonization

The Portuguese were the first Europeans to come to Africa. About 1500 they began to set up bases on the west coast. They needed stopping places for their ships on their way around the Cape of Good Hope to Asia. The Portuguese gradually gained control of Angola on the Atlantic Ocean and Mozambique on the Indian Ocean.

Spain, England, and Holland also began setting up bases for their ships. Few Europeans ventured inland beyond the coast.

At about that same time explorers from Portugal and Spain traveled to the West Indies and South America. There they set up sugar plantations. The working conditions were harsh and many workers died. In order to replace them, both countries began to import slaves from Africa's west coast. As other countries established plantations in the Western Hemisphere, the market for slaves increased.

This engraving of a slave auction shows a common scene in the age of European colonization. Between 1500 and 1800, more than 9 million Africans were sold as slaves.

The Slave Trade

In the early sixteenth century slavery was quite common. People of all races had been sold into slavery dating back to ancient times. Prisoners taken in war often became slaves. The selling of slaves was a profitable business.

From 1500 to 1800 more than 9 million Africans left their homelands as slaves. They were put aboard filthy, crowded ships for the hard journey to the Americas. Black African kingdoms such as Benin (be nin′) and Ashanti (ə shant′ē) controlled slave trade in their territories. They raided rival villages. Then they sold their captives to the European traders. The kingdoms grew rich. Elsewhere European slave traders captured Africans to sell at market.

Denmark was the first country to ban slavery. It passed a law against slavery in 1804. Soon other countries followed and the slave trade fell off. In 1808 Great Britain set up a colony called Sierra Leone (sē er′ə lē ō′nē) on the west coast of Africa. There it sent freed slaves from the slave ships of many nations. In 1821 a group of Americans opposing slavery bought land on the west coast from African chiefs. Freed slaves from the United States settled here. This land became the modern nation of Liberia.

The Lure of Africa

Some Europeans had a scientific interest in Africa. Explorers from France, Germany, and Great Britain began to journey through the interior of Africa. David Livingstone, a missionary from Scotland, traveled across Africa in the 1850s. His journey was widely reported in the newspapers. People in Great Britain became excited about the unusual sights he described. Africa seemed a wonderful, mysterious place. People from Europe decided to go to Africa for several reasons.

David Livingstone, a missionary from Scotland, traveled through Africa in the 1850s. This engraving shows him reading the Bible to some African men.

Missionaries

Missionaries wanted to teach the African people the Christian religion. The missionaries thought that by becoming Christians the Africans would become more like themselves. Missionaries began to arrive in Africa soon after hearing news of the explorers.

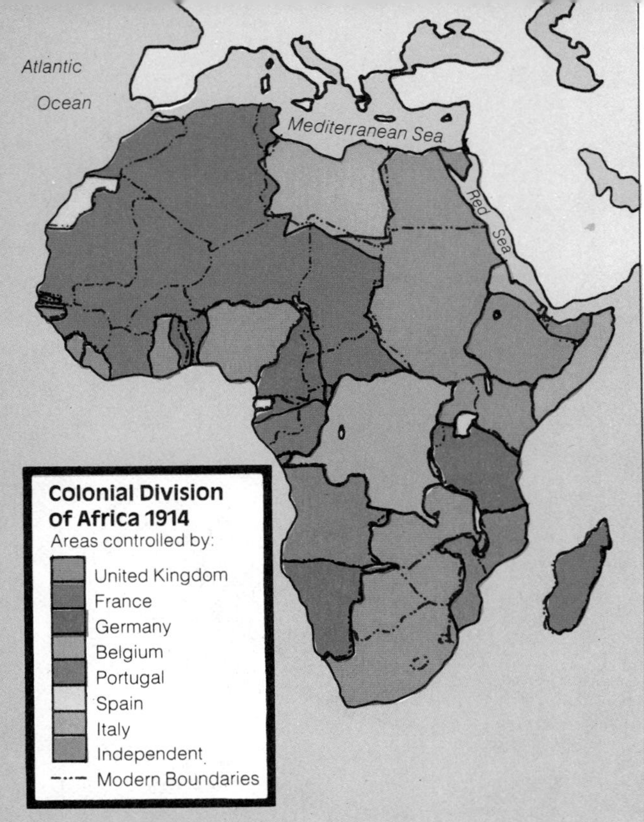

Africa had only two independent countries in 1914, Ethiopia and Liberia. Find these countries on the map. Which two European nations controlled the most area?

A Rush for Colonies

In the nineteenth century Europe grew richer. New industries sprang up. Governments had more money to spend. Europeans felt a sense of pride and a new spirit of adventure. They also needed raw materials for their factories and new markets for the products of the factories. Africa looked like a good place to set up colonies.

First to be colonized were the northern and southern parts of Africa. In the north, France moved into Algeria, Morocco, and Tunisia. In the south the Dutch had already set up a colony at Cape Town in 1798. Later, English settlers pushed the Dutch into the interior. There the Dutch fought with the Zulu people. The Zulu fought bravely. But their spears were no match against modern rifles and machine guns.

Every European power seemed to want a foothold in Africa. Italy took Libya. Germany and Great Britain divided up East Africa. France took over the island of Madagascar. Belgium controlled the lands of the Zaire River Basin (then called the Congo).

By 1914, nearly all of Africa was held by European powers. Whatever could not be taken by force was taken by trickery. Traders fooled African chiefs into signing away their lands. The only countries left free were Liberia and Ethiopia. The rest of Africa was carved up among world powers with little thought given to boundaries of tribes. Sometimes Europeans set boundaries that included rival tribes. Sometimes the boundaries separated members of the same tribe or ethnic group. This has caused trouble for many years and in some parts of Africa continues to be a problem today.

Do You Know?

1. What conditions beyond Africa led to an increase in the slave trade?
2. What was the first country to oppose slavery? When?
3. By 1914, how many countries in Africa were self-governing? Which countries were they?
4. Why was there a "rush for colonies" in Africa in the nineteenth century?

5
Independent Africa

The move to independence among African nations began after World War I. When the war began in 1914, nearly every African country was held by a European power. By 1977 nearly every nation was independent. Although each nation's history of independence is different, there are some common reasons for independence.

After Two World Wars

When Germany lost World War I, other European nations—Great Britain, Belgium, and France—took over its colonies. But there was a difference in the way they were run.

These nations agreed that African colonies would not remain colonies forever. They recognized that it was the duty of the colonizers to put the African nations on their own feet. Some African leaders took this to mean that their nations would soon be free.

During World War II, Africans fought along with Allied troops. They played a part in defeating the German troops in North Africa. When the Africans returned home, they felt their own lands should be as free as those they had fought to make free.

The wars had affected the colonial powers as well. Many people in those countries now favored self-rule for the colonies. Besides, the two wars had weakened the European countries. They could no longer afford the cost of ruling colonies.

The Demand for Freedom

During the colonial period, some Africans left their lands to study in foreign universities. There they met other black students from the United States and the West Indies. They exchanged ideas and returned to Africa with strong feelings about independence. One such native leader was Kwame Nkrumah (kwäm′ē en kroo′mə).

Ghana Leads the Way

At the end of World War II, the nation we now know as Ghana was called the Gold Coast. Talk of freedom had already caused the British to think about granting the nation independence. But Kwame Nkrumah thought it would take too long. He led many strikes and was thrown in jail. This made him a hero among his people and among Africans all across the continent. The people of the Gold Coast demanded full independence, which the British granted in 1957. The nation then renamed itself after the earlier West African kingdom of Ghana.

Nigeria Gains Independence

Ghana's success led to independence for Nigeria. In 1960 Great Britain granted Nigeria its independence. The situation there was much more difficult, however. Nigeria is a very large nation that includes many different tribal groups. Uniting the nation proved to be difficult because some tribes could not agree on who should run the government. One group,

In Kenya, many Masai still live a nomadic life. But Western ways prevail in Nairobi, the capital city of Kenya, where more than a half million people live.

composed mainly of Ibo, wanted to split off from the rest of Nigeria and form their own nation called Biafra (bē äf′ rə). A civil war resulted which brought much suffering before the rebels were defeated in 1970.

Kenya Fights for Freedom

Independence did not come easily to some colonies. Kenya was also a British colony. After World War II the population grew rapidly. The richest farmlands were owned by British settlers, while black Kenyans did not have enough to eat. Members of the Kikuyu tribe took the lead in forming a secret society, called Mau Mau (mow′mow′), that attacked the British settlers. The Mau Mau rebellion was finally put down by the British in 1959. But it convinced the British that Kenya should be made free. The leader of the Mau Mau movement, Jomo Kenyatta (jō′mō ken yät′ tə), became Kenya's first president after independence was declared in 1963.

North Africa Gains Freedom

After the war, France decided to give its colony Algeria some rights but not full freedom. France offered the people of Algeria representation in the French government. The Algerian people felt this was not enough. The best jobs in their own country seemed to be held by the French. Many Algerians left their nation to go to France to look for work. But they could not find good jobs there either.

Frustrations began to build. A group called the National Liberation Front fought the French army in Algeria for almost 8 years. In 1962 the French finally gave Algeria its independence.

Other countries in the area, Tunisia and Morocco, had also demanded independence for themselves. The French had agreed. Tunisia and Morocco became independent countries in 1956.

In similar ways other nations of Africa gained their independence. The success of one nation seemed to spark success in another.

The New Nation of Zimbabwe

For years a small European minority controlled the government of Rhodesia (rō dē′zhə). This was so even though only 3 out of every 100 residents were European. The black population pressed heavily for change. In 1979 a law was passed which gave the black population an equal vote. Soon afterward a black government took over. The country was renamed Zimbabwe, after the ancient kingdom, in 1980.

With the change of government in Zimbabwe, in the 1980s only two African nations remained with minority white governments. They were South Africa and Namibia.

Africa Today

Africa is made up of many different countries. The countries of Africa are changing. They are changing from traditional ways of living to modern ways. Countries that are changing in this way are called developing countries. As you know, the countries of Africa were under the control of modern nations for a long time. This caused problems that still remain.

Economic Problems

In the past, the British and French often changed the traditional governments in Africa. They put in place their own forms of government. But Africans remained loyal to their tribes and ethnic groups. Africans held fast to their local government and traditional chiefs. They were not used to thinking of themselves as part of a unified country.

As African nations became independent, many people joined the national governments. Government jobs seem to offer security. But few people are being trained for technical jobs. New universities have been developed, but education for elementary and high school students has been neglected. Books often teach young people about France and Great Britain, but not how to live in their own countries.

Many of Africa's natural resources are not in great demand in the rest of the world. For example, peanut oil is not as popular in America as corn oil and sunflower oil. African countries also need products they do not have, such as iron and steel. These products are needed for development. They are very expensive and must be imported.

The movement of people to cities is another economic problem. Cities have become crowded. There is not enough food to feed everyone. Famines occurred in the 1970s throughout much of Africa.

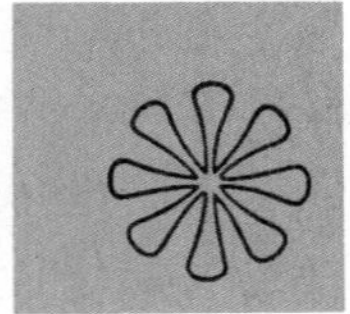

Dakar
Contrast of Culture

Much in Dakar, the capital of Senegal, might remind you of London or Paris. Planes bring passengers from every part of the world. European-made automobiles, driven mainly by Africans, jam the city's avenues. African men and women, some dressed in colorful hand-printed textiles and flowing robes and others wearing the latest European fashions, can be seen entering the modern hotels and government offices. Many of the people speak French.

At the same time there is a side to Dakar that is distinctly African. Many people live in family compounds alongside the modern buildings. These families spend much of their time outdoors—cooking, tending sheep, and conducting business with their neighbors. Dakar has large open markets where the women and men sell fresh food, clothes, and spices. They often bargain over the price of each item.

There is a tall mosque against the skyline, built with the help of Muslims from Morocco. Large storage bins of peanuts can be seen from a distance, and the smell of peanuts being roasted is everywhere. Alongside the Africans are merchants from Mauritania and Lebanon who tend small grocery stores and textile shops. The French government continues to send advisors to help with the development of Senegal. Dakar is a city of contrasts and of cultures. ■

Africans are working together to improve their country. A Nigerian student learns the fine points of surveying on a construction site in Ibadan, one of the nation's major cities.

Often there are few jobs in the cities. Women in rural areas have important roles in village life. They grow crops, manage family money, and raise children. They may get some cash from selling food and cloth. But an African woman who moves to the city leaves the fields and many of her responsibilities. Because she does not have an education or skills, she often cannot find work.

These economic problems may be solved. Mineral resources are being used up by the rest of the world. The minerals that remain in Africa will become more valuable. As the wealth of African nations grows, their governments will be able to improve living conditions. New irrigation projects have already begun. Africans will be able to grow more food. Countries with strong leadership and important resources, such as oil and copper, may be able to become modern and stable.

African Nations Work Together

The African nations have come to recognize their importance in the world. They realize they must work together. In 1963 representatives from 30 African nations met in Addis Ababa (ad′is ab′ə ba), the capital of Ethiopia. They set up the Organization of African Unity. Every year its leaders meet to talk over common problems, such as trade relations and ways to keep peace.

The key to Africa's future is its people. They have lived through periods of slavery and domination by other nations. Yet throughout their long and sometimes sorrowful history, the Africans' own strong cultures have endured.

Do You Know?

1. What happened to Germany's colonies in Africa after World War I?
2. Who was the leader of the modern nation of Ghana's struggle for independence?
3. What caused the civil war in Nigeria? How and when was it settled?
4. What is the Organization of African Unity?
5. What are three economic problems of modern Africa?

Nations of Africa

Country	Capital	Independence Gained (from)		Area (sq.km)	Area (sq.mi.)	Population
North Africa						
Algeria	Algiers	1962	(France)	2,381,741	919,595	20,250,000
Egypt	Cairo	1922	(Gt. Brit.)	1,001,450	386,661	43,000,000
Libya	Tripoli	1951	(Italy)	1,759,540	679,362	3,100,000
Morocco	Rabat	1956	(France; Spain)	445,050	171,835	20,500,000
Sudan	Khartoum	1956	(Gt. Brit.; Egypt)	2,505,813	967,500	18,750,000
Tunisia	Tunis	1956	(France)	163,610	63,170	6,500,000
West Africa						
Benin	Porto-Novo	1960	(France)	112,622	43,484	3,675,000
Burkina Faso	Ouagadougou	1960	(France)	274,200	105,869	7,100,000
Cameroon	Yaoundé	1960	(Gt. Brit.; France)	475,442	183,569	8,650,000
Cape Verde	Praia	1975	(Port.)	4,033	1,557	352,000
Equatorial Guinea	Malabo	1968	(Spain)	28,051	10,831	370,000
Gambia	Banjul	1965	(Gt. Brit.)	11,295	4,361	625,000
Ghana	Accra	1957	(Gt. Brit.)	328,540	92,100	11,750,000
Guinea	Conakry	1958	(France)	245,857	94,926	5,115,000
Guinea-Bissau	Bissau	1974	(Port.)	36,125	13,948	580,000
Ivory Coast	Abidjan	1960	(France)	322,463	124,503	8,500,000
Liberia	Monrovia	1847		111,369	43,000	1,920,000
Mali	Bamako	1960	(France)	1,240,000	479,000	7,100,000
Mauritania	Nouakchott	1960	(France)	1,030,700	397,955	1,675,000
Niger	Niamey	1960	(France)	1,267,000	489,200	5,550,000
Nigeria	Lagos	1960	(Gt. Brit.)	923,768	356,699	79,575,000
São Tomé and Príncipe	São Tomé	1975	(Port.)	964	372	87,000
Senegal	Dakar	1960	(France)	196,192	75,750	5,800,000
Sierra Leone	Freetown	1961	(Gt. Brit.)	71,740	27,699	3,560,000
Togo	Lomé	1960	(France)	56,000	21,600	2,600,000
East Africa						
Burundi	Bujumbura	1962	(Belgium)	27,834	10,747	4,650,000
Djibouti	Djibouti	1977	(France)	22,000	8,500	330,000
Ethiopia	Addis Ababa			1,221,900	471,778	32,000,000
Kenya	Nairobi	1963	(Gt. Brit.)	582,645	224,960	16,300,000
Rwanda	Kigali	1962	(Belgium)	26,338	10,169	5,200,000
Somalia	Mogadishu	1960	(Italy; Gt. Brit.)	637,657	246,155	3,750,000
Tanzania	Dar es Salaam	1961; 1963	(Gt. Brit.)	945,100	364,900	19,000,000
Uganda	Kampala	1962	(Gt. Brit.)	236,036	91,134	14,000,000
Central Africa						
Central African Republic	Bangui	1960	(France)	622,980	240,535	2,500,000
Chad	N'Djamena	1960	(France)	1,284,000	495,800	4,650,000
Congo	Brazzaville	1960	(France)	342,000	132,000	1,580,000
Gabon	Libreville	1960	(France)	267,667	103,347	550,000
Zaire	Kinshasa	1960	(Belgium)	2,345,409	905,567	29,450,000
Southern Africa						
Angola	Luanda	1975	(Port.)	1,246,700	481,350	7,250,000
Botswana	Gaborone	1966	(Gt. Brit.)	600,372	231,805	750,000
Comoros	Moroni	1975	(France)	2,171	838	399,000
Lesotho	Maseru	1966	(Gt. Brit.)	30,355	11,720	1,375,000
Madagascar	Antananarivo	1960	(France)	587,041	226,658	9,000,000
Malawi	Lilongwe	1964	(Gt. Brit.)	118,484	45,747	6,125,000
Mauritius	Port Louis	1968	(Gt. Brit.)	2,046	790	975,000
Mozambique	Maputo	1975	(Port.)	783,030	302,330	10,750,000
Namibia	Windhoek		(S. Afr.)	823,168	317,827	1,000,000
Seychelles	Victoria	1976	(Gt. Brit.)	375	145	68,000
South Africa	Cape Town; Pretoria; Bloemfontein;	1931	(Gt. Brit.)	1,223,404	472,359	28,280,000
Swaziland	Mbabane	1968	(Gt. Brit.)	17,363	6,704	550,000
Zambia	Lusaka	1964	(Gt. Brit.)	752,614	290,586	6,000,000
Zimbabwe	Harare	1980	(Gt. Brit.)	390,620	150,819	7,580,000

To Help You Learn

Words to Learn

vassal	oral tradition
dialect	apartheid
savanna	reserve

Number a paper from 1 through 6. After each number write the word or term that matches the definition.

1. A form of a language spoken by a particular group of people
2. A policy in South Africa of segregating or keeping apart different races
3. A broad, grassy plain
4. History and literature spoken rather than written and passed down from person to person
5. Something set aside for a special purpose, such as land
6. A person or state that owes allegiance to another

Finding the Facts

1. In what temperature zone does most of Africa lie?
2. What is the source of the Nile?
3. How much of Africa does the Sahara cover?
4. Describe the environment in a tropical rain forest.
5. What is Africa's tallest mountain?
6. Name three important mineral resources in Africa.
7. What areas in Africa have the greatest shortage of water? What area has the most water resources?
8. What mineral do monazite sands contain? What is it used for?
9. Name three countries that have established animal reserves.
10. About how many people live in Africa? What is the ancestry of the majority of these people?
11. What is unusual about the language of the Bushmen and Hottentots?
12. Which are Africa's fastest-growing cities?
13. What kind of housing is used by people who live in desert oases? By desert nomads?
14. How do the Mbuti make their living?
15. List the nations in which each of the following people live: Hausa; Kikuyu; Mbuti; Zulu; Ibo; Yoruba; Masai; Hottentot.
16. How do most of the young black men in South Africa make a living?
17. What two peoples merged to form the kingdom of Axum?
18. When did Axum (Ethiopia) become a Christian nation? Why did this change take place?
19. Who was Lalibela? What was his greatest achievement?
20. What group seized control of Ghana in 1076? Why?

21. What king of Mali defeated the last king of the Ghana empire?
22. When did Mansa Musa reign in Mali?
23. Why did Mansa Musa's visit to Cairo cause such excitement there?
24. Whom did Mansa Musa bring back with him from his visit to Mecca?
25. Why was Askia Mohammad a respected leader?
26. What was Timbuktu? Why was it famous?
27. What was remarkable about the stonework of Zimbabwe?
28. How did Zimbabwe become rich?
29. What two countries in Africa were established for freed slaves?
30. Who was David Livingstone? When did he travel in Africa?
31. Who was the first president of independent Kenya?
32. How long did the Algerians fight with France before they were granted independence?
33. Why is Dakar called a city of contrasts?
34. Why do Africans have problems finding work when they come to live in the cities?

Learning from Maps

1. Turn to the map of Africa on page 223. Between what parallels of latitude does the continent lie? Through what part of the continent does the equator pass? How much of the continent lies in the tropics, or low latitudes? How much lies in the middle latitudes? What does this tell you about the climate of Africa?
2. Look at the World Population map on page 26. What parts of Africa have less than 25 people per square mile? More than 250?
3. Look at the World Rainfall map on page 26. What parts of Africa have the most rainfall? The least rainfall?
4. Look at the map of West African Kingdoms and Sahara Trade Routes on page 244. Which was the largest of the three kingdoms? Which kingdoms reached to the Atlantic coast? Through what city passed most of the major trade routes?

Using Study Skills

1. **Time Line:** Place the following events in the proper order of time: Mali defeats Ghana; Axum Kingdom converts to Christianity; Askia Mohammad becomes Songhai leader; Slave trade begins; Muslims begin conquest of North Africa; British set up Sierra Leone colony for freed slaves; Ghana kingdom begins peak years; Americans set up Liberia for freed slaves.

   Copy the time line from page 221. Add these events to your time line.

   Study the completed time line and answer the following questions: Which religion, Christianity or Islam (Muslims), was the first to convert an African nation? By how many years? How long was ancient Ghana an important kingdom? How long was Mali?

   How many years did the African slave trade continue before Denmark took anti-slavery action? How many years later did the British set up Sierra Leone? A group of Americans set up Liberia?

How many years did it take after most of Africa was colonized for most of Africa to form independent nations?

2. **Graph:** Look at the graph of Africans taken away in the slave trade on this page. Now answer the following questions: What period of time is covered in the graph? What two population groups are shown? During which period of time were most slaves taken? During the period 1701–1810, about what percentage of the total were West Africans? For the entire period, about what percentage? What was the total number of Africans taken for the entire period?

Thinking It Through

1. Here are some African proverbs. What does each tell you about family life in Africa?

"A child who asks questions does not become a fool."

"A child breaks a snail's shell but does not break a tortoise's shell."

"It is a child who has never traveled away from home who says that only her mother can prepare tasty meals."

"The world is like the skin of a chameleon; it changes fast."

"The tongue never gets used to the sharpness of pepper."

2. Good housing must be made of materials easily available. It must be suited to the life of the people who live in it. And it must look right in its surroundings.

With this in mind, how would you rate the mud-brick houses of the Berbers, the tents of the Tuareg, the stick-and-grass huts of the Mbuti? Explain your answers.

3. The apartheid system in South Africa has been compared to the caste system in India. How do you think they are the same? How do you think they are different?

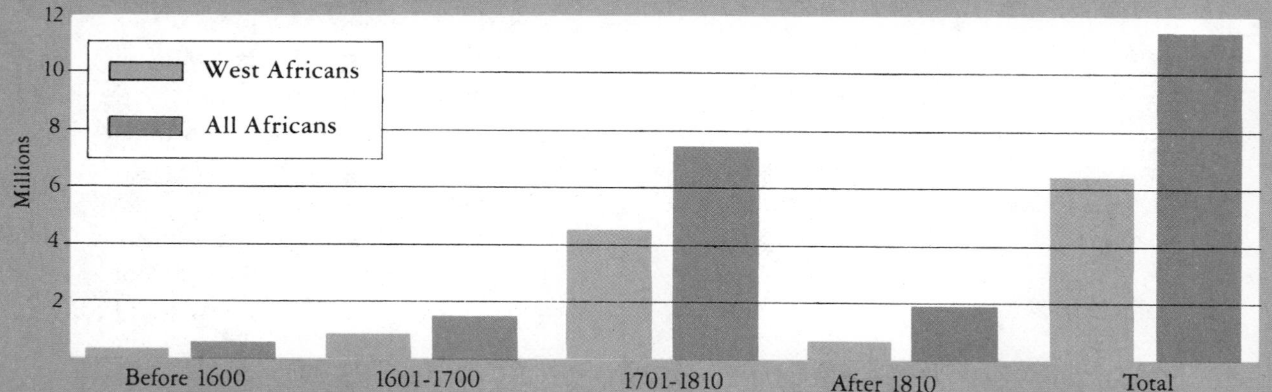

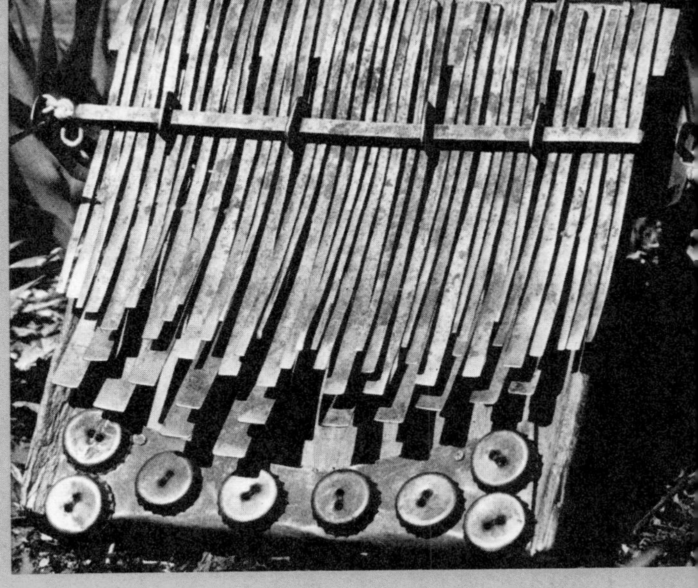

4. Improved medicines have saved the lives of both herders and their cattle in East Africa. Their population has increased, and the herders want more grazing land for their animals. Some of this land is used by elephants and other large animals. What should the government do in this conflict?

Projects

1. Until recently people went on an African safari (sə fär′ē), which is a kind of trip, to hunt wild animals. Now most people understand the need to protect the wild animals of Africa. Instead they go on photo safaris.

   Take your own African safari. Your trophies will be pictures of the animals of Africa you can find. Write a label for each picture giving the name of the animal and the kind of land area it lives in.
2. The mbira (em bē′rə) is an African musical instrument. It is also called a thumbpiano. Look at the photo on this page. The mbira is held in both hands and played by striking the reeds or thick metal strips with the thumbs.

   Ask your librarian to help you find recordings of African mbira music. If you can, find an mbira and show the class how it is played.
3. The Explorers' Committee might like to read more about the journey across Africa of Sir Henry Morton Stanley to look for David Livingstone. Trace both their journeys on a map.
4. You may have seen the television film "Roots." In the film the hero learned about his family's origin from a griot. Imagine that you are a griot. Learn from your parents the name of their parents and their grandparents and an event that happened to each. Memorize it.
5. The Research Committee might like to learn more about one of the following: the discovery of the source of the Nile river, the Zulu wars, or the life of the Kalahari Bushmen.
6. The Reading Committee will enjoy the stories and pictures in *Tales Told Near a Crocodile: Stories from Nyanza,* by Humphrey Harman. Nyanza is the African name for Lake Victoria. There are 10 stories in the book. Perhaps students could choose selections to tell the class. "The King of the Frogs" and "Onsongo and the Masai Cattle" are two interesting tales that can be retold around a campfire or in a classroom.
7. Ask your librarian about a recording of Hottentots or Bushmen speaking in their unusual "clicking" language.

8 Life in the Middle Ages

Unit Preview

The fall of Rome in the year 476 marked the end of the ancient world. The period between 476 and 1450 is known as the Middle Ages.

After the fall of Rome, Europe fell into a period of lawlessness. To bring about a safer way of life, people created a new kind of society, the feudal system. Under this system, people were divided into two main classes, the nobles and the common people. The nobles were warriors. The common people produced the food and did the other work. They were protected by the nobles and in times of war served in their armies.

The Christian religion spread through Europe in the Middle Ages and the churches served as centers of learning. Crusades were made to the Middle East to recapture the land where Christianity started. The Crusaders brought back to Europe the products they had seen on their journeys. The Europeans wanted more of the spices, fruits, silks, and other items. Trade developed between the Middle East and Europe.

The increased trade made marketplaces in cities and towns more important. As cities grew, the feudal system came to an end.

New inventions made it easier and safer for ships to sail long distances. The printing press made books available to more people. Discoveries and new ideas became the foundation of the modern age.

Things to Discover

If you look carefully at the picture, map, and time line on these pages, you can answer these questions.

1. What modern countries that you have already studied are on the continent of Europe?
2. The end of the Roman Empire marked the beginning of what historical period?
3. What invention came into use close to 1450?
4. The picture shows a scene on an estate in the Middle Ages. What tasks are the workers doing for their noble master?
5. Trade was an important reason for growth of towns. When did trade develop?

Words to Learn

You will meet these words in this unit. As you read, you will learn what they mean and how to pronounce them. The Word List will help you.

apprentice	manor
astrolabe	master
battlement	moat
cathedral	monastery
charter	page
compass	Renaissance
convent	serf
Crusade	squire
feudalism	tapestry
flying buttress	tenant
guild	tournament
knight	

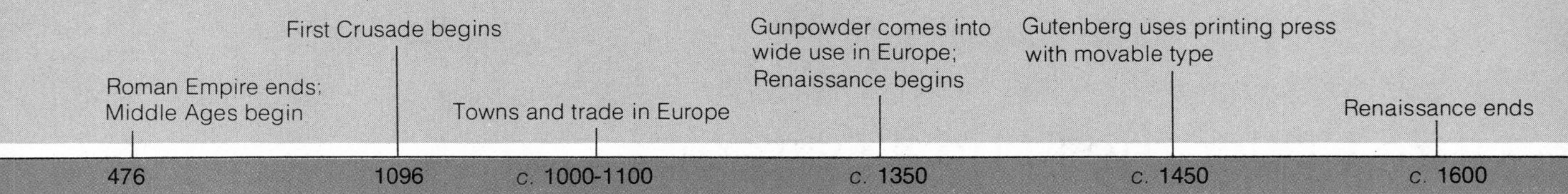

Arctic Ocean

Atlantic Ocean

EUROPE

ASIA

AFRICA

Indian Ocean

AUSTRALIA

Pacific Ocean

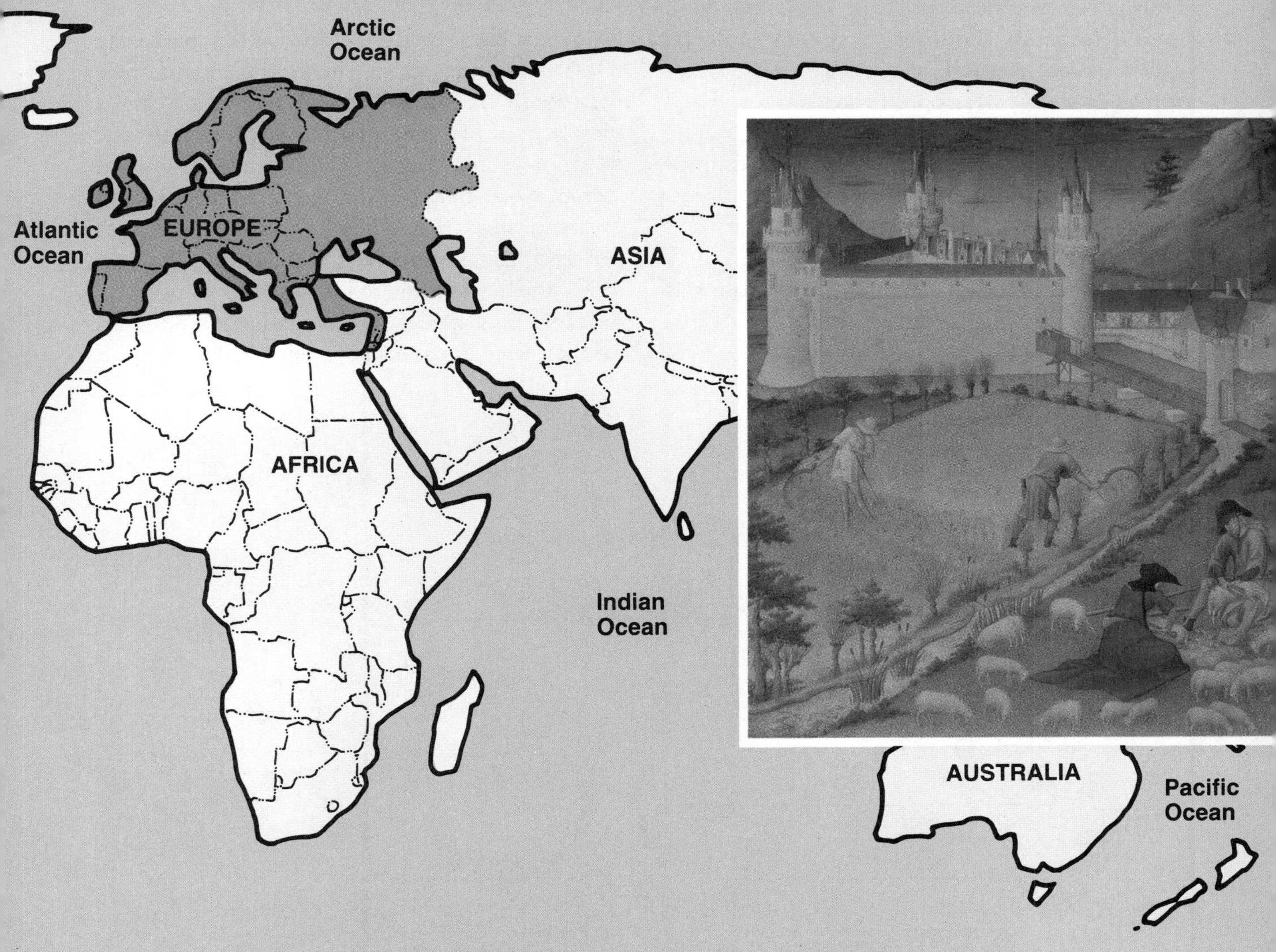

1
Life Under the Feudal System

During the Middle Ages, from about the sixth to the fifteenth centuries, a system of living called *feudalism* (fyo͞od′əl iz′əm) was widespread in western Europe. Feudalism was based on cooperation between two classes of people, the nobles and the commoners. Nobles provided land and protection to the commoners. In return, the commoners pledged military and other services to the lords.

Feudalism lasted a long time. Its purpose was to give the people protection in a time of disorder.

How Feudalism Worked

Between the years 500 and 1000, barbarian Germanic tribes from the north fought their way south. They came in search of homes and a new way of life. They settled down in different parts of western Europe. Their leaders, some of whom were called kings, were unable to keep order in their areas. They had no regular armies to send against enemies. Even if they had armies, there were few roads for them to use.

The kings appointed nobles to defend parts of their kingdoms. As payment for their help in

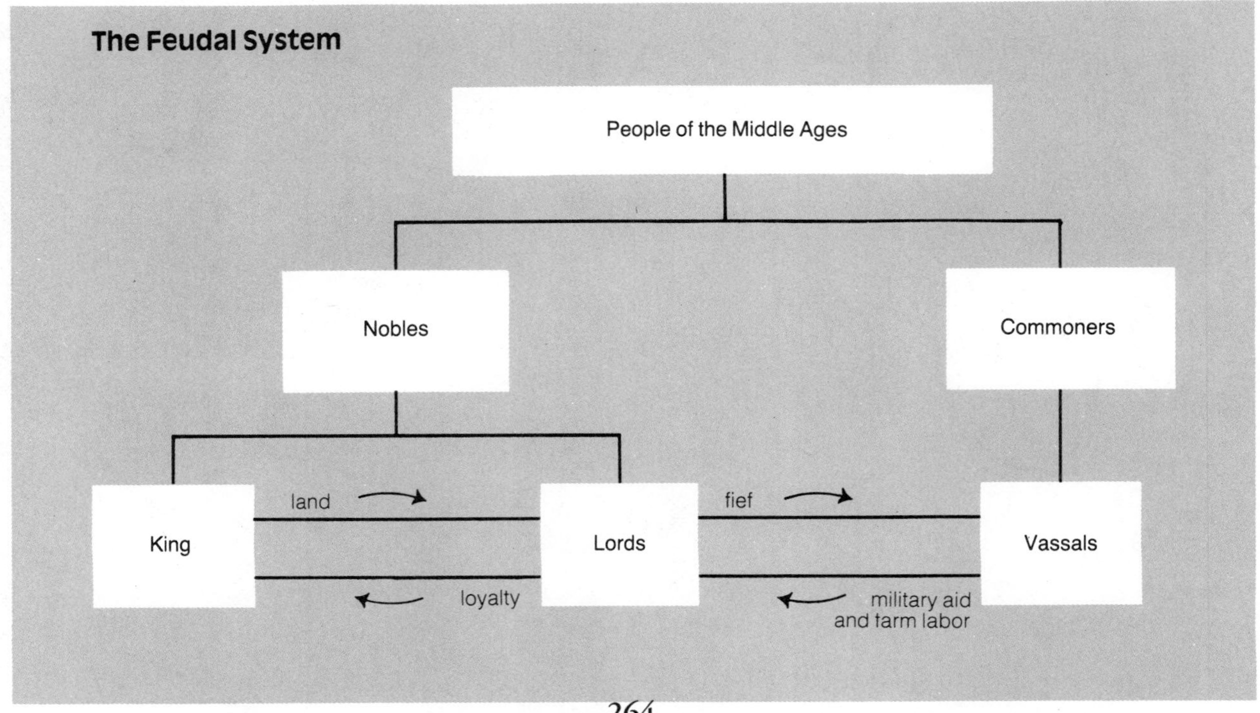

times of danger, the kings gave the nobles portions of land.

Each noble, in turn, divided his land. He was called a landlord, or a lord. Each man who received land promised to help the lord if called upon. He was called the lord's vassal (vas′əl). The land that was granted in this way was called a feud, or fief (fēf).

If the system worked well, everyone from king to commoner would get help and give help when needed.

However, the system did not always work smoothly. Some of the great lords, who lived far from the king, felt so important that they did as they pleased. They felt they could treat the common people as they liked. Sometimes these lords tried to rule even the king.

After the Germanic tribes had brought about the destruction of Rome, other groups of invaders came. From the east came hordes of Slavic peoples, who settled down in Central Europe. Vikings from Norway, Sweden, and Denmark sent their fleets to make raids on the coasts and rivers. One large group of Vikings made a settlement in what is now northern France. From regions north of the Black Sea bands of Huns rode on horseback. From the south came the Arabs who had conquered North Africa. They crossed the Mediterranean, entered Spain, and brought with them the Muslim religion. The Arabs settled down in Spain.

The people of Europe were not united to protect themselves against the newcomers. Often there were wars between the kings and lords. It sometimes seemed that the feudal system, which was intended to create order, was actually causing disorder. This was not true. The feudal system brought order to various regions and improved conditions in a time of danger.

Commoners depended on nobles for land and protection. In return, they provided the nobles with various services. What services are being performed in this scene?

Life in the Castles

The lords built strong castles for themselves. In these castles lived warriors called *knights* (nīts). The knights defended the castles and also followed their lords to war.

What the Castles Were Like

Castles were usually built on rocky cliffs or steep hills that were easy to defend. After a time the castle became a fort.

Castles can still be seen in many European countries. Some are preserved as museums or historic places. What parts of a castle can be identified in this picture?

The main tower of the castle was called the donjon, from which we get the word "dungeon." The high castle walls were surrounded by a deep ditch, or *moat* (mōt), usually filled with water. The entrance to the castle was over a drawbridge crossing the moat. The drawbridge could be drawn up by chains to keep enemies from crossing.

In an attack, a portcullis (pôrt kul′is) of heavy bars was lowered to close the gate. When the portcullis was down, no one could enter the castle. Around the roof were balconies, protected by walls, or *battlements* (bat′əl mənts), which had openings at certain points. The fighters could stand behind the battlements and defend the castle. At the same time they could see an approaching enemy.

Castles are beautiful, but they were not comfortable places in which to live. The windows were small, which made the rooms dark. The stone walls were always damp and chilly. To keep out drafts, the walls and windows were hung with heavy embroidered draperies, that are called *tapestries* (tap′istrēz). There were no chimneys so rooms were filled with smoke from the fireplaces.

Duties of the Lord of the Castle

The lord of the castle always had to be prepared for war. In battle he wore armor made of overlapping links of iron. The armor was heavy and clumsy to wear. But it protected the knight's body from the long, sharp weapon, or lance, of his enemy.

To keep fit for war, the young nobles were trained to jump, wrestle, and ride. As they grew older, they exercised with real weapons. They also kept in practice by having contests, called *tournaments* (toor′ne mənts). In a tournament each knight rode toward his opponent and used his lance to try to throw his opponent from the saddle.

Duties of the Lady of the Castle

The wife of the lord was called a lady. She had a great deal of work to do. She managed the household, cared for the children, and directed the servants. She supervised the training of the young pages. Since there were few doctors in the Middle Ages, she also might be called upon to attend the sick.

When the lord was away at war the lady had even more to do. She might have to defend the castle if it were attacked. If the lord was captured in a war, she would have to raise the money to pay for his release.

The Training and Duties of a Knight

The sons of the lords trained to be knights. A young man of noble family began his training at the age of 7 as a *page* (pāj) in a great lord's castle. The page waited on the table, ran errands,

A lady of a castle had many duties. In her spare time, however, she would sometimes practice needlework. This part of a *tapestry* shows a French lady sitting with her sewing basket in a garden.

and learned good manners. When he was 16 years old, he became a *squire* (skwīr) and followed his lord in the hunt and in battle.

When a lord thought that his squire was ready, he made the young man a knight. The new knight promised to be gentle and courteous to women. He also promised to protect weak and helpless people. The age of knights

Knights competing in a *tournament* would very often have to fight with swords. Their lances were easily broken.

belongs to times past. But knightly behavior still means bravery, consideration for others, and courtesy.

Village Life in Feudal Times

Most farms in the Middle Ages were large estates owned by lords. In England they were called *manors* (man′ərz). Few farmers owned land. Instead, most of them were *tenants* (ten′ənts) on the land. The tenants lived on the manor by permission of the lord. The lord's residence was a fortified manor house or a castle.

The tenants lived in cottages in a village. For safety and convenience the villages were near the castle. In an attack the villagers could seek the shelter of the castle and help defend it.

The Manor, an Independent Community

The tenants on the manor produced all the food, clothing, tools, and other goods. They ground their grain into flour at the lord's mill and baked bread in ovens. They wove cloth, tanned leather, and made tools. Officials supervised the work. Every village had a church, which was the center of the community, and a priest who served the church.

Freemen and Serfs

There were two classes of tenants in the Middle Ages. A few tenants enjoyed free use of parts of the land, for which they paid rent to the lord. Or perhaps they owned a few acres of land within the lord's estate. Tenants who served the lord faithfully sometimes received from him a grant of land as a reward. The produce tenants raised there was their own. These tenants were called freemen. The freemen could stay on the manor or leave if they wished. If they owned land, they could sell it or pass it on to their children. They were under the lord's command only while fighting.

Most of the tenants, however, were *serfs* (surfs), who were neither slaves nor freemen. They could not be sold like slaves because they were not owned by the lord. Instead the serfs belonged to the land on which they lived. They lived on the manor but could not leave it.

The serfs had a lowly place in feudal life. Though the life of a serf was hard, a wise lord knew it was profitable to treat serfs well. If they were treated fairly, they would be loyal to him.

Lords in France and England found that freemen worked better than serfs. So, as time went

Land on a *manor* was divided into areas for farming, livestock, dwellings for *serfs*, and living quarters for the lord. Mills run by water power were used to grind wheat and other grains.

on, there came to be more freemen and fewer serfs in these lands. In Central Europe, however, serfs did not become free for a long time. In Russia serfs were not freed until 1861.

A Visit to a Village Home

The home of a village family was usually a one-room house. It stood with similar houses at the foot of a hill below the castle. The water the family needed had to be carried from the village well. Back of the house was a shed for oxen and a small patch of ground for a garden.

Members of the family arose at daybreak, worked hard all day, and went to bed soon after dark. They had to work long hours just to survive. If they had any free time, they did not read because none of them knew how. The priests were almost the only ones who could read.

How Feudalism Ended

The feudal system lasted for hundreds of years. It disappeared gradually when kings grew strong enough to control the lords and to maintain order. People felt safer and were willing to leave the protection of the manor. They moved to towns. Cities grew up, trade increased, and people were paid in money instead of services.

Do You Know?

1. What was the purpose of feudalism?
2. Into what different groups were people divided?
3. How did the lives of serfs differ from slaves and freemen?

2 Towns and Cities in the Middle Ages

After the fall of Rome many of the small towns of the Roman Empire disappeared. The few large cities in western Europe grew smaller and lost most of their trade. The roads were poor, and there were so many robbers that people were afraid to travel. Towns and cities cannot grow without trade and travel.

The Revival of Town Life

Between the years 1000 and 1100 trade in Europe began to increase. Although land travel was difficult, sea travel improved. Population was increasing. Merchants began to visit settled parts of Europe. Old towns began to grow again, and new ones arose.

Let us look at an example of how the feudal system was replaced by town life. A large number of people might visit a castle. Some came to enjoy the lord's hospitality. Others were merchants who sold him goods.

Because it was not convenient to entertain all these people in the castle, the lord built inns to shelter and feed the travelers. Merchants then opened shops nearby. In a few years a busy town had grown up near the castle. The lord controlled the town, and the people who lived there paid him rent.

But the people in these towns began to feel important and wanted to be independent of the nobles. By paying sums of money and by fighting, they gradually gained their freedom. Finally, many towns became free to direct their own affairs.

The revival of town life during the Middle Ages was a prosperous time in Europe. Shown here is a scene from a Middle Ages bank.

When a town gained certain privileges, they were listed in a document called a *charter* (chär′tər). The lord had to swear that the privileges were guaranteed rights of the town, and he had to put his name or his seal to the charter.

Merchant *guild* halls built in the Middle Ages still stand in Ghent, Belgium, a city of splendid Gothic architecture. Ghent was once a great commercial port.

Markets in the Middle Ages

The people of the towns made and sold goods, while most of the people on the manor or lord's estate grew food. The more the townsfolk could sell, the more prosperous they were. Each town had one open space, the marketplace, where people met to buy and sell goods.

Once a week the country people came to the nearest town to sell their produce in the marketplace. When this was sold, they bought town goods. Refreshment stands were set up in the marketplace. Peddlers mingled with the crowd. Plays were performed. It was a busy, jolly time which brought profit to everyone. The larger towns had several marketplaces. In many lands market days are still common.

Fairs in the Middle Ages

Besides the markets, which helped trade, there were fairs. The fairs were important occasions, lasting for a week or longer. They brought together people from many distant lands.

Towns held their fairs at different times. But each town held its fair at the same time each year so that the traveling merchants could plan in advance to be there. A merchant could spend the whole year either selling goods at fairs or preparing for the fairs.

The people who attended a fair learned much by seeing the interesting articles that were brought from a distance. At the fairs, trading was easy. Strangers were made welcome, and people learned about other lands.

The Guilds

When towns grew and trade became important, the town officers could not direct trade properly. The richer merchants of some towns joined together in groups called merchant *guilds* (gildz). A guild was a group of merchants or skilled workers who organized to maintain standards of work and to protect their own interests. These guilds elected officers and drew up rules which they enforced. Sometimes a merchant guild took part in the government of the town.

The skilled workers formed their own groups called craft guilds. People who did one kind of work joined together. There were guilds for bakers, metalworkers, weavers, shoemakers, and many others. The earliest craft guild was the candlemakers' guild of Paris.

The member of a craft guild was called a *master* (mas′ter). The master was a skilled worker who could work at the trade independently. A young person who wanted to learn a trade had to become an *apprentice* (ə pren′tis) to a master. The apprentice lived in the master's house and served the master while learning the trade.

When the master notified the guild that the apprentice had learned the trade, the apprentice became a journeyman, and could then be paid wages for working. With enough experience and a little money, the journeyman could ask the guild to be declared a master. He had to prove his skill by showing a piece of work that he had done. This "masterpiece," as it was called, was a well-made article that he had spent a long time creating. In the weaver guild, for example, the masterpiece might be a finely woven piece of tapestry or altar cloth.

All the masters of one craft in a town lived near one another. The guild decided what hours during the day the shops in the town could be open. Inspectors belonging to the guild saw that the masters sold only articles of good quality. The guild set the prices, so one master could not sell at lower prices than another.

The Growth of Towns and Cities

There were differences between the town and the city in the Middle Ages. The city, because of its size, was stronger than the town. Some Italian cities, such as Venice, Genoa, and Florence, were free cities during the Middle Ages and never were ruled by a feudal lord. They were city-states, and they governed large areas of land outside their walls.

The citizens of important towns and cities had rights not enjoyed by the serfs. The guilds made the people feel pride in their town or city and in the work done there. Out of this two great ideas developed. One was that good work is more deserving of honor than noble birth. The second was that cooperation makes communities strong.

Some kings realized that the cities and their workers were opposed to the lords. So the kings began to favor the cities in order to weaken the power of the lords. The power of the kings, helped by the people of the cities, increased. With the growth of cities our modern world was beginning.

Do You Know?

1. Why did towns begin to grow in the late Middle Ages?
2. What was a guild? Name three.
3. How were cities different from towns in the Middle Ages?

Before You Go On

Using New Words

moat	knight	feudalism
master	tournament	guild
tenant	apprentice	page
serf	battlement	squire
manor	tapestry	charter

Number a paper from 1 through 15. After each number write the word or term that matches the definition.

1. A group of merchants or skilled workers who organized to maintain standards of work and to protect their own interests
2. A contest in which knights kept in practice for warfare
3. A farmer who lived on a manor by the lord's permission
4. The system of living in western Europe in the Middle Ages based on cooperation of nobles and commoners
5. A worker who belonged to the land and could not leave it
6. A document signed by a lord listing privileges given to a town
7. A large estate in England in the Middle Ages
8. A wall around the top of a castle with openings through which soldiers could see the enemy approach and defend the castle
9. A young boy who was beginning his training as a knight
10. Heavy, embroidered drapery fabric
11. A highly skilled worker who could work independently
12. A deep ditch, usually filled with water, surrounding a castle
13. A warrior in the Middle Ages
14. One who served a master worker for a certain time to learn a trade
15. A boy who followed his lord in hunting and in battle

Finding the Facts

1. What duties did a lord perform for a king? A vassal for a lord?
2. Name three groups of people who invaded western Europe after the fall of the Roman Empire.
3. Name the two stages a young man passed through in his training to become a knight.
4. Why were tenants' houses located near the manor house?
5. What were three drawbacks to living in a castle?
6. What brought about the end of the feudal system?
7. How might a town grow up around a manor house?
8. What activities took place at fairs? Why were fairs important?
9. What were some of the duties of the lady of the castle?

3
The Crusades

We have learned that the Muslims conquered the Middle East and North Africa. They held Palestine, or the Holy Land. To Jerusalem, the sacred city of the Christians, traveled many pilgrims. They made the long, hard journey to pray at the Holy Sepulcher (sep′əl kər), thought to be the tomb of Christ. For many years the Muslims allowed pilgrims to visit Jerusalem in peace.

The Story of the Crusades

Then, Muslim armies began to move westward again. Conquering as they went, they reached Asia Minor and threatened to take Constantinople. With the Eastern Empire in danger, the emperor in Constantinople asked the Pope to send help.

How the Crusades Began

The Pope had heard that the Turkish Muslims, who then held Palestine, were mistreating Christian pilgrims. He agreed that the Eastern emperor should have help. He called on the people of western Europe to fight the Muslims. He asked them to wage a holy war, or *Crusade* (kro͞o sād), to rescue the Holy Land from the Turks. The Crusades began in 1096.

In churches all over western Europe people heard the message of the Pope. In France a number of lords raised armies to go on Crusades. Thousands of people cried out, "God wills it!" They sewed crosses on their coats and set out for the Holy Land. They were called Crusaders, from a French word meaning "to take the cross."

The Capture of Jerusalem

The Crusaders traveled in groups by different routes to reach the Holy Land. In 1099 their armies captured Jerusalem. Most of the Crusaders went home when Jerusalem was captured. Those who stayed set up a kingdom in the Holy Land and three neighboring states.

Jerusalem was governed by Christians for nearly 100 years after the First Crusade. But war between the Christians and the Muslims went on.

Other Crusades

When the people of Europe realized that the Muslims might win back the Holy Land, they started the Second Crusade. But the armies from the different countries did not march together, and the Muslims defeated them one by one. Not long after this, the Muslims took Jerusalem again and the cities around it also.

The Third Crusade began. One of its leaders was Richard of England. He was called Richard the Lion-Hearted because of his bravery and daring. Richard was defeated in the Crusade. Later he was captured and put in prison by enemies. The Third Crusade failed also.

Other Crusades followed, until there were nine in all. But the Christians were never able to regain the Holy Land.

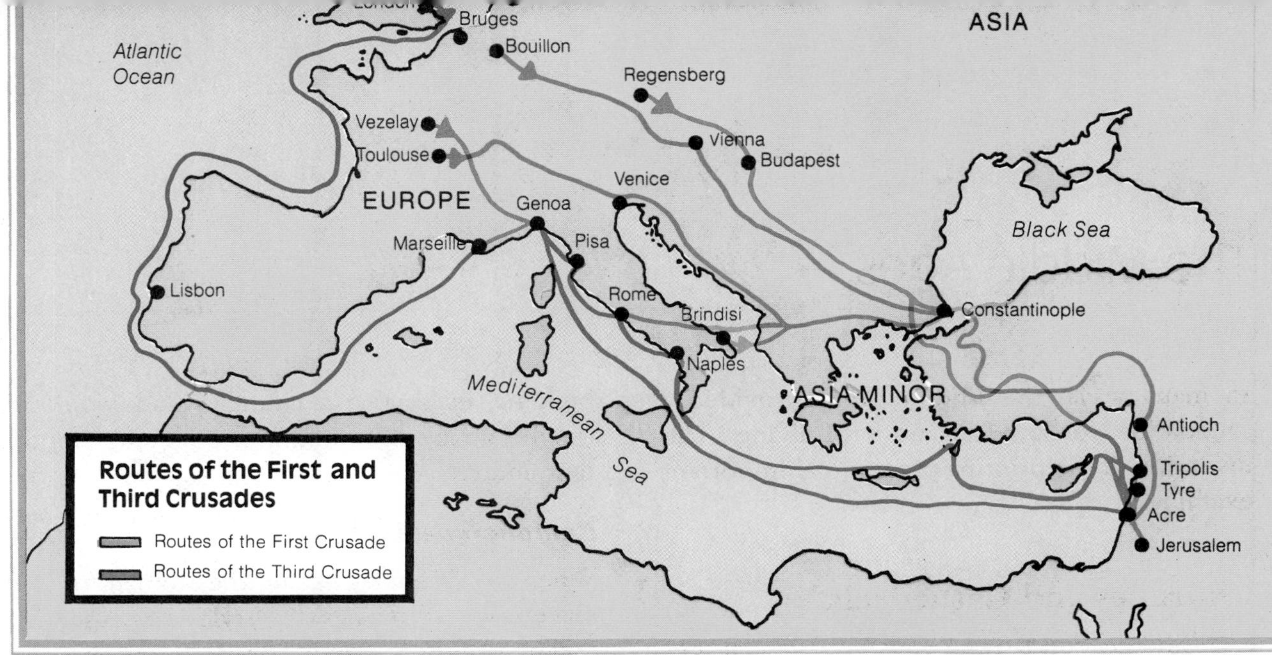

In the First *Crusade*, the routes were over land to Constantinople, then across Asia Minor to Jerusalem. Two routes of the Third *Crusade* were primarily by water. Where did these water routes begin?

The Crusades lasted more than 200 years. They are sometimes called the Holy Wars of the Middle Ages.

Results of the Crusades

The Italian cities of Venice, Genoa, and Pisa sent out trading ships before the time of the Crusades. Later, the ships carried supplies for the Crusaders in the Middle East. This greatly increased trade.

Before the Crusades no one in western Europe knew a great deal about the lands that lay beyond the forests or the sea. The Crusades took lords and squires, soldiers, sailors, and people of the Church to new countries.

The Crusaders helped Europeans learn about and understand people of other lands. The people of western Europe thought of Muslims as uncivilized. They found that these "unbelievers" were brave in battle and that many were just as courteous as the Crusaders themselves.

Crusaders found they could learn much about comfortable living from the homes of the Middle East. The people there had customs which Europeans could copy to their advantage.

The Crusaders learned new methods of warfare in the East. The battering ram and the siege tower were used to attack walled cities. The Crusaders first saw these used by the Eastern emperor's soldiers at Constantinople.

Do You Know?

1. How did the Crusades begin?
2. How many Crusades were there?
3. How did cities like Genoa and Venice benefit from the Crusades?

4
The Middle Ages

In many ways, the Middle Ages provided a foundation for modern ways of living. The invention of the printing press is one important example of this.

Churches and Cathedrals

The Middle Ages owed much to the ancient world, especially to Greece and Rome. But the invaders who came down from the north and broke up the Roman Empire brought new ideas and new energy. One way they expressed themselves was in new styles of building, especially in churches and *cathedrals* (kə thē′drəlz). A cathedral is a large or important church.

Romanesque Architecture

When the Crusades began, the Roman, or Romanesque (rō′mə nesk′), style was used in building churches and cathedrals. They were

Romanesque and Gothic architecture were used in building churches in the Middle Ages. A Romanesque church, shown left, has rounded arches. A Gothic church has pointed arches.

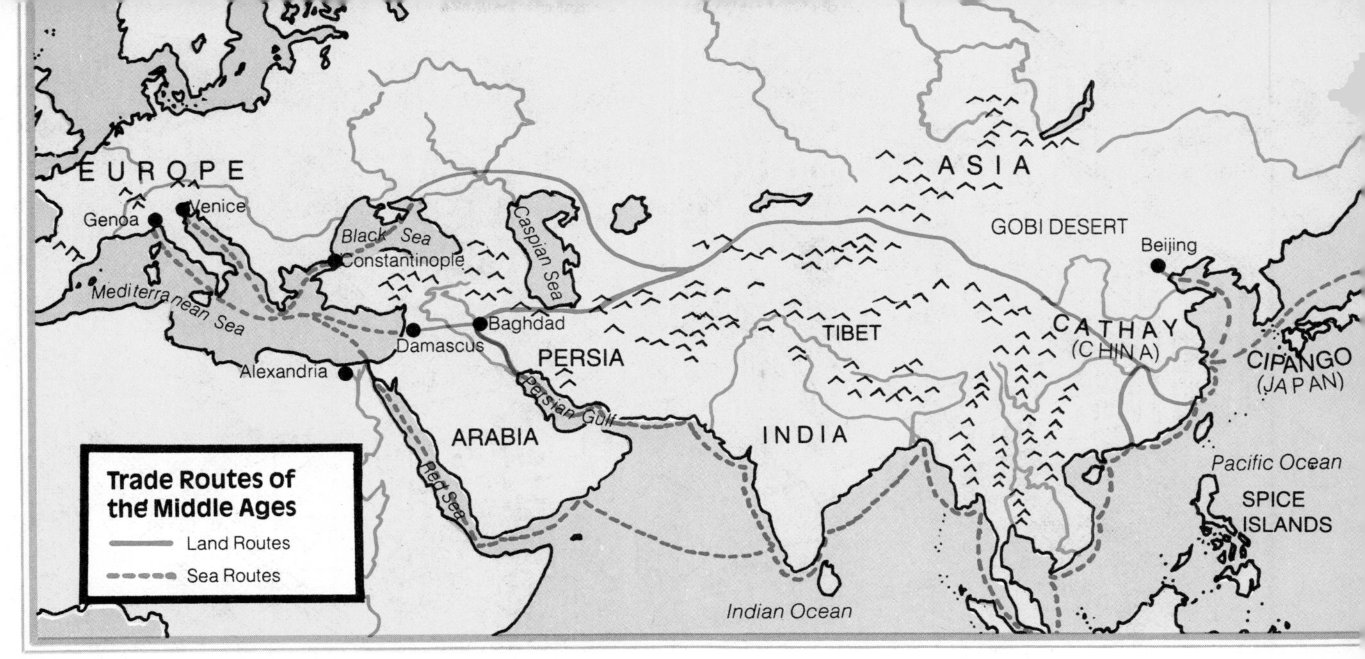

After the *Crusades*, trade increased. Ships from Venice and Genoa picked up goods brought to the Mediterranean by Arab traders. What other cities were important trading centers?

built of stone, with round arches above the doors and windows. Stone ceilings require strong walls to prevent the extra weight of the roof from pushing them apart. Architects built extra pillars to strengthen the walls. They protected the windows by keeping them small. A Romanesque church was dark on the inside.

The Gothic Cathedral

French architects worked out a new way of building churches. The new style of building was called Gothic (goth′ik). The Goths were Germans who had settled in many parts of western Europe. In place of round arches, the Gothic style used pointed arches. Instead of domes, it used ridged roofs. A new part of the Gothic cathedral was the *flying buttress* (flī′ing but′ris). The flying buttress was a heavy stone prop, or half of a pointed arch, placed outside the building.

With flying buttresses, the walls of the church could be made taller and thinner without weakening them. Architects could also put in as many windows as they wished. Some churches had so many large windows that it was sometimes said they had walls of glass. They also had towers and tall spires on the roofs.

Most of the windows of the cathedrals were made of stained glass. Colored glass kept out the glare of light and added to the beauty of the church. No glassmakers of today have been able to equal the marvelous shades of red and blue made by glassmakers of the Middle Ages.

The Growth of Trade

The Crusades failed to achieve their purpose. They did not permanently restore the Holy Land to the Christians. But they had good results in trade.

A feudal *monastery* is almost like a small city. Farms and vineyards around it provide food for the monks who study and produce manuscripts in the *monastery*.

The crusaders acquainted people with the products of the East. Sugar, rice, oranges, lemons, pepper, and cinnamon were brought to Europe by the crusaders. Other goods—such as perfumes, medicines, silk and cotton cloth, porcelain dishes and cups, fine rugs and carpets—were also imported. Thus, as a result of the Crusades, people in Europe enjoyed things they had never before known.

With the rise of cities and towns there was trade by land and sea. On land the old Roman roads were used again. Businesspeople became important citizens. The guilds pointed the way to our trade unions. People began to use the Arabic numerals instead of Roman numerals.

The Growth of Learning

In the Middle Ages some men and women wanted to live apart from others in order to devote themselves to a holy life. The men were called monks, and the women were called nuns. The buildings the monks lived in were called *monasteries* (mon′ə ster′ēz). The buildings the nuns lived in were called *convents* (kon′vents). The monasteries and convents were quiet places where those who had chosen to live a religious life could read, study, and do good works.

Schools of higher learning, called universities, were established in the Middle Ages. Law, religion, and medicine were taught in the universities. Latin was the language used by educated people of all countries in western Europe. They began to study books by Roman writers. Books in Greek and Arabic were translated into Latin and read by students.

After reading ancient books, many persons wanted to write books themselves. They wrote histories and stories of travel. They wrote about the lives of saints and the deeds of heroes. They also wrote amusing stories, or fables, in which animals were the principal characters.

Some modern nations had their beginnings in the late Middle Ages. In England, France, and Spain the rulers grew powerful and molded their countries into nations.

Several new languages developed. In Unit 6 we learned how the Romance languages came about when Latin became mixed with the languages of the regions under Rome's rule. In northern Europe several Germanic languages developed. German, Dutch, the Scandinavian languages, and English belong mainly to this group.

Important Inventions

Many things brought about the end of the Middle Ages. Among these were inventions which brought changes.

The Use of Gunpowder

Gunpowder began to be used in Europe in the Middle Ages. Gunpowder helped destroy feudalism. It made the foot soldier with a gun a better warrior than the knight on horseback with a lance. By 1350 three German towns had factories making gunpowder.

New Instruments Used in Sailing

Knowledge of geography was greatly increased by improved methods of sailing. From about 1200 two new instruments, or tools, aided sailors—the *compass* (kum′pəs) and the *astrolabe* (as′trə lāb′).

Using the compass, whose needle always points to the north, sailors always knew the direction in which they were going. The astrolabe measured the height of the sun in the sky. With this information sailors could find their latitude and know how far north or south of the equator they were. The new instruments helped people to sail more safely and to draw better maps and charts. Thus the way was paved for the age of exploration.

The Invention of Printing

Another invention which brought important changes at the close of the Middle Ages was a method of printing from movable type. Up to this time books were copied by hand on parchment. Parchment, a writing material made of sheepskin, was expensive. Few people could afford books of parchment.

The Chinese had invented wood-block printing hundreds of years earlier. In time the Europeans developed their own method, using movable type. The first European book was printed in Germany about 1450. Johann Gutenberg (go͞ot′ən bûrg′) used movable type to print it. The use of movable type made it possible to print hundreds of copies of books in a short time. Paper made from cotton rags had been developed about this time. Now there was a good, cheap material to print on. Books were printed in many languages. The reading of books was to become the privilege of many.

The Renaissance

The spread of ideas resulting from inventions and discoveries was part of a movement in Europe known as the *Renaissance* (ren′ə säns′). This word means "rebirth."

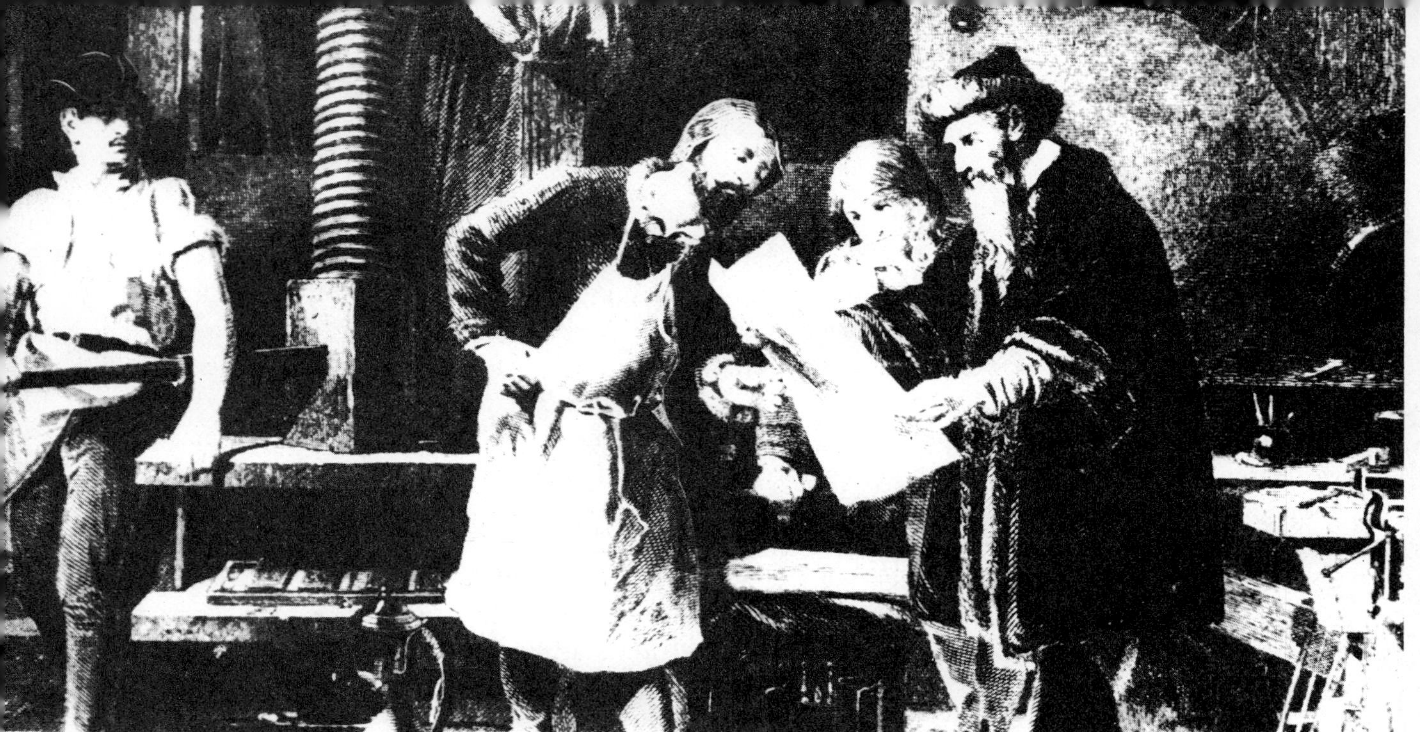

An important invention at the close of the Middle Ages was a way of printing with movable type. This method was developed by Gutenberg, a German inventor. He is shown holding a sheet printed on his press.

As ideas spread, more discoveries followed. One important scientist was the Italian, Galileo (gal′ə lē′ō). He built instruments through which he watched the moon and stars. He helped to prove that the earth rotates on its axis and that the earth moves around the sun.

During the time of the Renaissance people read eagerly the works of ancient Greek and Latin authors. They tried new ideas in painting. Michelangelo and Raphael were Renaissance artists.

The new interest in the writings of Greece and Rome began in Italy. From Italy, teachers of the "new learning" went to other countries of western Europe. Italy thus became the teacher of Europe, just as Greece had been many years before.

The Renaissance lasted from about 1350 to 1600. It marked the end of the Middle Ages and the beginning of modern times. We shall see the effects of the Renaissance as we follow the stories of modern nations.

Do You Know?

1. What two styles of building were used in churches in the Middle Ages?
2. How did printing from movable type help to spread learning?
3. What was the Renaissance? When and where did it begin?

To Help You Learn

Using New Words

manor	Crusade	flying buttress
guild	compass	convent
cathedral	feudalism	Renaissance
astrolabe	monastery	

Number a paper from 1 through 11. After each number write the word or term that matches the definition.

1. The building where a group of nuns live
2. A heavy stone prop placed outside a building to support it
3. The system of living in western Europe in the Middle Ages based on cooperation of nobles and commoners
4. An instrument used by sailors to measure the height of the sun in the sky so that they could find their latitude
5. The period of time, beginning about 1350, in which there was a new interest in art, learning, and discovery
6. A group of merchants or skilled workers who organized to maintain standards of work and to protect their own interests
7. An instrument with a needle that always points north
8. A holy war, undertaken to capture the Holy Land from the Turks
9. A large estate in England in the Middle Ages
10. A large or important church
11. The building where a group of monks live

Finding the Facts

1. How was feudalism based on cooperation?
2. How was a castle made strong to stand against attack by enemies?
3. Match the following words with the correct statements:
   donjon   moat   portcullis
   a. heavy, barred gate
   b. deep ditch, usually filled with water, around a castle
   c. main tower
4. How did guilds help their members? How did they help their customers?
5. What was an apprentice?
6. What was a free city?
7. Why did kings favor cities and towns?
8. What did the Crusades accomplish?
9. Why was stained glass used?
10. Name three inventions of the later Middle Ages.
11. Name four new languages that began in the Middle Ages.

Learning from Maps

1. Look at the map of the First and Third Crusades on page 275. Which Crusade traveled mainly overland to the Holy Land? Which by sea? If a knight left Bouillon on the First Crusade, what cities would he pass through on the way? If he left London on the Third Crusade?

2. Look at the map of Trade Routes of the Middle Ages on page 277. Imagine that you are a medieval merchant traveling from Venice to Beijing. Through what cities might you pass?

Using Study Skills

1. **Time Line:** Place the following events in the proper order of time: Compass in use, *c.* 1200; Holy Land conquered by Muslims, *c.* 640; Third Crusade, 1189; Muslim invasion of Spain, 711; First Viking raid, 790.

   Copy down the time line on page 263. Add these new events to your time line.

   Study the completed time line and answer these questions: How many years passed between the occupation of the Holy Land by Muslims and the First Crusade? Between the beginning of the First and Third Crusades? Which came into use first in Europe, the compass or the printing press? Were guns used in the crusades? How does the time line support your answer? Why?
2. **Diagram:** Study the diagram of the manor on page 269. What building is closest to the stream? Why? Did villagers live nearer the fields or nearer the manor house?
3. **Diagram:** Use the diagram of the monastery on page 278 to answer these questions: What kinds of work were done in a monastery? What rooms were part of the main building? Why would a monk have to leave the main building?

Thinking It Through

1. Why were the compass and the astrolabe, shown below, useful to navigators in the Middle Ages? What devices help airplane pilots today to fly safely?
2. What was the difference between a slave and a serf? Who had the better life? Support your answer.
3. People from Europe traveled far from home during the Crusades. They met different people and gained new ideas which changed their lives. People today visit all parts of the world. Does travel help to bring understanding among peoples? Explain your answer.
4. The Renaissance was a time when people began to do new things in art, science, and literature. Is our time like the time of the Renaissance? Explain your position.

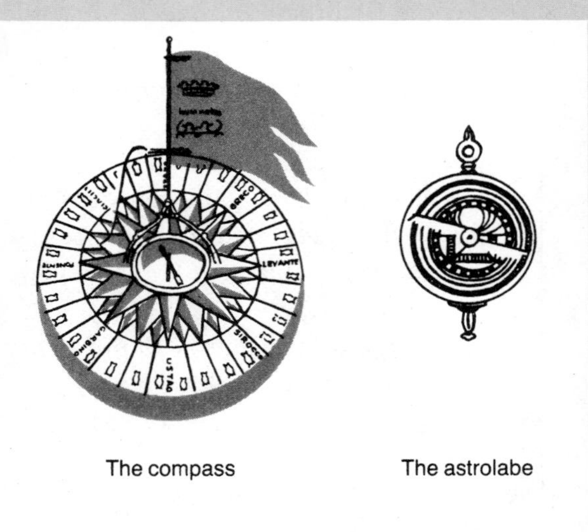

The compass The astrolabe

Projects

1. Today in a few occupations workers are still called "apprentices" while they are learning their trade. Ask a member of a labor union, such as a carpenter, baker, or mason, to tell you what it means to be an apprentice today.
2. Some churches in your community are probably built in the Gothic style. Do these churches resemble in any way the Gothic cathedral pictured on page 276?
3. Take a trip with some of your friends to a museum which has a collection of arms and armor of the Middle Ages. Report to the class on what you learn. If there is no museum that you can visit, consult books on the Middle Ages.
4. The Reading Committee might enjoy preparing a report on *The Door in the Wall* by Marguerite De Angeli. Include drawings to show how people lived in a monastery or castle in the Middle Ages.
5. The Research Committee might choose one of the topics discussed in this unit and find out more about it from an encyclopedia or other reference book. You might want to learn about armor, fairs, or the Crusades. You might want to read the exciting life of Richard the Lion-Hearted. Or you might want to know more about an invention like printing, gunpowder, or the compass. Share your knowledge with the class.
6. Use colored sheets of tissue and black construction paper to make "stained glass windows." Fold the construction paper in half and draw a design to cut out. Cut pieces of tissue paper to fill the spaces in the black paper form. The pieces should be larger than the spaces so that they can be glued down. Put a loop on the top and hang the completed design in the window so the sun can shine through it.
7. Plan a town fair. Display objects you have made as if they were for sale. Each member of the class can take the part of a person who might have been at a fair: merchants, townspeople, country folk, students, knights, monks, nuns. A group can prepare a song or dance suitable for the occasion. Another group can present a play. Still others can work on costumes and scenery. You may wish to share the fair with parents or with other classes.

9 Spain and Portugal

Unit Preview

The countries of Spain and Portugal are located on the Iberian Peninsula. This peninsula is the southwest corner of Europe. Spain occupies most of the peninsula. Portugal is on the western coast.

Like other parts of Europe, this area has known many conquerors. Beginning with the ancient Phoenician traders, sailing ships reached its shores. When Rome set out to conquer the world, the Iberian Peninsula became part of the Roman Empire. After the fall of Rome in A.D. 476, the peninsula was held by European tribes that had become Christian. Then, in 711, the Moors from the nearby African continent conquered most of Spain. The Moors brought with them the Muslim religion.

The Moors also brought great wisdom and beauty. Their university at Toledo was a center of learning for all Europe. Their knowledge of astronomy, geography, and medicine was respected. They were the dominant power in Spain for more than 500 years.

In the 1400s Spain and Portugal became strong seagoing kingdoms. They explored and conquered much of the Americas. For a while, they rivaled England on the seas. Then they gradually began to lose their overseas colonies.

Farming and fishing have always been important jobs in Spain and Portugal. Today, more manufacturing is being done in Spain.

Things to Discover

If you look carefully at the picture, map, and time line on these pages, you can answer these questions.

1. The area highlighted on the map is called the Iberian Peninsula. On what continent is it located? What ocean borders its west coast? Why is its location favorable for trading?
2. When did the Moors conquer Spain?
3. What country defeated Spain on the seas in 1588?
4. What South American country was once a colony of Portugal? When did it become a colony?
5. What important job of many workers in Spain and Portugal is shown in the picture?
6. Who became dictator of Spain in 1939? How long did he rule? Who became head of the government next?
7. Who was the explorer sent by Spain in 1492?

Words to Learn

You will meet these words in this unit. As you read you will learn what they mean and how to pronounce them. The Word List will help you.

armada	mercury
chemistry	merino
civil war	Moor
crop rotation	patio
latticework	

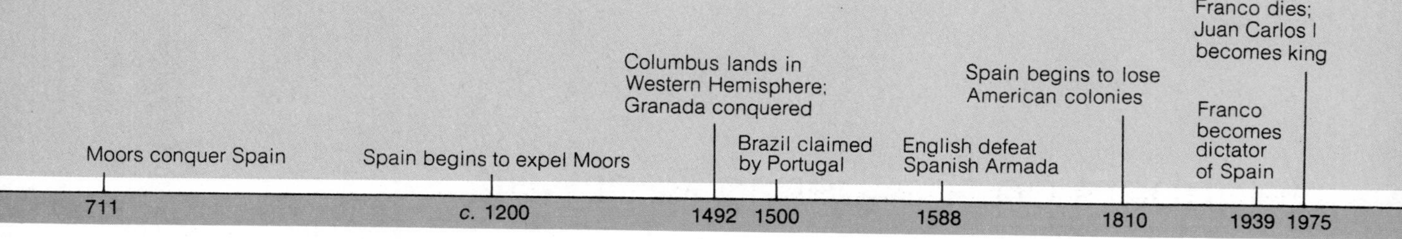

Arctic Ocean
EUROPE
Atlantic Ocean
ASIA
AFRICA
Pacific Ocean
Indian Ocean
AUSTRALIA

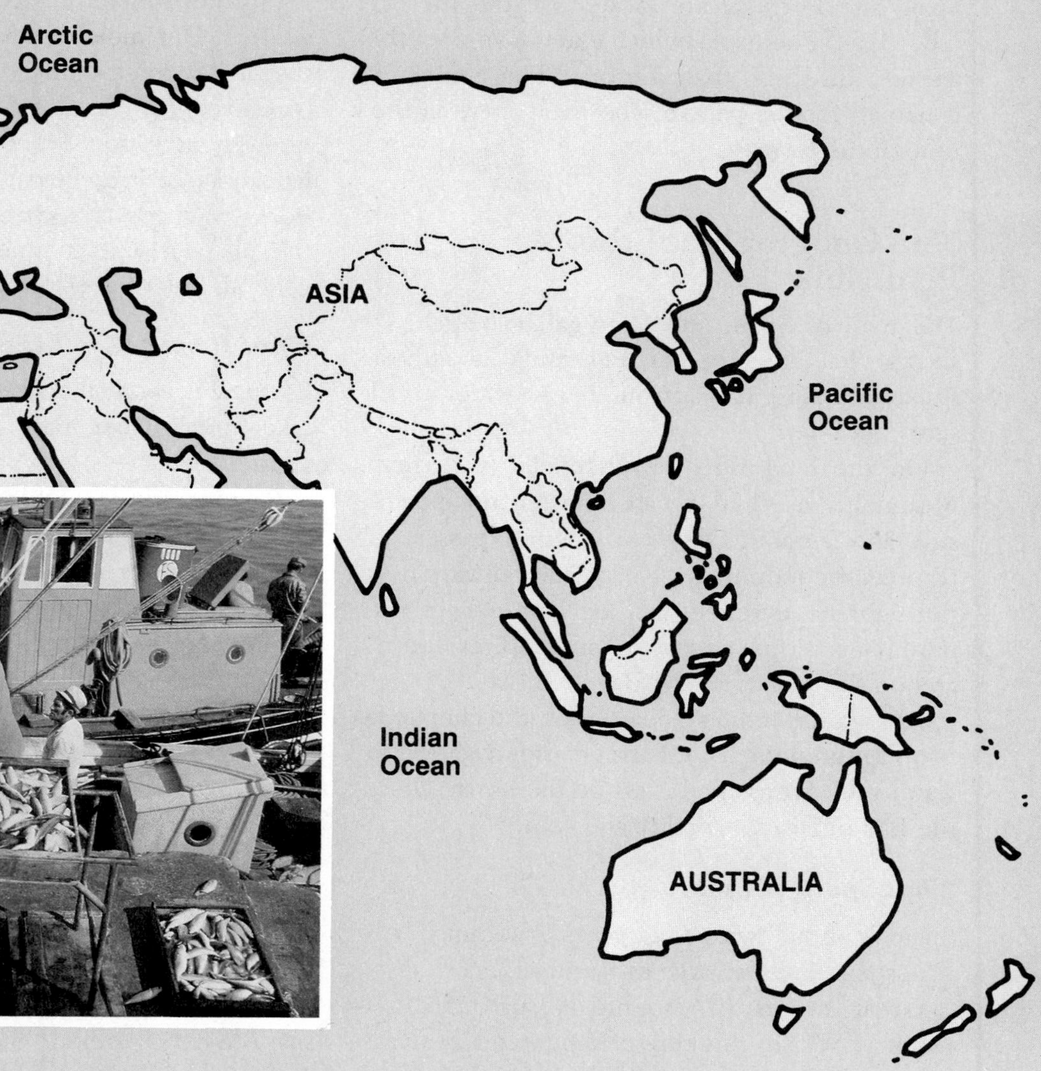

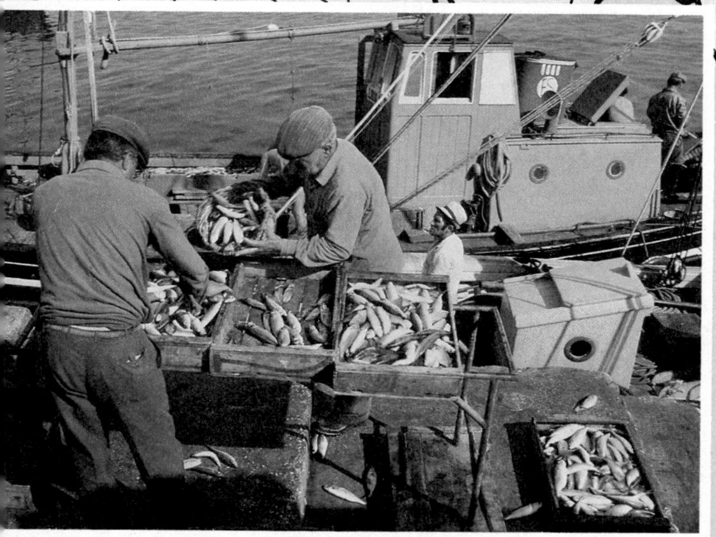

1

Neighbors on the Iberian Peninsula

Spain and Portugal are located on the Iberian (ī bēr′ ē ən) Peninsula, which extends in a southwestern direction from Europe. The peninsula is named for the people who lived there in the time of the Romans.

The Geography of the Peninsula

The map of Spain and Portugal on page 287 shows that the Iberian Peninsula is almost square in shape. It is surrounded by water on all sides but one.

On the land side the Pyrenees (pir′ ə nēz) Mountains rise like a wall between the peninsula and France. Only two natural passes go through the mountains. Roads and railways pass through the Pyrenees on the east, where the mountains slope down to the Mediterranean, and on the west near the Bay of Biscay.

Along the Mediterranean coast, the climate is good for growing fruit. Farmers use irrigation to water their crops. The coast on the north, along the Bay of Biscay, is rainy and cold.

What Spain is Like

Spain is about twice as large as Wyoming. It is almost six times as large as Portugal.

Great ranges of mountains surround the country. Within this ring of mountains is a vast plateau. The plateau covers more than half of Spain. The plateau itself is cut by many mountains and hills.

Northern Spain has cool summers and mild winters. But most of Spain is so high and dry that it is poor farming country. The plateau is bare except for gardens and fields that are watered by irrigation. Here and there are fields of wheat. Large stretches of land are good only for flocks of sheep and goats. Winters are cold on the plateau, and summers are hot. Spain, in general, lacks a comfortable climate.

What Portugal is Like

Portugal is about the size of our state of Maine. Like Spain, it has many mountains divided by many river valleys.

Portugal has a good location. It faces the Atlantic Ocean, which is favorable for carrying on overseas trade. The winds from the Atlantic make the climate rainy and mild in winter. In summer it is hot and dry, except along the ocean. Portugal has a pleasant climate, without the great differences that Spain has.

Do You Know?

1. What two nations occupy the Iberian Peninsula?
2. What natural barrier separates Spain from France?
3. What large body of water borders on Portugal? How does this help the overseas trade of the nation?

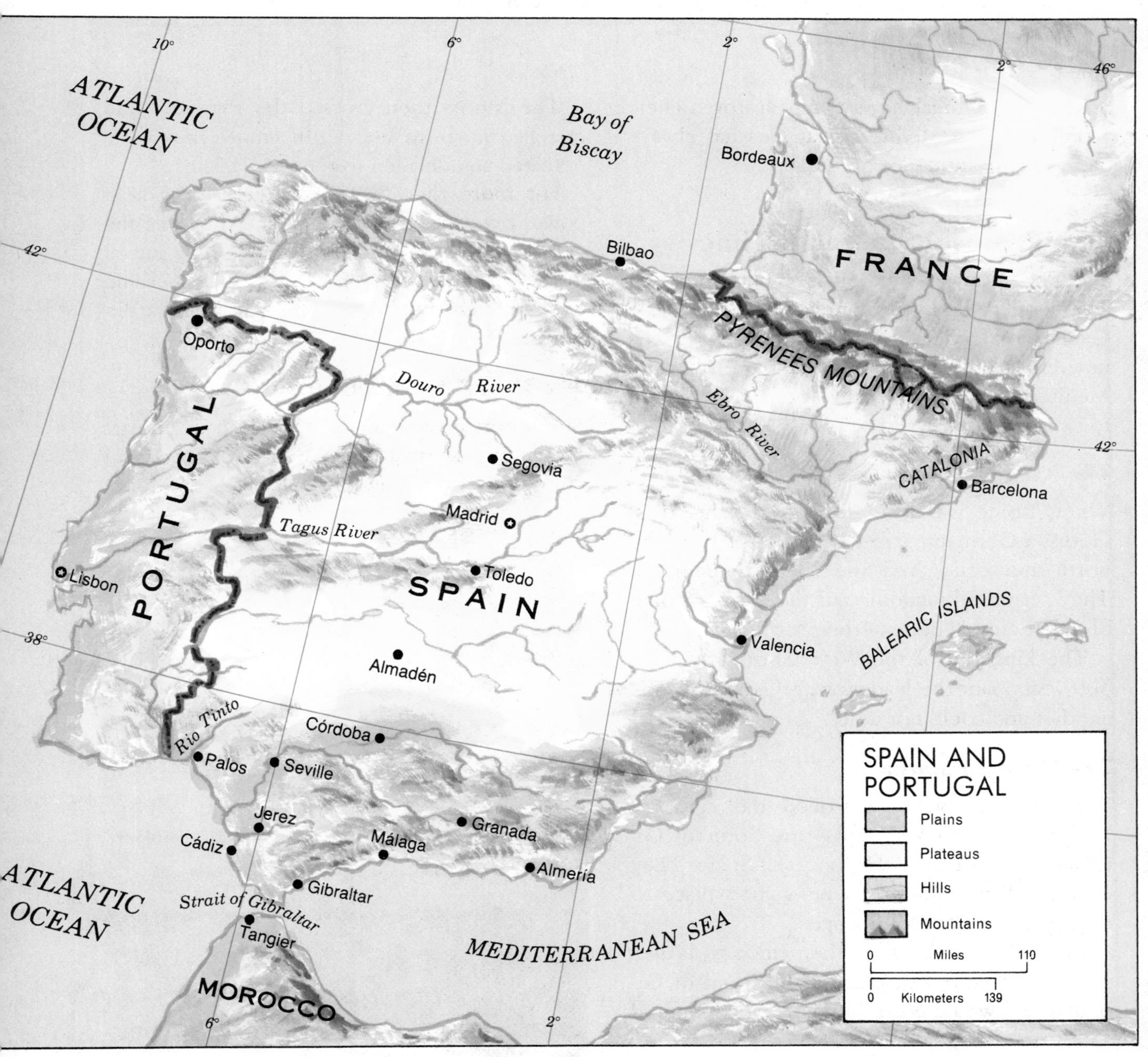

ATLANTIC OCEAN
Bay of Biscay
Bordeaux
FRANCE
Bilbao
PYRENEES MOUNTAINS
Oporto
Douro River
Ebro River
PORTUGAL
Segovia
CATALONIA
Barcelona
Madrid
Tagus River
Toledo
Lisbon
SPAIN
BALEARIC ISLANDS
Valencia
Almadén
Rio Tinto
Córdoba
Palos
Seville
Jerez
Granada
Cádiz
Málaga
Almería
Gibraltar
Strait of Gibraltar
Tangier
ATLANTIC OCEAN
MEDITERRANEAN SEA
MOROCCO
10°
6°
2°
42°
38°
46°
SPAIN AND PORTUGAL
Plains
Plateaus
Hills
Mountains
0 Miles 110
0 Kilometers 139

2
The History of Spain and Portugal

Spain and Portugal have a long history. Their position on the Mediterranean Sea has always been a major influence on them.

The Peninsula in Early Times

The Phoenicians visited Spain in ancient times. The people who lived there were related to the Gauls (gôlz), the early inhabitants of what is now France. When Rome gained control of the Mediterranean, it added most of the peninsula to its large empire.

The Kingdom of the West Goths

When Rome was losing its power, the West Goths, a Germanic tribe, swept down from the north and conquered the Iberian Peninsula. They set up a kingdom, and the native people of the peninsula became their serfs.

The kingdom of the West Goths lasted for 300 years. But the leaders were jealous of one another and could not unite.

The Moors in Spain

The Muslims, who controlled the coast of North Africa, looked across the Strait of Gibraltar (ji brôl′ tər) to the shores of Spain. They decided that Spain would be a good place to start their conquest of Europe.

In 711 the Muslims, or *Moors* (moorz) as they were called in Spain, crossed the Strait of Gibraltar and won a great battle. They conquered almost the whole peninsula.

The Moors then crossed the Pyrenees and marched north to France. In France they were defeated and decided to return to Spain.

For more than 500 years the Moors held power over that land. The northern part of the peninsula was too cold for them, so they stayed in the south. Under the Moors, Spain became one of the greatest centers of learning and art in Europe.

The Moors' Art and Culture

The Moors made many contributions to the art and culture of Spain. They built many beautiful mosques, universities, and libraries. The Moors

This palace near Granada, Spain, is considered to be the finest example of Moorish architecture in Europe.

had learned what the wise people of Greece and Alexandria knew. Their own scholars developed this learning still further and passed it on to others.

The Moors had a style of building new to western Europe. They used colored tiles and pointed archways with *latticework* (lat′is wurk′), or interlaced strips of stone or wood.

They had many good doctors. Their doctors mixed various medicines and found that the medicines changed when treated in certain ways. The study of these changes was called alchemy (al′kə mē). From the word "alchemy" we get the name for our modern science of *chemistry* (kem′is trē). Chemistry deals with the nature of substances and the changes they undergo.

At Córdoba (kôr′də bə) the Moors had a great university with a fine library. About the year 1200 Córdoba was the largest city in Europe except for Constantinople. Córdoba had more than half a million people. There were many public bathhouses and libraries. It had a mosque as large as St. Peter's Church at Rome. Not all the people were Muslims, but all were free to follow their own religious beliefs.

Spain was prosperous under the Moors, who had great skill in farming and gardening. They introduced many new plants into Spain. These included cotton, rice, sugarcane, palm trees, asparagus, and eggplant.

The Defeat of the Moors

While the Moors were peacefully working and studying, the Christians in the northwest of Spain were growing stronger. They organized armies. These Christian armies marched southward. After a time they defeated the Moors at Córdoba and Seville (se vil′).

Brightly striped archways form the inside of this mosque at Córdoba. Built by the *Moors* in the 700s, it is used today as a Christian church. More than 1,000 pillars of stone support its arches.

The city of Toledo now became the center of Moorish learning. The University of Toledo attracted many Christian students from Germany, Italy, and France. They respected the Moorish knowledge of medicine, astronomy, and geography. They learned Arabic in order to read Moorish books. They translated these books into Latin so they could be read by the learned people at home. Moorish Spain was a center of learning in Europe.

Queen Isabella was deeply interested in art and education. Here she listens carefully as Christopher Columbus tells of his plans to reach the Far East by sailing west.

In 1085 Toledo also was captured by Christian armies. By 1200 the Spanish began to push the Moors out of the country. But the Muslims continued to rule the small kingdom of Granada (grə nä′də), in southeastern Spain, for another 300 years.

The Rise of Spain

In 1469 a royal marriage united two important kingdoms, Aragon (ar′ə gon) in central Spain and Castile (kas tēl′) in eastern Spain. Both the future King Ferdinand and Queen Isabella were devout Catholics. They set out to make all of Spain a Catholic nation. The combined armies of Aragon and Castile moved against the Moors in Granada. With its fall in 1492 the last stronghold of the Moors in Spain was overcome.

In the years that followed, Spain became a powerful, united country. The other independent kingdoms followed the example of Aragon and Castile. Together they formed a nation.

Queen Isabella

Queen Isabella ruled the two kingdoms of Aragon and Castile jointly with her husband. She was known for her religious devotion and her support of learning and the arts.

Probably Queen Isabella's most important act was her support of Christopher Columbus's plans to reach the Far East by sailing west. He landed in the Western Hemisphere in 1492. This led to the growth of Spanish empires in the area later known as the Americas.

Queen Isabella hoped for a just rule in the new lands. At the time of her death in 1504 she was concerned about the rights of the Indians who had been brought to Europe from their native lands.

The Spanish in the Western Hemisphere

After Columbus's voyages Spanish adventurers rushed to the Western Hemisphere, seeking wealth and power. They explored and settled part of North America and most of Central and South America. Brazil was settled by the Portuguese. The Spaniards took back much gold and silver for the treasury of Spain.

Magellan (mə jel′ən), a Portuguese who sailed for Spain, was the first explorer to reach the Far East by sailing west. He went as far as the Philippine Islands, but lost his life there. Only one of his five ships completed the voyage around the world. But its return to Spain proved that the earth is round.

Ponce de León (pōns′dā lā ōn′), who explored Florida, was Spanish. So also were Cortés (kôr tez′), the conqueror of Mexico, and Hernando de Soto (her nän′dō dā sō′tō), who reached the Mississippi River. The first explorers to see the Grand Canyon of the Colorado River and the first European settlers of California were Spanish.

Spaniards had built hundreds of towns in America more than 100 years before the first lasting English settlement in America was started at Jamestown. They had set up missions to teach the Indians.

Spain left its mark on parts of the United States. Many buildings in our South and Southwest are Spanish in style. Many places there have Spanish names. The Spanish introduced their language and ways of living into Mexico, Central America, and South America. Today, in those areas except for Brazil, Spanish is spoken by most of the people. Spanish is also spoken in some islands of the Caribbean.

Spain's Loss of Power

In time, Spain lost its power. The precious metals which Spain took back from its explorations were used to pay for wars, not to create real or lasting wealth.

Meanwhile, England was growing in power on the sea. The Spanish king, Philip II, considered English ships a threat to Spain. So he fitted out a large fleet of armed ships, or *armada* (är mä′də). In 1588 this mighty fleet of 132 war vessels sailed up the English Channel. Spanish troops on the European shore just across the water from England were waiting to be taken aboard.

The English were ready for the Armada. They battered and crippled the Spanish fleet. They frightened the Spaniards with ships that were set on fire. The Spanish were unable to land troops on the English shore. The fighting lasted for a week. Many Spanish ships were sunk.

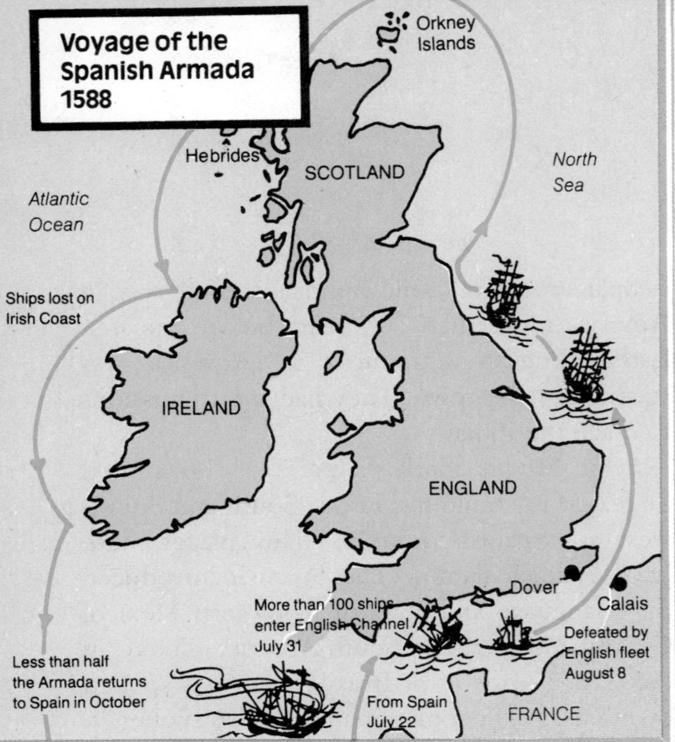

Trace the route of the Spanish *Armada.* What happened to the fleet in the English Channel? What other disasters did the fleet experience?

The Spanish vessels which were left tried to return to Spain by sailing around Scotland. But they ran into a storm, and many were wrecked. Less than half the ships of the Armada returned home. The Spanish were no longer a danger to England. Spain had begun to lose the power gained during the days of exploration.

Loss of American Colonies

About the time the United States won independence, the Spanish colonies in the New World began to grow restless. They felt that Spain just took wealth from them and was not really interested in their welfare. Finally they rebelled against Spain. One by one, beginning in 1810, all the Spanish colonies on the continents of North and South America won their independence.

The Rise of Portugal

Early in the 1300s ships from Venice and Genoa stopped for supplies in Lisbon. Portugal noticed that merchants in these cities were becoming rich by supplying Europe with spices from the Far East. The Portuguese set out to find their own route to the Far East by sailing south around Africa.

No one yet knew how far Africa extended to the south. For many years sailors traveled along the coast, each one going a little farther than the one before had dared to go. Then, one daring explorer succeeded in sailing around the stormy southern tip of Africa before he had to turn back. When he returned to Lisbon, he said that he had sailed around the "Cape of Storms."

"Not so," the king said. "We will call it the 'Cape of Good Hope.' "

The Portuguese in the Far East

In 1497 the Portuguese explorer, Vasco da Gama (väs′kō də gä′mə), sailed around the Cape of Good Hope and on to the west coast of India. There he built trading stations. He returned with a cargo of spices. Soon ships from Portugal sailed on to the East Indies Islands, and a large sea trade with these islands began. Portuguese colonies were also founded in Africa. Portugal became the greatest sea power in Europe.

The Portuguese in the New World

In 1500 a Portuguese captain reached South America by accident. The ship of Captain Cabral (kə bräl′), who had sailed for India, was blown off its course in a great storm. Cabral landed in what is now Brazil and claimed the land for Portugal. After a time Brazil was explored and settled by the Portuguese. This is why the people of Brazil today speak Portuguese.

Portugal's Loss of Power

In 1581 Spain took control of Portugal and ruled the land for 60 years. Meanwhile the Dutch attacked the East Indies and conquered most of the islands which the Portuguese had settled. Portugal regained its independence, but it never regained its former place of power in the world.

Portugal's large colony in South America, Brazil, sought its freedom. In 1821 Portugal granted Brazil its independence. Unlike the Spanish colonies, Brazil won freedom without a fight.

Gifts of Spain and Portugal

Spain and Portugal have had artists and writers who became famous. Spain also developed a style of building which is popular in America as well as in Europe. The early Spanish who settled in the Americas brought horses with them from Spain. They also brought sugarcane, cotton, and oranges. These things remind us of the Spanish and their gifts to us.

The *patio* (pat′ē ō′), or inner courtyard, is an idea in building which came from the Spaniards. Many homes in our Southwest are built around patios with gardens and fountains.

Two Famous Spaniards

Velásquez (və läs′kā) is a Spanish artist who is world famous. Some of his paintings are in the Prado (prä′dō) Gallery in Madrid. The Spanish writer Cervantes (sər vän′tēz) wrote one of the world's greatest books.

The Court Painter, Velasquez

Velásquez was born in Seville and began his painting there. When he was 23 years of age he went to Madrid. The Spanish king liked the paintings of Velásquez so much that he made

This painting by Velásquez shows a young Spanish princess surrounded by her maids of honor. The artist in the painting is Velásquez himself.

This drawing from Cervantes' *Don Quixote* shows Don Quixote and his squire, Sancho Panza, setting forth on a quest.

him the court painter. Velásquez painted more than 80 portraits of the king and other members of his family. Every one of his paintings was well done. He used beautiful colors, and he portrayed light and shadow in a way that is almost impossible for others to copy.

A Great Spanish Writer

One great Spanish writer wrote a book that will live forever. His name is Cervantes. The book, called *Don Quixote* (don'kē hō'tē), was published in 1615.

The main character in the book is Don Quixote. He was an old gentleman. As he had little else to do, he spent his time reading stories of old-time knights and their marvelous deeds. He decided to set forth on a quest like the knights he had read about and admired.

On his journey, Don Quixote had many accidents. He mistook windmills for giants, inns for castles, and country girls for highborn ladies. He even believed a flock of sheep was really an army he had to fight. His faithful squire, Sancho Panza (sän'chō pän'zä), saw things as they really were. He had a hard time trying to protect his master.

Cervantes meant to make the story of Don Quixote an amusing one. But he also hoped it would show Spain that it was wrong to cling to old-fashioned ways. This book, if the people had understood its meaning, could have given them a valuable lesson. *Don Quixote* is still read today because of its humor and the picture it gives of the life and times of the knights.

Do You Know?

1. When did the Moors conquer Spain? From what region did they come?
2. What lands in the Western Hemisphere did Spain and Portugal settle?
3. Why was the Spanish Armada built? What happened to it?

Before You Go On

Using New Words

patio chemistry
Moor latticework
armada

Number a paper from 1 through 5. After each number write the word or term that matches the definition.

1. The science that deals with the nature of substances and the changes they undergo
2. A large fleet of armed ships
3. An inner courtyard
4. One of the North African Muslims who invaded and conquered Spain
5. Interlaced strips of stone or wood

Finding the Facts

1. Where is the Iberian Peninsula located?
2. Why is most of Spain poor farming country? How are crops grown there?
3. Who ruled the Iberian Peninsula after the Romans left?
4. What happened to the Moors when they crossed over the Pyrenees into France?
5. Name three contributions Moors made to the culture of Spain.
6. After the fall of Córdoba, what city became the new center of Moorish learning?
7. About how long did the Moors rule in Spain?
8. What was the last stronghold of Moorish culture in Spain?
9. What two Spanish kingdoms were united by a marriage?
10. For what qualities was Queen Isabella known? What was her most important act?
11. What did the Spaniards bring back from the Western Hemisphere?
12. Name three Spanish explorers of North America.
13. What was Magellan the first to do?
14. Name two contributions Spanish explorers made to parts of the United States.
15. Why did the Portuguese attempt to sail around Africa?
16. What was the southern tip of Africa called by the sailors who first sailed around it? What was it renamed?
17. What did Vasco da Gama do when he reached India? What were the results?
18. What did Captain Cabral achieve for Portugal?
19. When did Spain conquer Portugal? How long did the Spanish rule there?
20. When did Brazil gain its independence?
21. Why is Cervantes remembered?

3
Spain and Portugal Today

In the countryside of Spain and Portugal most people work as farmers, miners, and fishers. In the cities, some work in factories.

The People of Spain

Many Spanish people earn their living from the land. They spend long hours tending vineyards, groves of olive and orange trees, and fields of grain, vegetables, and sugarcane. But Spain does not produce enough food to feed its people. Each year Spain must import, or bring in from other countries, large quantities of food. Spain does not have enough land that is level, fertile, and well-watered. More water is needed for irrigation and more fertilizer is needed.

Since 1960 Spain has changed from an agricultural to a manufacturing nation. Now more Spaniards work in manufacturing than in farming. Spain produces automobiles, ships, cement, chemicals, and shoes. Iron is the most important ore mined by the Spanish. Much of the ore is exported to Great Britain because Spain does not have enough steel mills to use it all.

Along the coasts, people fish for a living.

Manufacturing has become more important in Spain since 1960. Two of the country's products are automobiles and automobile parts. At this factory in Barcelona, seats are installed in cars.

They go out into the Mediterranean and Atlantic oceans to catch sardines, codfish, tuna, and other fish.

The People of Portugal

Portugal, like Spain, has many people who work as farmers and fishers. Here too people do not produce enough food to meet their needs. Portugal imports food.

The Portuguese mine some coal, tin, and copper but there are no factories to use these minerals. Portugal manufactures cloth, and some people make fine embroidery and lace.

The Cities of Spain

Spain has some interesting old cities. Among them are Barcelona (bär′sə lō′nə), Valencia (və len′sē ə), Madrid, and Seville.

Madrid, Capital of Spain

Madrid, the capital, is also the largest city in Spain. It has more than three and one-half million people.

Madrid is in the center of the nation. It is located on a high, barren plateau, which is cold in winter. But when summer comes, the weather is very hot. Madrid has fine public buildings, many of which were built by the Moors. It also has beautiful modern buildings and many lovely parks.

Seville, City of Old Spain

Seville is the leading city of the south. It represents the history and character of Spain better than any other city. Here are beautiful homes built in the Spanish fashion around courtyards. Bullfights are popular spectacles in Seville.

Madrid, the capital of Spain, has many beautiful old buildings. One of the city's most important industries is tourism. Many people from northern Europe come to Madrid for its hot summers.

Valencia, a Garden City

The country around Valencia, on the coast south of Barcelona, resembles a huge garden, although rain seldom falls in this region. Streams from the mountains are caught in large reservoirs. Water from these reservoirs, built by the Moors, fills the irrigation canals. The water is shared among the farmers.

Barcelona
Spain's Major Manufacturing City

The King and Queen of Spain greeted Columbus in Barcelona on his return from the New World. It is now the country's greatest port and most important modern industrial city. Skilled workers manufacture automobiles, textiles, chemicals, articles of glass and leather, and all kinds of machinery.

The people of Barcelona live in the region of Spain called Catalonia (kat′əl ō′nē ə). The Catalans are very proud. They have their own language, which is more like French than Spanish. Street signs in Barcelona are sometimes written in both Catalan and Spanish.

The Catalans boast that they are a hard-working people. As early as 1200 they made Barcelona an important city for trade and for textile manufacturing. Its location—on the far western end of the trade routes used during the Middle Ages—helped make it a trading center.

Today Barcelona draws millions of tourists. They come to sample nearby beaches on the Mediterranean Sea and the delicious seafood of waterfront restaurants. In Barcelona they find a city that, while becoming a great industrial center, has kept its Mediterranean charm.

Lisbon, Capital of Portugal

At the mouth of the Tagus (tā′gəs) River is Lisbon, the beautiful seaport capital of Portugal. The Tagus River rises in the mountains and flows across most of the peninsula. It is wide enough to be navigable through Portugal and far into Spain. Ships on the Tagus can carry inland products to and from Lisbon.

Lisbon, with its hills and green gardens, is a lovely city. Colored tiles, first used by the Moors, decorate many houses.

Products of the Peninsula

Both Spain and Portugal raise many crops, fruits, and animals. The peninsula also has useful minerals.

Farm Products of Spain and Portugal

Much wheat is grown in the valleys of Portugal and in central Spain. Trees are few because of light rainfall and cold, dry winters. There are a few forests in the mountains. In recent years Spaniards have begun to plant trees for shade and for the protection they give the soil.

The climate around Valencia is mild. Because of irrigation, the people can raise almost anything. They can even raise rice, which needs huge amounts of water. Their orchards of almond, apricot, and orange trees are famous. Date palms grow well, and there are large crops of corn and wheat. The farmers practice *crop rotation* (krop rō tā′shən). Different crops are planted in the same field from year to year to keep farmland fertile. In a field in which grain has been planted, beans or clover will be raised the next year. Beans and clover restore the soil's minerals.

At an orange-packing plant in Spain, workers inspect oranges as the fruit moves along conveyor belts. Then the oranges are packed in crates and shipped as exports.

Oranges, olives, grapes, and almonds make up a large part of Spain's exports. Spain's sweet oranges go to the British Isles and to other European markets. Oranges are grown along the lowlands in southern Spain and on the western coast of Portugal. Much of the olive oil that Spain and Portugal produce is sold to the United States.

Spain and Portugal produce most of the world's cork. Cork comes from the bark of the cork oak tree. The bark is stripped from the tree about once every ten years. It is dried in the sun.

The white or purple grapes that Spain sends abroad are called Málaga (mal′ə gə) grapes, from the name of the city on the Mediterranean. Grapes are also exported from Almería (al′mə rē′ə), east of Málaga.

In late winter the Balearic (bäl′ē ar′ik) Islands, in the Mediterranean, and the south Spanish coast are pink with almond blossoms. Spaniards eat the kernels of the green fruit as dessert. Spanish children enjoy candy made of almond paste.

Both Spain and Portugal are famous for cork. The cork oak trees sometimes live to be hundreds of years old. Every 10 years the bark of the cork oak can be stripped off. This does not harm the tree. Besides being used for stoppers in bottles, cork makes good life preservers. Ground up with linseed oil, cork is spread on burlap or canvas to make linoleum. Sometimes cork is used to make the soles of shoes.

Other Products of Spain and Portugal

Iron ore is mined near the northern coast of Spain. The ore is shipped from the city of Bilbao (bil bä′ō) to Great Britain, where it is smelted. In return, the English ships bring back to Spain cargoes of coal, for Spain does not have many coal mines.

In the south there are copper mines. These mines were known to the Phoenicians. The copper from these mines blackens the water of the river which flows past them, so that the river is called Rio Tinto or "ink river."

Almadén (al'mə dān'), north of Córdoba, has important *mercury* (mur'kyər ē) mines. Mercury is a silver-colored metal. It is commonly used in its liquid state in thermometers, but it has many other industrial uses.

Portugal has little coal, but a new iron-and-steel industry has been developed. Portugal has many swift mountain streams which furnish electrical power. Since it is a seacoast country, fishing is important. Sardines are canned and exported to many countries. Grapes are grown for wine making, Portugal's chief industry. Other products are cork and citrus fruit.

The Domestic Animals of Spain

One of Spain's important domestic animals is the donkey, whose stout back bears heavy loads and whose sure feet take it over steep mountain trails.

Spain has many sheep, but few cattle. Sheep can find food on rocky, dry ground and need little water. Southeast of Madrid a kind of sheep, the *merino* (mə rē'nō), is raised. They have a heavy coat of fine wool. Spain prized these sheep so highly in early times that none could be exported except by permission of the ruler.

Spain raises many goats. Even in large cities goats are driven through the streets each morning, so that householders may get their supply of fresh milk. The goat is hardier than the sheep, and its milk is more nourishing than cow's milk.

Many bulls are raised for bullfighting. Many Spaniards enjoy bullfights as much as some of the people in the United States enjoy basketball, football, and baseball. Every large city in Spain has its bull ring. Soccer is Spain's most popular sport. Jai alai (hī'lī') is also popular.

The Colonies of Spain

Most of Spain's former colonies now are independent. Morocco (mə rok'ō), which is separated from Spain by the Strait of Gibraltar, was granted independence in 1956. Farther south in Africa, on the Atlantic coast, was the former colony of Spanish Sahara. Spain withdrew in 1976 and the land was divided between Morocco and Mauritania (môr'ə tā'nēə).

Spain still owns the Canary Islands, near the coast of former Spanish Sahara. The birds called canaries came originally from these islands. Wild canaries were brown or green in color.

The Colonies of Portugal

Portugal used to own many colonies throughout the world. Portugal was powerful in India from 1500 to 1600. After 1600 Portugal lost most of its Indian possessions to the Dutch, the English, and the French. In 1961 India forced Portugal also to give up three trading stations it continued to hold there. The best known of these was Goa (gō′ə), a fine harbor on India's west coast.

On an island off the southeast coast of China is the Portuguese port of Macao (mə kou′). It formerly was a trade and fishing center. Because Macao's harbor is now rapidly filling up with soil, its trade is shrinking.

In Africa, Portugal used to own the large colony of Mozambique (mō′zəm bēk′), located on the east coast of Africa. But in 1975 Mozambique became independent. On the western coast of Africa, Portugal held Angola (ang gō′lə) until that country became independent in 1976. Several small islands in the Gulf of Guinea once belonged to Portugal, as did Guinea-Bissau (gin′ē bis au′).

Spain in Recent Times

In 1931 the king was overthrown by a revolution, and Spain became a republic. Many people opposed changes the government attempted. Under the leadership of General Francisco Franco, they revolted. A *civil war* (siv′əl wôr), which is a war between opposing groups within a country, broke out.

Each side in the war received aid from foreign countries and from people who acted on their own. More than 600 Americans fought against Franco. In 1939 General Franco won and made himself head of the government. He ruled as dictator.

In 1975 Franco died. Juan Carlos (hwän kär′lōs) became king. In 1976 a ban against political parties ended, and in the 1977 election, several parties competed for seats in Parliament. It was the first time since 1936 that voters were given a choice of candidates in an election.

Portugal in Recent Times

Portugal, like Spain, had been governed by a dictator for many years. The government was overthrown in 1974 and democracy was restored. In 1976 free elections were held for the first time in more than 50 years.

Do You Know?

1. What form of government did Spain have between the end of the civil war and Franco's death?
2. What form of government does Portugal now have?
3. In what ways is cork used?

To Help You Learn

Using New Words

merino chemistry armada
patio civil war crop rotation
mercury

Number a paper from 1 through 7. After each number write the word or term that matches the definition.

1. A silver-colored metal used in its liquid state to make thermometers and other products
2. Planting different crops in the same field from year to year to keep farmland fertile
3. A large fleet of armed ships
4. A war between opposing groups within a country
5. The science that deals with the nature of substances and the changes they undergo
6. A kind of sheep with a heavy coat of fine wool
7. An inner courtyard

Finding the Facts

1. What kind of climate does Portugal have in winter? In summer?
2. How long did the West Goths rule Spain? Why did they lose their power?
3. Name three plants introduced by the Moors into Spain.
4. When was the city of Toledo captured by Christian armies?
5. Who led the two kingdoms that united to defeat Granada?
6. What did Magellan's voyage prove to the world?
7. Who was the first explorer to sail around Africa and on to India? When?
8. Why do the people of Brazil speak Portuguese?
9. Why are the paintings of Velásquez so much admired?
10. Who was Don Quixote? Who wrote his story?
11. What are the four main occupations of the Spanish and Portuguese?
12. How do Spain and Portugal get enough food to feed their people?
13. Why does Spain export much of its iron ore to Britain?
14. Match each city below with a phrase that describes it:

    Madrid Barcelona
    Seville Valencia
    Lisbon

    a. capital of Portugal
    b. Spain's major manufacturing city
    c. a city of history
    d. a garden city
    e. capital of Spain
15. Name four farm products exported by Spain.
16. What is cork? How is it gathered?
17. What is Portugal's chief industry?
18. From what city is iron ore shipped to Great Britain? What do the boats bring back in return?

19. Why is the Rio Tinto called the "ink river"?
20. Where is mercury mined? How is it often used?
21. Why does Spain have more sheep and goats than cattle?
22. Name two popular sports in Spain.
23. What leader came to power after Spain's civil war? When did he rule?
24. What significant event occurred in Portugal in 1976?

Learning from Maps

1. Look at the map of Spain and Portugal on page 287 and answer these questions: What mountains separate Spain from France? What strait separates Spain from Africa? How much of the peninsula is mountainous? How much is plateau? What parallel of latitudepasses through central Spain? What meridian passes through Seville? How far is it from Oporto to Madrid? Lisbon to Valencia?
2. Study the product map of Spain and Portugal on page 301. What minerals are shown? What products do you suppose are shipped from Bilboa? Oporto? Barcelona? Valencia?

Using Study Skills

1. **Time Line:** Place in the proper order of time the following events: Marriage of Ferdinand and Isabella; Brazil granted independence; Capture of Toledo; Córdoba becomes the second largest city in Europe; Vasco da Gama sails around the Cape of Good Hope.

   Copy the time line from page 285. Add these events to your time line.

   Study the completed time line and answer the following questions: How many years passed between the marriage of Ferdinand and Isabella and the defeat of Granada? Between the Portuguese arrival in Brazil and Brazil's independence? How long did Franco rule? How many years passed between the Moors' entry into Spain and the capture of Toledo? Between the beginning of the Moors' expulsion from Spain and the defeat of Granada?
2. **Chart:** Make a chart showing former and present Spanish and Portuguese colonies in Asia and Africa. The chart has been started for you below.

	Spain	Portugal
Former:	Morocco	
Present:		

3. **Graph:** On page 305 is a circle graph. Because each section resembles a piece of pie, it is sometimes called a pie graph. A circle graph is useful to show how much of a total (or 100 percent) is used in a particular way. Study this graph and answer these questions:

   What uses are made of land in Spain? Do the forests take up more or less than half of the land in Spain? Arrange the uses of land in the order of their importance. Next to each, write the percent you find on the graph. Find the sum. What does it total?

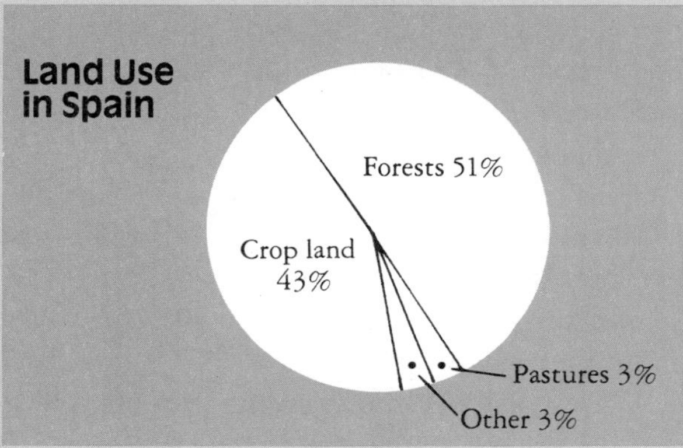

Thinking It Through

1. Under the Moors, Spain developed in the fields of learning and art more than any other part of Europe. How do you explain this?
2. Spain received much gold and silver from the Americas. It used most of these riches to carry on wars. But by 1600 Spain had begun to lose its power. Would Spain have been better off, perhaps, if it had used its money for the good of the Spanish people and of the Spanish colonists in the Americas? Give reasons for your answer.
3. Many of the new ideas and products that the Spanish brought to the Americas were first introduced into Spain by the Moors. What differences would it have made in your life if the Moors had not conquered Spain?
4. How do you think the history of the world would have been different if Queen Isabella had not supported Christopher Columbus?

Projects

1. Many places in the United States have Spanish names; for example, El Paso, Los Angeles, and Santa Fe. Find these on a map. Locate other places also and make a list to present to your class.
2. Arrange a program of Spanish songs and dances. Use phonograph records, or have someone sing the songs or play them on an instrument.
3. The Explorers' Committee might choose one of the Spanish and one of the Portuguese explorers and tell their stories. On a map show where they traveled.
4. The Research Committee might plan to be guides in Spain and Portugal for a travel bureau. Select places of interest in each of five cities. Use the encyclopedia and the library to find out more about the cities. Prepare "tourist talks" for the class.
5. Here are some words which came to us from the Spanish language: *bronco, barbecue, canyon, corral, adobe, plaza, tornado.* Look up these words in a dictionary. Use each word in a sentence that explains its meaning.
6. Find out more about one of these: cork, Portuguese lace, merino sheep, mercury, sardines, jai alai. Make a report to your class. Pictures or samples of the products or a demonstration of the sport might make your report more interesting.

10 France

Unit Preview

Before the year 51 B.C., the Gauls, a warlike people, roamed about the part of Europe that is highlighted on the map. In 51 B.C., Roman armies conquered the Gauls. The Romans kept order until after Rome fell. For many years after, Gaul, or France, was torn by wars. Then in A.D. 800, the emperor Charlemagne gained enough power to rule this region.

During the Middle Ages, France was divided into small states under the feudal system. English kings claimed portions of France. In 1429 the English were defeated at the Battle of Orléans. France became a powerful and united kingdom. The richest and most powerful of French kings was Louis XIV.

Not long after the American Revolution, the common people of France revolted against their king. Then a young soldier named Napoleon Bonaparte became dictator and emperor of France. He tried to conquer Europe, but failed.

During World Wars I and II, France became a battlefield. The French suffered many losses, but they managed to rebuild their country. After World War II, France gave up its possessions in Africa and Asia.

Today France is famous for its fine foods and wines, its fashions and perfumes. Visitors come from all parts of the world to see the beautiful city of Paris. They visit the museums to see the paintings of French artists.

Things to Discover

If you look carefully at the picture, map, and time line on these pages, you can answer these questions.

1. France is highlighted on the map. What areas of this country border a sea or ocean?
2. What was France called in early times?
3. How long did the Romans stay in France after the fall of Rome in A.D. 476? Why did they leave?
4. Who were two famous French emperors?
5. What French woman became a famous military leader?
6. The picture shows the Arc de Triomphe or Arch of Triumph in Paris. This great monument was begun by Napoleon in 1806. When did Napoleon become the French emperor?
7. What French colony in Africa became independent in 1962?
8. When was Charlemagne crowned emperor of the Holy Roman Empire?

Words to Learn

You will meet these words in this unit. As you read, you will learn what they mean and how to pronounce them. The Word List will help you.

bacteria	pasteurize
boulevard	premier
guillotine	radioactive
Impressionist	radium
lycée	

- 51 B.C. — Gaul becomes a Roman province
- 486 A.D. — Barbarian Franks defeat Romans
- 800 — Charlemagne crowned emperor
- 1429 — Joan of Arc leads French in Battle of Orléans
- 1643 — Louis XIV becomes king
- 1789 — French Revolution starts
- 1804 — Napoleon crowns himself Emperor of France
- 1944 — France liberated in World War II
- 1958 — De Gaulle elected president
- 1962 — Algeria wins independence from France

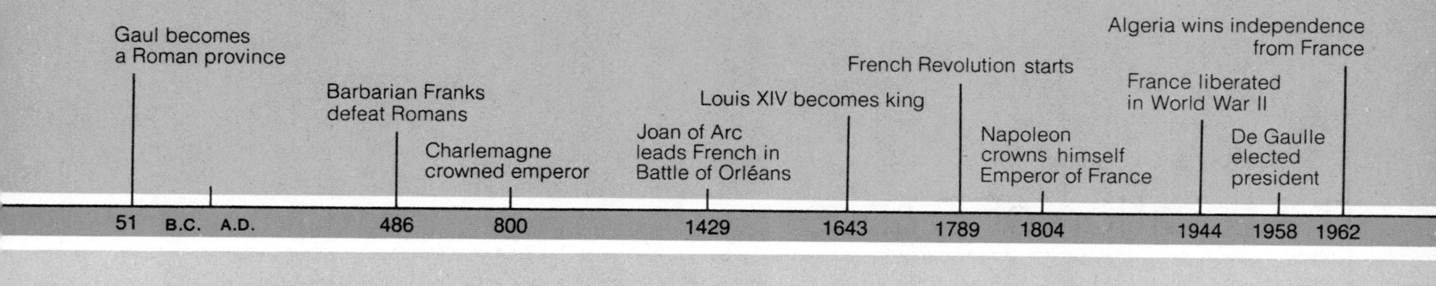

Arctic Ocean
Atlantic Ocean
EUROPE
ASIA
AFRICA
Pacific Ocean
Indian Ocean
AUSTRALIA

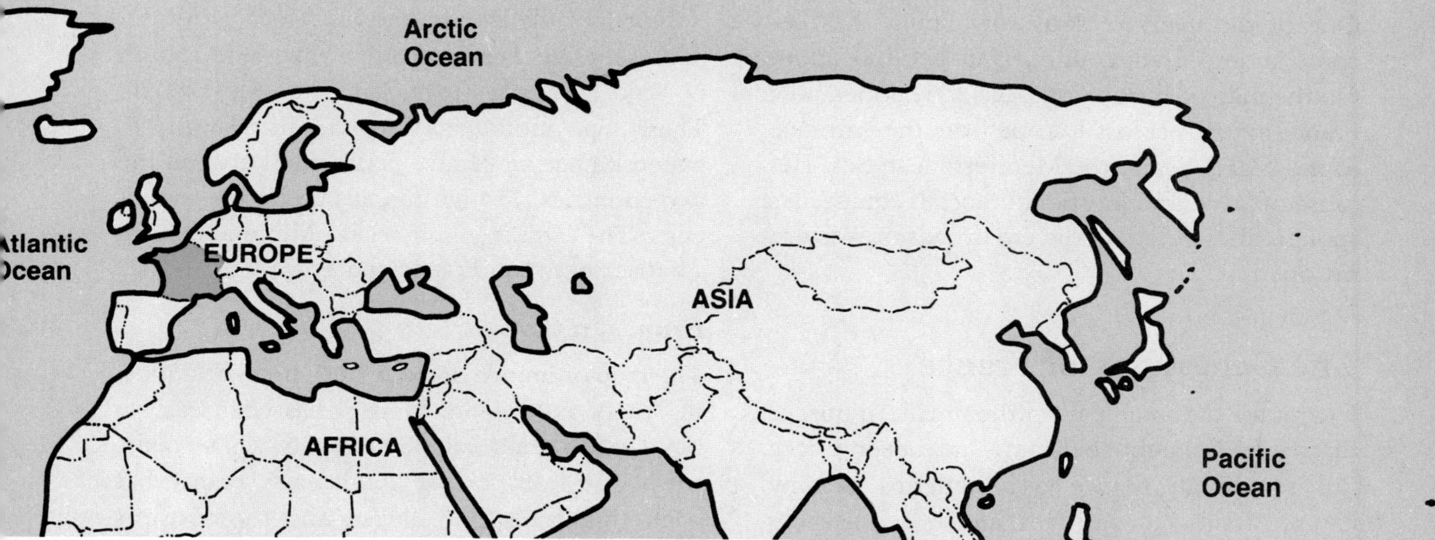

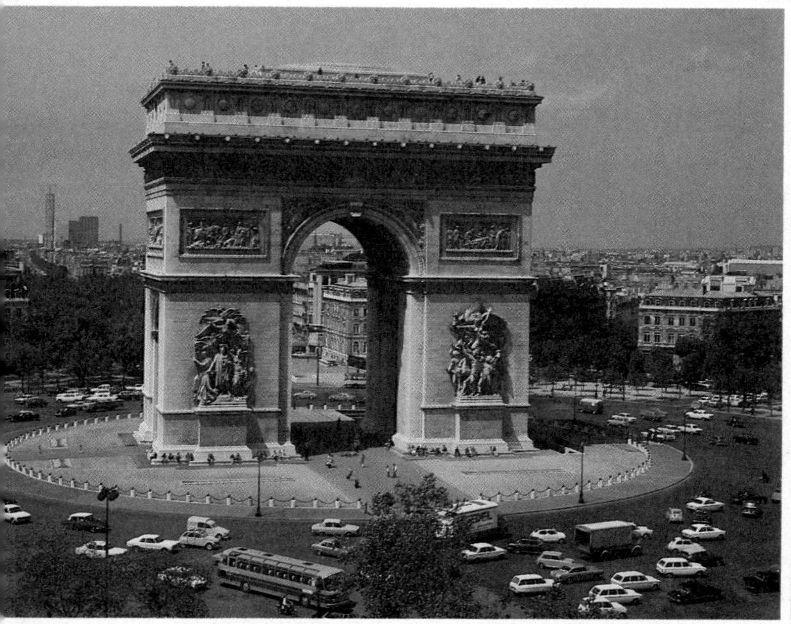

1
The Location of France

One of the many reasons why France has become an important country is its good location. On the map of Europe on page 161, notice how France extends across Europe from the entrance to the North Sea to the Mediterranean Sea. Because of its central location, France is sometimes spoken of as being on the crossroads of western Europe.

The Geography of France

Except for the small part of the northern border that faces Belgium (bel′jəm) and Luxembourg (luk′səm burg′), France has boundaries made by nature. Its long coastlines and good harbors have helped France have a large sea trade.

The Rivers and Mountains of France

Into the English Channel flows the Seine (sān) River. The Seine is not large, but the French have made it useful by building locks, dams, and canals. Paris, the capital of France, is on the Seine.

Two other rivers, the Loire (lwär) and the Garonne (gə rän′), flow into the Bay of Biscay. On the banks of the Loire are vineyards, wheat fields, and beautiful old castles. Garonne is long, but ships can use it only for a short distance near its mouth.

The Rhone River rises in the mountains of Switzerland, flows across France, and empties into the Mediterranean. This river has the power to turn many mills.

North of the Rhone, the Jura (joor′ə) Mountains separate France from Switzerland. South of Lake Geneva (jə nē′və), the Alps begin. These high mountains form a natural wall between France and Italy. Trains run between the two countries through tunnels under the mountains. The Pyrenees (pir′ə nēz) Mountains form a barrier between France and Spain.

France, a Great Plain

The map of France on page 309 shows that most of France is lowland. Here it has been easy to build roads, railroads, and canals which make travel and transporting goods easy. France has some highlands and mountains too. Forests grow in many parts of France.

The lowlands in the north of Europe form a broad, easily traveled plain. Travelers can go from the eastern Soviet Union to the English Channel without crossing a single mountain. From the Mediterranean the Rhone Valley also offers travelers an easy road northward across France.

Connecting many of the rivers of France is a network of canals. The building of the canals was begun about 300 years ago. As time went on, they were enlarged and lengthened. Today France has more than 6,000 miles (9,600 km) of waterways.

By means of this system of canals the French ship large quantities of coal, iron ore, chemicals, building materials, and other heavy freight. The barges carrying these things move slowly, but

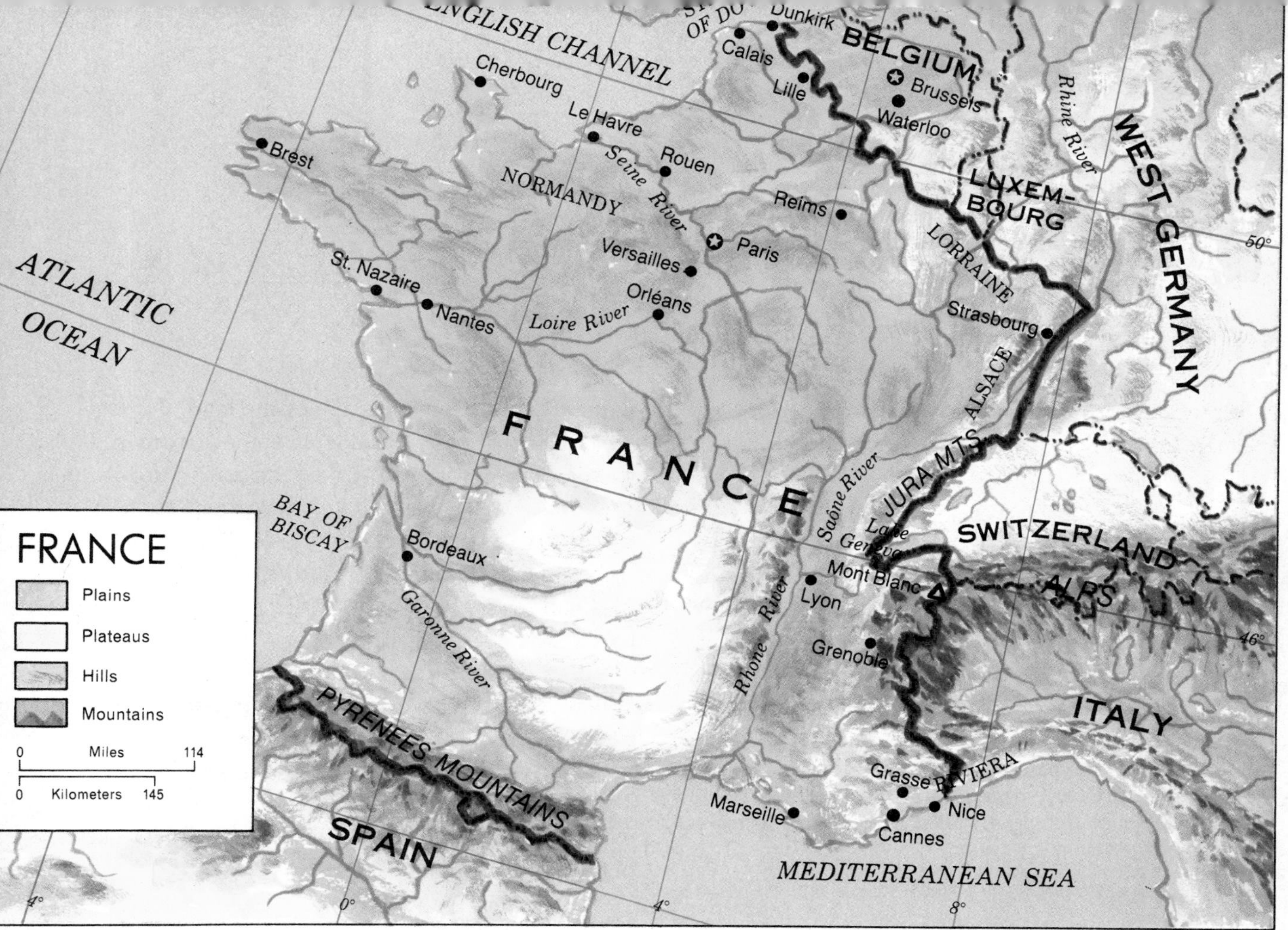

they cost little to operate. It is cheaper to send freight along the waterways than by train or truck.

France, a Crossroads

Easy routes of travel made France a center of trade in the Middle Ages. Today so many airplane routes go in and out of Paris that they look like the spokes of a wheel on an airline map. France carries on trade by barges, ships, railroads, trucks, and airplanes.

At times, however, France has also suffered from its location. It has been easy for armies to march across France. Many battles have taken place on its soil. The French people have worked hard to overcome the destruction left by wars.

Do You Know?

1. What bodies of water and mountains form the boundaries of France?
2. How much of France is lowland?
3. Why can heavy freight be shipped easily from one part of France to another?

2
The History of France

France has had a long history. Our study of France begins during the early years of the Roman Empire.

France in Early Times

In Roman times the country now known as France was part of a land called Gaul. The Gauls lived in huts among great forests. Julius Caesar, the Roman general, conquered this wild region. Gaul became a Roman province in 51 B.C.

These paintings show scenes from the life of Charlemagne. They illustrate a manuscript that tells about Charlemagne's reign as emperor.

Gaul as a Roman Province

Roman civilization spread over the land. Forests were cleared away. Roads stretched from sea to sea. The people observed Roman customs. Many cities that were important then, such as Bordeaux (bôr dō′), Lyon (lē ōn′), and Marseille (mär sā′), are important today. The capital of Gaul was Lyon, where four great Roman roads crossed.

For about 400 years Gaul belonged to Rome. When Rome's power faded, other peoples invaded Gaul. One tribe, the Franks, set up a kingdom after defeating the Romans in 486. The Gauls and the Franks became one people with one language. The land was called Francia, or the land of the Franks.

Charlemagne, King of the Franks

The land of the Franks covered most of the country which is France today and a part of western Germany. In the year 800 Charlemagne (shär′lə mān′), king of the Franks, was crowned emperor of the Holy Roman Empire by the Pope. The name Charlemagne means Charles the Great.

Charlemagne was a strong, wise king. He wished to bring order and unity to western Europe. He wanted it to become a great empire such as Rome had been centuries earlier.

For nearly 50 years Charlemagne worked and fought to carry out his plan. He united the peoples of western Europe and made them keep peace.

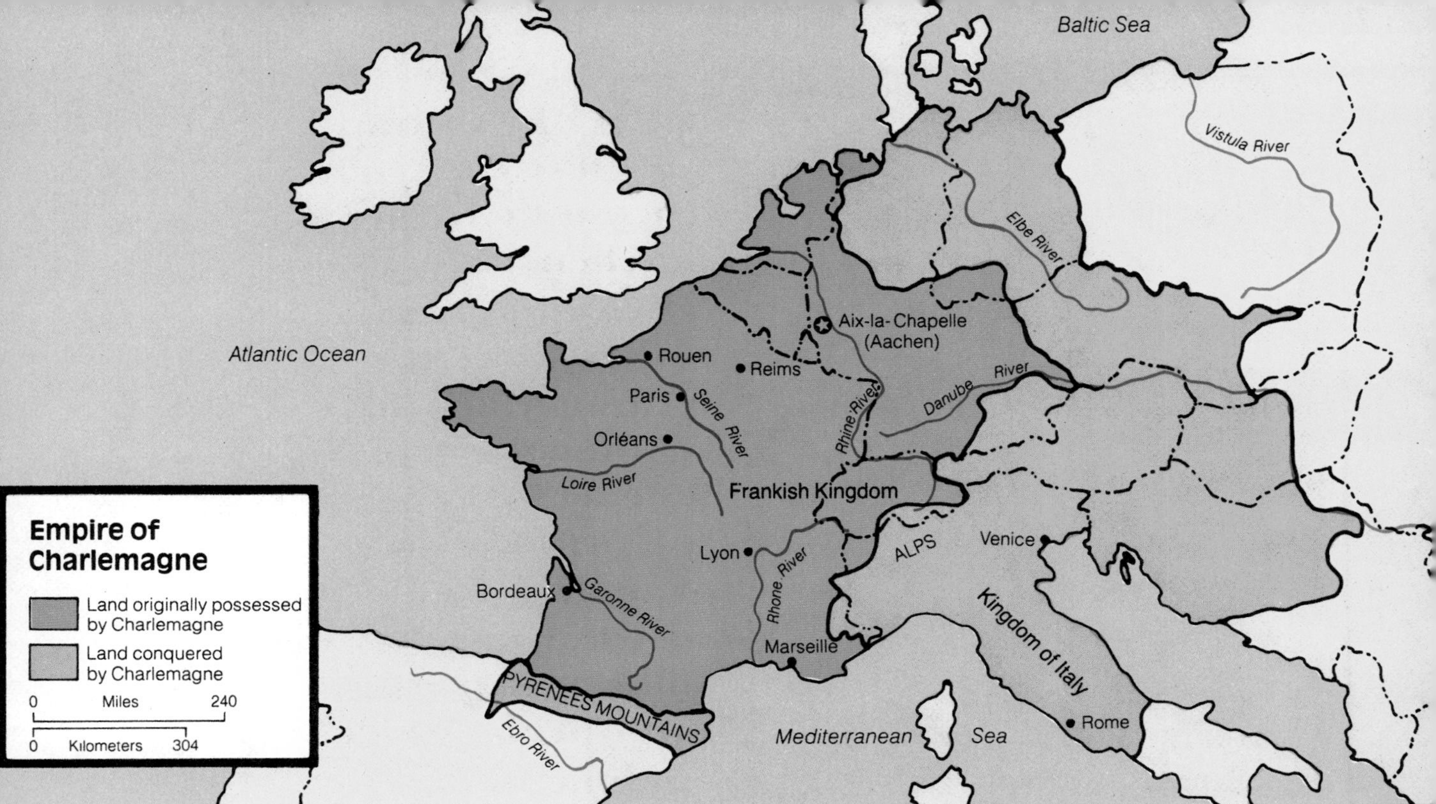

Charlemagne wished to unite western Europe and make it into an empire such as the Romans had created hundreds of years before.

Charlemagne had great respect for learning. He spoke several languages, but he never learned to read or write. While he lived, he kept order throughout his empire. When he died, his empire was divided. But Charlemagne, the great king, is remembered in the stories written about him long after his death.

The Coming of the Normans

After Charlemagne's empire broke up, daring Vikings sailed up the Seine to rob and plunder. They came from the lands which are now Denmark and Norway. They settled in the part of France now known as Normandy (nôr′mən dē). They were called Normans.

France in the Middle Ages

In the Middle Ages the land of the Franks was divided into many feudal states. Each was ruled by a count, a duke, or a baron.

France as a Kingdom

In 987 a group of French lords chose Lord Hugh Capet (că pā′) as their king. He arranged for his eldest son to succeed him as king. Members of the Capet family were kings of France for 800 years.

Although Hugh Capet had been elected king, he had trouble with some of the lords. He cleverly avoided claiming too much power, and he made sure of his strength before he quarreled

Joan of Arc is shown riding into battle at Orléans, where the English were defeated, in this painting from an old manuscript.

with any noble. Under the Capet kings, France gradually grew stronger.

When the French king died in 1328 without an heir, his nephew, the English king, claimed the French throne. This resulted in a long war, known as the Hundred Years' War, between the English and the French. At times it seemed that France would come under the control of England. But a peasant girl helped rescue France.

Joan of Arc

Joan of Arc was born in a village far from Paris. When she was not quite 17 years old, she heard a voice which she believed was from heaven. This voice told her to leave home and help her country. She dressed as a boy and rode through winter weather for nearly 300 miles (480 km). Finally, she reached the castle where she met Charles, the timid heir to the throne.

In 1429 Joan persuaded Charles to let her lead a small army to the city of Orléans (ôr′lē ənz) on the Loire. Orléans was the last French stronghold in the northern half of France still resisting the English.

At Orléans the French troops followed Joan into battle, and the English were defeated. After that Joan was called "the Maid of Orléans." The French felt a new spirit of hope and bravery. Victory followed victory. After the English

The Palace of Versailles, built by Louis XIV, is now a national museum. Each year thousands of visitors enjoy its beautiful gardens and splendid fountains.

were driven out of Reims (rēmz) Joan saw Charles VII crowned in the cathedral of Reims. Joan, who had been wounded twice, now wished to go back to her quiet village. But the king would not permit this.

A year after her victory at Orléans, Joan was captured by the English invaders. After a year in prison she was tried as a witch. She was condemned and burned to death in the city of Rouen (rōō än′) in northern France.

The work that Joan started was completed 20 years later. The English were driven out of France. Today the story of the Maid of Orléans is proudly told. Our city of New Orleans is named for the city that Joan saved for France.

France in Later Times

The Hundred Years' War was a terrible time for France. But during that period the French learned to work together and to be proud of being French.

The Reign of Louis XI

When Charles VII died in 1461, his son Louis XI inherited the throne. Louis XI knew that a great France must be a united France. He reduced the power of the feudal lords, killing or imprisoning those who opposed him. He set up a postal service. He established uniform weights and measures and laws throughout France. He built new roads and canals.

In Paris, Louis XI founded a school of medicine. In Bordeaux he started a law school. He knew the value of education to a nation.

Louis realized that manufacturing and trade also make a nation great. He increased the number of fairs held for trade. To encourage the French to weave rugs and tapestries, he would not allow the import of these products from the East. He encouraged the raising of silkworms and the weaving of silk.

During his reign Louis XI increased the size of France. He established peace and order. The kingdom of France now rested upon a strong foundation.

The Reign of Louis XIV

In 1643 another strong king, Louis XIV, came to the throne. During the 70 years that Louis XIV reigned, France grew to about the size that it is today.

Louis XIV was called the "Sun King" because of the splendor in which he lived. The nobles were forced to spend much time and money making the court more beautiful. He built a splendid palace with beautiful gardens at Versailles (ver sī′), near Paris. He encouraged painters, sculptors, and architects to beautify Paris and his palaces.

Other European rulers of the time admired the "Grand Monarch." They learned French, which became the fashionable language in most of Europe. They copied the rich court dress of France, and France became the center of styles.

The great cost of Louis's court, however, meant crushing taxes for the country. The nobles at court had little time to think about the hard life that the peasants were forced to live.

After the death of Louis XIV, France's power declined. Louis XIV had kept a large army and had waged many wars to extend boundaries. These wars and the money spent in supporting the court weakened France. The kings who succeeded Louis XIV continued to live in ease and to spend money freely. By the time Louis XVI became king, the government was almost bankrupt. However, he would not accept reforms. The glory of the court meant great suffering for the people.

France was drawn into wars against England over its possessions in America and in India. France was beaten and in time had to let go of its colonies on the mainland of North America. The largest of these, New France (later called Canada), fell to England. France also lost to England almost all of its lands in India.

The French Revolution

In 1789, the people of France revolted and swept away the power of the king and his nobles. Louis XVI, who was then king, Marie Antoinette (mə rē′ an′twə net′), his queen, and many others lost their heads under the knife of the *guillotine* (gil′ə tēn′). The guillotine was a new kind of machine for beheading persons.

The French Revolution was a long, hard struggle carried on with bloodshed and violence. A republic was formed, but it was weak. There was trouble also from outside France because the kings of some other countries were afraid that they also might lose their thrones. To prevent this, these rulers waged war on France.

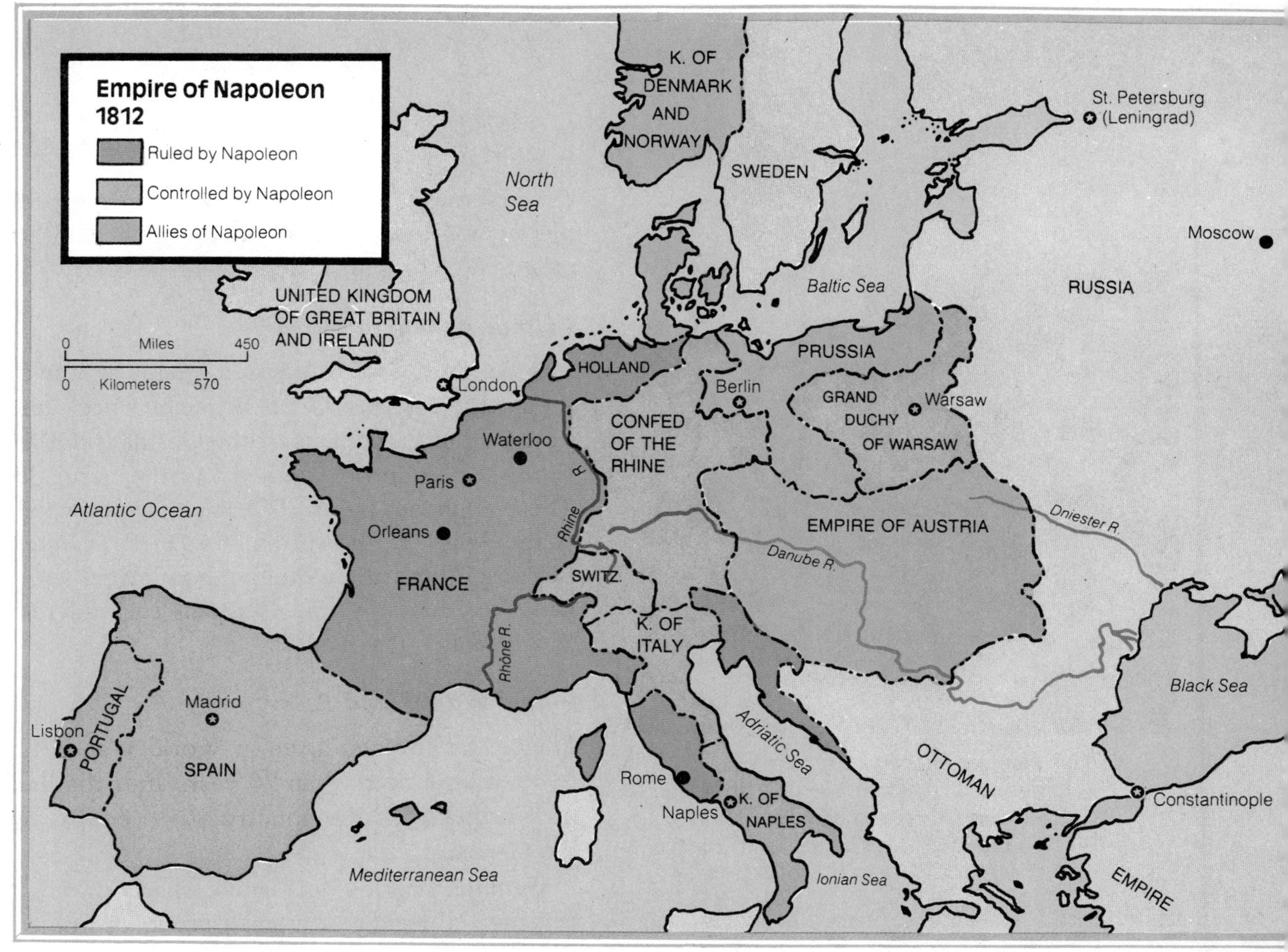

At one time Napoleon controlled most of Europe. He ruled some of this territory as part of the French Empire. Some areas became allies. He controlled others by appointing their rulers.

France under Napoleon

After much disorder and bloodshed, a young general, Napoleon Bonaparte (nə pō′lē ən bō′ nə pärt′), took control of the government. Napoleon had been in the army since the age of 16. He studied battles of the past to learn how they had been planned. Napoleon inspired his troops to win many battles.

He made himself dictator. Then, in 1804, he had himself crowned emperor of France. Although Napoleon controlled most of Europe, Great Britain continued to oppose the French emperor.

Napoleon kept on fighting to gain more power. He planned to invade England but was prevented by the British fleet. Then Napoleon

This painting shows the retreat of Napoleon's army from Moscow after the city was burned by the Russians. Napoleon, on a white horse, leads the retreat across the icy plains of Russia.

marched into Russia and captured Moscow, one of its greatest cities. But the Russians burned the city, leaving the French army without shelter. It had to retreat in the middle of winter.

On the slow journey back across the icy plains most of the French army perished. This was the beginning of Napoleon's downfall. Countries that he had conquered rebelled. In 1815 he was defeated at Waterloo, in Belgium. Napoleon spent the last years of his life as a prisoner of the English on a lonely island in the South Atlantic.

After the overthrow of Napoleon, France moved back and forth from a monarchy, which is a country ruled by a king, to a republic, or country ruled by a person elected by the people. It was a republic when the great conflict called World War I began.

France in World War I

In 1914 the Germans invaded France by way of the northern plains. Great Britain at once came to the aid of France against the Germans. Other European countries joined in the struggle. Those countries fighting Germany were known as the Allies. In the spring of 1917 the United States sent its army to help. About a year and a half later, in 1918, the Germans surrendered. World War I was over.

World War II and After

France was invaded again in World War II. In 1940, a little more than 20 years after the end of World War I, the country was occupied by the Germans.

General Charles de Gaulle (shärl′ də gōl′) became the leader of a small group of French who did not surrender to the Germans. He escaped to England, which became the headquarters of the "Free French" movement.

In 1944 American and British troops landed on the French beaches in Normandy. After desperate fighting France was freed from German control. The French once more governed themselves.

France, as a battlefield in two world wars, suffered great loss of life and damage to its cities and its land. Rebuilding the country was a difficult task. With the help of money from the United States and hard work by the French people, France rebuilt its factories and farms.

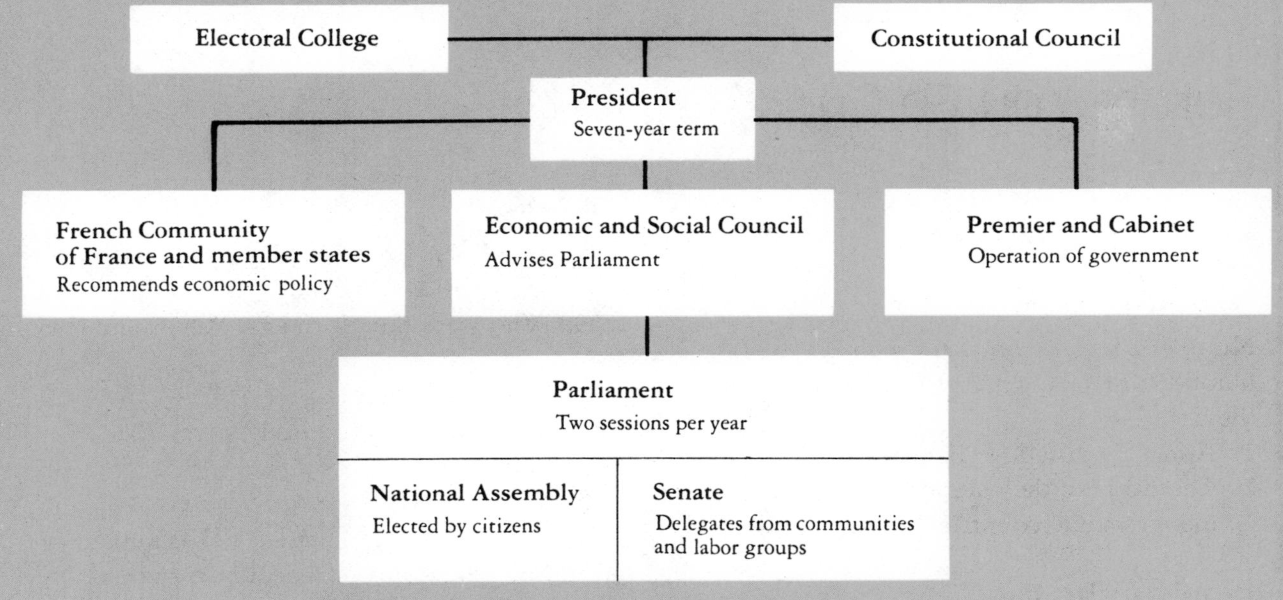

Under the direction of the French Constitutional Council, the Electoral College elects the President. The President chooses the Premier and Cabinet.

The Government of France

France is a republic. Its people elect representatives who meet in Paris to make the laws of the nation. In this city, too, are the offices of the nation's highest officials, its president, and its *premier* (pri mēr′). In some countries the chief officer of government is called a premier. Premier is a French word meaning "first in rank." But in France, the chief officer of the government is the president.

Like the United States, France has two legislative branches or houses of government. One house is the National Assembly. The less powerful house is the Senate.

A new constitution adopted in 1958 gives the president greater power than before. The president can help settle disputes in the Assembly. General de Gaulle, the hero of World War II, was elected the first president under the new constitution. He remained in office from 1958 until 1968, two years before his death.

Do You Know?

1. Who conquered the region of France for Rome?
2. Who was Charlemagne?
3. In what two wars of modern times was France invaded? By whom?
4. What form of government does France have?

Before You Go On

Using New Words

premier guillotine

Number a paper from 1 through 2. After each number write the word or term that matches the definition.

1. A machine used for beheading persons
2. The name of the chief officer of government in some countries

Finding the Facts

1. Why is France sometimes spoken of as the crossroads of western Europe?
2. What two physical features help France have a large sea trade?
3. On what river is Paris located?
4. What two rivers flow into the Bay of Biscay?
5. What mountains separate France from Switzerland? From Italy? From Spain?
6. What was France called in Roman times?
7. Name three modern French cities that were important in Roman times.
8. Who were the Franks?
9. When was Charlemagne crowned emperor of the Franks?
10. Who were the Normans? Where did they come from?
11. Who was Hugh Capet?
12. What was the Hundred Years' War? How did it come about?
13. What did Joan of Arc do for France?
14. Who succeeded Charles VII as king?
15. How did Louis XI encourage rug and tapestry weaving in France?
16. Who was the "Sun King"? Why was he given that name?
17. What was Versailles? Who built it?
18. How did other European monarchs show their admiration for Louis XIV?
19. How did the court of Louis XIV affect the peasants?
20. What was the French Revolution?
21. Who was Napolean Bonaparte?
22. When was Napolean defeated? Where?
23. Who came to France's aid in World War I?
24. Who were the "Free French" in World War II? Who was their leader?

3
What France Is Like Today

France is a nation with both fertile farms and busy industries. It is a country which produces a wide variety of foods and factory goods to supply its needs.

A Visit to Normandy

Normandy is an area in the northwest corner of France. It is like a large garden. Although Normandy is in the lowland of France, it is not flat. There are many hills and valleys. The winds from the Atlantic bring plenty of gentle rain. Thus the summer is seldom hot, and the winters are mild and rainy. The moisture and the mild climate make everything grow well.

A Farm in Normandy

Most of the farmers live in villages and drive to their farms each work day. The village is surrounded by farms, but few farms have houses on them. All through Europe we find this arrangement. Many of the farmers live in villages

Stacks of hay dry in an open field near the coast of Normandy. A farmer will drive out and collect them for livestock food. In the distance you can see one of France's most famous cathedrals.

The southern coast of France is a popular resort region. Summers there are warm and sunny. Most of the buildings in this picture are hotels. Can you spot one being built?

where they have more social life. They sometimes travel several miles to work on their land.

Behind many farmhouses is a shed that holds a big cage, or hutch, for rabbits. Rabbits are easy to raise, for they live on cabbage stalks and left-over green things. Norman farmers often have rabbit stew or rabbit pie for dinner.

Normans are good dairy farmers. They are thrifty and take good care of their cows. In the pasture, the farmer drives a row of stakes into the ground and ties each cow to a stake. The cow crops the grass in a neat half-circle around her. When the cow has eaten the grass as far as she can reach the farmer moves her to a fresh bit of pasture. Thus the pasture is not wasted. To shelter the cows in winter, thick hedges divide the fields and break the wind. In other places, bundles of straw are used for shelter.

The farmer milks the cows after the herd is driven home. Part of the milk is sold to a cheese factory in the village. The French are fond of cheese. In France people serve cheese and fruit for dessert in their homes and in restaurants.

The Products of Normandy

Normandy is famous for its cows, horses, and apples. The apples are used to make cider. At restaurants in Normandy there is always cider on the table. You will have to ask for water if you want it.

The strong Percheron horses are descended from the war horses that carried armored knights in battle during the Middle Ages. In some places where the rocky soil makes using modern farm machinery difficult, farmers use horses to help with their work.

A Normandy Fair

One day a week most Norman towns have a fair. The traveling merchants put up their booths. They sell all sorts of inexpensive articles. Farmers bring livestock to sell at the fair.

There are many amusements also, such as the Punch-and-Judy puppet show and the carousel (kar′ ə sel′). A carousel is a merry-go-round.

Southern France

A visitor to France sees few vineyards in the northern half of the nation. But from the heart of the country on to the south, vineyards are a familiar sight. A map sprinkled with dots to show grape production becomes almost black along the Mediterranean. On the Mediterranean coast, too, are many groves of olive trees.

A Resort Region

The part of France that borders the sparkling, blue waters of the Mediterranean Sea is a sunny region. For this reason it attracts many tourists. They come to enjoy the bright, mild days. Rain falls during the winter but almost never during the summer. The days seem to be made for enjoying the warm Mediterranean sun.

Farming in the South

This weather delights visitors and is good for the kind of farming carried on near the Mediterranean coast. Groves of silvery-gray olive trees and rows of grapevines cover the lowlands and valleys and spread up the hillsides.

The olive trees and the grapevines get just enough moisture from winter rains to help them grow. They continue to grow during dry summer days. The hot sun brings forth the fruit and ripens it for the harvest. The olives are packed in jars or pressed into olive oil. The grapes are hauled to nearby wineries.

Cities of France

Some of the important cities of France are busy ports and manufacturing centers. Others are famous resort cities. Many of the French cities have wide, often tree-lined avenues. These are known as *boulevards* (bool′ ə vardz′).

Marseille, France's Greatest Port

Marseille is the busiest port on the Mediterranean Sea. Next to Paris, it is France's largest city. It is the seaport for the Rhone River. The towns at the mouth of the Rhone are not good seaports because the delta of this river is so marshy. Ships carrying goods to or from the

Many French cities have buildings that were constructed in the Middle Ages. A Gothic cathedral towers over the wood-crossed houses of Strasbourg.

Rhone dock at Marseille, 25 miles (40 km) east of the Rhone's mouth.

Southern France produces many olives. Marseille has always been a trading center for olive oil and other vegetable oils. Factories in the city use the oil to make soap. Rice is another important crop.

Nice, City on the Riviera

Nice (nēs) is east of Marseille on the Mediterranean coast of France. This region is called the Riviera (riv′ē er′ə). Riviera means "seashore." Nice is a famous resort and is usually crowded with tourists.

In the hills above the Riviera there are large fields of flowers—roses, violets, carnations. In the nearby city of Grasse (gras), factories make the flowers into the fine perfumes for which France is famous.

Southeast of France, in the Mediterranean, is Corsica (kôr′ si kə). On this rocky island Napoleon was born. Corsica belongs to France, but it is so near Italy that the Corsicans speak more Italian than French.

Lyon, a Manufacturing Center

Lyon, the third largest city in France, is important for silk weaving. The raising of silkworms in the warm Rhone Valley began in the Middle Ages. Lyon had a very early start in the silk industry. The silks manufactured there were used all over the world. Many other industries have sprung up since then. Cotton and synthetics (sin thet′iks) are more important now.

Strasbourg, Center of Trade

The city of Strasbourg (stras′burg) is a gateway between France and Germany. In times past both countries have claimed the land between the Rhine and the mountains west of that river. Strasbourg is on a trade route. The trade along the Rhine and the trade across the Rhine meet at Strasbourg.

Bordeaux, City Among Vineyards

Bordeaux is the port for southwestern France. Built on the Garonne River, 70 miles (112 km) from the sea, Bordeaux has a fine position as a shipping center. The map of France on page 309 shows there is no other large French port nearby to compete with it.

Around Bordeaux the banks of the Garonne are lined with vineyards. After the harvest, the grapes are made into fine wines. Immense storerooms along the city wharves contain barrels of wine, brought down to be exported. Ships from South America and western Africa find Bordeaux the most convenient place to unload their cargoes for western Europe.

Le Havre, a River Port

Le Havre (lə hä′vrə) is one of the many cities that benefit from the use of France's rivers and canals. It is at the mouth of the Seine River, which is an important part of France's network of waterways.

The name Le Havre means "the harbor." Soon after the explorer Columbus sailed to America, the king of France realized that the mouth of the Seine needed a good port. What had been a little fishing village was turned into the busy port of Le Havre.

Today many freighters crossing the Atlantic end their voyages there. In large warehouses products from many foreign lands are stored at Le Havre before being shipped by boat or by rail to other parts of France.

Lille, a Great Manufacturing Center

In northern France quite near Belgium is Lille (lēl), a large manufacturing city. In this region are rich beds of coal. Coal furnishes power to run machines. A number of cities in that district have become centers for the manufacture of iron and steel, for weaving, and for other industries. This portion of France is a very important region in trade and industry.

Do You Know?

1. Why do most French farmers live in villages?
2. What are the chief farm products of Normandy? Of southern France?
3. What is one of France's busiest seaports?

Paris
Crossroads of France

In the Roman Empire all roads led to Rome. In modern France all roads lead to Paris.

The list of important activities throughout France that are controlled by people in the capital is long. Paris is more than the center of French government. It is the center of French education, business, art, music, and many other activities. Few cities dominate a country the way Paris dominates France.

The people of France are proud of their beautiful city. Its great wide boulevards and magnificent buildings are landmarks. The Arc de Triomphe (ärk də trē ōnf′), the Louvre (lo͞o′vre) Museum, and Notre Dame (nô′trə däm′) Cathedral are famous throughout the world. Paris is also known as a world center of art and fashion.

Today France is changing, and Paris is changing with it. Expressways have been built to speed traffic through and around the city. Although Paris still has hundreds of fine small shops, there are also many supermarkets and large department stores.

Outdoor cafés line the streets, and beautiful old bridges cross the Seine. People fish along the banks of this river. Unlike many modern cities, Paris is not yet a city of skyscrapers. It is felt that in central Paris tall buildings would spoil the skyline. So tall buildings are not permitted here. Paris changes, but much about it remains the same. It continues to be the crossroads of France and one of the world's most beautiful cities. ■

4

France and the World

France is famous throughout the world for its industry and for its customs. The country is also well known because it is the home of famous people.

French Industry

About the year 1700 European nations began to build factories to produce different kinds of goods. They needed raw materials for these factories. France was one of the European nations that hoped to obtain these raw materials from colonies in other parts of the world.

The French made their first settlement in the Western Hemisphere about the same time as the English did. As the colonies of these countries grew, there were clashes over territory. For many years England and France fought in both North America and Europe. By 1763 France had lost Canada and most of its possessions in India to England. France sold Louisiana to the United States in 1803. It kept only a few islands in the West Indies and a small colony in South America.

In time, France grew powerful again. It gained new colonies in Africa and Southeast Asia. These colonies also provided France with a source of raw materials and a marketplace for its goods. France ruled these territories until after World War II when small nations all over the world began to demand their independence. France was forced to withdraw from Indochina in 1954. That same year Algeria began fighting for its independence, which it finally achieved in 1962. The last of France's African colonies, the Afars (äf′ ärz′) and Issas (ē säz′) Territory, achieved independence in 1977 and changed its name to Djibouti (jə büt′ē). France is no longer a colonial power. But it has maintained trade agreements with many of its former colonies.

France today is a country of many industries. Lyon produces textiles. Mills in the northeast make cotton, woolen, and linen goods. The French have set high standards for their manufactured products. Making wines and perfumes and manufacturing automobiles and airplanes are big industries in France.

The French take pride in doing good work. As work is a large part of life, they say, why not do it well? Although there are many factories, people still value things made by hand like delicate lace and fine silk items.

French Ways of Living

For many years France was the center of art, learning, and manners in Europe. Today France is visited by many tourists who have come to enjoy the French way of life.

French Food

French food is famous throughout the world. In the United States restaurants often employ French chefs, or cooks. We say "Let us see the menu." Menu is the French word for the card which lists the food served in a restaurant. Even on our own menus, some dishes are listed by their French names. French chefs are famous for the preparation of delicious food. The French eat little at breakfast. But they enjoy a lunch and dinner with many courses.

French coffeehouses and restaurants are called cafés. At some cafés little tables are placed outdoors along the sidewalks. The French like to sit at these cafés and read their newspapers as they sip coffee or chocolate.

French Fashions

Paris has long been known as a fashion center. Its styles influence clothes throughout the world. France is also famous for fine cosmetics, leather goods, perfumes, and jewelry. To many persons a Paris label on a dress or a bottle of perfume means that the article is of high quality.

Chanel, Designer for the Masses

At one time only the very rich could afford to buy Paris fashions. A dress was often "one-of-a-kind," and each designer worked hard to think up something more unusual than the next. A woman designer, Gabrielle Chanel (gā′brē əl shə nəl′), changed all that.

Gabrielle was the daughter of a peasant. She opened up her first dress shop just before 1914. She found that many women wanted uncluttered, well-designed clothes. Chanel became known for her beautiful but simple dresses and suits, which were easy to mass-produce. In this way good design could be made available to many people at a reasonable cost. She was also responsible for a popular perfume, charm bracelets, and large, chunky jewelry.

Gabrielle Chanel, a famous French clothing designer, extended the pleasure of fashionable dressing to many who could not afford it before.

The Schools of France

France has strict schools. The school days are long, and the teachers are thorough. Many lessons must be learned by heart. Almost all French boys and girls go to grade school, but they often attend separate schools and study different subjects.

After attending grade school, a student may go to the *lycée* (lē′sā′), or high school. After students graduate from the lycée, they may de-

One of Millet's most famous paintings is "The Gleaners." The artist painted it while he worked at Barbizon.

cide to go to college. To be admitted to one of the agricultural or engineering colleges or to the university, they must pass difficult examinations in many subjects.

Some Famous French People

France has had many famous people who have given their talents to their country and to the world.

A Famous French Writer

One of France's well-known writers was Victor Hugo (hū′gō), whose home is kept as a museum. Among his books is a novel, *Les Misérables* (lā mē′ze rä′blə). This title is a French phrase which means "the poor people."

In *Les Misérables* the hero is Jean Valjean (zhän′ val zhän′), an escaped convict who changes his life and becomes a respected citizen. A police officer suspects that Jean is the convict he is looking for and follows him. Wherever Jean goes, the police officer is able to find him. On one occasion Jean flees through the Paris sewers. We feel great pity for this man who cannot escape the law even though he has become a good man.

Famous French Artists

France is famous for art. Among the best French artists are those of the Barbizon group. Barbizon (bär bi zōn′), a little village east of Paris, stands at the edge of a large forest. A number of artists who loved nature discovered this place where they could paint country life.

One of the leading members of this group was Jean François Millet (zhän′ frän swä′ mi lā′). Millet was born a peasant. In his boyhood he had worked in the fields with hoe and pitchfork. His pictures, such as "The Gleaners" and "The Man with the Hoe," tell the story of the hardworking peasants.

Form and shape were of primary importance to Cézanne. What basic shapes did he use in his "Basket of Apples"?

Pierre Auguste Renoir (pyer′ ō goost′ ren′ wär) was a French artist who liked to paint seashore scenes. He also painted people well. The women in his pictures have bright, happy faces and wear beautiful clothes. Renoir was born of a poor family. When he was 13 years old, he became an apprentice to a painter of chinaware. Later he studied art. Among his best-known works are "At the Seashore" and "Madame Charpentier (shar pän′ tē ā′) and Her Children."

Renoir and the painters of his time are called *Impressionists* (im presh′ ə nists). The Impressionists were nineteenth-century painters who were interested in depicting color and light at various seasons and at different times of day. An Impressionist might paint the same scene in summer and winter, at noon and twilight.

Paul Cézanne (sā zan′) learned about color from the Impressionists. But he was also interested in the shape and form of things. He and the other artists of his time are called Post-Impressionists. Cézanne is known for his paintings of apples and oranges.

Paris has many beautiful statues. One of the finest Parisian sculptors was Auguste Rodin (ō goost′ rō dan′). All of Rodin's statues express strong ideas. Rodin's "The Thinker" represents a man seated on a bench, deep in thought. It is one of the finest modern works of art. Rodin's former studio in Paris is now an art museum.

A Leading French Scientist

One of the world's greatest scientists was Louis Pasteur (lo͞o′ ē pas tur′). He discovered that microscopic organisms, called *bacteria* (bak tēr′ ē ə), cause changes in liquids and foods so that they become spoiled. Pasteur also discovered that bacteria cause many diseases.

Through experiments he learned how to kill many forms of bacteria and thus saved the lives of many people. He helped the silkworm raisers, the farmers, and the vineyard owners, whose businesses were being harmed by disease or blight.

We enjoy the results of Pasteur's research every day when we use *pasteurized* (pas′chə rīzd) milk. Milk or other food is pasteurized by heating it to a temperature high enough to kill the harmful bacteria. Thanks to Pasteur many diseases are now held in check. He helped to make the world a better and safer place for people and for animals. At the Pasteur Institute scientists now carry on research.

Pierre and Marie Curie

Years ago a young Polish woman came to Paris to study science. One of her teachers, Pierre Curie (pyer′ kyoor′ē), also wished to devote his life to making experiments in science. Before long they were married.

Pierre and Marie Curie had almost no money. While they were working on experiments, they were not earning money to live on. They almost starved, but they continued their work. They were interested in certain minerals that were *radioactive* (rā′dē ō ak′tiv). That is, the minerals sent out energy in the form of rays. What material was this from which the rays came, they wondered.

After years of work, the Curies succeeded in separating this material from the ore. They called it *radium* (rā′ dē əm). Radium is an element that is radioactive. Pierre died, but Marie Curie continued to find out more about radium. Radium is used in many ways today. We all have seen objects, such as the hands of clocks, that are covered with radium paint so they can be seen in the dark. The rays from radium are useful in treating certain diseases. But radium is still so scarce that it is one of the most costly substances on earth.

France and Other Nations

France is a member of several international organizations, including the Common Market. France also has defense agreements with other nations. It is a political, but not military, member of the North Atlantic Treaty Organization (known as NATO).

Some French people are afraid France might lose some of its independence by relying too much on other nations. Thus, France at one point withdrew from some defense agreements. It has at times refused to cooperate with other nations in trade and money matters.

France was one of the first western nations to establish friendly relations with The People's Republic of China. At the same time it was friendly with China's communist rival, the Soviet Union.

Do You Know?

1. Name three products manufactured in France.
2. Who was Victor Hugo?
3. Name two French artists.
4. Who was France's rival for colonies in the Western Hemisphere? Who won in the end?

To Help You Learn

Using New Words

radium
lycée
premier
bacteria
boulevard
pasteurize
radioactive
Impressionist
guillotine

Number a paper from 1 through 9. After each number write the word or term that matches the definition.

1. A French high school
2. The name of the chief officer of government in some countries
3. One of the painters of the nineteenth century interested in depicting color and light at various seasons and times of day
4. A machine used for beheading persons
5. A wide, often tree-lined avenue
6. Microscopic organisms that cause changes in liquids or foods
7. To heat milk or other food to a temperature high enough to kill harmful bacteria
8. A radioactive element
9. A type of mineral that sends out energy in the form of rays

Finding the Facts

1. Into what body of water does the Seine flow?
2. How has France suffered because of its location?
3. Why was Lyon important in Roman times?
4. How long did Gaul belong to Rome?
5. How long did Hugh Capet and his successors rule France?
6. Why was Joan of Arc called the "Maid of Orléans"?
7. Name four contributions Louis XI made to France.
8. What happened to Louis XVI?
9. What happened when Napoleon captured Moscow?
10. What is the National Assembly?
11. When was the last constitution of France adopted? What changes did it have over the previous constitution?
12. How are cows in Normandy sheltered during the winter?
13. Name three things Normandy is famous for.
14. What drink will you always find in restaurants in Normandy?
15. If you were to go to a fair in Normandy, what entertainment would you find?
16. What is the Riviera?
17. Name three things France is famous for.
18. Where is Barbizon? Why is it remembered?
19. Who was Paul Cézanne? Rodin?
20. Name two ways radium is used.
21. When did the last of France's colonies gain its independence?
22. How and why is milk pasteurized?

23. Match each of the following towns with the phrase that best describes it:

Marseille	Lyon	Paris
Strasbourg	Nice	Le Havre

a. The most important port on the Mediterranean
b. A famous resort
c. Gateway between France and Germany
d. A busy port on the Seine
e. Capital of France
f. An important silk-weaving center

Learning from Maps

1. Turn to the map of France on page 309 and answer these questions: What mountains form France's boundary on the southeast? On the east? How much of France is lowland? Use the map scale to find out about how far it is from Le Havre to Paris in miles. In kilometers.
2. Look at the map of the Languages of Europe on page 535. What language groups are spoken in France? In what other countries are these same language groups spoken?
3. Look at the map of Napoleon's empire on page 315 to answer these questions: What countries were independent of Napoleon? What countries were allies? Which were ruled directly? Which were controlled by Napoleon?

Using Study Skills

1. **Graph:** Study the bar graph below and answer these questions: What product is compared here? What countries are being compared? How much cheese did each produce? How much more cheese did France produce than Italy? How much more than West Germany?

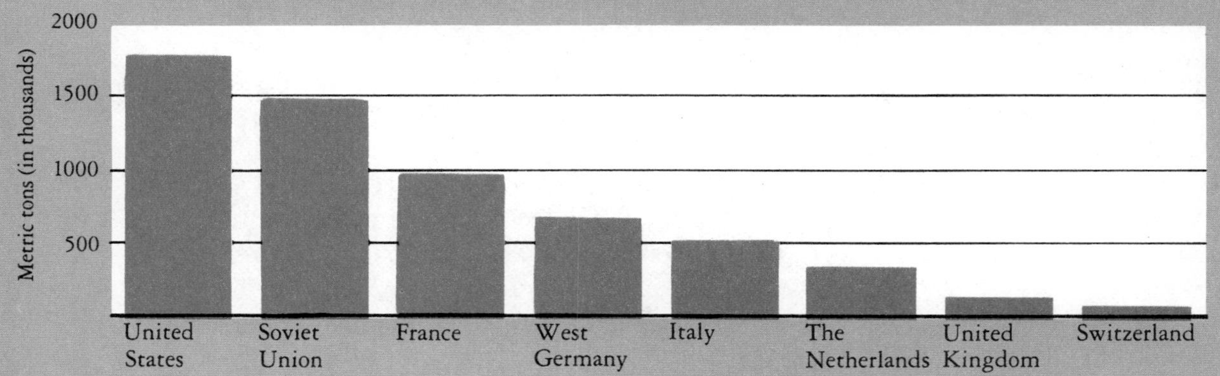

2. **Time Line:** Place the following events in the proper order of time: Louis XI took the throne; Hugh Capet crowned king; Germans invaded France in World War II; Napolean defeated at the Battle of Waterloo; Germans invaded France in World War I.

   Copy the time line from page 307. Add these events to your time line.

   Study the completed time line and answer the following questions: Was Napoleon emperor of France before or after the Revolution? How many years passed between the time he was crowned emperor and he was defeated at Waterloo?

   Who ruled earlier, Louis XI or Louis XIV? By how many years? How long was it between the two German invasions of France?

Thinking It Through

1. In New Orleans, Louisiana, and in the province of Quebec in Canada, the French language and customs are still used by many people. Why do you think this is so?
2. What do we mean when we say someone has "met his (or her) Waterloo"? How do you think this phrase came into use?
3. When Joan of Arc left her village to meet the French heir to the throne, she cut her hair short and dressed like a boy. Why do you suppose she did this? Could a woman become a military leader in the United States as Joan did in France? Support your answer.

Projects

1. Imagine that you are to spend a month in France. Would you travel from the United States to France by ship or by plane? Find the length of time each means of travel would take. List the places you would visit. Arrange your route with the help of the map of France on page 309. Collect travel leaflets and posters. Make a report on your planned trip to the class.
2. Many of the territories which belonged to France are now independent countries. Select one of those countries and find out as much as you can about the problems it faced as a new nation and what it is doing to solve its problems. Then make a short report to the class on what you have found.
3. France is famous for art. The Research Committee might use the encyclopedia to find out more about the great French artists mentioned in Unit 10. They might collect postcards or other illustrations of paintings and statues by these artists.
4. The stamp and coin collectors in the class may show their French collections.
5. Many famous stories were made popular by French writers. The fairy tales of "Cinderella," "The Sleeping Beauty," "Puss in Boots," and "Little Red Riding Hood" were all written by Charles Perrault, who lived during the days of Louis XIV.
   Find out more about Perrault. How did he become interested in fairy tales? An artist named Gustave Doré illustrated many of Perrault's stories. Try to find one of his drawings.

11 Great Britain

Unit Preview

The islands highlighted on the map are the British Isles. The history and culture of these islands have influenced the life of almost every person on earth today. England covers most of the largest island. At one time, English rulers controlled a vast empire. England, Scotland, and the tiny land of Wales form Great Britain. With Northern Ireland, they form the United Kingdom. Northern Ireland is on the north-eastern tip of the smaller island highlighted on the map. Ireland, an independent republic, occupies the rest of the island.

In the 1800s, England had possessions in so many different parts of the world that people said "the sun never sets on the British Empire." The English language spread across the globe. Parliamentary government, in which the people have a voice, began there. Trial by jury and ideas about law also came from England. New ways of making large numbers of products started in England with the invention of new machines.

With an uneven coastline, the British Isles have many good harbors. Trade is important to this island nation. Because of the country's climate and size, farmers do not produce enough food. Manufactured goods are traded for food imports.

The many colonies that once formed the British Empire are almost all independent now. Today some of them are united with Great Britain by trade and defense agreements.

Things to Discover

If you look carefully at the picture, map, and time line on these pages, you can answer these questions.

1. What ocean is west of Great Britain?
2. Name three conquerors of the British Isles.
3. The British flag shown in the picture is flying over the group of stone buildings called the Tower of London. William, Duke of Normandy, built one tower as part of his palace. It later became a prison. When did William conquer Britain?
4. For how many years was Great Britain involved in World War II?
5. What important resource has been found in the North Sea close to Great Britain?
6. When did Southern Ireland become independent? What form of government does it have?

Words to Learn

You will meet these words in this unit. As you read, you will learn what they mean and how to pronounce them. The Word List will help you.

absentee landlord
baron
Commonwealth
cricket
dominion
factory
Industrial Revolution
merchant marine
parliament
peat
prime minister
protectorate
Sinn Fein
spinning jenny

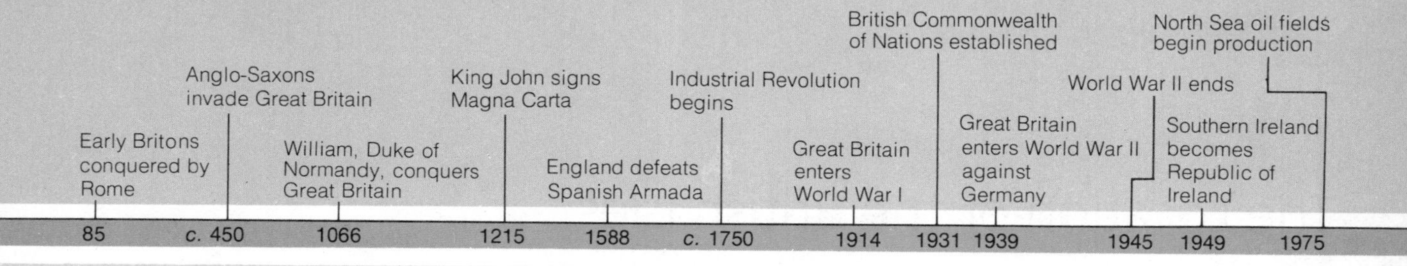

Arctic Ocean
Atlantic Ocean
EUROPE
ASIA
AFRICA
Pacific Ocean
Indian Ocean
AUSTRALIA

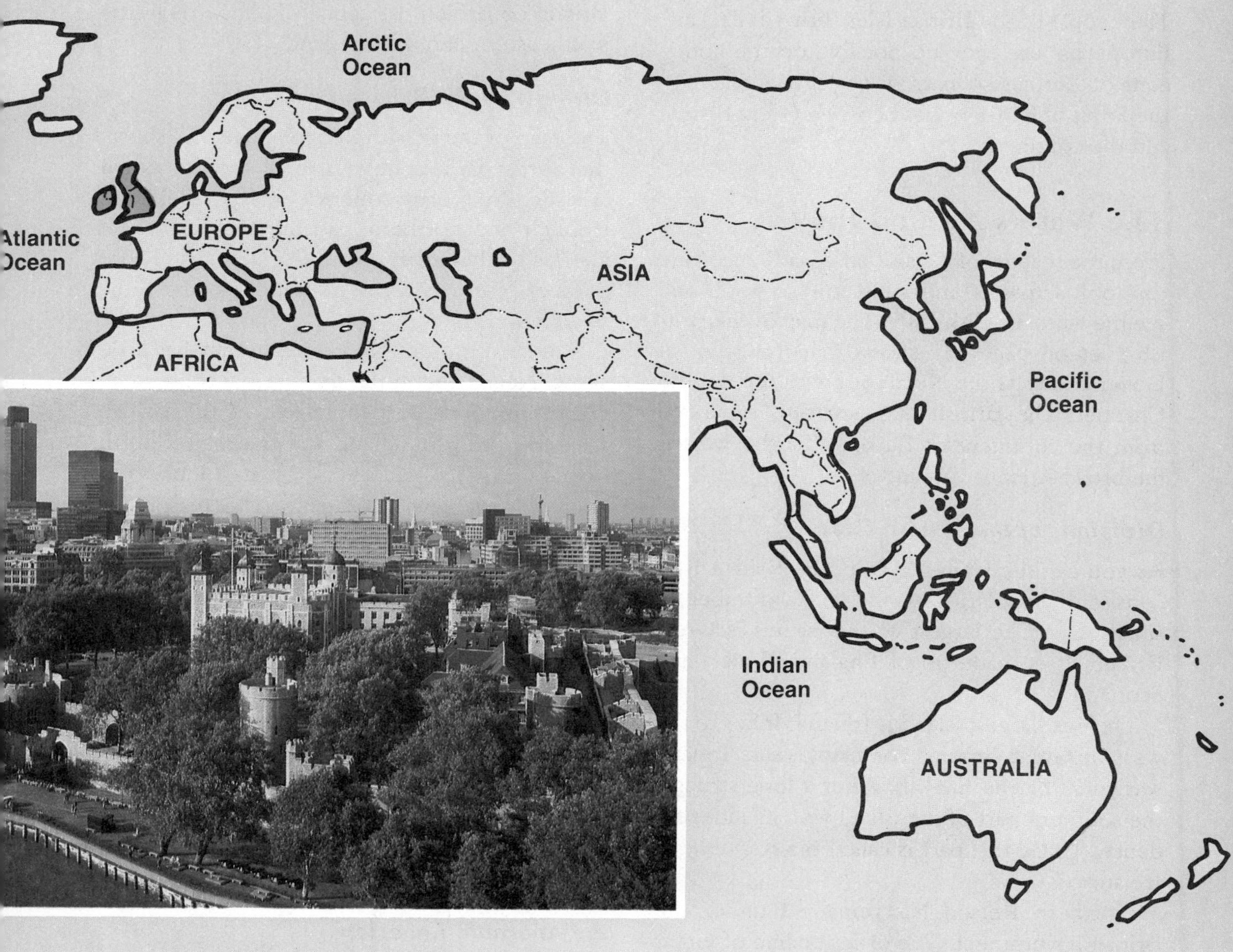

1

The Location of the British Isles

The people of the British Isles (brit′ish īlz′) are Europeans, but they do not live on the continent of Europe. A narrow passage of water—the Strait of Dover—lies between Great Britain and the continent.

The Waters Around the Isles

From the seaport of Calais (kal′ā) in France, one can look across 20 miles (32 km) of water and see the white English cliffs. The map of the British Isles on page 337 shows that the Strait of Dover connects the North Sea with the English Channel. The British Isles are thus separated from the continent of Europe. To the west is the broad Atlantic Ocean.

Divisions of the British Isles

As you can see from the map, the British Isles consist of two large islands and a number of small ones. The largest of the islands is Great Britain. It is made up of England, Wales, and Scotland.

The next largest island is Ireland. It lies to the west of Great Britain. For many years Ireland was ruled by the English. After a long struggle the southern part of the island won its independence. Today this part is called the Republic of Ireland.

Northern Ireland has remained under the British government. The official name of Great Britain and Northern Ireland together is the United Kingdom. But people refer to it as Great Britain or Britain. Its capital, London, is in the southeastern part of the island.

Climate of the British Isles

The map of the British Isles on page 337 shows that Great Britain lies north of the 50° north latitude. In North America this parallel goes through the northern part of Newfoundland and far to the north of the Great Lakes. These parts of North America lie under ice and snow in winter.

Southern England, however, usually has little snow. Near London the grass remains green all winter. Millions of people live in the British Isles. But Newfoundland and the region north of the Great Lakes, because of their long, cold winters, have few inhabitants. The reason for the great difference in climate is found in the winds that blow over the two regions.

Most of the winds that blow over the British Isles come from the southwest. These winds pass over the ocean before they reach the land. The ocean is warmer in winter and cooler in summer than is the land. The winds take their temperature from the ocean. Thus, the winds warm the land in winter. The British Isles have a more temperate climate than do the North American regions of the east coast at the same latitude.

A Favorable Location

The British Isles have an uneven coastline. The many bays along the coast provide harbors.

THE BRITISH ISLES
Plains
Hills
0 Miles 95
0 Kilometers 120
SHETLAND ISLANDS
ORKNEY ISLANDS
OUTER HEBRIDES
INNER HEBRIDES
SCOTLAND
Aberdeen
Dundee
River Clyde
Edinburgh
Glasgow
Tweed River
PRIME MERIDIAN
NORTH SEA
Londonderry
NORTHERN IRELAND
Belfast
Newcastle
Durham
ATLANTIC OCEAN
ISLE OF MAN
PENNINE CHAIN
Lancaster
Leeds
IRISH SEA
Bradford
IRELAND
Liverpool
Manchester
Sheffield
Dublin
Chester
Stoke-on-Trent
Boston
Rugby
River Shannon
Birmingham
Derby
ST. GEORGE'S CHANNEL
Cork
Lee R.
WALES
ENGLAND
Thames River
Cardiff
London
Bristol
Dover
Southampton
Hastings
STRAIT OF DOVER
Calais
ENGLISH CHANNEL
Cherbourg
Le Havre
Rouen
GUERNSEY
CHANNEL ISLANDS
JERSEY
FRANCE
10°
5°
0°
60°
55°
50°

Many people in Britain make their living from the sea. Britains's 4,000–mile (6,400–km) coastline provides fine harbors for the merchant and fishing fleets that operate in the country.

Good harbors make it easy for people to be fishers, sailors, and traders. For this reason many British people have depended on the sea for their livelihood.

The location of the British Isles is favorable for carrying on trade. They lie on or near important trade routes between Europe and other continents. They are especially well placed for sharing in the valuable trade between Europe and North America.

For many hundreds of years the waters around the British Isles also helped to protect them. Nations on the continent could be invaded by land, but it was difficult for an enemy to cross the waters and set foot on British soil. Until airplanes and rockets came into use, the British Isles were fairly safe from attack.

Farms and Industries

The location, size, and resources of Great Britain helped make it a nation of industries, rather than of farms. Because of its location, it has cool summers and heavy rainfall. Such a climate is not good for some crops. Also, much of the land is suitable only for the grazing of cattle and sheep. The English must buy much of their food from other countries.

To pay for their imports, the people depend on manufacturing. With their own resources and with those that are imported, they manufacture a wide variety of products.

Great Britain is thus a leading nation in both industry and trade. Ships leaving its shores carry manufactured goods to many parts of the world. Ships return with cargoes of food and raw materials.

Do You Know?

1. Where are the British Isles located?
2. What large islands make up the British Isles?
3. What is the United Kingdom?
4. What is the coastline of Great Britain like? How does this encourage fishing and trading?

2
The Early History of Britain

When Julius Caesar conquered Gaul in 58-51 B.C., he heard of the Brythons, or Britons. They were a people who were related to the Gauls. Caesar led his armies across the channel and won some battles. But the Romans did not stay on the island of Great Britain at that time.

Great Britain in Roman Times

One hundred years later Roman armies invaded Great Britain again. In A.D. 85 they took possession of the island as far north as the part now called Scotland. For 300 years Great Britain remained a Roman province.

Many towns grew up in Great Britain. Some towns had names ending in "caster," "cester," or "chester." This meant that a Roman camp—called "castrum" in Latin—had been placed there. On the map of England we find such names as Lancaster (lang′kəs tər), Chester, and Manchester.

Across the northern part of the island the Romans built a wall to keep out the barbarians. The Britons felt safe under Roman protection. They even learned the Latin language. They built forums, temples, and public bathhouses in their cities. Some cities were protected by walls. Roads were built, linking Roman cities.

When Rome began to have trouble near home, its legions left Great Britain. They were needed to fight the barbarians who threatened Rome. Then fierce tribes from what is now Scotland swarmed over the wall built by the Romans. From Ireland came other warriors who overran Great Britain.

Anglo-Saxon Britain

Danger also threatened Great Britain from the south and east. About the year 450 many ships, crowded with fair-haired warriors, raided the eastern coast of the island. They came from lands now part of Denmark and Germany. These invaders were the Angles, the Saxons, and the Jutes.

While in Great Britain, the Romans built a 74–mile (118–km) wall to keep out barbarians. Parts of the wall, 6 feet (1.8 m) high and 8 feet (2.4 m) thick, are still standing.

Settlement of the Island

The Britons resisted, but the ships kept coming. Some of the warriors were eager only for plunder, but many liked the country and settled there. In time, most of Great Britain was occupied by these invaders. The Angles settled in the central part of the island. The Saxons and the Jutes settled in the southern part.

Many Britons fled to the mountains and forests in the region now called Wales and to the Channel Islands. Some stayed and mixed with the conquerors.

About the year 600 a Roman priest, named Augustine (ô′gəs tēn′), came to England. Augustine was well received by King Ethelbert (eth′əl bərt′), whose wife was a Christian. Slowly Ethelbert's people began to learn the ways of Christianity. We call the English people of this time the Anglo-Saxons. Most persons who live in England today are descended from these Anglo-Saxons.

The Britons who found safety in mountainous Wales are called Welsh. Even today the Welsh are a people apart. Many of them still speak their ancient language. Their towns have such names as Llangollen (lan gäl′ən), Pwllheli (pül hel′ē), and Ffestiniog (fes tin′ē äg′). The Welsh are a musical people, and their singing festivals are famous.

The Raids of the Vikings

About 200 years after Augustine had brought Christianity to England, the land of the Anglo-Saxons was invaded again. Vikings who came from Denmark and Norway attacked England.

The Vikings, or Danes, as they came to be called, were fierce fighters. With their battle-axes they drove the Anglo-Saxons into retreat. After defeating the Anglo-Saxons, the Danes occupied a part of the land. In England today many cities have the Saxon ending of "ham" or "ton." Some of these are Birmingham, Boston, and Southampton. Others with names ending in "by" were founded by the Danes, such as Whitby, Derby, and Rugby.

The Great King Alfred

After a time a great leader whose name was Alfred became the English king. King Alfred built England's first fleet. He forced the Danes to stay in the northeastern part of England. The Danes settled down, became Christians, and merged with the English. King Alfred, who was a man of learning, had the Anglo-Saxon laws written down. He also improved the courts. Before he died, his country was at peace. For these reasons, he is known as Alfred the Great, the only king of England with this title.

England Under the Normans

Soon after the Danes and the Saxons settled their quarrels, a new invader appeared. He was William, Duke of Normandy. As you know, some of the Vikings, or Normans, settled on the coast of France. Their land was called Normandy. Here the Vikings had quickly adopted the French language and French ways of living.

The Norman Conquest

Duke William was master of Normandy. He also claimed the throne of England. In 1066 the

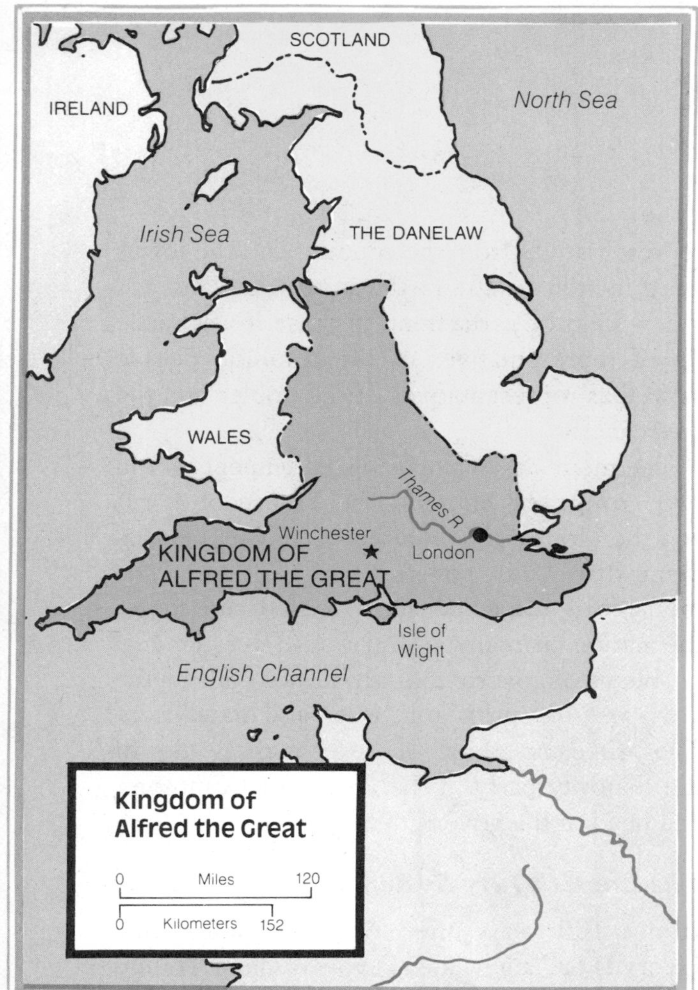

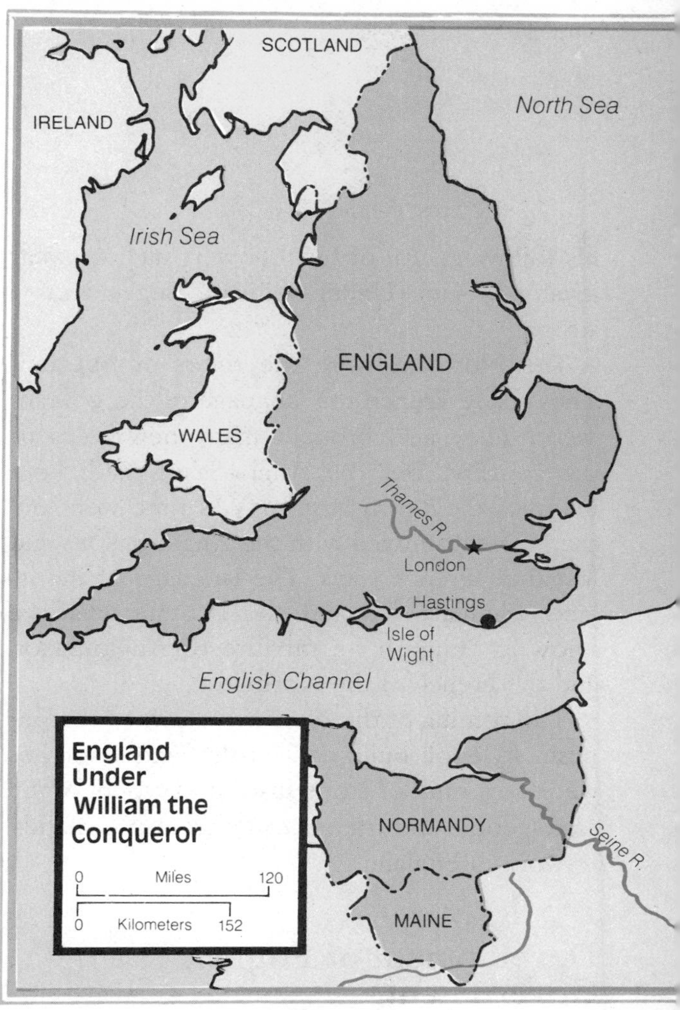

The map at the left shows how England was divided under Alfred the Great. What areas were not under his control? The map at the right shows England under William. Find Normandy on the map. What were the capitals of these kingdoms?

duke sent a powerful army to conquer England. He landed his troops at Hastings, on the south shore of England. There he met the army of Harold, king of England. The Normans were victorious, and Harold was killed. William then marched to London and was crowned king in Westminster Abbey. He is known as William the Conqueror.

The Influence of the Normans

William kept about half of England as his own property and divided the rest of the land among his followers. All of his followers had to swear loyalty to him. Under William, England grew strong.

The Normans were the rulers of England. They made French the language of the government. They also brought many new ideas to the country. But the Anglo-Saxons still kept many of their own customs. As time went on, the Normans mixed with the Anglo-Saxons and lost their French ways. The language of the island gradually changed and became what we know as "English," a mixture of Anglo-Saxon and the French of the Normans.

The coming of the Normans changed the English style of building. Castles and churches were now built of stone instead of wood. Many craftspeople and traders came from Normandy to work in England.

Development of English Government

William and most of the Norman kings who came after him were able and powerful. They ruled England with a firm hand, and they helped to unite the people.

English Representative Government

When the early kings of England wanted advice, they called together some of the nobles and the high church officers. This body of advisers was called the Great Council. Later the council came to be called a *parliament* (pär lə mənt). A parliament is an assembly that makes the laws of a country. The word is based on the French word "parler," meaning "to speak." After some time representatives from the counties and the towns were invited to attend the meetings. This was a new kind of parliament, because it was made up of representatives of the common people as well as representatives of the nobles and the church.

The members of England's Parliament met in two groups, or houses—the House of Lords and the House of Commons. Today it is Parliament that really governs Great Britain. The monarch is respected and honored and serves the nation in many useful ways. But the real problems of government are worked out by the *prime minister* (prīm′ min′is tər) and his advisers. The prime, or "chief," minister is the leader of the majority party in the House of Commons, and head of the government.

The English Jury System

About 100 years after William's time, King Henry II had a new idea in government. To find out who was guilty of a crime, he questioned people who lived near the place where the crime had been committed. The people whom he selected had to swear to tell the truth.

In our courts today jurors listen to both sides of a case when there is a dispute or when a suspected criminal is being tried. Then they decide which side is right. This is called a trial by jury. In England and in the United States the right to a trial by jury is an important part of our government.

The Great Charter

Henry's son John thought that because he was king he could do just as he pleased. A group of his *barons* (bar′ənz), who were the lowest ranking of the nobles, banded together to stop his high-handed way of ruling. The armies of the barons defeated the King's forces. Then King John agreed to give the barons the rights they demanded.

In a meadow not far from London, the barons met the king in the year 1215. They presented him with a list of their demands and forced him to place the royal seal upon it. This document was called "Magna Carta," or the "Great Charter." It marked the first time an English king's power had been limited.

The Great Charter required the king to respect the rights of the nobles. The charter stated that some of the privileges given to the barons must be granted to the common people also. The charter guaranteed "no taxation without representation." It also promised that no one should be imprisoned without a trial. The English call the Magna Carta "the cornerstone of English liberty." King John never got over his anger. When he died of a fever the next year, people said, "Magna Carta killed him." Never again has an English king been called by the name of John.

King John was forced by his *barons* to sign the Magna Carta in 1215. This document limited royal powers and gave certain rights to the common people.

English Government Today

Trial by jury, government by elected representatives, a two-house Parliament, change of prime ministers when necessary—all these things are prized by the British people. They have a royal family and nobles with titles, but they feel their government is just as democratic as ours. Many of our ideas of law originated in England.

Do You Know?

1. Why is King Alfred called "the Great"?
2. When did the Normans conquer England? Who was their leader?
3. What was the Great Council? In later times, what did it become?
4. Why is the Magna Carta called "the cornerstone of English liberty"?

3
Great Britain as a World Power

For many years Spain was the strongest nation in Europe. At the height of its power in 1588, Spain sent the Armada against England and lost an important sea battle. After this defeat, Spain's influence declined. English sea power began to grow.

England prospered as a world power under Queen Elizabeth I. During her reign, Great Britain ruled the seas.

Great Britain's Rise to Power

At the time of the important sea battle with Spain, Queen Elizabeth I was the ruler of England. The queen and her advisers knew that their fleet had saved them, so they spent a great deal of money on ship-building. This was the beginning of Great Britain's power on the sea. After the battle with the Spaniards, England enjoyed a period of peace during Elizabeth's long reign.

In times of peace people have a chance to think and to write. Many poets and writers developed their skills during Elizabeth's reign. Among them were playwrights and poets like William Shakespeare (shāk′spēr), Christopher Marlowe, and Ben Jonson. The works of these writers, who lived more than 300 years ago, are still enjoyed today.

William Shakespeare

The greatest of these British writers was William Shakespeare. Many consider him the best writer of plays of all time. He was born in the city of Stratford-on-Avon in 1564. Like other children of his time, Shakespeare studied Latin and probably read the works of Virgil. For a while he worked as an apprentice. In 1582 he married Anne Hathaway.

By the 1590s he was living in London as a well-known writer and actor. He would act in his own plays along with groups of actors who went from theater to theater. Audiences went to these theaters as we go to movies today.

Shakespeare wrote histories, tragedies, and comedies. His plays are still popular today, partly because he understood people so well. His characters, whether rulers or pickpockets, are as interesting to modern audiences as they were to audiences of Queen Elizabeth's time. Many of his lines are quoted in daily speech.

English Colonies in the Western Hemisphere

During the reign of Queen Elizabeth I many nations sent explorers and settlers to the Western Hemisphere. Sir Walter Raleigh was one of Queen Elizabeth's friends who organized expeditions to America. Raleigh did not succeed in founding a permanent colony, but others who followed him did.

In 1607 Jamestown was founded in Virginia. Several others followed soon afterwards. These colonies became the United States of America after the Revolutionary War.

The English Merchant Marine

Not only did England have a strong navy but also a *merchant marine* (mur′chənt mə rēn′). A nation's merchant marine is its fleet of trading ships. The English merchant marine sailed on many seas and carried rich cargoes.

For about 250 years Great Britain had the strongest navy in the world and many trading ships. Large trading associations such as the East India Company sent their vessels to India and China. They brought back tea and silk, spices and drugs, cotton goods and jewels. Through its strong navy Great Britain took possession of many foreign regions.

This portrait of William Shakespeare was printed inside the first collection of his plays. The book was published in 1623.

The Industrial Revolution in Britain

People in Great Britain have raised sheep since early times. Long ago England's woolen cloth became so good that other nations were glad to buy it. At first all the spinning and weaving were done by hand in the homes of the workers.

About 1750, people developed new inventions that would transform the lives of people in Great Britain and throughout the world. As a result of these inventions, hand tools were replaced by machinery. This machinery was driven first by water power, then by steam, and later by electricity. New machines brought many changes in the way people lived and worked. This period of change is called the *Industrial Revolution* (in dus′trē əl rev′ə lo͞o′shən).

An important invention of the Industrial Revolution was the *spinning jenny* (spin′ing jen′ē). This machine was invented in 1764. For many years people had been using the spinning wheel to make thread. It twisted the fibers of

With a *spinning jenny* one person could spin many threads at one time. How do you think this machine affected the textile industry in Britain?

wool into a long thread of yarn. It could form only one thread at a time. With the spinning jenny many threads could be spun at the same time. Although the first spinning jenny was turned by hand, it was a great improvement. Using the new machine, one person could spin as much as 16 persons could by hand.

The Use of Water Power

After the spinning jenny was improved, it needed more power to run it. Wheels turned by falling water provided that power. Soon, along many streams, dams were built. The water flowed through a narrow channel and turned a splashing wheel. As the wheel turned it moved shafts which ran the machines.

The spinning machines turned out yarn or thread more quickly than the weavers could use it. A new weaving machine, or loom, was made. It was also driven by water power. As improvements followed, a race began between spinners and weavers to turn out the most material. This resulted in great quantities of cloth.

The Beginning of the Factory System

As the production of cloth increased, more buildings were built along streams. Machinery was installed in these buildings. Workers operated these machines. The building was called a *factory* (fak′tər ē) because it manufactured, or made, goods.

Soon almost all the spinners and weavers of Britain were laboring in factories. Sometimes there were hundreds of workers in one building. The factories could turn out more and cheaper cloth than had ever been made before.

The Rise of Steam Power

Water power has much force, but to make use of it factories have to be close to rivers and streams. Steam power can be used in more places. People had been thinking about steam power but had not used it much. Then a Scot named James Watt improved the steam engine and made it workable. At once factory owners saw that a factory could be run by steam anywhere, not just along a water course.

Steam engines need coal to heat the water, and England had plenty of coal. Many new factories using steam power sprang up. Now not only cloth but also many other things were made in factories.

Because coal is heavy to carry, the first factories run by steam were built near coal fields. Soon railroads, using steam-driven locomotives, carried coal to distant parts of England. England built many factories and became one of the great manufacturing nations of the world.

The Importance of Coal in Great Britain

Coal played an important part in making Great Britain rich and powerful. Without coal the machines and locomotives necessary for business could not run. Without coal Great Britain could not have had its fleets of steam-driven warships and merchant vessels. Coal filled the needs of the nation's industries.

One of England's coal fields lies near the city of Newcastle. At one time, the city had so much coal that it has given rise to a famous saying. When people talk about doing a useless thing, they say, "That would be carrying coals to Newcastle." Coal does go to Newcastle now. Much of its high-grade coal already has been mined. England now has to import high-quality coal to keep the machines in its factories turning.

One of Great Britain's energy resources is oil from the North Sea. Platforms like this one support drills that pump oil from the sea floor.

Near the city of Glasgow (glas′gō), Scotland, there are also coal and iron mines. Glasgow is the center of steel and shipbuilding industries in the British Isles.

British coal used to go to many countries. Ships came into British ports with raw materials from both tropical and temperate countries. The raw materials from these countries were used in British factories. Great Britain is now producing oil and gas from the North Sea. These products will help the British to meet future energy needs.

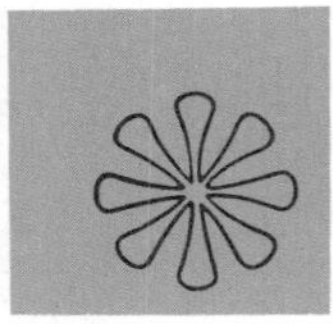

London
New Things in a Historic City

In all of England there is no better place for a city than where London is situated. At this point the Thames River is still deep enough for ocean-going ships. Today more goods are shipped in and out of London than any other port in the world except for New York City and Rotterdam.

A good place to begin a London visit is at the site where the Roman walled town once stood. This district, called "The City," has long been the center of money dealings in Great Britain. One of London's historic buildings, the ancient Tower of London, is in this area.

Across "The City" to the west of the Tower is Saint Paul's, one of the world's finest cathedrals. Its architect, Sir Christopher Wren, built more than 50 churches and other beautiful buildings throughout London.

All over London new architecture is taking its place beside the old. Skyscrapers stand near the Houses of Parliament and Westminster Abbey. Every English king and queen since William the Conqueror has been crowned in this famous church.

London is an international city where people from many nations live and work. The West End of London is an international center for the arts. Here concerts, plays, ballets, operas, and musical comedies are performed almost every night. The people of London have preserved their history while setting the pace of modern life for others to follow. ■

The Importance of Iron Ore

In industry coal and iron are important resources for industry, and Great Britain has both. The iron mines of England are found in the central and northern parts of the country. Coal and limestone are found nearby. Coal is used as fuel for the furnaces. Limestone makes iron melt more easily.

Long ago ironworkers used charcoal from the English forests to keep their furnaces going. Then, as wood grew scarce, they found out how to make coal into coke. Coke is even better than coal as a fuel for use in the manufacture of iron.

Manufacturing Cities

Great Britain has many manufacturing cities. Usually the factories that make the same kind of goods are near each other.

The Thread and Cloth Districts

The factories that spin and weave cotton cloth are centered in northwestern England. Manchester, with the towns around it, is the busiest cotton cloth district in the world. All Great Britain's raw cotton comes from other lands. But factories in Great Britain make synthetic fibers. Fibers such as polyester (pol'ē es'tər), which is made from petroleum, are produced in mills.

A range of hills divides the cotton weaving district of England from the wool weaving district. Leeds and Bradford are the chief woolen cloth cities. Much of the wool used comes from Africa, Australia, and South America.

Wool is also woven in Scotland. Many years ago, each Scottish clan, or group of families descended from the same ancestor, wore wool woven in a special pattern that identified the clan. These patterns, called plaids (pladz), are popular in the United States.

The Iron and Steel District

South of the two great weaving districts of England is an area called the Midlands. Look at the product map of Great Britain and Ireland above. The map will show you the reason for this name. Products from the Midlands are shipped out to other countries from London and Liverpool.

The region is dark with soot and smoke from factory chimneys. The largest city is Birmingham with more than one million people. This city is an iron and steel center like Pittsburgh. Hardware, automobiles, and machinery pour out of the factories of Birmingham and towns nearby.

Sheffield, between Birmingham and Leeds, has been a steel-making center for hundreds of years. In early days its steel went into knives and swords. Later the steel was used for razors, scissors, and surgical instruments. For many years steel for ships has come from Sheffield.

The Pottery Districts

Halfway between Sheffield and Birmingham are towns that make pottery and china. These towns are known as Stoke-on-Trent. "Wedgwood" and "Spode" are two famous brands of fine china made in these towns. Both types are named after the men who developed them.

Edinburgh

Edinburgh is the capital and second largest city in Scotland. It is a city of culture and industry. Edinburgh is a center of publishing, banking, and insurance as well as the home of breweries and distilleries and paper and textile mills. This city on hills is overlooked by Castle Rock, on which Edinburgh Castle stands. Parades of people in kilts playing bagpipes are a frequent sight. The beautiful flower clock of Princes Street Gardens is in the center of the city. Many of the great buildings of Scotland line the main street, Princes Street.

The Farming and Dairy Regions

The eastern part of England, which is drier than western England, has been a wheat-growing region. But in recent years the wheat grown there has been more expensive than wheat imported from Canada. Many of the wheat farmers have changed to dairying. Today Great Britain produces only a small part of the wheat it uses. And although many cattle and sheep are raised, the country produces only half the meat it uses.

To get the food it needs, Great Britain must rely on imports. The British pay for this food by selling manufactured goods to other countries.

British Art Treasures

The National Gallery in London is the home of many famous paintings. These include portraits by such artists as Joshua Reynolds (ren′əldz) and Thomas Gainsborough (gānz′bur′ō). Both were fond of children and painted them well.

The British Museum is also in London. Art treasures from all over the world are here, many of them from ancient times. Statues from the Parthenon, described in Unit 5, are in the British Museum.

Cricket

The game of *cricket* (krik′it) was originally an English game. Cricket is played with bats, ball, and wickets, usually between sides made up of 11 players each. A cricket match may go on for several days.

Cricket was introduced by the English to the colonies they governed. Today it is played throughout the world. It is particularly popular in the West Indies, Pakistan, and India. The game of cricket has come to stand for sportsmanship. English fans watching a game may call out, "Well played!" at a good hit or a good catch regardless of which team they are for. A player who tries hard but fails hears, "Well tried!" The game is played so politely that the word "cricket" is often used to mean "fair." Thus, when people see someone being unfair, they may say, "That's not cricket."

British Music

Great Britain has produced some of the world's finest music. Henry Purcell, Sir Edward Elgar, Ralph Vaughan Williams, and Benjamin Britten are all famous composers of classical music. During the late 1960s, the Beatles, a group of composers and performers, gained world-wide recognition for their contribution to popular music.

Great Britain in World War I and World War II

Great Britain entered World War I in 1914 after Germany invaded the neutral country of Belgium. David Lloyd George, the British prime minister at that time, helped write the Treaty of Versailles, which ended World War I. The treaty gave Great Britain control over colonies in Africa.

In 1939 Adolf Hitler, the German leader, sent his troops to attack Poland, a country to the east of Germany. Because Great Britain had promised to help Poland in case of attack it declared war upon Germany. Great Britain also sent armies to help France when it was invaded by Germany the next year.

The Germans, who had long been preparing for war, defeated the French army. They trapped a large British force on the north coast of France at Dunkirk (dun′kurk′). To free the British troops and bring them home, people in Great Britain used every boat they could find. The men, women, and children of Great Britain risked their lives sailing across the channel in small boats, but they brought most of the British army safely back home.

If Hitler had sent his armies across the English Channel at that moment, he might have overcome Great Britain. However, he waited and his chance was lost. The British people kept up the fight on sea and on land under the leadership of their great prime minister, Winston Churchill. "There'll always be an England," they cried. By "England" they meant the whole United Kingdom. Soon other countries of the Commonwealth and the United States joined Great Britain in its fight against the Axis. The war finally came to an end in 1945.

Do You Know?

1. How did Great Britain become a sea power?
2. Name an important invention of the Industrial Revolution.
3. How did coal help British manufacturing and trade grow?
4. What happened at Dunkirk?
5. What is a major advantage in using steam power instead of water power to run factories?

Before You Go On

Using New Words

Number a paper from 1 through 8. After each number write the word or term that matches the definition.

factory	spinning jenny
parliament	prime minister
cricket	Industrial Revolution
baron	merchant marine

1. A game of English origin, played with bats, ball, and wickets
2. The period when new machines, such as the steam engine, brought many changes in the way people lived and worked
3. An assembly that makes the laws of a country
4. A noble of the lowest rank
5. A building equipped with machines, in which goods are made
6. A nation's fleet of trading ships
7. The head of the majority party in the House of Commons and of the government in Great Britain
8. A machine used for making thread

Finding the Facts

1. Name the two largest of the British Isles. Why do they have a favorable location?
2. What is the climate of the British Isles like?
3. Why is the climate of the British Isles different from that of the east coast of North America at the same latitude?
4. What was Britain like in Roman times?
5. How did the Normans change England?
6. Explain how representative government works in England.
7. What does a jury do?
8. What was the Magna Carta?
9. Why do the British think highly of the Magna Carta?
10. Why was Elizabeth's reign an important time in English history?
11. Who was William Shakespeare? What kind of plays did he write?
12. Who was James Watt?
13. What product is Newcastle known for? Glasgow? Birmingham? Manchester? Sheffield?

4
Ireland: The Emerald Isle

The island of Ireland is the farthest west of any large division in Europe. The Irish are related to the Scots, and the Irish language is similar to the Scottish. The Irish language is called Gaelic (gā′lik). It is the official language of the Republic of Ireland.

The History of Ireland

A short time before the Angles and Saxons came to Great Britain a priest named Patrick came to Ireland as a missionary. He and other missionaries brought the Christian faith to the Irish people.

English Rule in Ireland

About 100 years after Duke William of Normandy came to England, an Irish chief was driven from his land. He went to England to ask help of the English king, Henry II, but the king was in France. However, some of Henry's lords sent their men to defeat the chief's enemies. In return, the English lords received large estates in Ireland.

When Henry II went to Ireland later, he found it easy to persuade the English lords in Ireland to swear loyalty to him. He granted lands to his friends among the English nobles, and many of them settled in Ireland. Later English kings and queens called themselves king or queen of Ireland as well as of England.

The English monarchs wished to make Ireland like England. But since the Irish had clans, or groups of families, and were neither townspeople nor farmers, the two ways of life did not agree. The Irish rebelled. England then sent settlers to take over the lands.

Later, people from Scotland settled in North Ireland, in the province of Ulster (ul′stər). The religion of the Scots was like that of the English who founded our Plymouth and Boston. It was different from the Catholic religion of the rest of the island.

Irish Rebellions Against the English

The English and the Irish people did not get on well together in Ireland. One reason was the difference in their religions. Harsh laws were made against the Irish Catholics. Although there was an Irish Parliament, only Protestants could be elected to it.

Some of the Irish plotted to set up an Irish republic with the aid of French ships and French troops. When their plan failed, England did away entirely with the Irish Parliament. After this all the laws for Ireland were made by the British Parliament, in London.

Irish land came to be held by *absentee landlords* (ab′sen tē′ land′lôrdz′), or owners who did not live on their estates. If the people who rented the land could not pay the rent, the absentee landlords or their managers had them put out of their homes. Many of the absentee landlords were English, and their harsh treatment of the Irish was another reason why the two peoples did not get along well together.

Most Irish people were poor and depended on the potato crops for a large part of their food. Beginning in about 1840 one potato crop after another failed, and food became very scarce in Ireland. Thousands of people starved to death. In this time of great suffering, many Irish decided to leave their homeland.

Many people left Ireland and went to live in the United States. Between 1845 and 1900 the number of persons living in Ireland dropped by nearly half. Both those who left the country and those who stayed were unfriendly toward England. After a time, however, the English passed laws which did away with absentee landlords. Ireland then became a country of small landowners.

After 1900 a new political party grew up in southern Ireland. Its members wished to separate Ireland entirely from Great Britain and to make it a republic. They wanted to revive the old Irish, or Gaelic, language. These Irish called themselves the party of *Sinn Fein* (shin′ fān′). In Gaelic, Sinn Fein means "we ourselves." The Sinn Fein party became very important in the independence movement of Ireland.

Most of the people of northern Ireland, however, depended on manufacturing and on trade

Ireland is called the "Emerald Isle" because it has broad, green fields. The chief products of Ireland are potatoes, flax for linen, and livestock. Many farm families live in simple stone houses.

Peat is a common fuel in rural Ireland. It is important because firewood and coal are scarce. *Peat* is made when decayed grass from bogs is cut into blocks and dried in the sun.

with Great Britain. They refused to help the Sinn Fein members of southern Ireland, who depended mainly on farming and stock raising.

The Republic of Ireland

After World War I the Irish declared their country independent and chose a president. The British government objected. For more than two years there was fighting between the Sinn Feiners and the British troops.

At last Great Britain yielded and agreed that southern Ireland should be an independent country, like Canada. It elected a president and parliament and called itself the Irish Free State. Dublin was the capital. Six counties of northern Ireland chose to remain under the British government and to send their representatives to the Parliament in London. In 1949 southern Ireland became the Republic of Ireland, and cut its ties with Great Britain.

Thus, after nearly 800 years of quarrels and rebellion, most of Ireland became independent. A large part of the island's exports continued to go to Great Britain. But the new nation had a chance to work out its own trade agreements with other countries.

Rural Ireland

Many of the homes in the Irish countryside are one-story stone buildings with three rooms. Their whitewashed walls stand out against the green grassy land. On many days the western winds bring rain. The rain and mild climate keep the grass green all winter. Because of this, Ireland is sometimes called "The Emerald Isle."

Peat, an Important Source of Fuel

Ireland has little or no snow in winter, but many days are chilly. Large piles of brownish material, called *peat* (pēt), are stored in sheds. Decayed vegetable material, such as grass or moss, has formed peat. A few pieces of peat, laid on the fire, furnish much heat.

A peat bog is soft ground from which the peat is dug. After peat is dug from the peat bog, it is dried and sometimes made into bricks. If the peat had been pressed down and heated by underground layers of rock, it would have turned into coal in a few hundred years. But Ireland has little coal.

Ireland is shaped like a saucer, with mountains around most of the edge and flat ground in the middle. It has many lakes and peat bogs.

Because Ireland has little coal, few forests, and no oil, peat has been used for fuel. In recent years, the government has built large harvesting machines which slice the peat from the bogs. The peat is then taken to processing plants, where it is compressed into small bricks which are slow burning.

The Great River Shannon

Electricity is produced by water power from the Shannon River. The Shannon is the longest river in Ireland. A great dam across the Shannon furnishes the water power to make the electricity Ireland needs.

Important Cities

Dublin is the capital and largest city of the Irish Republic. The industrial center of Belfast is the largest city in Northern Ireland. Belfast is known for the production of linen.

Ireland and Northern Ireland Today

In recent years in Northern Ireland there has been much bitterness between the Catholics and Protestants. There has been much fighting and many people have been killed.

Dublin lies on the east coast of the Irish Republic, at the mouth of the Liffey River. Ships travel up and down the river, making Dublin the country's chief port.

Since 1955 the Irish Republic has encouraged companies from other countries to build factories in Ireland. Thousands of Irish people work in these new plants to produce many kinds of manufactured goods.

Do You Know?

1. How did Ireland become an English possession?
2. Why did many people leave Ireland for America between 1845 and 1900?
3. What is the largest city in the Irish Republic? In Northern Ireland?
4. Why is the River Shannon so important?

5
The Commonwealth of Nations

Since the Norman Conquest, Great Britain has had more than 800 years of settled government. In that time no enemy has successfully invaded the island. Even Napoleon, with his great army and powerful fleet, did no more than to plan an attack on Great Britain.

Britain in Modern Times

Great Britain built up the strongest navy in the world. Under the protection of the fleet, British merchant vessels visited all the ports of the world. Great Britain was the leader in the Industrial Revolution and needed raw materials and markets for the products of its factories.

Forming the British Empire

When vessels driven by steam came into use, there had to be coaling stations on all the seas. These were places where ships could load fresh coal. To secure coaling stations, Great Britain began making treaties, or agreements, with certain countries and received parts of their land. It sent expeditions to explore unknown regions and claim them. Great Britain also arranged with certain rulers to give their countries protection in return for special trading rights. Such countries, which depend upon an outside nation for their defense, are called *protectorates* (prə tek′tər itz) of the stronger nation. These countries became a part of the British Empire.

Thus Great Britain formed an empire which reached around the earth. At one time, one fourth of the people on earth were ruled by Great Britain.

New Nations Formed

For a long time the British government and other strong nations held the idea that colonies existed to bring wealth to the ruling country. Colonies were supposed to furnish raw materials for manufacture and to buy manufactured goods from the country that governed them. Great Britain tried to keep its American colonies from developing their own manufacturing. This was one reason why it lost the colonies which became the United States of America.

After World War II colonies were no longer profitable for countries like Great Britain. If a country owned a colony, it was responsible for protecting it, for building roads and hospitals, and for educating its people and helping them earn a living. Colonies began to cost more than the money they brought in.

Many of the British colonies felt they should have self-government. Great Britain worked with its colonies to prepare them. Almost all British colonies have become independent.

Cooperation in the Commonwealth

Several countries that were once a part of the British Empire chose to form an organization called the *Commonwealth* (kom′ən welth′) of Nations.

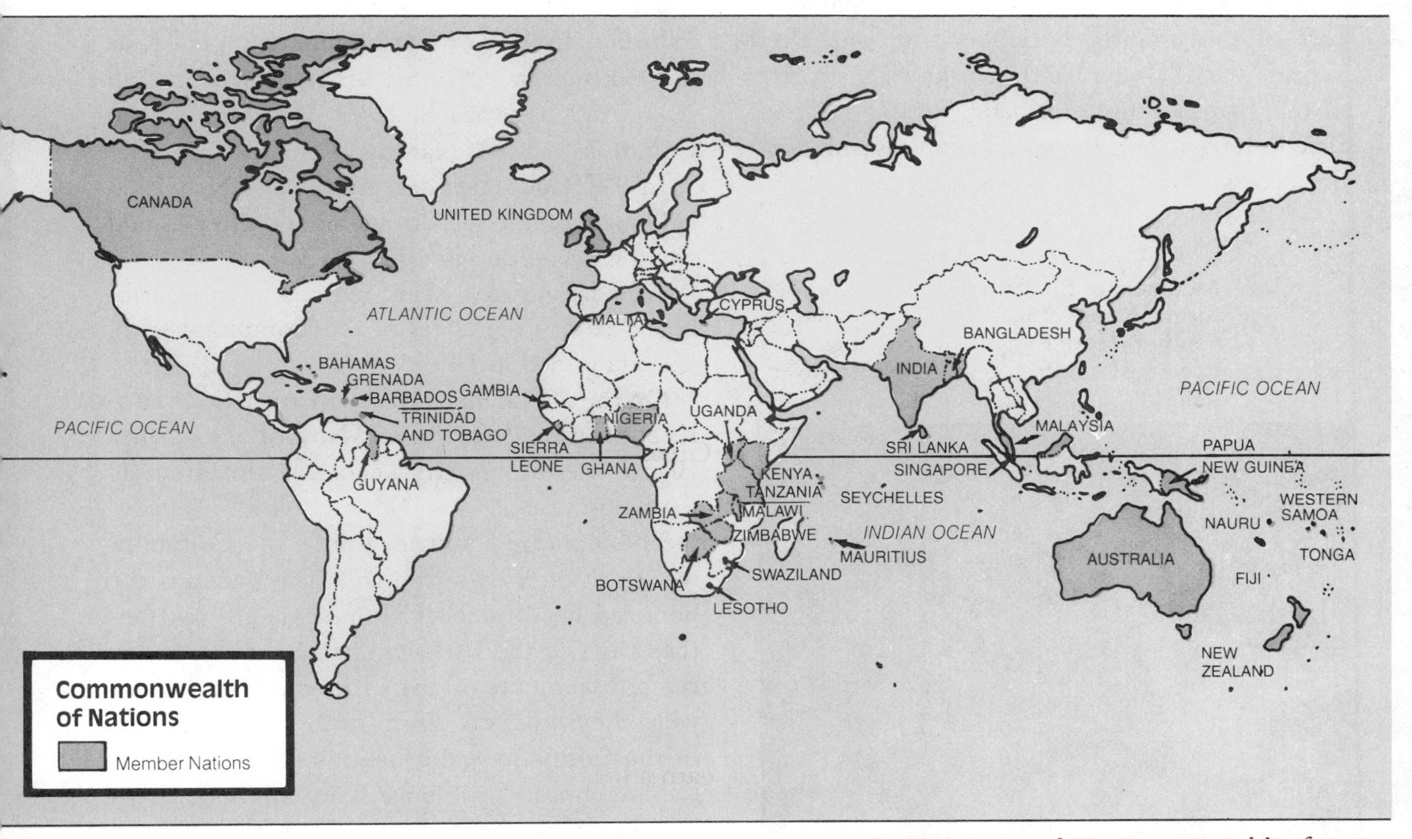

The countries of the *Commonwealth* of Nations cover about one-fourth of the earth's land surface. They form the world's largest trading organization.

The Commonwealth of Nations is a family of free nations, many of which are united for their own welfare in matters of defense and trade. The members feel that they and Great Britain should work together for the benefit of all.

When Great Britain declared war against Germany in 1939, each of the *dominions* (də min′ yənz), or self-governing states of the Commonwealth, made its own declaration of war. Each member sends its own representatives to other nations. Members receive special privileges in their trade with Great Britain and with other Commonwealth members. Representatives from member countries meet for discussions.

India, Pakistan, and Sri Lanka, which were part of the empire, became dominions after World War II. India had been the richest prize in the British Empire. Finally, in 1947, Great Britain recognized two new nations as independent parts of the Commonwealth of Nations—the Dominion of India and the Dominion of Pakistan. In 1950 India became a republic, as did Pakistan in 1956. Sri Lanka became free in 1948, and Malaysia in 1963. They joined the Commonwealth of Nations.

Members of the British *Commonwealth* form a family of nations that help one another. Here English and Nigerian experts search for oil in the Niger River delta.

In the South Pacific, Australia and New Zealand are Commonwealth members. They joined when it was set up in 1931.

Canada and two island nations in the Caribbean are also members of the Commonwealth. Canada joined in 1931.

On the continent of Africa many nations have recently gained freedom. Many of the former British colonies in Africa chose to remain in the Commonwealth.

The member countries joined the Commonwealth of their own free will. The queen is the honored head of the Commonwealth, but neither she nor the Parliament in London can tell the governments of any of its member nations what they must do. From time to time leaders of the Commonwealth nations meet to discuss their common problems. The continuance of the Commonwealth proves that trust among nations is stronger than force.

Do You Know?

1. How was the British Empire formed?
2. Why did Great Britain want colonies?
3. What led to Great Britain's loss of its colonies after World War II?
4. What is the Commonwealth of Nations?

To Help You Learn

Using New Words

peat	prime minister
parliament	protectorate
dominion	absentee landlord
Commonwealth	Industrial Revolution
Sinn Fein	

Number a paper from 1 through 9. After each number write the word or the term that matches the definition.

1. A self-governing state of the Commonwealth of Nations
2. The period when new machines, such as the steam engine, brought many changes in the way people lived and worked
3. The head of the majority party in the House of Commons and of the government in Great Britain
4. A family of free nations united for their own welfare in matters of trade and defense
5. An owner who does not live on his or her estate
6. An assembly that makes the laws of a country
7. Decayed vegetable material which is burned for heat
8. A country which depends upon an outside nation for its defense
9. A party in Ireland which wanted the country to separate from Great Britain and become a republic

Finding the Facts

1. What is the largest of the British Isles? What is it made up of?
2. Why is Great Britain a nation of industries, rather than one of farms?
3. Who were the Britons? The Angles, the Saxons, and the Jutes?
4. What happened at Hastings in the year 1066?
5. What languages combined to form English?
6. Into what two groups is parliament divided?
7. How did the Magna Carta help common people?
8. Who were Shakespeare, Marlowe, and Jonson?
9. What kind of power drove machines in early factories? What was the next source of power?
10. Why was coal important to Great Britain?
11. Name the great textile cities of England.
12. Name England's iron and steel center.
13. What would we find at the National Gallery in London?
14. Why did Great Britain declare war on Germany in 1939?
15. Which part of Ireland is an independent republic?
16. Which part is still governed by Great Britain?

17. Why is Ireland called the Emerald Isle?
18. What is the queen's role in the Commonwealth?

Learning from Maps

1. Look at the map of the British Isles on page 337. What is the capital of England? On what river is it located? What meridian runs through that city? What body of water must a boat cross to get from Hastings to Calais, France? From Liverpool to Belfast? What is the capital of the Republic of Ireland?
2. Look at the product map of Great Britain and Ireland on page 350. In which area is most manufacturing done? Where are sheep raised? Where is coal mined? Where is barley grown?

Using Study Skills

1. **Chart:** Fill in the chart below showing all the countries or peoples who have tried to defeat Great Britain. Show what year they tried, who their leader was (if the leader is mentioned in this unit), and the results.

Attempts at Defeating Great Britain

Countries or People	Year	Leader	Result
Romans	58-51 B.C.		stayed a short while
Romans		—	
tribes from Scotland	—	—	
warriors from Ireland	—	—	overran Great Britain
		— — —	settled in central part settled in southern part Britons fled to Wales and Channel Islands
Vikings	c. 800	—	defeated Anglo-Saxons, occupied part of land
Normans			crowned king of England
		—	England defeated Armada
Germany	1939		Germany was defeated

2. **Time Line:** Place in the proper order of time the following events: Jamestown in Virginia founded; Potato crop failures in Ireland begin; William Shakespeare born; Spinning jenny invented.

   Copy the time line from page 335. Add these events to your time line.

   Study the completed time line and answer the following questions:

   How long after England defeated Spain was Jamestown founded? How long was it between the signing of the Magna Carta and the beginning of the Industrial Revolution? The invention of the spinning jenny and the potato crop failure in Ireland?

Thinking It Through

1. Suppose that in the House of Commons the question arose: "Can Great Britain produce more of its own food?" What answer would you give if you were a member of the House? Explain to your class why you would take that side.
2. The United States fought Great Britain to gain its independence. Yet the countries have been friends and allies for many years. How do you explain this?
3. In what ways has the Industrial Revolution affected the way you live today?

Projects

1. Read a story or poem or learn a song about one or two of the nations in the Commonwealth. Have a program in which the stories, songs, and poems are given in class. You might invite another class to enjoy it with you.
2. Act out the scene in which the English nobles forced King John to agree to the Magna Carta.
3. Compare an election in the United States with one in Great Britain. How are they alike? How different?
4. The Explorers' Committee might lay out an automobile trip to take through Great Britain. Show the class this route and give your reasons for visiting each place. Invite suggestions from the class.
5. The British Isles have a more irregular coast than France has. Do they have a greater number of important seaports than France has? Prove to your class the correctness of your answer.
6. Follow the news about the British Isles in the newspapers. Watch particularly for news about the conflict in Northern Ireland.
7. The Reading Committee might find the book *Tales from Shakespeare* by Charles and Mary Lamb in the library and share some stories with the class.

12 Belgium, The Netherlands, Luxembourg

Unit Preview

Much of the land in Belgium, the Netherlands, and Luxembourg is below sea level. The land is so low that unless it is protected it will be overrun by sea water. The people protect their land from the sea by building dikes. Dikes are walls of earth or stone. Even in Roman times, people in these lands built dikes. Because so much of the land is close to sea level, Belgium, the Netherlands, and Luxembourg are called the Low Countries.

When the Middle Ages began, the city-states of Italy were the leading trading centers. Toward the end of that period trade began to shift to the north. The city of Bruges in Flanders, a part of Belgium, became active as a trading center.

Later on the Dutch in Holland, which is now known as the Netherlands, also became active traders. They hired an English captain named Henry Hudson to explore North America. Along the river named after him, the colony of New Amsterdam was founded. This would later become the city of New York.

Trade is still very important to the Low Countries. Textiles, electronics, iron and steel are major industries. Making pottery, cutting diamonds, and growing flowers are other jobs. Dairy farms in the Netherlands produce milk, butter, and cheese. When these foods are processed, they are exported.

The Netherlands, Belgium, and Luxembourg have joined together to make trade easier among the three countries. They also cooperate with other countries in the Common Market.

Things to Discover

If you look carefully at the picture, map, and time line on these pages, you can answer these questions.

1. On what continent are the Low Countries located?
2. The picture shows a scene in the Netherlands. Because land is so flat there, hydroelectric power cannot be used. What kind of power can be used? Is this type of power being tried in other countries?
3. Who was the explorer sent by the Dutch to North America in 1609?
4. What important resource was discovered in the Netherlands in 1964?

Words to Learn

You will meet these words in this unit. As you read, you will learn what they mean and how to pronounce them. The Word List will help you.

Benelux	pile
carillon	polder
dike	telescope
microscope	underground resistance
neutral	yacht
oceanic climate	

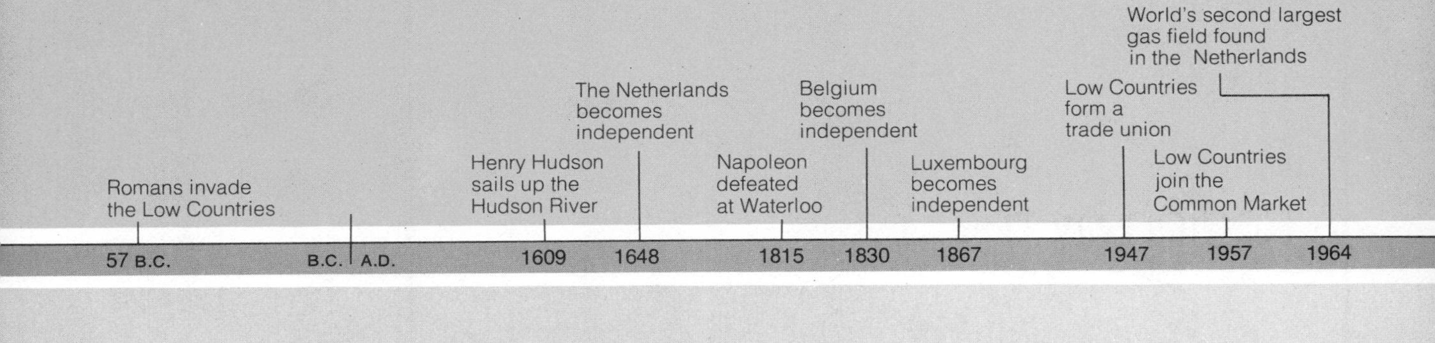

Arctic Ocean
antic
ean
EUROPE
ASIA
AFRICA
Pacific Ocean
AUSTRALIA

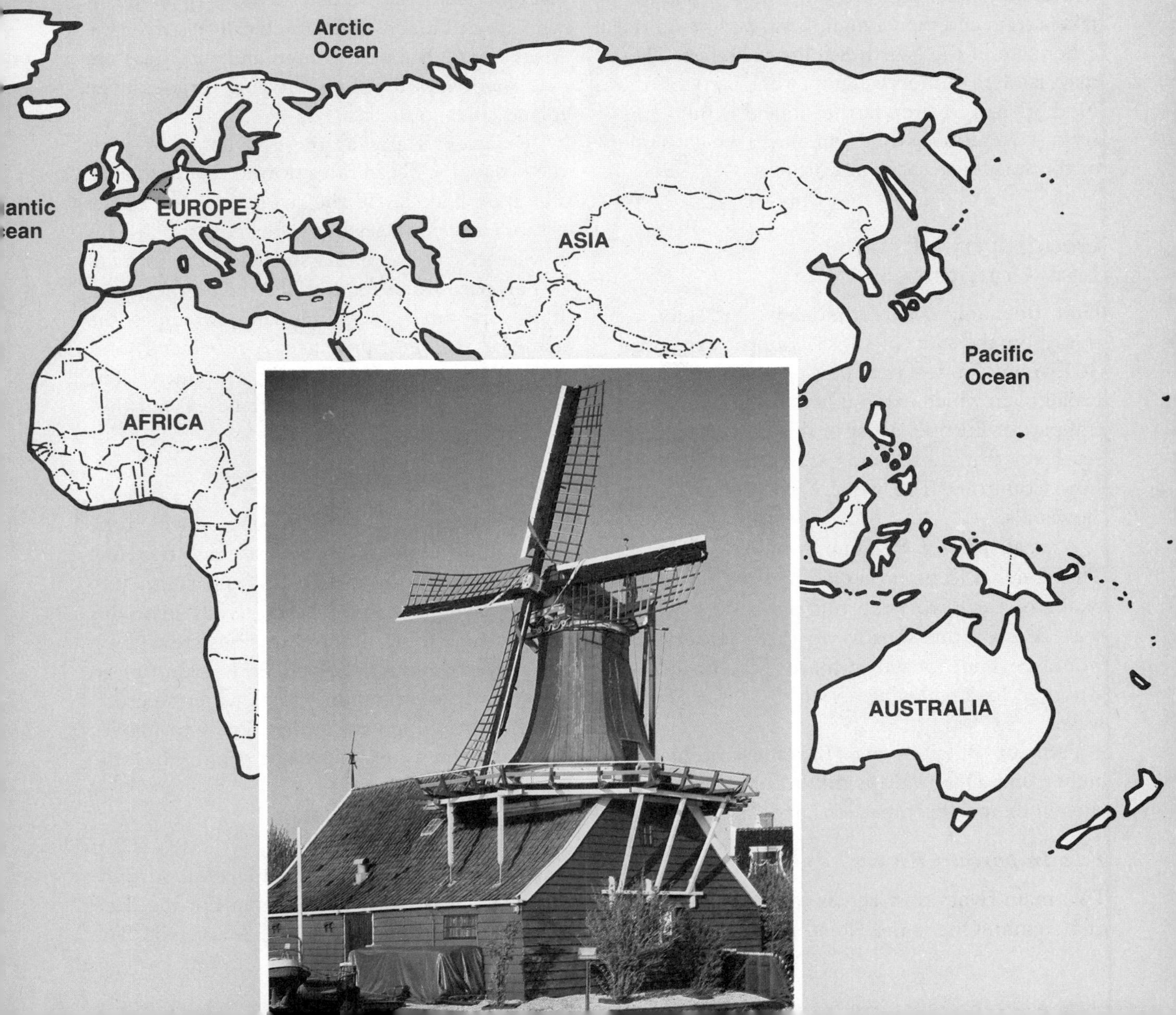

1
A Region by the Sea

Travelers can eat their evening meal in London, take a train and then a night boat, and be on the other side of the North Sea for breakfast. They may land in either Belgium (bel′jəm) or the Netherlands. A little farther inland is the country of Luxembourg (luk′səm burg′) which is one of the smallest nations in Europe.

Geography of the Low Countries

Find Belgium, the Netherlands, and Luxembourg on the map of those countries on page 367. You can see that they are a part of the broad plain which extends across the north central part of Europe. Most of this plain is so near sea level that these lands are often called the Low Countries. The word Netherlands means "lowlands."

A small part of Belgium is below sea level. This area has to be protected by *dikes* (dīks), or banks of earth, to keep out the waters of the sea. Almost one-fourth of the Netherlands would be under water if there were no dikes. Another fourth lies at about the level of the waves.

Parts of Belgium and Luxembourg lie on higher land. Deep valleys cut through the mountains in the northern part of Luxembourg.

Two Important Rivers

Two main rivers flow across the lowland north of Belgium. One is the Rhine River. The other river is called the Meuse (myo͞oz) by Belgians who speak French. The Dutch call this river the Maas (mäs). Both the Rhine and the Maas are fine waterways for ships carrying cargoes from inland cities to the sea.

In ancient times as these rivers came near the ocean, the ocean tides slowed their currents. The mud and clay in the rivers dropped to the bottom and blocked the water courses. In this way large stretches of marshy land were formed.

This part of Europe is called the Netherlands. It is sometimes called Holland, which is the name of its largest province. A province (prov′ ins) is a political division of a country. The people call themselves Netherlanders, but they are better known as Dutch.

A Great Trade Route

The great central plain of Europe on which the Low Countries are located allows easy traveling from Russia to the North Sea and south into France. Belgium and the Netherlands lie on this natural trade route. Important cities grew up on the trade route and helped both countries to prosper. At one time the Dutch were the greatest seafaring people in Europe. Trade from over both land and water helped the country become prosperous.

Three Small Neighbors

Belgium, the Netherlands, and Luxembourg are three of the smallest countries in Europe. Belgium is a little larger than Maryland. The

BELGIUM, THE NETHERLANDS, AND LUXEMBOURG
Plains
Plateaus
Hills
Mountains
0 Miles 55
0 Kilometers 70
DENMARK
NORTH SEA
ENGLAND
THE NETHERLANDS
Edam
Haarlem
Amsterdam
The Hague
Leiden
Delft
Rotterdam
Strait of Dover
Ostend
Bruges
Ghent
Antwerp
BELGIUM
Brussels
Waterloo
Liege
Scheldt River
Meuse River
Maas River
Rhine River
WEST GERMANY
EAST GERMANY
Bonn
LUXEMBOURG
Luxembourg
Moselle River
Paris
FRANCE
0°
2°
4°
6°
8°
10°
54°
52°
50°
48

Netherlands is about as big as the areas of both Connecticut and Massachusetts. Even though Belgium and the Netherlands are very small, they have played a large part in the history and trade of the world.

Luxembourg is a little smaller than Rhode Island. A car trip across this country takes less than a half hour. Luxembourg is one of the oldest independent countries in Europe.

Do You Know?

1. What are the "Low Countries"? Why are they called this?
2. Which two rivers flow across the lowland north of Belgium?
3. How did the location of the Low Countries help cities to grow up?

2 The History of the Low Countries

As we have learned, the Low Countries lie on a natural trade route in Europe. When cities began to grow during the Middle Ages, many of the important ones were in the Low Countries. Ghent (gent) and Bruges (br o͞o zh) in western Belgium, which was then called Flanders, became well known. The region now called the Netherlands had important cities then too. Among them were Haarlem (här′ləm), Leiden (lī′dən), Amsterdam, and Rotterdam. Find these cities on the map of Belgium, the Netherlands, Luxembourg, on page 367.

The History of the Netherlands

We first hear of the Dutch in the days of the Roman Empire. In 57 B.C. Julius Caesar found the early tribes of the Netherlands living in the midst of swamps. These people were patient and hard-working. Little by little they had built dikes around the low mounds of land on which they lived to keep out the sea. They cut channels to drain the marshes. In time, the country could support many people, and prosperous cities grew up.

The Netherlands Under Spain

The Spanish Emperor Charles V inherited the Low Countries from his father and Spain from his mother. From Madrid, his capital, he ruled over vast lands. All of them were Catholic in religion except the Low Countries. Because many of the people there were Protestants, he dealt with them harshly.

Philip II of Spain followed Charles, his father, on the throne. Philip decided to root out

Drainage canals extend across Holland, the largest province of the Netherlands. Water from the marshy land is pumped into these canals.

the Protestant faith in the Low Countries. He took away many of the rights enjoyed by the cities and collected heavy taxes from the people. You will remember that he was the king who sent the Spanish Armada against England.

How the Netherlands Gained Freedom

Philip's harsh measures drove the Low Countries to rebel. War broke out. After many towns were ruined and many people killed, the southern provinces made peace with Spain. The northern provinces, now the Netherlands, were protected by their swampy land. Enemy ships could sail to the shores, but troops found it difficult to land.

The hero of the Dutch rebellion was William. He was Prince of Orange, a part of the Netherlands. Time and again he and his followers seemed to be crushed. But after each defeat he took another step toward victory. In 1584 William was killed. However, his son and other Dutch leaders carried on. When Philip II and the Armada were defeated in 1588, England and Holland were saved.

In 1609 a truce, or agreement to stop the fighting, was arranged. In that same year an English captain, Henry Hudson, was sent out by the Dutch to explore North America. The river that he explored is known today as the Hudson River. Along this river grew the colonies of New Netherland, which later became part of New York state.

The Dutch gained their freedom in 1648. Explorers and traders established colonies in many parts of the world. They built a navy to protect their colonies and their trade.

The History of Belgium

At one time Ghent was one of the largest cities of northern Europe. Bruges, a center for trading in wool, was not far behind. Ghent and Bruges were cities of canals, known for their skillful workers. The cities of Flanders grew to be rich and important centers of trade.

The people who lived in the area now called Belgium did not consider themselves Dutch. Their land had once been the home of a tribe of Gauls, known as the Belgians. The people called themselves by this name.

Belgium was taken by one nation after another until Napoleon conquered it for France. In 1815, the British and the Germans defeated Napoleon in a battle at Waterloo in Belgium.

After the battle of Waterloo, Belgium and the Netherlands became one country. However, the languages and customs of the two peoples were different and kept them from feeling united. Moreover, the Belgians thought the Dutch had too much power in the government.

In 1830 the Belgians rebelled. After a period of fighting, a group of larger European nations made the Dutch agree that Belgium should be independent. The stronger nations also promised that in case of war, troops would not be sent over Belgian land.

The History of Luxembourg

In times past, the area that now makes up Luxembourg belonged first to one nation and then to another. Among the countries that controlled this region were Spain, Austria, Belgium, and the Netherlands. After the Belgians gained their freedom in 1830, a peace conference recognized Luxembourg as independent.

Today Luxembourg is ruled by a grand duke and a parliament elected by the people. The country was declared *neutral* (no͞o′trəl) in 1867. That meant it would not take sides in a war. Even though Luxembourg was neutral, it was still overrun by armies of larger nations in times of war.

Do You Know?

1. What cities grew up in Belgium in the Middle Ages? In the Netherlands?
2. Who led the Dutch against Spain?
3. Why did the Belgians rebel against the Netherlands?
4. How is Luxembourg ruled today?

3

The Netherlands as a Nation

A visitor to the Netherlands is impressed by its dikes and canals, its flowers, its farms and cities, and its busy people.

The Geography of the Netherlands

The Netherlands is a small kingdom in northwestern Europe. Look at the map of Belgium, the Netherlands, Luxembourg, on page 367, and note how much of the Netherlands is bordered by the sea.

The Importance of Dikes

Half of the area of the Netherlands has been drained and made into firm ground. The drained lowlands are called *polders* (pōl′dərz). If the sea were not kept out of the polders by dikes, the waves would roll over land that now supports farms and towns.

The sea has been a foe as well as a friend to the Dutch. In one great storm the North Sea burst through the sand hills on the coast. When the storm ended, a bay covered one-seventh of the Netherlands. The Dutch called this bay the Zuider Zee (zī′dər zē′), or the "Southern Sea," because it was south of the North Sea.

The Dutch have built more than 1,000 miles (1,600 km) of dikes. The largest of these is 100

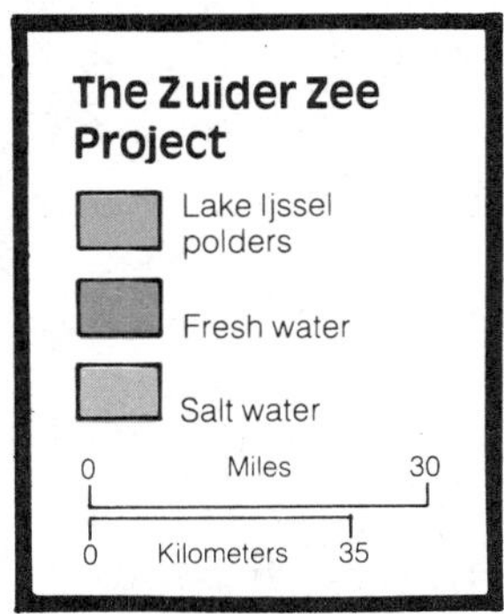

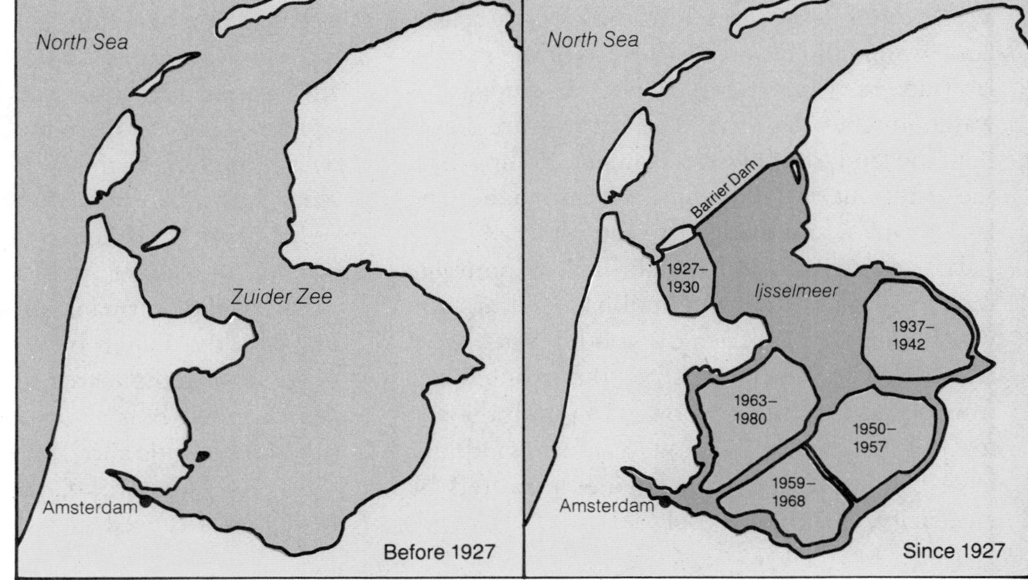

The Dutch worked hard to reclaim farm land from the Zuider Zee. A very large and strong *dike*, or sea barrier, was built. Salt water behind the *dike* was replaced by fresh water from the Ijssel River.

This *dike* built of earth and stone helps keep water from flooding the city of Amsterdam in the Netherlands. The city's many *dikes* have created beautiful canals.

feet (30 m) wide. Guards watch them day and night to check for leaks and to find places needing repairs. Some of the dikes are so broad and straight that roads and railroads are built on top of them.

The Importance of Pumps

While dikes keep the sea from flooding coastal land, water collects on the surface of the marshy land across which rivers flow. To remove this water, ditches are dug. The ditches are lower than the land, so the water flows in. Pumps force the water out of the ditches, and into higher and larger canals, and finally into the ocean.

For many years the Dutch did the pumping with windmills. Each windmill had four arms to which vanes, or a series of wooden slats, were attached. The vanes, turned by the strong winds from the sea, furnished power to pump the water out of the fields. Today, most windmills have been replaced with engines powered by electricity, steam, or diesel fuel.

The Draining of the Zuider Zee

For hundreds of years the Dutch have been adding land to their country because the number of people living there has grown. They decided to drain most of the arm of the sea called the Zuider Zee. By building a dam 18 miles (29 km) long, they closed off this body of water from the ocean. Then beginning in 1927, they worked to drain two-thirds of the Zuider Zee, and turned the deepest part into Lake Ijssel (ī′səl).

Hundreds of square miles of land were added to the nation in this way. Part of the Zuider Zee, however, was allowed to remain. This helped fishers to remain in business. Look at the map of the Zuider Zee Project on page 371.

When the Germans invaded the Netherlands in 1940, the Dutch blew up some of the dikes to try to stop the marching troops. Later the Allies dropped bombs on the German forces in the Netherlands and damaged other dikes.

As the dikes broke, the water poured over the land and caused great losses in crops, cattle,

Colorful fields of tulips are a common sight in the Netherlands. Gardeners sell the bulbs of the flowers to tulip growers in other countries. The Netherlands is also known for its many windmills.

and homes. When the war was over, the Dutch set to work rebuilding their dikes. Then they treated the soil to remove the salt left by the ocean so that crops could grow again.

In 1953 a great storm caused a flood. Many dikes were damaged, and islands in the southwestern part of the Netherlands were covered with water. It took a year to repair the dikes and reclaim the islands. To prevent similar floods, the government has built heavy dams.

Occupations in the Netherlands

The Dutch have learned valuable lessons from their history and their land. They have learned to work together and use their resources.

How the Dutch Use Canals

With so much lowland and water, the Dutch have made many canals for transporting goods easily and cheaply. Barges carry heavy loads of freight to most parts of the land. There are also canals for ships. One of these is wide enough to be used by the largest ship afloat. Canals are a cheap means of transportation. Because freight is carried by barges on the canals, the railroads in the Netherlands are used chiefly for passenger travel.

Dairying in the Netherlands

The moist pasture lands of the Netherlands are especially good for dairy cattle. With their fine herds of cows, the Dutch produce great quantities of milk, butter, and cheese. They process these foods and export them to other countries. But they still have plenty for their own use.

Flower-Growing in the Netherlands

On the western border of the country, the sand of the shore mixes with the moist clay of the fields. Flowers grow well in this soil. Here gardeners raise tulips, narcissuses, and hyacinths. The bulbs of these flowers are shipped to flower

Rotterdam has the best harbor in the Netherlands and is a major European port. Shipbuilding is an important industry in Rotterdam, and many shipping companies have their headquarters there.

growers in other lands. The Dutch also sell the seeds for garden vegetables.

The Famous Delft Pottery

The soil of the Netherlands has much clay. The Dutch put the clay to work. They build many houses of brick. They also make beautiful pottery. The city of Delft (delft) is famous for its blue-and-white dishes, plates, vases, tiles, and ceramic figurines. Some designs were copied from the Chinese, with whom the Dutch once did much trading.

Diamond Cutting in the Netherlands

Many Dutch are skillful diamond cutters. At about the time Columbus visited America, the gem polishers of Bruges formed a guild. Later, Antwerp (ant′wərp), in Belgium, and Amsterdam, in the Netherlands, became the centers of gem cutting and polishing. Amsterdam is still a diamond-cutting center.

Industry in the Netherlands

Manufacturing is the most important economic activity in the Netherlands. There are large iron and steel factories. The iron and coal for this industry have to be imported. The steel is used to build ships in Amsterdam and Rotterdam.

One of the world's largest electronics factories is in Eindhoven (īnd′hōv ən). It produces household appliances, radios, and television sets. The textile industry produces cotton, linen, wool, and synthetic fibers.

In 1964, a natural gas field was discovered. It is the second largest in the world. There are also large refineries.

Three Famous Dutch Cities

Let us take a bus from Leiden to Rotterdam. A student from the University of Leiden points out places of interest. Near Rotterdam we see long canals, flat green meadows, and dikes.

The Peace Palace in The Hague was built during the early 1900s as a meeting place for representatives of all nations. People hoped to prevent war by settling disputes there.

Rotterdam, a Great Trading City

Soon we come to the city of Rotterdam, a thriving center of trade. Rotterdam is built on strong beams of wood called *piles* (pīlz). Thousands of timbers support each important building and form a solid foundation in the marshy soil. Canals connect the city with the Rhine River and the North Sea. Thus barges bring goods from Germany and Switzerland to be exported to other countries by ocean vessels. Incoming ocean ships, in turn, unload their cargoes onto the barges to be carried throughout Europe. Rotterdam profits from this trade on water and land.

Amsterdam, Capital of the Netherlands

Amsterdam, northeast of Rotterdam, is the largest Dutch city. Like Rotterdam, Amsterdam, too, is built on piles.

Amsterdam is a great business and manufacturing city. It is also a large trading center. Tin, quinine, rubber, coffee, and tobacco from the Far East are brought to Amsterdam. A wide and deep canal allows ocean-going vessels to come into the heart of the city, so Amsterdam is an inland port.

The Hague, and the Peace Palace

Now we turn southward along the coast and come to a city which English-speaking people call The Hague.

Our guide is happy to show us The Hague. "Amsterdam is really our capital," she tells us, "but The Hague is so pleasant that our queen lives here."

She leads us to a huge building. "This," she says, "is the Palace of Peace, the most interesting building in The Hague. It was built in 1913 with the money of one of your citizens, Andrew Carnegie. Long before this palace was erected, The Hague had been a place where European nations gathered to discuss their problems. Many agreements were signed here.

"Today the palace is a permanent meeting place for the settlement of disputes. The World Court is here. The Hague has become a kind of world capital."

Important Dutch Inventions

Because the Dutch were so skillful at grinding gems, they became expert in making glass lenses. These lenses magnified, or made larger, the things seen through them.

This self-portrait by Rembrandt, a famous Dutch painter, shows the artist's skillful use of light and shadow.

The Telescope and the Microscope

A Netherlander named Hans Lippershay (li′pər shā′) improved the *telescope* (tel′ə skōp′), an instrument which magnifies objects seen at a distance. He made a telescope 300 feet (90 m) long. He used it to find new bodies in the heavens.

Zacharias (zak′ə rī′əs) Janssen made a special lens to help the eye see unusually small objects. An instrument with a lens of this kind is called a *microscope* (mī′krə skōp′). The microscope made it possible to discover the bacteria that cause disease.

The Yacht, a Dutch Invention

In the year 1660 King Charles II of England received a gift from the Netherlands. It was a trim little sailing vessel to be used for pleasure cruising. The Dutch called it a *yacht* (yot). Since that time yachts have been used for pleasure trips all over the world.

Art in the Netherlands

Soon after the Dutch became independent, a group of Dutch painters became world famous. They liked to paint people at work and play, and views of the tidy rooms inside Dutch homes. They also painted the flat Dutch fields, the canals, and the roads.

Many of the artists painted scenes exactly as they saw them. We call such paintings "realistic," because they show people and things as they really appear.

Two Famous Painters

Among Dutch painters Rembrandt (rem′brant) is given first place. Rembrandt painted fine portraits of the rich and poor. He covered large canvases with group portraits for guild halls. We know what Rembrandt looked like because he painted his own portrait several times. No one ever used light and shadow in painting the way Rembrandt did. The colors in his pictures seem to glow from within. Each year many people visit the museum at Amsterdam to see Rembrandt's famous painting, "The Night Watch."

Another fine Dutch painter was Frans Hals (fränz′ häls′). Like Rembrandt, Hals painted many portraits. The people in Hals's paintings are so lifelike they seem to step out of their frames. Hals's "Laughing Cavalier" and "Merry Lute Player" are two of his best paintings.

Anne Frank, a Young Writer

Anne Frank, a young Jewish girl, was another sort of artist.

When the Germans took over the Netherlands during World War II, Anne and her family hid from them in rooms behind a warehouse in Amsterdam. They knew the Germans would send them to a prison camp if they were found, because they were Jewish. The Frank family hid there for 2 years. A group of people who had worked for Mr. Frank brought them food, but finally the Germans found them. They were sent to prison camps, where all but Mr. Frank died. Anne was only 15 when she died.

While the family lived in the Amsterdam room, Anne kept a diary of their lives. Her father obtained the diary after the war and had it published. The book is called *The Diary of a Young Girl.* Even though Anne and her family lived in fear and poverty in Amsterdam, she believed people were really good. Today the rooms in which the Frank family hid is a museum.

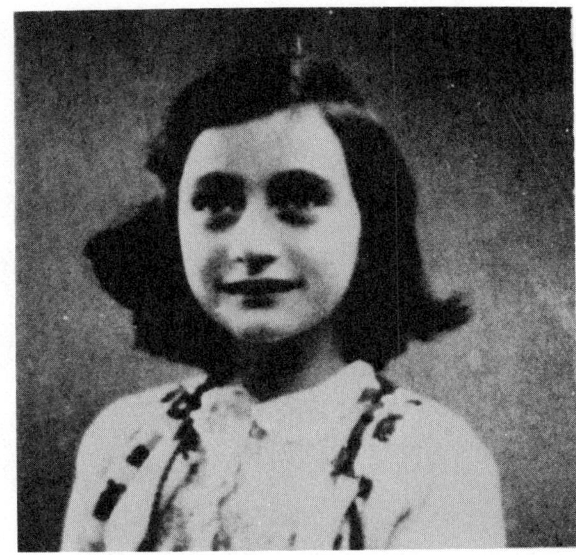

Anne Frank became famous after her diary was published. The diary describes two years she and her family hid from the Germans.

The Netherlands in Modern Times

During World War II, nearly half of the factories of the Netherlands were destroyed. Many farms, homes, and dikes were ruined, too. Since then, the Dutch have worked to rebuild them. They have also built new industries that produce chemicals and airplanes.

Today, the number of citizens is growing fast. To provide homes, jobs, and security for them, the Netherlands has joined several trade and military groups. NATO, the North Atlantic Treaty Organization, is one. It has 15 members, who promise to help one another in times of war. The Common Market is another. It is made up of nine European nations who trade with one another without charging import fees or tariffs.

The modern-day Dutch elect a parliament to run their country. They also have a queen, whose name is Beatrix. She advises the parliament on matters of state.

Do You Know?

1. How was the Zuider Zee formed?
2. Why did the Dutch build windmills?
3. What happened to many dikes in World War II?
4. What are the main occupations of the Dutch?
5. What are three important Dutch cities?

Before You Go On

Using New Words

dike	telescope
yacht	microscope
polder	neutral
pile	

Number a paper from 1 through 7. After each number write the word or term that matches the definition.

1. A trim sailing vessel used for pleasure cruising
2. An instrument which magnifies objects seen at a distance
3. Low land that has been drained
4. A bank of earth built up to keep out water
5. An instrument with a lens that helps the eye see unusually small objects
6. A strong beam of wood that supports a building
7. A nation that does not take sides in a war

Finding the Facts

1. Name two important cities in Belgium.
2. Who built the first dikes?
3. Who led the Dutch during the war with Spain?
4. Describe the government of Luxembourg today.
5. What is used now instead of windmills to pump water from land in the Netherlands?
6. Where is a modern center of diamond cutting?
7. What industry is headquartered in Eindhoven? What products are manufactured there?
8. Describe the city of Rotterdam.
9. What is the most important building in The Hague? How is it used?
10. What kind of government does the Netherlands have? What does the Queen do?
11. Name two of the Netherlands' most famous artists.
12. What is NATO?
13. What does the word "Netherlands" mean?
14. What are the most important economic activities in the Netherlands?
15. Who was Anne Frank? Why is she famous?

4
Belgium as a Nation

Belgium is another small country in northwestern Europe. Like the Netherlands, it is also a kingdom.

Geography of Belgium

Belgium is small, but it has a great many people. There are nearly 14 times as many people to the square mile in Belgium as in the United States. To prosper under such crowded conditions, the Belgians have made the land work for them. Belgium has an *oceanic climate* (ō′shē an′ik klī′mit), with cool summers, mild winters, and plenty of moisture.

A line drawn east and west across Belgium near Brussels would divide the country into two fairly equal parts. In the north are the people of Flanders, who speak Flemish. Flemish is a language somewhat like Dutch. In the south are the Walloons (wo lo͞onz′), who speak French.

Antwerp, in northern Belgium, is a Flemish city. Brussels is south of Antwerp.

Occupations of the Belgians

The Belgians are good farmers. About one-third of their land is taken up by pastures and crops, but the farms are small.

Farming in Belgium

One of Belgium's main crops is potatoes. Another crop is sugar beets. On the sandy soil around Ghent flowers and vegetables are grown for export. There are also large greenhouses where winter flowers, vegetables, and fruits are grown. Even though the Belgians are successful farmers, they still must import more food.

Flax grows in the southern part of Belgium. In slow-flowing streams, bundles of flax stalks are "retted," or allowed to rot, until only the fine inside fibers remain. Linen cloth is woven from these fibers.

Manufacturing in Belgium

Thickly populated countries need industry as well as farms. Belgium has many industries. It has been called "the workshop of Europe."

Belgium has coal mines along its border with France. At one time, the Belgians also mined iron ore, but this ore is almost gone. The fields of iron ore in the area around Liège (lē ezh′) are still mined. Liège produces locomotives and rails, tools, and machines.

The weavers of Flanders have been famous for nearly 1,000 years. When William the Conqueror invaded England, the greatest wool market in Europe was Bruges. Ghent, supported by its wool weaving, was five times as large as London. Today, Ghent also produces steel.

The Cities of Belgium

Fifty miles (80 m) up the Scheldt (shelt) River from the sea lies the old city of Antwerp. See the map of Belgium, the Netherlands, Luxembourg on page 367.

Brussels
A Common Market Capital

Brussels has long been a center of administration in the Low Countries. Today, Brussels is a capital to many nations. It is the capital city of Belgium. It is the administrative and military headquarters of NATO. When the European Common Market made Brussels its headquarters in 1957, the city also became a trade capital for other nations of Western Europe.

Brussels, a city of more than a million people, is growing fast. Its location in the middle of a rich farming area has helped the city attract many food-processing industries. There are also textile, leather, and metal industries here. Why do you think many goods manufactured in Brussels are likely to be sold in such nations as France and Italy? Do you think these goods will be priced so that many French and Italian people can afford them? Why?

Even though Brussels is an industrial city, its elaborately decorated old guild houses and wide streets and parks give it an old-fashioned charm. It looks like a city designed for elegant and comfortable living. The many foreign officials of the Common Market agencies enjoy the city's quiet charm.

Brussels' appearance reminds you of a city of the old Europe. However, as a Common Market capital, it represents the spirit of cooperation that marks the new Europe. ■

What Antwerp is Like

Antwerp developed as a seaport in the late Middle Ages. It soon became the leading port in Europe and one of the world's richest cities. During the Netherlands' revolt against Spain, Spanish troops nearly destroyed the city in 1576. In 1795, Napoleon conquered it for France.

Napoleon saw the importance of Antwerp as a port facing his greatest enemy, England. He ordered great docks built. A canal built through the Netherlands allowed barges to go from Antwerp into Germany. Today Antwerp is a trade center for all of western Europe.

Art and Music in Belgium

Many famous painters called Belgium home, and it was there that a special musical instrument was invented.

Two Great Artists of Belgium

In art museums all over the world there are pictures by many Flemish painters, including Peter Paul Rubens and Anthony Van Dyck (van dīk). They lived in Antwerp.

Rubens studied painting in Italy. He came home to paint rich costumes, great buildings, and people in action. With a group of pupils, he painted more than 2,000 pictures.

Anthony Van Dyck studied painting under Rubens, but his style was different. Rubens was fiery and loved bright colors while Van Dyck was quiet and used cool tones. So many men in his paintings wore small pointed beards that we now call such beards "Vandykes".

Belgium, the Home of the Carillon

Inventors in Belgium developed the *carillon* (kar′ə lon′). A carillon is a musical instrument made up of a set of bells, large and small. The bells are struck by hammers operated from a keyboard like a small organ. On festive days, the sounds of the carillons are heard in Belgian towns and cities.

Belgium in Two World Wars

Belgium became independent in 1830. It has never had a large army or navy, but the other nations of Europe respected its rights for about 100 years.

Then in 1914 World War I began. The German troops took the easiest path to attack France. This was across Belgium. Through years of war, the Germans occupied most of Belgium.

In World War II, which began in 1939, Belgium was again overrun by the Germans. But throughout this war many Belgians were part of the *underground resistance* (un′dər ground′ rɪ zis′təns). This was a group that worked in secret to overthrow the enemy occupying their country.

Since World War II, Belgium has become one of the most industrialized nations in Europe. It now has many new factories, modern expressways, and office buildings and hotels of bold design. Even though it is tiny, Belgium has international influence. It is the seat of NATO, the Common Market, and the Supreme Headquarters Allied Powers in Europe.

Belgium is ruled by a king, ministers, and a parliament.

Luxembourg is a small country of great charm and natural beauty. It has many small towns surrounded by forested hills. This town, called Dudelange, is in the southern part of the country.

Little Luxembourg

The country of Luxembourg is so small on the map of Europe that it can easily be overlooked. But Luxembourg ranks high as a producer of iron and steel. The nation's other industries make cloth, pottery, tires, and chemicals.

Luxembourg has regions that are very different from each other. The north is rugged and forested. Lumbering is done there. Where there are pastures, herders keep dairy cattle. In the south are farms where grain, potatoes, sugar beets, and wine grapes are raised.

To carry on trade, Luxembourg depends on the Moselle River and on railroads that connect it to neighboring countries. Luxembourg has many good roads and bicycle paths.

The Benelux Nations

Take the first letters of Belgium, the first of the Netherlands, and the first of Luxembourg. Put these letters together and you form the name *Benelux* (ben′ ə luks′). This is the name of the organization these countries formed in 1947.

The purpose of Benelux is to promote trade. The members of Benelux do this by lowering or removing the taxes on goods which they import from each other.

How does this encourage trade? When the price of a product is high, few people can afford to buy it. When the price is lower, more people are able to purchase it. As the Benelux countries reduced import taxes, goods could be sold for less so more people could buy more things.

As you learned earlier, these three countries are also joined with seven other countries of western Europe in a larger trade group, called the Common Market. The partners are France, West Germany, Great Britain, Denmark, Ireland, Greece, and Italy. The members of the Common Market continue to cooperate in both trade and industry.

Do You Know?

1. What kind of climate does Belgium have?
2. What languages do Belgians speak?
3. What happened to Belgium in World War I? In World War II?
4. How do the Benelux countries promote trade with one another?

To Help You Learn

Using New Words

Benelux	underground resistance
dike	carillon
polder	oceanic climate

Number a paper from 1 through 6. After each number write the word or term that matches the definition.

1. A climate with cool summers, mild winters, and plenty of moisture
2. A musical instrument composed of bells
3. An organization formed by Belgium, the Netherlands, and Luxembourg to promote trade
4. A bank of earth to keep out water
5. A group that works in secret to overthrow the enemy occupying their country
6. Low land that has been drained

Finding the Facts

1. Explain the meaning of the name "the Low Countries." How were the lands of these countries formed?
2. How did the Netherlands become an independent nation?
3. Discuss the importance of dikes in the history of the Netherlands.
4. Name the crops grown in Luxembourg.
5. Why do the Dutch use canals?
6. What is a "realistic" painting?
7. How do the Dutch people earn a living?
8. How are the Dutch now adding to the land of their country?
9. What are the major means of transportation in Luxembourg?
10. Name some important Dutch inventions.
11. How does the location of Rotterdam help make it a great trading city?
12. Who are the Walloons? What language do they speak?
13. Why are the Dutch replacing the windmills they needed in the past?
14. Who are some famous Dutch artists?
15. What languages are spoken in Belgium?
16. Who invented the microscope? Who improved the telescope?
17. How did Belgium gain independence?
18. List Luxembourg's two most important industrial products.
19. How is linen produced? What country produces it?
20. How do the Belgians earn a living?
21. Name two cities of Belgium. Give an important fact about each one.
22. What is the city of Brussels like?
23. What makes Amsterdam an important city?
24. Why was Benelux formed?
25. What is "The Night Watch"?
26. Describe the two regions in Luxembourg and tell about the type of work done in each.
27. What was Bruges famous for 1,000 years ago?
28. What is a neutral country? Are any of the Low Countries neutral?

29. What was Flanders?
30. How does a windmill look? How does it work?
31. How many people live in Brussels?
32. What did the Belgians do when the Germans invaded in World War II?
33. How are Van Dyke's paintings different from Rubens's?
34. How did Napoleon help develop the port of Antwerp?
35. What do the citizens of Liège manufacture?
36. What nation is nicknamed the "workshop of Europe"?

Learning from Maps

1. On the map of Belgium, the Netherlands, Luxembourg on page 367, locate Luxembourg. What is its capital city? What river forms one of its borders? What countries form its other borders?
2. Look at the map of the Zuider Zee Project on page 371. What major city is near the Zuider Zee? What is the name of the dam? How many polders have been made? How many years did it take to make them?
3. On the map of Belgium, the Netherlands, Luxembourg on page 367, find Belgium. Name the river that flows past Liège. Where does it come from? Where does it go? Name the river that flows past Ghent. What important city is south of the capital of Belgium? What battle took place there? Why was it important?

   Is The Hague closer to Rotterdam or Amsterdam?

   Are there any plateaus in Luxembourg? Any plains? Any mountains?

   Do you find hills in Belgium? If so, where?

Using Study Skills

Time Line: Place the following events in the proper order of time:
First polder begun; Germans invade the Netherlands; Peace Palace completed.

Copy the time line from page 365. Add these events to your time line.

Study the completed time line and answer the following questions: How many years passed between the time the Netherlands became independent and the world's second largest gas field was found? Between the time the polders were begun and the Germans invaded the Netherlands? Between the time Belgium gained independence and joined Luxembourg and the Netherlands in the Common Market?

Thinking It Through

1. It has been said that the sea has been a foe as well as a friend to the Dutch. How would you prove this statement?
2. Why is it cheaper to ship goods by water than by land?
3. Why is it important for nations to meet at The Hague?
4. If you wanted to live in the Netherlands and be successful in business, what skills would you learn? Explain why you named the skills you did.

5. How have the telescope and the microscope benefited us?
6. In one respect, the Benelux countries are like states in the United States. Explain what that similarity is.
7. If you were a farmer, would you rather live in Belgium or the Netherlands? Give reasons for your choice and tell what crops you might raise.
8. It has been said that much of the Netherlands is the gift of the Rhine. Explain this sentence. Does it apply to Belgium also?
9. Why do you think Belgians joined the underground resistance to fight the Germans in World War II?

Projects

1. To farm the land in the past, Belgian farmers bred a special horse called a Belgian draft. Find a picture of this horse and learn how it differs from other kinds of horses.
2. Ask some florists if they have ever imported flower bulbs from Belgium or from the Netherlands. If so, find out why and tell your class.

   Look in garden catalogs for pictures of flowers from the Low Countries for a classroom display.
3. With some of your classmates, form a committee to paint designs of tiles for a frieze for your classroom. The designs should represent features of Dutch life. Tulips, dairy cattle, windmills, canal boats, bridges, and ships furnish good subjects.
4. Arrange a display of prints of pictures by Dutch artists. Be sure to include Rembrandt, Vermeer, Van Gogh, Hals. To represent Belgium, try to find some prints of paintings by Van Dyck and Rubens.
5. Photographers today often use what is called "Rembrandt lighting." Find out what this is and report on it in class.
6. Ask your librarian to locate records of music with a part for the carillon. Find out which composers use this instrument most often, and the kind of music best suited for the carillon.
7. Ask at your grocery store if cheeses from the Netherlands are sold there. If so, find out the names of the cheeses and which ones people who go to that store seem to like the best.
8. Ask the Research Committee to plan a class vacation through the three Low Countries, visiting all three capital cities. Show the route to take, describe the main sights to see, and explain how much time to allow for the trip.

13 Scandinavia and Finland

Unit Preview

The Scandinavian countries of Sweden and Norway make up the largest peninsula in northern Europe. Finland and Denmark touch the European mainland. Denmark is a peninsula by itself. The large island at the top of the map is Greenland, and the small island is Iceland. Both of these islands were colonized by the Scandinavians, or the Vikings as they were called in early times. Leif Ericson, a Scandinavian explorer, is known to have reached the continent of North America.

Norway is on the western side of the Scandinavian Peninsula, and Sweden is on the eastern side. Denmark is really on a separate, smaller peninsula of its own, jutting off Europe. Denmark is also made up of many islands.

In 1397, Denmark, Norway, and Sweden, were united as Scandinavia under Queen Margrete of Denmark. Sweden broke away in 1523. Norway and Denmark had one ruler until 1905. In that year, Norway chose its own king.

Finland is not considered a Scandinavian country because its people migrated from Asia, not from Europe. Also, the Finnish people speak a different kind of language from the people of Scandinavia. The Finnish language is similar to Hungarian. Because of its location, however, Finland is included in our study of northern Europe. Its history is closely related to that of the Scandinavian countries. For more than 600 years Sweden controlled Finland.

Things to Discover

If you look carefully at the picture, map, and time line on these pages, you can answer these questions.

1. On what continent are the Scandinavian countries and Finland?
2. What ocean is north of these countries? What ocean is west?
3. In what year did one person rule Norway, Sweden, and Denmark?
4. The picture shows what much of the coastline of Norway is like. The sea flows into narrow inlets. What kind of land borders many of these water channels?
5. Roald Amundsen was a famous Norwegian explorer. Where did he go in 1911?
6. In what year did Sweden become independent? Norway?

Words to Learn

You will meet these words in this unit. As you read, you will learn what they mean and how to pronounce them. The Word List will help you.

cooperative union	sardine
drift	sauna
dynamite	smelting
ecology	smorgasbord
fiord	Swedish gymnastics
nitroglycerine	Swedish massage
Nobel Prize	tanker

- c. 1000 A.D. — Vikings roam Europe
- 1397 — Scandinavian countries of Norway, Denmark, and Sweden unite under Margrete
- 1523 — Sweden becomes independent
- 1867 — Alfred Nobel tests dynamite
- 1905 — Norway becomes independent
- 1911 — Amundsen arrives at South Pole
- 1917 — Finland declares independence from Russia
- 1939 — Finland-Soviet Union war beings; World War II begins
- 1945 — World War II ends
- 1975 — Helsinki Agreement

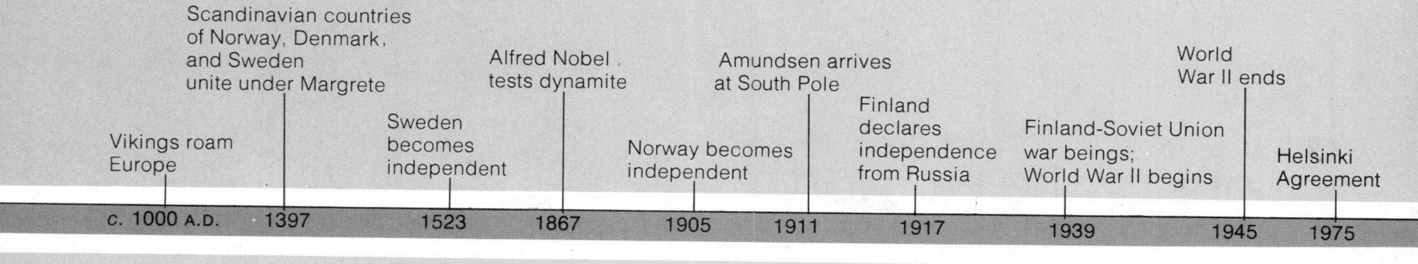

Arctic Ocean
Atlantic Ocean
EUROPE
AFRICA
ASIA
Pacific Ocean
Indian Ocean
AUSTRALIA

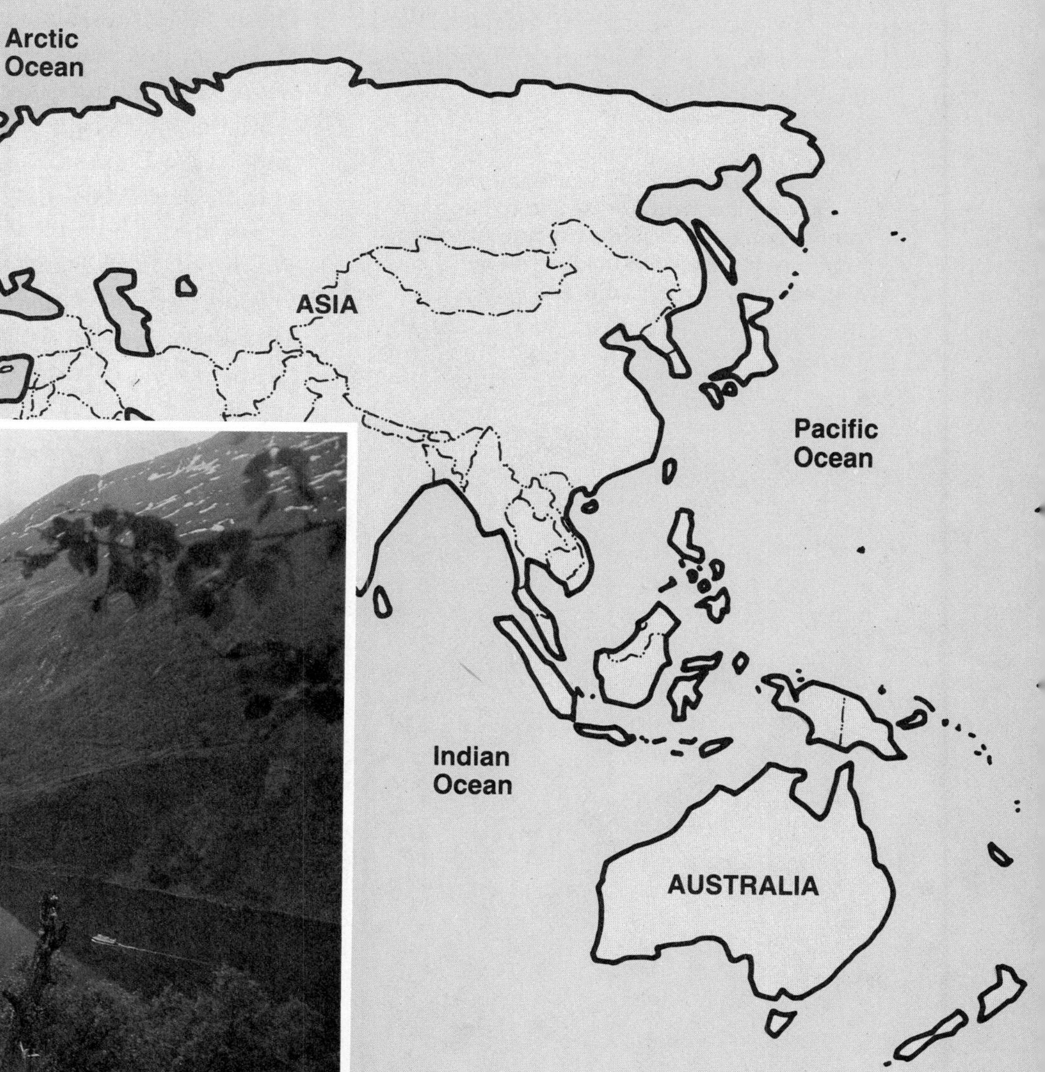

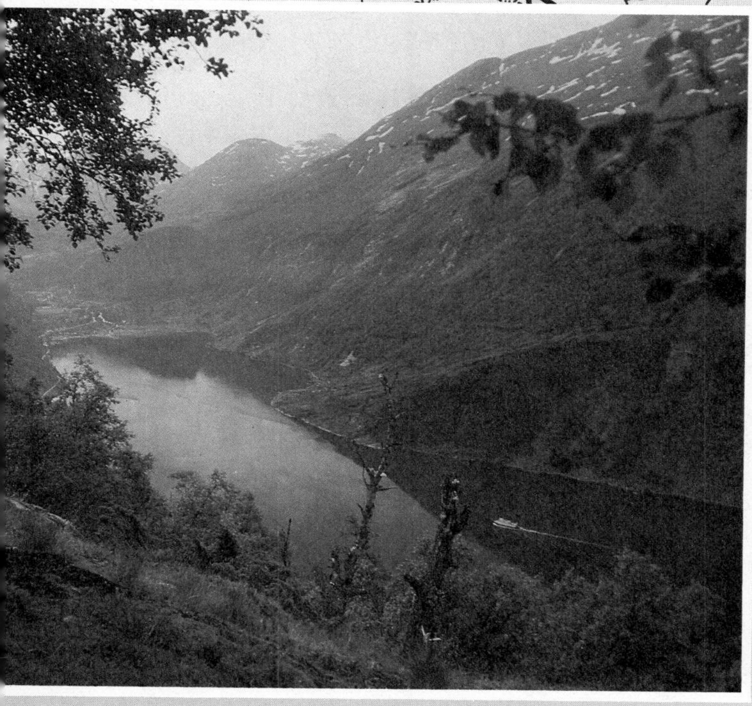

1

Nations of the Far North

Scandinavia (skan′də nā′vē ə) and Finland are surrounded by gulfs, seas, and oceans. Find these bodies of water on the map of Scandinavia and Finland on page 389.

The coast of Norway has many *fiords.* These inlets from the sea were cut from high banks by rushing streams and sheets of moving ice. The *fiords* provide excellent natural harbors.

A Region of Peninsulas

These nations of northern Europe are made up of several peninsulas. Denmark is a small peninsula, with offshore islands. It extends from the continent of Europe into the North Sea. This land of the Danes lies between the North Sea and the Baltic (bôl′tik) Sea.

North of Denmark is a larger peninsula. It is almost cut off by water from the rest of Europe. Through it, like a huge backbone, stretch high mountains. On the Atlantic, or western, side of this peninsula is Norway. On the eastern side is Sweden.

On the north, both Norway and Sweden shares boundaries with Finland. As the map of Scandinavia and Finland shows, Finland is at the base of the peninsula that Norway and Sweden occupy. Farther south a gulf separates Sweden from the peninsula of Finland.

Rugged Norway

Norway has a very jagged coastline. Rushing streams and sheets of moving ice have cut deep, narrow valleys between high banks on the coastline. Norway has many such inlets, or *fiords* (fyôrdz). The sea has entered these fiords, flowing inland at some places 100 miles (160 km).

Forested Sweden

As the map shows, Sweden is larger than Norway and extends farther south. Sweden has more farmland than Norway. But half the country is covered with forests, and there are many

SCANDINAVIA AND FINLAND
Plains
Plateaus
Hills
Mountains
0 Miles 140
0 Kilometers 177
ARCTIC OCEAN
OCEAN
North Cape
LOFOTEN IS.
Narvik
PETSAMO
Murmansk
ARCTIC CIRCLE
NORWEGIAN SEA
NORWAY
SCANDINAVIAN HIGHLANDS
SWEDEN
GULF OF BOTHNIA
FINLAND
ATLANTIC
Bergen
Oslo
Stavanger
Lake Vanern
Göta Canal
Stockholm
Helsinki
Viipuri
Lake Ladoga
Leningrad
GULF OF FINLAND
Tallin
NORTH SEA
DENMARK
Göteborg
GOTLAND
SEA
ÖLAND
Copenhagen
Malmö
BALTIC
Riga
SOVIET UNION
WEST GERMANY
EAST GERMANY
POLAND
Kalingrad
5°
10°
15°
20°
25°
30°
55°
60°
65°
70°

An early means of record-keeping in Scandinavia were stones inscribed with an ancient alphabet. Many of these stones can be found there today.

lakes. Snow lies on the ground in Sweden for about 4 months of the year.

Finland, Land of Lakes

Norway, Sweden, and Finland have many lakes and rivers. But Finland has so many of them that its people call their homeland Suomi (swô′mē). That means "land of lakes." Look at the lakes on the map of Scandinavia and Finland.

Denmark with Its Islands

Although it occupies its own small peninsula, much of Denmark is made up of islands. Copenhagen (kō′pən hā′gən), the capital, is on one of these islands. It is at the entrance to the Baltic Sea. Denmark has the flattest surface of the four northern lands.

The Scandinavian Nations

Norway and Sweden together occupy the Scandinavian Peninsula. However, Denmark is also a Scandinavian country. The name "Scandinavia" came from the Romans, who talked of an island in the Baltic Sea called Scandia. The "island" was actually southern Sweden, which the Swedes still call Scandia.

The three Scandinavian countries have fish and water power, but few mineral resources. The people of the three countries speak similar languages. In 1960 the Scandinavian nations joined with other countries in a trade association somewhat like the Common Market.

The Union of Scandinavia

In early times, Scandinavian warriors, called Vikings, brought terror to England and to France. Soon after the year 1000 the Scandinavians became Christians. Then they settled down and formed three national communities: Denmark, Norway, and Sweden.

In 1397 the three countries united under Margrete, queen of Denmark. They formed the largest kingdom in Europe at the time. Margrete was a good queen, but her successors were harsh rulers.

Sweden, Once a Great Power

The Swedes revolted against a cruel Danish king and set up their own kingdom in 1523 under Gustavus (gus tā′vəs) I. A hundred years later, Gustavus Adolphus (ä däl′fus) became king. He made Sweden strong.

While England was founding colonies in what is now the United States, Sweden was one of the great powers of Europe. During this period Sweden conquered much of northern Europe.

Some Swedes also sailed to North America. Many settled along the Delaware River in "New Sweden," the site of Wilmington, Delaware, and Philadelphia, Pennsylvania, today.

But Sweden fought many wars. In a war with Russia, Sweden lost. After this Sweden lost its position as a great power in Europe.

Norway, an Independent Kingdom

Norway and Denmark were ruled as one country for 400 years. Norway then came under the rule of the Swedish king. In 1905 Norway chose a king of its own and became completely independent.

Finland, a Republic

Finland's history was for many years, closely united with that of its Scandinavian neighbors. It was controlled by Sweden for more than 600 years. After Sweden was defeated in a war with Russia, the Finns lived under Russian rule for a time. In 1917 Finland gained its independence and became a republic.

Do You Know?

1. Which two countries occupy the Scandinavian peninsula? Which country is larger? Which extends farther south?
2. Where is Denmark located? What landforms make up this country?
3. What do the Finns call their land?
4. Who was Gustavus Adolphus? Queen Margrete?

2 Denmark, Land of the Danes

There is no place in Denmark that is more than 50 miles (80 km) from the sea. This makes the climate cool in summer and warm in winter. It gives the country a long coastline and good fishing grounds.

Making a Living in Denmark

For a long time Denmark was a poor country. Its soil was not good for growing wheat or other grains. It was hard for Danes to make a living as farmers.

The dairy industry plays a major role in Denmark's economy. Danish farmers show their cattle at agricultural events like the one seen here.

Denmark, a Dairy Country

Danish scientists studied the resources of the country to see how they could best be used. They decided that Denmark could become a good dairy country. They made a plan to show how this could be done. Schools were established to teach both the old and the young how to operate dairies.

Dairying requires more work than general farming, but it brings in more profit and makes the soil rich. Danish farmers plant clover and other crops which feed cows and also are good for the soil. The well-fed cows produce much milk. The Danes make such good butter that most of it is eagerly bought by the English. It is also canned and shipped to tropical countries.

Denmark is also famous for other products such as cheese, eggs, and pork. So many eggs are exported that there is a saying, "If Danish farmers have only one egg, they send it abroad." Millions of eggs are sent abroad to join Danish ham and bacon on English breakfast tables.

Denmark still has many schools that train young people in the best farming methods. It led the Scandinavian countries in providing education for adults and in giving pensions to aged people who could not work. Danish farmers have formed *cooperative unions* (kō op′ ər ə tiv yo͞on′ yənz). Like the guilds of former days, these unions secure fair prices for their members' products. They see that the quality of products is kept high. They buy goods for farmers in large amounts at low prices.

A Danish woman who had been living in England went back to Denmark on a visit. Near her old home she remembered a windy stretch of sand hills along the coast. To her surprise she found a thriving forest, which acted as a windbreak. What had been a sandy wasteland was now a pasture. This is an example of how land can be improved. It is a lesson in *ecology* (ē kol′ ə jē). Ecology is the study of how living things relate to their environment.

Denmark's Industries

The city of Copenhagen, which means "merchants' haven," has an excellent harbor. Long ago the people of this city learned that large profits could be made from carrying goods. As a result, they built many ships.

Almost half of the Danes earn a living in manufacturing. Danish factories make radios, television sets, diesel engines, ships, machinery, and furniture.

The people of Denmark are skillful in making articles which are beautiful as well as useful. Their silverware is famed for its fine design. They make excellent pottery and a kind of porcelain, or fine china, called Royal Copenhagen. This china, which is often patterned in blue, is delicate in design and is highly prized.

Copenhagen, Capital of Denmark

Copenhagen is built on Sealand (sē′land), which is an island between the Danish peninsula and Sweden. Ships sailing from the North Sea directly into the Baltic use this narrow waterway. For hundreds of years Denmark made every ship that passed Copenhagen pay a tax. To avoid the tax many captains sailed their ships through the channels west of the island. After a time the tax was removed. Copenhagen lost the tax money, but it continued to be prosperous.

The queen of Denmark lives in Copenhagen. The royal palace is one of four that surround an open square.

Today one-third of Denmark's people live in Copenhagen. It is a fine city with open-air flower markets and beautiful suburbs. In the suburbs, homes stand on plots of land, surrounded by gardens, grass, and trees. Few European cities have garden suburbs of this kind.

Denmark's Tivoli Gardens, above, is a world-famous amusement park that includes rides, circus acts, and concerts. Christiansborg Palace, below, is the seat of Denmark's parliament.

Some Famous Danes

Many Danish kings have been named Christian. This was also the middle name of one of the most famous men of Denmark, the great storyteller, Hans Christian Andersen.

Hans Christian Andersen

As a child, Hans lived with a gloomy father and a neglectful mother in a single room. They were poor, so Hans found happiness in a make-believe world. The other children made fun of him as an awkward fellow with big feet. When he was 14 years old, he went to Copenhagen to seek work. He was not successful, but generous friends sent him to school.

Soon Hans began to write down stories. Both children and grownups loved the stories and the man who wrote them. On the waterfront of Copenhagen stands a bronze statue of "The Little Mermaid," to remind people of one of Andersen's best stories. Another of his famous stories is "The Ugly Duckling."

A World-Famous Sculptor

Another gifted Dane was Bertel Thorwaldsen (bər tel′ thôr′wôld sən). His father was a woodcarver, and Thorwaldsen learned this skill. He had the chance to go to art school, and won many prizes. Finally, he was sent to Italy to work as a sculptor in marble.

Thorwaldsen did not win fame quickly. The people of Rome admired his work, but they did not buy it. Just as he was ready to give up and return home, orders began to come in. He was kept so busy that it was many years before he could go home.

Thorwaldsen admired the old Greek statues so much that he used the Greek style in his own sculpture. Thorwaldsen's most famous work is a carving of a lion in Lucerne, Switzerland. It was cut into solid rock. Many of Thorwaldsen's sculptures are in a museum in Copenhagen.

Denmark in Recent Times

When World War II began, peace-loving Denmark had only a small army and navy. In April 1940, a German army marched in and occupied the country. Against the mighty German army the Danes could do little to defend themselves. The Danes became prisoners in their homeland. The Germans forced Denmark to give them much of the food it produced. But the Danes never willingly helped the Germans during the war. Denmark was the only country that consistently protested the Germans' cruel treatment of the Jews.

After the war the country turned its attention to peaceful living. Today its farmers continue to be world leaders in the production of milk, butter, eggs, bacon, ham, and pork. The country's chief industries are iron and metal production, food processing, and paper making.

Denmark is a kingdom, but it is a democratic country. The people elect their lawmakers and take a keen interest in government. This is one reason why Denmark has many laws providing for the well-being of its citizens. In Denmark the government pays for schools, pensions, medicine, and hospital treatment.

The people of Denmark are proud of Queen Margrete II and her family. She is the first queen to reign in 600 years. The queen and parliament share power. The actual head of the government is a prime minister. He forms a cabinet, called a council of state.

Greenland and Iceland

Small Denmark has had two island colonies. They are Greenland and Iceland. Iceland is now independent.

What Greenland Is Like

Greenland, the world's largest island, lies west of Iceland. It is part of Denmark. The capital city is Godthaab (got′hôb).

Greenland is not a good name for this large, cold island. Most of it is covered by a huge sheet of ice which is slowly pushing its way to the sea. Only a part of the southwest coast of Greenland can be inhabited.

The people who live on Greenland are mostly Eskimos. But many Danes live there too. The Eskimos hunt seals, but fishing and fish processing are the main industries.

During World War II, Greenland was a base for weather stations and was also useful to the Allies as a base for warships and planes. From Greenland, Allied air and naval forces protected ships on the Atlantic against enemy attack.

What Iceland Is Like

More than 1,000 miles (1,600 km) northwest of Denmark is Iceland, which touches the Arctic Circle. Find it on the map of Europe on page 161. Iceland is twice as large as Denmark.

Iceland has long winters and such high winds that there are few trees. The only crops are potatoes, turnips, and hay. Yet Iceland is a land of fire as well as ice, for it has many volcanoes. Underground heat has produced spouting geysers of hot water and many hot springs. The hot water is used to warm homes, to wash clothes, and to heat greenhouses.

Small fishing villages are scattered along the rocky coast of Greenland. Fishing and fish processing are Greenland's main industries.

Iceland has few natural resources and cannot support many people. Most of the people live in the southwestern part of the island, where the land is lowest and the weather is warmest. Their winters, though long, are not colder than those of Boston.

The people raise sheep, but only in small numbers, since the hay crop is not large enough to feed large flocks through the winter. Potatoes and turnips are raised during the short summer, when the days are long.

The ocean around Iceland swarms with fish, and fishing is a very important industry. Iceland's fishing fleet uses modern radar (rā′där) instruments to find the fish. Radar is a way of using radio waves to locate moving objects.

Reykjavik (rā′kyə vēk′) is Iceland's capital and largest city. It is also the main seaport. Through this port fish and fish meal are shipped to other nations. Fish products are over 75 percent of Iceland's exports. Through Reykjavik, too, lumber, coal, petroleum, grains, and manufactured goods are brought into Iceland.

Iceland was a Danish possession for almost 600 years. Then during World War II the people of Iceland voted to become independent. Denmark granted them their freedom. Iceland then became an independent republic.

Do You Know?

1. Why did Denmark become a dairy country?
2. What is Copenhagen like?
3. Who was Hans Christian Andersen?
4. What does this mean: "Iceland is a land of fire as well as ice"?
5. When did Iceland become independent? What form of government does it have?

3 The Land of Norway

Norway is not a rich land. Much of Norway lies beyond the Arctic Circle, and much of it is mountainous.

The Climate of Norway

The ports of Norway are ice-free in the winter. But Greenland's waters, in the same latitude as Norway, are full of ice all summer.

Why are conditions on Norway's coast so favorable? Why are Norway's ports ice-free in winter? The answer is that west winds, blowing across the Atlantic, drive a mass of warmer water, called a *drift* (drift), along Norway's shores. The warm drift keeps the water from freezing. Winds blowing over the drift lessen the winter's cold on land. Thanks to the drift, the sea lies open to Norwegians all year long.

Making a Living in Norway

The ocean helps make Norway the kind of country it is. It influences both the climate and the people's way of living. Shipping and fishing are two important industries.

The Fisheries of Norway

With little good farm land and an open sea, many Norwegians make their livelihood by fishing in the ocean. Around the rocky islands of Norway swim millions of fish. Fish furnish a large share of Norway's food and exports.

In spring the herring come up the fiords and into the streams to lay their eggs. Thousands of pounds of herring are caught during this time. Before the herring season is over, it is time for the codfishers to go to the waters around the Lofoten (lō′fō′tən) Islands, above the Arctic Circle. Codfish are even more important to Norway than herring. Some of the codfish are salted for export. Some are dried in the sun. The liver of the cod contains an oil from which a useful medicine is made.

Norwegian waters are also full of small fish called *sardines* (sär dēnz′). Sardines are canned, smoked, or packed in oil, and carried in Norwegian ships all over the world.

Norway's Great Merchant Fleet

Long ago the Vikings set out from this land in their sailing ships on long voyages. They reached the shores of America nearly 500 years before Columbus.

Many Norwegian ships still sail to foreign countries. Norway today has one of the largest merchant fleets in the world. About half the

The economy of Norway depends greatly on fishing. The main catches include herring and cod. These herring have been hung from racks and smoked.

Norway has the greatest number of waterfalls in Europe. They are used to provide electric power for the country's homes and industries.

Norwegian ships are *tankers* (tang′kərz). A tanker has large tanks below its decks, used for carrying oil or other liquids. Norway's tankers often haul petroleum from the Middle East to ports in Western Europe.

Ships are also needed to link the cities and towns that dot the coast of Norway. Ships carry supplies from town to town. There are also ferries that cross the many fiords.

Farming in Norway

Most of Norway is mountainous and covered by trees. Less than one-fourth of the land can be used for farming. Because the growing season is short, only a few kinds of crops can be raised.

Raising enough food is not as big a problem as it once was. Norway is following the example of Denmark in farming. By selecting better kinds of plants and animals and by adding fertilizers to the soil, Norway is able to produce more food. It even exports some food, such as potatoes. By draining ponds and marshes and by clearing off forests, Norway has increased its farmland.

Norway's Waterfalls

Melting snow, heavy rains, and mountainous country make Norway a land of rivers, lakes, and waterfalls. Falling water, when controlled, produces electric power.

Norway has more waterfalls than any other country in Europe. By using them, the country is improving its industries. Most of Norway's factories are now run by electric power. Two-thirds of the farm homes have electric lights and use electricity in other ways. By means of cheap electric power Norway has become a manufacturing country.

Near the largest of Norway's waterfalls stands a chemical factory. Here the invention of a Norwegian engineer is used to take a gas called nitrogen from the air. By means of electric power the nitrogen is combined with other materials, such as lime, to form fertilizer. This is used to make Norway's fields rich. Factories have been built where such useful materials are manufactured. The way air and water are used to produce the gas and electricity is an example of wise use of resources.

Norway's Forests

Forests cover about one-fourth of Norway. They provide raw material for factories where the wood is ground into pulp. Much of the pulp is made into paper. Some of the pulp, however, is given special treatment and is made into rayon (rā′yon). Rayon is used for clothing and for household articles.

Life in Norway

About half of all Norwegians live in towns and cities. They are very proud of Oslo.

Oslo, Norway's Capital

Before 1924 the capital of Norway was called Christiania. In that year Norway decided that its capital should take the old Norse name of Oslo (os′lō). Oslo is Norway's greatest seaport. One-tenth of the people of Norway live in Oslo. The best farming land of Norway lies around it. Many visitors come to Oslo every year. It is one of Europe's most important shipping and trading centers.

Education in Norway

Everybody in Norway can receive an education. Norwegians are great readers. Libraries and bookstores are everywhere. Norway was one of the first countries to build public libraries. A law requires every city and village in the nation to provide at least one free library.

Skiing, a National Sport

Long ago, in their snow-covered lands, the Norwegians learned to use skis. With these slim runners strapped to their feet they made amazing journeys. They made skiing a sport and held ski races and ski jumps. Many countries today have adopted skiing as a winter sport.

Norway's Famous People

Many Norwegians are famous. The best known are musicians and explorers.

Great Musicians of Norway

In the city of Bergen (ber′gən) stands the statue of a violinist named Ole Bull (ō′lē bull′). He was loved and honored by multitudes in Europe and the United States.

Ole made two concert tours in the United States. He liked our country so much that he dreamed of it as a place where poor Norwegians might own their own land and live in plenty. In Pennsylvania he bought a great tract of land and called it Oleana (ō lē′a nə). It was to be a place of freedom for all. The plan did not succeed, but Norwegians have not forgotten Ole Bull and his dream.

Ole met a musically gifted boy by the name of Edvard Grieg (ed′värd grēg′), who also lived in the town of Bergen. He persuaded Edvard's parents to send the boy to study music in Germany. Edvard then went to Copenhagen where he studied the tunes which had been sung and played since early times. He began to write musical works which used these folk tunes. Grieg became famous for his truly Norwegian music.

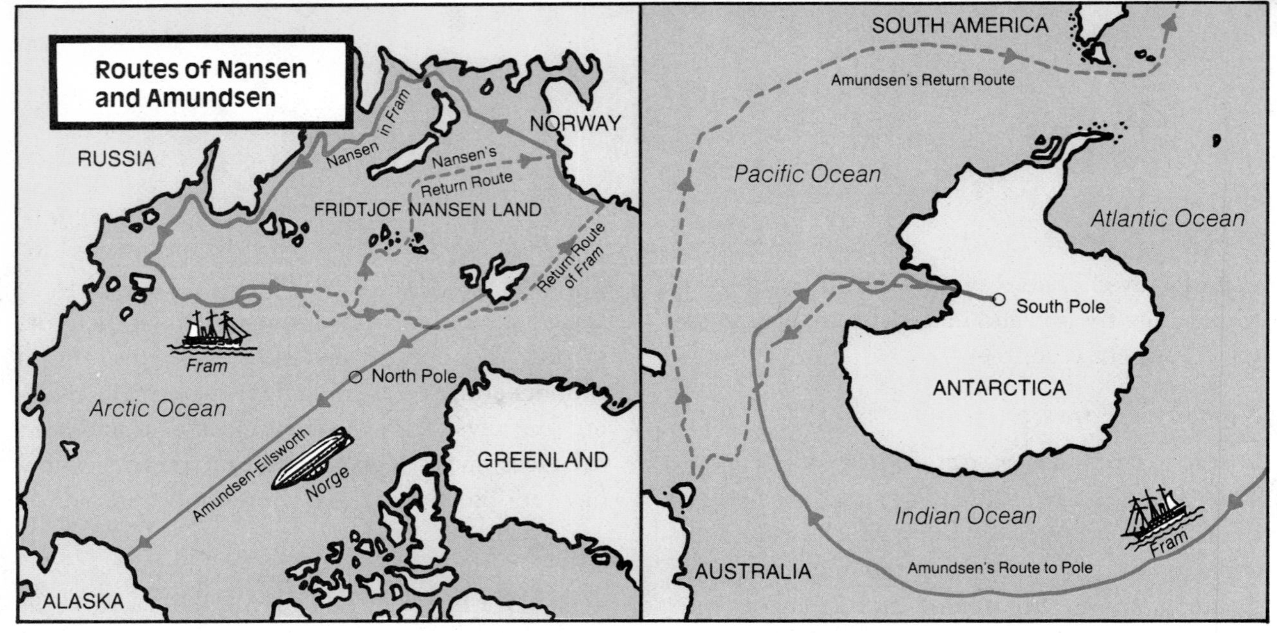

Neither Nansen nor Amundsen set foot on the North Pole, but their expeditions were important scientific contributions. After many hardships, Amundsen reached the South Pole. Before leaving, he raised the Norwegian flag over it as a marker.

Norway's Explorers

The map of the Routes of Nansen and Amundsen on this page shows that far north in the Arctic Ocean is a group of islands called Fridtjof Nansen (frit′yôf nan′sən) Land. The islands are named for a famous Norwegian explorer. At the age of 27, this Norwegian athlete succeeded in crossing icy Greenland by means of sled and ski.

Next, Nansen tried to reach the North Pole. Because driftwood from Siberia floated northward, Nansen believed that a ship might also be carried northward across the pole. He fitted out a stout vessel, called the *Fram* (fram), a name meaning "Forward." The ship carried Nansen and a companion slowly toward the north. In the winter they were frozen fast in the ice. When spring came, the boat, now ice-free, was helped on its way by the drift of the water toward the north.

After 18 months Nansen and his friend left the *Fram* and started on dog sleds for the pole. Before the cold forced them to turn back the two men came nearer to the North Pole than any earlier explorer had done. They spent the winter on the islands now known by Nansen's name. His adventures made Nansen one of the greatest explorers of the time.

A young friend of Nansen's, Roald Amundsen (rō′äl ä′mən sən), was another heroic explorer. In 1911 Amundsen set out for the South Pole. With his companions he traveled across a plateau 11,000 feet (3,300 m) high and crossed the dangerous Antarctic regions. The dangers were soon forgotten when the men reached the South Pole. They were the first to do so.

Amundsen then became an aviator. His flight with his American friend, Lincoln Ellsworth, and his Italian pilot was one of the first made over the North Pole.

Norway in Recent Times

Like Denmark, Norway was occupied by Germany during World War II. Since then, Norway has become a strong, industrial nation with one of the highest standards of living in Europe.

Norway in World War II

At the same time that German troops marched into Denmark in World War II, German warships sailed into Norway's fiords. Soldiers from German airplanes landed in Norway and captured its airfields.

The people of Norway were taken by surprise. Though their army fought bravely, the Germans were stronger. The Norwegians were angry because one of their army officers, named Quisling (kwiz′ling), became a traitor and helped the Germans. Because of this we sometimes speak of a traitor as a "quisling."

After the Germans took over the country, the Norwegians continued to oppose the enemy in every possible way. All Norway's ships went to aid the Allies. Many of its young men left for England to serve as pilots and as soldiers. They made raids upon the Germans in Norway. In 1945 Norway was freed. After the war, loans from the United States helped Norway rebuild its merchant fleet and industries.

Norway's Government

When Norway became independent, the people had to decide whether to have a president or a king. They voted to have a king. Haakon (hô kən′) VII became ruler. He was succeeded by his son Olaf (ō′läf) V. The king is the head of state but the people elect the parliament.

Norway's Industries

The biggest industries in Norway make ships and metal products, chemicals, and electrical machinery. Other big industries are those which process the country's forest and fish products. These factories make wood into pulp for paper and rayon, can and pack fish, and produce furniture.

Fishing has long been the main way of making a living in Norway's northland. Haddock, cod, herring, and mackerel are among the fish caught. But not all the fish is processed for eating. Much of it is ground into fish meal to feed to livestock.

In 1968, huge oil and gas deposits were found in the Norwegian section of the North Sea. The first oil began to flow from these fields in 1971. Now refined oil and chemicals total 8 percent of Norway's exports.

Do You Know?

1. How does the drift influence the climate and ways of living in Norway?
2. How does Norway use its waterfalls?
3. What products are made from the wood of Norway's forests?
4. Which Norwegian explorer reached the South Pole?
5. What happened to Norway in World War II? What did the Norwegians do in this war?

Before You Go On

Using New Words

ecology	tanker
drift	fiord
sardine	cooperative union

Number a paper from 1 through 6. After each number write the word or term that matches the definition.

1. A great ship with tanks below its decks for carrying petroleum
2. A wind-driven mass of water
3. A small fish, often canned
4. The study of how living things relate to their environment
5. A narrow inlet of the sea between high banks or cliffs
6. Farmers who have joined together to keep prices fair and the quality of products high

Finding the Facts

1. How are the Scandinavian nations alike in geography?
2. How are the Scandinavian nations different in geography?
3. When did Sweden become independent? Norway? Finland?
4. How do the Danes make a living?
5. What kind of government does Denmark have?
6. How are Iceland and Greenland alike? How are they different?
7. Why was Greenland important to the Allies during World War II?
8. Why are Norway's port cities free of ice in the winter?
9. Why are Norway's waterfalls considered a natural resource?
10. What is the capital of Norway? What is it like?
11. Name the major industries of Norway.
12. Who were Norway's greatest musicians?
13. Describe Nansen's accomplishments.
14. Where did Roald Amundsen lead a group of explorers in 1911? Where else did he go?
15. Who was Quisling?
16. What natural resources were recently discovered by Norwegians?

4
The Land of Sweden

East of Norway lies Sweden. The location of Sweden is the most favorable of the three Scandinavian countries.

Sweden, a Prosperous Land

Among the Scandinavian countries, Sweden is first in size, in number of people, and in wealth. Its total population is about 8 million.

More than half of Sweden is covered with forests. Much of the rest is covered with water in the form of lakes. Only a few regions in Sweden have land that is good for farming.

Farming in Sweden

A small part of southern Sweden is flat and almost all cultivated, like Denmark. Here turnips and potatoes are grown. In all northern lands, where the summers are short, potatoes are a major crop. Farmers give special attention to dairying and raising livestock. Sweden has fewer farmers than it once had, but by using good farming methods, the farmers produce more than in previous years.

Using Other Resources

Sweden makes good use of its natural resources. Timber from its many forests gives Sweden a large lumber industry. Iron ore from northern Sweden is the nation's most important mineral. Sweden has more water power than any other European country except Norway. Northern and southern Sweden are connected by power lines more than 1,000 miles (1,600 km) long. Thus the vast water power of the north supplies electricity for farms and industries in the south.

A Trip Through Sweden

To get an idea of what Sweden is like, we can imagine taking a trip there. We will visit some of its important cities and farming regions.

On the Göta River Canal

At Göteborg (yoo′tə bôr′yə), a seaport on the Göta (yoo′tə) River, a tall, blond man comes up to us. As he addresses us, we are surprised to find that the man speaks excellent English.

"I am from Minnesota," he says, "but my parents were Swedish. They went to the United States from Sweden before I was born. I am about to take an inland voyage to the Baltic. Would you like to go along?"

"What is an inland voyage?" we ask with interest.

"Come with me and you will see," answers our new friend, Peter Hallborg.

We soon find that we are to travel on a canal, because Göteborg is on the Göta Canal. The city was built by a king who decided Sweden needed a "window on the Atlantic." He called Dutch engineers to build a port on the western coast of Sweden opposite the northern tip of Denmark. Being Dutch, these engineers put canals in the new city like those they had at home.

Göteborg still finds the canals very useful.

Sweden produces large amounts of lumber. These workers tie logs together to form floats, which will be transported down the river to the lumbermills. Much of the wood will then be shipped abroad.

The city has grown more important as Atlantic trade has increased and as Sweden has enlarged its factories which supply goods for export.

At a wharf Peter Hallborg leads us aboard a trim little boat. "This is to be our home for 3 days," he remarks. Soon the vessel moves off, and we find ourselves in a canal. We pass through one lock after another. Each lock takes our boat to a higher level. The boat follows the course of the Göta River.

The canal goes through woodland and past beautiful farms. We pass a large power station where the rapidly flowing Göta River is used to make electricity. Then we come out upon a big lake. This is Lake Vanern (vä′nərn), almost as large as our Great Salt Lake in Utah.

"North of this lake," our friend informs us, "there are great forests. On the shore are sawmills, pulp and paper mills, and other factories which use wood. The Swedish government makes sure that new trees are always planted in place of those that have been cut."

Northeast of Lake Vanern lies a great deposit of high-grade iron ore. From this ore some of

Steel made in Sweden is of a fine grade. In a Swedish factory, steel rings for ball bearings are sent through a small blast furnace.

the world's finest steel is made. Swedish steel is used for ball bearings, tools, machinery, and automobiles.

In the far north of Sweden, beyond the Arctic Circle, there are even richer deposits of iron ore. Some of this ore is shipped out of the country to be smelted. *Smelting* (smel′ting) is the process of melting ore and extracting the pure metal from it. Electric trains carry the ore across the mountains to the Norwegian seaport of Narvik (när′vik). The port of Narvik remains free of ice throughout the year.

Our boat passes through Lake Vanern and continues through the canal. Soon the locks lower our vessel. We descend toward the Baltic. After passing through dozens of locks, we reach Stockholm.

In the Swedish capital, we visit a restaurant. First comes the *smorgasbord* (smôr′gəs bôrd′), which in Swedish means "bread-and-butter table." The smorgasbord is spread out on a separate table and consists of a variety of appetizers such as cheese, seafoods, sausage, and pickles. We serve ourselves, in cafeteria fashion. The main course and dessert are still to come.

We find beautiful handmade articles of silver, copper, and glass in the shops of Stockholm. In a gymnasium we can see people doing the body-

Many Swedes are skillful craftworkers. This Swedish woman is learning to operate a loom in a weaving class. Other craftworkers in Sweden make glassware and items from silver and copper.

building exercises known as *Swedish gymnastics* (jim nas′tiks). A way of treating the body by rubbing, called *Swedish massage* (mə säzh′), is used to improve circulation, relax the nerves, and help tone the muscles.

Famous People of Sweden

Sweden, like Denmark and Norway, has had its share of famous people. Some of them have done their work in science.

Alfred Nobel

Alfred Nobel (nō bel′) was a chemist and engineer who became interested in the making of explosives. In Stockholm he experimented with a new powerful explosive that he thought would be useful to engineers and builders. It was called *nitroglycerine* (nī′trə glis′ər in).

One day some of the nitroglycerine exploded and killed five people. Nobel saw that something had to be done to control it. He mixed the explosive with other materials and succeeded in changing it into *dynamite* (dī′nə mīt′), which is less dangerous. Nobel's many inventions made him a very wealthy man.

Nobel's explosives gave the world new materials for warfare, but he was interested chiefly in peace and progress. When he died, Nobel left a large sum of money to be given in prizes. The *Nobel prizes* (prī zəz) are given to people whose work in science, literature, and the furthering of peace is considered of most benefit to humanity.

Stockholm
A City of Islands

Around the year 1200, people of the islands of southern Sweden were often raided by pirates. At that time, a powerful leader built a castle where Stockholm (stok′hōm) now stands. From the map of Scandinavia and Finland on page 389 tell why this was a good place to build a fort.

Today, Stockholm spreads across 15 of these islands and parts of the mainland. Because of its beautiful waterways and cliffs, the people of Stockholm realized they would have to plan carefully. More than 330 years ago they set up a special office to plan for the orderly growth of their city.

As Sweden's center of government and leading commercial and industrial city, why do you think Stockholm might be the nation's fastest-growing city? For a long time before the rise of Göteborg, a port in southwest Sweden, Stockholm was also Sweden's main seaport. Ships can still sail to the heart of Stockholm to load and unload their cargoes.

If you were to visit Stockholm, you might not notice one of its outstanding features. This city is famous for something it does not have! Despite its many industries and its fast growth, Stockholm is a city without slums. The people of Sweden have voted to pay taxes for the well-being of all the people. They have voted for free medical care, free lunches for school children, and free university education for most students.

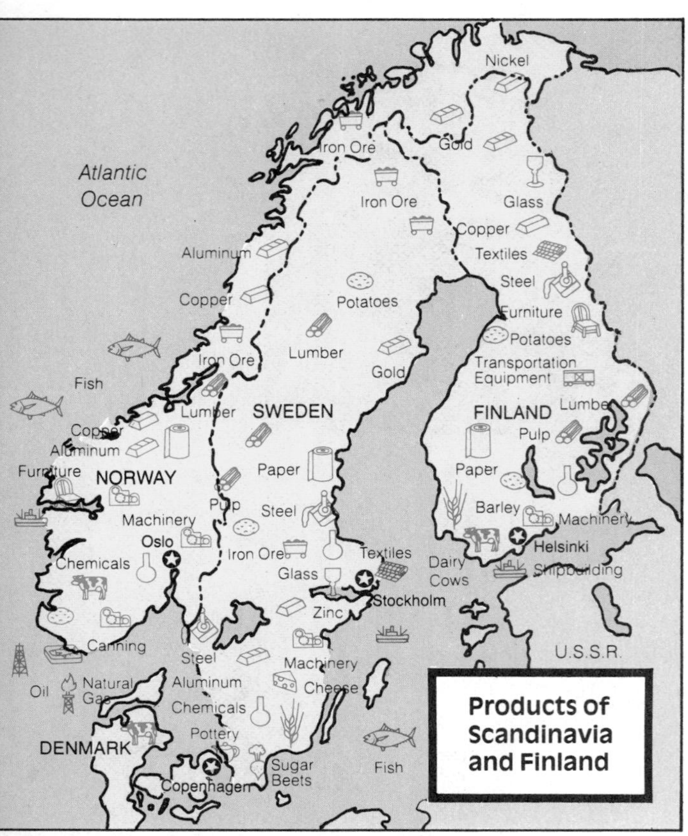

The Safety Match, a Swedish Invention

The safety match was invented by Gustave Pasch, a Swedish chemist. The first matches were made with heads of the mineral phosphorus (fos′fər əs). Because phosphorus catches fire easily when it is rubbed or heated, these matches were highly dangerous. Pasch had the idea of separating the chemicals in the match. He took some of the chemicals out of the match heads and put them on the rough surface of the match box or match book. The match head had to be scratched on this special surface containing the chemicals before it would burst into flame. This invention is the safety match. Why has this invention been important in homes throughout the world?

Sweden in Recent Times

Germany chose not to attack Sweden in World War II, and Sweden's government decided to remain neutral. A neutral nation is one that does not take sides in a war. Because countries respected Sweden's decision to remain neutral, it came through the war free of damage. The Swedes realized how fortunate they were to be unharmed. Since the war they have given aid to many countries.

Today Sweden has a high standard of living. It has much iron ore and lumber. Among its products are wood pulp, glass, ships, airplanes, machinery, and electrical products. Its chief farm products are cheese and butter. Handmade products by Swedish artisans are also highly appreciated in Sweden and abroad.

Sweden, like Norway and Denmark, has a monarch. Sweden's king is greatly respected by the people, but he has little power. The people elect the representatives to a parliament led by a prime minister.

Do You Know?

1. Why is Sweden a prosperous land?
2. How does Göteborg provide Sweden with a "window on the Atlantic"?
3. Why was Stockholm built where it is?
4. What are two of the products made from Swedish steel?
5. Who was Alfred Nobel?

5
The Land of Finland

East of Stockholm across the Gulf of Bothnia (both′nē ə) lies Finland. Like Sweden, it has great forests and many lakes. "Half land and half water" is one description of Finland. Like Norway, Finland has much land that is rocky and barren.

The History of Finland

Some historians believe that the early Finns may have come from Asia. They speak a language that is not quite like any other in Europe. Wherever the early settlers of Finland came from, the Finns today are much like the people of Western Europe in their ways of living.

Finland Under Foreign Rule

Sweden held Finland for more than 600 years. The Swedes brought the Christian religion to Finland. All educated Finns learned the Swedish language and manners. Yet the Finns continued to speak Finnish and to consider themselves a separate people.

Then Russia, a powerful neighbor to the east, took Finland away from Sweden. Russia held Finland for a period of about 100 years.

Finland, an Independent Nation

During World War I, Finland saw its chance to gain independence. In 1917 Finland declared itself independent from Russia. It gave its towns their old Finnish names.

When Finland became independent, it was given a small section of land on the Arctic. This region, called the Petsamo (pet′sə mō) region, is 200 miles (320 km) north of the Arctic Circle. The area can be reached by a motor road from Finland for 6 months of the year. Ships can reach it at any time. On the Gulf of Finland, 700 miles (1,120 km) south, huge icebreakers are needed to keep the harbor of Helsinki open during the winter. But the Petsamo region is warmed by the drift current. Mines there furnish nickel.

Because forests cover about three-quarters of Finland, most of its exports are wood products. These include lumber, paper, and pulp, which is used in making paper.

Finland became one of the world's most progressive republics. The Finns had fine schools. They led in music and sports.

The Russian-Finnish Wars

In 1939 Russia made war on Finland. The Finns fought bravely. But there were 50 Soviet soldiers for each Finnish soldier, and the Finns were beaten. Finland lost much of its best land, bordering on Russia. The largest timber export city, Viipuri (vē′pə rē), on the Gulf of Finland, went to the Soviet Union. Lake Ladoga (lad′ə gə), the largest lake in Europe, became Soviet. The Soviet Union secured a bigger window on the Baltic.

When Germany invaded the Soviet Union in 1941, the Finns, who considered the Soviets enemies, took the German side. German troops

The people in Helsinki can buy fresh vegetables and several kinds of fish at a large outdoor market along the city's waterfront.

came into Finland in order to fight the Soviets more easily.

With the defeat of Germany, the Finns had to yield to the Soviet Union's demands. They lost not only the Arctic region, Petsamo, but also their nickel mines. The Soviet Union set up a naval base on the Gulf of Finland almost at Helsinki's door, which they maintained for 12 years, until 1956. The Finns had to pay money to the Soviets. They also had to help the Soviets drive the German troops out of Finland. The country was exhausted. But the Finns still had faith in their nation and set out to rebuild it.

Helsinki, the Finnish Capital

Stockholm and the Finnish capital of Helsinki lie in almost the same latitude. But a fairly large part of Sweden lies south of Stockholm, while Helsinki is on the southern border of Finland. (Find their locations on the map of Scandinavia and Finland, page 389.)

Helsinki and Stockholm are much alike. Each has a group of islands near it. Each has many landing places for ships. Helsinki is a quiet city. Cars are forbidden to sound their horns except in emergencies. Factories are not allowed to blow whistles. This freedom from noise is not only pleasant but it also helps to prevent traffic accidents.

Helsinki prides itself on being a modern city with well-designed buildings. Near the harbor are flower and fruit vendors, and fishers selling the catch of the day. Shoppers walk along the row of boats to choose what to buy. The city has good schools, a fine university, a famous art museum, and beautiful parks. Though it is a compact city, nearly 500,000 people live there.

One of the islands near Helsinki is the home of a zoo. Another has an outdoor museum. Still another has fine homes.

In 1975 Helsinki was the site of an important international conference on human rights, out of which came the Helsinki Agreement.

Finnish Education and Culture

All children in Finland are provided with free education. Ninety-nine out of 100 persons can read and write.

The Finnish Language

The Finnish language differs from the languages of the other Scandinavian nations. It is similar in origin to the Hungarian language.

Historians think the Finns came to Finland from an area between the Baltic Sea and the Volga (vol′gə) River. Find this area on the map of the Soviet Union on page 473. Why might Finnish be similar to Hungarian?

Finnish Health Education

The health of its people is a national concern in Finland. Physical training is important in Finland, as it is in Sweden. The Finns are a nation of athletes. They say, "We were born on skis." Finnish athletes have often set records in foot races. They are expert sailors.

The Finns and other Scandinavians enjoy the *sauna* (sou′nə). A sauna is like a steam bath but the bather is surrounded by hot and dry air.

Finland's Music and Literature

The music of a great Finnish composer, Jan Sibelius (si bə′lē əs), is often played in the United States and other countries. One of his best works is called *Finlandia* (fin lənd′ē ə). *Finlandia* expresses the poetic feeling and the national spirit of the Finnish people.

The Finns also like to remember that our poet Longfellow patterned his "Song of Hiawatha" upon a Finnish poem.

Finland in Recent Times

Finland lost much in World War II, but the Finns rebuilt their country rapidly. Softwood trees are used to make pulp, paper, veneer, and furniture. These are the products of Finland's most important industry.

Finnish factories also produce iron and steel, locomotives, luxury liners, and icebreaking ships. Other industries include chemicals, glass, electronics, textiles, pewter, and beer brewing. Finland's merchant fleet is larger than ever before in its history.

Finland is a republic and has a president. The Finns elect representatives to make the nation's laws. Their leaders try especially hard to stay on friendly terms with other nations. Finland paid heavily for its part in past conflicts and now refuses to take sides in disputes between other nations. That means that it is a neutral country.

Finland has an agreement with the Soviet Union that it will not let any other countries use its land to invade the Soviet Union. In spite of this agreement, Finland is attached to the West in culture and trade.

Do You Know?

1. What countries have ruled Finland? When did it become independent?
2. What are Finland's chief exports?
3. What makes Helsinki a modern city?
4. Who was Jan Sibelius?
5. To what language is Finnish similar?
6. What is Finland's form of government?

To Help You Learn

Using New Words

fiord	dynamite	Nobel Prize
drift	cooperative union	smorgasbord
sardine	Swedish gymnastics	ecology
tanker	Swedish massage	smelting
sauna	nitroglycerine	

Number a paper from 1 through 14. After each number write the word or term that matches the definition.

1. A powerful explosive
2. A ship with large tanks below its decks for carrying oil or other liquids
3. A narrow inlet of the sea between high cliffs or banks
4. Farmers who have joined together to keep prices fair and the quality of products high
5. A way to improve circulation, relax the nerves, and help muscle tone by rubbing the body
6. A wind-driven mass of water
7. A small fish, often canned
8. A variety of Swedish foods, such as seafoods, cheese, sausage, and pickles
9. Money awarded to persons whose work in science, literature, and the furthering of peace benefits humanity
10. The process of melting an ore and extracting the pure metal from it
11. A type of body-building exercise
12. Nitroglycerin mixed with other materials to make it safer to handle
13. The study of how living things relate to their environment
14. A bath similar to a steam bath, but with hot, dry air

Finding the Facts

1. Name the Scandinavian nations.
2. Why is Finland called the "land of lakes"?
3. Under whose leadership did Sweden become a world power?
4. When did Norway gain freedom?
5. How do the Danes make a living?
6. Why did the location of Copenhagen help the city to become wealthy?
7. Name two famous Danes. What did they do to make us remember them?
8. What are some of Norway's natural resources? How are they used?
9. Name three famous Norwegians. Tell what each did.
10. How does Sweden use its resources?
11. Why are canals important to Sweden?
12. Why is Alfred Nobel remembered?
13. When did Finland gain freedom?
14. Compare Helsinki and Stockholm.
15. Name a famous Finnish composer.
16. Which of the three Scandinavian countries and Finland are monarchies? Which is a republic?
17. Where did the name Scandinavia originate?

18. Where do the people of Greenland live?
19. What is Norway's national sport?
20. Who is Norway's head of state?
21. Who was Gustav Pasch? Why do we remember him?
22. What is an important type of farming for both Sweden and Denmark?
23. In what two ways is Finland different from the Scandinavian countries?
24. Why did Finland lose much of its best land?
25. Name the capital of Finland. What is it like?
26. What kind of conference took place in Helsinki in 1975?
27. What natural resource is the basis of Finland's biggest industry?
28. What benefits does the Danish Government pay for?
29. Why is Iceland called the land of fire and ice?
30. Who lives on Greenland?
31. Which Scandinavian country has the most people?
32. Why was Göteborg built?
33. What are Sweden's most important products?
34. Where do some historians believe the Finns came from?
35. How much of Finland is covered with forests?

Learning from Maps

1. What does the map of Scandinavia and Finland on page 389 tell you about land surfaces in these northern countries? Which country has the most mountains? The most plains?

   Between what parallels of latitude do the northern countries lie? Which extends farthest north? What lines of longitude pass through these countries? Compare Oslo and Helsinki in latitude.
2. Look again at the map of Scandinavia and Finland on page 389. What is the name of the gulf that separates Sweden and Finland? Finland and the Soviet Union? What Norwegian city is closest to the Lofoten Islands? Name the city in Sweden that is closest to Copenhagen.

Using Study Skills

1. **Time Line:** Place the following events in the proper order of time: German occupation of Denmark; name of Norway's capital changed to Oslo; Norway found oil in the North Sea.

   Copy the time line from page 387. Add these events to your time line.

   Study the completed time line and answer the following questions: How many years elapsed between the time when the Scandinavian countries were united under

Queen Margrete and Sweden and Norway gained their independence? Between the time Nobel invented dynamite, a safer explosive, and World War II ended?

2. **Time Line:** Look at the time line below and answer the following questions: How many years elapsed between the time Finland was taken by Sweden and it declared independence? Between Swedish control of Norway and its independence?

c. 1155	Finland conquered by Sweden
1397	Union of Sweden, Denmark, and Norway
1523	Swedish independence
1630	Sweden made military power
1638	Swedish settlement in Delaware
1809	Finland taken by Russia
1815	Norway given to Sweden
1905	Norwegian independence
1917	Finnish independence
1939	Russian-Finnish War
1945	World War II ends

3. **Chart:** Look at the chart comparing Finland and Scandinavian countries on page 415 and answer the following questions: Which Scandinavian country has the most people? How many more people does it have than the least populated of the four countries? How many more square miles does Sweden have than Denmark? If you wanted to live in Scandinavia and make a good living, which country would you choose?

Thinking It Through

1. The Scandinavian countries provide many services for people. However, the citizens pay high taxes for these services. What are the advantages and disadvantages of a government providing extensive services for people?
2. Iceland's fishers use radar to find fish. Name some other uses of radar.
3. Which of the Scandinavian countries would take the longest to cross from east to west by car? Explain why you named the country you did.
4. Why did Finland side with Germany against the Soviet Union in World War II?

Projects

1. Look in newspapers and magazines for pictures of arts and crafts from Sweden and other countries in this unit.
2. Read Andersen's *Fairy Tales.* Dramatize or retell one of them in class.
3. Plan a musical program in which you include recorded selections by Grieg and

Scandinavian Countries Compared

	Area sq. miles (sq. km)	Population	1980 Per Capita Income	Imports billions	Exports billions
Denmark	17,028 (44,272)	5,130,000	$12,956	$14.77	$11.85
Finland	130,119 (338,309)	4,800,000	$10,477	$ 7.85	$ 8.54
Norway	125,181 (325,470)	4,150,000	$12,432	$11.40	$10.04
Sweden	173,665 (451,529)	8,330,000	$14,821	$20.47	$21.74

Literacy rate for all four countries is 99%.

Sibelius and other northern composers. Have one pupil introduce each record and tell something about it.

4. The Research Committee could find out the names of this year's Nobel Prize winners and what they did to win the prize. With an almanac they could make a list of Nobel Prize winners in one field (medicine or peace, for example). Then they could write the names of the persons, the countries they came from, and the year they received the award. The lists could be made into posters for a classroom display.
5. The Explorers' Committee could find out more about Roald Amundsen's journey to the South Pole. Amundsen was not the only explorer who was trying to reach the South Pole in 1911. Robert Falcon Scott, a British explorer, and his companions were also making the dangerous journey. What preparations did the two men make for their expeditions? How did their plans differ?
6. The Reading Committee could find books of folk tales from Finland and the Scandinavian countries to share with the class.

14 Germany

Unit Preview

Germany lies in the center of Europe, east of France and Belgium, and south of the Scandinavian Peninsula.

Long after other countries in Europe were united under strong monarchs, the Germans still lived as they had in the Middle Ages. Slowly, feudal lands expanded into states, but these states did not group together to form a nation.

Until the state called Prussia became very powerful in the 1800s, no one German state was strong enough to lead the others. Prussia's king, Wilhelm, had a strong prime minister, Otto von Bismarck. Bismarck made Prussia strong by rallying other German states to war against France. It was victory over France that finally united Germany.

In the twentieth century, Germany tried to conquer all of Europe. In World War I the Germans were defeated.

The Germans worked to rebuild their country after the war. Germany became a great industrial nation. In World War II Adolf Hitler led the Germans to defeat. After this war, Germany was divided into a communist East Germany and a democratic West Germany. Even Germany's main city, Berlin, was divided. In 1961 the East Germans built a wall in Berlin to clearly separate the two areas. Germany remains a divided nation today.

Things to Discover

If you look carefully at the picture, map, and time line on these pages, you can answer these questions.

1. Germany is highlighted on the map. Does this country have a coastline?
2. The picture shows the Rhine River, the longest waterway in Germany. How is the land along the Rhine used? What is an important use of the river?
3. The castle in the picture was built during the Middles Ages. When did feudal lands become small states in what is now Germany?
4. How long did it take Bismarck to unite Germany?
5. Who was the first emperor of Germany?
6. What French leader defeated the German states in 1806? How many years later was France defeated by Germany?
7. When was Germany divided ?

Words to Learn

You will meet these words in this unit. As you read you will learn what they mean and how to pronounce them. The Word List will help you.

concentration camp
lignite
opera
Protestant
Reformation
swastika
symphony

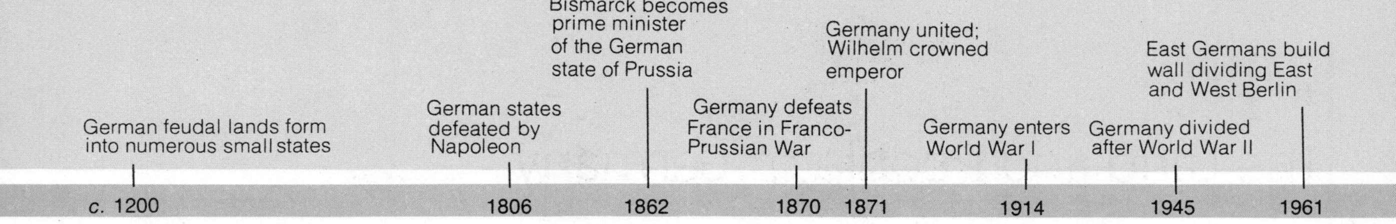

Arctic Ocean

EUROPE

tlantic
cean

ASIA

Pacific Ocean

Indian Ocean

AUSTRALIA

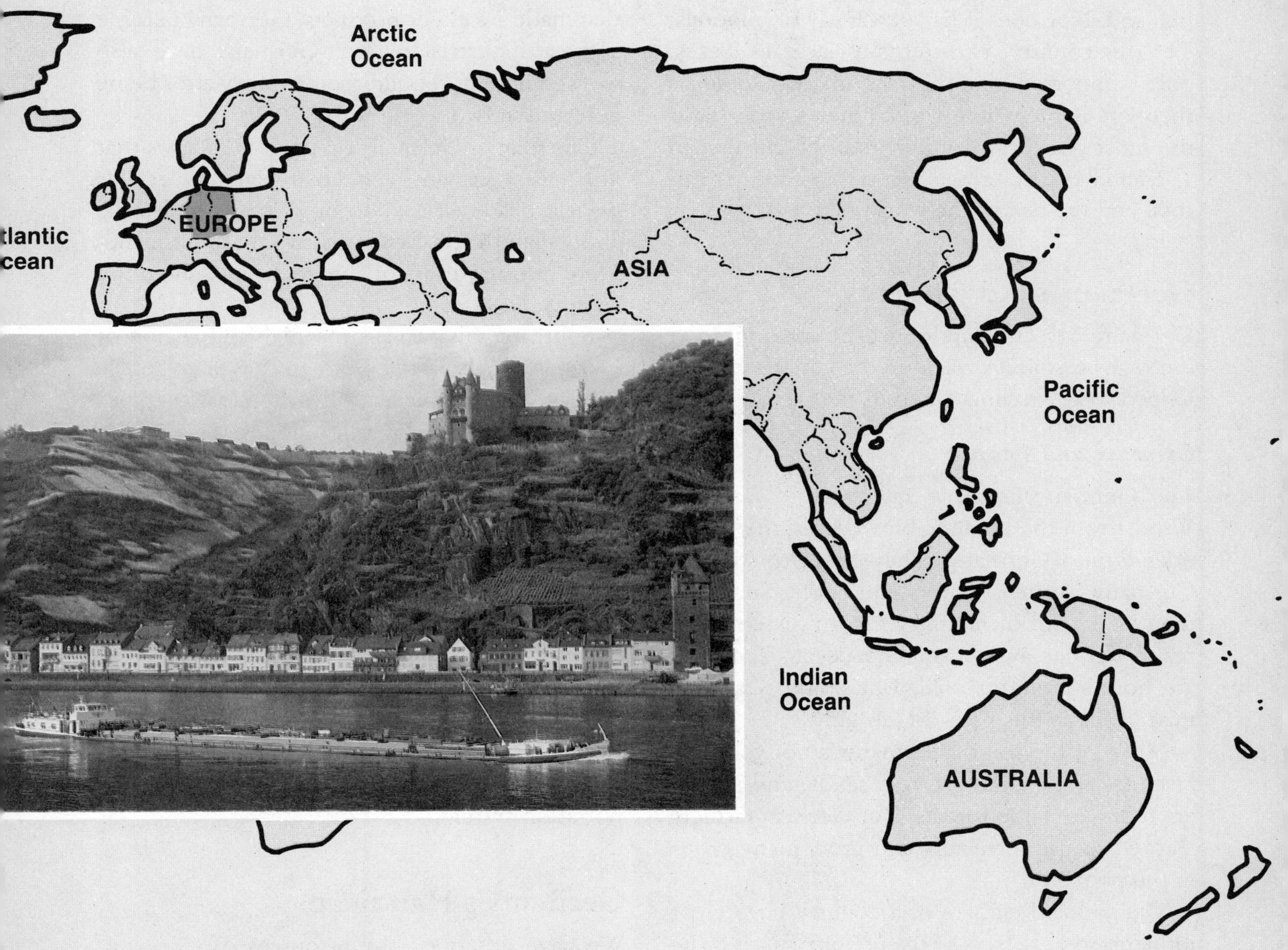

1
The Land and People of Germany

Germany does not possess many large areas of rich soil. Nor does it have a variety of minerals. Yet this country, two-thirds as large as Texas, once supported one-third as many people as there are in the whole United States. It was also the most powerful country in all of Europe. In 1914 and 1939 Germany set out to conquer Europe and the rest of the world.

Germany's Advantages

Germany rose to importance by making good use of its resources. Among the conditions that helped were its climate and its people.

Climate and People

The German climate is favorable to farming. Winds from the Atlantic blow across the Netherlands into Germany. They bring to western Germany warmer winters and cooler summers than the rest of the country has. In eastern Germany, farther away from the ocean, summers are hot and winters cold. But farmers can still raise crops in this part of Germany.

Much of the soil of Germany is not good for farming. Some areas are very sandy, and in others there are large forests. But German farmers learned to use fertilizers and grow many crops in the poor soil.

The soil and climate of a country have great influence on the lives of the people. But it is the people themselves who really make a country what it is. The Germans turned their attention to manufacturing. They built many factories that made excellent products. Germany became a great industrial nation. Germans have also worked hard to rebuild their country after being defeated in two world wars.

The map of Germany on page 419 shows that northern Germany is a great plain. Over this plain it has been easy to build roads, railroads, and canals. Here is Germany's best farmland. Here also are most of the great manufacturing centers.

South of this plain is the highland region of Germany. This part of Germany has many fertile valleys. The people who live here raise grapes on some of the river valley slopes. This region is ideal for grapes. The sun can reach the vines, but the vines are sheltered from cold winds. Germans raise cattle here. They also work in the cities and the forests that cover the hills and mountains of central and southern Germany.

Large Rivers

Four large rivers flow north through Germany. From west to east, they are the Rhine, Weser (vā′zər), Elbe (el′bə), and Oder (ō′dər). These rivers are an important part of Germany's transportation system.

Germany's Handicap

We have described the resources of Germany as if they belonged to one country. But we must remember that Germany is a divided nation.

Copenhagen
SWEDEN
DENMARK
BALTIC SEA
NORTH SEA
54°
Hamburg
Cuxhaven
Wittenberg
Elbe River
Bremen
Oder River
POLAND
Amsterdam
THE NETHERLANDS
Weser River
PRUSSIA
West Berlin
East Berlin
Hannover
GERMAN DEMOCRATIC REPUBLIC (EAST GERMANY)
52°
Essen
Duisburg
Ruhr River
HARZ MTS.
Düsseldorf
Leipzig
Dresden
Wroclaw (Breslau)
BELGIUM
Cologne
Brussels
Bonn
SAXONY
GERMAN FEDERAL REPUBLIC (WEST GERMANY)
RHINELAND
ORE MTS.
LUXEMBOURG
Prague
50°
CZECHOSLOVAKIA
Mannheim
Nuremberg
SAAR
Saar River
Stuttgart
LORRAINE
BLACK FOREST
Danube River
FRANCE
BAVARIA
Rhine River
Munich
Vienna
AUSTRIA
48°
GERMANY
Plains
Plateaus
Hills
Mountains
0 Miles 75
0 Kilometers 95
Bern
SWITZERLAND
ALPS
46°
ITALY
6°
8°
10°
12°
14°
16°

The northern plain and the southern highlands extend across the two parts of Germany. West Germany has the Rhine and Weser rivers. The Elbe flows out of East Germany into the West. The Oder forms part of the eastern boundary of East Germany. Find these rivers on the map of Germany on page 419.

The people of each region have to get along without part of the resources they had as a united country. Even Berlin, the capital of Germany before World War II, is divided.

Do You Know?

1. What is the climate of Germany like?
2. Which four rivers flow north through Germany? Into what large body of water does each river flow?
3. Name the advantages Germany enjoys. Name its major handicap.

2
How Germany Became a Nation

During the Middle Ages, from about 1200, the region we now call Germany was made up of hundreds of states. These states were formed out of feudal lands. They were ruled by dukes, counts, kings, princes, barons, bishops, and archbishops.

The Rise of Germany

Germany became a nation much later than did England, France, and Spain.

The Beginnings of German Unity

It was Napoleon of France who first awakened national feelings in the Germans. He fought the largest German states and defeated them in 1806. Napoleon then made some relatives and friends rulers of these German lands.

The Germans did not like to be ruled by the French. As a result, clubs and secret societies sprang up to work against Napoleon. Patriotic Germans tried to make the German people proud of their language and their history. Poets wrote stirring songs that built up German spirit.

The Union of German States

After Napoleon's defeat in 1815, representatives of European governments met in a peace congress. This congress formed the German states into a loose union, with Austria (ôs′trē ə)

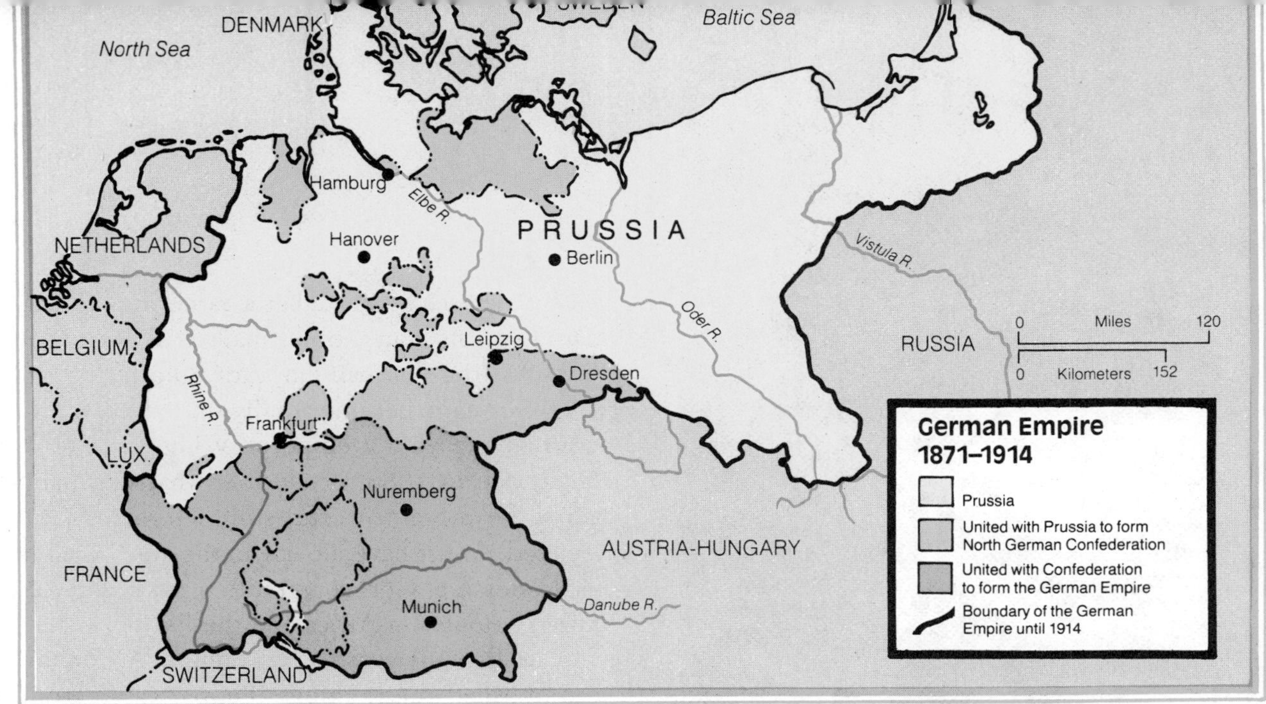

Prussia became the largest German state. Its power and leadership convinced other states to join the North German Confederation. By 1871 what had Germany become?

at its head. A parliament, representing the German states, set up a few strong rulers instead of many weak ones. Germans began to feel they were a nation.

Germany as an Empire

Before Germany became a united nation, one of its states would become powerful enough to control the others. At one time it looked as if Austria would become the leader of Germany.

The Rise of Prussia

One of the states of Germany gradually grew in strength until it challenged Austria's leadership. This state was Prussia (prush′ə), in northern Germany. Its king and his nobles ruled the people with a hard hand. Each Prussian ruler tried to make Prussia bigger and more powerful.

In time, Prussia built up a strong army. The greater Prussia grew, the more it directed the affairs of all Germany. The states in southern Germany disliked Prussia and its cruel ways. Because it was so powerful, however, they had to follow its lead.

The Leadership of Prussia

To make the country stronger, the Prussian king, Wilhelm I, decided to enlarge the army. When lawmakers refused to give him the money he needed, he asked Otto von Bismarck (ot′ō von biz′märk) to become the prime minister in 1862. Bismarck was a bold man who helped the king get what he wanted.

Bismarck wanted to create a great united Germany, with Prussia at its head. He did not care how this was brought about. "It will be decided by blood and iron," he said.

Under the leadership of Emperor Wilhelm II Germany became a powerful nation. German industries grew. The army and navy were strengthened. It was during his reign that World War I began.

Under Bismarck the powerful Prussian army grew mightier yet. He defeated Austria so soundly that Austria had little power in German affairs. Then Bismarck turned the Prussian army against France.

Formation of the Empire

In 1870 war broke out between Germany and France. Because Germany had begun to industrialize, the Prussian army was the best equipped in Europe. But the French emperor, Napoleon III, thought his army was as strong as the Prussian army. He also thought that the south Germans disliked Prussia so much that they would refuse to join in the war. But he was wrong. All the Germans joined together. Led by Prussia, they defeated the French.

In the palace at Versailles a gathering of German generals and nobles hailed Wilhelm of Prussia as the German emperor. On this day in 1871 Germany became solidly united.

When the young emperor Wilhelm II took the throne in 1888, he decided that Germany had to be more powerful still. "Germany," he declared, "must have a place in the sun." Under his leadership Germany built a navy and acquired colonies in Africa and the Pacific.

In its first 40 years as an empire, Germany accomplished many things. People came from other countries to see its well-governed cities. They enjoyed German music and art.

Some Famous Germans

Germany has had many great religious leaders, writers, musicians, and artists.

Luther, a Religious Leader

One of Germany's most noted people was Martin Luther (lo͞o′thər). Luther was born in 1483 in Saxony (sak′sə nē). He showed an eagerness for learning as a young man. After his graduation from the university he became a monk, but he was not sure that the Catholic Church was always right. He studied the Bible. In doing so, he found a new view of religion.

In 1517 Luther protested against some of the activities of the Catholic Church. He wrote out his beliefs and posted them on the church door in the city of Wittenberg (wit′ən burg) where everyone could see them. Soon people all over Germany learned about Luther's action. Many agreed with him.

Martin Luther began a protest against the Catholic church by nailing a list of his beliefs on the door of the Wittenberg Cathedral.

A few years later Luther broke with the Catholic Church. Most of the German princes and nobles agreed with Luther because they no longer wanted to be under the Pope, who was an Italian. At this time groups of peasants in southern Germany rebelled against their rulers. The princes punished them cruelly. While this stopped the rebellion, the peasants remained angry. They did not become followers of Luther as their rulers did.

Germany was divided. The northern states followed Luther. Those in the south rejected his beliefs and remained Catholic. The followers of Luther called themselves *Protestants* (prot′is tənts) because they acted in "protest" against certain beliefs and practices of the Catholic Church. The religious movement Luther started is called the *Reformation* (ref′ər mā′shən). Because of the Reformation there are Protestant as well as Catholic churches today.

Luther translated the Bible into German so that people could read it for themselves. He also wrote many hymns to be sung in church services.

Great Writers of Germany

One of Germany's greatest writers was Wolfgang von Goethe (vôlf′gäng vôn goo′tə). We remember him best for his great drama, *Faust* (foust). Faust was a man who, in return for earthly pleasures and glory, agreed to sell his soul to the devil. His adventures brought sorrow to others and to himself.

Friedrich Schiller (frē′drik shil′ər) was another German who won fame as a writer and poet. One of Schiller's best-known plays is *William Tell,* a play about the Swiss people and their struggle for freedom from the powerful Hapsburgs (haps′burgs).

Great Musicians of Germany

Many splendid musical works have been written by German composers. Felix Mendelssohn (mend′əl sən) wrote many beautiful musical selections. In one he wrote music to accompany Shakespeare's play *Midsummer Night's Dream*. It contains a march which is often played at weddings.

Another great German composer was Richard Wagner (väg′nər). Wagner gained fame by

Ludwig van Beethoven was a German composer and pianist. He also taught students how to play the piano. He sometimes wrote music for his students.

writing *operas* (op′ər əs), a kind of musical play in which the actors sing instead of speak. A group of Wagner's operas, called *The Ring of the Nibelungs* (nē′bi lungs), set many German myths to music.

Beethoven, a Giant of Music

Ludwig van Beethoven (lo͞od′wig vän bā′tō′vən) was one of the most important composers of his time. He was also one of the finest pianists.

Beethoven was born in Bonn in 1770. He was a professional musician at age 11. As a young man, Beethoven moved to Vienna, the center of the musical world. Vienna was his home for 34 years. Beethoven wrote nine *symphonies* (sim′fə nēz), as well as piano concertos (kən cher′tōz), quartets (kwôr tets′), and an opera. A symphony is a musical work to be played by a large orchestra.

The early compositions of Beethoven were written in the style of the day. As time went on, his music became more dramatic. This dramatic style did not always please his audiences. Beethoven completed some of his most important works after becoming deaf.

A Famous Artist

Albrecht Dürer (äl′brekt door′ər) was a great German artist. He was born in Nuremberg (noor′əm burg′), where he worked with his father at the goldsmith's trade. At the age of 15 he decided to become a painter. He went to study, first in Venice and later in the Netherlands. In these countries he learned how to use color in a marvelous way. He also painted fine portraits.

Do You Know?

1. How did Prussia become the leader of Germany?
2. What wars did the Prussians carry on before Germany was united?
3. What was Bismarck's dream?
4. Who was Martin Luther? Albrecht Dürer? Beethoven? Goethe?

Before You Go On

Using New Words

Protestant	symphony
opera	Reformation

Number a paper from 1 through 4. After each number write the word or term that matches the definition.

1. The name of a follower of Martin Luther who acted in protest against certain practices of the Catholic Church
2. A kind of musical play in which the actors sing instead of speak
3. The religious movement started by Martin Luther
4. A musical work to be played by a large orchestra

Finding the Facts

1. Name the four large rivers that flow through Germany. In what direction do they flow?
2. What foreign conqueror first awakened national feelings in the German people?
3. Who was Otto von Bismarck?
4. Why is Germany's climate good for farming?
5. Where was Prussia? How was it important to Germany?
6. When did Germany really become a nation?
7. Where did most of Martin Luther's followers live?
8. What did Wilhelm II accomplish?
9. Name two of Martin Luther's most important contributions.
10. What is *Faust?*
11. Who was Albrecht Dürer?
12. Name Germany's great opera composer. What did he set to music in one group of his operas?
13. What well-known play did Friedrich Schiller write?
14. What was Beethoven's handicap?
15. What is an important product of Germany's highland region?
16. Where is Germany's best farmland?

3

World War I and Its Results

The spirit of national unity was strong among Germans after 1871. In that year, Germany had become an empire. The country grew more powerful. Germany's industries produced more goods and weapons. It built up a strong army and navy. It had a fine overseas trade. But still Wilhelm II was not satisfied. He wanted to make his nation the strongest in Europe. This led to World War I.

The Story of World War I

Long before it happened, Bismarck had said that a world war would come. He said that it would begin in the small Balkan countries. He was right.

Compare this map of Europe just before World War I with the map of Europe on page 161. Which large European country existed in 1914 that is no longer a nation?

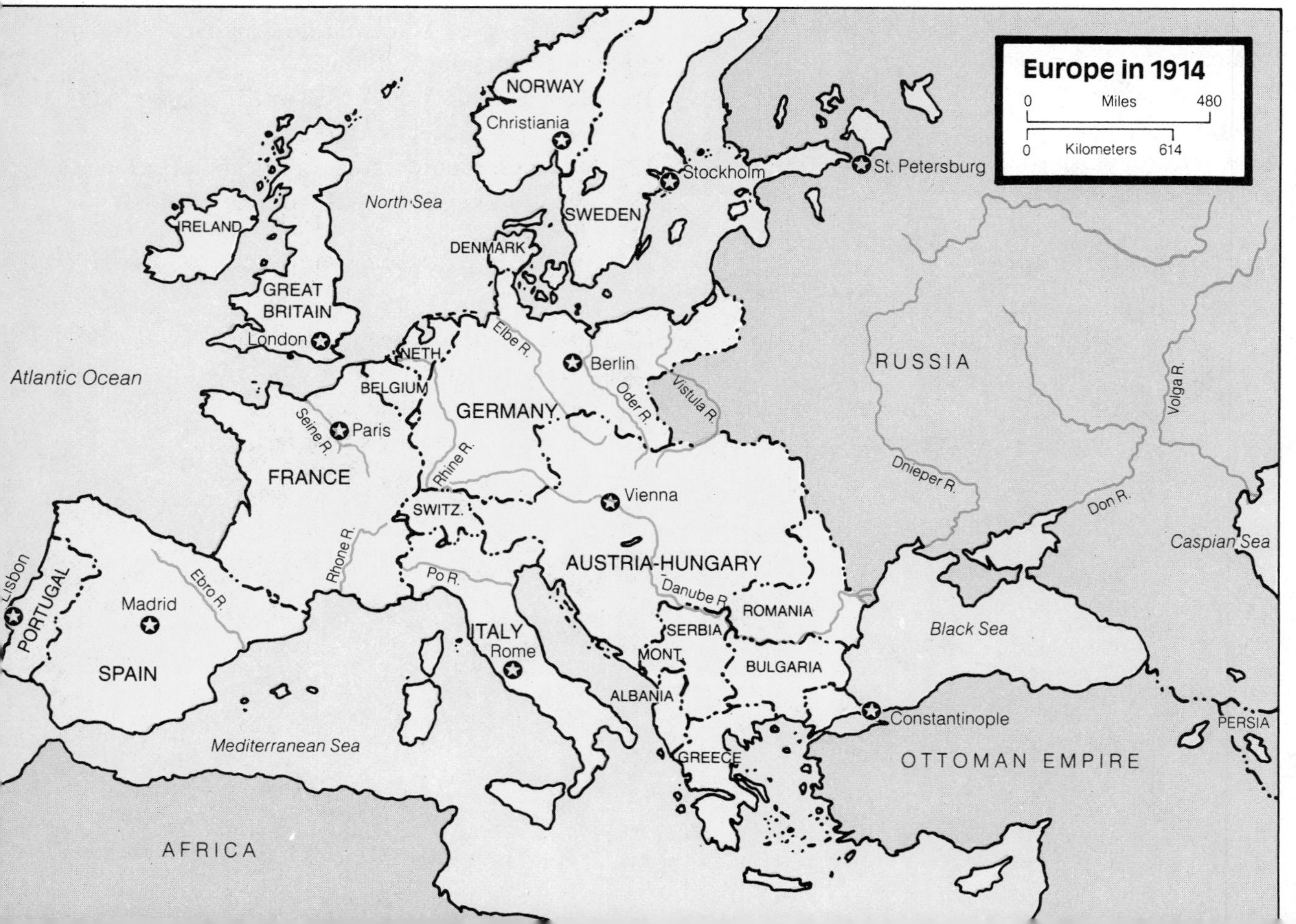

The peace treaty that ended World War I was signed at the palace of Versailles, in France, in 1919. Many Germans thought that the terms of the treaty were harsh.

How the War Began

In a part of the Balkans which belonged to the empire of Austria-Hungary, a student from Serbia (sur′bē ə) shot and killed the heir to the throne of Austria-Hungary. The government leaders of Austria-Hungary were very angry. As a result, they decided to take over the country of Serbia.

Germany sided with Austria. Great Britain, France, and Russia opposed Austria. The Germans were so eager to use their army that they began the war, first by striking at Russia, then at France. Great Britain quickly came to the aid of France. Later Italy joined the French and British. The Ottoman (ot′ə mən) Empire joined Germany.

A Worldwide Struggle

The war spread over most of Europe. Millions of people opposed each other. After the war had been going on for more than 2 years, the United States entered it against Germany. More than 2 million members of the armed forces went overseas and the German army was defeated. This war, later called World War I, lasted from 1914 to 1918.

The Results of the War

Germany had been the leader in starting the war. The group of nations which had opposed Germany—known as the Allies—intended to make a peace that would prevent any future wars. In 1919 the Treaty of Peace was signed at the palace of Versailles near Paris. The Versailles treaty, as it came to be called, took away from Germany its colonies. The treaty also took from Germany some of its land in Europe. Its army and navy were put out of business. The Allies thought that a weak Germany would not be dangerous to world peace.

The German Republic

The German emperor fled to the Netherlands, and the German empire ended. In 1919 the people elected a National Assembly. The assembly met at Weimar (vī′mär), a city in central Germany, and drew up a constitution for a republic. But the Germans were not united. The times were bad after the war. There was little trade and the people suffered. Realizing the bad conditions, the Allies tried to make things easier for Germany. For a time conditions improved. But the republic lasted for only 15 years.

Do You Know?

1. When did World War I begin? What events led to it? How did it end? How did the peace treaty affect Germany?
2. What form of government did Germany adopt after World War I? Why did it fail?

4 Germany in World War II

For 15 years under the Republic, Germany had a democratic government. But because the German armies had surrendered before the Allied soldiers reached German soil, the Germans claimed, "We were not defeated."

Many Germans began to say that Germany should again take a leading place in the world. Germany's nearly 70 million people, they declared, must have their "place in the sun." By this they meant that Germany must be stronger than it was in 1914.

The Nazi Party

A new party, called the National Socialist German Workers' Party, was organized. Members of the party were called Nazis (nät′sēz). The party's leader was Adolf Hitler.

The Nazi Party in Power

Adolf Hitler became a dictator and began to increase the size of the army. He declared that Germany would gain greater power because the Germans were "a master race."

At the height of his power, Hitler was supported by millions of people. Here the people of a town in Czechoslovakia salute the dictator.

Hitler organized the whole nation for war. Sports events were held to produce hardy soldiers. In school, children were trained to love marching and fighting. They were not allowed to think for themselves but were taught to accept the teachings of the Nazis without question. Speeches and radio broadcasts repeated what the Nazis wanted people to believe.

Life Under the Nazis

The kinds of freedoms which our Constitution promises us were not permitted in Germany. Newspapers could publish only what the government permitted. People were not allowed to speak their minds. Secret police were ready to arrest anyone who did not follow Hitler's teachings or who failed to salute the *swastika* (swos′ti kə) emblem on the Nazi flag. The swastika was a cross with the ends bent at right angles.

During World War II the Nazis built many prison camps for all those who disagreed with them and those people they believed were inferior to the "master race." Such fenced camps, used to confine political prisoners, are called *concentration camps* (kon′sən trā′shən kamps). In these camps men, women, and children were kept behind barbed-wire fences. They were taken from their homes because they had displeased the Nazis in some way. Many of these people died through torture or starvation because Hitler wanted to get rid of all people who opposed the Nazis.

Hitler stirred up the most bitter hatred against the Jews. He believed they were his worst enemies and he hated them. He sent millions of Jews to concentration camps to die or be killed. Today, this tragedy is called the Holocaust (hol′ə kôst′). Holocaust is the word used to describe the near elimination of all European Jewish people. About 4½ million Jews died in the camps. Another 2 million died of disease and starvation.

The other nations of Europe looked on anxiously while Germany prepared for war. They did not want war again, and they granted many things to Germany in the hope that war might be avoided. France fortified itself behind a strong line of defenses. Great Britain increased its fleet. But Germany was not stopped by their actions. Hitler put the nation's factories and farms to work preparing for war.

Germany's Industries

Germany had factories, skilled workers, farms, and important minerals. This helped Hitler carry out his plans.

The Mineral Wealth of Germany

Germany has a great deal of coal. Large coal fields are found in the Ruhr (roor) Valley in western Germany. There are also coal fields near the Rhine, the Elbe, and the Oder rivers.

Some of the German coal was very good. From it coke, which is needed in smelting iron and steel, could be made. But a large amount was *lignite* (lig′ nīt), or soft brown coal. The lignite was used to make electricity.

In 1940 only about one-fourth of the iron ore Germany used came from its own mines. It was using great quantities to produce war materials.

Much of the iron ore that Germany imported came from Sweden. But much also came from Lorraine (lə rān′). Lorraine and its rich iron mines had been French. In 1871 the Germans had seized Lorraine. After the defeat of Germany in World War I the French got it back. When the Germans overran and conquered France in 1940, they again seized Lorraine. With the resources of Lorraine and Sweden to draw upon, the Germans could keep their armies well supplied.

The Industries of the Saar Valley

Bordering Lorraine is the valley of a little river, the Saar (sär). The Saar Valley has rich coal fields. For a time, following World War I, France controlled the Saar Valley. After a while its large population, mostly Germans, were allowed to decide who would rule them. They voted in favor of Germany, and Germany received this valuable region again.

The Industries of the Ruhr Valley

Farther north, near the point at which the Rhine flows out of Germany into the Netherlands, a small stream unites with the river. This stream is the Ruhr. The valley of the Ruhr has even more coal than the Saar has. The Ruhr Valley became a great manufacturing center.

To the coal fields of the Ruhr was brought iron from Lorraine. This created the greatest center of iron and steel manufacturing in Europe. All types of iron and steel products were made there. These included locomotives, beams for bridges and buildings, tools, and machines.

The great Krupp (krup) mills, which were located in the city of Essen (es′ən), were famous for the making of cannons. The giant guns were made from steel cast in the Krupp factories.

The Outbreak of World War II

In 1938, 6 years after coming to power, Hitler and his advisers felt strong enough to begin conquering Europe.

The Beginning of World War II

To strengthen Germany, Hitler began to seize land from his neighbors. Early in 1938 Nazi troops conquered Austria. Later in the same year they took part of Czechoslovakia (chek′ə slə vä′kē ə), a neighboring country, and the next year swept up all of Czechoslovakia. Italy by then was on Germany's side.

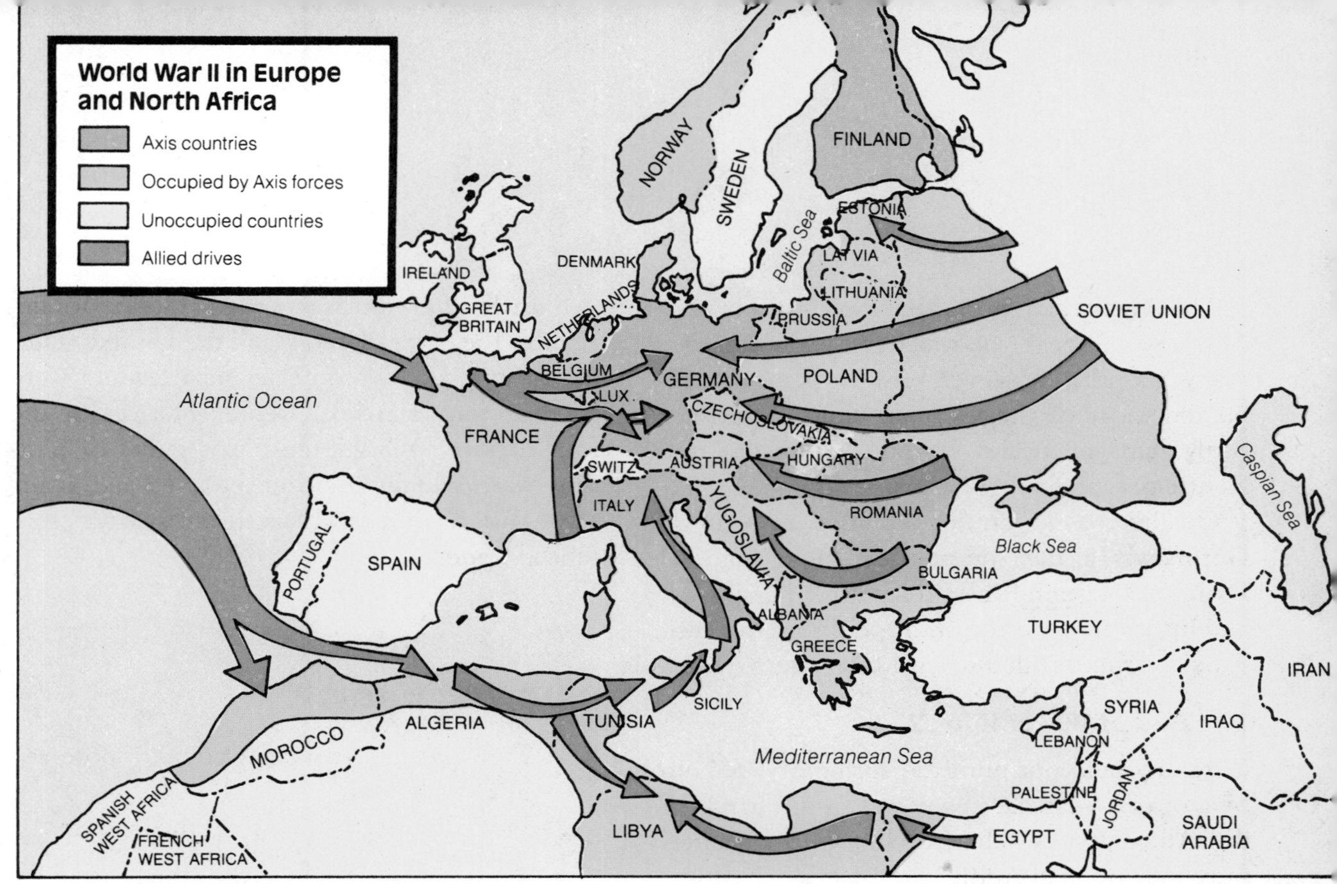

What European countries were Axis powers during World War II? From what country did Allied forces attack Axis powers from the east?

Then, in the summer of 1939, Germany invaded Poland. World War II had begun.

German armies took over a great part of the continent. One nation after another fell. France surrendered in 1940. Some of the countries were united with Germany. Some were merely controlled through puppet rulers.

The Soviet Union, which had made a peace pact with Germany, kept out of the war for a time. But in June 1941, Hitler suddenly turned his armies against the Soviet Union also. Now Germany was at war with both the Soviet Union and Great Britain.

The Great Struggle

The years 1940 and 1941 were filled with bad news for the Allies. Hitler's armies swept over much of western Europe and North Africa. Near the end of 1941 the United States joined the struggle against Germany and its partners, Italy and Japan. Many other Western countries also entered the war on the side of the Allies.

The Allies were slow in gathering their forces, but the tide gradually began to turn. After 1943, Italy was no longer a threat. The full power of the Allied forces could then be turned against Germany.

The Nazis had promised their people that Berlin would never be touched by a bomb. For many months, however, Allied planes bombarded most of the German cities. The raids badly damaged Berlin, Hamburg, Dresden, the Ruhr cities, and many others.

On the ground, armies began to move in on Germany. In the summer of 1944, General Dwight D. Eisenhower directed the massive Allied invasion of western Europe. From the east, Russian armies rolled toward Germany.

The End of World War II

Germany held out until the spring of 1945. In May of that year, Germany was in the hands of the Allied forces. Most of the German cities were in ruins, and Adolf Hitler had died in Berlin. More than 5 years after it had begun, World War II had ended.

In the Far East, Japan fought on alone. When the Japanese signed surrender terms in September, World War II was over.

Shortly after the war ended, Great Britain, France, the Soviet Union, and the United States held a trial in Nuremberg. Nazi leaders were tried as war criminals. Representatives of the four nations found some Nazis guilty of plotting war, killing innocent people, and using slave labor. Several Nazi leaders were sentenced to death.

Do You Know?

1. How did the Nazi party come to power in Germany?
2. How did the Germans get the iron ore they needed for war?
3. Who fought with Germany in World War II?
4. When did Germany surrender? When did Japan surrender?

5
Germany Today

After Berlin fell, millions of Germans surrendered. The Nazi government was gone, and Germany had no government of its own. The Allies took charge. Territory Germany had seized during the war was taken away. War industries were dismantled.

Germany Under the Allies

The Allies took away part of eastern and northeastern Germany. Some of the land went to the Soviet Union, whose troops had taken it in battle. The Oder River valley and the city of Breslau (bres′lou) became part of Poland.

The rest of Germany was divided by the Allies into four parts, called zones. The Soviet Union governed the eastern part, or what is now East Germany. South Germany, including Bavaria (bə ver′ē ə), was governed by the United States. The British controlled the northwestern part. The French had an area in the southwest along the Rhine.

The Communists in East Germany

After the war, the Soviets made East Germany into a Communist country with East Berlin as its capital. Only German Communists were allowed to hold office in the government. Secret police were organized to spy on people. Those who did not support the Communists were imprisoned.

German factories were taken apart and shipped to the Soviet Union. During the war, Germany had caused great damage to the Soviet Union. The Soviets took the factories to help in rebuilding their nation. They also took some of the food produced in East Germany. Much food was used to feed the Soviet armies who lived among the Germans to keep order. Life became very hard there.

In 1949 elections were held in East Germany. But the elections were not free. People could vote only for Communists. East Germany had become a puppet state under strict Soviet control.

West Germany After the War

West Germany was divided into three zones. These zones were controlled by the United States, Great Britain, and France.

The three western Allies wanted to make their part of Germany a democratic nation. Under the Marshall Plan the United States gave money and other aid. The Allies helped rebuild bombed cities and brought in food. German schools were reorganized to educate the children in democratic ways.

Berlin After the War

The city of Berlin was also divided into four parts. The Soviet Union, Great Britain, France, and the United States each controlled a part. The British, French, and American zones came to be known as West Berlin. The Soviet-controlled part of the city is called East Berlin.

East Germany Today

In East Germany, the German Communists worked with the Soviets in setting up a government. The official name of this country is the German Democratic Republic. But it is not a democracy. East Germany does not have free elections. The government is really a dictatorship under Soviet control. The capital of East Germany is East Berlin.

East Germany is about the size of our state of Virginia and has a population of more than 16 million people. East Germany has fewer factories than West Germany. During the 1950s, the people greatly increased their industrial output. One of East Germany's biggest problems was that so many people were unhappy under Communist rule. More than 3 million fled to West Germany by crossing over from East Berlin to West Berlin. To keep people from leaving the

The Berlin Wall, 28 miles (45 km) long, was built in 1961 by the Soviets to prevent people from crossing into West Germany. The barrier has become a symbol of a divided Germany.

country, the Soviets built a high concrete wall in 1961 to separate East and West Berlin. This wall is closely guarded. Anyone trying to cross it is shot.

Since the wall was built in 1961, however, 50,000 more people have escaped from East Germany.

In the 1960s, a new economic system was tried in East Germany. This system let factories make profits, the money left over after all costs are paid. The factories could keep the profits if they agreed to use the extra money to buy more machines or if they gave it to the workers. The plan worked. By the 1970s, East Germany was the world's ninth biggest industrial nation. In the early years of East Germany's existence, few goods were produced for consumers. Now there are more goods produced to make life comfortable. But East Germans still do not enjoy the freedoms of the West Germans.

In 1972, people from West Germany were allowed to visit East Germany. Since then millions have crossed the border to see families and friends. In 1974 the United States recognized East Germany as a nation. Now the two countries have opened diplomatic relations.

West Germany Today

After 4 years under Allied control, the people of West Germany were allowed to form their own government. In 1949 a constitution was adopted.

Berlin
A Divided City

In the west, the glass-walled office buildings are tall and gleaming. Workers are busy manufacturing delicate scientific instruments and other small lightweight articles. The 2 million people here shop in stores well-stocked with every item, including goods from France and Italy. Streets crowded with well-dressed people tell you of West Berlin's prosperity.

A long gray wall, topped by barbed wire, has left a dark shadow across the city of Berlin since 1961. East Berlin, like West Berlin, has modern factories, office buildings, hotels, and shops. But it seems dull compared to West Berlin. It lacks the lively atmosphere of West Berlin.

Why are two parts of a city that was once united so different? You might answer that East and West Berlin have different governments. West Berliners elect the officials who govern them. They are free to live and work wherever they wish. East Berliners live under Communist domination. All newspapers and broadcasts present only the Communist point of view. The Berlin Wall divides not only a city, but also families and friends. What do you think it would it be like if a wall were built across your own community? ■

The superb vineyards of the Rhine Valley have been a source of pride to Germans for centuries. Wines made from the grapes are exported to other countries.

West Germany became officially the German Federal Republic. Its capital is at Bonn (bon), a small city on the Rhine. Citizens vote freely in national elections. A chancellor (chan′sə lər), who is an official like a prime minister, and a parliament run the country.

West Germany is about the size of the state of Oregon and has more than 62 million people. Since 1945 West Germany's population has greatly increased. This is because of the flow of refugees from Communist countries.

The Rhine, Germany's Largest River

The Rhine River flows north for over 800 miles (1,280 km). For a long time it has marked the boundary between the nations of France and Germany.

During most of its course through Germany the Rhine River is bordered by high slopes. For 80 miles (128 km) along the Rhine these hills narrow into a deep valley. From the rocky slopes the ruins of old castles look down. The hills are covered with grapevines.

The Rhine is also a river for trade. From Antwerp and Rotterdam and from Central Europe come hundreds of barges bearing heavy goods. Ships crowded with passengers sail up and down stream. Large cities like Mannheim (män′hīm), Cologne (kə lōn′), and Düsseldorf (doos′əl dôrf′) stand along its course. Factories dot its shores. The Rhine is a waterway of many uses. Canals connect it with the Rhone River, thus allowing barges to carry cargo all the way to the Mediterranean.

Hamburg, Germany's Greatest Port

About 50 miles (80 km) from the mouth of the Elbe stands the large city of Hamburg. It was famous as one of the free cities that rose to importance in the Middle Ages. This city, a little larger than Detroit, is Germany's greatest port and its second largest city. The canals which cross the city in all directions are lined by warehouses. To these warehouses small boats bring goods from the harbor.

The river is too narrow for the largest ocean vessels to come up to Hamburg, so passengers and heavy freight are taken off at the mouth of the Elbe, at Cuxhaven (kux′hä vən). Smaller ships or railroad cars take the passengers and freight the rest of the way.

Hamburg is a great shipbuilding center. It is famous, too, for its manufacture of bicycles,

Hamburg is Germany's greatest port and an important shipbuilding center. From Hamburg are shipped goods manufactured in German factories. To Hamburg come in the raw materials for these goods.

sewing machines, textiles, ironware, and automobiles.

Bremen, a Center of World Trade

Bremen, not quite as large as Hamburg, occupies a place on the Weser River like that of Hamburg on the Elbe. Bremen, too, rose to importance as one of the free cities of the Middle Ages. In modern times it became one of Germany's chief ports for international trade. Raw products, such as tobacco, rice, and cotton, are imported from America and tropical lands. Bremen has many factories which process these raw materials into goods.

Munich, the Capital of Bavaria

Bavaria is a state in southeast Germany. Munich, the capital of Bavaria, is Germany's third largest city. It stands on a high plain not far from the Alps. This is the greatest center of German beer brewing and a center of art and culture.

In their leisure, the Bavarians like to visit the Alps. This is a beautiful and famous scenic region. Here snowy mountains rise above forests and pastures, and glaciers and waterfalls decorate their heights. People come from all over the world to see the many castles, ornate churches, and little villages.

German Farming

Germany raises most of the food it needs. Farmers grow crops which suit the soil and enrich it. Almost every kind of land in Germany is suited to some one crop.

The soil in the southern part of the German plain is good for raising beets. In the days before World War II, the government encouraged farmers to raise them. A German scientist discovered that a certain kind of beet was very sweet. By careful work, the Germans developed and raised beets so full of sweet juice that they were one-sixth sugar. They used them to make sugar for their own needs. The people of Germany also used to export sugar to other countries.

The climate and soil of Germany are also good for raising potatoes. But the German people eat less than half of the crop. They feed

East and West Germany Compared

	Area (sq. km)	Population	Population Largest City	Per Capita Income (1980)
East Germany	40,646 (105,680)	16,700,000	1,145,743 East Berlin	$ 5,945
West Germany	95,815 (249,119)	61,700,000	1,896,230 West Berlin	$10,509

some of them to pigs and cows. And some potatoes are made into fine flour.

About two-thirds of Germany's meat comes from pigs. The German farmers raise more pigs than the farmers of any other European country except Denmark. Since Germany's climate is not hot enough to grow corn, farmers raise barley to feed their pigs and to brew beer.

German Industry

West Germany has done a good job of making itself prosperous again. A period of prosperity began in 1950 and continued for over 20 years. In recent years this boom has slowed somewhat, and some workers have had trouble finding jobs. But West Germany is still the fourth greatest industrial nation in the world.

West German factories produce steel, machinery, cars, electrical engineering products, and chemicals for German use and for export. Foods and raw materials, such as meat, grain, cotton, rubber, and oil are imported.

In 1967 oil began to be brought into West Germany through a new pipeline. This pipeline carries Middle Eastern oil from the port of Trieste (Trē est′) on the Adriatic (ā′drē at′ik) Sea, across the Alps and into Germany.

West Germany cooperates with its neighbors in western Europe and with the United States. It is an important Common Market member.

A United Germany?

During the years since the close of World War II Germany has been a divided nation. People in both East and West Germany would like to be united under one government. However, efforts to bring the two regions together have failed. Germany thus remains a divided nation. Despite their differences, East and West Germany do carry on active trade with one another.

Do You Know?

1. Into how many zones was Germany divided after World War II? Which countries occupied Germany?
2. What kind of government does East Germany have today?
3. What kind of government does West Germany have? What city is its capital?
4. Why is Berlin a divided city?

To Help You Learn

Using New Words

concentration camp	symphony
swastika	Protestant
lignite	Reformation
opera	

Number a paper from 1 through 7. After each number write the word or term that matches the definition.

1. A cross with the ends bent at right angles, used on the Nazi flag
2. A fenced camp, used to confine political prisoners
3. The name of the followers of Martin Luther who acted in protest against certain practices of the Catholic Church
4. A musical work to be played by a large orchestra
5. Soft, brown coal
6. A kind of musical play in which the actors sing instead of speak
7. The religious movement started by Martin Luther

Finding the Facts

1. What nations sided with Germany in World War I? What nations fought Germany in World War I?
2. How did Wilhelm II contribute to the beginning of World War I?
3. What event sparked the beginning of World War I?
4. What happened to Germany at the end of World War I?
5. What happened at Weimar in 1919?
6. Who were the Nazis?
7. Who was the leader of the Nazis?
8. Who went to concentration camps?
9. What was the Holocaust?
10. What was life like under the Nazi government?
11. Name the places in Germany that have coal reserves.
12. Where did Germany's iron ore come from?
13. Name the first three countries Germany invaded in World War II. What years did the invasions take place?
14. What two nations did Germany go to war with in 1941?
15. What countries fought on the side of Germany in World War II? What was the name given to the countries that fought against Germany in World War II?
16. Who was the American general whose armies invaded Europe in 1944?
17. When did World War II end?
18. What happened to Adolf Hitler?
19. What happened in Nuremberg?
20. Who controlled Germany after World War II?
21. What was the Marshall Plan?
22. Describe what happened to Berlin after the war.
23. What was made in the Krupp mills?

24. What is the official name of the country of East Germany? What is its capital?
25. Why was a wall built in East Berlin?
26. What is the official name of the country of West Germany? What is its capital? What kind of government does it have?
27. What is Germany's largest river? Why is it important?
28. Name three German cities and give one important fact about each one.
29. What crops do German farmers grow?
30. Name Germany's most important industrial products.

Learning From Maps

1. Look at the map on page 431. Name the countries in Europe that fought with Germany in World War II.
2. On the map of Germany on page 419, locate each of these places: Munich, Bonn, Lorraine, the Saar, Berlin, Hamburg, Bremen, and Essen. Tell whether they are located on plains or plateaus, or in hills or mountains.
3. Turn to the map of Berlin on page 435. Into how many parts or sectors was Berlin divided after World War II? What nations occupied these sectors? Does the whole city of Berlin lie in East Germany or West Germany? If you are not sure, look at the map of Germany on page 419.
4. Look again at the map of Germany on page 419. Name the countries that border East Germany. Name the countries that border West Germany. Martin Luther was born in Saxony. Is it in East or West Germany? Is Bavaria in the north or south, east or west of Germany? Is Hamburg closer to Berlin or to Munich? Is Bonn closer to Berlin or Nuremberg? Are there mountains in East Germany? What river flows past Bonn? What other big cities does it pass?

Using Study Skills

1. **Time Line:** Study the time line for Germany below. How many years were there between the union of the German states (under a diet or parliament) and the formation of the empire? Between World War I and World War II? When was the present German republic formed?

2. **Time Line:** Place the following events in the proper order of time: Treaty of Peace ending World War I signed; Weimar Republic ends; World War II ends; the years Germany seizes Lorraine; Nazis march into Austria; Allies invade west coasts of Europe; U.S. recognizes East Germany; Luther protests activities of Catholic Church.

   Copy the time line from page 417. Add these events to your time line.
3. **Chart:** Use the chart comparing East and West Germany on page 438 to answer these questions. How many more people live in West Germany than in East Germany? Do workers in East or West Germany make more money? What is the difference in size between East and West Germany? What is the difference in population between East Germany's largest city and the largest city in West Germany?

Thinking It Through

1. Bismarck said he would unite Germany by iron and blood. What did he mean?
2. In a dictionary, you will find the word holocaust defined as a great or complete destruction. Explain why this word describes the experience of the Jews in World War II.
3. Why do you think Wilhelm II felt it was important for the young German nation to have colonies?
4. When Hitler became leader of Germany, he didn't allow the Germans to have the freedoms we enjoy. Why do you think he did this?
5. After the Allies bombed Nazi Germany in World War II they helped rebuild the country. Do you think that was a good idea? Why?

Projects

1. Together with three of your classmates, choose one of these dates for each of you—1871, 1918, 1940, 1944. In proper order, each of you should tell your class what the relationship was between Germany and France at the date selected.
2. Conduct an exhibit of pictures of German scenes, found in books and magazines. Frame these in cardboard or paper and place them on the bulletin board. Put a caption on each scene.
3. The operas of Richard Wagner, based on stories drawn from German myths, are often sung in America. Ask your librarian to help you find some of these stories. You also might like to read the stories in Grimm's *Fairy Tales.*

15 Central Europe

Unit Preview

From the air, the land of Central Europe looks like a patchwork quilt of mountains, plateaus, and plains. Here are Poland, Austria, Hungary, Czechoslovakia, and Switzerland. To the west of these countries lie Germany and France. On the east is the Soviet Union. Italy and the Balkan countries are to the south.

The people of Central Europe have Germanic and Slavic ancestors. The Huns were a Germanic tribe who settled in the area near the Danube River. Then the Magyars invaded and set up a kingdom in Hungary. In Austria, the Hapsburg family became powerful rulers. They ruled most of Central Europe, except for Poland and Switzerland. Austria and Hungary united to form an empire. It lasted until World War I. After Austria and Hungary were defeated in World War I, part of their lands became Czechoslovakia.

Poland is one of the largest countries in Europe. Because of its location, it has often been invaded. Switzerland is one of the smallest European countries. It has refused to take sides in wars and has remained independent.

Poland is the only one of the central European countries that has a seacoast. Ships can travel from the Baltic to the North Sea and then to the Atlantic Ocean. Important rivers flow through Czechoslovakia, Hungary, Austria, and Switzerland. These waterways are trade routes. Railroads and highways connect river ports to inland cities.

Farming, mining, lumbering, and manufacturing are major industries in Central Europe.

Things to Discover

If you look carefully at the picture, map, and time line on these pages, you can answer these questions.

1. The picture shows an area in Switzerland. What landforms can be seen in this Central European country?
2. The Hapsburgs ruled much of Central Europe at one time. When did they become powerful?
3. Was Switzerland conquered by Hapsburg armies?
4. When was the country of Poland divided? How many years later did it once again become a united nation?
5. What two countries of Central Europe were once joined together as an empire?
6. What country was invaded by the Soviet Union in 1947?

Words to Learn

You will meet these words in this unit. As you read, you will learn what they mean and how to pronounce them. The Word List will help you.

appeasement	international
canton	League of Nations
corridor	pass

Magyars invade Hungary
c. 900
Hapsburg family rises to power
1186
Swiss unite
1291
Polish nation divided
1795
Court of the Hapsburgs rules
c. 1850
World War I ends; Austria-Hungary empire broken up; Poland restored as nation
1918
Germany invades Poland and Czechoslovakia
1939
World War II ends
1945
Soviet Union controls Czechoslovakia
1947
Uprising in Hungary crushed
1956
Soviet Union ends Hungarian revolution
1968
Polish workers win right to establish labor unions
1980
Solidarity is outlawed
1982

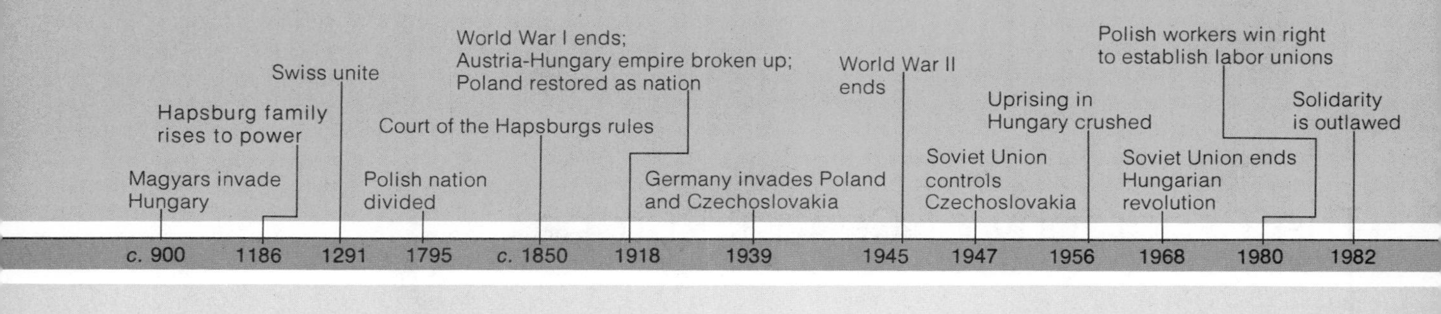

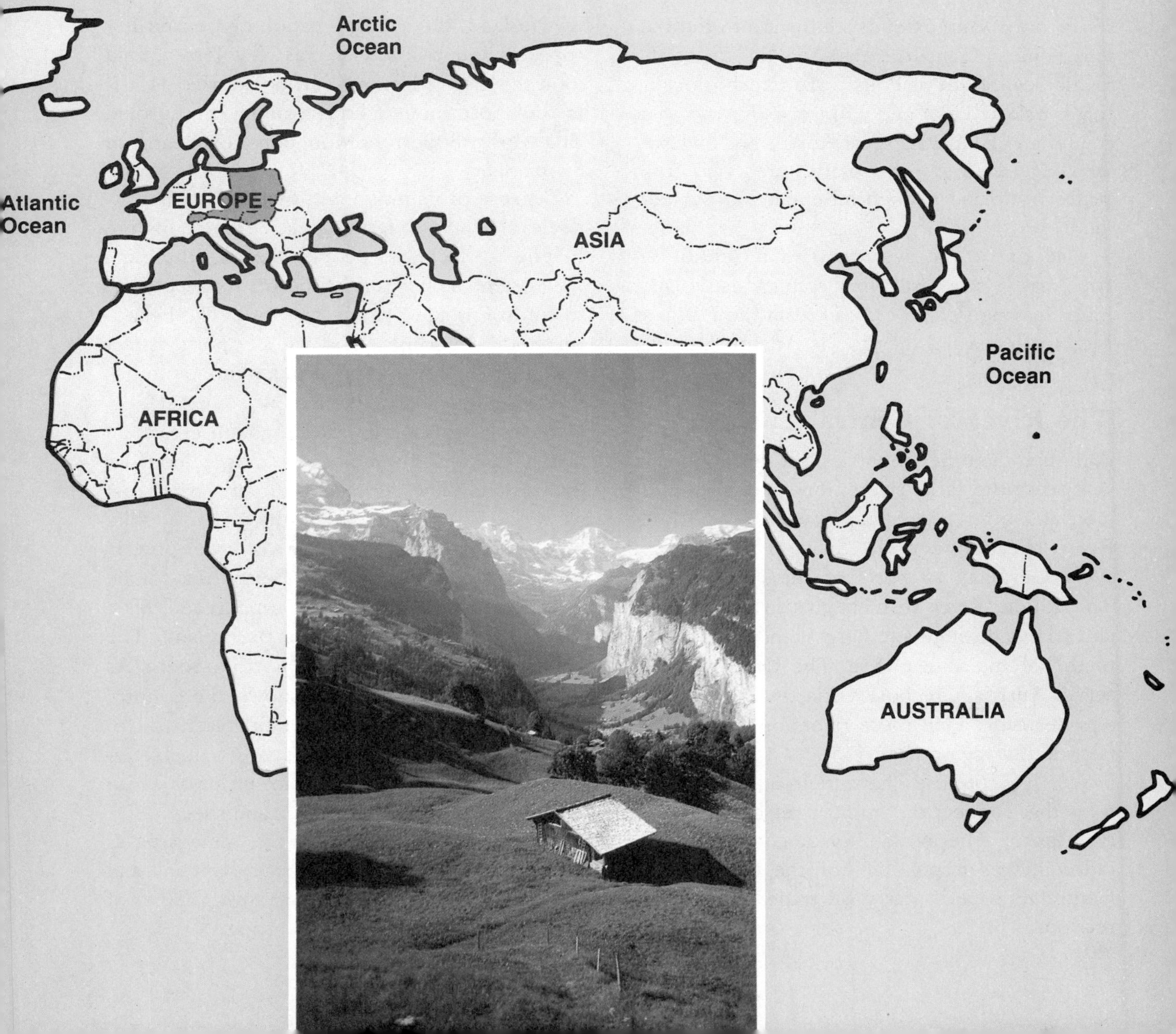

Arctic Ocean
Atlantic Ocean
EUROPE
ASIA
AFRICA
Pacific Ocean
AUSTRALIA

1
The Geography of Central Europe

Central Europe begins at the Baltic (bôl′tik) Sea in the north, and extends southward to the Balkan Peninsula and the Alps. Poland faces the Baltic Sea. South of Poland are Czechoslovakia (chek′ə slə vä′kē ə) and Hungary. To the west of Hungary, in the Alps, lie Austria and Switzerland. The land surfaces of this area vary from plains in Poland to high mountains in Switzerland.

Only one of the five countries in Central Europe has a seacoast. This country is Poland. Ships leaving Poland can sail from the Baltic to the North Sea and then to the Atlantic Ocean.

The Rivers of Central Europe

Although the other countries of Central Europe lack seacoasts, large rivers flow through the region and offer fine transportation. The Rhine River (rīn) flows from Switzerland through West Germany to ports of the Netherlands. The Rhone River (rōn) begins in Switzerland and passes through southern France on its way to the Mediterranean Sea. The Danube River serves Austria, Czechoslovakia, and Hungary as a trade route. Find these rivers on the map of Central Europe on page 445.

All five countries have railroads and highways that connect the interior regions with the river ports. The availability of good transportation makes it possible for the countries of Central Europe to carry on trade in many directions.

Natural Resources

Switzerland, the smallest nation of Central Europe, is about twice as large as New Jersey. Find it on the map of Central Europe on page 445. It is the most mountainous country in Europe. The Alps and the Jura Mountains cover most of Switzerland.

Because of its mountains Switzerland has little level land for farming. Yet mountains are helpful to the Swiss people. Streams tumbling down steep slopes furnish power for electricity to run trains and operate factories. The beautiful mountain scenery and winter sports attract visitors. The visitors spend much money in hotels, restaurants, and shops.

Austria, which is a little larger in area than South Carolina, is almost as mountainous as Switzerland. The Alps cross Austria from east to west, covering much of the country. Like Switzerland, Austria has plenty of water power.

Austria is rich in minerals. Beneath its soil lie valuable deposits of iron ore, copper, and oil.

Hungary is about the size of Indiana. The Danube River crosses it from north to south. As the map of Central Europe shows, the country occupies a great plain. The rich, black soil of this treeless plain is Hungary's most valuable resource. Its fertile farms produce crops of wheat and potatoes, beef cattle, hogs, and sheep.

Czechoslovakia has about the same area as North Carolina. It has rugged mountains and rolling plains. It also has the greatest number of natural resources in Central Europe.

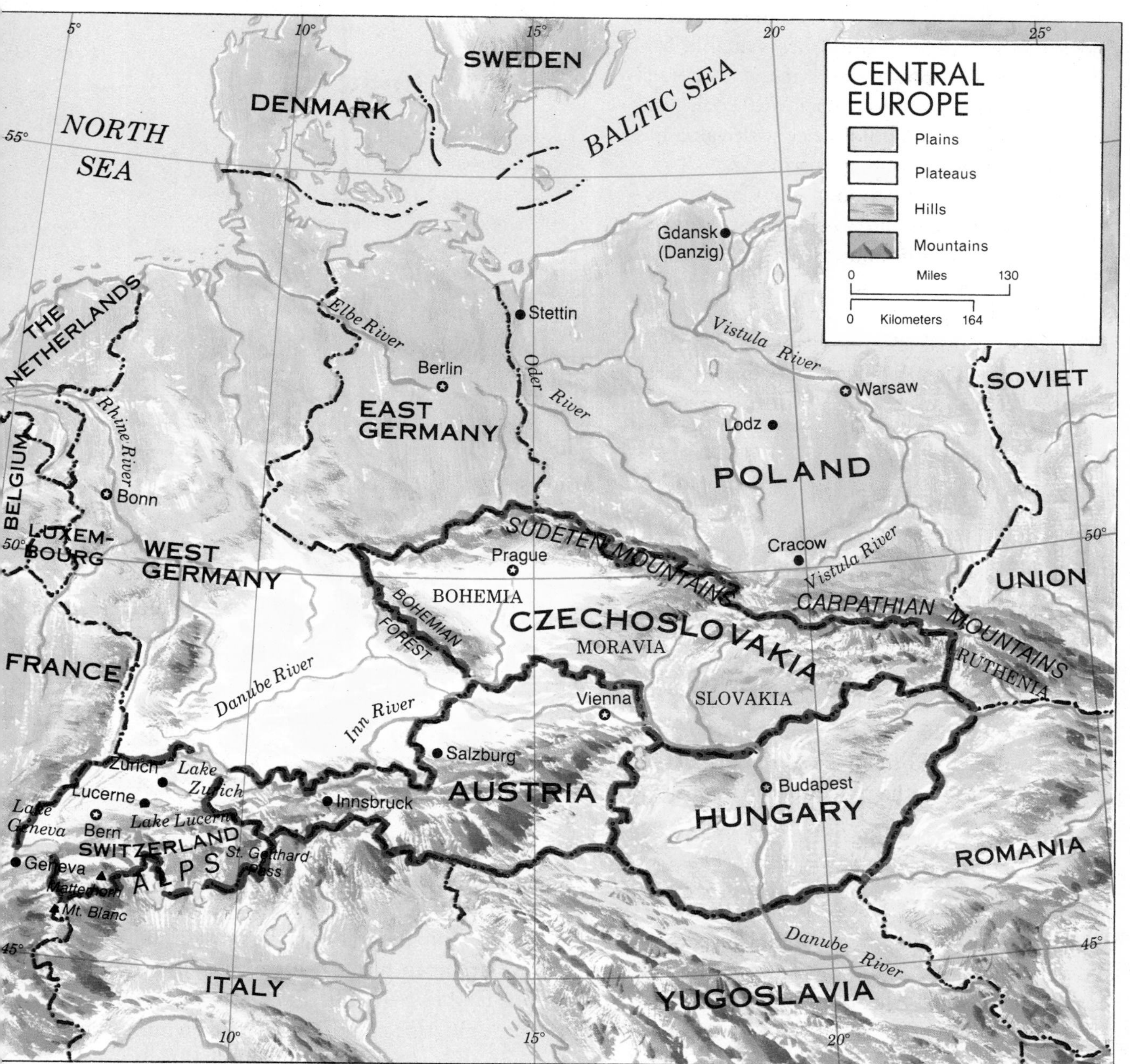
CENTRAL EUROPE
Plains
Plateaus
Hills
Mountains
0 Miles 130
0 Kilometers 164
SWEDEN
DENMARK
NORTH SEA
BALTIC SEA
THE NETHERLANDS
BELGIUM
LUXEMBOURG
FRANCE
EAST GERMANY
WEST GERMANY
POLAND
SOVIET UNION
CZECHOSLOVAKIA
BOHEMIA
MORAVIA
SLOVAKIA
RUTHENIA
AUSTRIA
HUNGARY
ROMANIA
YUGOSLAVIA
ITALY
SWITZERLAND
Gdansk (Danzig)
Stettin
Berlin
Warsaw
Lodz
Bonn
Prague
Cracow
Vienna
Salzburg
Innsbruck
Budapest
Zurich
Lucerne
Bern
Geneva
Elbe River
Oder River
Vistula River
Rhine River
Danube River
Inn River
SUDETEN MOUNTAINS
CARPATHIAN MOUNTAINS
BOHEMIAN FOREST
ALPS
Lake Zurich
Lake Lucerne
Lake Geneva
St. Gotthard Pass
Matterhorn
Mt. Blanc
5°
10°
15°
20°
25°
55°
50°
45°

Almost half the land in Czechoslovakia is good for farming. The nation has valuable forests, much water power, and many minerals. Among its underground riches are coal, uranium, lead, silver, and gold. Czechoslovakia has many raw materials for its industries.

Poland, the largest country in Central Europe, is almost the same size as New Mexico. As you can see by the map of Central Europe on page 445, most of Poland is a plains region. Poland, like Hungary, has many farms.

The most valuable minerals in Poland are coal and zinc. The Polish people export large quantities of coal to other countries.

Do You Know?

1. Which countries in Central Europe have no seacoast?
2. Lacking seaports, how do these countries carry on trade?
3. Which countries in Central Europe have many mountains? Which have plains?
4. What mountains are in Switzerland?

2 Switzerland, a Land of the Alps

The peaks and valleys of mountainous Switzerland have influenced the lives of the Swiss people. This was true in the past, and it remains true today.

The Geography of Switzerland

Switzerland is a land of mountains, sparkling lakes, and rushing rivers. From the melting snow on the Swiss Alps, streams flow in four directions. To the north flows the Rhine. To the west the Rhone rushes toward France. On the south the Ticino (ti chē′nō′) flows into Italy. Eastward the Inn River hurries to the Danube.

The Importance of Mountain Passes

When early travelers crossing a continent came to a range of mountains, instead of climbing the lofty peaks, they looked for an opening, or *pass* (pas), through the range. These natural paths are important in history, especially in a mountainous land like Switzerland.

The high Alps stand like a wall dividing the Mediterranean lands from Central Europe. As the cities of Germany, Belgium, and the Netherlands grew, highways for trade with the south were needed. Road builders explored the passes through the Alps to see which could be used as highways.

In the southern Alps a pass was found which led toward the Italian lake region. This pass, called the St. Gotthard (got′hard) Pass, was to prove important in Swiss history.

The St. Gotthard Pass

The St. Gotthard Pass offered a direct road from Germany to Italy. Travelers could reach Lake Lucerne (lo͞o sərn′) without going over high mountains. This was the only point in the Alps where a single pass led from one country to the other. During the Middle Ages it became an important trade route.

A road was first built through the St. Gotthard Pass some time after the year 1100. In those days the king of the German states called himself the emperor. The emperor wanted to be sure that the pass would not be seized by powerful nobles. So the emperor put the Swiss living near Lake Lucerne in charge of the pass. This area was divided into three districts, called *cantons* (kan′tənz). The people liked the plan, for it meant they had to serve no lord except the emperor himself. And the German emperor was far away. They still had freedom.

Glaciers carved many valleys through the mountains in Switzerland. The Swiss have built their homes and villages along the steep mountainsides.

The History of Switzerland

The three cantons were proud of their freedom. As time went on, however, they began to fear that they would lose it. Their concern was caused by the rise of a powerful family whose stronghold, called Hapsburg, was in the mountains above Lake Lucerne. The Hapsburg family seized more and more land. The people of the cantons feared that the emperor could not protect their lands.

In 1291 the leaders of the three cantons met in a mountain meadow. They promised to work and to fight together for their freedom. The union of the three cantons was the beginning of the nation we now call Switzerland. One by one more cantons and free cities joined the union.

Defeat of the Hapsburgs

The united cantons had to fight to keep their freedom. The Hapsburg family, against whom

Zurich is the largest city in Switzerland. Parts of it are hundreds of years old. Which do you think is older, the cable car or the road?

they had united, took over Austria and claimed many other lands.

For 200 years powerful armies from Austria attacked the Swiss again and again. But in one great battle after another, the Swiss defeated them. During the struggle with Austria, the Swiss took over land south of the St. Gotthard Pass. Some of this land is still part of Switzerland. You can find it on the map of Central Europe on page 445.

Switzerland as a Republic

Switzerland today is made up of 23 cantons. As a republic for more than 600 years, it is the oldest in the world. Its capital is Bern.

The Swiss form of government is somewhat like ours in the United States. The 23 cantons elect a body of lawmakers called the Federal Assembly. Like our Congress, it has two branches, or houses. Each year the lawmakers choose a person who serves for 12 months as president of Switzerland.

Swiss laws are published in three languages—German, French, and Italian. These languages as well as Romansch are spoken in different parts of Switzerland today. Even though not everyone speaks the same language, the Swiss are a united people.

Switzerland has good schools. Students come from many foreign countries to study in Swiss universities.

The mountains of Switzerland help protect it from invasion by other countries. Since 1515 Switzerland's geography has helped to keep it from going to war.

The Cities of Switzerland

Three important cities of Switzerland are Zurich (zoor′ik), Lucerne, and Geneva (jə nē′və). All three are on lakes. Zurich and Lucerne are cities where German is spoken. In Geneva the people speak French.

Zurich, the Largest Swiss City

Zurich, on a long, deep lake, is about the size of Atlanta, Georgia. It has factories run by electricity which is produced by water power.

The city of Lucerne, above, has many charming old streets. A hillside castle overlooks Lake Geneva, Switzerland's largest lake, right.

Zurich is a noted center of learning. Its university is one of the greatest in Europe.

Lucerne, City of the Three Cantons

Lucerne is a city on a winding narrow lake among the mountains. These mountains overshadow almost the whole length of the lake.

Tourists visiting Lucerne like to ride on the lake steamers. From the deck of the boat they can see railroads leading to the tops of mountains. A fine highway, part of it cut out of solid rock, runs along the shore.

At one place, according to an old story, William Tell led the Swiss in a fight against a cruel officer of the Hapsburgs. In the end Tell is said to have shot the Hapsburg officer with his crossbow.

At the far end of the lake is the point at which the St. Gotthard Highway begins. Here automobiles can follow a good road to Italy. A quicker way is by train through a tunnel under the pass.

The St. Gotthard tunnel is almost 10 miles (16 km) long. This and other tunnels serve as important trade routes from Switzerland to the Middle East, Italy, and Greece.

Geneva, a World Center

Lake Geneva, about 50 miles (80 km) long, is the largest Swiss lake. At its southern end lies the city of Geneva. Many foreign visitors come to Geneva. This is because many *international* (in′tər nash′ən əl) groups, or organizations, have had their headquarters in Geneva. "International" means "among nations."

Geneva lies on the French border. A favorite excursion from Geneva is a trip to nearby France to view the great Mont Blanc (blänk), or "White Mountain." Mont Blanc is the highest mountain in the Alps.

How Switzerland Became Prosperous

Switzerland is a landlocked country. The Swiss have little farmland and no coal or other minerals. Yet they are comfortable and prosperous. They have developed special skills to make a good living.

Switzerland, a Manufacturing Nation

Nearly half the workers of Switzerland are engaged in manufacturing. The Swiss import raw materials such as the metals from which they make watches, scientific instruments, and other valuable articles.

A watch is small and takes little material to make, but it must be put together with great skill. Scientific instruments also must be made with care. These special kinds of manufacturing are carried on in Switzerland.

The Swiss also manufacture some heavy machinery. They make electrical equipment and electric locomotives. The Swiss are also well known for their cheese and chocolate.

Before World War I, Switzerland imported coal to run its factories. It was so hard to get coal during the war that the Swiss decided they would no longer depend on it. They built dams across their rivers and mountain streams. Water released through the dams turned machinery to make electricity. Since that time Swiss factories and trains have been run by electric power.

Tourism in Switzerland

For many years people from other lands have visited Switzerland. To take care of their guests, the Swiss built hundreds of hotels. The tourists bring a great deal of money into the country.

The Swiss have made it easy to view their fine scenery. They have built electric railways by which visitors can reach the tops of high mountains. For those who like to climb mountains, guides lead the way up snowy, rocky peaks. At some points overnight shelters are provided.

The clear, dry air of Switzerland is healthful. People enjoy winter sports such as skiing, bobsledding, tobogganing, and ice skating.

The Farms of Switzerland

The Swiss are good farmers. The plateau of Switzerland is warm during the summer. The Swiss can raise enough fruit and potatoes for themselves, but most other kinds of food must be imported.

Around the larger lakes, such as Zurich and Geneva, the slopes facing the sun are lined with terraces covered with grapevines. No other country has vineyards so high above sea level.

Both in the valleys and high on the mountain slopes, dairy cattle feed. They graze on the green pastures at the very edge of snow fields. Herds of goats eat grass in places too steep even for Swiss cattle to climb safely. Goats produce rich milk.

Home of International Societies

Switzerland has never taken sides in the wars of other nations. For this reason it is the meeting place for representatives of nearly 100 international organizations.

The Matterhorn, a famous mountain peak, can be viewed from the train station at Zermatt, an old mountain village in Switzerland. The top of the Matterhorn is always covered with snow.

The Red Cross Society

In 1864 Switzerland became the birthplace of the International Red Cross Society. Its headquarters are in Geneva. Most of its thousands of workers are Swiss.

In wartime the International Red Cross Society watches over the welfare of all prisoners of war. It sends workers to inspect the places where the prisoners are held. The Society sees that prisoners receive their mail and sends messages to their families. It tries to locate persons who have been driven out of their countries as a result of war.

More than 70 nations have formed Red Cross societies. Our own American Red Cross and Junior Red Cross help those in need in peacetime as well as during a war.

The League of Nations

After World War I, a group of countries interested in preventing war formed the *League of Nations* (lēg ov nā′shənz). About 60 nations joined it. The League had its home in Geneva.

For 20 years the League carried on much useful work. But it was not strong enough to keep the nations at peace. At the beginning of World War II, people had to admit that the League had failed in carrying out its purpose.

The world now has an organization somewhat like the League, called the United Nations. The United Nations was formed at the end of World War II. The home of the United Nations is in New York City. The League buildings in Geneva are now the European headquarters of the United Nations.

What We Can Learn from Switzerland

Switzerland shows how well people can live in a land with few natural riches. The Swiss have prospered by making the best use of what they have as a nation. They have also benefitted from the long periods of peace they have enjoyed as a neutral nation.

Switzerland also presents an example of compassion. People driven from other lands have often found refuge among the Swiss.

Do You Know?

1. What is the St. Gotthard Pass? Why was it important in Swiss history?
2. Which languages are spoken in Switzerland?
3. What kind of government does Switzerland have?
4. Why is Geneva called a world center?

3 The Story of Austria and Hungary

In 1914 the map of Europe showed a large country near the center of the continent. It was called Austria-Hungary. On the west Austria-Hungary touched Germany and Switzerland. On the east it bordered Russia.

Today Austria and Hungary are separate countries. Each is smaller than it was years ago.

The Empire of Austria-Hungary

The Hapsburgs extended their control over a large part of Central Europe. With Austria as the center of their empire, they ruled many different peoples. In this empire were the people living in the region we now know as Hungary.

Union of Austria and Hungary

More than 100 years ago the power of the Hapsburgs began to crumble. The Hungarians then demanded an equal place in the empire. Austria agreed that Hungary should be treated as a partner. The two countries were united and called Austria-Hungary in 1867.

Austria lay to the west and Hungary lay on the east. Each had its own capital on the Danube River—Vienna (vē en′ə) for Austria and Budapest (bo͞o′də pest) for Hungary. Each had its own parliament and managed its own home affairs. But in matters dealing with foreign nations they were united. The Austria-Hungary empire had just one army and one navy.

Austria had factories, but on its mountainous land it could not raise the food it needed. Hungary was mostly farming country and needed manufactured articles. The two countries exchanged their products, and both profited by the trade.

The People of the Empire

The Hapsburgs over a long period of time had brought many smaller states under their rule. Austria was thus a strange assortment of peoples. Within its borders were Germans, Czechs (cheks), Poles, Italians, Serbs (surbz), Romanians (rō mā′nē ənz), and Slovaks (slō′vaks). In the Parliament at Vienna, 11 different languages were spoken. Hungary, too, was made up of a variety of people.

The Hapsburgs were Germans and tried to make the empire as German as possible. The Czechs and the Poles were not Germans and did not wish to become so. They were Slavs.

In southern Austria there were millions of other Slavs who did not like the Germans. They felt that the Germans treated them unfairly.

The Empire in World War I

In June 1914, the Austrian government sent Archduke Francis Ferdinand, heir to the throne, on a tour along the Serbian border. The Serbs, who are Slavs, had no love for Austria. At a little town in southern Austria the archduke was shot and killed by a young Serb.

The Austrian government demanded that Serbia take the blame. Now is the time, Austria thought, to gain power over Serbia.

When the Serbs did not immediately agree to Austria's demands, Germany backed Austria. Russia began assembling troops to defend the Serbs. Germany too assembled troops and declared war. Soon other nations were drawn in, and the conflict became a world war.

World War I lasted 4 years, from 1914 to 1918. In the end Austria, Hungary, and Germany were defeated.

After World War I

Austria-Hungary was hard hit by World War I. Near the end of the war people throughout the empire were rebelling. Hungary declared itself independent. At the peace conference at the end of the war, the Allies took away much of the land that had belonged to the twin empire. The empire became two separate countries. See the map of Austria-Hungary Before and After World War I on page 457.

Austria lost other lands. New nations were created from its former territory. Four former Austrian provinces were made into a new country called Czechoslovakia. Most of Austria's factories were in the territory assigned to Czechoslovakia. Austrian territory on the northern Adriatic coast, including the port of Trieste, now belonged to Italy. Yugoslavia was formed from the Austrian territory on the eastern coast of the Adriatic.

Austria was now a little country about the size of Maine. Hitler marched his troops into Austria and made it a part of Germany in 1938.

Vienna
A Cultural Center, Past and Present

For centuries, Vienna competed with Paris in grandeur and as a center for the arts. In the heart of Vienna is the Ringstrasse (ring′sträs′ə), a great circular boulevard lined with parks and plazas and grand old buildings. On the Ringstrasse are beautiful public buildings. Nearby are the palaces, concert halls, art galleries, museums, and cathedral that once helped make Vienna the cultural capital of Europe. Haydn, Mozart, Beethoven, Schubert, and Brahms (brämz) all lived and wrote music in Vienna. During the 1800s the city became identified with romantic waltzes of the Strauss family.

Although the twentieth century saw Vienna's political importance ebb, the city has retained its intellectual vitality. Its great university continues to attract distinguished scientists. Many came to consult Sigmund Freud (sig′mənd froid′), the doctor who made many discoveries about how the human mind works. Twentieth-century composers, such as Alban Berg, wrote music that sounded unusual, because it used the tones of the scale in a new way. This new-sounding music was presented in the same concert halls where Mozart's works were first performed. Vienna, the capital of a small country, has maintained its role as a center for music for the entire world. ■

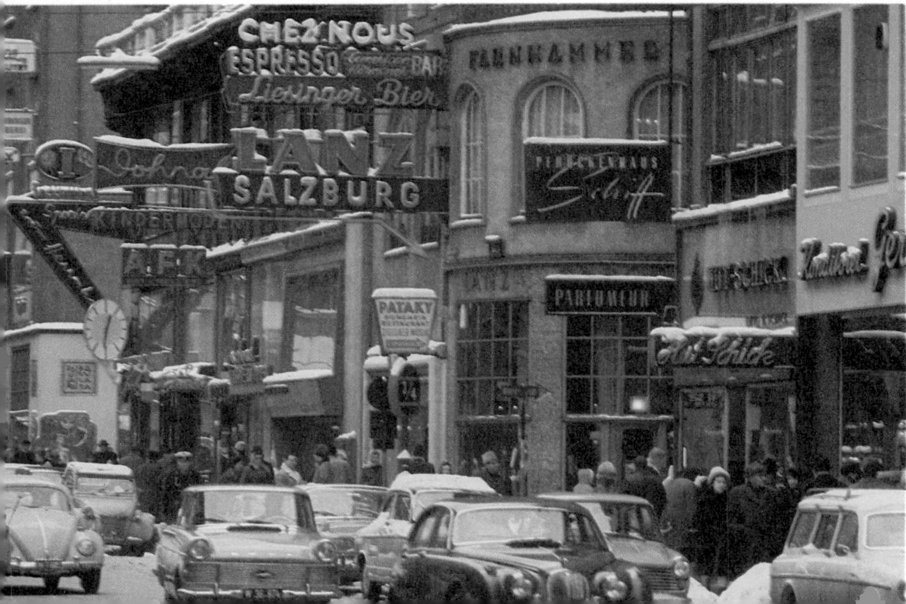

At Innsbruck, Austria, people dressed in national costumes enjoy a spirited, traditional dance.

Austria After World War II

After the defeat of Germany in World War II, Austria became a separate country again. But it was not given full independence right away. British, French, Soviet, and American soldiers controlled Austria. In 1955 the Allied nations withdrew their troops. Austria joined the free nations of the world.

Austria Today

Since regaining its freedom, Austria has made steady progress. Its factories are busy making glassware, pottery, cars, textiles, and machinery. The forests furnish wood for a variety of products. From beneath its soil the nation draws oil, iron ore, and other minerals. Austria's farms can supply most of the food that the nation needs.

Austria, like Switzerland, attracts many tourists. Each year they come to enjoy the mountain scenery, the pleasant cities, and the music festivals for which the nation is famous. Money spent by the tourists helps to keep Austria's economy stable.

The people of Austria elect their lawmakers and their president. The lawmakers in turn choose one person to serve as prime minister. The prime minister is the real head of government and has more power than the president.

The History of Hungary

The earliest settlers of the region now known as Hungary were called Huns. The Huns were warlike tribes who had come from Asia.

The Magyars in Hungary

During the early part of the Middle Ages, in the early 900s, a host of warriors from the Russian plains rode across the Carpathian (kär pā′thē ən′) Mountains. They saw before them more plains (see the map of Central Europe on page 445). Down into these plains along the Danube they rushed. These invaders were called Magyars (mag′yärz).

The Kingdom of Hungary

The Magyars conquered the Huns and set up a kingdom in Hungary. For a time Hungary was the strongest nation in Central Europe. Then the nobles began to quarrel and fight among themselves, and the country grew weak.

The Turks invaded Hungary and pushed the Magyars back to Austria's border. The Turks controlled Hungary until the late 1600s. The Magyars asked for and received Austria's protection. As a result, the Magyars became part of

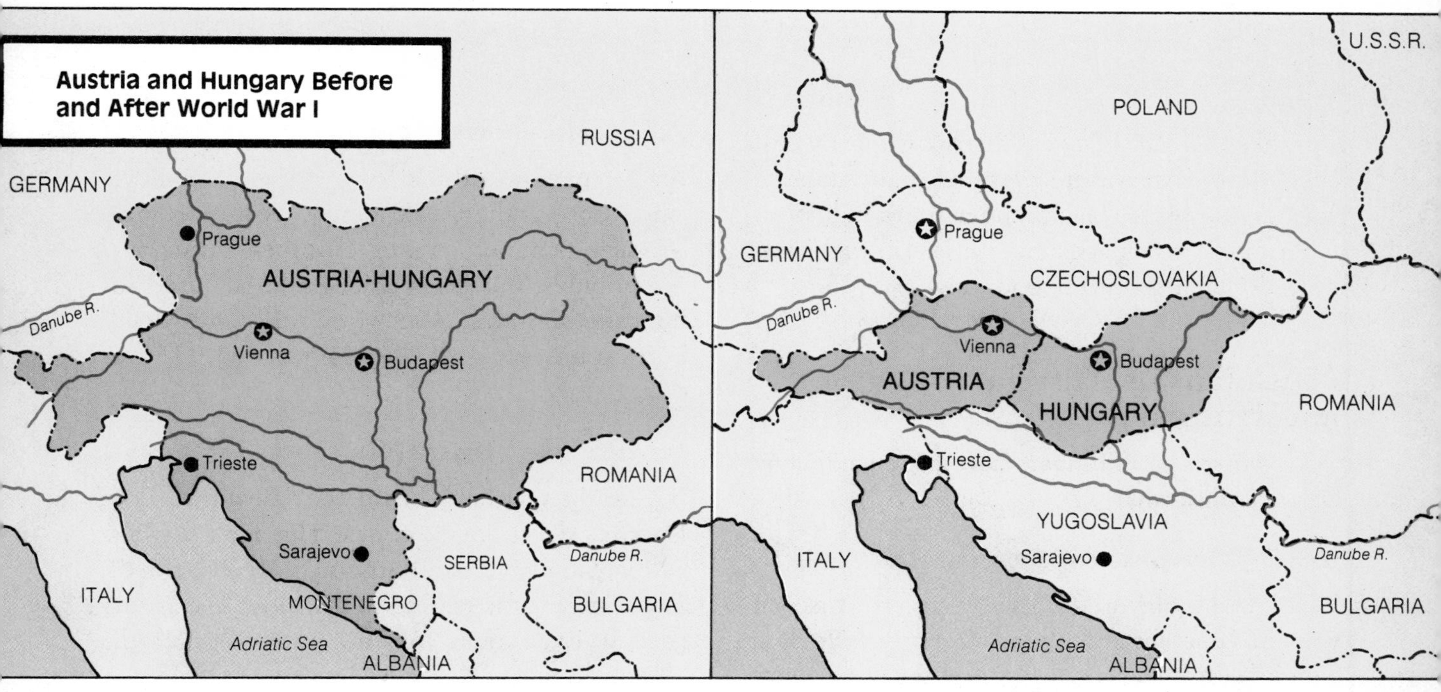

Before World War I, Austria-Hungary included areas that became several different countries after the war. What are these countries? What became of Serbia and Montenegro?

the Hapsburg empire. Since that time many other groups have come to Hungary, but the majority are still Magyars.

Hungary Today

Present-day Hungary, with a population of more than 10 million, is about the size of the state of Indiana. Its capital is Budapest. Hungary has a Communist government and follows policies much like those of the Soviet Union. In 1956 the people of Hungary revolted and there was much fighting. Thousands left the country. The Soviets sent tanks to help the government, and the uprising was stopped.

The Products of Hungary

Most of Hungary is flat. In winter, cold winds sweep across the land, but in summer the weather is hot. The climate makes it easy to raise corn. The Danube Valley, including parts of Hungary, Romania, and Yugoslavia, is Europe's corn belt.

Hungary's factories produce chemicals, machinery, steel, textiles, and transportation equipment.

Budapest

Budapest lies on a broad curve of the Danube River. On the west bank are the medieval churches and palaces which reflect the city's long history. The business district is on the east bank. Budapest is noted for the many mineral springs nearby. Over half the nation's industries are located in Budapest, and it is also the transportation center for the country.

Musicians of Austria and Hungary

Both Austria and Hungary have produced many famous musicians.

Haydn, Composer of Symphonies

Franz Josef Haydn (hīd′ən) was an Austrian who became famous as a composer. He was widely admired. Haydn composed fine symphonies. Haydn's symphonies showed how the sounds of many instruments could be blended in a pleasing way.

Mozart, Child Composer

Wolfgang Amadeus Mozart (wo͞olf′gang ä′mə dä′əs mōt′särt) began to compose and play little musical pieces of his own when he was 4 years old. When he was 6, he was invited to the palace in Vienna to play for the emperor.

Salzburg (sälz′burg), a city near the boundary line of Austria and Germany, was Mozart's birthplace. After composing more than 600 works, Mozart died at the early age of 35. He received few honors and died poor.

But Mozart's work will never die. You may enjoy hearing some of his operas, such as *The Magic Flute* and *The Marriage of Figaro* (fēg′ə rō). The city of Salzburg is now famous for its yearly Mozart festival.

Schubert, and His Songs

Many persons think that Franz Schubert (sho͞o′bərt) is the musician who best represents Vienna. Schubert wrote chamber music and symphonies, but he is chiefly remembered for his tuneful songs. The world still sings Schubert's songs. He died when he was only 31 years of age.

Strauss, the "Waltz King"

No doubt you have heard the "Beautiful Blue Danube Waltz" many times. This famous waltz was written by Johann Strauss (yō′hän strous′). It was meant for people to dance to, and it succeeded! Even today Johann Strauss is called the "Waltz King."

Liszt, and His Folk Dances

Franz Liszt (list), of Hungary, had two musical talents. He played the piano wonderfully well. He also put the tunes of Hungarian folk dances into musical works that all Europe loved. His Hungarian melodies are still popular.

Do You Know?

1. Why did Austria and Hungary unite to form a twin empire?
2. What river flowed through the empire?
3. What happened to the empire after World War I?
4. Who was Mozart? Schubert? Liszt?

Before You Go On

Using New Words

canton	international
pass	League of Nations

Number a paper from 1 through 4. After each number write the word or term that matches the definition.

1. An international organization, formed after World War I, of nations interested in preventing war
2. A term that means "among nations"
3. A natural path through a mountain range
4. A Swiss district or state

Finding the Facts

1. Which countries in Central Europe have valuable minerals?
2. Which country has the most natural resources?
3. What are three important rivers in Central Europe? Through what countries do they flow?
4. What is the Swiss Federal Assembly?
5. Why are Swiss laws printed in different languages?
6. How does the Red Cross Society help prisoners of war?
7. How do the Swiss make a living?
8. How was Austria-Hungary involved in World War I?
9. What is the highest mountain in the Alps?
10. What is the largest lake in Switzerland?
11. Who were the Huns? Who were the Magyars?
12. What happened to Austria after World War II?
13. What attracts tourists to Austria?
14. Why do people remember Franz Josef Haydn and Johann Strauss?

4

The Story of Czechoslovakia

Czechoslovakia occupies a region that is rich in raw materials. It is also a region that has known many conquerors.

The Early History of the Czechs

At one time the land of the Czechs was called Bohemia (bō hēm′ē ə). It was protected by mountains on three sides. On the southwest were the highlands of the Bohemian Forest. To the northwest were the Ore Mountains. On the northeast rose the Sudeten (so͞o dāt′ən).

Who Are the Czechs?

The people of Bohemia were Slavs. They had come from the eastern plains of Europe, the land later called Russia. Pressing westward, they reached the Baltic Sea and the Adriatic Sea.

The land of the Czechs, almost surrounded by mountains, was a natural fortress. The kingdom of Bohemia grew strong. The Moravians (mor āv′ē ənz), a people living to the east, united with the Bohemians. During the Middle Ages important trade routes passed through Prague (präg), the Bohemian capital. One of the oldest universities in Europe was established in Prague. The people of the country were known to the world as Bohemians, but they called themselves Czechs.

This view from the Old Town Hall shows some of the buildings in the historic center of Prague, the capital city of Czechoslovakia.

The Religion of the Czechs

Some of the Czechs did not agree with all of the teachings of the Catholic Church. When their religious leader, John Huss, was burned at the stake, the people rose in rebellion.

After a time most of the Czechs again became Catholics. But some followers of Huss set up their own church. They called themselves the Moravian Brethren. Later many Moravians settled in Pennsylvania and Texas.

The Czechs Under Hapsburg Rule

Unfortunately the Czechs quarreled among themselves. They lost their strength. Finally they came under Hapsburg rule.

After a time the Czechs rebelled against the Hapsburg emperor and chose a Protestant king. His reign was short. After one year the Hapsburg army defeated the Czechs. The Czechs lost most of their rights. But they never gave up their desire to be free.

Czechoslovakia as a Nation

Bohemia was under the rule of the Hapsburgs until 1918, when Austria-Hungary was defeated in World War I.

At the end of World War I, the Czechs were freed. A new nation was created by the treaty of peace following that war. It was given the name of Czechoslovakia. It occupied a long narrow piece of land, taken partly from Austria and partly from Hungary. Besides Bohemia and Moravia, Czechoslovakia included Slovakia and Ruthenia (roo thēn′ē ə). It reached as far east as the Carpathian Mountains.

The new nation was a mixed group of people. Half of the 15 million inhabitants were Czechs, about one-fourth were Germans, and one-sixth were Slovaks. Each group spoke its own native language. Czechoslovakia's task was to unite these different peoples, just as Switzerland had united its people.

Prosperous Czechoslovakia

The Czechs were the natural leaders of the new nation. They had great respect for education, for they realized that only educated people can make progress.

So many languages were spoken in Czechoslovakia, it was hard to provide schools for all. But the Czechs managed to open schools for the children of the different language groups.

Before World War I, Bohemia made most of the manufactured articles used in Austria-Hungary. The Czechs now set to work to develop even more industries. They had coal and iron, forests and farmland, and they used these to good advantage.

Czechoslovakia exported sugar made from beets, beautiful glass and chinaware, machinery, chemicals, woven goods, and shoes. The people of Czechoslovakia became very skillful in producing beads, toys, and costume jewelry.

The Conquest by Hitler

For 20 years Czechoslovakia went its way, following the motto "We must educate ourselves and work." But to the north, Adolf Hitler was gaining power in Germany. Czechoslovakia stood between Hitler and the German-speaking country, Austria.

The Powder Tower still serves as an entrance to one section of Prague. This historic tower was constructed during the 1400s.

Hitler took over the land inhabited by the Germans of Czechoslovakia. These Germans wished to become a part of Germany, so they put up no defense. The Czechs were ready to fight Hitler, but France and Britain would not support them. France and Great Britain had decided to practice a policy of *appeasement* (ə pēz′ ment). Appeasement is a policy of giving in to a strong power in order to maintain peace. France and Great Britain thought that by giving in to Hitler they would discourage him from further aggression.

Hitler soon sent his troops into Prague and took over all of Bohemia and Moravia. The Germans set up concentration camps in Czechoslovakia where they imprisoned many Czechs. Hungary now took over Ruthenia.

The Rebirth of Czechoslovakia

Although Germany crushed Czechoslovakia, the people never gave up hope. When Hitler took over the country, their president escaped to London. During World War II, he encouraged his people to look for the day when they should again be free. Then in 1945, 6 years after the Germans had taken over the country, the Czechs were freed.

Changes in territory were made. Ruthenia, which had been only a small part of the old Czechoslovakia, was taken over by the Soviet Union. Bohemia, Moravia, and Slovakia were united in the new Czechoslovakia.

The Conquest by Russia

Soon after World War II the Communist party, which had been until then secretly at work in

Czechoslovakia, suddenly seized the government. The Communists did this with the help of the Soviet Union. They then did everything that the Soviets told them to. So, although Czechoslovakia was called a free country, it had really lost its freedom for the third time. It was now under the control of the Soviet Union.

Czechoslovakia Today

Czechoslovakia is one of the European countries which have Communist governments. Others are East Germany, Poland, Yugoslavia, Hungary, Romania, Bulgaria, and Albania. Find these nations on the map on page 445.

Czechoslovakia's mines, forests, farms, and factories continue to produce abundantly. Many of its products are exported to the Soviet Union.

In 1968, a more liberal Communist government came to power. But in a short time, the Russians restored the older, harsh type of Communist rule.

Famous People of Czechoslovakia

Some people of Czechoslovakia have been world famous. Among them were a teacher and a musician.

Comenius, a Great Teacher

In Moravia about 300 years ago there lived a poor boy, whose name was Johann Komensky (yō′hän kaw mən′skē). His name later was changed to Comenius (kə mē′nē əs). Johann grew up to become a minister of a church.

Comenius wanted to improve schools. He wrote books to help students learn. In some of his books pictures were added. These were the first picture books for school use.

Dvořák, a Great Composer

The city of Prague rivaled Vienna in its love for music. In Prague was born Anton Dvořák (än′tōn dvôr′zhäk), who made his native land famous in the world of music. He grew up among Bohemian peasants, and learned to love their folk songs so much that he used them in many of his musical works. Such pieces as "Moravian Duets" and "Gypsy Melodies" included the folk music played in the villages.

After gaining fame in Europe, Dvořák was invited to become director of a music school in New York. In a symphony, called *From the New World,* Dvořák used some of the American melodies that he had learned in this country. One of the best-loved melodies in the symphony is "Going Home."

Do You Know?

1. Where was the first homeland of the Czechs? To what group of people did they belong?
2. When and how did Czechoslovakia become a nation?
3. How did it become prosperous?
4. Who were some famous Czechs?

5

The Story of Poland

About 300 miles (480 km) northeast of Prague is the large city of Warsaw. It stands in a fertile plain on the bank of the Vistula River (vis′chə lə). More than once Warsaw has been partly ruined by enemy attacks. It is the capital of Poland.

Poland's Early History

Just before our country gained its freedom from England, the kingdom of Poland was a large and important country. By 1770 Poland had grown weak. This was because the country lacked natural boundaries and its people disagreed among themselves.

The map of Central Europe on page 445 shows that Poland lies on the north central plain of Europe. On the north it stretches out to the Baltic, where the city of Gdansk gives Poland a seaport. To the east and the west Poland has no natural boundaries, such as mountains or bodies of water. Because of Poland's position, it has always been difficult to defend the borders against enemies.

The Government of Poland

In addition to the Poles, Poland was made up of Germans, Russians, and others. These groups disagreed among themselves. To keep order, Poland needed a strong government. But the government was weak.

The Polish king had little power. He was elected by the Polish national assembly, which was made up of nobles. Meetings often broke up in disorder. The Poles could not seem to agree or work together. Poland grew weaker and weaker.

The Division of Poland

Three powerful neighbors of Poland realized that the country was weak. These countries were Austria, Prussia, and Russia. They decided that each of them would take some Polish territory. Poland was so weak that between 1772 and 1795 the invaders simply divided the country as they saw fit.

Austria took over southwestern Poland. Prussia had the Baltic lands, with the city of Danzig (dan′sig) (or Gdansk, as the Poles called it). Russia got the greatest part of what used to be Polish territory.

Poland in Modern Times

In 1918, after World War I, the Allies made Poland a nation again nearly 150 years after it had been divided.

The Republic of Poland

The new Poland reached to the Baltic, into which the Vistula flows. Danzig was inhabited by Germans, not Poles. But Poland needed "a window on the Baltic," and Danzig was that window. A strip of land 50 miles (80 km) wide, laid out through German territory, gave the Poles a road to Danzig. This narrow strip of land was called the Polish *Corridor* (kor′ə dər). A corridor is a passageway.

Most of the land of the new Poland was farming country. But in the part which had belonged to Germany there were many factories.

The first head of the new republic was Ignace Paderewski (ēn yäs′ pad′ə ref′ skē), a Polish patriot. He was also one of the world's greatest pianists. Poland began to prosper. Some of the large estates were divided among the peasants. The city of Lodz (looj) became the center of the Polish textile industry.

The new country had received about one-fourth of Germany's coalfields. This enabled Poland to smelt iron and to carry on manufacturing. It had rich zinc mines. Zinc, melted with copper, makes brass. It is also used to make paints.

The Problems of Poland

The new nation had many problems to meet. The Polish people were not united. They spoke different languages. Germany and the Soviet Union were unfriendly to the new nation. So many political parties grew up that none was strong enough to elect officers to govern the nation. After a while a military government took control of the country.

In the late 1930s, Hitler's government in Germany demanded that some land, including Danzig, should be returned to Germany. Six months after invading Czechoslovakia in 1939, German soldiers marched into Poland.

Great Britain and France had promised to aid Poland in case it was attacked. They declared war on Germany. But they were so far away that their armies could not reach the Poles in time to help them. In a few weeks the Polish army was defeated. Warsaw was in ruins.

Poland has large coal deposits, and mining plays an important role in the nation's economy.

When Germany had almost finished conquering Poland, the Soviet soldiers marched in and took over eastern Poland. Now the country was divided for a fourth time. Western Poland was held by the Germans and eastern Poland by the Soviet Union. In western Poland the Nazis set aside special camps. Jews and all other Poles who could not be used as laborers were crowded together in these concentration camps. Hundreds of thousands died or were killed.

The old part of Warsaw, above, was destroyed during World War II and rebuilt afterward. The new parts of Warsaw, right, include many modern buildings.

Poland After World War II

At the end of World War II, Poland again became free. But the nation was not the same as it had been. Millions of Poles had died while German troops occupied the country. There had been several million Jews in Poland and now only a small number were left.

The Soviet Union held the Polish territory that its soldiers had taken over early in the war. In return, the Allies agreed that Poland was to have the eastern part of Germany up to the Oder River.

The new Poland was smaller than before the war, but its people were almost all Polish. It now included the whole course of the Vistula River between Czechoslovakia and the Baltic. It had Danzig (renamed Gdansk by the Poles) and other good ports, together with a stretch of seacoast. This change meant moving many Germans out of the new Poland and bringing in many Poles. This region is rich in resources and industries.

Poland Today

Since World War II, Poland has lived under a Communist government. Its capital is at Warsaw, but its policies are often directed by the Soviet Union. In 1956 many Polish people showed their bitter dislike of their rulers by rioting. Soldiers quickly put down the rebellion, but the people did win a small victory. After their revolt, they found the Communist rulers a little less harsh. In 1980, there were again riots and strikes to demand more rights. The government allowed a labor union called Solidarity to be established in 1980. But Solidarity was outlawed in 1982.

Poland produces machinery, textiles, and iron and steel. It has large coal deposits.

Some Famous Polish People

Poland has had a number of people who are world famous. Among them are scientists, musicians, writers, and religious leaders.

Copernicus, a Great Astronomer

About the time that Columbus discovered America, a Polish lad of 18 entered the University of Cracow (krak′ou), in Poland. His name was Nikolaus Copernicus (nik′ə lā′əs kə pur′ni kəs). Later Copernicus was made a professor of mathematics in Rome. At that time most people believed that the earth was the center of the universe, around which the sun, moon, and stars revolved.

Copernicus wrote a book on the motions of the heavenly bodies. He stated that the earth and the other planets moved about the sun. Other scholars followed his ideas in studying the heavenly bodies. Copernicus, a Pole, thus became the "father of modern astronomy."

Chopin, a Master Musician

Frederic Chopin (fred′ər ik shō′pan) was born near Warsaw. While a child, he showed great talent for playing the piano. As he grew older, he gave concerts in Prague and Vienna. Finally he settled in Paris.

Chopin's music was written chiefly for the piano. It is filled with the rhythm of Polish dances.

Joseph Conrad, a Famous Novelist

A Polish boy wandered away from home at the age of 13 and became a sailor. After his ship visited England, he began to study English. He had read Shakespeare's plays in Polish. Then he learned to read them in English. Twenty years later, while recovering from a fever, he wrote the story of some of his adventures at sea.

The author's name was Jozef Konrad Korzeniowski (jō′zef kon′rad kô′zhən yôf′skē). Later he dropped his last name and was known as Joseph Conrad. His books are based on his own experiences. They are tales of the sea and faraway lands and people. He is one of the world's greatest writers of adventure stories.

Pope John Paul II, Religious Leader

Karol Wojtyla (kä′rōl wō tē′yə) was born in Poland in 1920. He became a priest and later an archbishop. He pursued the craft of poetry throughout his religious training. In 1978 he was elected Pope, the head of the Catholic Church. He changed his name to John Paul II. The Pope lives and works in Vatican City, near Rome. Pope John Paul greeted millions of people when he visited the United States, Poland, and other countries in 1979 and 1980. He speaks to world leaders about the need for human rights and religious freedom. The people of Poland are very proud of John Paul, the first Polish Pope.

Do You Know?

1. What natural boundaries did Poland have when it was a great nation?
2. When did Poland become a republic?
3. What large cities are on the Vistula River?

To Help You Learn

Using New Words

canton	international
pass	League of Nations
corridor	appeasement

Number a paper from 1 through 6. After each number write the word or term that matches the definition.

1. An international organization, formed after World War I, of nations interested in preventing war
2. A passageway
3. A term that means "among nations"
4. A natural path through a mountain range
5. A Swiss district or state
6. The policy of giving in to a strong power in order to maintain peace.

Finding the Facts

1. What natural resources does Switzerland have? How do the Swiss use them?
2. What minerals does Austria have?
3. Why is Hungary a good farming area?
4. What natural resources have enabled Czechoslovakia to build up industries?
5. How did Switzerland gain freedom? What kind of government does it have?
6. Name three Swiss cities. Give one important fact about each.
7. What international societies make their home in Switzerland?
8. What happened to Austria-Hungary after its defeat in World War I?
9. How did Austria unite with Germany?
10. Who were the Magyars?
11. What are Hungary's chief products?
12. What kind of government does Hungary have? What happened there in 1956?
13. Describe Poland's government today.
14. Name four famous Polish people. Why do we remember them?
15. How did Czechoslovakia lose its freedom?
16. What two countries divided Poland after 1939?
17. Who was Paderewski?
18. What is the largest country in Central Europe?

Learning from Maps

1. Turn to the map of Central Europe on page 445. What are the five countries of Central Europe and their capitals?
2. Turn again to the map of Central Europe on page 445. What rivers are important highways of trade through these countries? Where are the best farming areas? Which country has the least amount of land suitable for farming? Why?

Using Study Skills

1. **Time Line:** Place the following events in the proper order of time: Czechoslovakia becomes a nation for second time; First road built through St. Gotthard Pass; Hungary revolts against Communist government; Austria and Hungary united; Austria added to Germany; World War I begins.

   Copy the time line from page 443. Add these events to your time line.
2. **Chart:** Make a chart showing the area, population, and capital city of each Central European country. Use the Reference Table on page 592 to help you. Then answer these questions: Which country has the largest population? The smallest? Which has the largest area?

Thinking It Through

1. The Red Cross, which began in Switzerland, is now worldwide. How does the American Red Cross help people?
2. Why are Polish-Americans proud of Pulaski and Kosciusko? You will find the stories of these men in an American history book and in the encyclopedia.
3. At different times in their history, both Poland and Czechoslovakia were weakened because they quarreled among themselves. What happened to each country as a result?

Projects

1. For hundreds of years people could travel across the Alps only through mountain passes. In 1964 the Great St. Bernard tunnel, a two-lane tunnel leading from Switzerland to Italy, was opened. The Research Committee might use the library to find out how the tunnel was built and how it helps trade in Europe.
2. Plan a music festival. Divide into small groups. Use records or tapes of music by Mozart, Schubert, Chopin, Johann Strauss, and Dvořák. Introduce each composer by presenting some facts about his life.
3. The Reading Committee could find out more about the legend of William Tell and share the story with the class.
4. The Explorers' Committee could find out about the first mountain climber to reach the top of the Matterhorn.
5. Some students might prepare a program of Central European folk songs and dances.

16 Union of Soviet Socialist Republics

Unit Preview

No other country in the world covers as much land area as the Union of Soviet Socialist Republics. This country, also called the Soviet Union, was known as Russia until the Communists took over the government in 1917.

The Ural Mountains divide the European part of the Soviet Union from the Asian part. You can see on the map the long coastline on the Arctic Ocean. As most of the Arctic Ocean is frozen over most of the year, Russia has always been interested in getting year-round ports.

The people who first settled northeastern Europe also settled Russia. The Tartars invaded Russia from eastern Asia. Under Ivan the Great, the Tartars were expelled and pushed back to Asia. Under Czar Ivan the Terrible, Russia began to expand to the east and to the west. By 1680 Russian power had reached the Pacific Ocean. Czar Peter the Great continued Russia's expansion and also tried to make the country more modern, like the other nations in Europe. He was also a great builder of cities. With Peter, Western ideas began to reach Russia. But the life of the common people did not improve. For this reason, the people revolted in 1917.

Today, the Soviet Union is a major industrial country. New factories are being built east of the Ural Mountains. This area's natural resources are being developed.

Things to Discover

If you look carefully at the picture, map, and time line on these pages, you can answer these questions.

1. On what continents is the Soviet Union located?
2. What people invaded the Russian states? How long did they stay in power?
3. Who was Russia's first czar? How long did the czars rule? Who followed them in power?
4. The picture shows a church in the city now called Leningrad. The city used to be known as St. Petersburg. When was St. Petersburg founded? Who founded it?
5. When did the Soviet Union send the first satellite into space? How many years later did the United States and the Soviet Union work together on a space project?

Words to Learn

You will meet these words in this unit. As you read, you will learn what they mean and how to pronounce them. The Word List will help you.

asbestos	platinum
ballet	socialist
Bolshevik	soviet
collective	steppe
czar	Tartar
iron curtain	tundra
magnesium	

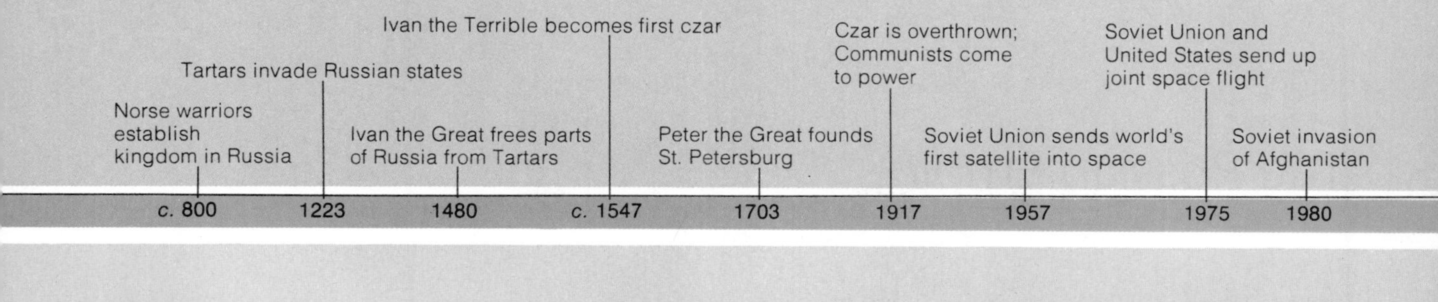

EUROPE

Atlantic Ocean

ASIA

Pacific Ocean

AFRICA

Indian Ocean

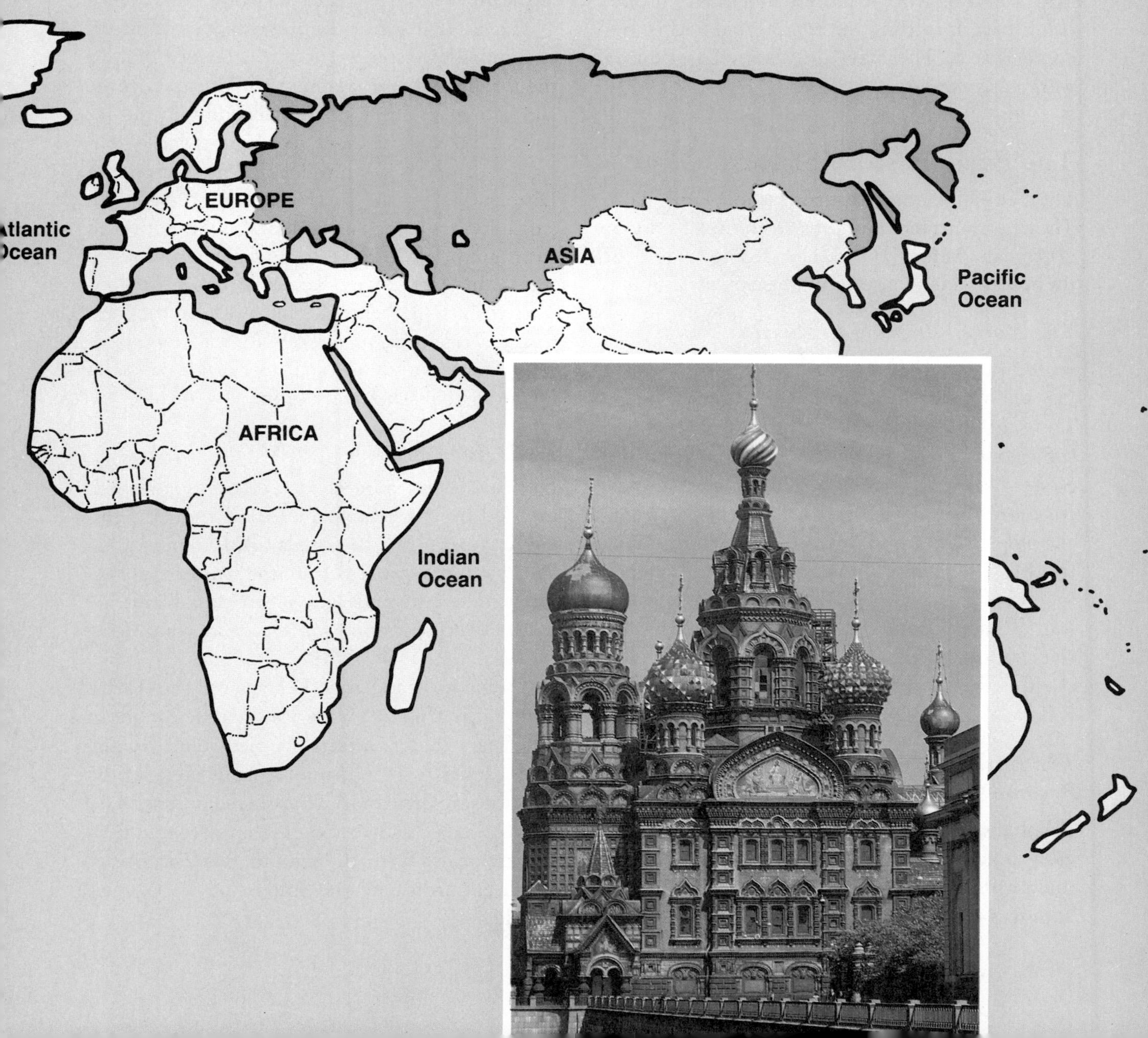

1
The Russian Empire

The Vikings, who explored much of Europe, had a part in settling the region that was to become Russia. The Slavs of eastern Europe also were early settlers.

The Early History of Russia

The people of northeastern Europe were Slavs. They began to move into western Europe about 200 years before the fall of Rome. Some of them settled in what is now the Soviet Union.

The Norse Kingdom in Russia

In the 800s a bold Norse leader named Rurik led his warriors into the land of the Slavs. They established a kingdom at Novgorod (nōv′gô rôt). Find Novgorod on the map of the Soviet Union on page 473. This kingdom lasted for more than 300 years.

Some of Rurik's followers explored the country. Moving inland, they arrived at the Dnieper (nē′pər) River, on which they traveled southward. They conquered the Slavs along that river, took possession of Kiev (kē′yef), and made it the capital of the Norse possessions in Russia.

The Early Russians Become Christians

Throughout southern Russia little governments grew up, some Norse, some Slav. They were ruled by dukes and princes. One powerful kingdom was that of Kiev.

In the 980s the ruler of Kiev was Prince Vladimir (vlad′ə mir). Representatives of different religious groups tried to convert him to their religions. He listened to Muslims, Jews, and Roman Catholics. After listening to the reports of people he sent to observe these religions, Prince Vladimir decided to accept the Eastern Orthodox faith. He was impressed with stories about the great cathedral of St. Sophia in Constantinople and the beautiful ceremonies of the faith. Also, many Russians had trade contacts with the Byzantine empire where the faith was practiced. Soon after Vladimir converted, many Russians followed. Later, many beautiful Orthodox churches were built.

The Tartar Conquest of Russia

Before Russia had a chance to develop, it was invaded by powerful armies from the east. Beginning in 1223, vast armies of Mongols, called *Tartars* (tär′tərz), overran the eastern plains. They rode across the grassy, treeless plains, or *steppes* (steps), conquering and destroying along the way.

Unable to stand together against the Tartar armies, the Russians were conquered. For about 200 years these Eastern peoples ruled Russia. The Tartars were not interested in developing the cities or farmlands. They were content to let the Russians do so, as long as they received tribute, or taxes. With the tribute, the Tartars set up an empire called the empire of the Golden Horde.

UNION OF SOVIET SOCIALIST REPUBLICS
0 100 200 400 600 800 Miles
0 161 322 644 966 1287 Kilometers
National Capitals
Other Cities
Mountains
Hills
Plateaus
Plains
Permanent Ice Pack
ARCTIC OCEAN
ARCTIC CIRCLE
SVALBARD
BERING SEA
SEA OF OKHOTSK
Kamchatka Peninsula
Sakhalin
Kuril Islands
PACIFIC OCEAN
SOVIET UNION
SIBERIA
RUSSIA
TUNDRA
EUROPE
NOVGOROD
URAL MOUNTAINS
KAZAKHSTAN
UZBEKISTAN
TURKMENISTAN
KIRGHIZIA
TADZHIKISTAN
ESTONIA
LATVIA
LITHUANIA
BYELORUSSIA
UKRAINE
MOLDAVIA
GEORGIA
ARMENIA
AZERBAIJAN
CAUCASUS MTS.
BLACK SEA
CASPIAN SEA
ARAL SEA
Lake Balkhash
Lake Baikal
Ob River
Yenisey River
Lena River
Angara R.
Amur River
Volga River
Don
Dnepr
Ural River
Amu Darya
London
Paris
Bonn
Berlin
Oslo
Stockholm
Helsinki
Leningrad
Murmansk
Arkhangelsk
Moscow
Gorkiy
Odessa
Rostov
Sverdlovsk
Chelyabinsk
Novosibirsk
Vladivostok
Istanbul
Ankara
TURKEY
SYRIA
LEBANON
ISRAEL
Jerusalem
JORDAN
IRAQ
Baghdad
Basra
SAUDI ARABIA
IRAN
Tabriz
Tehran
Meshed
AFGHANISTAN
Kabul
Islamabad
Rawalpindi
Lahore
PAKISTAN
Indus R.
New Delhi
INDIA
Bombay
Calcutta
Ganges River
Bay of Bengal
NEPAL
Kathmandu
Mt. Everest 29,028 ft. (8080 m)
HIMALAYA MOUNTAINS
PLATEAU OF TIBET
Lhasa
BHUTAN
BANGLADESH
Dacca
Brahmaputra River
BURMA
Irrawaddy
Mandalay
Rangoon
THAILAND
LAOS
Hanoi
Mekong
VIETNAM
MONGOLIA
Ulan Bator
GOBI
CHINA
Huang River
Chang River
Beijing
Tianjin
Nanjing
Shanghai
Wuhan
Chongqing
Guangzhou
Victoria
HONG KONG
TAIWAN
SOUTH CHINA SEA
EAST CHINA SEA
YELLOW SEA
SEA OF JAPAN
N. KOREA
Pyongyang
S. KOREA
Seoul
Shenyang
JAPAN
Tokyo
Osaka
Kitakyūshū
PHILIPPINES
Manila
20°
40°
60°
80°
100°
120°
140°
160°
50°
30°
© Rand McNally & Co.

The Old Russian Empire

In about 1390 the empire of the Golden Horde itself was challenged from the east. A central Asian leader named Tamerlane (tam′ər lān) began attacking the Tartar settlements. By 1395 he had conquered the last Tartar stronghold. He withdrew to the south, leaving the Tartar empire mortally weakened.

The Independence of Russia

Under the leadership of Ivan, the Grand Duke of Moscow, the Russians in 1480 drove the Tartars back toward Asia. Ivan then took charge of the government set up by the Vikings many years earlier and laid the foundation of the Russian nation. He is sometimes called "Ivan the Great."

Russia's Growth into Asia

In the 1500s another ruler by the name of Ivan came to power. He is called "Ivan the Terrible." As a warrior Ivan was merciless, often killing the people of whole villages. In the late 1540s he became Russia's first *czar* (zär), from the Latin name Caesar, meaning "emperor." Czars were the emperors of Russia until 1917.

The nobles of the czar's court imitated the Tartars who had governed Russia so long. They wore long Chinese robes and turbans, making the court seem more Asian than European.

Ivan brought about many changes which curbed the power of the nobles. He enlarged the borders of Russia eastward. The Volga became a Russian river.

The land east of the Ural (yo͞or′əl) Mountains was held by many roaming Mongol tribes. One of these tribes had its center at a place called Sibir (sə bēr′). Rich traders of Russia received Ivan's permission to make war against this tribe. The traders gained the victory and sent word to the czar in 1582 that Sibir now belonged to him. The city of Tobolsk (tə bôlsk′) stands where Sibir once stood, and the entire region is called Siberia.

From that time on, explorers and fur traders pushed eastward. In fewer than 100 years, they carried Russian power across Asia to the Pacific.

The Rule of Peter the Great

Peter I, known as "Peter the Great," was one of Russia's most influential rulers. As a boy, he lived in a part of Moscow where many Europeans lived. There he met English, French, and German artists and technicians who worked for the czar. Fascinated by what he heard, he began to travel to Western Europe. He saw that Russia lagged behind the West in industry and modern warfare.

Soon after he came to the throne, Peter sent 50 young Russians to England, the Netherlands, and Italy to learn European ways. Then he went to the Netherlands himself and studied shipbuilding, navigation, and manufacturing. When he returned to Russia, he took with him a group of people skilled in many lines of work. Russia was to become a modern nation.

It took all of Peter's energy to carry out his plans for Russia. He tortured and killed thousands of those who opposed him. He ordered the Russian nobles to shave off their bushy beards. He made them put on European clothes instead of the long robes worn since the time of the Tartars. He dropped the Old Russian calendar and replaced it with the Roman, or Julian, calendar which we learned about in Unit 6.

Russia's Seaport on the Baltic

When Peter became czar, Russia had no seaport leading to the ocean. The nation was shut off from the Baltic Sea because Sweden held the land along the Baltic. Without such a seaport Russia could not trade or take part in world affairs. Peter made war on Sweden, conquered its army, and seized the strip of land on the Baltic. Russia now had a "window" toward the West.

St. Petersburg, the New Capital

Peter wanted the world to know Russia as a Western power. He also wanted to show Russia's hold on the Baltic Sea. To do so, in 1703 he ordered a new capital to be built.

The waters of Lake Ladoga reach the Gulf of Finland and the Baltic Sea by means of a short river known as the Neva (nē′və). Near the river's mouth, Peter began to build a city. The land around it was low and swampy. There was plenty of timber nearby, but no stone.

As in Venice, the land was so marshy that long poles, or piles, had to be driven into the ground to support the heavy buildings. In 10 years Peter had a fine capital. He called the new city St. Petersburg, after himself. The city is now called Leningrad (len′in grad), after V. I. Lenin, the Soviet leader.

Russia's Seaport on the Black Sea

Peter wanted to extend his country as far south as the Black Sea, but he was not able to drive out the Turks. Later on, however, Russia did gain a seaport on that sea and so secured a second "window" from which to look out on the world. Before he died, Peter knew that Russia was on the way to becoming a strong nation.

Writers of Old Russia

About 200 years after the death of Peter the Great, Russia had a period when great literature was produced. Several writers of this time became world famous.

Alexander Pushkin

One of the brightest stars in Russian literature is Alexander Pushkin. In his short life he wrote

A statue of Alexander Pushkin stands in Pushkin Square in Leningrad. A master of realism, he is often called the founder of modern Russian literature.

many of Russia's finest poems, novels, and plays. Because of some of his beliefs, the Russian government sent him away to southern Russia. During his 4 years there he learned to write better than ever. The government welcomed him back and paid him to write the life of Peter the Great. When he was killed in a duel, there was great sorrow.

Leo Tolstoy

One of the best known Russian novelists is Leo Tolstoy. His finest book is *War and Peace.* It tells of Napoleon's attack on Russia, a bitter war in which the French army was finally defeated.

Tolstoy was more interested in showing the awful effects of war than he was in telling about a Russian victory. Tolstoy, though a noble, also had sympathy for the peasants. He dressed like them, set up schools for them, and did all he could to help them.

The *ballet* of Russia is admired throughout the world. Here in Moscow a Russian dancer is honored after a performance of the *Nutcracker Suite*.

Musicians of Old Russia

In most parts of Europe, composers learned their trade by writing music for the church. But in Russia the Eastern Orthodox church did not allow the playing of music in church. Russian composers thus were at a disadvantage. By the middle of the 1800s, however, Russian composers began to gain world attention.

Peter Ilyich Tchaikovsky

One famous Russian composer was Peter Ilyich Tchaikovsky (il′yich chī kôf′skē). His symphonies, operas, and music for dance are played often by orchestras around the world. He wrote more than 100 separate pieces of music. One work you may have heard is the *Nutcracker Suite.*

Nikolai Rimsky-Korsakov

Another fine Russian composer was Nikolai Rimsky-Korsakov (nik′ə lī rim′skē kôr′sə kôf′). The spirit of the Russian folk songs runs through his melodies. They are often lively tunes. Perhaps you have heard his *Flight of the Bumble Bee,* which sounds very much like the humming of a bee. One of his best works, based on *The Arabian Nights,* is called *Scheherazade* (shə her′ə zäd′).

The Russian Ballet

The Russian *ballet* (ba lā′) is known all over the world. A ballet is a dance that tells a story through graceful movements accompanied by music. A ballet is sometimes given as a program in itself. Ballets are also often performed as part of an opera or between acts of an opera or play. Ballet dancers are highly trained and have to begin studying while still very young.

The best Russian painters made scenery for the stage on which the ballets were presented. The result was a fine combination of music, dancing, color, and acting.

The ballet reached its greatest glory in Russia in the work of Anna Pavlova (pav lō′ və). Anna entered the ballet school at the court of the czar when she was 10. She learned rapidly, and soon was making up her own dance patterns. She toured the United States and Europe, where she delighted audiences. Later she formed her own dance company.

Anna Pavlova's most famous ballet performance was in *Swan Lake.* In it, as she danced to music, she portrayed a dying swan. The Russians still excel in ballet dancing. Their performers are much admired.

Do You Know?

1. Which people invaded Russia from the West in the 1200s?
2. What did Ivan the Great and Ivan the Terrible do for Russia?
3. Why did Peter the Great want a "window" toward the West? Did he get it?
4. Who was Leo Tolstoy? Anna Pavlova? Peter Tchaikovsky?

2
How the Soviet Union Developed

The Soviet Union, or the Union of Soviet Socialist Republics, covers nearly one-sixth of the earth's surface. It is two and one-half times as large as the United States. It is sometimes called the U.S.S.R.

Geography of the Soviet Union

The Soviet Union is bounded on the north by the Arctic Ocean. On the south its boundaries are formed by the high Caucasus (kô′kə səs) Mountains and the Caspian and Black seas. It reaches from the Baltic Sea, on the west, across Europe and Asia to the Pacific, on the east.

Its eastern coast is divided from North America only by the Bering Strait. At this point fewer than 60 miles (96 km) separate the Soviet Union from Alaska.

Surface and Climate

The map of the Soviet Union on page 473 shows that the great mass of land making up the Soviet Union is mostly a plain. The plain covers

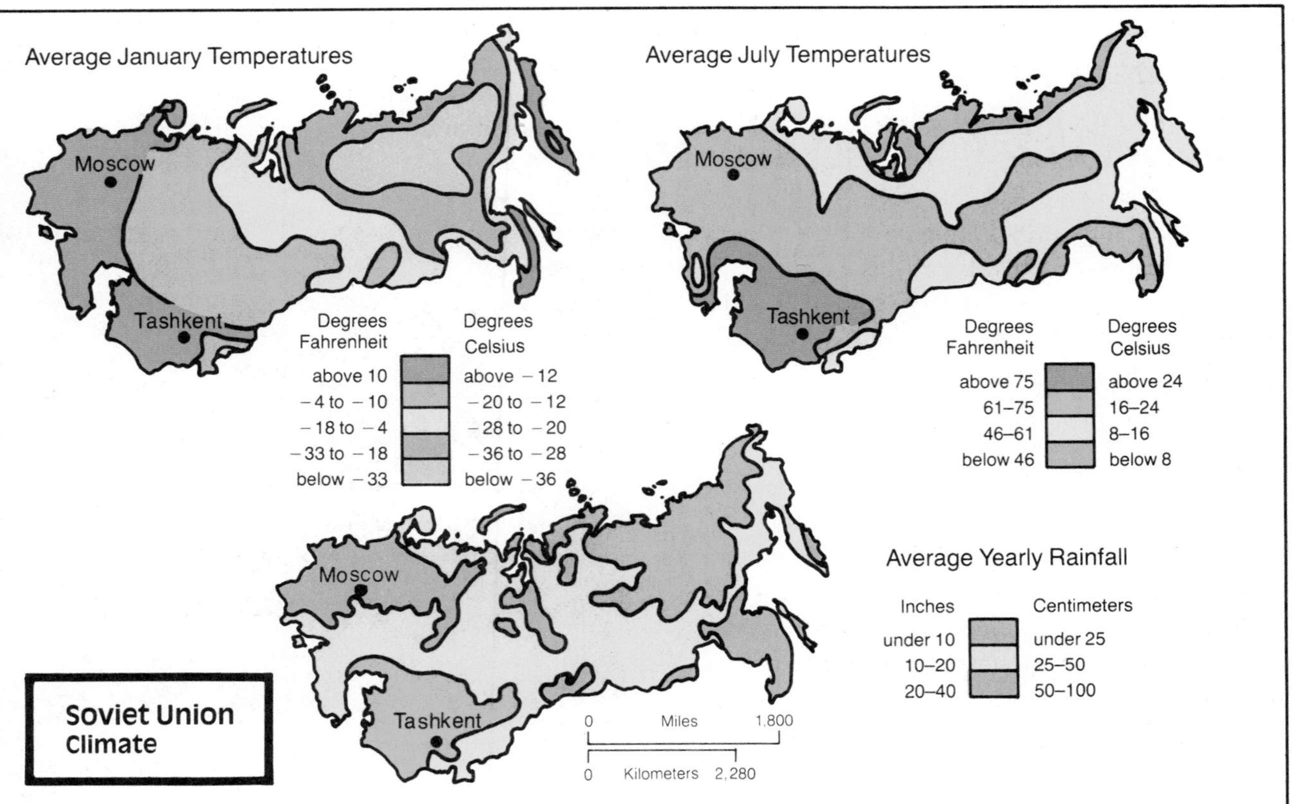

Soviet Union Climate

the northern part of Asia and northern Europe.

The only important break in the plain is made by the Ural Mountains. Find these mountains on the map on page 473. East of the Urals is Asia. The Urals are not high or difficult to cross.

The Soviet Union is so large that it has every kind of climate except a tropical one. The weather in some parts is like that of the far north of Canada. Other regions have the kinds of climate that are found in the different areas of the United States. Most of the land is not densely populated.

People and Languages

The Soviet Union is the home of many different peoples. More than half of the people live in the European part of the Soviet Union. Most of these people are Slavs and they speak Russian, a Slavic language. The Asian part is inhabited by many Oriental peoples. More than 170 languages are spoken in the Soviet Union. Russian is used by the largest number of people and is taught in schools to all children.

The Russian Revolution

In Old Russia the czars, the nobles, and a few other people were wealthy. They led comfortable lives. The rest of the people were poor and uneducated. Reforms, or improvements, were made at times, but most Russians remained poor. The czar ruled Russia much as he pleased.

There were some people, however, who had other ideas of how Russia should be governed. They thought that the government should own and operate the factories, farms, railroads, and mines. These people were known as *socialists* (sō′shə lists). Some of the socialists were willing to have the changes which they sought come about gradually. Others wanted to bring about the changes all at once by revolution.

How the Revolution Began

In 1914, when World War I broke out, Russia declared war on Austria and Germany. At first, the Russians were successful against Austria, but later Germany crippled the Russian armies. While Russian soldiers were being killed in battle, there was great suffering in many of the Russian cities.

A severe shortage of food in St. Petersburg brought matters to a head. The city workers went on strike. The soldiers who were ordered to fire on the strikers refused to do so. A revolution began. Officials of the czar were removed from office, and some were imprisoned.

The czar, who now realized that the army was not on his side, gave up his throne. The czar and his family were put in prison and later shot.

A Short-Lived Republic

After the czar lost his throne, Alexander Kerensky (kə ren′skē) became the head of the government. Kerensky and a group working with him established a republic. They hoped to build a government in which the people of Russia would have a part.

The republic, however, lasted for only a short time. Some of the socialists wished to change the government more swiftly and completely. In the fall of 1917 they overthrew the republic.

Lenin and the Bolsheviks wanted Russia's wealth to be divided equally among all its people. In taking power, however, they did not treat everyone fairly.

Results of the Revolution

The people were tired of war. So Russia made peace with Germany and the nations fighting on Germany's side. Russia lost one-fourth of its land and more than half of its coal and iron.

Soviets (sō′ vē ets′), or councils made up of peasants, workers, and soldiers, took over the government. The soviets became powerful. In the end, a revolutionist known as V. I. Lenin became the head of the government. The followers of Lenin were called *Bolsheviks* (bōl′ shə viks). The Bolsheviks under Lenin seized the property of the rich. The nobles were stripped of their wealth, and their land was given to the peasants. Some nobles were shot. Many were imprisoned or sent to Siberia, a harsh, cold region in the north of Russia. Others fled from the country. Secret police roamed the country and cities, spying on those who opposed the Bolsheviks.

Organization of the Soviet Union

The Bolsheviks now called themselves Communists and waved a red flag as their sign of revolution. On the flag was a hammer and a sickle, representing the workers and the peasants. St. Petersburg was no longer the capital, for it brought back memories of the czars. Moscow, the old capital, was made the center of government once again.

As time went on, the nation was divided into areas called Soviet republics. All together these republics form the Union of Soviet Socialist Republics. There are now 15 of these republics. Find them on the map of the Soviet Union on page 473.

How the Soviet Union Works

After Lenin died, Joseph Stalin (stä′ lin) headed the government. Stalin was a cruel dictator. Anyone who opposed him or his plans was killed or imprisoned. While he ruled, hundreds of thousands of people in the Soviet Union were killed.

The Five-Year Plans

Stalin set up a program of work which was to be finished within 5 years. By means of this "Five-Year Plan" Stalin hoped to make his country advance as most of the countries of Western Europe had done. During this period the people of the Soviet Union would learn to use the coal, oil, and water power of the nation. They would learn to use machinery, produce more food, and build schools.

To carry out this five-year plan, Stalin brought in experts from other lands. The Soviet people worked hard. They underwent great hardships because of the difficulty of obtaining food and housing in the new industrial centers. At the end of this five-year period the Soviet Union was on the way to becoming a manufacturing country.

Other five-year plans followed. By the end of the third plan, in 1943, the "machine age" had come to the Soviet Union. It had grown strong at a faster rate than anyone outside the country had dreamed possible.

Communism in the Soviet Union

The government is all-powerful in the Soviet Union. Under the Communist plan all workers are in the employ of the Soviet government. A highly skilled man or woman may earn better wages than a less skilled person. People may own such things as furniture and clothing, but cannot own businesses. All the factories, mills, mines, banks, railways, and telephone and telegraph systems belong to the nation. That is, they are said to belong to all the people.

The Soviet Union has only one party, the Communist Party. Citizens must either vote for candidates selected by the Communist Party

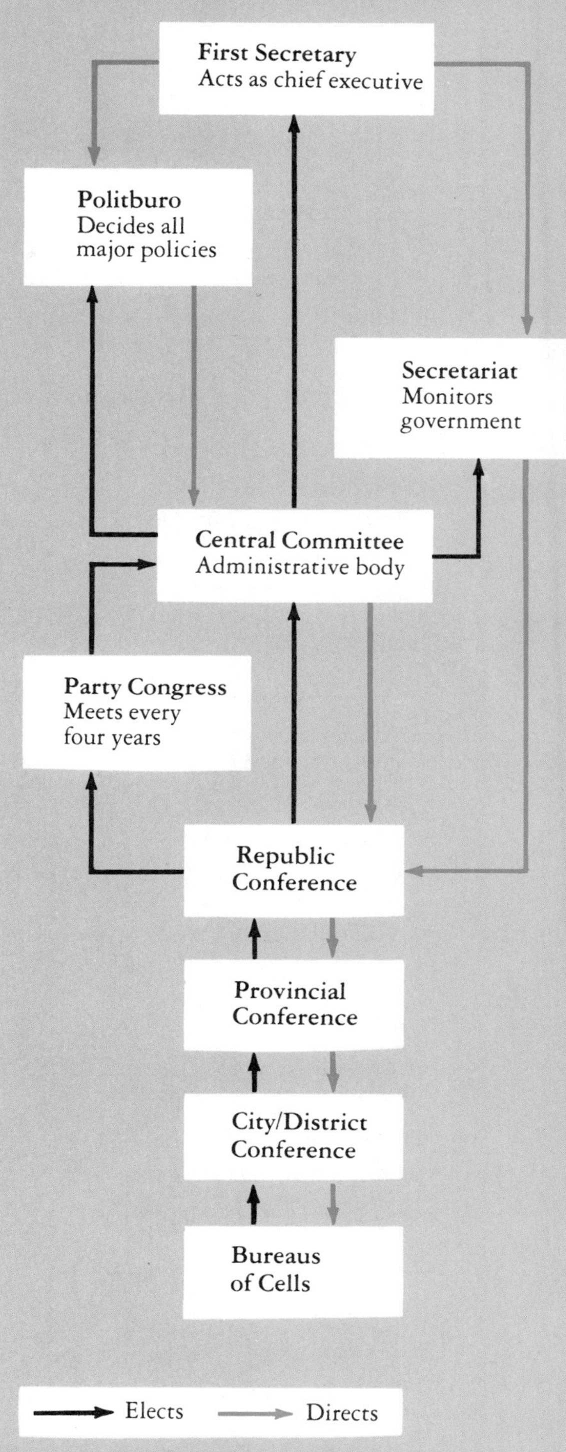

This chart shows the organization of the Communist Party. The arrows show how party members are chosen and directed. What levels choose the Central Committee? Who controls the entire party?

Soviet Union Government

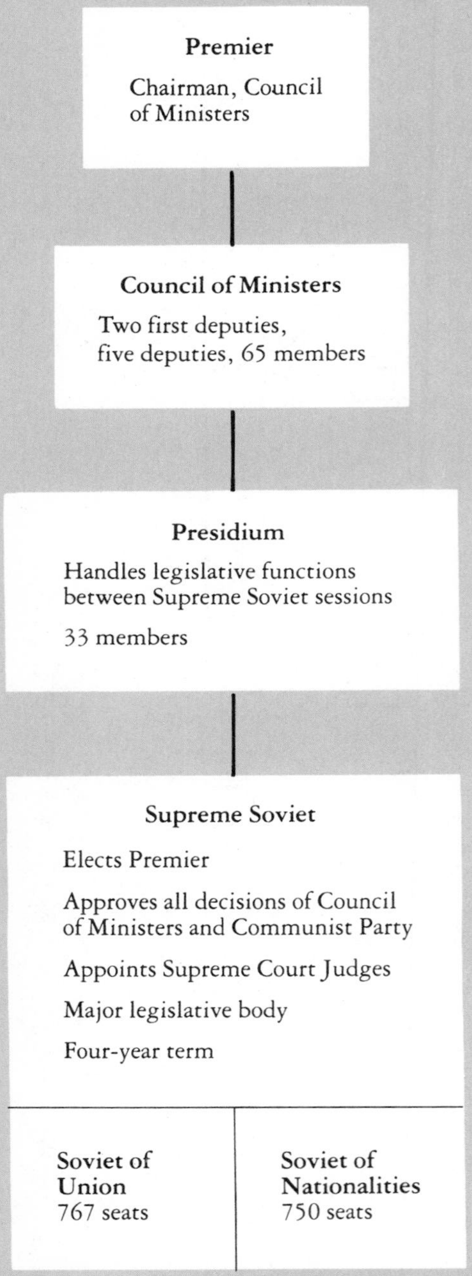

The government of the Soviet Union is led by the Premier. The Council of Ministers executes laws. What does the Supreme Soviet do?

or not vote. The people cannot criticize decisions made by their government. The party decides all important questions. Only a small percentage of people belong to the Communist Party.

The running of the government is in the hands of a small but powerful group. Stalin led this group until his death in 1953. After he died, there was a struggle for leadership for 3 years. In 1956 Nikita Khrushchev (ni kē′tə kroosh′chef) won.

He was replaced in 1964 by Leonid Brezhnev (lā′ō nēd brezh′nev) as Communist Party leader and by Aleksei Kosygin (ä lek′sā ko sē′gin) as the country's premier.

How Communism Differs from Democracy

The Communists want their country to lead the world in science, industry, and farming. They want the Soviet Union to be a truly modern nation. They also want the Soviet Union to have the world's most powerful armies. They are using their knowledge of science and their great natural resources to achieve these goals.

The people of the Soviet Union have no real choice in all this. The Communist leaders have the power to decide how the nation's resources will be used.

Americans, for example, have the right to vote for any party or candidate. In the Soviet

Union people can only vote for the candidates of the Communist Party.

Also in the United States there is freedom of the press. This means that newspapers may print what they consider to be the truth. In the Soviet Union only what the government considers to be the truth may be printed.

Thousands of workers are needed to harvest grain in the Soviet Union's vast fields. This land is part of a large *collective* farm.

Life on a Collective Farm

Many people of the Soviet Union live and work on large farms called *collectives* (kə lek′tivz). The collectives are owned and controlled by the government.

How the Collectives Started

Before the revolution, farmers cultivated their own pieces of land. The Communist governmend did away with the private ownership of land in 1928. Collectives were established to make the farming more efficient. The collectives followed some of the practices used by large farms in other countries. Now nearly all the farmlands of the Soviet Union belong to one large collective or another.

When some farmers tried to hold on to their land, they were executed. Others were sent to labor camps.

How Work Is Done on a Collective

The government decides what crops are planted on the collective and how many acres in each crop. The government supplies the tractors and other machines needed. Most of the crop is taken by the government. The rest is divided among the workers.

Family Farming

During World War II many families had private gardens and raised animals. This is against the Communist plan, but some family farming is still allowed.

Behind each house on the collective farm is a small piece of land which the members of the family may use. If the family can spare part of what they raise on this land, they sell it. The produce of the private plots accounts for a large part of Soviet farm output.

Do You Know?

1. How many republics make up the Soviet Union?
2. Who were the Bolsheviks? What are the Bolsheviks called today?
3. What were the "Five-Year Plans"? How were they carried out?
4. How does voting in the Soviet Union differ from voting in the United States?

Before You Go On

Using New Words

czar	steppe	soviet
collective	Tartar	Bolshevik
ballet	socialist	

Number a paper from 1 through 8. After each number write the word or term that matches the definition.

1. A dance that tells a story through graceful movements, accompanied by music
2. A large farm owned by the government
3. A council made up of peasants, workers, and soldiers
4. A grassy, treeless plain
5. The title of the Russian emperors from the time of Ivan the Terrible until 1917
6. A member of the tribe of Mongols who overran Russia's eastern plain in the 1200s
7. A person who thinks that the government should own and operate the factories, farms, railroads, and mines
8. A follower of Lenin

Finding the Facts

1. What two main groups of people first settled in Russia?
2. What is the name of the Christian religion first adopted in Russia?
3. What was the empire of the Golden Horde?
4. What Russian leader defeated the Tartars?
5. What Russian leader was responsible for gaining the territory now known as Siberia?
6. What is Russia's "window toward the West"? Who was responsible for building it?
7. What Russian author wrote about Russia's war with France?
8. Why did the development of Russian music at first lag behind that of Western European countries?
9. Who was Anna Pavlova?
10. What physical feature separates European Russia from Asian Russia?
11. What is the most widely spoken language in the Soviet Union?
12. How did World War I help to bring about the Russian Revolution?
13. Who led the Bolsheviks?
14. What is the name of the only political party in the Soviet Union?
15. Who in the Soviet Union decides what crops are to be planted on the collectives?
16. What two men succeeded Nikita Khrushchev as leaders of the Soviet Union?

3
Soviet Europe

The European part of the Soviet Union covers more than half of Europe. It is more than half the size of the United States. To go from its most northern point on the Arctic Ocean to the Caucasus Mountains on the south, a person would travel 2,000 miles (3,200 km).

The Geography of Soviet Europe

Most of the Soviet Union's European land is a great plain. In the north reindeer graze. In the south there are camels.

The Northern Plains

The northern plain is so cold that people cannot support themselves by farming. The part along the Arctic Ocean has almost no trees.

Tundra (tun′drə) is the name given to the treeless plains of the Arctic region. Moss, on which reindeer can feed, covers the tundra. For most of the year the surface of the earth is covered with snow. The reindeer dig away the snow with their hoofs and feed on the moss.

During the short summer the snow melts, but just below the surface the ground is still frozen. For this reason most of the water cannot soak in, and the region becomes a swamp.

South of the tundra are forests of evergreen trees. In the northern part of this forest the trees are small and scattered, but farther south the tree growth is thicker. Few people live in the far north.

The Forest Regions

From Leningrad southward the forest is different. The summers are longer here and the evergreen forest is mixed with broad-leaved trees such as oaks and birches. Many people live in these wooded areas. They have cleared away much of the forest so they can raise crops. This is called the Open Forest or Mixed Forest. Farmers in this region raise rye, oats, and potatoes. In winter, when the farmers cannot work in the fields, they cut down trees for lumber.

The Grasslands of the South

The southern part of Soviet Europe receives little rain. Trees grow only along the streams. Here are great steppes. The western part of the steppes, north of the Black Sea, has more rain than the eastern. There is not enough moisture for trees to grow well. But the farmers can raise wheat and big fields of sunflowers, whose seeds make good feed for animals.

Over a period of many years the long grass of the steppes has fallen to the ground and decayed. The decayed grass has enriched the ground and caused large areas of the western steppes to have fertile, black soil. These fertile steppes are much like our wide plains of Texas. Most of the collective farms are in this region.

Winters are colder than those of western Europe. In Moscow the ground freezes in October and stays frozen until April. Even in the far south, along the Black Sea, snow may lie on the ground for a month or more.

Moscow
Vital Hub of the Soviet Union

All the great changes that have occurred in the Soviet Union over the past 50 years are reflected in the city of Moscow. From Moscow the numerous railways and highways spread out to tie the huge country together. More industry is found in and around Moscow than in any other Soviet city. Factory workers turn out household appliances, foods, cloth, and other consumer goods.

Moscow is an exciting city with a lively interest in the arts. The Bolshoi (bul shoi′) ballet company and the Moscow Art Theater are famous throughout the world.

Most important, Moscow is the center of government for the Soviet Union. The Kremlin was built by the czars as a fortress. From behind its walls Soviet Union officials rule the nation. Here also are magnificent churches and government buildings. Outside the Kremlin there is an open area called Red Square where important celebrations are held. At one end of the square is GUM, a huge state-owned department store.

Moscow has many large squares and wide boulevards. During the long winters these streets and boulevards are covered with heavy snow. ■

The canal that flows through Leningrad connects the city with ocean trade routes. What can you identify that shows Leningrad's past?

The Largest Soviet Republic

Most of Soviet Europe is a part of the Russian Soviet Federated Socialist Republic. The capital of this republic is Moscow. This immense division stretches from the Baltic Sea on the west through the Ural Mountains, across Asia, to the Pacific. Leningrad and Moscow are its chief European cities, and the Volga is its great river in Europe. Find this republic and its cities on the map of the Soviet Union on page 473.

Leningrad, Old Russian Capital

In the days of the czars, the city of Leningrad was called St. Petersburg. It was the capital of the Russian Empire. It was famous for its fine palaces and its broad streets along the Neva River.

Today Leningrad is still an important city. It has about 4 million people. Because there is no coal or iron near the city, it has little heavy manufacturing. But skilled workers in its factories make many small things such as field glasses, watches, and electrical instruments. A ship canal connects Leningrad with the Baltic Sea, which leads to the Atlantic.

The Great River Volga

The Volga is the longest river in Europe. It flows south for about 2,300 miles (3,680 km). Find it on the map of the Soviet Union on page 473. When the water is not frozen, boats can travel for thousands of miles on the Volga and its branches.

On the Volga's banks are several large cities. The most important is Volgograd (vol′gə grad′), formerly Stalingrad. At Stalingrad, in one of the bloodiest battles of World War II, the Russian army turned back the German invaders.

Kiev, the capital of the Ukraine, is an important cultural center. Here is the Opera and Ballet Theater of Kiev. Many performances are staged here.

The Ukrainian Republic

On the shore of the Black Sea is the Soviet republic called the Ukraine (yo͞o krān′). Its capital is Kiev, on the Dnieper River.

The name "Ukraine" means "borderland." This border region protected the rest of the country from the Tartars and the Turks. Bands of Ukrainian horsemen, known as Cossacks, fought the invaders. The Cossacks, who were expert fighters, were famous in the defense of Russian borders.

The Ukraine was independent for a short time following the Russian Revolution. But in 1923 it became one of the republics of the Soviet Union.

Products of the Ukraine

The Ukraine is known as a "bread basket" because so much wheat is grown there. Most of the soil of this republic is so rich that it is black. Excellent crops can be raised on such soil. The Ukraine is also called a "sugar bowl," because so many sugar beets are grown here. Ukrainian farmers also raise vegetables and livestock.

The Ukraine is a center of coal and iron mining, too. Its coal deposits are immense. The Ukraine produces a large part of the Soviet Union's coal, steel, and machinery. It is an important industrial area.

People of the Ukraine

The Ukrainians are the second largest of the Slav groups. Their language is quite different from the language spoken by the people of Moscow.

Rivers of the Ukraine

Through the middle of the Ukraine flows the Dnieper River. The Ukrainians speak of it as "Father Dnieper."

The Dnieper River is the third largest in Europe. On the Dnieper the Soviets constructed

The capital of Estonia is the city of Tallin. Like many Soviet cities, Tallin has both old and new parts. This view of old Tallin shows the Baltic Sea.

an enormous dam. Then they built a chain of giant factories along the Dnieper to use electric power developed by the dam. When the Germans invaded the Soviet Union in World War II, the Soviets themselves blew up this dam so that the Germans could not use its resources.

On the Dnieper stands the city of Kiev. This city is one of the oldest in the Soviet Union. It is the capital of the Ukraine. Around the city are vegetable gardens and orchards. Kiev has many sugar refineries, for the city is almost surrounded by sugar beet fields. In World War II, many of the city's splendid parks, streets, and buildings were destroyed by German bombs. But the Ukrainians rebuilt Kiev from the ashes.

In the southeast the land rises to a rolling plateau through which the Donets (də nets′) River flows. The Donets basin contains the richest coal fields in Europe. Salt and mercury, lead, and zinc are also mined here.

Other Soviet Republics in Europe

Of the 15 republics which make up the Soviet Union, 9 lie entirely or partly on the continent of Europe.

Byelorussia

Northwest of the Ukraine is the republic of Byelorussia (byel′ō rush′ə). Byelorussia, also called White Russia, is a little larger than the state of Kansas.

Most people in this republic earn their living by farming. But most land in the region is covered by swamps. The government is showing people how to make better use of their land. Swamps are being drained and put to use.

The Baltic Republics

Along the Baltic Sea are three small republics, Estonia, Latvia, and Lithuania (lith′o͞o wā′nē ə). Russia controlled these nations before World War I, but their people are not Russian. They each have independent histories and speak their own languages, unrelated to Russian.

After World War I the Baltic states became independent nations. But their factories were not up-to-date enough to compete with those of larger nations, so they followed Denmark's example and took up dairying. This proved very profitable.

Early in World War II the three Baltic States were taken over by the Soviet Union. Their factories make many things that the Soviets need. The products of their dairy industry go to cities like Leningrad and Moscow within the Soviet Union.

The Republic of Georgia

Separated from the largest Soviet republic by the Caucasus Mountains is the small republic of Georgia. Georgia's capital is Tiflis (tif′ləs).

The Soviet Union has the world's greatest deposits of manganese (mang′gə nēz′), the mineral used to harden and toughen steel. Great deposits of manganese are found in the republic of Georgia, near the eastern end of the Black Sea.

Pipelines bring oil from the rich Soviet oil fields in the Caucasus Mountains to Batumi. At Batumi, on the Black Sea, the oil is refined and shipped.

Do You Know?

1. Where is the tundra region? The Open Forest? The Steppes?
2. What is the capital of the Soviet Union? What is the Kremlin?
3. What is the longest river in Europe?
4. Why is the Ukraine so important to the Soviet Union?
5. What mineral is found in Georgia?

4
Soviet Asia

East of the Ural Mountains lies the Asian part of the Soviet Union, which is three times as large as Soviet Europe. Much of Soviet Asia is called Siberia.

What Siberia Is Like

Soviet Asia, especially the northern part of Siberia, is much colder than Soviet Europe because it gets none of the winds from the Atlantic. More than half of it cannot be farmed because of the cold. In this vast region, valuable mineral resources have been discovered.

Siberia is so large that it has a belt of good land nearly as large as the farming area of Soviet Europe. The Ob (ōb) River flows north, like all the great Siberian streams. On this river is Novosibirsk (nō′vō sə birsk′), a name which means "New Siberia."

Novosibirsk has been called the Chicago of Siberia. The rich prairies around it support many farmers. These farmers raise millions of pigs and cattle. They raise grain to supply faraway peoples. So, in spite of bitter winters and hot summers, Novosibirsk has grown to be a large trade and industrial city.

The Trans-Siberian Railroad

Find on the map of the Soviet Union on page 496 the railroad that extends from Moscow all the way across Soviet Asia. This is the Trans-Siberian Railroad. "Trans" means "across."

The long railroad is Siberia's lifeline. Except along the Urals, where cities have spread north and south from it, the railroad marks the location of most of the Siberian cities. It is more than 6,000 miles (9,600 km) long, and the world's longest railroad.

The Development of Siberia

The czars thought of their Asian land chiefly as a place to send convicts. The Soviet government has imprisoned millions of people there, too. But it has also done much to develop the resources of Siberia—its soil, minerals, timber, and furs. On the Pacific there are fisheries.

The Trans-Siberian Railroad is the longest in the world. In the late 1970s, new sections of rail were added. Ceremonies marked the opening of the new tracks.

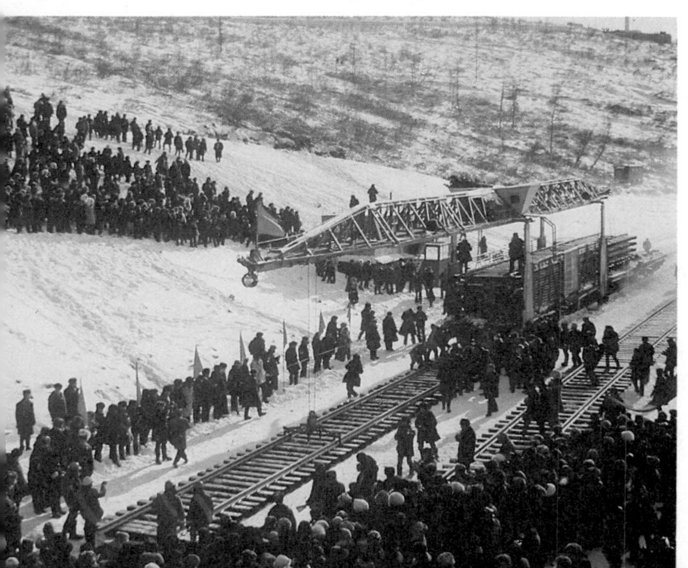

Scientists traveled over most of Siberia and took stock of its value. In the years that followed, millions of people settled there.

During World War II, the Soviet government moved many factories eastward into the Ural Mountains and the land beyond. With the factories went workers, who were forced to settle near the factories.

The Siberian factories were safe from enemy attack. They turned out much war equipment to help the Soviet forces halt the German armies. Since the war the Soviet Union has continued to build up the industries of Siberia.

At a place south of the Trans-Siberian Railroad, a scientist found that his compass pointed far away from the north. Its needle was attracted by a mountain of magnetic iron ore. Soon the Soviet Union built at that spot the first modern steel plant in the Urals. Magnitogorsk (mag nēt′ə gôrsk′), which means "Magnet Mountain," became a large city and a large producer of steel.

Twelve hundred miles (1,920 km) east of Magnitogorsk is Novokuznetsk (nō′vō kooz netsk′), formerly called Stalinsk. In this region are thick layers of coal.

A rare mineral found in the Urals is *platinum* (plat′ən əm). Platinum is a soft, silvery metal which has many industrial uses. It is also used in the tips of fountain pens and in watch chains and rings. The fields have not yet been fully explored, but rich deposits of manganese, chrome, nickel, zinc, and gold are lying in the Urals.

Sverdlovsk (svurd lôfsk′), near the place where the Trans-Siberian Railroad crosses the Urals, is the great city of the mining region.

Here are bauxite mines. Aluminum is made from this red mineral. Here also are copper ores and a kind of rock from which *magnesium* (mag nē′zē əm) is taken. Magnesium is a light, white metal which resembles aluminum. Also abundant is *asbestos* (as bes′təs), a mineral used in fireproof products.

Soviet Republics of Central Asia

In Central Asia there are five Soviet republics. Find this region on the map of the Soviet Union on page 473.

Central Asia has no rivers that flow to the ocean. The Caspian Sea, and the smaller Aral Sea to the east of the Caspian, have no outlets. In this region are steppes and deserts.

This Central Asian region has mountain walls on the south. These high mountains divide it from Iran, from India, and from China.

Cities on an Ancient Trade Route

In early times traders going west from China toward the Mediterranean Sea had to follow the oases near the foot of the great mountains. On this trade route grew up such important cities as Tashkent (tash′kent), Bokhara (bô khä′rä), and Samarkand (sam′ər kand′). In these cities were the shops of craftspeople who traded with the caravan travelers. Irrigated fields near the cities produced much food and helped to make the cities prosperous.

Samarkand was the capital of the great conqueror, Tamerlane. Tamerlane was a Muslim who once controlled a vast empire.

Tamerlane conquered most of Asia. Central Asia, part of India, and Persia paid him tribute. He extended his rule to the Ural and the Volga rivers. He ruled as a conqueror and a dictator.

In the time of Tamerlane Samarkand was a pleasant place. Orchards and mulberry groves flourished along the irrigation canals, and water from the river was brought into the houses. The people of Samarkand made fine paper and beautiful cloth. Many traders came to Samarkand to buy these products.

When Tamerlane died, in the year 1405, his empire fell apart. Samarkand and other cities of Central Asia like Tashkent and Bokhara were almost forgotten until the Soviet government brought new activity to the region.

Central Asian Cities Today

Today these Central Asian cities, all of which are in the Uzbek (ooz bek′) Republic, are prosperous. Tashkent is now the largest city of Central Asia. It is about the size of Houston, Texas. Here, in the grain market shaggy camels wait beside trucks to receive their loads. Low houses of sun-dried brick made up the old parts of the city. But the newer portions of Tashkent have modern factories and homes.

Samarkand now is about the size of Oakland, California. It has tile-covered buildings which date from Tamerlane's time. But it also has modern cotton mills, silk factories, and theaters.

Bokhara has kept its old Asian ways. It has many little shops, many craftspeople, and many water carriers who supply their customers from skin bags. Yet even in Bokhara a new city is growing up.

New growth can be seen in many old Central Asian cities as shown by this modern library building in Tashkent. In Samarkand one of the most famous ancient buildings is the tomb of Tamerlane.

A Region Helped by Irrigation

What has made these cities grow? Irrigation is the answer. The chief crop in these irrigated valleys is cotton. The Soviet government expects to grow enough cotton for the country's needs. An irrigation project near Tashkent brings water to 500,000 acres (600,000 ha) of land, known as the Hungry Steppe. Farmers, working on collectives, raise cotton, fruit, vegetables, and wheat there.

Cotton takes much richness out of the soil. Soviet farmers have learned how to meet this problem by growing sugar beets. In addition to producing sugar, the beets provide feed for cattle, whose manure furnishes fertilizer to make the soil rich again.

Warm sun and abundant water produce especially fine fruit. Apricots and peaches, apples and cherries, plums and melons, fill the city shops and supply the country tables. In the hot sunshine grapes are dried into raisins. There are large fruit-canning factories in Central Asia.

Today Central Asia is one of the three great manufacturing regions east of the Ural Mountains. More water has given it new life. The old caravan trade has been replaced by trade on highways and railroads.

Do You Know?

1. Where does the Trans-Siberian Railroad run?
2. Why did the Soviets move factories east of the Urals during World War II?
3. What is the chief crop raised in the irrigated valleys of Central Asia?

5
The Soviet Union's Place in the World

The Soviet Union is one of the great powers in the world today. It has so much land that there is room for its population of about 260 million to grow even larger.

Since the end of World War II the Soviet Union has turned its attention to manufacturing and developing its resources. It has worked to modernize its farming methods and increase crop production.

Soviet Industry and Science

The Soviet Union, as you know, has made great advances in industry and science since World War II. It is second only to the United States in

This graph compares the number of people in the United States, in the Soviet Union, and in China, with the amount of land in each country. Which has more people? Which has more land? Which has a higher population density?

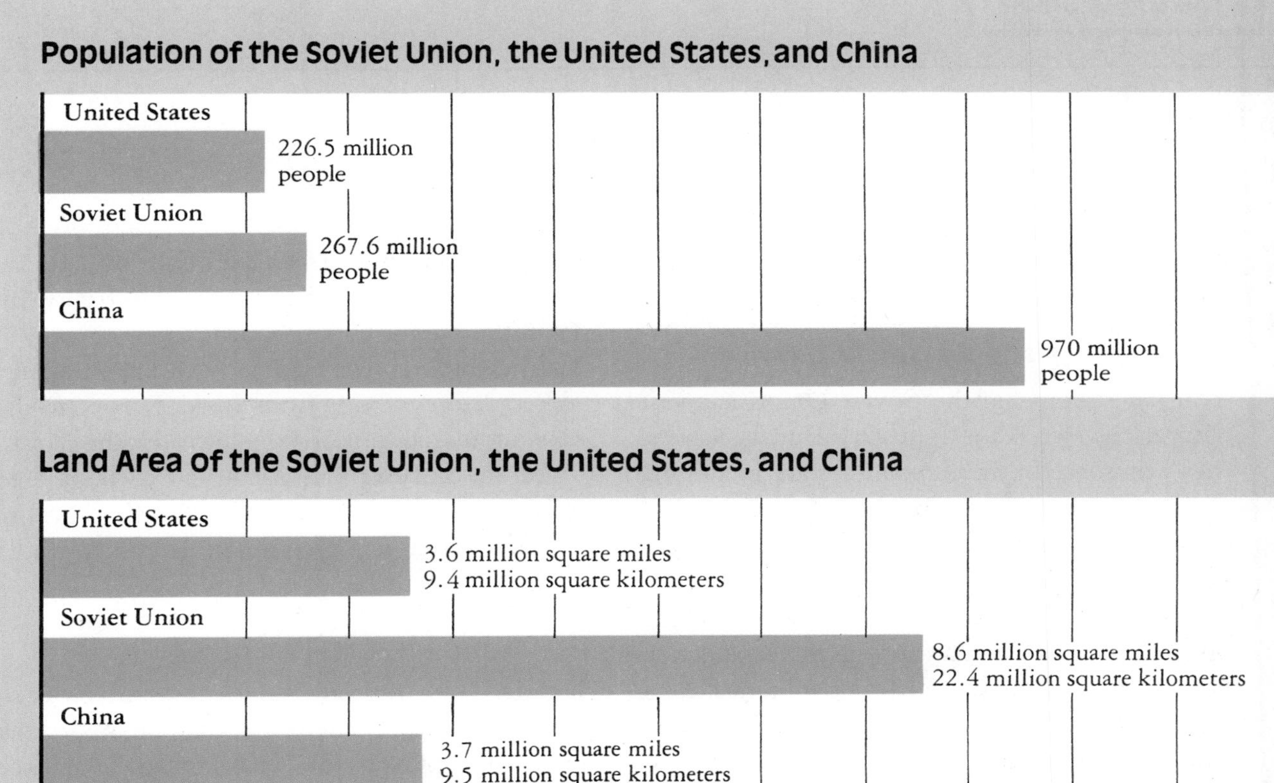

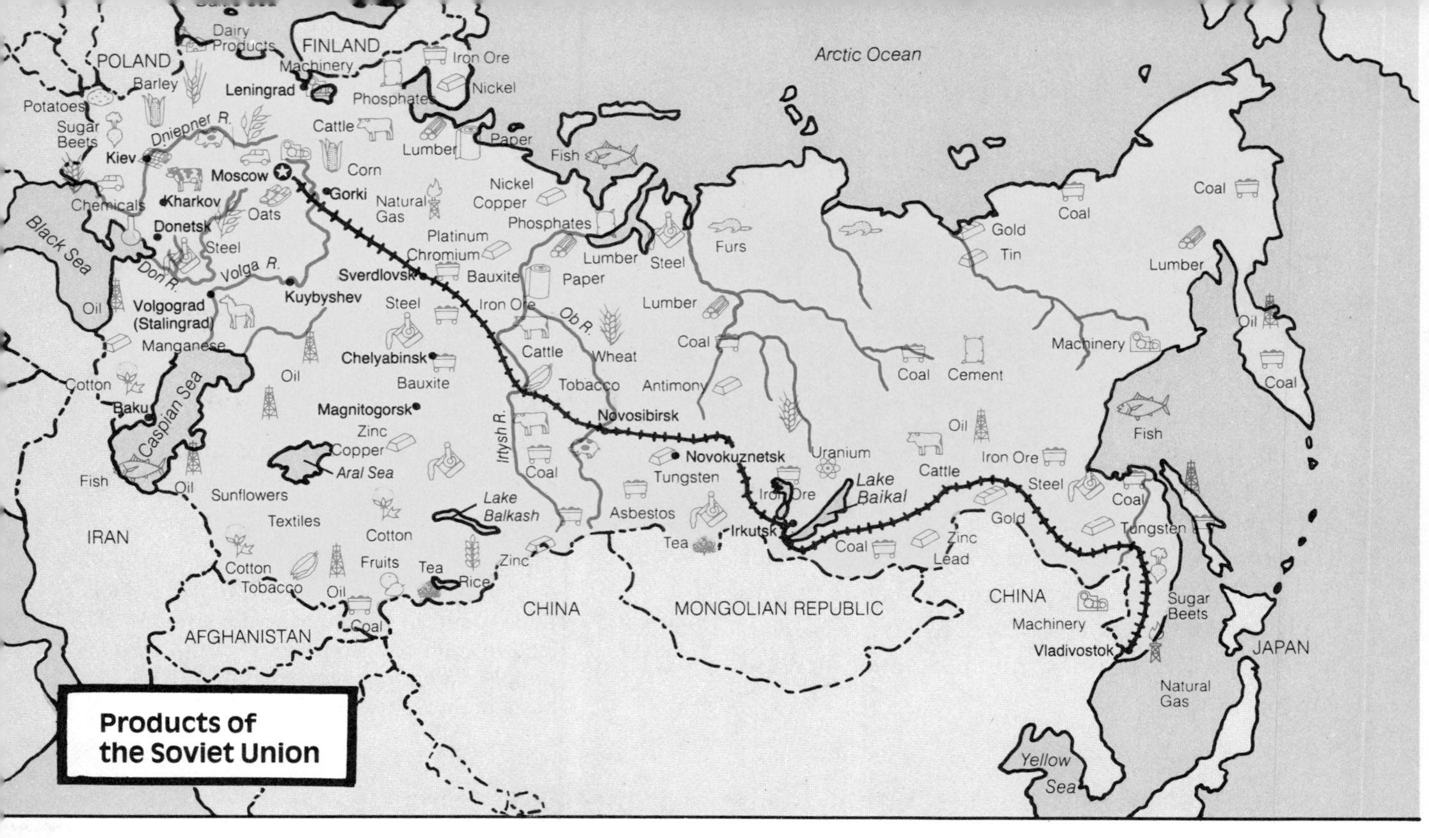

Products of the Soviet Union

industrial production. And the nation has made enormous strides in space exploration.

New Industries in the Soviet Union

You have seen that the Soviet Union has vast natural resources for industry. But as vast as they are, some of these resources are beginning to disappear, especially in Soviet Europe.

As a result, Soviet industry has been moving beyond the Urals into Soviet Asia. Find Lake Baikal (bī kôl′) on the map of the Soviet Union on page 473. The region around this lake is rich in iron ore, uranium, and other minerals. Several new industrial cities have been built there. The Trans-Siberian Railroad is the main means of transportation for this area. The Soviet Union is using the streams around Lake Baikal for water power to help make electricity. In 1966 the Soviet Union built the world's largest hydroelectric power plant west of Lake Baikal.

People are moving from Soviet Europe to the new industrial settlements beyond the Urals. Once the government had to force people to move there. Now people go willingly, because they know that the government pays high wages in the new factories.

Science in the Soviet Union

Not far from the industrial center of Novosibirsk is a small city called Akademgorodok (ək ə dəm gor′ə dək), which means "Science Town." It was built especially for scientists. The

Science has special importance in the Soviet Union. Two successful projects are the "Science Town" studies and the space program. Shown left are complex controls at "Science Town." Astronauts completed a major mission in 1975.

scientists who live and work there are concerned with everything from the study of plants and animals to experimenting with new forms of transportation and energy.

Scientific study in the Soviet Union is especially important. In Soviet schools science and mathematics are stressed more than other subjects. Soviet scientists and mathematicians are paid well and have special privileges.

Soviet scientists have been quite successful in space exploration. The Soviet Union sent up the first space satellite in 1957, and later the first astronaut. In 1975 the United States and the Soviet Union undertook a joint space mission. While orbiting the earth, Soviet and American spacecraft met in space. After docking, astronauts from both nations carried out scientific experiments.

The Spread of Communism

Leaders of the Soviet Union once said that the Communist way of life must be spread throughout the world. After World War II, the Soviet Union set up Communist governments in a number of European countries. Find these Communist countries on the map of the Spread of Communism in Europe and Asia on page 498. It was said that the people of these countries lived behind the *iron curtain* (ī′ərn kur′tin), because they were allowed little contact with the non-Communist world.

The Soviet Union seemed eager to take over countries in other parts of the world. These moves were opposed by the United States. The United States and the Soviet Union, which had been allies in World War II, entered into a period of distrust. This unfriendly relationship

You can see from these maps that large areas of Europe and Asia have become Communist since World War II. Which European countries are Communist today? Which Asian countries?

between the two countries became known as the Cold War.

Both the United States and the Soviet Union realize, though, that a war fought between them with the terrible weapons developed since World War II might destroy the earth. In recent years, the Communist and non-Communist nations have tried to work together. In the 1970s there was greater trade and exchange of information between them.

There have also been the Strategic Arms Limitations Talks (SALT) between the United States and the Soviet Union. The two nations are trying to agree to put limits on the weapons they will produce. These talks were interrupted in 1979.

Relations between the Soviet Union and the United States became strained after the Soviet Union invaded Afghanistan in late 1979 and early 1980. Some Americans were afraid that the Soviet Union wanted the oil of the Persian Gulf, south of Afghanistan. Others thought that by invading the Muslim nation of Afghanistan, the Soviet leaders hoped to keep their own Muslim people from rebelling. Whatever the reason for the invasion, the act caused a serious disagreement between American and Soviet leaders. The United States responded by leading a boycott of the 1980 summer Olympic games in Moscow.

Do You Know?

1. In what part of the Soviet Union are the newest industries being built?
2. In what scientific field have the Soviet Union and the United States cooperated?
3. What are the Strategic Arms Limitations Talks?

To Help You Learn

Using New Words

asbestos	platinum
collective	magnesium
ballet	iron curtain
socialist	tundra

Number a paper from 1 through 8. After each number write the word or term that matches the definition.

1. A dance that tells a story through graceful movements, accompanied by music
2. A light, white metal
3. A mineral used in fireproof products
4. A treeless plain in the Arctic region
5. A soft, silvery metal
6. A person who believes that the government should own and operate all factories, farms, railroads, and mines
7. A large farm owned by the government
8. A term used to describe the lack of contact between Communist and non-Communist countries after World War II

Finding the Facts

1. Where was a Norse Kingdom set up in Russia?
2. When did the Tartars invade Russia?
3. Who laid the foundation of the Russian nation?
4. How did Russia expand into Asia?
5. How did Russia gain territory on the Baltic? Under whose leadership?
6. Name two famous writers of Old Russia.
7. What is the correct name for Russia?
8. What different kinds of climate does the Soviet Union have?
9. What language do most people speak in the European part of the Soviet Union?
10. When did the Russian Revolution begin? Who started it?
11. What was the purpose of the "Five-Year Plans"?
12. What event caused an increase in tension between the United States and the Soviet Union during 1979 and 1980? How did the United States respond to this event?

Learning from Maps

1. Look at the map of the Soviet Union on page 473. Find the Arctic Circle. What Soviet port lies north of it? This port is open all year round. Why? *Hint:* reread page 396.
2. Look at the map of the Soviet Union on page 496. Locate the route of the Trans-Siberian Railroad. Which cities does it go through?
3. Study the products map of the Soviet Union on page 496 and list the chief crops and animals.
4. Look at the map of the Spread of Communism in Europe and Asia on page 498. List the European Communist countries. Which country is divided in two, one Communist, the other not?

5. Look at the climate map of the Soviet Union on page 478. What is Moscow's average temperature in January? In July? How much rain does it get in a year? How does Tashkent's climate compare to Moscow's?

Using Study Skills

1. **Time Line:** Place the following events in the proper order of time: Tamerlane attacks Tartar settlements; Soviet troops invade Afghanistan; the "machine age" comes to the Soviet Union; World War I begins; Soviet Union builds world's largest hydroelectric plant.

   Copy the time line from page 471. Add these events to your time line.

   Study the completed time line and answer the following questions: How long was it between the overthrow of the czar and the building of the world's largest hydroelectric plant? Between the beginning of World War I and the "machine age" in the Soviet Union? Between the invasion of the Tartars and the attack on the Tartars by Tamerlane? Between the world's first space satellite and joint Soviet Union–United States space flight?
2. **Diagram:** Look at the diagram of the organization of the Communist Party in the Soviet Union on page 481. Who leads the party? Who chooses the leader? What two bodies are just below the leader? Who chooses the Central Committee?
3. **Diagram:** Now look at the diagram of the government of the Soviet Union on page 482. What is the highest government office? What body is this official the chairman of? What does the Presidium do? What is the legislature, or law-making body, called? What are its two houses?

Thinking It Through

1. What geographical feature of the Soviet Union makes its "window" toward the West so important?
2. Why do you think the plots of land behind Russian farmers' houses might be more productive than the land on Russian collectives?
3. You have learned that the Soviet Union is a Communist nation. Communism is not only a political system, it is an economic system, too. The economic system in the United States is the free enterprise system. How is making a living in the Soviet Union different from making a living in the United States?

Projects

1. Plan a program of music by Russian composers. Use the phonograph or have someone play the selections on the piano. Have the announcer tell something about each selection and each composer.
2. List the most important minerals that the Soviet Union has. Then find out how the United States compares with the Soviet Union in the same minerals.

3. The Explorers' Committee might like to plan a journey on the Trans-Siberian Railroad from Moscow to Vladivostok. List the cities on the railroad line. Describe the kinds of land you would see.
4. Make a chart in which you compare life in the United States with life in the Soviet Union. The headings of your chart should include: Population, Political Parties, Kind of Elections, and Rights of Citizens.
5. Look through recent newspapers and magazines for articles about the Soviet Union. Have a class discussion on current events in the Soviet Union.

17 Nations of the Pacific

Unit Preview

The Pacific Ocean covers more area than all the land on the surface of the earth. It reaches from the frozen lands of Alaska and Siberia in the north to Antarctica in the south. It reaches from the United States halfway around the world to China. The Pacific separates, sometimes with narrow channels, sometimes with vast expanses, islands of great variety.

The Philippine Islands are in the southwestern part of the Pacific Ocean. More than 7,000 islands make up this nation. The climate of the Philippines is tropical. There is plenty of rainfall, so rice grows well. Coconuts are another important crop. The United States took over the Philippines in 1898. After World War II, the island nation became independent.

The islands of Indonesia are in the Pacific Ocean off the coast of southeastern Asia. In the rich soil of these islands, crops like coffee, tea, and rice grow well. Tin and oil have been found.

Many islands are scattered throughout the Pacific Ocean east of Indonesia. They are parts of island groups called Micronesia, Melanesia, and Polynesia. Some of these islands are stopping places for ships and planes that cross the Pacific. In the past, the people of Asia and Europe explored and conquered many of these islands.

Australia and New Zealand are two island countries in the Southern Hemisphere. Australia is so vast that it is a continent. Sheep and cattle graze on huge ranches. Wheat is the most important crop. Raising sheep is also important in New Zealand.

Things to Discover

If you look carefully at the picture, map, and time line on these pages, you can answer these questions.

1. The picture shows a scene in the group of islands northeast of Australia called the Solomons. What things in the picture suggest that these islands have a tropical climate?
2. What explorer reached the Philippine Islands in 1521?
3. For how many years were the Philippines controlled by the United States? What country governed them before 1898?
4. What form of government does Australia have? When was it established?
5. What sea captain came to Australia in 1770? What country did he come from?

Words to Learn

You will meet these words in this unit. As you read, you will learn what they mean and how to pronounce them. The Word List will help you.

abaca	kangaroo	kookaburra
aborigine	koala	platypus
batik	echidna	quinine
breadfruit	eucalyptus	taro
copra		

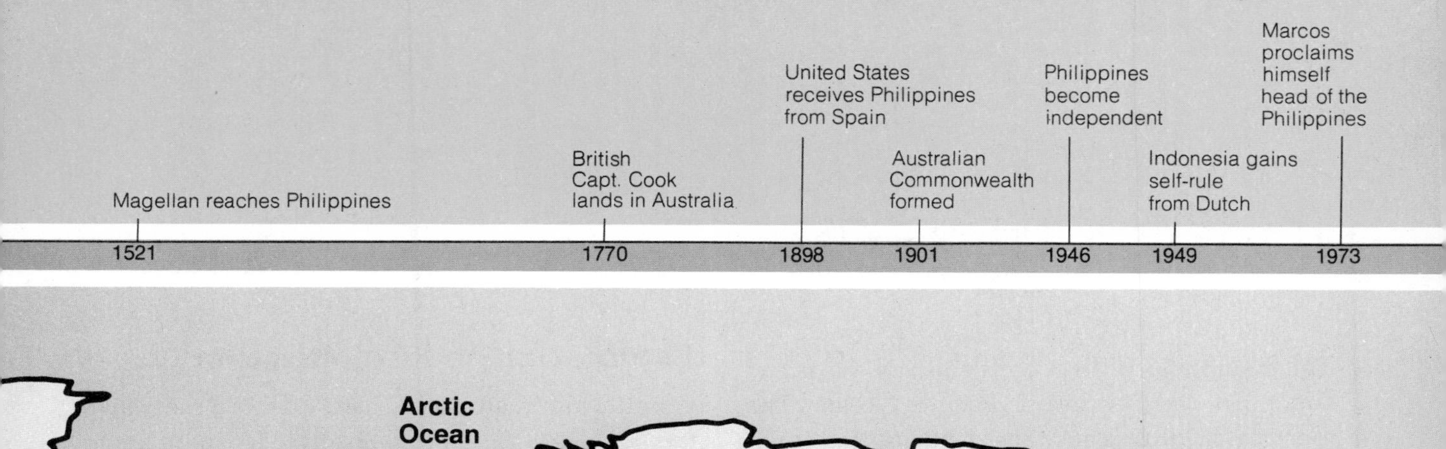

Arctic Ocean
Atlantic Ocean
EUROPE
ASIA
Pacific Ocean
AFRICA
Indian Ocean
AUSTRALIA

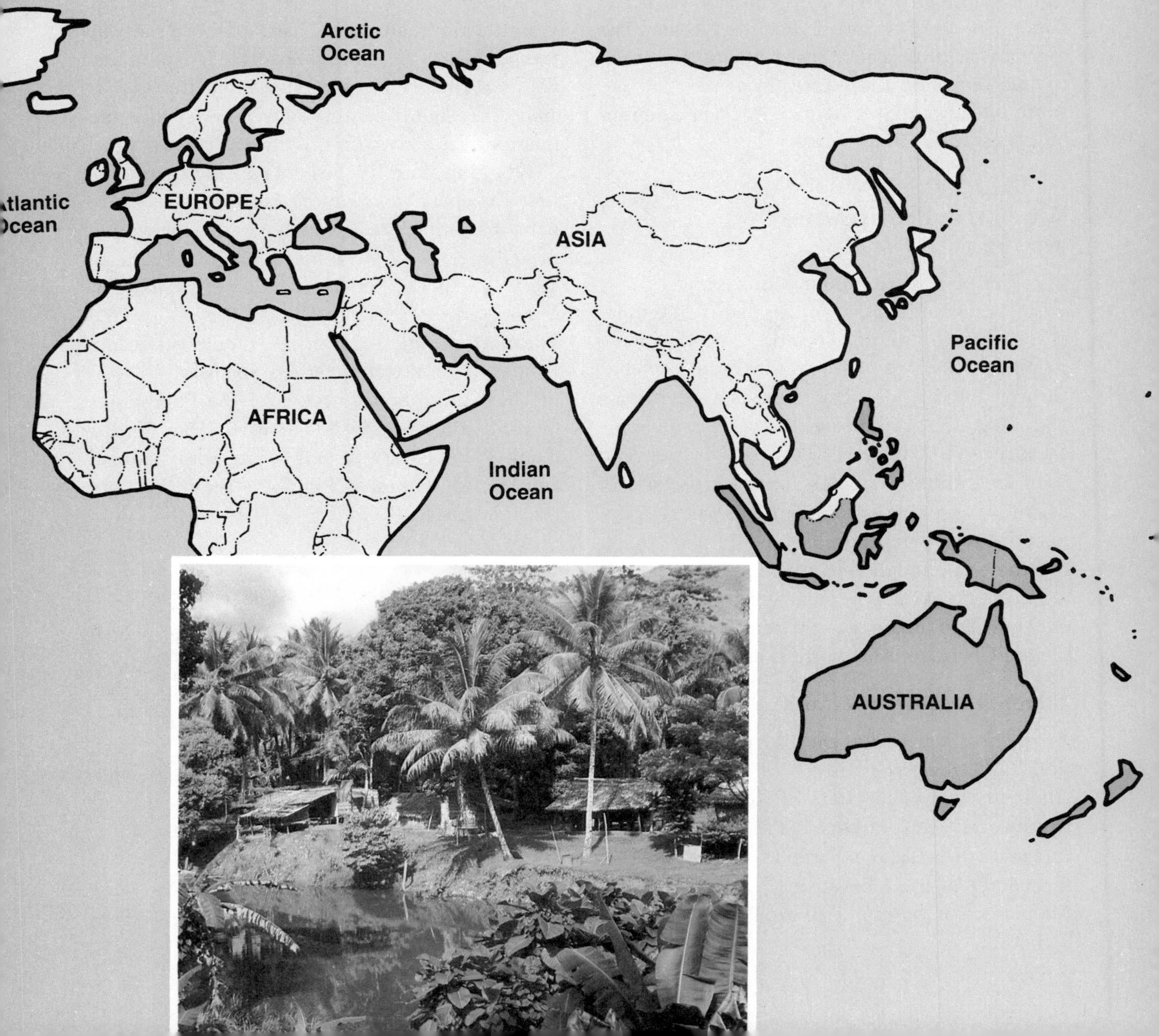

1

The Philippine Islands

The Philippine (fil′ə pēn) Islands are an island nation in the southwest Pacific Ocean. The more than 7,000 islands that make up the country lie north of Indonesia (in′də nē′zhə) and south of Taiwan. See the map of Pacific nations on pages 506–507.

What the Philippines Are Like

The Philippines are mountainous islands, partly volcanic, extending over more than 1,000 miles (1,600 km) of water. They lie entirely in the tropics. There is little temperature change throughout the year. But there is a wet season and a dry season. During the wet season some areas receive 80 inches (203 cm) of rain per year.

In area, the Philippines are twice the size of Michigan and almost four times as thickly populated. More than 48 million people live there, but there is enough land for more. The people are made up of many groups which speak different languages. More than 90 percent of the people are Christian. Many others are Muslims.

Luzon, the Largest Island

At the northern end of the Philippines is Luzon (lo͞o zon′), the largest island in the group. It is about the size of the state of Kentucky. In the southwestern part of Luzon is the city of Manila (mə nil′ə). Manila is as large as Philadelphia. It is a center of trade because of its large harbor. Manila is also the capital of the Philippines.

Exploration and Colonization

People from many lands have affected the way the people of the Philippines live. Japanese and Chinese traders have been visiting the islands since the eighth century. Arab merchants and missionaries arrived in the fifteenth century.

Not long after, in 1521, Magellan became the first European to visit the islands. They were named by the Spanish in honor of the young prince who became Philip II, King of Spain, in 1556. The people of the islands were called Filipinos. Spain held the islands for 300 years. During that time most of the Filipinos became Roman Catholics and learned Spanish.

The United States took over the Philippines in 1898, after winning a war with Spain. Today many Filipinos speak and write both Spanish and English as well as Pilipino, the official national language.

Products of the Philippines

The Philippines have plenty of rain, which means rice grows well. To Filipinos rice is as important as it is to the people of Asia. Other foods of the Filipinos are fish and vegetables, especially sweet potatoes and bamboo sprouts. The sprouts are cooked and eaten somewhat like asparagus. Pork is also a favorite food.

Philippine Exports

The Philippines are a leading coconut-growing country. Ships leaving Manila carry hundreds of

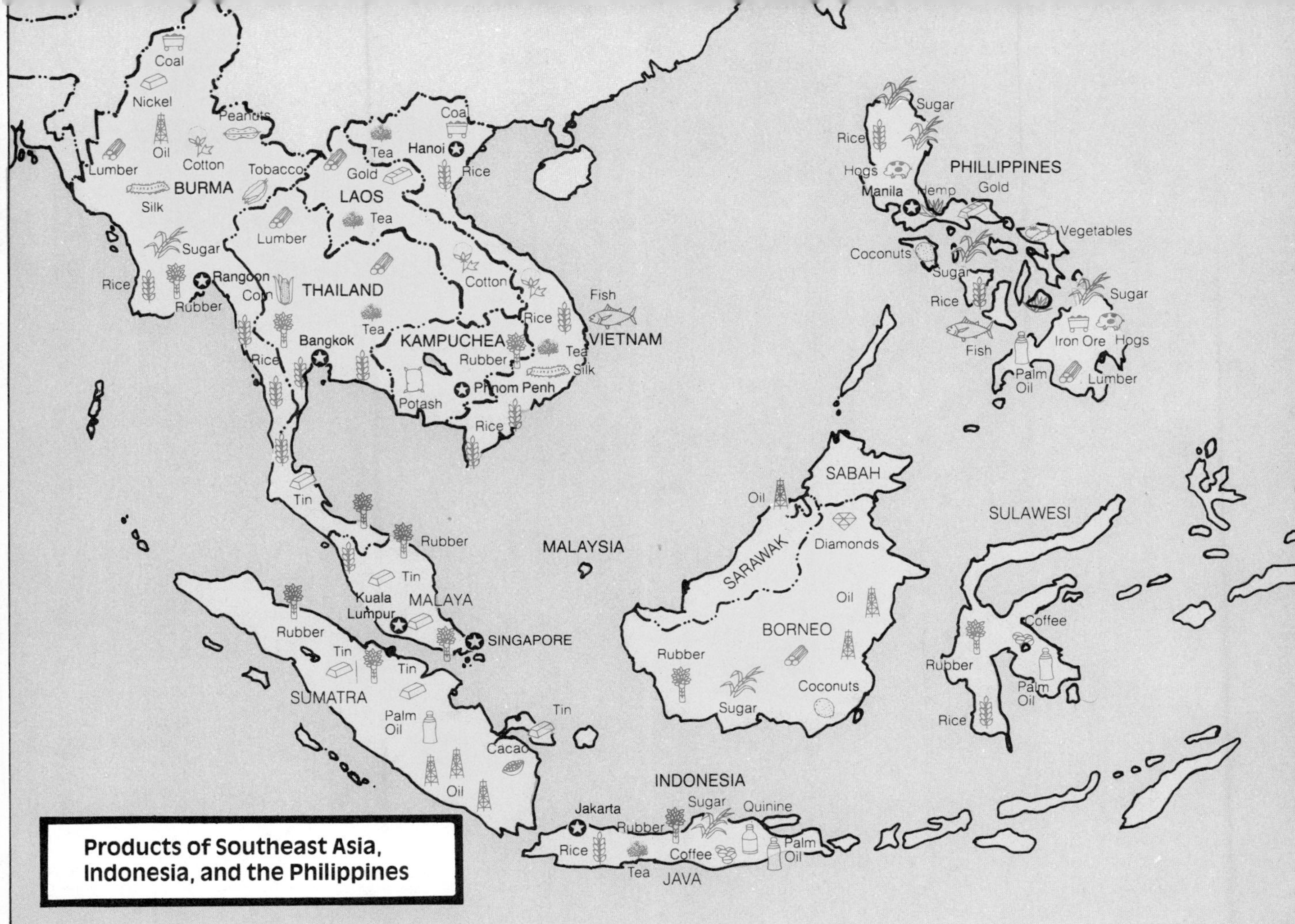

barrels of coconut oil, used to make salad oils and soaps. Ships also carry raw sugar, gold, and the best iron ore in the Orient.

Another article exported is *abaca* (ab′ə kä′), or Manila hemp. The abaca fibers are twisted together to make twine or rope. Abaca is highly prized by sailors. It is the only rope that can be soaked in salt water without rotting. Abaca is also woven into hats, slippers, rugs, and made into wrapping paper.

Philippine Independence

When the United States took over the islands, it promised the Filipinos independence as soon as they could govern themselves. The Filipinos became better educated. They developed leaders to hold important government positions. Under a constitution adopted in 1935, they were almost completely self-governing. The United States continued to handle only matters of foreign relations and defense.

NATIONS OF THE PACIFIC
Plains
Plateaus
Hills
Mountains
National Capitals
Other Capitals
Other Cities
0 Miles 750
0 Kilometers 950
90°
120°
150°
30°
0°
CHINA
NORTH KOREA
SOUTH KOREA
JAPAN
Beijing
Pyongyang
Seoul
Tokyo
Nanjing
Shanghai
Chongqing
Taipei
TAIWAN
TROPIC OF CANCER
INDIA
BANGLA-DESH
Calcutta
BURMA
Guangzhou
Hanoi
Hong Kong (Br.)
LAOS
Bay of Bengal
Rangoon
THAILAND
VIETNAM
Bangkok
KAMPUCHEA
Phnom Penh
Ho Chi Minh City
SOUTH CHINA SEA
PHILIPPINE SEA
LUZON
Manila
PHILIPPINES
MINDANAO
MARIANA ISLANDS (U.S. Trust)
GUAM (U.S.)
CAROLINE ISLANDS (U.S. Trust)
PALAU (U.S. Trust)
MICRONESIA
EQUATOR
BRUNEI
MALAYSIA
Kuala Lumpur
SINGAPORE
SUMATRA
BORNEO
INDONESIA
Jakarta
JAVA
BALI
TIMOR
IRIAN JAYA
PAPUA NEW GUINEA
NEW IRELAND
NEW BRITAIN
Port Moresby
SOLOMON ISLANDS
ARAFURA SEA
TIMOR SEA
Darwin
INDIAN OCEAN
CORAL SEA
GREAT BARRIER REEF
GREAT DIVIDING RANGE
NORTHERN TERRITORY
GREAT SANDY DESERT
QUEENSLAND
TROPIC OF CAPRICORN
WESTERN AUSTRALIA
AUSTRALIA
GIBSON DESERT
SOUTH AUSTRALIA
GREAT VICTORIA DESERT
Brisbane
Darling River
Lake Eyre
NULLARBOR PLAIN
NEW SOUTH WALES
Newcastle
Sydney
Perth
Great Australian Bight
Murray River
Adelaide
Canberra
VICTORIA
Melbourne
Bass Strait
TASMAN SEA
TASMANIA
Hobart

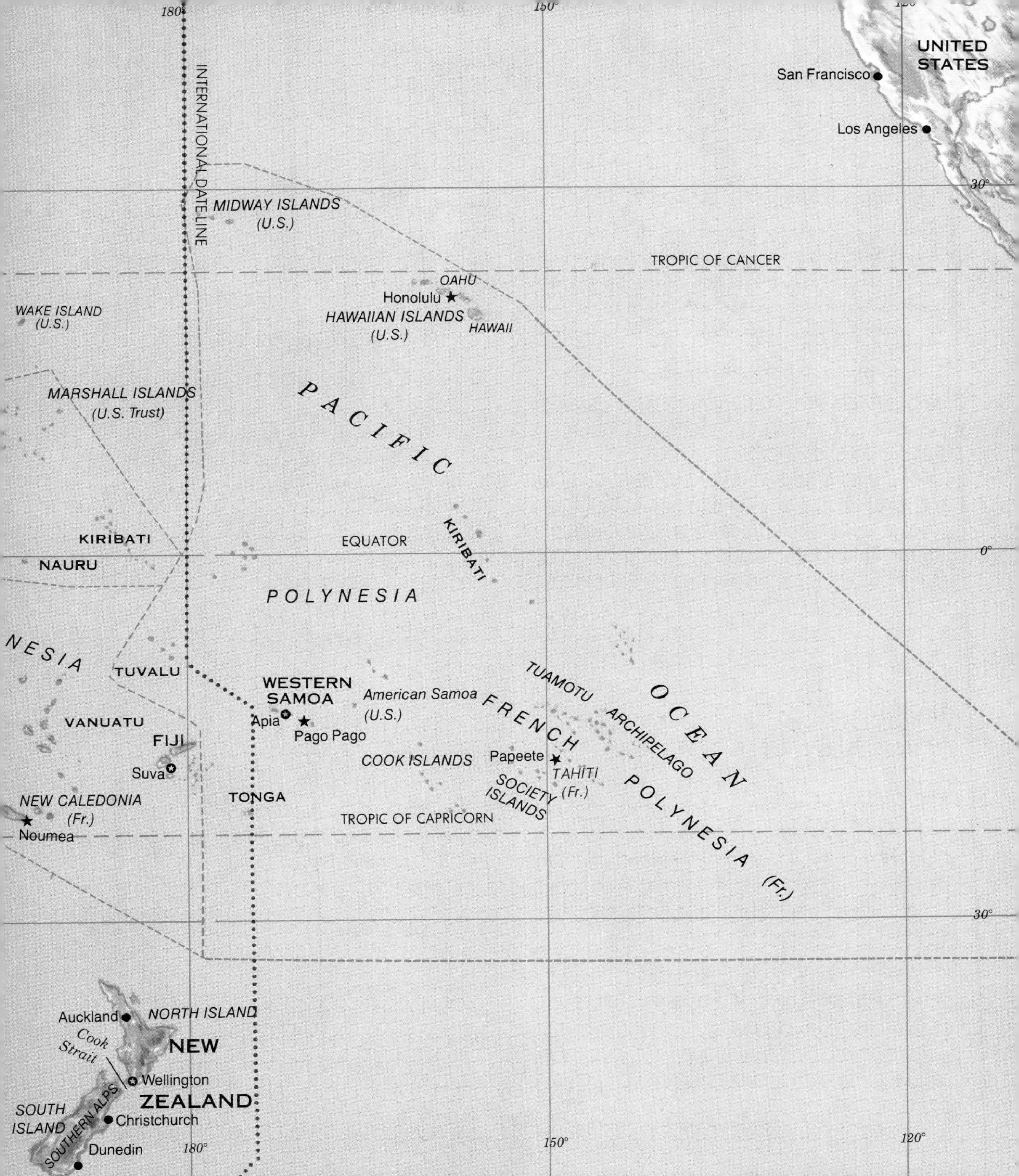

180°
150°
120°
UNITED STATES
San Francisco
Los Angeles
30°
INTERNATIONAL DATE LINE
MIDWAY ISLANDS (U.S.)
TROPIC OF CANCER
OAHU
Honolulu
HAWAIIAN ISLANDS (U.S.)
HAWAII
WAKE ISLAND (U.S.)
MARSHALL ISLANDS (U.S. Trust)
PACIFIC
KIRIBATI
NAURU
EQUATOR
KIRIBATI
0°
POLYNESIA
NESIA
TUVALU
WESTERN SAMOA
Apia
American Samoa (U.S.)
Pago Pago
TUAMOTU ARCHIPELAGO
OCEAN
FRENCH POLYNESIA (Fr.)
VANUATU
FIJI
Suva
COOK ISLANDS
Papeete
TAHITI (Fr.)
SOCIETY ISLANDS
NEW CALEDONIA (Fr.)
Noumea
TONGA
TROPIC OF CAPRICORN
30°
Auckland
NORTH ISLAND
Cook Strait
NEW ZEALAND
Wellington
SOUTH ISLAND
SOUTHERN ALPS
Christchurch
Dunedin
180°
150°
120°

The Philippines in World War II

When the Japanese conquered the islands in World War II, the Filipinos proved their loyalty to the United States. Their guerrilla fighters continued to resist the Japanese until the islands were freed in the late summer of 1945.

The Republic of the Philippines

After World War II the United States kept its promise, and on July 4, 1946, granted the Philippines independence.

Poverty, unemployment, and opposition to the government by violent Muslim and Communist groups have created serious problems for the Philippines in recent years. In 1973 Ferdinand E. Marcos proclaimed a new constitution with himself as both president and prime minister. His government has tried to suppress the opposition, but violence has continued. Many people have been killed.

Do You Know?

1. Who was the first European to reach the Philippines?
2. Which is the largest island in the Philippines? What is the capital?
3. What are the chief exports of the Philippines?
4. When did the Philippines get their independence?

2 Indonesia

The country of Indonesia is made up of three large islands, parts of two others, and thousands of smaller ones. The islands once belonged to the Dutch and were known as the East Indies because the Dutch East India Company controlled the trade of most of the islands.

The Geography of Indonesia

Look at the map of the Nations of the Pacific on pages 506 and 507. South of the peninsula of Malaya is the big island of Sumatra (soo mä′trə). East of it are Java (jäv′ə), Borneo (bôr′nē ō′), and New Guinea (no͞o gin′ē). Stretching beyond over thousands of square miles of water are the other islands.

What Java Is Like

Java is about the size of the state of New York, but has more than four times as many people. This makes it one of the most heavily populated areas in the world. Java's largest city, Jakarta (jə kär′tə), was built by the Dutch in the early 1600s.

A market square in Jakarta is a busy place where people can buy food and other goods. What kinds of transportation do you see in the picture?

Jakarta is the capital of Indonesia. A grand canal forms its main highway. On each side of its many canals are ships and red-roofed houses.

In the hot climate of Java, where there is abundant rain, crops grow quickly. The soil, enriched by ashes from the island's volcanoes, is fertile. Java has always been a land of forests, flowers, and fruits.

Rice, coffee, and tea are important products. In the hills many forests of cinchona (sin kō′ nə) trees have been planted. Cinchona bark gives us the bittertasting medicine called *quinine* (kwī′ nīn), which is used for the treatment of certain fevers. Java produces almost all of the world's quinine.

Java has a fine network of roads and railways, built by the Dutch when they ruled the island.

What Sumatra Is Like

The island of Sumatra is more than three times the size of Java. Sumatra has great plantations of rubber, and of oil-yielding palms. Sumatra also has rich deposits of tin.

What Borneo Is Like

Borneo is the third largest island in the world. It is owned partly by Indonesia and partly by Malaysia. Borneo has rich deposits of petroleum. Diamonds have also been found in many places. Many of the people of Borneo still live in much the same way as they have for centuries.

What New Guinea Is Like

New Guinea is a large tropical island in the Pacific, north of Australia. It has two political

Indonesian dancers of Bali are famous for their graceful movements and elaborate costumes. Dancers begin training at a young age. They often use fans to help express emotion.

units. Irian Jaya (ir′ē än′ jī′yə) covers the western half. It is a part of Indonesia. The independent state of Papua (pap′yə wə) New Guinea occupies the eastern half. Gold and copper are produced in Papua New Guinea. An important resource of Irian Jaya is oil.

Much of the island's interior is covered by rugged, snow-capped mountains. The coastal lowlands are hot and humid. Many of the people live in traditional ways in small villages. The island has crocodiles, snakes, and many beautiful birds and butterflies.

The Culture of Indonesia

Most Indonesians are Muslims, though many continue to observe local religious customs and beliefs as well. This local tradition is based in part on Hinduism. This is because Hindu traders and priests were important in Indonesia in the first to the eighth centuries. Elaborately carved Hindu and Buddhist temples are still found on some islands.

Dances and Puppets

Indonesia is rich in the arts. The royal court dances of the island of Bali (bä′lē) are famous for their grace and pleasing hand movements. This dance tradition has been continued in modern times.

Another lively art uses puppets to tell stories. The puppets are made of flat pieces of leather. The puppets are moved with sticks. Only the puppets' shadows are seen by the audience. The storyteller sits behind a white screen and sings and tells stories. The storyteller also moves the puppets to throw their shadows up onto the screen.

The Art of Batik

Indonesian artists make a kind of design on cloth called *batik* (bə tēk′). Batik is printed by putting a wax coating on those parts of the cloth that are not to be dyed. When the cloth is dipped into the dye, that part covered by the wax resists the dye and is not colored. The rest of the cloth picks up the color of the dye. This process is also called resist dyeing. After the dyed cloth is dry the wax is removed with boiling water.

Designs of more than one color can be made by dipping the cloth in progressively darker colors. New coats of wax are applied between the dye baths.

Java is a center of this craft in Indonesia. The best batiks are brilliantly colored with complex designs of birds and flowers. Long pieces of the decorated cloth are worn by both men and women as clothes.

The East Indies in Recent Times

The Japanese occupied the Dutch East Indies from 1942 to 1945 during World War II. The Japanese wanted the oil, tin, and rubber found on the islands.

A New Indonesian Nation

After World War II the people of the East Indies wished to be self-governing. They fought the Netherlands for their independence. In 1949 the Dutch agreed that the islands should become self-governing. The country is now called the Republic of Indonesia. It has a president as its head.

The Future of Indonesia

Indonesia is fortunate in having rich soil. Good crops of rice, corn, coconuts, tea, coffee, and rubber are produced in the islands. Indonesia also has valuable deposits of tin and oil. Oil production has recently expanded. These bring money to the nation and provide work for its people.

When the Dutch left the islands, few Indonesians had experience in doing the work of government. The number of trained persons is growing, but many more are needed.

Indonesia also needs to build up a greater unity between the islands. Because the Indonesians live on different islands and speak a variety of languages, they sometimes forget that they live under one government. They often feel a greater loyalty to their separate islands than they do to their nation. This has caused some problems in the early years of the republic.

Do You Know?

1. To whom did the islands of Indonesia belong before they gained independence?
2. Name four islands of Indonesia.
3. Which island produces most of the world's quinine?

3

The Islands of Micronesia, Melanesia, and Polynesia

East of Indonesia, for thousands of miles, the ocean is dotted with specks of land. These islands fall into three main groups. Micronesia (mī'krə nē'zhə), which means "small islands," is made up of 1,400 islands. Micronesia lies between the Philippines and the 180th meridian

To the south and east of Micronesia is the island group known as Melanesia (mel' ə nē'zhə). Melanesia means "black islands." They are called this because so many of their people have black skin. East of the 180th meridian is a very large group of islands, called Polynesia (pol'i nē'zhə). Polynesia means "many islands." Locate these three large groups of islands on the map of the Nations of the Pacific on pages 506–507.

What Micronesia Is Like

Micronesia includes four large island groups: the Marianas, Carolines, Marshalls, and Gilberts. Guam (gwam), a United States territory, is also part of this region. The two independent island countries of Micronesia are Kiribati (kir'ə bas) and Nauru (nä o͞o'ro͞o). Coconuts, the chief crop, are shipped out in the form of *copra* (kop'rə). Copra is dried coconut meat from which coconut oil is extracted.

Nauru island consists mainly of a coral plateau rich in phosphate. The phosphate was formed over centuries by the droppings of sea birds, which had a chemical interaction with the coral limestone of the island.

How Micronesia Is Governed

Micronesia is governed in part as a trust territory of the United Nations, administered by the United States. Guam and Wake Island are United States' possessions. Nauru is an independent country.

What Melanesia Is Like

Melanesia lies just south of the equator. It reaches from New Guinea on the west to the Fiji (fē'jē) Islands on the east. Melanesia includes New Ireland, New Britain, the Solomon Islands, New Hebrides (heb'rə dēz'), Fiji, New Caledonia (kal ə dō'nyə), and many other scattered islands. New Guinea is sometimes considered a part of Melanesia.

Fiji, the Solomon Islands, and Papua New Guinea are independent nations. In 1980, the New Hebrides became the independent nation of Vanuatu (və no͞o'ə to͞o). France governs New Caledonia. Other Melanesian islands are ruled by Great Britain.

The People of Melanesia

Melanesia is made up of many separate groups of people who speak hundreds of different languages. Sometimes those tribes who live next to each other are separated by thick jungle or steep mountains. Until well into this century

People living in this Solomon Island village use some modern machinery, such as motors for boats. Houses near the water are built on stilts. Why do you think this is necessary?

tribes were almost constantly at war with one another.

In recent times new ideas of law and order have been introduced by European administrators and by Christian and Muslim missionaries.

Products of Melanesia

In these islands the chief foods are the banana, the coconut, the yam, and the *breadfruit* (bred′ froot). This is a fruit which, when roasted, tastes like bread.

Another important source of food is provided by the *taro* (tär′ō) plant. It has a starchy root which is good to eat when cooked. The processing of sugarcane is the main industry of Fiji. New Guinea produces much gold, and New Caledonia has rich mines of nickel. It also exports copra, cacao, and coffee.

What Polynesia Is Like

East of Melanesia thousands of islands, most of them small, dot the vast South Pacific. They are called Polynesia. As you will see from the map on pages 506–507, many of these islands seem to be arranged in groups.

How Polynesia Was Settled

Several hundred years before Columbus landed in America, it is believed that groups of people from southeastern Asia set out on voyages seeking new homes. With stone tools they built big double canoes whose planks were not nailed but sewed together with coconut fibers. They joined the two canoes by a platform on which there was a cabin to hold their belongings. Sixty persons could travel in one such boat.

The daring explorers found and settled the large group of islands now called Polynesia.

Paul Gauguin painted scenes of everyday life in Polynesia. He used vibrant colors in this picture, "The Big Tree."

These people had no compasses or other instruments to guide them in finding new lands. But they were wonderfully skillful in reading the signs of the sea. They studied the stars. They followed birds. They knew when land was near from the appearance of clouds and waves.

Finally the Polynesians settled every island north of New Zealand to Hawaii. They carried with them their food plants—the breadfruit tree, yam, taro, and coconut—and animals.

How Polynesia Is Governed

France, Great Britain, and the United States control most of the Polynesian islands. Tahiti, a territory of France, has been visited by many tourists since a jet airport was built in 1965.

Hawaii became a United States possession in 1898 and the fiftieth state of the Union in 1959. The eastern part of Samoa (sə mō′ə) has been administered by the United States since 1900. Pago Pago (päng′ō päng′ō) is the capital of

American Samoa. This city lies on the shipping route between the United States and Australia. Many ships stop for supplies.

Western Samoa, Tonga (tong′gə), and Tuvalu (too vä lo͞o′) are independent nations. The Cook Islands are a self-governing territory of New Zealand.

The People of Polynesia

The Polynesian people are remarkably alike even though they live scattered throughout a vast ocean area. They tend to be tall, athletic, and skilled seafarers. Women have an important position in society and can become rulers.

Queen Salote (sə′lō′tā) ruled Tonga from 1918 until her death in 1965. Queen Salote encouraged the traditional crafts of Tonga. These crafts include making fine reed mats and decorated barkcloth.

Tonga women still practice traditional crafts. Here an islander sits on a fine mat while she pounds out barkcloth, which is made from the bark of the mulberry tree.

Products of Polynesia

Like other lands near the equator, Polynesia grows tropical products. The most valuable of these is the coconut palm.

The Valuable Coconut Palm

On almost every Polynesian island grow many coconut palms. The trunk of the tree forms timber for building furniture, houses, and boats. The leaves cover roofs and are woven into baskets and screens. From the fiber the Polynesians make sails, matting, rope, and nets.

Coconut oil is used for lighting and cooking. The nut, before it is ripe, contains a liquid which is good to drink. The meat of the ripe nut is a nourishing food.

Copra, the Chief Money Crop

The chief money crop of the islands is copra. All through Polynesia piles of dried, broken coconut meat lie on the docks near the water's edge waiting to be bought and carried away. Copra is shipped to France, Great Britain, Australia, and the United States.

The walls of Samoan houses can be opened when the weather is very hot. Ocean breezes blow through the house and keep it cool. This house belongs to a chief. It is used for meetings and ceremonies.

Future of the Islands

Many nations have an interest in the islands that are sprinkled across the broad Pacific Ocean. Certain of the islands are useful in world transportation. They serve as stopping places for ships and airplanes which are crossing the Pacific. Such island bases are necessary to trade and travel in an ocean where distances are so great.

Several nations gained independence in the years following World War II.

Daily life in a tropical climate can be calm and peaceful. Most homes are built on stone or earth platforms. The walls are wooden frames covered with leaves. When cool breezes blow, the walls on one or more sides can be left open. On many islands food is plentiful, as close as the nearest coconut palm or the fish in the sea. If trouble arises, family members are expected to help one another. Now more and more islanders are traveling to other countries for schooling or on business. Conflicts may arise between those who want to keep the traditional ways and those who would like to see more modern customs adopted.

Do You Know?

1. Where are the islands of Melanesia? Of Polynesia?
2. How are the Pacific islands useful in world transportation?
3. What three western countries continue to rule over some Polynesian islands?

Before You Go On

Words to Learn

batik	taro
quinine	breadfruit
abaca	copra

Number a paper from 1 through 6. After each number write the word or term that matches the definition.

1. A tropical fruit which, when roasted, tastes like bread
2. Manila hemp, used to make rope and other products
3. A medicine made from the bark of the cinchona tree used to treat certain fevers
4. A design on cloth made by putting a wax coating on those parts that are not to be dyed
5. Dried coconut meat from which coconut oil is extracted
6. A tropical plant with a starchy root that is used for food

Finding the Facts

1. How many islands make up the Philippines?
2. What peoples visited the Philippines in the eighth century? In the fifteenth century? In the sixteenth century?
3. Why do many Filipinos speak Spanish and English in addition to their own languages?
4. Name four foods commonly eaten in the Philippines.
5. Why is abaca rope valued by sailors?
6. Who controlled the Philippines during World War II?
7. What is the capital of the Philippines?
8. What is the capital of Indonesia?
9. Name three important products of Java.
10. Why are cinchona forests planted in Java?
11. What two countries own portions of Borneo?
12. Name the major natural resource of Borneo.
13. What are the two parts of New Guinea? How do their governments differ?
14. What type of art is the island of Java best known for? The island of Bali?
15. What two problems does the Republic of Indonesia face?
16. Name four clusters of islands in Micronesia.
17. What is the chief crop in Micronesia?
18. Why is Nauru rich in phosphate?
19. What are three important food products of Melanesia?
20. What is the main industry of Fiji?
21. How long was Hawaii a United States possession before it became a state?
22. Who was Queen Salote? When did she rule?

4

Australia and New Zealand

Two important countries in the Pacific Ocean lie south of the equator in the Southern Hemisphere. They are Australia and New Zealand.

Australia, the Hidden Continent

While North and South America were being explored and settled, a great mass of land lay entirely unknown to Europeans. For thousands of years Australia, now called a continent because of its great size, had been cut off from other parts of the world. Its few people were simple hunter-gatherers. They used stone tools. Some of the animals and plants there were not found anywhere else in the world.

The Exploration of Australia

Dutch explorers learned that there was a large island in the South Pacific. When they sailed to its shores, they called it Terra Australia, which means "southern land."

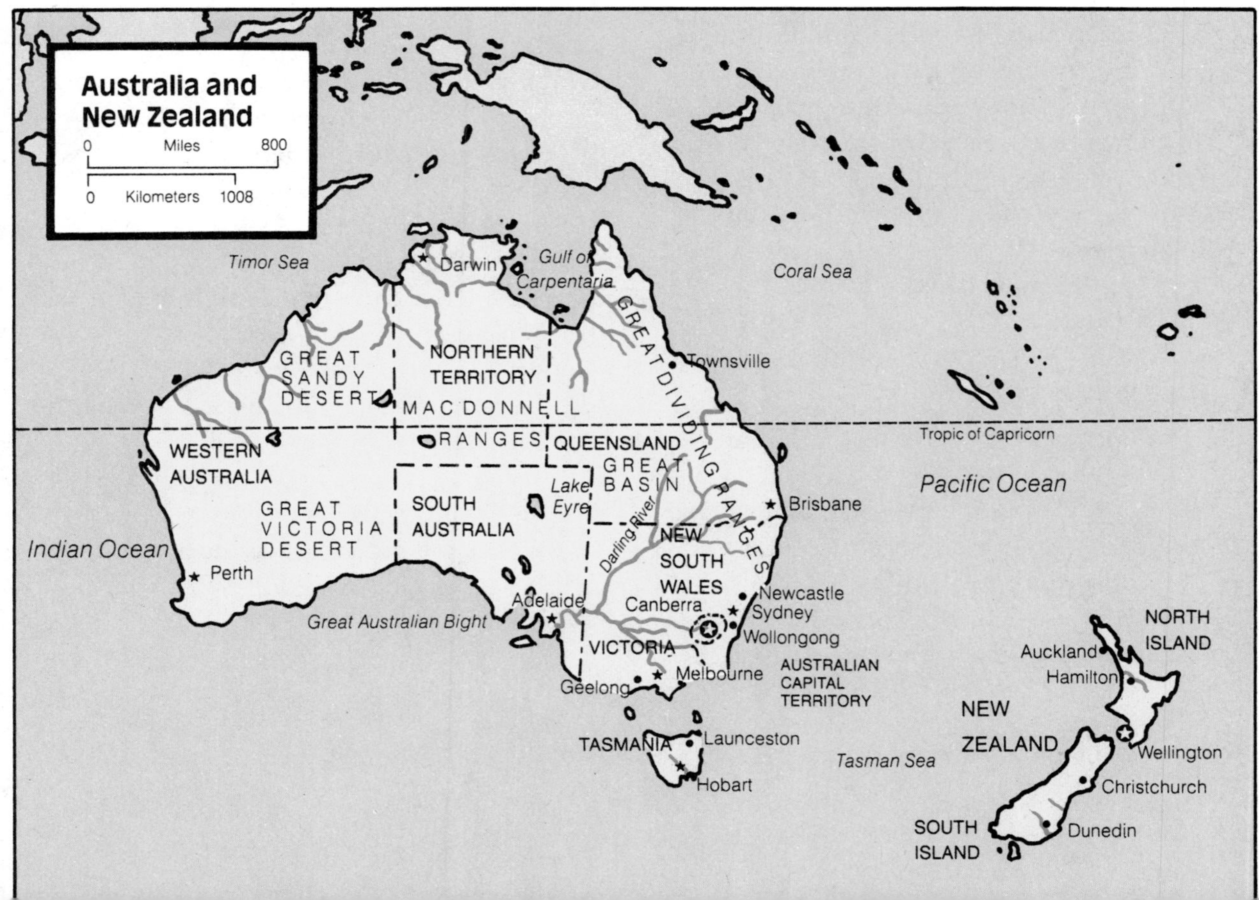

In 1770 an English officer, Captain James Cook, came to the eastern coast of Australia. He took possession, in the name of Great Britain, of a great tract of land which he called New South Wales. Sir Joseph Banks, a student of botany, or the science that studies plants, was with him. Sir Joseph found so many new plants that Captain Cook called the harbor in which the ship was anchored Botany Bay.

The Settlement of Australia

Some years later Great Britain decided to get rid of a group of lawbreakers by sending them out of the country. The first group arrived in Australia in 1788 and were settled on the beautiful inlet where Sydney now stands. The colony was under the charge of an English governor. More criminals were sent out later.

After they had served their terms, some of the former prisoners obtained land, began to till the soil, and built up colonies. After a time these colonies became semi-independent states.

The discovery of gold in the 1850s caused many people from England to throng to Australia. Many who came for gold stayed as settlers. Some settlers raised wheat. Others had large flocks of sheep or herds of cattle.

At last the states of Australia decided to unite. In 1901 Victoria, New South Wales, Queensland, South Australia, and Western Australia, together with the island of Tasmania (taz mā′ nē ə), formed the Australian Commonwealth. A sixth part of the Australian mainland, the Northern Territory, is not much developed. Australia is an independent nation and a member of the British Commonwealth of Nations.

Koalas live in *eucalyptus* trees. They are able to sleep safely high above ground by clinging with sharp claws to branches.

Outdoor Life in Australia

Most of Australia lies in a warm region. The people enjoy outdoor life throughout the year. Those who like nature study find unusual plants and animals to observe there.

Australia's Unusual Animals

The *koala* (kō ä′ lə) is an Australian animal whose young is carried in its mother's pouch. The koala looks like a small teddy bear but is not actually a bear.

The *kangaroo* (kang′gə ro͞o′), moves about by jumping instead of walking or running. The baby kangaroo, also, is carried in its mother's pouch. The largest male kangaroos stand nearly

Melbourne is the capital of the state of Victoria, Australia. Its factories make cars, aircraft, and clothing. Shown here is the Melbourne Exhibition Building.

7 feet (2.1 m) high and can jump forward as fast as the average horse can gallop.

The duckbill, or *platypus* (plat′ə pəs), is an egg-laying mammal with a flat bill like a duck's. The soft fur of the platypus is silvery-dark like that of a mole.

Another mammal that lays eggs is the *echidna* (i kid′nə) or spiny anteater. When frightened, the echidna curls up like a porcupine to protect itself. It has a long tapering snout for poking into anthills.

Among Australia's unusual birds are its black swans and the *kookaburra* (kook′ə bur′ə). The kookaburra has a cackling, braying call.

An Important Australian Tree

Australia has some kinds of trees and shrubs which are not found any place else in the world. One of the trees is the *eucalyptus* (yo͞o′kə lip′ təs). It is often called the gum tree because of the gum, or resin, which oozes from it.

Some eucalyptus trees grow more than 300 feet (90 m) tall. They are beautiful as well as useful trees. The flowers of the eucalyptus look like white bells. The wood is good for making ships, railroad ties, telegraph poles, and fences.

The eucalyptus sheds its bark as well as its leaves. An oil from its leaves is useful in the treatment of coughs and colds.

Some varieties of the eucalyptus will grow in dry ground. Spain and California have imported the eucalyptus tree.

Australian Sports

Australia is one of the world's most sports-minded countries. Its athletes have held many world titles in tennis, swimming, boating, track, and golf.

Almost every type of sport is a favorite in Australia. Surfing, fishing, and boating are popular. In the winter thousands enjoy snow skiing in the southern part of the continent. Another popular sport is Rugby. This is a rough-and-tumble team game something like football.

Australia's People

Australia is almost as large as the United States without Alaska and Hawaii. But Australia has fewer people than our one state of California.

Where the People Live

More than half of the Australians live in the southeastern part, where there are mild winters, warm summers, and plenty of rain. Here are most of the railroads, the farms, the heavy manufacturing, and about all of Australia's coal lands. Here also are the great cities of Sydney and Melbourne (mel′bərn). Each of these cities has a population close to that of Cleveland.

Why Australia Has Few People

About half of Australia will probably never have many people. One reason for its small population is that great stretches of stony desert lie in its center. The temperature is hot there. In the day it is almost never less than 100°F (37.8°C).

At first the Australians did not want their country to have too many settlers. They thought that the coming of people with other ways of living would introduce problems. But in recent years Australia has tried to attract more settlers, by offering farmland, jobs, and homes.

Australia's Early People

Thousands of years before the British people came, tribes of *aborigines* (ab′ə rij′ə nēs) lived in Australia. Aborigines are the earliest known inhabitants of a region. There are about 200,000 aborigine descendants there today. In earlier days they were hunter-gatherers. Today most of them live in modern ways.

Australia's Chief Products

Some vessels leaving Australian ports are loaded with wheat. Others are packed with bales of wool or rabbit skins. Refrigerator ships hold mutton, beef, and rabbit meat. Since the 1960s, iron ore, oil, nickel, and uranium have increased as exports.

A descendant of an Australian *aborigine* paints tree bark, probably from the *eucalyptus* tree. About 200,000 *aborigines* live in Australia today.

Australia's Mines

Australia has produced much gold. It also has large amounts of good coal. Its largest coal fields lie near the largest city, Sydney.

Australia has valuable deposits of lead, silver, zinc, iron, nickel, copper, and uranium. Gas and oil deposits have been discovered.

Australia's Industries

During most of its history Australia has depended on farming for its income. But in recent years manufacturing has rapidly gained in importance.

The island now has many factories which make a variety of small and large products. The Australians manufacture clothing, railroad equipment, automobiles, and machinery. There are also many plants which process foods.

Wheat

Wheat is the great crop of the continent. Nearly three-fourths of all the farming land is used to grow wheat. Wheat grows best in regions that

Today sheep are more easily herded with motorcycles or jeeps. It has been said that "Australia rode to prosperity on a sheep's back." Can you explain why?

have a moist winter or spring and a dry summer. This is true of both southeastern and southwestern Australia.

Sheep and Cattle

Australia has more sheep than any other country. For many years sheep in Australia were raised for wool, not meat. When refrigerator ships were invented, it was found that meat could be exported at a profit.

Sheep raising proved so profitable that it spread northward into dry regions. Even in those semi-desert lands, sheep raisers found that by sinking wells they could get water.

Because Australia lies in the Southern Hemisphere, the northern regions are warmer than the south. North Australia is hot. It has a rainy season and a dry season. In the dry season the pasture is poor. In this part of Australia sheep do not thrive, but cattle can endure dampness and heat. On these great stretches of pasture land are many cattle ranches.

Australia's Rabbits

Soon after the first settlements were made in Australia, new settlers took with them crates of rabbits. Some rabbits escaped. Rabbits quickly increase in number and soon millions of rabbits were devouring pasture needed for sheep.

The government of New South Wales has spent great sums of money to get rid of the rabbits. But Australia has also found uses for these animals. It sells rabbits to England for food. It also sells rabbit skins to England and the United States. Felt hats and fur coats are made of the rabbit skins.

Tasmania and New Zealand

The Dutch, in their voyages to the Pacific, explored new lands. Among these were New Zealand and Tasmania.

Dutch Exploration

One of the early Dutch captains who explored the southern seas was Abel Tasman. He discovered the large island south of Australia which is named for him. This fruit-raising, sheep-raising island is now a part of the Commonwealth of Australia.

Sailing on toward the east, Tasman came upon two large and mountainous islands about 1,200 miles (1,920 km) southeast of Australia.

The people on these islands were tall and strong. When his ship anchored, they came out in large war canoes, each carrying 100 men, and surrounded the ship. These islands were a part of New Zealand.

Settlement by the English

After Australia was settled, the British spread out gradually over the islands to the southeast, where Tasman had encountered the fierce people known as Maoris (mou′rēz). The Maoris were Polynesians. There were conflicts between British settlers and Maoris, but in time peace was made.

What New Zealand Is Like

The two principal islands of New Zealand are North Island and South Island. Look at them on the map of Australia and New Zealand on page 518. They are 1,000 miles (1,600 km) long and have about the same area as the British Isles.

The islands were settled by English missionaries, who converted the Maoris to Christianity. In time, these islands were brought under the rule of the British government. Today they are a part of the British Commonwealth.

Along the western side of the twin islands are mountains called the Southern Alps. Some of these are volcanoes that send out steam.

The westerly winds bring plenty of rain to New Zealand. The eastern parts of the islands are drier. Wheat is raised there, but most of the land is in pasture. In the mild climate, cattle can stay outdoors even during the winter.

This is a fine land for sheep. New Zealand exports more mutton than does any other country, but Australia produces more wool. Dairying is very important too.

Swift mountain streams help New Zealand produce much electricity. Although power is plentiful, manufacturing has not become important. New Zealand lacks the raw materials needed to supply factories.

The chief industries are those which process farm products. Many of the processing plants are located in Wellington, the capital, and in Auckland (ôk′lənd), the largest city.

New Zealand Today

New Zealand is working hard to protect its environment and to create more jobs. One of its special interests is to create more jobs for Maoris. Maoris are integrated with the rest of the population in schools, although there are some special schools for Maori children. Because of the great distances in rural areas, some schools teach by radio and by mailing lessons to children. New Zealand is also trying to develop markets for its industries in other lands.

Do You Know?

1. Why do most people live in the southeastern part of Australia?
2. How was Australia settled?
3. What are its chief industries?
4. Name three unusual animals found in Australia.
5. Which islands make up New Zealand?

To Help You Learn

Words to Learn

koala	aborigine	copra
abaca	eucalyptus	echidna
platypus	kookaburra	kangaroo
taro		

Number a paper from 1 through 10. After each number write the word or term that matches the definition.

1. An Australian bird with a cackling, braying call
2. An egg-laying mammal of Australia, also called the spiny anteater
3. An Australian animal that looks like a teddy bear and whose young is carried in its mother's pouch
4. An egg-laying mammal of Australia with a flat bill like a duck's
5. Dried coconut meat from which coconut oil is extracted
6. An Australian animal that moves about by jumping and whose young is carried in its mother's pouch
7. A tropical plant with a starchy root used for food
8. An Australian tree that oozes gum, or resin
9. One of the earliest known inhabitants of a region
10. Manila hemp fiber used to make rope and other products

Finding the Facts

1. In what temperature region are the Philippines?
2. How did the United States gain control of the Philippines?
3. What is the official language of the Philippines?
4. How did the Philippines gain their independence?
5. What is the capital of Indonesia?
6. What are two products of Sumatra?
7. Why did the Japanese want control of Indonesia during World War II?
8. How and when did the Indonesians gain their independence?
9. How is Guam governed?
10. What is the chief product of Nauru?
11. Name three independent Melanesian nations.
12. Who settled Polynesia? How did they reach the islands?
13. What is the capital of American Samoa? Why is its location important?
14. Name two traditional crafts of Tonga.
15. Name four separate parts of the coconut tree that are used by Pacific islanders.
16. Australia and New Zealand are located in what hemisphere?
17. When did Captain Cook arrive in Botany Bay? Why did he give the harbor that name?

18. What event in the 1850s caused many people from England to rush to Australia?
19. When was the Australian Commonwealth formed?
20. Name four exports of Australia.
21. Where are Australia's largest coal fields?
22. Who are the Maoris?
23. Name three farm products of New Zealand.

Learning from Maps

1. Look at the map of the Nations of the Pacific on pages 506 and 507 to answer these questions: Which includes the largest area, Micronesia, Melanesia, or Polynesia? Which has the greatest number of large islands? Find the distance between Melbourne and Jakarta. Between Melbourne and Sydney. Between Jakarta and Manila.
2. Look at the map of Australia and New Zealand on page 518 and answer these questions: In what temperature region is the northern half of Australia? The southern half? What imaginary line separates these two regions? Where are most of the cities? In what temperature region is New Zealand?

Using Study Skills

1. **Time Line:** Place in the proper order of time the following events: Beginning of Japanese occupation of Dutch East Indies; Hawaii becomes fiftieth state; First British colony founded in Australia; Philippines almost completely self-governing; All Pacific islands freed from Japanese occupation; United States acquires Hawaii.

   Copy the time line from page 503. Add these events to your time line.

   Study the completed time line and answer the following questions: How many years was it between Captain Cook's arrival in Australia and the founding of the first British colony there? Between the Philippine's almost complete self-government and independence? Between the Philippines' release from Japanese occupation and independence? How long were the Dutch East Indies occupied by the Japanese? How long was Hawaii governed by the United States before it became a state? Which came first, Philippine independence or Hawaiian statehood? By how many years?
2. **Outline:** Outline the steps in making a batik print using three colors: pink, red, and black. The outline has been partially completed for you below.

   I. Pink design
      A. Dip the cloth in pink dye
   II. Red design
      A. Apply the wax to the pink area of the design
      B.
      C. Remove the wax with boiling water
   III. Black design
      A. Apply the wax to the pink and red areas of the design
      B.
      C.

France	Great Britain	United States	Independent
			Philippines Indonesia

3. **Chart:** Make a chart showing the present governments of Pacific nations. The chart has been started for you above. Add to it: Nauru, Tahiti, Guam, New Hebrides, the Solomon Islands, New Caledonia, Fiji, and Tonga.

Thinking It Through

1. Imagine that you are a southeast Asian of long ago and are getting ready to start on a sea journey which will take you to the Polynesian islands. You are traveling by a double canoe with a storage platform in between. What will you load on the platform?
2. Modern Philippine culture and language has been influenced by that nation's past rule by Spain and the United States. In its long history Chinese, Japanese, and Muslim Arabs were also important visitors. What kind of clues would you look for to decide the influence of these peoples on the Philippines?
3. Australia's first settlers were lawbreakers from England's prisons. What kinds of problems do you think this might have caused the first governor of the colony?
4. Rabbits in Australia are an example of how the manipulation of an environment by the introduction of new animals or plants can cause new problems. What other examples can you give?

Projects

1. You may wish to learn more about the unusual animals found in Australia. Make a report to your class on one of the following: platypus, echidna, kangaroo, koala, kookaburra. Pictures will help make your report more interesting. If you live near a museum or zoo make a visit to see these animals.
2. The Explorers' Committee might like to learn more about the voyages of Captain Cook. Read about him and trace his route through the South Pacific on a map.
3. Present a shadow play. Cut out figures of birds, animals, or people from heavy cardboard. With tape attach a stick at least 12 inches (30 cm) long as a handle. Make a stage by hanging a sheet above a table and putting a light a few feet behind the table. Scenery can be made of cardboard and set up on the table behind the sheet. The puppets must be moved between the light and the sheet. The storytellers and musicians can sit on the floor behind the sheet while they move the puppets across the stage.
4. See how many objects you can find in your home that came from the Pacific islands or are made of Pacific island products. Set up a display in your classroom.

Learning About Maps and Globes

Maps and globes are special tools. They help us to understand our earth and the people, places, and things on it. Maps and globes are useful tools only if we know how to use them. The lessons in this section will help you improve your skills in using maps and globes. These map and globe skills will help you to better understand the world around you.

Words to Learn

You will meet these words in this unit. As you read, you will learn what they mean and how to pronounce them. The Word List will help you.

barrier
boundary
distortion
economic activity
Great Circle
grid
majority
minority
partition
per capita
projection
scale

1 Map Projections and Latitude and Longitude

The only truly accurate, or correct, likeness of the world is a globe. This is because a globe, like the earth, is a sphere. It is not always practical, however, to use a globe. It cannot be folded or easily carried. Maps are needed for this purpose.

Maps have some drawbacks also. They are never completely accurate. Showing the round earth on a flat surface is difficult. It is like trying to flatten a rubber ball or the peel of an orange. Part of the surface must be stretched. This change of shape is called *distortion* (dis tôr′ shən).

Many geographers have worked at the problem. They have figured out many ways of making maps from globes. These different ways of showing the world on a flat surface are called *projections* (prə jek′shənz).

Two different kinds of projections are shown on the right. Each gives a fairly accurate picture of a part of the earth. Some regions, however, are shown more accurately than others. The regions near the center of each map are accurate. The regions away from the center are distorted.

The map of the Western Hemisphere, to the right, shows the equator as a line halfway between the North Pole and the South Pole. Regions near the equator are shown fairly accurately. This is because the map is centered on the equator.

Look at the map on the lower right. It is centered on the North Pole. Where is the equator on this map?

Pilots sometimes find polar projections useful for plotting air routes. Note how simple it is to see the most direct routes between major cities in the Northern Hemisphere. Find the shortest route to Moscow from Chicago. Would you fly by way of London or over the Arctic Circle?

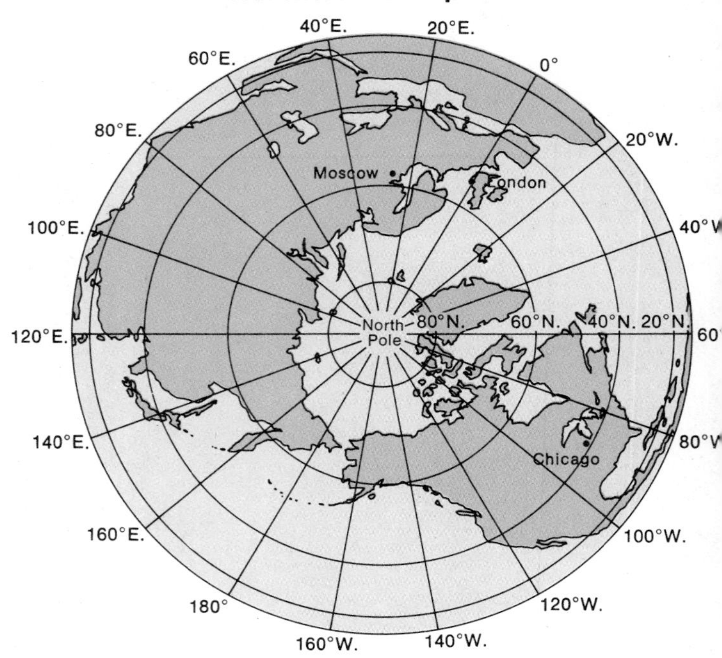

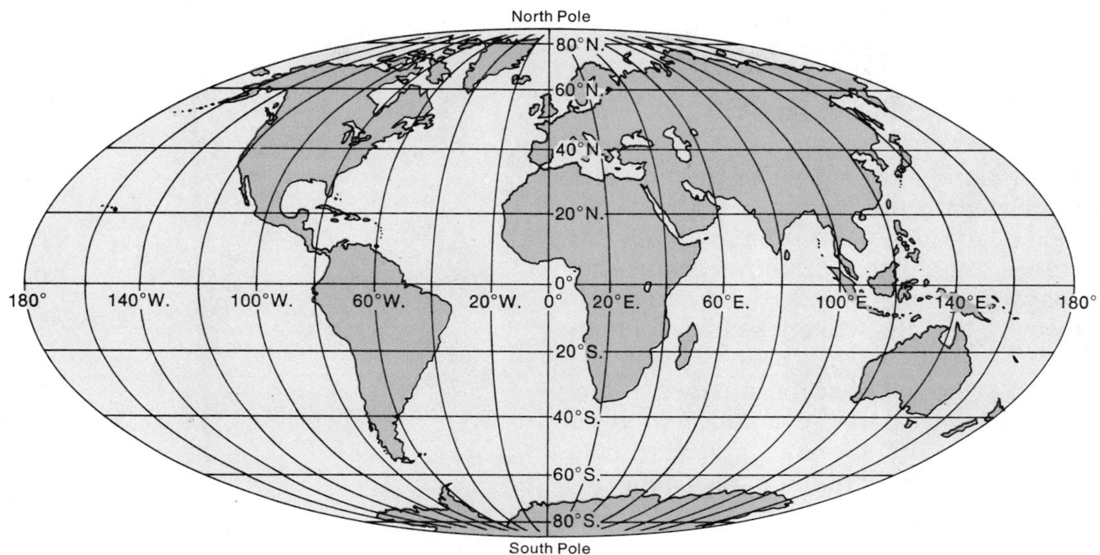

The map above shows all of the earth's continents and oceans. It shows the whole world on one map. From north to south it is centered on the equator. From east to west it is centered on Europe and Africa. These continents, especially the areas near the equator, are shown most accurately here.

The east-and-west lines on this map are latitude lines. Latitude is measured in degrees north or south of the equator. These guidelines are drawn parallel to, that is, at an even distance from, the equator. Therefore, they are called parallels of latitude or, more simply, parallels. Parallels show how far a place is north or south of the equator.

The distance between parallels is measured in degrees. From the equator to one of the poles is 90 degrees. The equator is zero degrees, or zero latitude. The parallels on this map are shown at 20 degrees, 40 degrees, 60 degrees, and so on.

The north-and-south lines on the map are also guidelines for locating places. They are called meridians of longitude, or simply meridians. These meridians meet at both poles. They, too, are measured in degrees. The degrees help to measure distance east and west. The numbering starts from an imaginary line called the prime meridian, which runs through Greenwich, England. It is at 0 degrees.

Parallels of latitude and meridians of longitude form an intersecting pattern called a *grid* (grid). A grid helps us locate any place in the world in terms of degrees.

Look at Africa. Its northernmost part is located halfway between 30 degrees and 40 degrees. We say it is at 35 degrees north latitude. Its tip is located at 35 degrees south latitude. Its western "bulge" is at about 19 degrees west longitude. And its eastern "horn" is at about 50 degrees east longitude.

Between which parallels and meridians is your home located?

Between which parallels and meridians is Australia located?

At what latitude is the North Pole?

2 Globes Show the Shortest Distance Between Places

Ship and airplane navigators like to know the shortest possible route from one place to another. They can't use most ordinary maps for this purpose. Maps, as you know, distort distances between places on the round earth. The easiest way to find true distances is by using a globe.

On a globe, the shortest route between any two places is always part of a *Great Circle* (grāt sur'kəl). A Great Circle is any circle that cuts the earth in half. You can find many Great Circles by doing a simple exercise.

Take a string, wrap it tightly around the globe at the equator. Mark the distance on the string. You have just measured the largest circle possible on a globe. It is one of an endless number of Great Circles. Next, wrap the string from the North Pole to the South Pole and back again to the North Pole. You will find this distance the same. It, too, is a Great Circle. Now take your string and wrap it tightly around the globe in any direction. So long as the distance is the same as the equator's distance, you have found another Great Circle.

You can measure other circles around the globe, but they will be smaller. For example, wrap your string around any parallel of latitude except the equator. Notice that you must hold the string more loosely than before. Is the circle shorter or longer than a Great Circle? Circles which are not Great Circles are more curved than Great Circles. A Great Circle route is shorter because it is less curved than a smaller circle's route.

Now you are ready to measure a Great Circle route between any two places on earth. You can find this route without measuring a whole Great Circle. Anytime you hold your string really tight between two places on a globe, you are measur-

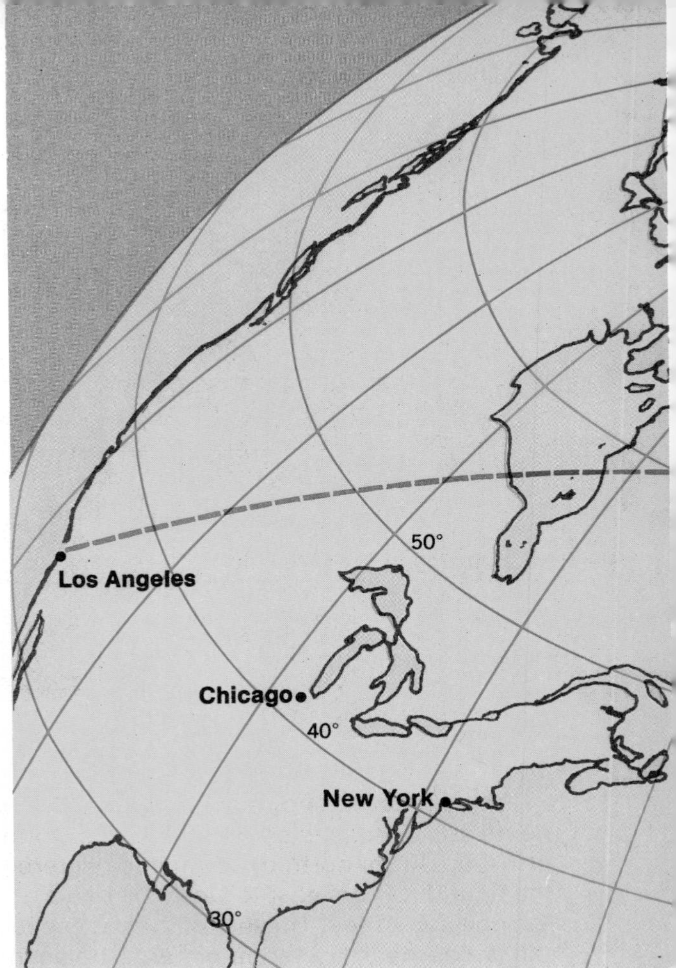

ing the shortest distance. And the shortest distance is always part of a Great Circle.

Use the "tight string trick" on a globe to answer the following questions:

Suppose you are planning to fly from Chicago to Moscow in the Soviet Union. You want to go the shortest way. Will your plane fly over Greenland?

Charles Lindbergh was the first pilot to fly alone from New York to Paris, France. Naturally, he wanted to go the shortest way possible. Therefore, he chose a Great Circle route. Over what water and land areas did he fly?

When you fly a Great Circle route, you may change directions many times. This is especially true when you fly between places at the same latitude. Look at the map. Los Angeles and Rome are at about the same latitude. If you flew from Los Angeles, what would your direction be at first? What direction would you fly in the last part of your trip?

Now suppose you are flying from the east coast of the United States. You start from a place located at 40 degrees north latitude. You are flying to a place on the west coast of the United States at the same latitude. During the latter part of the trip you will fly southwest. In what direction will you fly at first?

3 Comparing Distribution Maps

All over the world, people work to earn a living. There are millions of different jobs. But it's impossible to show them all on a map. The map of the Eastern Hemisphere on the right-hand page shows only six general kinds of work or *economic activity* (ek′ə nom′ik ak tiv′ə tē). The label, "manufacturing and commerce," for example, covers many jobs. Can you name some?

What other patterns do you see on this map? Why, for example, are there places with little economic activity? Compare the map with the World Vegetation map on page 27 to find some reasons.

Comparing economic activity with average

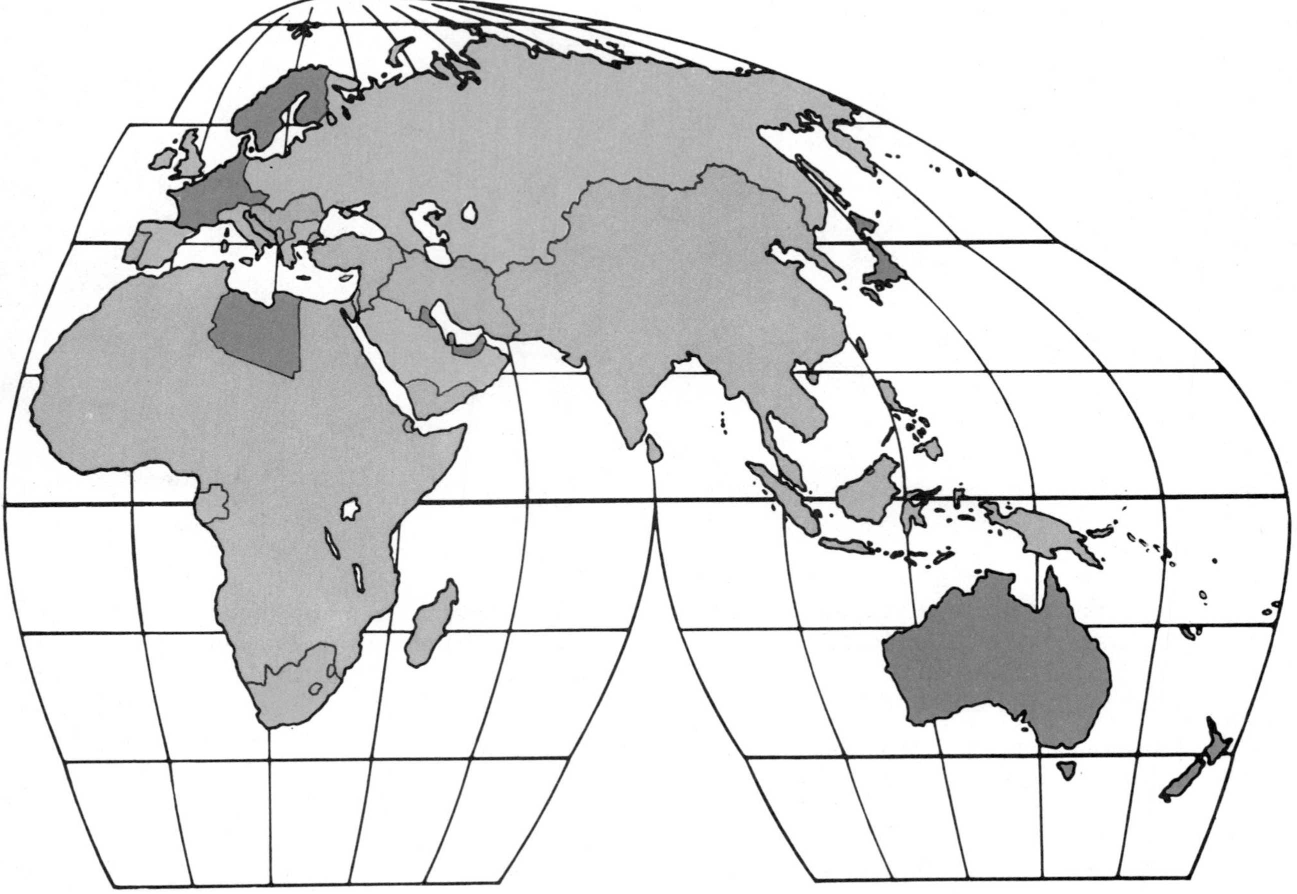

Per Capita Income

(Average yearly income per person in U.S. dollars)

0–1000

1001–2000

2001–4000

more than 4000

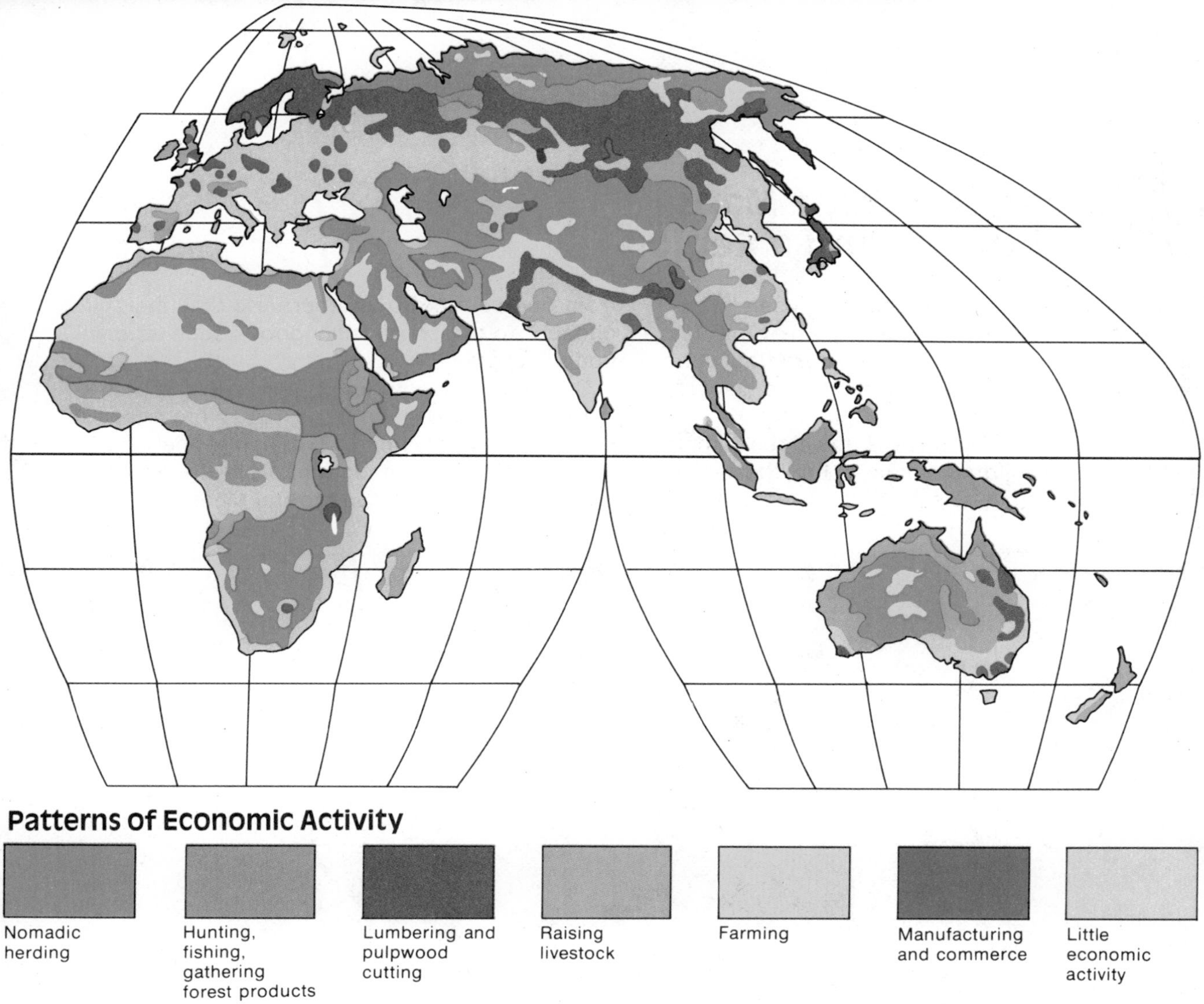

Patterns of Economic Activity

Nomadic herding

Hunting, fishing, gathering forest products

Lumbering and pulpwood cutting

Raising livestock

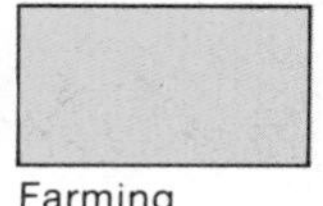

Farming

Manufacturing and commerce

Little economic activity

per capita income (pur kap′i tə) gives even more facts about working. Per capita means per person. Some kinds of work seem to make countries, and people, richer than other kinds.

Average income is a useful way of measuring how well people live. But remember, it's only an average. For example, you can find the average height of pupils in your class. Just add up everyone's height. Then divide that number by the number of pupils. The answer you get will be the average height of pupils in your class. But it probably won't be the same as your height.

Look at countries where the average income is $4,000 and over. What is the major kind of economic activity in most of these countries? In general, do Europeans, or Africans, or Asians have higher average per capita incomes?

These two maps give only part of the story. They don't tell you how many people live in each country. Some countries in the Middle East receive much money from oil. In addition, very few people live in these countries. Low population and valuable oil make the average income very high. However, other countries such as India must divide their resources among many people. Is India's average per capita income high or low? Are incomes in Europe high or low?

4 Using Different Maps to Understand a Region

Some things can draw people closer, while other things keep them apart. The map on this page shows a network of transportation connections in Europe. Connections join people, places, or things together.

Long ago, the Europeans developed their waterways by building canals to link the rivers. These rivers and canals make it easier to travel from one country to another. And they make it cheaper to transport bulky goods such as ore, coal, and grain.

Compare the waterways map with the political map of Europe on page 161. Which countries have a lot of canals? Which ones have very few? Find canal connections from the Atlantic Ocean and the North Sea to the Mediterranean

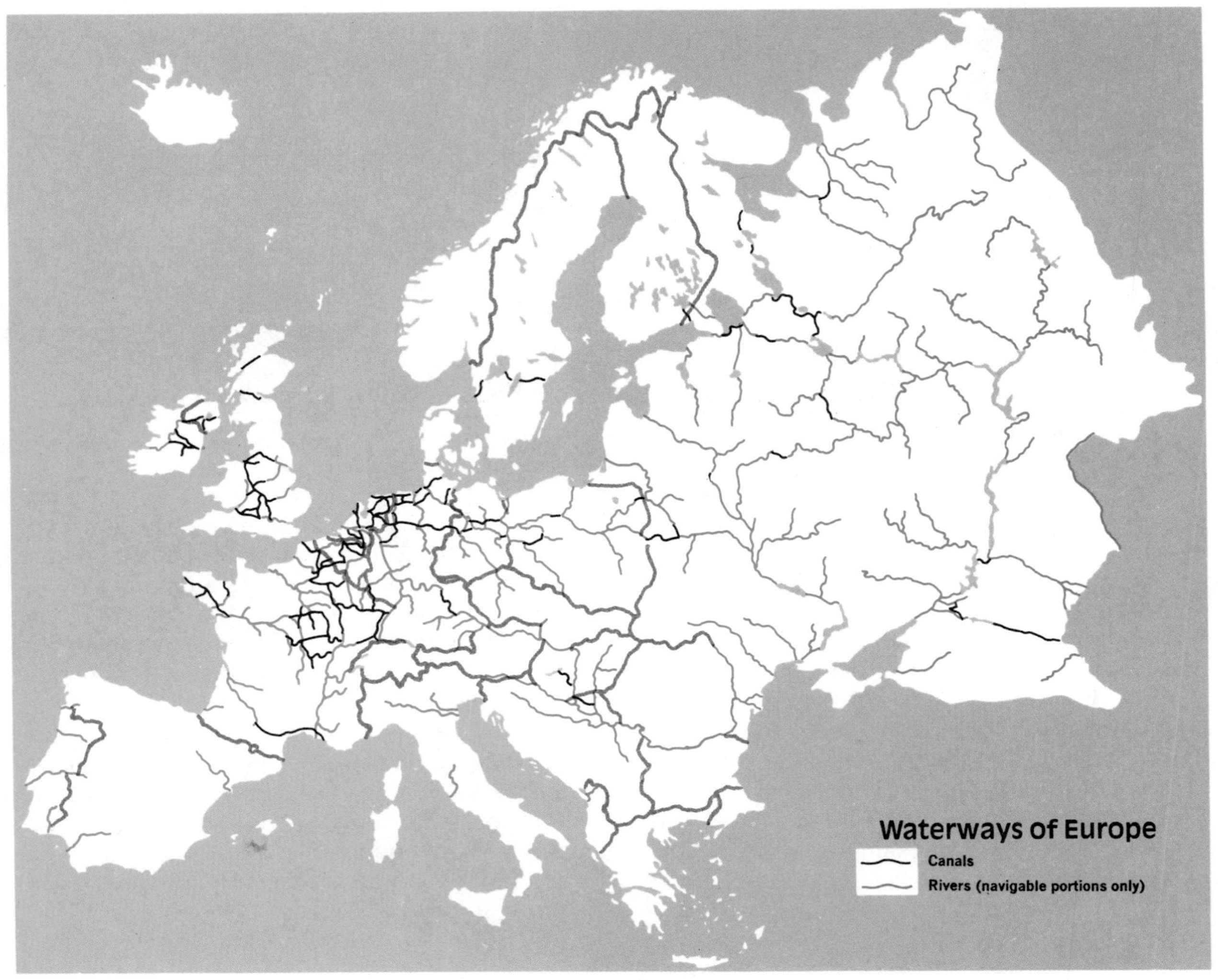

Languages of Europe

Sea. Find waterways that connect the White Sea and the Baltic Sea with the Black Sea.

Barriers (bar′ē ərz) are the opposite of connections. They separate people, places, and things instead of linking them together. A barrier can be easy to see, such as a wall or a mountain. Or it can be invisible, such as people not being able to speak and communicate with other people.

Look at the languages map on this page. In how many countries are Romance languages spoken in Europe? In how many are Germanic languages spoken? Do you think language is a bigger barrier between France and Italy or France and Germany? Why? Why do you suppose school children in Europe study more than one language? Capital letters have been used on the map to show the languages spoken in some small areas. What letter is shown for Switzerland?

5 Comparing Maps at Different Scales

You have already seen how two maps may look alike but show different things. On pages 532 and 533, two maps of the Eastern Hemisphere were used to compare both economic activity and average per capita income.

On these pages, only one subject is shown: religions. But the *scale* (skāl), or relative size, of the map below is quite different from the scale of the map on the next page.

Sometimes people need a map that shows a subject in a general way. In that case, a small-scale map like the one below is most useful. One inch (2.5 cm) stands for thousands of miles on the earth. This map is used to show the religions that the *majority* (mə jôr′ə te) of the people in each country practices. A majority is any number greater than half the total number.

What major religions are shown for the United States? Does that mean that no other religions are practiced here?

What major religions are shown on the world map? Some *minority* (mə nôr′ə te) religions are not shown. A minority is any number less than half the total number.

Other things you cannot see on this map are the different branches of a religion. The Christian religion, for example, is shown as the majority religion in the United States. But you cannot tell from the map that the Christian religion includes both Catholics and Protestants.

To get more details about a subject, you need a different map. The map of the Middle East is

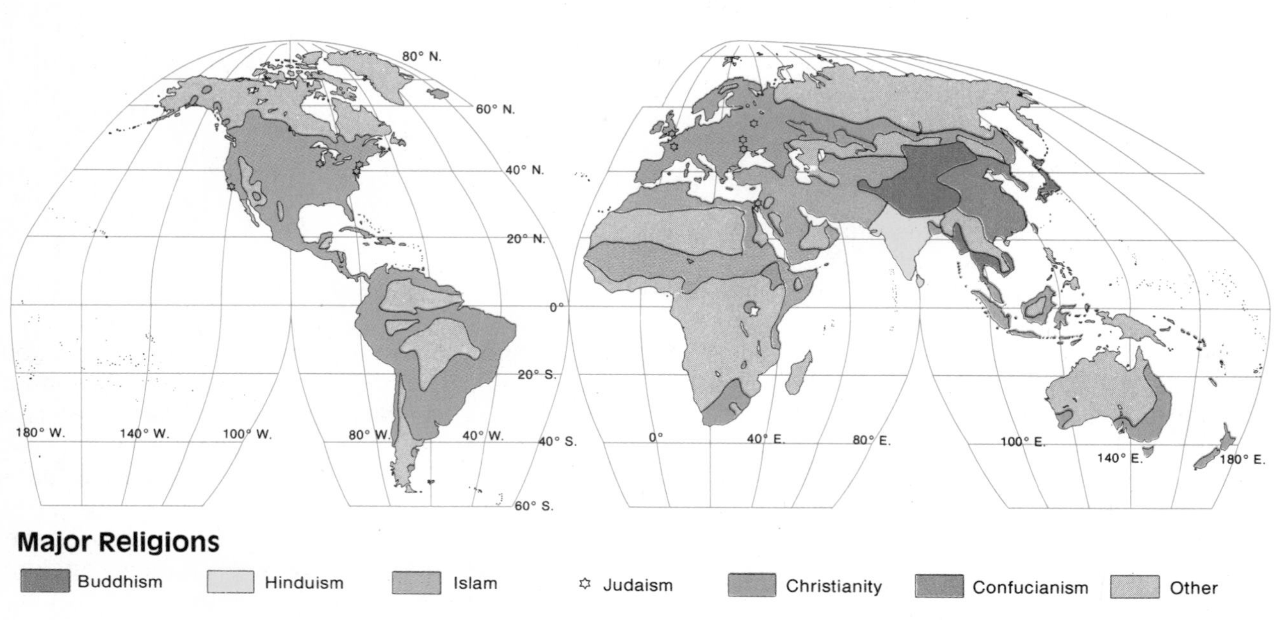

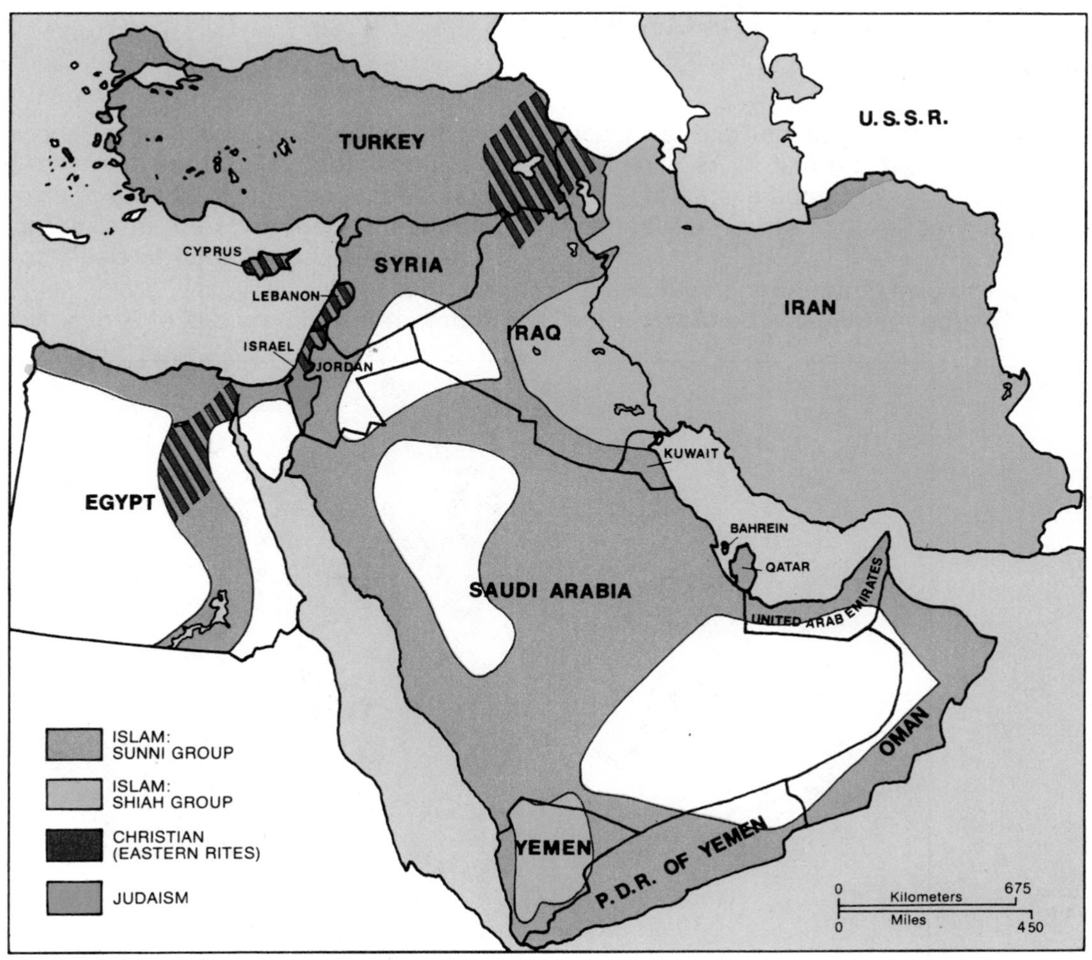

an example. On this map, one inch (2.5 cm) stands for far fewer miles on earth. This map is a large-scale map.

This large-scale map of the Middle East shows that people who believe in Islam are divided into two main groups. They are the Sunni (soon′ē) and the Shiah (shē′ə). In what countries is the Shiah group of Moslems in the majority? What other religions are practiced there? In what countries do you find Judaism? (The map does not show all minorities within each country.) In which countries do you find the Christian religion?

6 Using Maps to Understand History: Africa

Maps showing different time periods can teach you something about the history of a region. These maps of Africa are good examples. They show who has controlled Africa at different times.

Maps can also give information about changing *boundaries* (boun′dar ēz). A boundary is the line drawn between one country and another. As political control in Africa changed, political boundaries sometimes changed also. Some countries became different in size and shape. Sometimes a colony was divided into several countries.

Look at the three maps of Africa. Notice the

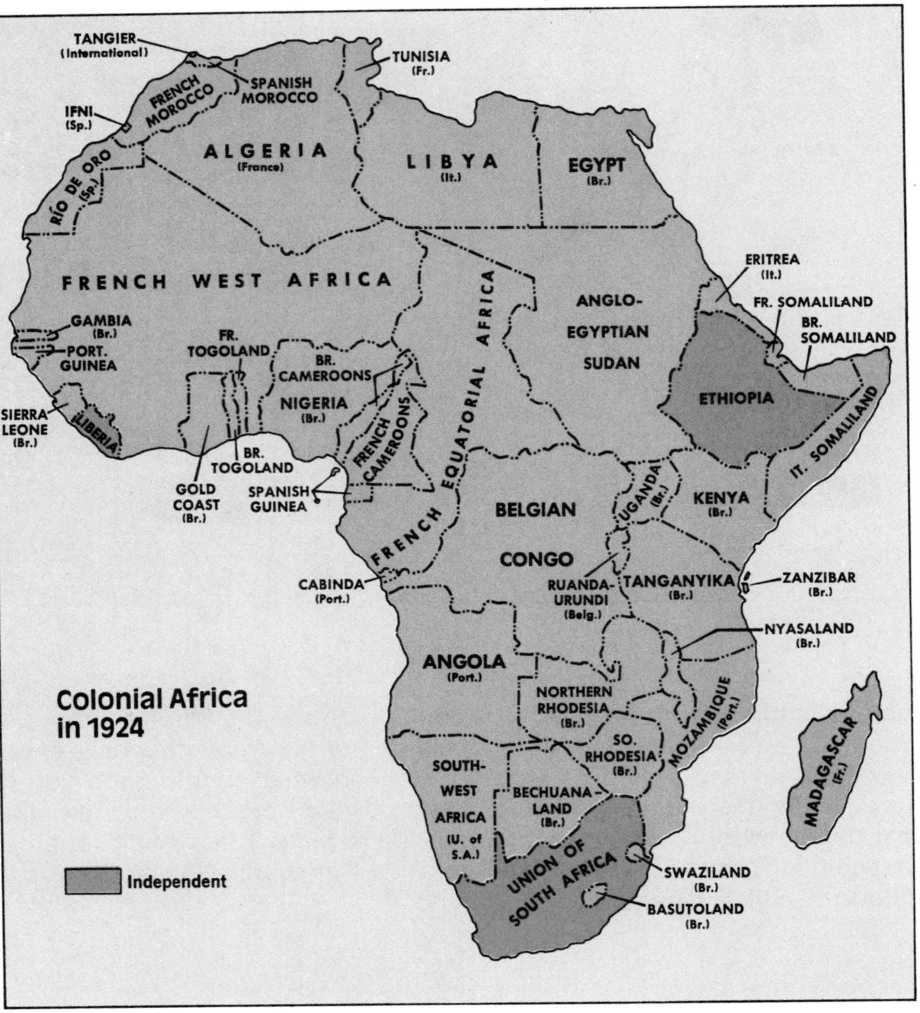

Colonial Africa in 1924

Independent

years they represent. During that time, great changes happened. The map of Africa on page 232 of your textbook gives an up-to-date picture of the continent.

Before the times shown here, Africa was divided differently. It was divided largely into ethnic, or culture, groups. Then several hundred years ago, people from Europe came to Africa. They divided the continent to suit their own needs. Mainly, they wanted slaves and they wanted Africa's natural resources for factories back in Europe. To ship these resources, Europeans built ports along the coast. They claimed the land around those ports. These areas were known as European colonies. The control by foreign countries was called colonialism (kə lō′ nē ə liz′əm).

After 1950, many African colonies began to gain independence. The Africans formed new governments and sometimes gave their nations new names. Many of these nations, however, kept their old boundaries. Sometimes, many different ethnic groups became fellow citizens of a new nation. But their customs and languages often remained completely different.

Look at the three maps. In general, what do they tell you about Africa's history in the twentieth century?

What European countries controlled Africa in 1924? What countries were independent at that time? Compare Africa in 1950 with Africa in 1924. What changes had taken place?

What changes took place in Africa between 1950 and 1968? How much of a change was there on the continent?

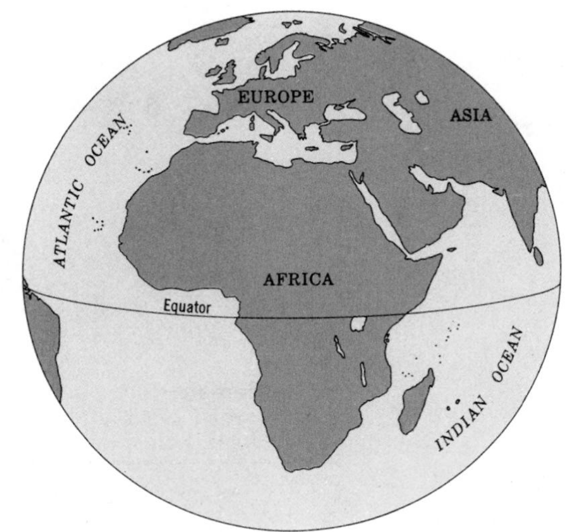

7 Using Maps to Understand History: Poland

In the last map skill lesson, you saw how a huge continent—Africa—changed in just a few years. The three maps on these pages show how the boundaries of a single country have changed many times in the last 200 years.

The many sizes and shapes of Poland were the result of history and geography. Poland is located on a low, fertile plain in central Europe. Except for mountains in the south, it has no natural barriers to protect it from invaders. A natural barrier is anything that separates one country from another. It may be a mountain range, a thick forest, a desert, or a rugged coastline. For centuries, neighboring countries

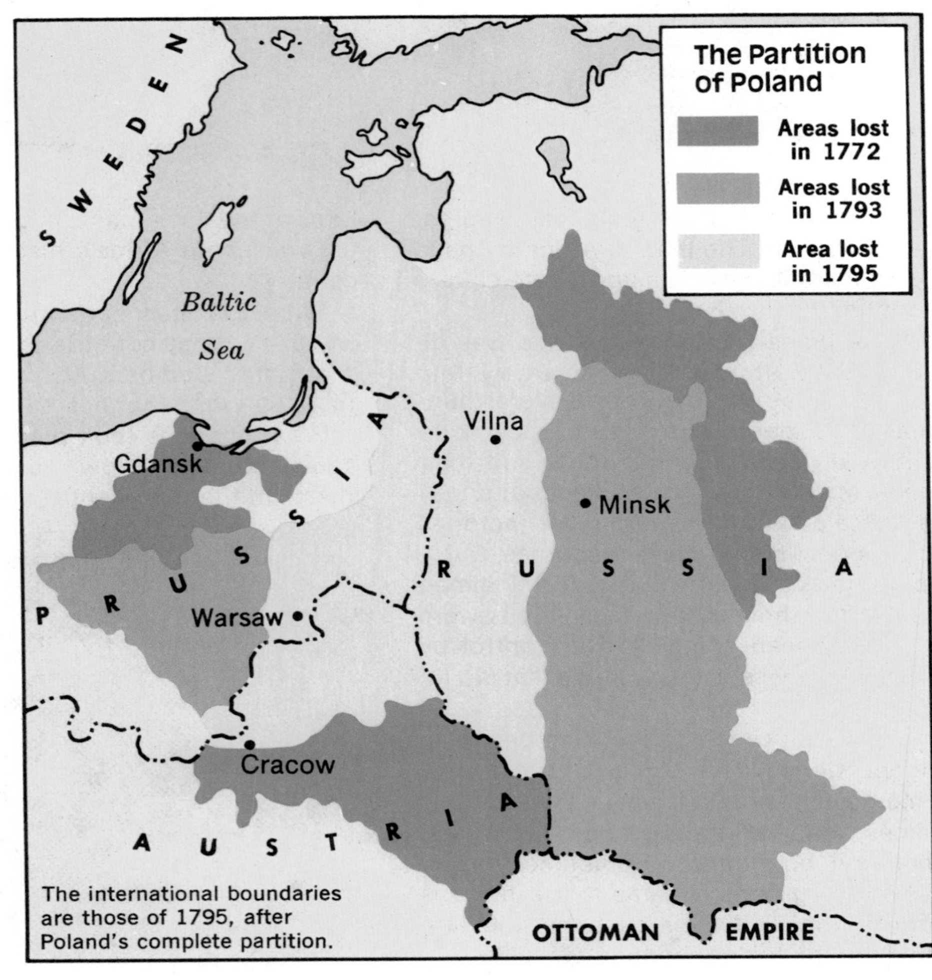

have marched over Poland's hard-to-defend borders. Often Poland has fought back. But several times it has actually disappeared from the map.

In the eighteenth century, three countries carved up Poland three times in less than 25 years. In 1772, Poland was divided the first time. Parts of it went to Austria, Russia, and Prussia. (Prussia is now part of Germany.) Prussia and Russia took even larger chunks of the country in 1793. At that time, a group of Polish people fought hard to keep their country. But they were finally defeated by their neighbors. In 1795, the complete *partition* (pär tish′ ən), or division, of Poland had taken place. The country was swept off the map.

Poland lived only as a dream in the minds of the Polish people for almost 125 years. Finally, Poland became a country again in 1918. Germany had just lost World War I. The winners—Great Britain, France, Italy, and the United States—created a new Poland. The map at the right, above, shows what Poland looked like in 1921.

During World War II (1939–1945), Poland once more disappeared completely. Germany invaded Poland and took complete control. After the war, which Germany lost, Poland was reborn. What country gained a large part of what had been Poland? What country lost a large area that became a part of Poland? Since that time, the Polish government has been closely controlled by the Soviet Union.

8 Maps Show a World of Water

The oceans of the world cover over 75 percent of the earth's surface. As you can see on a globe, they are actually one big global ocean. However, we usually think of them as four separate oceans: the Atlantic Ocean, the Pacific Ocean, the Indian Ocean, and the Arctic Ocean. You can see their shapes clearly on the opposite page. Which ocean is the largest?

Does the Pacific Ocean extend over more than a hemisphere? How is the Arctic Ocean shown on the large, wide map?

For centuries, oceans were great barriers between the continents. It took courage and good geographic guesswork for early explorers to leave home. Gradually sailors learned to locate places accurately. Methods of transportation improved.

Today, we say our world is "shrinking." What does that term really mean? The real size of the earth cannot change. What has changed is the

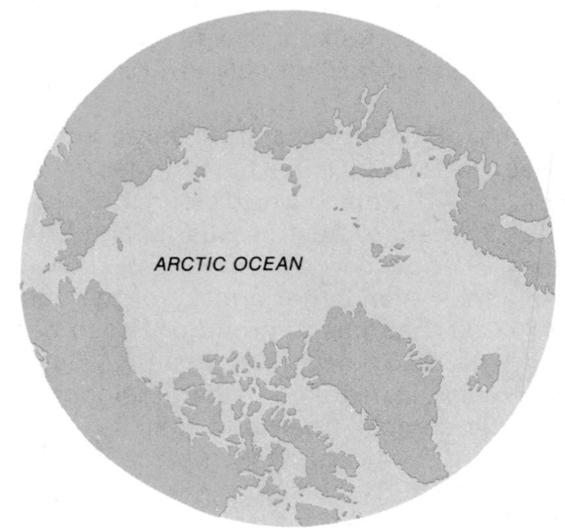

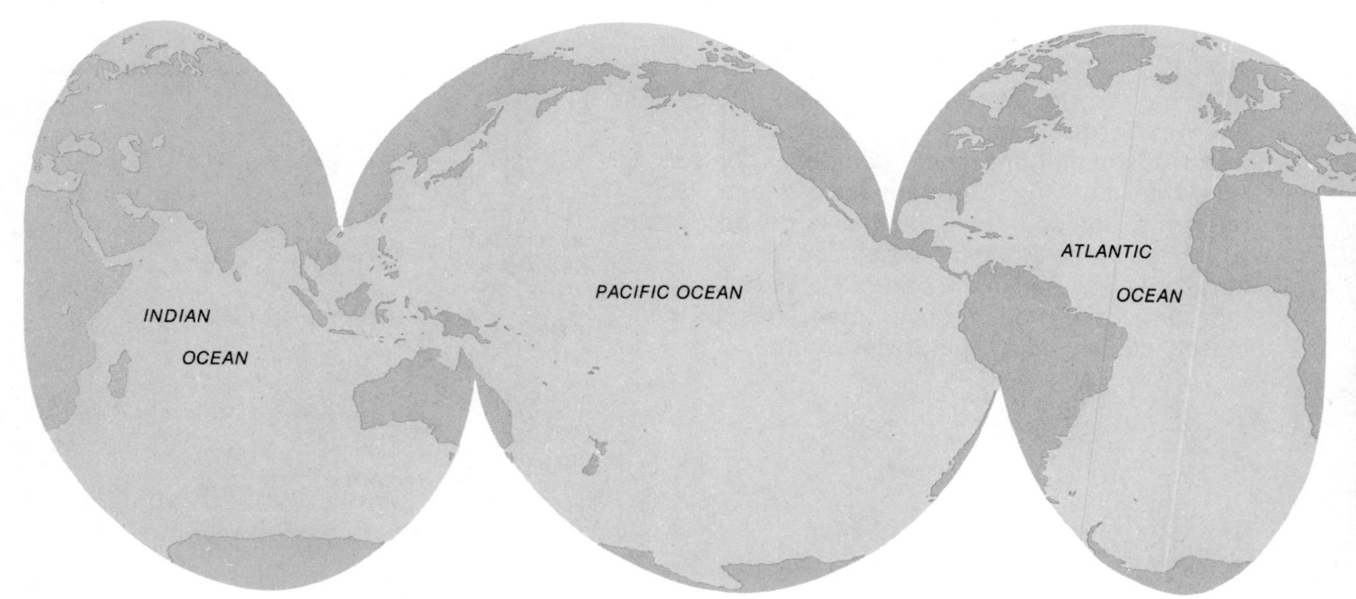

Oceans of the World

time it takes to travel. Every new improvement in shipbuilding has made travel time shorter. Airplanes have become faster and faster.

Here is an example of the changes in travel time. In 1927, an American, Charles Lindbergh, made the first solo flight from New York to Paris. The flight took more than 33 hours. Today, over 50 years later, a fast jet flies the same distance in 4 hours. Suppose we measured distance in hours rather than miles. The large globe below shows the size of the earth measured by Lindbergh's flying time. Compare it with the small ball below it, which shows the size of the earth measured by a jet plane's flying time.

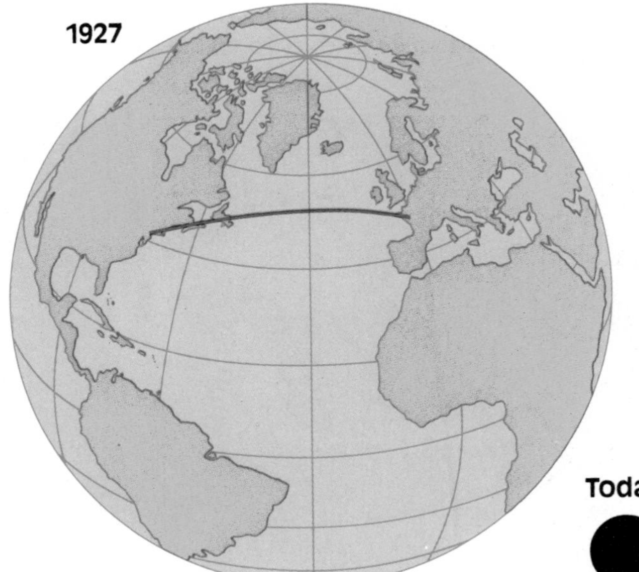

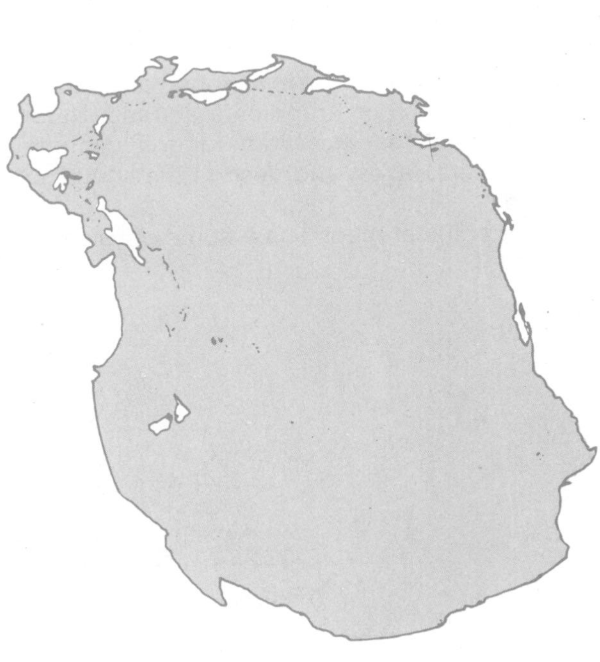

9 Using an Atlas

You probably have used an atlas before and know that it is a book of maps. Your book has a special reference section called an atlas. This atlas can be a valuable source of information if you know how to use it. You can find the atlas by referring to the table of contents.

To use the atlas in your book, you must know what parts of the world the maps show and what each map tells about the area shown. The map titles will help you. How many world maps are there in your atlas? What continents or regions are shown on the other maps?

Maps often are grouped according to the kind of information they show. Your atlas includes political maps, physical maps, and special-purpose maps.

Political maps are used to show countries, states, and other political divisions. Most political maps also show capitals and other cities. Physical maps help you understand how the earth looks. Colors and shading are used to show landforms or to indicate altitude. Natural features such as mountain ranges, mountain peaks, rivers, lakes, and deserts are shown and labeled.

Most political maps show some physical features and almost all physical maps include political features. Maps that show both political and physical features often are called physical-political maps. **Map A** below shows part of one of the physical maps in your atlas. What political features are included on this map?

Maps that show such things as population, precipitation, climate, vegetation, and products are called special-purpose maps. **Map B** on the next page is one of the special-purpose maps in your atlas. What does **Map B** show?

When you study the maps in your atlas, you will have to use what you have learned about direction, latitude, longitude, and scale. You will need to know some common map symbols and how to interpret, or understand, color keys.

Many maps have a compass rose or a north arrow to show directions. Remember, if you know which way north is, you can find the other cardinal directions and the intermediate directions. Even if there is no compass rose or north arrow on a map, you can still find directions. It is a general practice to print maps so that north is toward the top of the page. Look at **Map A.** What country is north of Namibia? In what direction is Madagascar from Tanzania?

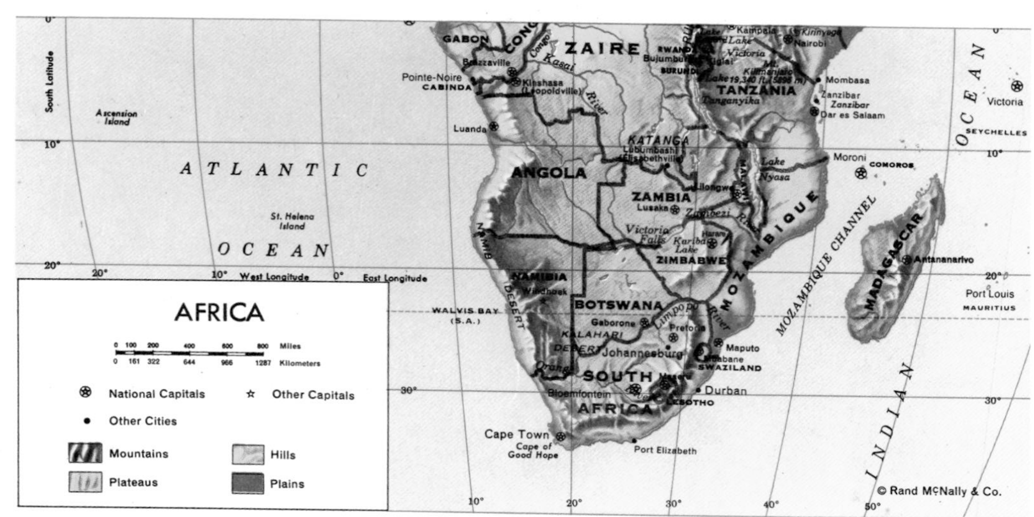

Map A

World Vegetation

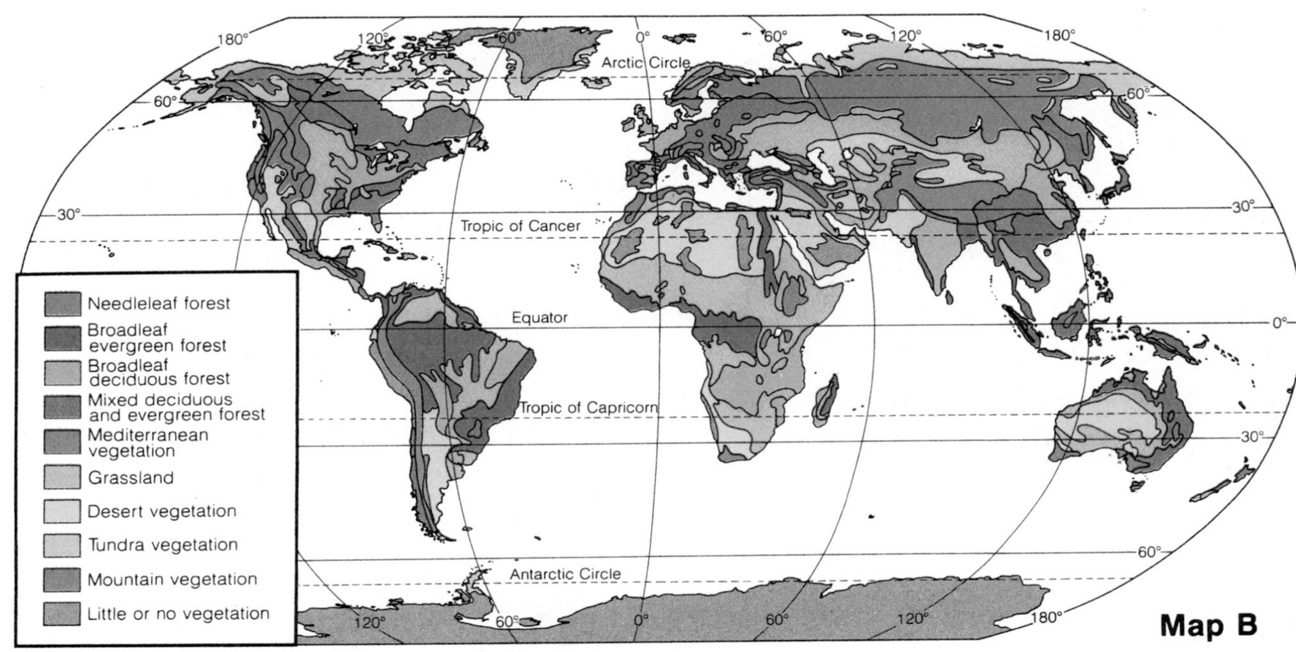

Lines of latitude and lines of longitude on a map also can help you find directions. You know that lines of latitude run east and west. Lines of longitude run north and south. What lines of longitude are shown on **Map B?**

The map grid formed by lines of latitude crossing lines of longitude can help you find locations as well as directions. You can tell exactly where any place on the earth is by knowing its latitude and longitude. Remember that latitude and longitude are measured in degrees. Use **Map A** to find the location of Kinshasa, Zaire, in degrees. What city is located at 26° south latitude and 28° east longitude?

Scale is relative size. The scale of a map tells you what actual distance on the earth's surface is represented by a given distance on the map. A scale bar is one way of showing scale. How many miles are represented by each of the black and white divisions on the scale bar of **Map A?** How many kilometers? About how long is Lake Tanganyika?

Much information on maps is shown by symbols. Symbols are sometimes explained in a key. What does the symbol ✪ stand for on **Map A?** Common map symbols are not always explained in a key. You will find some commonly used map symbols on page A–15 of your book.

Color is a special symbol used on maps. The same color may mean different things on different maps. It is particularly important to correctly interpret the color keys on special-purpose maps. For example, the color blue is commonly used to represent water. Is it used to show water on **Map B?** There are two shades of blue on **Map B.** What does each stand for?

ENRICHMENT

UNIT 7

UNIT 8

UNIT 9

UNIT 10

UNIT 11

UNIT 12

UNIT 13

UNIT 14

UNIT 15

UNIT 16

UNIT 17

Reviewing the Text

To follow page 28

Number a paper from **1** through **12**. After each number, write the letter of the correct answer.

1. A continent that lies entirely within the Southern Hemisphere is ______.
   a. Africa
   b. Australia
   c. South America
   d. Asia
2. Day and night are of unequal length on earth because of the ______.
   a. rotation of the earth
   b. revolution of the earth
   c. tilt of the earth's axis
   d. seasons
3. The sun is directly above the Tropic of Capricorn on ______.
   a. June 21–22
   b. September 22–23
   c. December 21–22
   d. March 20–21
4. The longest day of the year in the Southern Hemisphere is ______.
   a. June 21–22
   b. September 22–23
   c. December 21–22
   d. March 20–21
5. All of the following can affect climate *except* ______.
   a. distance north or south
   b. altitude
   c. winds
   d. distance east or west
6. Lines of longitude ______.
   a. never meet
   b. run north and south
   c. cross one another
   d. are measured from the equator
7. The South Pole is at ______.
   a. 0° latitude
   b. 90° south latitude
   c. 90° east longitude
   d. 0° longitude
8. Latitude is measured from the ______.
   a. prime meridian
   b. North Pole
   c. equator
   d. Tropic of Cancer
9. The only place in the United States where the sun is directly overhead is ______.
   a. Hawaii
   b. Alaska
   c. New York
   d. California
10. The sun is directly over the equator at noon ______ time(s) a year.
    a. one
    b. two
    c. three
    d. four
11. Maps that show features such as state and national boundaries are ______ maps.
    a. physical
    b. population
    c. vegetation
    d. political
12. The map scale on page 49 indicates that one inch on the map stands for ______.
    a. 328 kilometers
    b. 259 miles on the earth
    c. 259 miles on another map
    d. 1 mile on the earth

Writing Captions

To follow page 37

Captions are words, phrases, or sentences that help explain illustrations. Most of the photographs, charts, graphs and diagrams in your book have captions. Write a caption of two or three complete sentences for each of the illustrations below. Number each caption.

1.

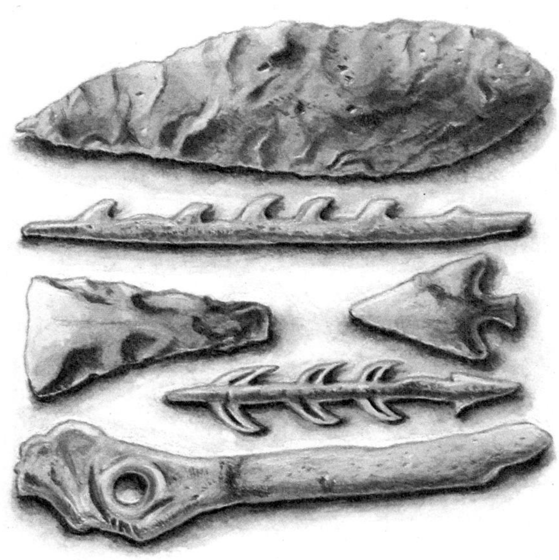

3.

2.

4.

The Ice Age in North America

To follow page 45

Read the paragraph below and study the table and map. Then number a paper from **1** through **6**. After each number, write the answer to the question.

Rather recently in geologic time, ice sheets, or glaciers, covered about one-third of the earth's land surface. These glaciers existed during a period of time known as the Pleistocene Epoch (plis′te sen′ep′ek). The Pleistocene Epoch is sometimes called the Ice Age. When scientists first studied the Ice Age, they thought that there were four periods of ice formation and three periods between the ice formations (interglacials). The names of these ages in North America are given in the table. Today it is believed there may have been many more periods of glaciers during the Pleistocene Epoch. Scientists think that the Ice Age began about 1,500,000 years ago. It is estimated that it ended between 10,000 and 20,000 years ago.

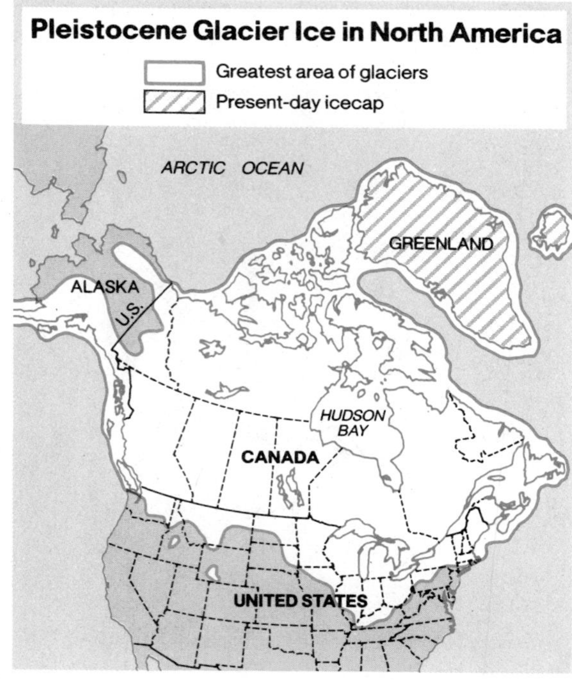

Pleistocene Time

Epoch	Age
Pleistocene	Wisconsin Glacial
	Sangamon Interglacial
	Illinoian Glacial
	Yarmouth Interglacial
	Kansan Glacial
	Aftonian Interglacial
	Nebraskan Glacial

The oldest age is at the bottom of the table, the youngest at the top.

1. What is the name of the geologic epoch that is known as the Ice Age?
2. About how long ago do scientists think the Ice Age began?
3. What is another name for a sheet of ice and snow?
4. What is the oldest period of glaciers shown in the table? The youngest?
5. How much of Canada was covered by glaciers during the Ice Age? About how much of Alaska was covered?
6. What area is still covered by ice and snow today?

To follow page 81

Political cartoons are drawings that express feelings or opinions about current events or about people in the news. These cartoons usually are amusing, but they can also be serious.

In your book you have read about OPEC (Organization of Petroleum Exporting Countries) and learned that many of the countries of the Middle East belong to this organization.

Look at the political cartoon below and think about what it is saying. Then number a paper from **1** through **5**. After each number, write the word or words in parentheses that correctly complete each statement.

1. A good title or caption for this cartoon is ("OPEC Increases Production," "Oil Production by OPEC Falls").
2. The figure in the cartoon represents (OPEC countries, non-OPEC countries).
3. The situation presented in the cartoon is (amusing, serious) for the OPEC countries.
4. The oil tower carried by the figure in the cartoon turns down at the end to show that (there is no more OPEC oil, the production of oil by OPEC countries has been decreasing since 1979).
5. From 1973 through 1981, (OPEC, non-OPEC) countries supplied more than half of the world's oil.

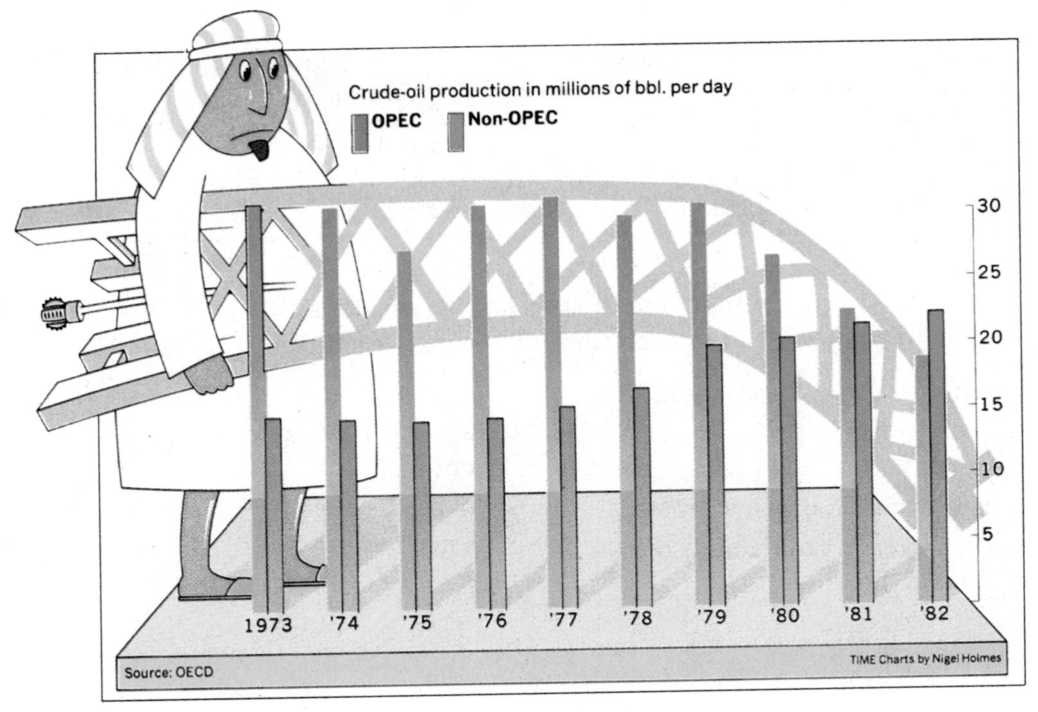

Making and Using a Time Line

To follow page 97

The time line below shows several events related to Egyptian history. Copy the time line on a sheet of paper. Add the events listed below to the time line in the correct order. Be sure to give the date for each event.

City of Cairo started
Howard Carter discovers Tutankhamen's tomb
Britain gives up most of its power in Egypt
Lower Egypt and Upper Egypt united
Death of King Tutankhamen
Egypt becomes a republic
Aswan High Dam completed

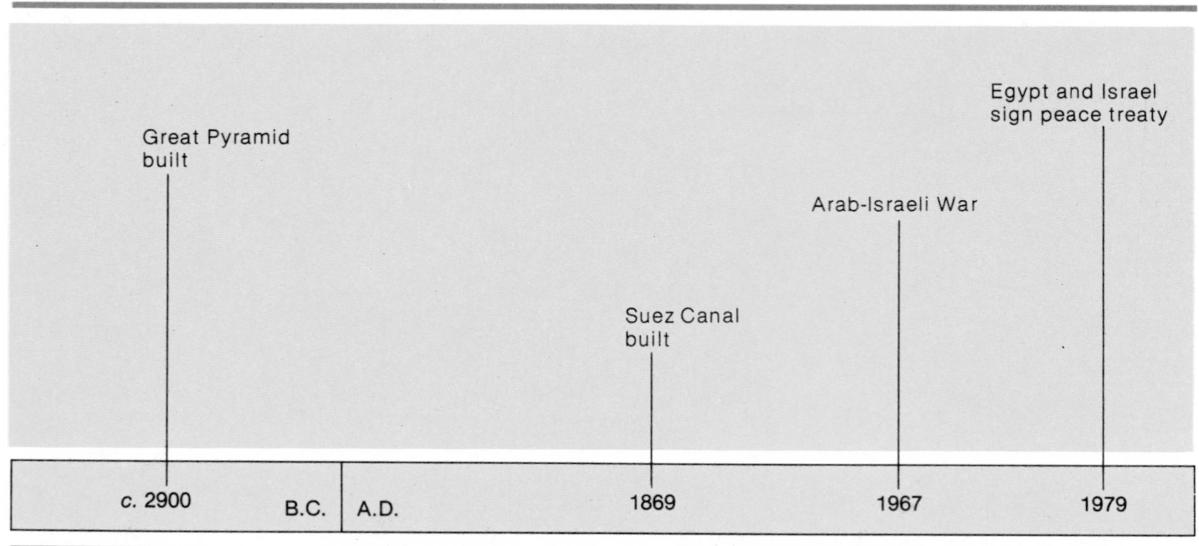

Now use your completed time line to answer the questions that follow. Number a paper from **1** through **6**. Next to each number, write the answer to the question.

1. When was the city of Cairo started?
2. How long after the Great Pyramid was built was the Suez Canal completed?
3. What two events happened in 1922?
4. How long after Tutankhamen died was his tomb discovered?
5. How long after Britain gave up most of its power in Egypt did Egypt become a republic?
6. In what year did Egypt and Israel sign a peace treaty?

Reading a Product Map

To follow page 116

Refer to the map below to answer the questions that follow. You may also need to refer to the map on page 101. Number a paper from **1** through **9**. After each number, write the answer to the question.

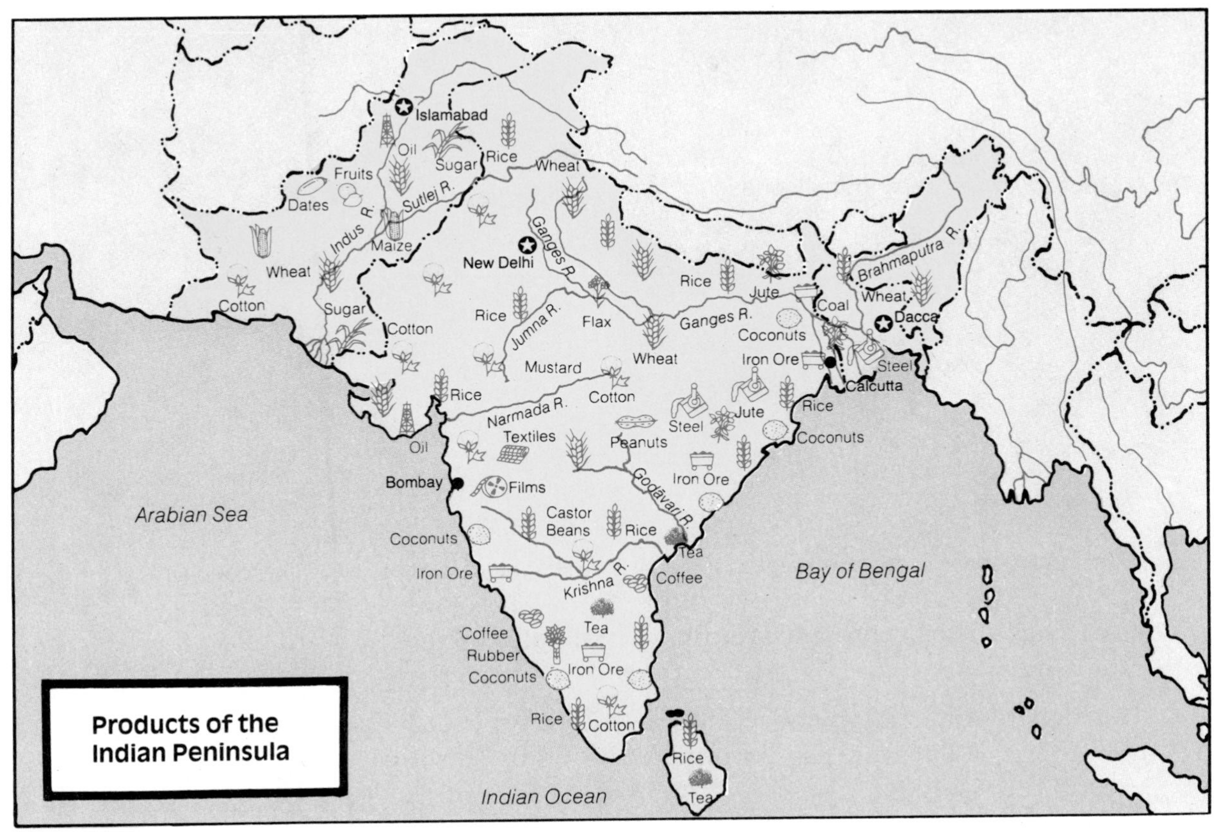

1. What does this map show?
2. What products are important in Sri Lanka?
3. What important things are produced in Bangladesh?
4. In what countries of the Indian Peninsula is oil an important product?
5. Name two important crops grown along the Jumna River.
6. Briefly explain where coconuts are grown in India.
7. What important grain crops are raised between the Ganges River and the Himalaya Mountains?
8. What city would you suppose is an important textile-producing center?
9. What grain is an important crop in Pakistan but not in India?

ENRICHMENT

Reviewing the Text

The highest mountain peak in the world

Leader of the independence movement in India

His name means the Enlightened One

Number a paper from **1** through **11**. After each number, write the word or words that complete the sentence.

1. The highest mountains in the world are the ______. The highest mountain peak in the world is ______.
2. Another name for the Far East is ______.
3. The largest peninsula that extends south from the continent of Asia is the peninsula of ______.
4. Winter is a ______ season in most of southern Asia. The winter monsoon blows from the ______ to the ______.
5. The people who invaded and conquered much of India in about 1500 B.C. were known as ______.
6. An Indian prince named ______ came to be known as the Buddha.
7. In 1950, the ______ system was outlawed in India.
8. The East India Company was organized by people from ______.
9. The leader of the independence movement in India after World War I was ______.
10. When it became independent in 1947, India was divided into the two countries of ______ and ______.
11. The famous ______ Pass leads from Afghanistan into Pakistan.

Using an Index

An index is a list of subjects discussed in a book, showing the page or pages where each subject is found. An index appears at the back of a book. Each subject listed in an index is called an entry. Main entries are general subjects. They are printed in heavy, or **boldface**, type. Subentries are specific topics under general subjects. They are indented and printed in lightface type. Main entries are listed in alphabetical order. Subentries are listed in alphabetical order under main entries. The number or numbers of pages following an entry tell the page on which information on that subject can be found. Sometimes an index gives other information, such as where illustrations and maps can be found. In the index of your book the traditional English spellings of Chinese names are included.

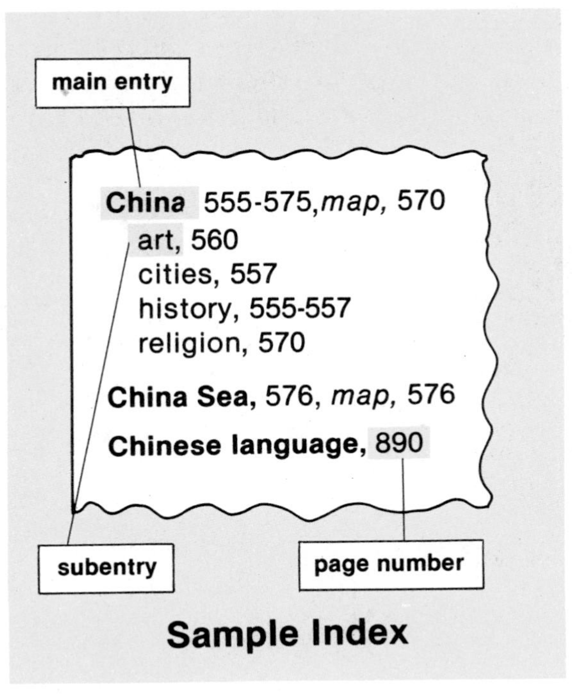

Sample Index

Use the index in your book to answer the questions that follow. Number a paper from 1 through 5. After each number, write the answer to the question.

1. On what pages can you find general information about China?
2. What subentries are found under the main entry **China**?
3. What is the traditional English spelling of Chongqing? Beijing? Guangzhou? Huang River?
4. On what pages can you find information on the Great Wall of China?
5. Suppose you wanted to find out about growing tea in China. If you do not find a subentry on tea under China, where would you look next? On what page in your book is there information on tea in China?

ENRICHMENT

Features of China and Japan

To follow page 157

The features of the earth can be divided into two groups. **Natural features** are landforms and bodies of water. **Constructed features** are things made by people. Number a paper from **1** through **14**. After each number write **NF** for natural feature or **CF** for constructed feature. Then write the letter of the phrase that describes the feature.

1. Hokkaido
2. Great Wall
3. Ginza
4. Huang
5. pagoda
6. terrace
7. Himalayas
8. Mount Fuji
9. Grand Canal
10. Chang
11. Yellow Sea
12. Forbidden City
13. Kyoto
14. Taiwan

a. a river of North China, often called the Yellow River

b. the world's highest mountains

c. a building with many stories, each of which has a roof overhanging the roof below

d. one of the four main islands of Japan

e. city that was once the capital of Japan

f. the fifth longest river in the world

g. the brightly lit main street of Tokyo

h. an old part of Beijing that is sealed off by a moat and walls

i. a waterway that connects the Huang with the Chang

j. a large body of water lying between China and the Korean Peninsula

k. barrier that was begun about 200 B.C. as a defense against invaders

l. a snow-capped mountain that is a dead volcano

m. an island off the coast of China, once known as Formosa

n. a raised level platform of earth on a hillside

The map of Athens below shows some of the points of interest of the city. The map has a grid to help you find places and to help you tell where places are. Remember that each square is referred to by its letter and number. For example, the uppermost left square is A-1.

Number a paper from **1** through **8**. After each number, write the answers to the questions that follow. You will need to refer to the map and the map key.

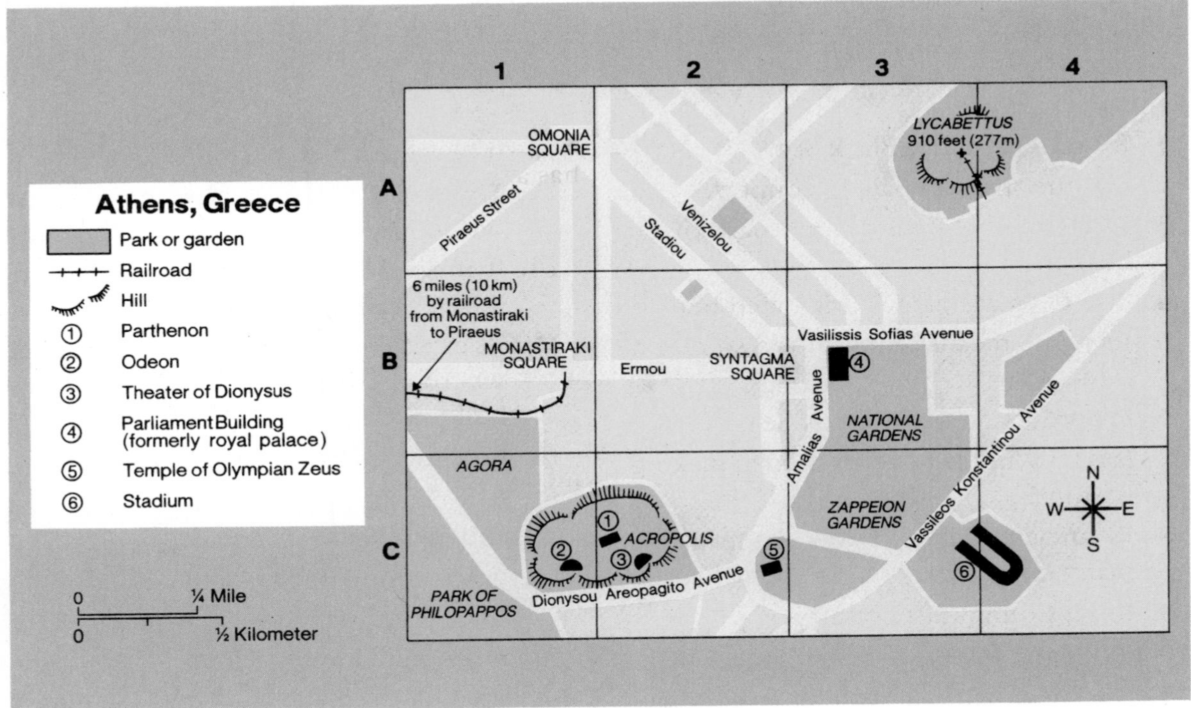

1. Life in Athens centers on the three squares named on the map. What are they?
2. What are the green areas shown on the map?
3. Athens uses the port of Piraeus on the Aegean Sea. In what direction is Piraeus from Monastiraki Square? How far is it? How could you go from Monastiraki to Piraeus?
4. What two hills are shown on the map? On which hill is the Parthenon situated?
5. What important building is situated in B-3? What was this building in former times?
6. In what direction is the Stadium from the Temple of Olympian Zeus? About how far apart are they?
7. About how far is Syntagma Square from Omonia Square? In what direction is Omonia Square from Syntagma Square?
8. The Agora was the market place of ancient Athens. Describe its location in two different ways.

What Country Is It?

To follow page 187

Look at the words in the box. Then number a paper from **1** through **20**. After each number, write the name of the country or countries that the sentence describes.

Greece	Romania	Albania
Bulgaria	Yugoslavia	

1. It borders on the Black Sea.
2. It is the smallest Balkan country.
3. The Danube River forms part of its borders.
4. The Olympic games originated here.
5. Its name means "land of the southern slavs."
6. It borders on the Adriatic Sea.
7. It is famous for its roses used in making perfume.
8. In ancient times, it was made up of many city-states.
9. It is a Communist country.
10. Its capital was once called "little Paris."
11. It is the northernmost Balkan country.
12. It became a republic in 1973.
13. Tito was head of its government after World War II.
14. It is divided into northern and southern halves by the Balkan Mountains.
15. Its capital has a hill called the Acropolis where there are ruins of many fine buildings.
16. It borders on the Aegean Sea.
17. It leads Europe in the mining of lead and bauxite.
18. It was conquered by the Romans in 146 B.C.
19. It has valuable oil fields.
20. Hippocrates lived here about 400 B.C.

The Appian Way

To follow page 196

Read the paragraphs below and study the map. Then number a paper from **1** through **7**. After each number, write the answer to the question.

The Appian Way is the oldest and most famous of ancient Roman roads. Its Latin name is Via Appia. The Romans, who were proud of the Via Appia, called it the "queen of long-distance roads." It was begun as a military highway in 312 B.C. It started in Rome, and at first ran only to ancient Capua. Later, it was extended south to Brindisi, reaching it in about 244 B.C. The trip from Rome to Brindisi took from 10 to 15 days.

In A.D. 109 the Emperor Trajan decided to build a new section of the road to avoid a difficult route through the Apennines. This new section was called the Via Appia Traiana in Trajan's honor. The older part of the road then became known as the Via Appia Antica. (Antica means old.) The Via Appia Traiana ran from Beneventum to Barium, then down the Adriatic coast to Brindisi. It saved a day's travel time.

Today the Appian Way is mostly in ruins. Only widely separated parts of the original roadbed and paving can be seen.

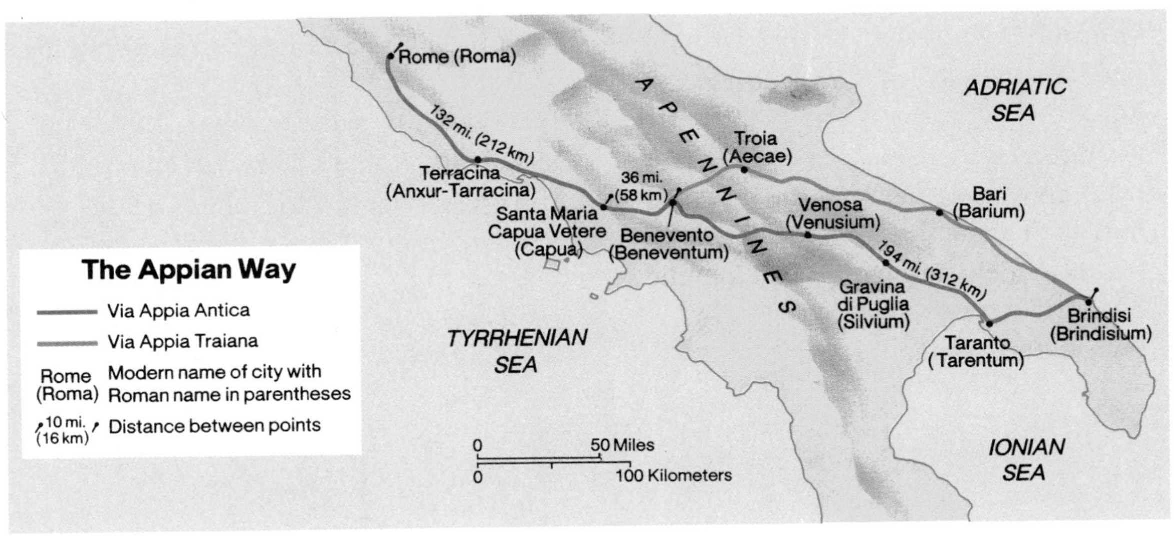

1. What is the Latin name for the Appian Way?
2. When was the Appian Way begun? From what city did it start?
3. What two cities on the map are the farthest apart? How far apart are these cities traveling by the Via Appia Antica?
4. What mountains did both sections of the Appian Way cross? Why was the Via Appia Traiana built?
5. At what two cities did the Via Appia Antica join the Via Appia Traiana?
6. What seas did the Appian Way reach?
7. What was the Roman name for Bari?

Who Am I?

To follow page 205

Number a paper from **1** through **18**. After each number, write the name of the person listed in the box that the phrase describes. You will need to use some names more than once.

Cincinnatus	Horatius	Hannibal	Julius Caesar
Octavian	Homer	Virgil	Constantine

1. I was the first Roman emperor.
2. I introduced the Egyptian calendar of 12 months to Rome.
3. I was a Roman farmer who became a general.
4. I was a Greek poet admired by the Romans.
5. I led the armies of Carthage against Rome.
6. I conquered the Gauls.
7. I was given the title "Augustus" by the Roman Senate.
8. I built a new Roman capital on the Bosporus.
9. I wrote the *Aeneid*.
10. I took elephants across the Alps to help my troops.
11. I was made dictator for life by the Roman Senate.
12. I was a Roman hero in the war between the Romans and the Etruscans.
13. I brought part of Britain under Roman rule.
14. I gave my name to the month of July.
15. I made Rome a Christian empire.
16. I was a nephew of Julius Caesar.
17. I reigned during Rome's "Golden Age."
18. I gave my name to the month of August.

Can You Match These?

To follow page 219

Number a paper from **1** through **13**. After each number, write the name of the place listed in the box that matches the phrase. Then write the letter on the map where the place is found. The maps on pages 191 and 199 will help you.

Sicily
Sardinia
Naples
Genoa
Venice
Messina
Mount Etna
Rome
Carthage
Mount Vesuvius
Pompeii
Florence
Milan

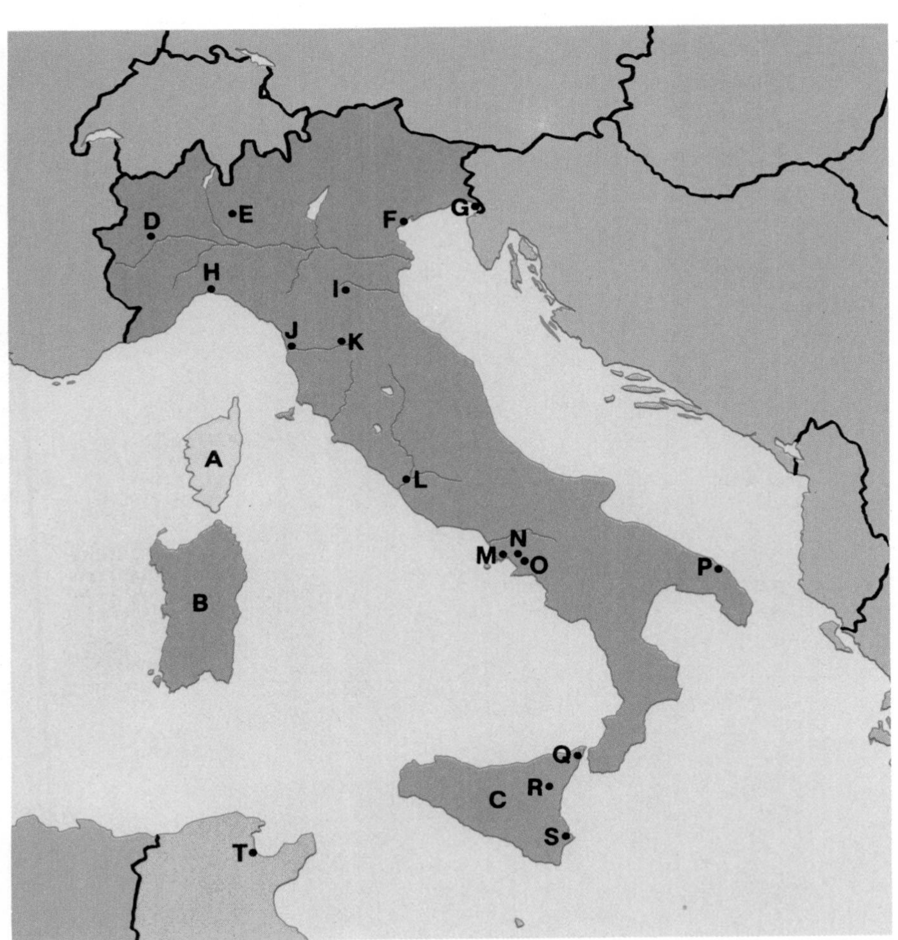

1. sometimes called the "Eternal City"
2. buried under ashes and lava in A.D. 79
3. once an important place for mining sulfur
4. an important art city north of Rome
5. Italy's largest and busiest port
6. a seaport in Sicily
7. Italy's second largest island
8. a volcano not far from Naples
9. built on a series of low islands
10. a Phoenician city destroyed by the Romans around 146 B.C.
11. an important banking city
12. Italy's southernmost island
13. a city known for its beautiful bay

Kenya's Parks and Reserves

To follow page 227

Kenya, like several other African countries, has set aside lands as parks and reserves where its unique variety of wildlife can roam freely. Since 1978 Kenya has had a complete ban on hunting. The map on this page shows the names and locations of Kenya's parks and reserves. The pictures show some of the animals that can be seen in these areas.

Number a paper from **1** through **6**. After each number, write the answers to the questions that appear on page 563.

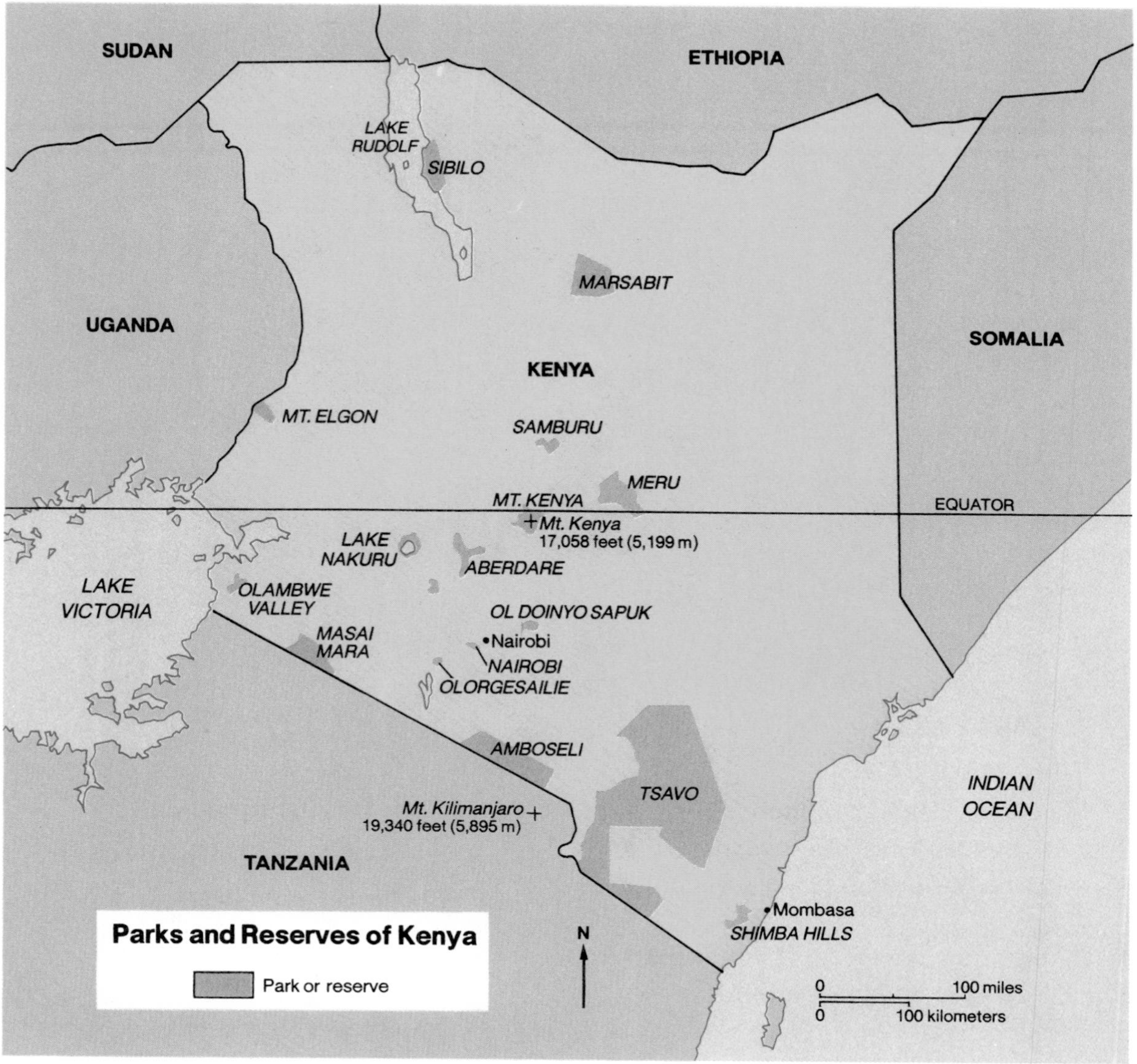

1. How many parks and reserves in Kenya are shown on the map? What is the largest park or reserve?
2. The equator passes through two of Kenya's national parks. Which ones are they?
3. The last stronghold of rhinoceros herds left in Kenya is Aberdare National Park. In what direction from Nairobi is this park?
4. Mt. Kenya is the highest peak in Kenya. In what park or reserve is it situated?
5. Mt. Kilamanjaro is the highest peak in Africa. In what country is Mt. Kilamanjaro? From what parks or reserves in Kenya would you probably be able to see this mountain?
6. Lake Nakuru National Park is famous for its millions of flamingos. What natural feature of this park makes it a good place for these birds?

Elephants, giraffes, and flamingos make their home in Kenya.

Learning About Swahili

To follow page 241

Swahili is spoken in more parts of Africa than any other language. Study the chart below to answer the questions that follow. Number a paper from 1 through 4. After each number, write the answer to the question.

Letter in Swahili alphabet	Swahili word beginning with letter	Meaning of word
A		
B	baba (bä′ bä)	father
C	chakula (cha ko͞o′ lä)	food
D	dawa (dä′ wä)	medicine
E		
F		
G		
H		
I		
J	jambo (jam′ bō)	hello
K	karibu (kä rē′ bo͞o)	welcome
L		

Letter in Swahili alphabet	Swahili word beginning with letter	Meaning of word
M	mama (mä′ mä)	mother
N	ngoma (n gō′ mä)	drum and dance
O		
P	punda (po͞on′ dä)	donkey
R	rafiki (rä fē′ kē)	friend
S	shule (scho͞o′ lä)	school
T	tembo (tem′ bō)	elephant
U		
V		
W	watoto (wä tō′ tō)	children
Y		
Z		

1. How many letters are there in the Swahili alphabet?
2. What letters are part of the English alphabet but do not occur in Swahili?
3. What does the Swahili word *jambo* mean in English? *Rafiki*? *Shule*?
4. What is the Swahili word for food? Father? Mother?

To follow page 247

Number a paper from **1** through **24**. After each number, write the word or words that belong in the blank. Choose the words from the list that appears in the box below.

salt	Mecca	mortar
Mansa Musa	Ethiopia	Lalibela
Cushites	King Sundiata	Zulu
oral tradition	Bantu	Askia Mohammad
gold	spices	Almoravids
learning	Muslims	Ghana
Timbuktu	kingdoms	North Africa
southern	Portuguese	Christianity

Many important empires, or __1__, grew up in Africa long ago. We know about these empires through reports of early travelers, through monuments and art, and through __2__.

The kingdom called Axum was formed about A.D. 300 in the country that is now __3__. The people who founded this kingdom were Arabs and __4__. The wealth of Axum was based on the trade of incense and __5__. After about A.D. 330 the religion of Axum was __6__. Several hundred years later the Arabs, who were __7__, drove the people of Axum into the interior. Here the modern country of Ethiopia began to develop. Here also an early king named __8__ ordered the now famous rock-cut churches to be built.

In West Africa, three powerful kingdoms developed. The oldest of these was __9__. This kingdom traded __10__, ivory, and honey in return for __11__. Eventually, the capital of the kingdom was conquered by a Muslim group called the __12__. Although the city was recovered, the last king of the empire was defeated in 1235 by __13__ of Mali. Mali expanded its territories and became very wealthy. In 1324 the king of Mali, __14__, made a famous pilgrimage to __15__. Mali declined after this king died. The Songhai Empire began with the capture of the Mali city of __16__. Under the leadership of __17__, the Songhai Empire flourished. Timbuktu became a center of __18__ and trade. In 1591, Muslims from __19__ captured the city, and the Songhai Empire began to decline.

One of the few large kingdoms that grew up in __20__ Africa was Zimbabwe. The ruins of Zimbabwe are remarkable for the granite buildings built without __21__. It is believed that Zimbabwe was built by a people who spoke a __22__ language. In the 1500s, the __23__ learned about Zimbabwe and began to control its trade. In the 1830s, it was attacked by the __24__.

Writing Captions

To follow page 269

Study the drawings below and write a caption for each one. Each caption should be two or three sentences long. Number each caption:

1.

3.

2.

4.

Is It True?

To follow page 269

Number a paper from **1** through **8**. After each number, write **True** if the statement is true. Write **False** if the statement is false. Then write your reason for each answer in a complete sentence.

1. The Middle Ages lasted about 900 years.
2. Feudalism was based on cooperation between two classes of people.
3. Under feudalism, land granted by a lord in return for services was called a vassal.
4. The feudal system caused disorder.
5. Castles were comfortable places in which to live.
6. Young nobles did nothing to keep themselves in practice for battle.
7. When a page reached the age of 16, he became a knight.
8. Serfs were neither slaves nor freemen.

Using the Card Catalog

To follow page 283

A card catalog is a list on cards of all the books in a library. There are three different cards for each book. One is a **subject card**, one is an **author card**, and one is a **title card**. The first line on each card gives the subject, the author, or the title of the book. All the cards are arranged in alphabetical order in drawers in cabinets. The drawers are labeled with the first three letters of the first and last subject, author, or title cards they contain.

Cards in a card catalog list the author's last name first, followed by a comma and the first name. The cards also tell the name of the book's publisher and the place and date of publication. The abbreviation *illus.* means that there are illustrations in the book. The number on the bottom of the card is the **call number**. This number tells you on what shelf to look for the book. The shelves are numbered with the first and last numbers of the books they include.

Refer to the sample catalog cards below to answer the questions that follow. Number a paper from **1** through **6**. After each number, write the letter of the correct answer.

CARD I	CARD II	CARD III
MIDDLE AGES Bishop, Morris Horizon Book of the Middle Ages New York: 1968. American Heritage Pub., 416 pp. *illus.* 940.1 B	Bishop, Morris Horizon Book of the Middle Ages New York: 1968. American Heritage Pub., 416 pp. *illus.* 940.1 B	Horizon Book of the Middle Ages Bishop, Morris New York: 1968. American Heritage Pub., 416 pp. *illus.* 940.1 B

1. Card I is ______ card.
   a. a subject **b.** an author **c.** a title
2. If you knew only the title of the book, you would look for Card ______.
   a. I **b.** II **c.** III
3. The name of the author of this book is ______.
   a. Bishop Morris **b.** Morris Bishop
   c. neither of the above
4. Card III would be found in a drawer marked ______.
   a. ALG–ATW **b.** HAG–HIR
   c. HEM–HUM
5. This book has ______ pages.
   a. 940 **b.** 1968 **c.** 416
6. This book would be found on a shelf numbered ______.
   a. 800–849 **b.** 400–499 **c.** 900–999

Reading a Graph

Radio and television stations and newspapers often report the highest and lowest temperatures recorded in a place during a 24-hour period. These daily highs and lows can be used to give an average monthly high and low temperature for a given place. The graph below shows such information for two cities in Spain.

Refer to the graph to answer the questions. Number a paper from **1** through **7**. After each number, write the correct answer.

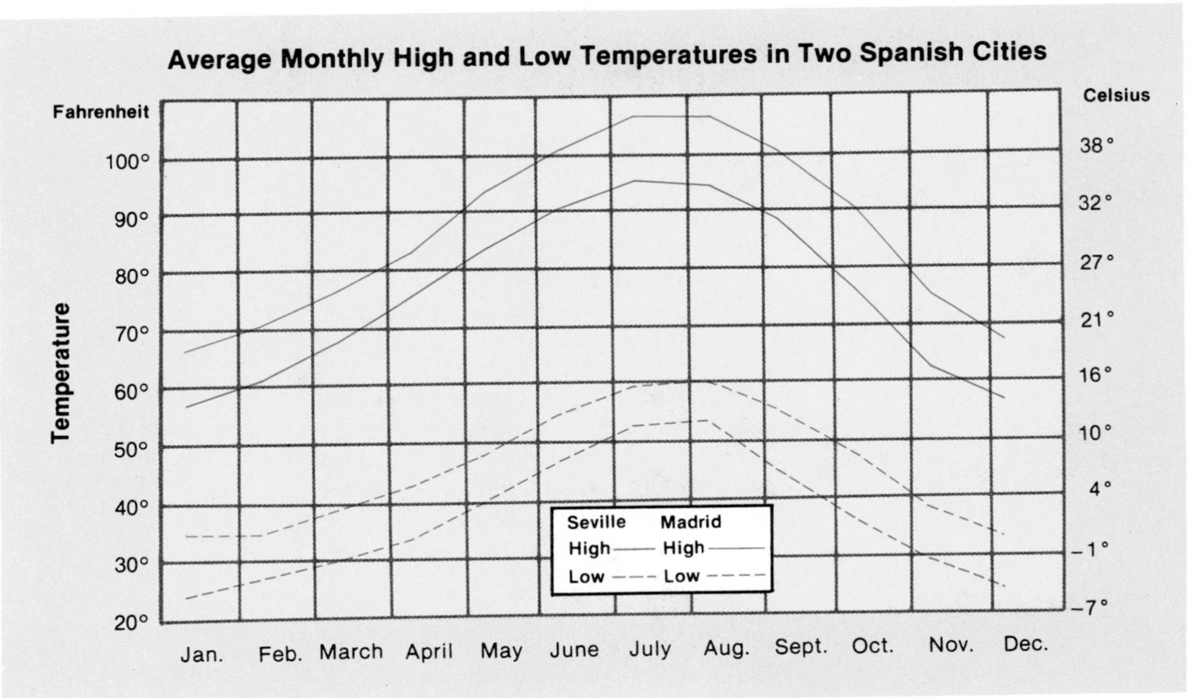

1. What kind of graph—circle, line, or bar—is shown above?
2. For what two cities in Spain is information given?
3. What color is used to show the temperatures in Seville? In Madrid? How are the average monthly high temperatures shown for each city? The average monthly low temperatures?
4. Which city is hotter throughout the year?
5. What is the average high temperature in Seville in July?
6. In what month is the difference between the high temperature in Madrid and the high temperature in Seville the smallest?
7. How many degrees difference is there between the average high and low temperatures in Madrid in May?

Writing a Paragraph

To follow page 295

Read each group of words below. Then on a piece of paper, write a short paragraph using each group of words. Before you begin, think what the main idea of each paragraph will be. Remember that each sentence in the paragraph should be related to the main idea. Number each paragraph.

1.

Iberian Peninsula	Pyrenees Mountains	Bay of Biscay
Atlantic Ocean	Mediterranean Sea	

2.

Phoenicians	Romans	Goths
Moors	Christians	

3.

Ferdinand	Isabella	Castile
Aragon	Catholic	

4.

Columbus	Magellan	Ponce de León
Cortés	Hernando de Soto	

5.

Vasco da Gama	Cape of Good Hope	India
trade	Africa	

6.

Don Quixote	Cervantes	Sancho Panza
Spanish	knight	

What's the Right Order?

To follow page 317

Louis XIV, the Sun King

The events below are not listed in the order in which they happened. Number a paper from **1** through **10**. After the numbers, list the events in the order in which they happened. Then after each event write the date when it took place.

Napoleon was defeated at the Battle of Waterloo.
Charlemagne was crowned emperor of the Holy Roman Empire.
Joan of Arc led an army to the city of Orléans.
Gaul became a Roman province.
American and British troops landed in Normandy.
The French Republic adopted a new constitution.
Louis XIV came to the throne of France.
Hugh Capet was chosen king by a group of French lords.
The French Revolution began.
Napoleon was crowned emperor of France.

Paris—Changes in Population

To follow page 325

The line graph below shows how the population of Paris has changed over the years. Use the graph to answer the questions that follow. Number a paper from 1 through 7. After each number, write the answer to the question.

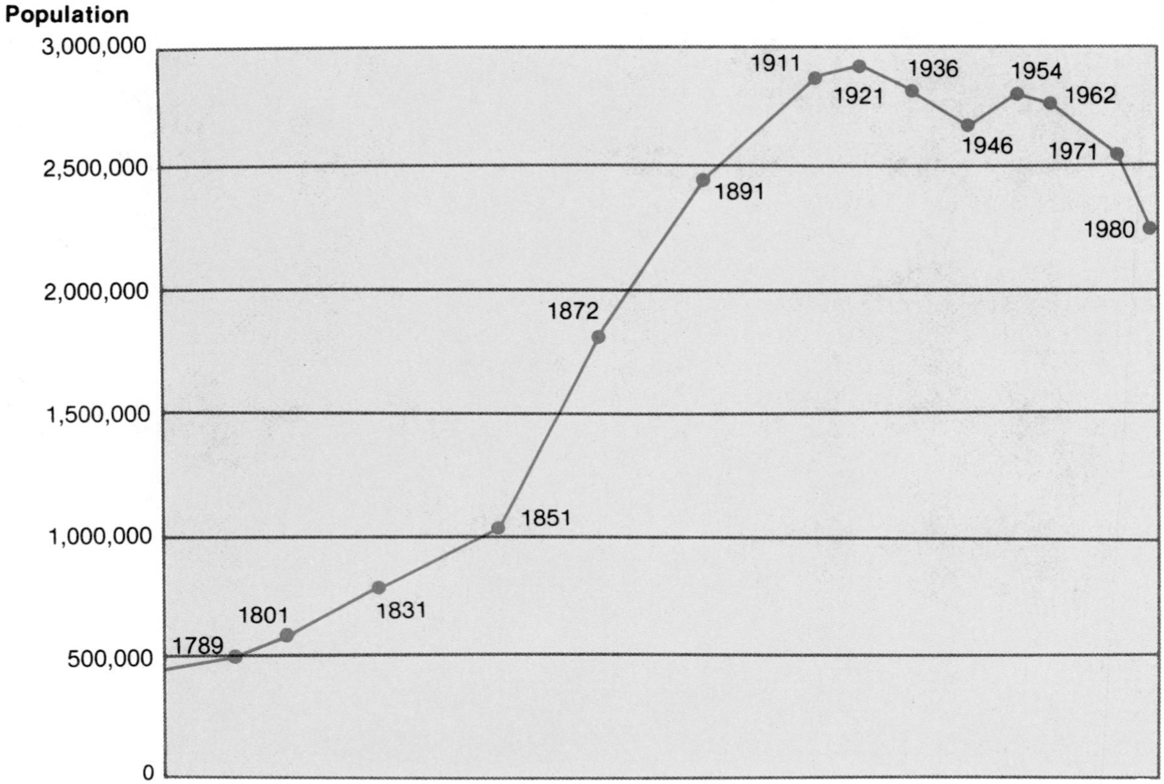

1. What would be a good title for this graph?
2. How many years are covered by this graph? Are the periods of time between the years shown the same or different?
3. In what year was the population of Paris 500,000? By what year had the population roughly doubled?
4. In what period did the population of Paris increase most rapidly? What was the population of Paris at its highest?
5. What happened to the population of Paris between 1921 and 1946? Between 1946 and 1954? Has the population of Paris been increasing or decreasing since 1954?
6. Was the population of Paris in 1980 greater or smaller than it was in 1891?
7. How much smaller was the population of Paris in 1980 than it was when it was at its highest?

Refer to the maps below to answer the questions that follow. Number a paper from **1** through **5**. After each number, write the answer to the question.

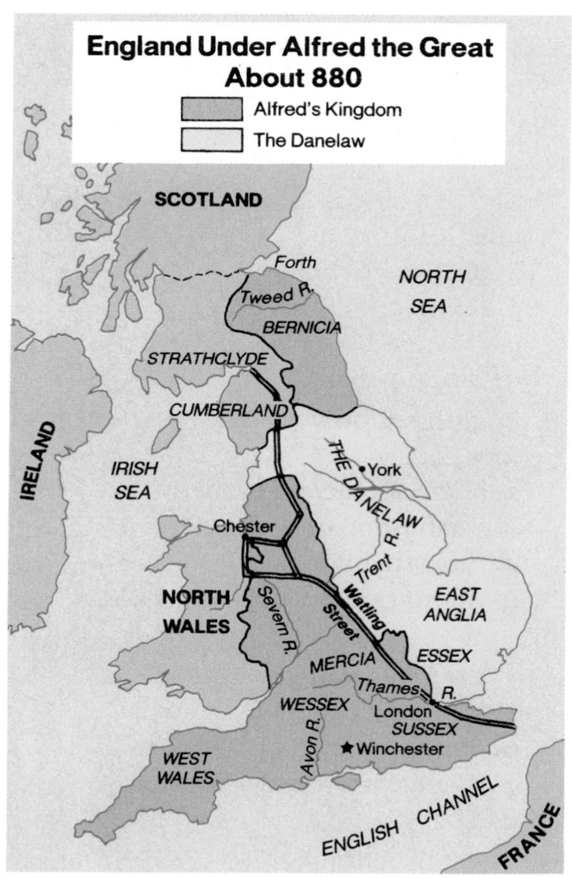

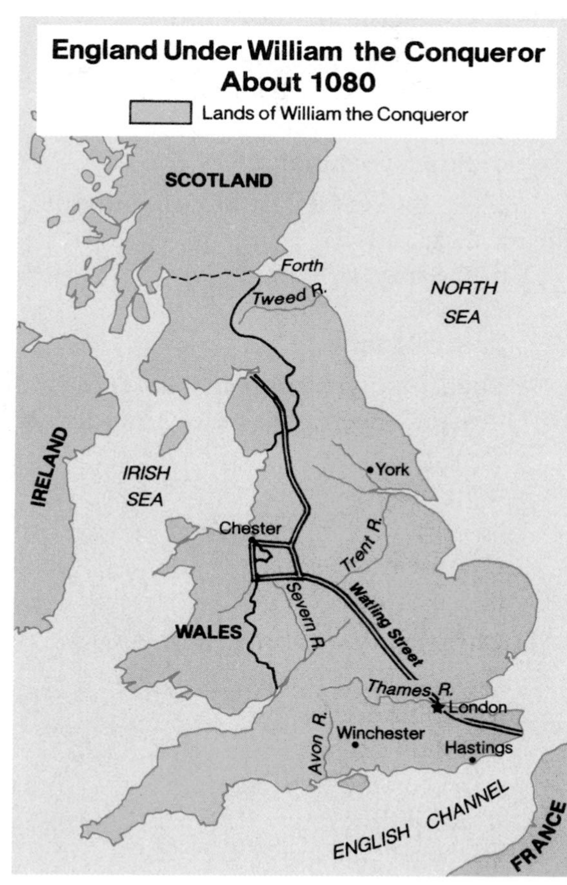

1. At what time does the map on the left show England? The map on the right? How many years passed between the map on the right and the map on the left?
2. Where besides Great Britain did William the Conqueror hold lands? What body of water separated this land from Great Britain?
3. What was the name of the region that separated the two parts of King Alfred's kingdom?
4. Watling Street was a road built by the Romans to make travel easier in Great Britain. What other purpose did Watling Street serve in the 880s?
5. Which king, Alfred or William, controlled more land in Great Britain?

Reviewing the Text

To follow page 353

Number a paper from **1** through **10**. After each number, write the letter of the correct answer.

1. The _______ lies between Great Britain and the continent of Europe.
   a. Irish Sea
   b. St. George's Channel
   c. Strait of Dover
   d. Strait of Gibraltar
2. _______ is *not* a part of Great Britain.
   a. England
   b. Ireland
   c. Wales
   d. Scotland
3. English towns with names ending in "caster" were probably founded by the _______.
   a. Romans
   b. Jutes
   c. Danes
   d. Saxons
4. Christianity was brought to England by _______.
   a. King Alfred
   b. Julius Caesar
   c. Augustine
   d. King Ethelbert
5. William the Conqueror was _______.
   a. a Dane
   b. a Norman
   c. an Anglo-Saxon
   d. a barbarian
6. England's Parliament is made up of _______ group(s), or house(s).
   a. one
   b. two
   c. three
   d. four
7. The Magna Carta _______ royal power in England.
   a. did away with
   b. limited
   c. extended
   d. did not change
8. English sea power began to grow after the _______.
   a. reign of Queen Elizabeth
   b. establishment of Jamestown
   c. Industrial Revolution
   d. defeat of the Spanish Armada
9. _______ did *not* play an important part in the Industrial Revolution.
   a. The steam engine
   b. Sheep raising
   c. The factory system
   d. Coal
10. Winston Churchill was one of Great Britain's great _______.
    a. generals
    b. composers
    c. prime ministers
    d. cricket players

Writing a Paragraph

To follow page 363

Read each group of words below. Then on a piece of paper, write a short paragraph using each group of words. Before you begin, think what the main idea of each paragraph will be. Remember that each sentence in a paragraph should be related to the main idea. Number each paragraph.

1.

British Isles	Great Britain	United Kingdom
Ireland	Northern Ireland	

2.

King John	Magna Carta	liberty
nobles	privileges	

3.

Queen Elizabeth I	William Shakespeare	writers
reign	Sir Walter Raleigh	

4.

Industrial Revolution	factory system	steam engine
coal	spinning jenny	

5.

British Empire	colonies	independent
dominion	Commonwealth of Nations	

Using a Primary Source

To follow page 377

Reread the section "Anne Frank, a Young Writer" on page 377. Then read the Introduction and the passage from *The Diary of a Young Girl* below. When you have finished, number a paper from 1 through 6. After each number, write the answer to the question.

Introduction: In July 1942, Anne Frank, her parents, and her older sister Margot went into hiding from the Germans. Anne called the rooms they occupied above a warehouse in Amsterdam the "Secret Annex." Here the Franks were soon joined by Mr. and Mrs. Van Daan, the Van Daan's teenage son Peter, and Mr. Dussel. The Franks, the Van Daans, and Mr. Dussel lived in the "Secret Annex" until August 1944, when they were captured by the Germans. During this time, Anne kept a diary. The entries in the diary were in the form of letters to an imaginary friend, Kitty. To the right is an entry from Anne's diary.

Friday, 23 July, 1943

Dear Kitty,

Just for fun I'm going to tell you each person's first wish, when we are allowed to go outside again. Margot and Mr. Van Daan long more than anything for a hot bath filled to overflowing and want to stay in it for half an hour. Mrs. Van Daan wants most to go and eat cream cakes immediately. Dussel thinks of nothing but seeing Lotje, his wife; Mummy of her cup of coffee; Daddy is going to visit Mr. Vossen first; Peter the town and a cinema, while I should find it so blissful, I shouldn't know where to start! But most of all, I long for a home of our own, to be able to move freely and to have some help with my work again at last, in other words —school.

Yours, Anne

1. How many people lived in the "Secret Annex" in Amsterdam?
2. How many years did the people in the "Secret Annex" hide from the Germans?
3. When was the diary entry above written? How long had Anne been in hiding when she wrote it?
4. Who was Kitty?
5. What things did Anne wish for?
6. In your own words, describe how you think Anne felt when she wrote the diary entry above.

What's the Main Idea?

To follow page 382

The main idea of a selection tells what the selection is all about. It tells what is most important about what you have read. Read the three paragraphs in the selection below, which comes from page 382 in your book. Then number a paper from **1** through **4**. Next to each number, write the letter of the correct answer.

Paragraph 1

Take the first letters of Belgium, the first of the Netherlands, and the first of Luxembourg. Put these letters together and you form the name *Benelux* (ben′e luks′). This is the name of the organization these countries formed in 1947.

Paragraph 2

The purpose of Benelux is to promote trade. The members of Benelux do this by lowering or removing the taxes on goods which they import from each other.

Paragraph 3

How does this encourage trade? When the price of a product is high, few people can afford to buy it. When the price is lower, more people are able to purchase it. As the Benelux countries reduced such import taxes, goods could be sold for less so more people could buy more things.

1. What is the main idea of Paragraph 1?
   a. The name Benelux comes from the first letters of Belgium, the Netherlands, and Luxembourg.
   b. Benelux was formed in 1947.
   c. Benelux is an organization formed by Belgium, the Netherlands, and Luxembourg.
2. What is the main idea of Paragraph 2?
   a. Benelux promotes trade by lowering or removing taxes.
   b. The Benelux countries import goods from one another.
   c. Benelux countries lower taxes.
3. What is the main idea of Paragraph 3?
   a. Few people can afford to buy high-priced products.
   b. Many people can buy low-priced goods.
   c. Reducing taxes lowers the price of goods so that more people can buy more goods.
4. What is the main idea of the entire selection?
   a. Benelux is an organization that promotes trade by removing or lowering taxes so that more people can buy more goods.
   b. Many people in Belgium, the Netherlands, and Luxembourg can afford to buy low-priced goods.
   c. Benelux was formed so that Belgium, the Netherlands, and Luxembourg could import goods.

Roald Amundsen, Polar Explorer

To follow page 400

Reread page 400 in your book. Then read the paragraphs below and study the maps. Number a paper from **1** through **4**. After each number, write the answer to the question.

Roald Amundsen was a famous Norwegian explorer of both the Arctic and the Antarctic. He hoped to become the first person to reach the North Pole by sailing across it in the *Fram*. When he learned that Robert Peary had reached the North Pole on April 6, 1909, Amundsen decided to try for the South Pole instead. He sailed the *Fram* south to the Ross Sea and landed in Antarctica in 1911. Traveling by dog sled, Amundsen and four companions reached the South Pole on December 14, 1911. Amundsen is credited as being the first person to reach the South Pole.

Years later, Amundsen decided to try again for the North Pole, this time by air. On May 12, 1926, Amundsen, with Lincoln Ellsworth of the United States and Umberto Nobile of Italy, succeeded in crossing the North Pole in the motor-driven air ship *Norge*. Their crossing came three days after Richard Byrd and Floyd Bennett made the first flight over the North Pole.

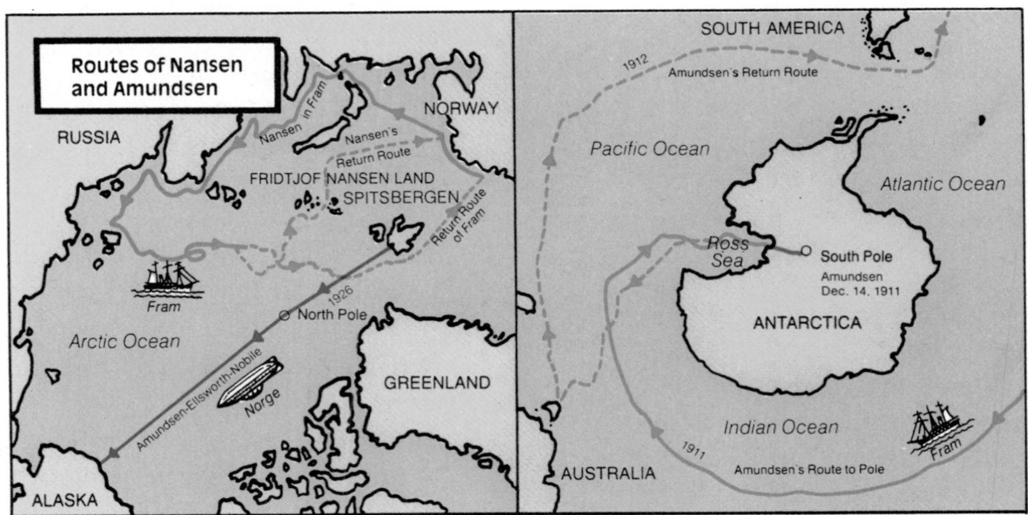

1. Who was Roald Amundsen? How many people joined him in the first expedition to reach the South Pole?
2. How did Amundsen reach the South Pole?
3. In what year did Amundsen arrive in Antarctica?
4. How many years passed between Amundsen's arrival at the South Pole and his flight over the North Pole?

What Country Is It?

To follow page 415

Look at the words in the box. Then number a paper from **1** through **24**. After each number, write the name of the country or countries that the sentence describes.

Denmark	Norway	Iceland
Sweden	Finland	

1. It is part of Scandinavia.
2. It occupies a peninsula.
3. It shares a boundary with Finland.
4. It has land that touches or lies north of the Arctic Circle.
5. It is famous for its dairy products.
6. It was invaded by Germany during World War II.
7. It includes the island of Greenland.
8. It was part of the Kingdom of Denmark under Queen Margrete.
9. It has many volcanoes, geysers, and hot springs.
10. It has one of the world's largest merchant fleets.
11. It was the home of the musician Edvard Grieg.
12. Much of its land is covered by forests.
13. It has a king or queen as its ruler.
14. It has important iron ore deposits.
15. It was colonized by the Vikings.
16. It has been described as "half land and half water."
17. It occupies the largest peninsula of northern Europe.
18. It has coasts on the North Sea and on the Baltic Sea.
19. It was once a colony of Denmark.
20. It has more waterfalls than any other country in Europe.
21. It was the home of the founder of the Nobel prizes.
22. It became independent in 1917.
23. It is a republic.
24. It is the largest and most populous country of northern Europe.

To follow page 415

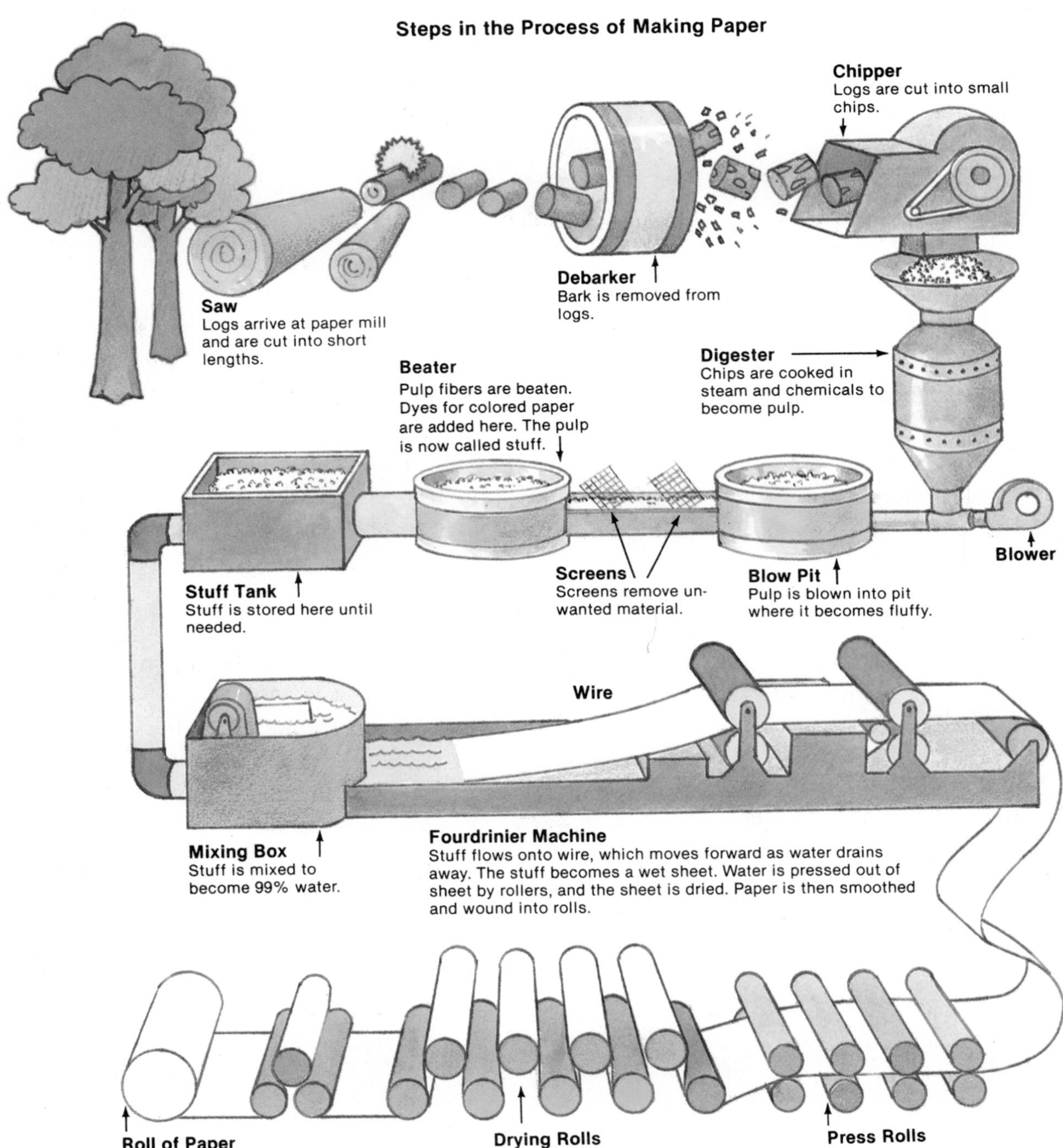

Study the diagram on page 580 and use it to answer the questions below. Number a paper from 1 through 7. After each number, write the answer to the question.

1. What does this diagram show?
2. What is the name of a factory that makes paper?
3. What happens to the logs in the debarker?
4. What happens to the chips in the digester?
5. What happens to the pulp in the blow pit?
6. What machine performs the final steps in making paper?
7. If the paper is to be colored, is the dye added before or after the pulp is bleached?

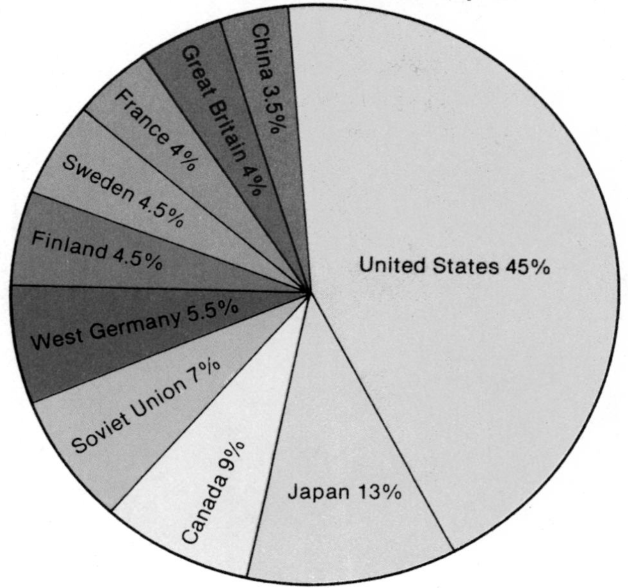

Refer to the graph above to answer the questions that follow. Number a paper from **8** through **12**. After each number, write the answer to the question.

8. What kind of graph is shown above? What does it show?
9. What country leads the world in the production of paper and paperboard?
10. What countries that you studied in Unit 13 are represented on the graph?
11. How much of the world's paper and paperboard do Sweden and Finland produce together? What single country produces this percentage of paper and paperboard?
12. Do Sweden and Finland together produce more or less paper and paperboard than the Soviet Union? Than Japan?

Berlin—A Divided City

To follow page 435

Number a paper from 1 through 9. Refer to the map below to answer the questions that follow.

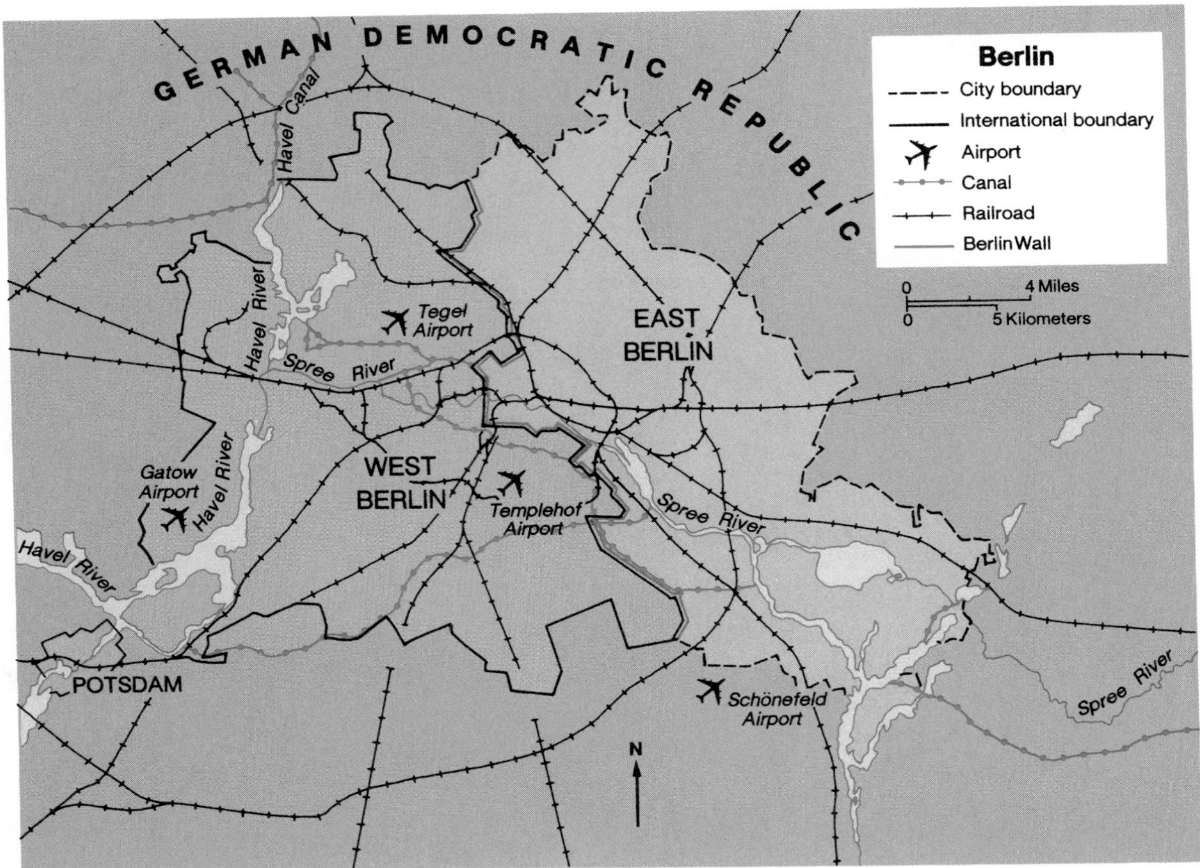

1. Into what two parts is Berlin divided?
2. In what country is East Berlin located? What country surrounds West Berlin?
3. Find the Berlin Wall on the map. What two boundaries are marked by the Berlin Wall?
4. In what general direction does the Berlin Wall run?
5. What river runs through both East Berlin and West Berlin?
6. Name the airports that are situated in West Berlin.
7. According to the map, how many railroad lines cross the boundary between East Berlin and West Berlin?
8. What does the symbol —•—•— indicate on this map?
9. In addition to East Berlin and West Berlin, what city is shown on the map? Describe its location.

Reviewing the Text

To follow page 441

Number a paper from **1** through **15**. After each number, write the word or group of words in parentheses that correctly completes the sentence.

1. Northern Germany is a (plateau, plain); to the south is a (highland, lowland) region.
2. The four large rivers that are important to Germany's transportation system are the Rhine, the Elbe, the Oder, and the (Saar, Weser).
3. After Napoleon's defeat in 1815, the German states were formed into a union with (France, Austria).
4. Bismarck became the (king, prime minister) of Prussia in 1862.
5. The leader of the Reformation was (Martin Luther, Wolfgang von Goethe).
6. In 1871, Germany became (an empire, a republic).
7. World War I began when the heir to the throne of (Germany, Austria-Hungary) was shot and killed.
8. After World War I, Germany became a (republic, colony).
9. Important coal fields are found in the Saar Valley and (Lorraine, the Ruhr Valley).
10. In World War II, the Soviet Union eventually sided with (Germany and Italy, Great Britain and the United States).
11. After World War II, Germany was divided into four zones controlled by France, Great Britain, the United States, and (Italy, the Soviet Union).
12. (East, West) Germany is larger than (East, West) Germany and has more people.
13. The official name of East Germany is the (German Federal Republic, German Democratic Republic).
14. (Hamburg, Bremen) is West Germany's second largest city and its greatest port.
15. The Rhine River forms the boundary between West Germany and (the Netherlands, France).

Changing Boundaries

Look at the maps below. Then number a paper from **1** through **4**. After each number, write the answers to the questions that follow.

A.

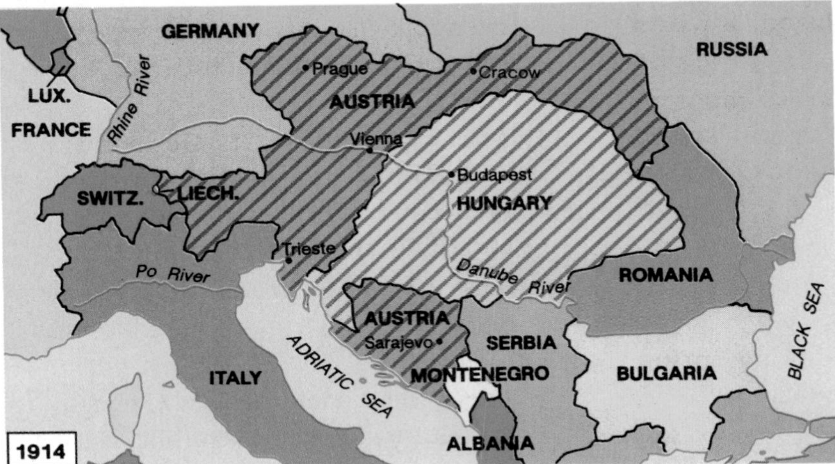

Austria and Hungary Before World War I

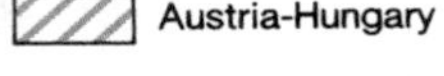

GERMANY
POLAND
SOVIET UNION
LUX.
FRANCE
Rhine River
Prague
Cracow
CZECHOSLOVAKIA
Vienna
AUSTRIA
Budapest
HUNGARY
SWITZ.
LIECH.
ROMANIA
Po River
Danube River
YUGOSLAVIA
Sarajevo
BLACK SEA
ADRIATIC SEA
ITALY
BULGARIA
ALBANIA
1919

Austria and Hungary After World War I

Boundary of Austria-Hungary in 1914

Boundary of Russia in 1914

1. What happened to Austria-Hungary after World War I?
2. World War I began after the Austrian Archduke Francis Ferdinand was killed at Serajevo. In what country was Sarajevo in 1914? In 1919?
3. What countries had disappeared from the map by 1919? What countries had appeared by 1919?
4. What three countries gave up land in 1919 that became part of Poland?

Completing and Using Bar Graphs

To follow page 469

One of the graphs below compares the population of five Central European countries. The other graph compares the land area of the same countries. The graphs are not completely labeled. You can supply the missing labels by referring to the reference table on pages 592-593 of your book. Number a paper from 1 through 12. After each number, write the correct label for the numbered blank on the graph. Choose the labels from the list in the box below. Remember that each name of a country will be used twice.

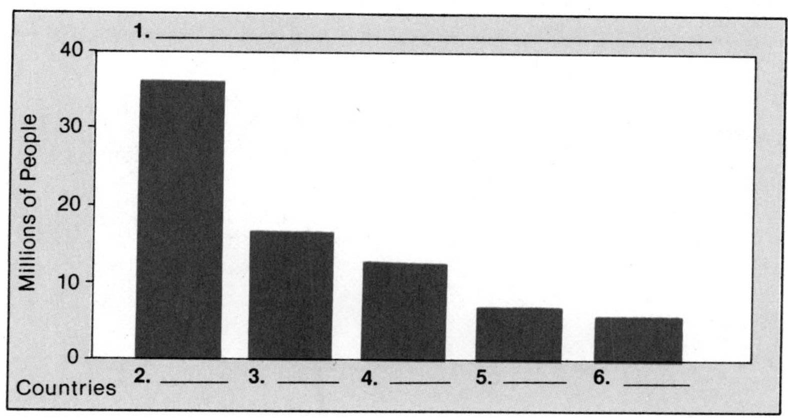

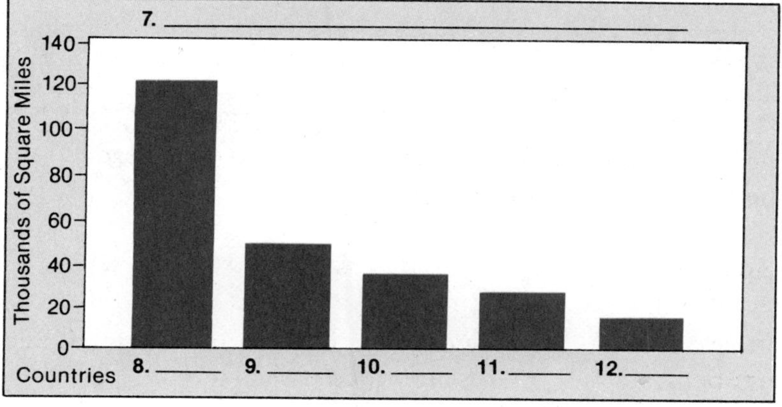

Continue numbering your paper from 13 through 15. After the numbers, write the answers to the questions below.

13. What two Central European countries have nearly the same area?
14. About how many times larger than Switzerland is Czechoslovakia?
15. Is the rank in size for each of the five countries the same or different from its rank in population?

Making and Using a Time Line

To follow page 469

Copy the time line below showing some of the dates and events from the time line on page 443 of your book. Leave plenty of space so that you can add more events and dates. Now add the following dates to your time line in the proper order. For each date, describe the important event that is mentioned in your book. Name two events for 1914. For help, refer to pages 444-467.

1100, 1864, 1867, 1914, 1920, 1938, 1978

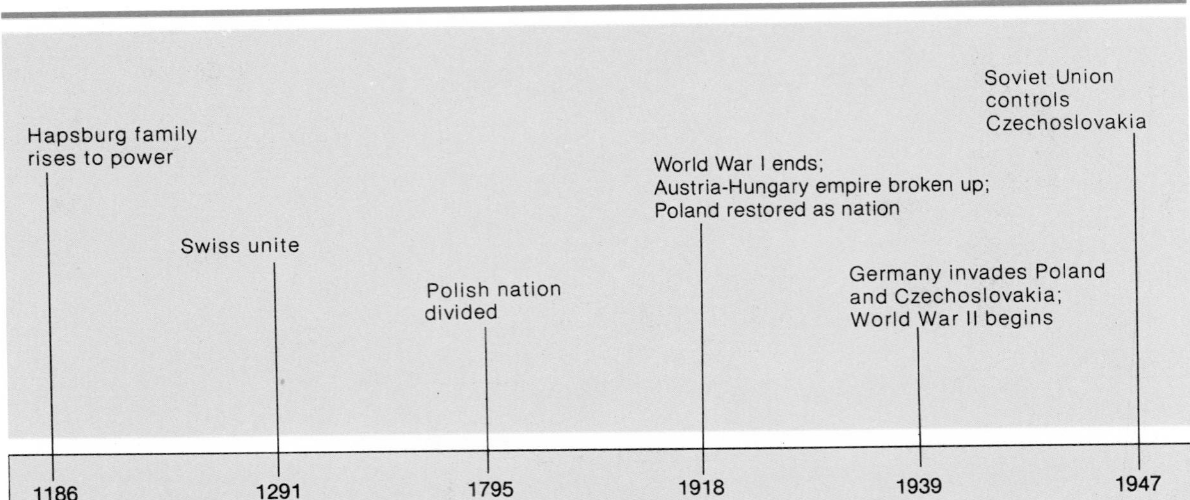

When you have finished the time line, number a paper from **1** through **8**. After each number, write the answers to the questions that follow.

1. What two important events happened in 1914? How were these events related?
2. Was the road over the St. Gotthard Pass built before or after the Swiss became united? How many years before or after?
3. The Hapsburg family lost its power when the empire of Austria-Hungary was broken up. How many years did this family stay in power?
4. How many years after Czechoslovakia was invaded by Germany was it invaded by the Soviet Union?
5. How old was Karol Wojtyla when he became Pope?
6. In what year was the International Red Cross founded?
7. How long after Austria became part of the Austrian-Hungarian empire did it become part of Germany?
8. For how many years was the Polish nation divided?

Fact and Opinion

To follow page 484

Some things you read are facts and others are opinions. It is important to be able to tell the difference between facts and opinions. A **fact** is something that is true or something that actually happened. An **opinion** is something that a person feels is true. Facts can be proven to be true; opinions cannot be proven to be true.

Read the statements below and decide which are facts and which are opinions. Then number a paper from **1** through **16**. After each number, write **fact** if the statement is a fact and **opinion** if the statement is an opinion.

1. The Soviet Union is the largest country in the world.
2. Most of the Soviet Union is a plain.
3. The Soviet Union should increase its population.
4. Too many languages are spoken in the Soviet Union.
5. Before the Russian Revolution, the czar ruled much as he pleased.
6. Governments should own and operate factories, farms, railroads, and mines.
7. There is only one political party in the Soviet Union.
8. There are 15 republics in the Soviet Union.
9. Stalin was a cruel dictator.
10. The followers of Lenin were called Bolsheviks.
11. The Soviet people wanted the five-year plan to succeed and worked hard to carry it out.
12. No part of the Soviet Union has a tropical climate.
13. Under the Communist plan, all workers are employed by the Soviet government.
14. The people of the Soviet Union are content to let the government make all important decisions.
15. People in the Soviet Union can vote only for candidates of the Communist Party.
16. Collective farms are more efficient than privately owned farms.

Making an Outline

To follow page 494

Copy the incomplete outline below. Complete the outline by referring to pages 485-494 in your book.

The Soviet Union

I. Soviet Europe
  A. Russian Republic
    1. Important cities
      a.
      b.
    2. Important rivers
  B.
    1. Important cities
    2.
      a. Dnieper River
      b.
  C. Other Soviet Republics
    1. Byelorussian Republic
    2.
    3.

II. Soviet Asia
  A. Siberia
    1.
      a. Novosibirsk
      b.
      c.
      d.
    2. Trans-Siberian Railroad
  B. Soviet Republics of Central Asia
    1. Important cities
      a. Tashkent
      b.
      c.
    2. Agriculture

The Winter Palace is located in Leningrad on the River Neva.

Reading a Population Map

To follow page 517

A population map compares the number of people living in different areas. The map below shows the average number of persons per square mile (or square kilometer), for each of the eight main islands of Hawaii. Number a paper from **1** through **6**. After each number, write the answers to the questions that follow by referring to the map.

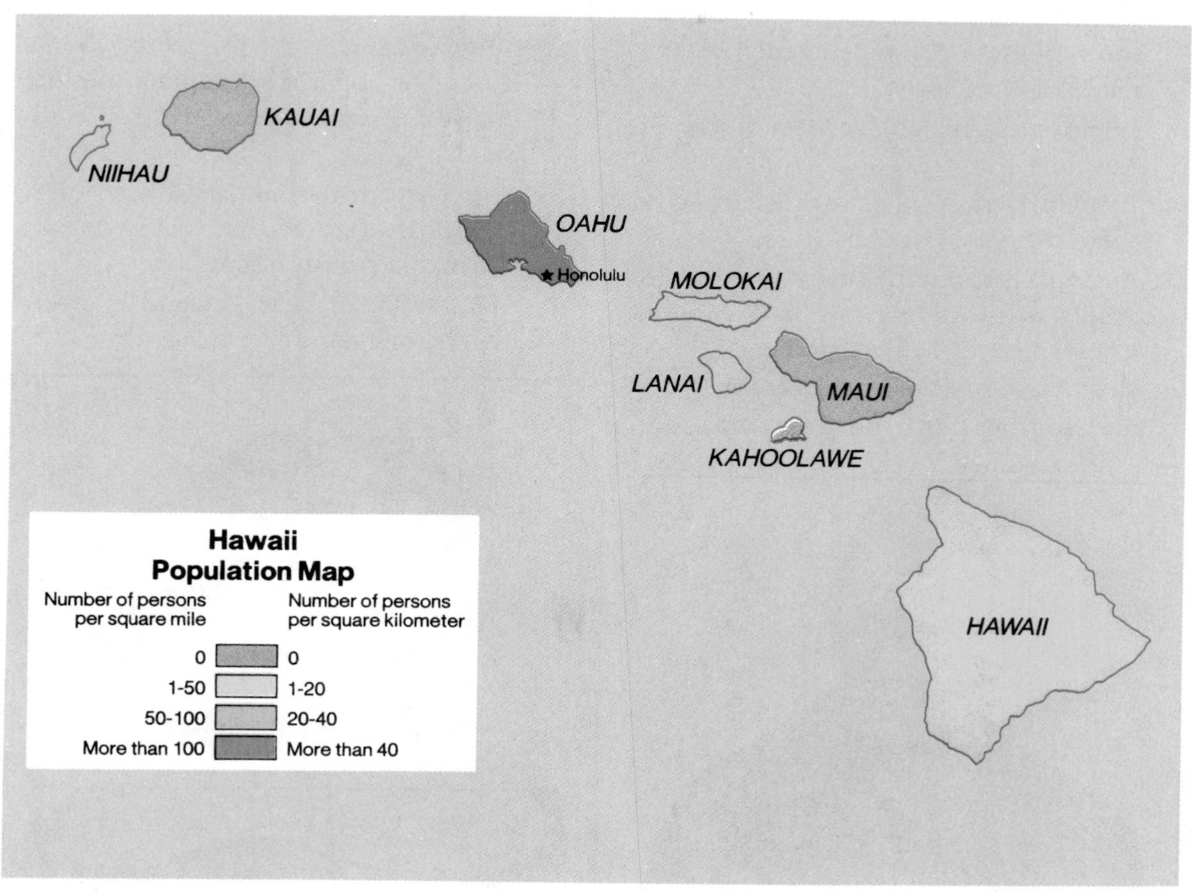

1. How many people per square mile does the color yellow represent on the map? How many persons per square kilometer?
2. What color is used to show the areas of densest population?
3. How many people per square mile (per square kilometer) live in Oahu?
4. What island has about the same population as Kauai?
5. Name the islands that have a population of 1 to 50 people per square mile (1 to 20 per square kilometer).
6. Is the island of Kahoolawe inhabited or uninhabited? How do you know?

Reviewing the Text

Number a paper from **1** through **10**. After each number, write the word or words in parentheses that correctly complete each statement.

1. Australia and New Zealand are in the (Northern, Southern) Hemisphere.
2. (Captain James Cook, Sir Joseph Banks) took possession of Australia in the name of Great Britain.
3. (Victoria, Tasmania) is an island state of Australia.
4. Baby (platypuses, koalas) are carried in their mothers' pouches.
5. Australia is about the size of (the United States without Hawaii and Alaska, California and Texas together).
6. Most of the people of Australia live in the (southeastern, northwestern) part of the country.
7. About three-fourths of the farming land in Australia is used to grow (rice, wheat).
8. New Zealand was discovered by (a Dutch, an English) sea captain, but the first European settlers were (Dutch, English).
9. The two principal islands of New Zealand are North Island and (Tasmania, South Island).
10. The capital of New Zealand is (Wellington, Auckland).

The English officer who took possession of Australia

A kookaburra

A kangaroo

Making a Chart

To follow page 526

Copy and complete the chart that has been started for you below. For help, refer to pages 504–523 in your book. The map on pages 506–507 will also be useful.

Some Nations, Islands, and Island Groups of the Pacific				
Nation, Island, or Island group	Check if Independent	Controlled by	Capital City	Check if partly or wholly in tropics
Philippines	✓		Manila	✓
Indonesia				
Marianas				
Carolines				
Marshalls				
Nauru				
Solomon Islands				
Fiji				
New Caledonia				
Papua New Guinea				
Tahiti				
American Samoa				
Western Samoa				
Tonga				
Tuvalu				
Australia				
New Zealand				

Country	Area (sq. km)	Area (sq. mi.)	Population	Capital
Africa				
(see page 257)				
Europe				
Albania	28,478	11,100	2,800,000	Tirana
Andorra	453	175	30,000	Andorra la Vella
Austria	83,849	32,374	7,515,000	Vienna
Belgium	30,513	11,781	9,870,000	Brussels
Bulgaria	110,912	42,823	8,875,000	Sofia
Cyprus	9,251	3,572	635,000	Nicosia
Czechoslovakia	127,869	49,370	15,400,000	Prague
Denmark	44,272	17,028	5,130,000	Copenhagen
Finland	338,309	130,119	4,800,000	Helsinki
France	547,026	211,208	53,950,000	Paris
Germany, East	105,680	40,646	16,700,000	East Berlin
Germany, West	249,119	95,815	61,700,000	Bonn
Gibraltar	6	2.25	30,000	
Great Britain	244,019	94,216	55,900,000	London
Greece	131,944	50,944	9,700,000	Athens
Hungary	93,030	35,919	10,725,000	Budapest
Iceland	103,000	39,800	235,000	Reykjavik
Ireland	70,283	27,136	3,460,000	Dublin
Italy	301,225	116,304	57,150,000	Rome
Liechtenstein	157	61	30,000	Vaduz
Luxembourg	2,586	998	365,000	Luxembourg
Malta	316	122	350,000	Valetta
Monaco	1.5	0.6	30,000	Monaco-Ville
Netherlands	40,844	15,770	14,250,000	Amsterdam
Norway	325,470	125,181	4,150,000	Oslo
Poland	312,677	120,725	35,900,000	Warsaw
Portugal	92,082	35,553	10,000,000	Lisbon
Romania	237,500	91,700	22,500,000	Bucharest
San Marino	61	24	20,500	San Marino
Spain	504,782	194,897	37,750,000	Madrid
Sweden	451,529	173,665	8,330,000	Stockholm
Switzerland	41,288	15,941	6,375,000	Bern
Vatican City	0.44	0.2	1,000	
Yugoslavia	255,804	98,766	22,550,000	Belgrade
Asia				
Afghanistan	647,500	250,000	16,250,000	Kabul
Bahrain	622	240	400,000	Manama
Bangladesh	142,776	55,126	90,700,000	Dacca
Bhutan	47,000	18,147	1,325,000	Thimphu
Burma	678,033	261,790	34,350,000	Rangoon
China	9,527,200	3,691,500	970,000,000	Beijing
Hong Kong (G.B.)	1,034	339	5,156,000	Victoria
India	3,287,590	1,269,346	683,810,000	New Delhi
Iran	1,648,000	636,932	37,400,000	Tehran
Iraq	434,924	167,925	13,400,000	Baghdad
Israel	20,700	7,992	4,000,000	Jerusalem
Japan	372,197	143,706	117,650,000	Tokyo
Jordan	97,740	37,738	3,300,000	Amman
Kampuchea (Cambodia)	181,035	69,898	9,000,000	Phnom Penh
Korea, North	120,538	46,540	18,350,000	Pyongyang

Reference Tables *Continued*

Country	Area (sq. km)	Area (sq. mi.)	Population	Capital
Korea, South	98,477	38,022	38,800,000	Seoul
Kuwait	20,118	7,768	1,440,000	Kuwait
Laos	236,800	91,429	3,800,000	Vientiane
Lebanon	10,400	4,015	3,230,000	Beirut
Macao (Port.)	15.5	6	280,000	Macao
Malaysia	332,633	128,430	14,000,000	Kuala Lumpur
Maldives	298	115	150,000	Malé
Mongolia	1,565,000	604,247	1,725,000	Ulan Bator
Nepal	140,797	54,362	14,325,000	Kathmandu
Oman	212,457	82,030	920,000	Muscat
Pakistan	804,772	310,724	85,000,000	Islamabad
Qatar	11,000	4,249	230,000	Doha
Republic of China	35,981	13,892	18,000,000	Taipei
Saudi Arabia	2,153,090	831,313	8,650,000	Riyadh
Singapore	581	224	2,420,000	Singapore
Southern Yemen	287,683	111,075	1,950,000	Aden
Sri Lanka	65,610	25,332	15,000,000	Colombo
Syria	185,408	71,586	9,325,000	Damascus
Thailand	514,000	198,456	48,175,000	Bangkok
Turkey	780,576	301,382	45,500,000	Ankara
U.S.S.R. (Soviet Union)	22,402,200	8,649,490	267,600,000	Moscow
United Arab Emirates	82,880	32,000	850,000	Abu Dhabi
Vietnam	332,559	128,402	53,550,000	Hanoi
Yemen	195,000	75,290	6,100,000	San'a
Australia and Pacific Island Countries				
American Samoa	197	76	33,500	Pago Pago
Australia	7,686,848	2,967,909	14,900,000	Canberra
Cook Islands (N.Z.)	241	93	18,200	Rarotonga
Fiji	18,272	7,055	625,000	Suva
French Polynesia	4,000	1,544	160,000	Papeete
Guam (U.S.)	549	212	105,800	Agaña
Indonesia	1,919,270	741,034	155,300,000	Jakarta
Kiribati	754	291	60,000	Bairiki
Nauru	21	8	8,000	Yaren
New Caledonia	18,998	7,355	150,000	Nouméa
Vanuatu	14,763	5,700	110,000	Vila
New Zealand	268,676	103,736	3,150,000	Wellington
Papua New Guinea	461,691	178,260	3,250,000	Port Moresby
Philippines	300,000	115,830	49,000,000	Manila
Solomon Islands (G.B.)	28,446	10,983	225,000	Honiara
Tonga	699	270	100,000	Nuku'alofa
Tuvalu	10	3.9	7,000	Funafuti
Western Samoa	2,842	1,097	160,000	Apia

Word List

a bad	i it	oo wood	u cup	ə *stands for*
ā cake	ī ice	o͞o food	ur turn	a *as in* ago
ä father	j joke	oi oil	yo͞o music	e *as in* taken
b bat	k kit	ou out	v very	i *as in* pencil
ch chin	l lid	p pail	w wet	o *as in* lemon
d dog	m man	r ride	wh white	u *as in* helpful
e pet	n not	s sit	y yes	
ē me	ng sing	sh ship	z zoo	
f five	o hot	t tall	zh treasure	
g game	ō open	th thin		
h hit	ô off	t͟h that		

A

abaca (ab′ə kä′): Manila hemp, used to make rope and other products

aborigine (ab′ə rij′ə nē): the earliest known inhabitants of a region

absentee landlord (ab′sen tē′ land′lôrd′): an owner who does not live on his or her estate

acacia (ə kā′shə): an umbrella shaped tree; the African species is a source of gum arabic

alloy (al′oi): a metal formed by combining two or more metals

altitude (al′tə to͞od′): the height of a place above sea level

amphitheater (am′fə thē′ə tər): a large, round building with rows of seats around a central space, used for sports and spectacles

apartheid (ə pär′tīd): a policy in South Africa of segregating or keeping apart different races

appeasement (ə pēz′mənt): the policy of giving in to a strong power in order to maintain peace

apprentice (ə pren′tis): in the Middle Ages, one who served a master worker for a certain time to learn a trade; one learning a trade

aqueduct (ak′wə dukt′): a pipe or channel used to carry water long distances

arena (ə rē′nə): in ancient Rome, the central space of an amphitheater, where the events took place

armada (är mä′də): a large fleet of armed ships

asbestos (as bes′təs): a mineral used in fireproof products

astrolabe (as′trə lāb′): an instrument formerly used by sailors to measure the height of the sun in the sky so that they could find their latitude

axis (ak′sis): the imaginary rod on which the earth seems to turn

B

bacteria (bak tēr′ē ə): microscopic organisms that cause changes in liquids or foods

ballet (ba lā′): a dance that tells a story through graceful movements, accompanied by music

bamboo (bam bo͞o′): a giant, treelike grass

baobab (bā′ō bab′): an African tree with a thick trunk that stores water and a gourdlike fruit used for food

barbarian (bär ber′ē ən): in ancient times, a foreigner who was not part of Greek or Roman civilization

baron (bar′ən): a noble of the lowest rank

barrier (bar′ē ər): something that separates people, places, and things

batik (bə tēk′): a design on cloth made by putting a wax coating on those parts that are not to be dyed; the cloth printed with the design

battlement (bat′əl mənt): a wall around the top of a castle with openings through which soldiers could shoot at approaching enemies

bauxite (bôk′sīt): the mineral from which aluminum is made

bazaar (bə zär′): a marketplace or street lined with shops

Benelux (ben′ə luks′): an organization formed by Belgium, the Netherlands, and Luxembourg to promote trade

Bolshevik (bōl′shə vik): a follower of Lenin

boulevard (bool′ə värd′): a wide, often tree-lined, avenue

boundary (boun′dar ē): a line or thing that limits or marks a separation, such as between one country and another on a map

breadfruit (bred′fro͞ot′): a tropical fruit which, when roasted, tastes like bread

breakwater (brāk′wô′tər): a wall built to protect a harbor from the force of waves

Buddhism (bood′iz′əm): a religion based on the teachings of the Buddha that began in India and spread to China and Japan

C

canton (kan′tən): a Swiss district or state

capital (kap′it əl): the top of a column or pillar

caravan (kar′ə van′): a group of merchants or travelers who cross the desert together

carillon (kar′ə lon′): a musical instrument composed of bells

caste system (kast sis′təm): a social system that keeps each person in a certain class or group for life

cathedral (kə thē′drəl): a large or important church

census (sen′səs): the counting of people in an area

charter (chär′tər): a document signed by a lord, listing privileges granted a town; a document setting out the rules and purposes of an organization

chemistry (kem′is trē): the science that deals with the nature of substances and the changes they undergo

circumference (sər kum′fər əns): the distance around a globe

city-state (sit′ē stāt′): a city that rules a large area of surrounding land

civil war (siv′əl wôr): a war between opposing groups within a country

civilization (siv′ə li zā′shən): a stage of development of a society; a way of life of a particular people, place, or time

clan (klan): a group of families who claim descent from the same ancestor

climate (klī′mit): the weather of a certain place over many years

collective (kə lek′tiv): a large farm owned by the government

comedy (kom′ə dē): an amusing play with a happy ending

Common Market (kom′ən mär′kit): an organization of European nations, formed for the purpose of buying and selling goods among themselves

Commonwealth (kom′ən welth′): a family of free nations united for their own welfare in matters of defense and trade

commune (kom′yo͞on): a group of people who live, work, and own property together

communism (kom′yə niz′əm): a system of government in which property and goods are controlled by the government

compass (kum′pəs): an instrument with a needle that always points north

concentration camp (kon′sən trā′shən kamp): a fenced-in camp, used to confine political prisoners

consul (kon′səl): in ancient Rome, one of the highest officials of the republic

continent (kont′ən ənt): a large body of land

convent (kon′vent): the building where a group of nuns live

cooperative union (kō op′ər ə tiv yo͞on′yən): a group of farmers or others who have joined together to keep prices fair and the quality of products high

copra (kop′rə): dried coconut meat, from which coconut oil is extracted

corridor (kor′ə dər): a passageway

cricket (krik′it): a game of English origin played with bats, ball, and wickets

crop rotation (krop rō tā′shən): planting different crops in the same field from year to year to keep farmland fertile

Crusade (kro͞o sād′): during the Middle Ages, a holy war undertaken to capture the Holy Land from the Turks

culture (kul′chər): learned behavior of a group of people
cuneiform (kyo͞o nē′ə fôrm′): writing on clay with wedge-shaped symbols
custom (kus′təm): a social habit that people living together have followed for a long time
czar (zär): the title of the Russian emperors from the time of Ivan the Terrible until 1917

D

delta (del′tə): a stretch of land built up at a river's mouth by the mud and sand brought down by the river
democracy (di mok′rə sē): rule by the people
dialect (dī′ə lekt′): a form of a language spoken by a particular group of people
dictator (dik′tā′tər): in ancient Rome, a leader given absolute power in time of war; in modern times, a ruler who has absolute power and authority
dike (dīk): a bank of earth to keep out water
discus (dis′kəs): a circular plate made of stone or metal, thrown by athletes
distortion (dis tôr′shən): change of shape
dominion (də min′yən): a self-governing state of the Commonweath of Nations
drift (drift): a wind-driven mass of water
dromedary (drom′ə der′ē): a camel with one hump
dynamite (dī′nə mīt′): an explosive made of nitroglycerine mixed with other materials to make it safer to handle

E

echidna (i kid′nə): an egg-laying mammal of Australia, also called the spiny anteater
ecology (ē kol′ə jē): the study of how living things relate to their environment
economic activity (ek′ə nom′ik ak tiv′ə tē): work
empire (em′pīr): a government that holds power over many countries
endangered species (en dān′jərd spē′shēz): type of animal or plant that is in danger of dying out
epic (ep′ik): a long poem about a great hero
equator (i kwā′tər): an imaginary line circling the earth midway between the North and South poles
eucalyptus (yo͞o′kə lip′təs): an Australian tree that oozes gum, or resin

F

fable (fā′bəl): a tale about animals that teaches a lesson
factory (fak′tər ē): a building, equipped with machines, in which goods are made
Fascist (fash′ist): the party formed after World War I which wanted to make Italy a powerful country; any similar movement
feudalism (fyo͞od′əl iz′əm): the system of living in western Europe in the Middle Ages based on cooperation of nobles and commoners
fiord (fyôrd): a narrow inlet of the sea between high cliffs or banks
flint (flint): a hard stone with sharp edges used to make weapons and to strike fire
flying buttress (flī′ing but′ris): a heavy stone prop placed outside a building to support it
forum (fôr′əm): in ancient Rome, an open space where markets and public festivals were held
frieze (frēz): a band of carved marble around a building

G

glacier (glā′shər): a great sheet of ice
gladiator (glad′ē ā′tər): in ancient Rome, an armed man who fought to amuse the people
gondola (gon′də lə): a long, flat-bottomed boat used on the canals of Venice
government (guv′ərn mənt): a plan under which people live together in an orderly way, obeying laws
Great Circle (grāt sur′kəl): in mapmaking, any circle that cuts the earth in half
grid (grid): in mapmaking, an intersecting pattern formed of parallels of latitude and meridians of longitude
guerrilla (gə ril′ə): a civilian fighter
guild (gild): a group of merchants or skilled workers who organize to maintain standards of work and to protect their own interests
guillotine (gil′ə tēn): a machine used for beheading persons

H

hemisphere (hem′is fēr′): half of a globe
Hinduism (hin′do͞o iz′əm): a religion and a way of life in India

Holocaust (hol′ə kôst′): a great destruction, especially referring to the killing of many Jews during World War II

hydroelectricity (hī′drō i lek tris′ə tē): energy produced by water

I

Impressionist (im presh′ə nist): one of the painters of the nineteenth century interested in depicting color and light at various seasons and times of day

Industrial Revolution (in dus′trē əl rev′ə lo͞o′shən): the period when new machines, such as the steam engine, brought many changes in the way people lived and worked

international (in′tər nash′ən əl): a term that means "among nations"

iron curtain (ī′ərn kur′tin): a term used to describe the lack of contact between Communist and non-Communist countries after World War II

isthmus (is′məs): a narrow strip of land connecting two larger bodies of land

J

jade (jād): a white or green stone used for jewelry and art objects

Japan Current (jə pan′ kur′ənt): a stream of water in the Pacific Ocean which has a warming effect on Japan and many other Pacific Islands

javelin (jav′lin): a kind of spear

junk (jungk): a large Chinese sailing vessel

jury (joor′ē): a group of impartial persons who listen to both sides of a case and decide it

jute (jo͞ot): a plant with strong fibers used to make rope and burlap

K

kangaroo (kang′gə ro͞o′): an Australian animal that moves about by jumping and whose young is carried in its mother's pouch

knight (nīt): a warrior in the Middle Ages

koala (kō ä′lə): an Australian animal that resembles a teddy bear and whose young is carried in its mother's pouch

kookaburra (kook′ə bur′ə): an Australian bird with a cackling, braying call

L

lacquer (lak′ər): a kind of varnish that gives wood a smooth hard surface that can be carved

landlocked (land′lokt′): a word describing a country that has no seacoast

latex (lā′teks): the milky white juice of the rubber tree

latitude (lat′ə to͞od): the distance north or south of the equator, expressed by degrees measured from the earth's center

latticework (lat′is wurk′): interlaced strips of stone or wood

law (lô): a rule for social conduct made by the leaders of a group

league (lēg): a union of governments which agree to work together

League of Nations (lēg ov nā′shənz): an international organization, formed after World War I, of nations interested in preventing war

legion (lē′jən): a large division of ancient Roman troops

lignite (lig′nīt): soft, brown coal

longitude (lon′jə to͞od): measurement of distance east and west on the earth's surface

lycée (lē′sā′): a French high school

M

magnesium (mag nē′zē əm): a light, white metal

maharaja (mä′hə rä′jə): the title of a former ruler in India

majority (mə jôr′ə tē): any number greater than half the total number

mandate (man′dāt): the responsibility given a powerful country to control and protect a weaker one

manioc (man′ē ok′): a plant grown for its starchy roots, which are used for food

---

a bad, ā cake, ä father; e pet, ē me; i it, ī ice; o hot, ō open, ô off; oo wood; o͞o food, oi oil, ou out; u cup, ur turn, yo͞o music; ə ago, taken, pencil, lemon, helpful

---

manor (man′ər): a large estate in England in the Middle Ages

master (mas′tər): a highly skilled worker, qualified to work at a trade independently

Mediterranean climate (med′ə tə rā′nē ən klī′mit): a climate with rainy cool winters and hot, almost rainless summers

merchant marine (mur′chənt mə rēn′): a nation's fleet of trading ships

mercury (mur′kyər ē): a silver-colored metal used in its liquid state to make thermometers and other products

meridian (mə rid′ē ən): an imaginary line on the earth's surface reaching from pole to pole

merino (mə rē′nō): a kind of sheep with a heavy coat of fine wool

microscope (mī′krə skōp′): an instrument with a lens that helps the eye see unusually small objects.

millet (mil′it): a grasslike plant that people can use as food

minaret (min′ə ret′): a tower on a mosque

minority (mə nôr′ə tē): any number less than half the total number

moat (mōt): a deep ditch, usually filled with water, surrounding a castle

monastery (mon′əs ter′ē): the building where a group of monks live

monsoon (mon so͞on′): a wind of southern Asia, that blows from the southwest in summer and from the northeast in winter

Moor (moor): one of the North African Muslims who invaded and conquered Spain

mosque (mosk): a building where Muslims worship

N

neutral (no͞o′trəl): a nation that does not take sides in a war

nitroglycerine (nī′trə glis′ər in): a powerful explosive

Nobel prize (nō bel′ prīz): money awarded to persons whose work in science, literature, and the furthering of peace benefits humanity

nomad (nō′mad): a member of a group that moves from place to place in search of food or grazing land for their animals

O

oasis (ō ā′sis): a green and fertile spot in a desert

oceanic climate (ō′shē an′ik klī′mit): a climate with cool summers, mild winters, and plenty of moisture.

open city (ō′pən sit′ē): in wartime, a city that is not to be made a scene of fighting

open-door policy (ō′pən dôr pol′ə sē): opening ports for trade to all nations

opera (op′ər ə): a musical play in which the actors sing instead of speak

oral tradition (ôr′əl trə dish′ən): history and literature spoken rather than written and passed down from person to person

P

page (pāj): in the Middle Ages, a young boy who was beginning his training as a knight

pagoda (pə gō′də): a high temple with a series of roofs

parliament (pär′lə mənt): an assembly that makes the laws of a country; Parliament, the legislature of Great Britain, made up of the House of Commons and the House of Lords

partition (pär tish′ən): division of a country

pass (pas): a natural path through a mountain range

pasteurize (pas′chə rīz): to heat milk or other foods to a temperature high enough to kill the harmful bacteria

patio (pat′ē ō′): an inner courtyard

patrician (pə trish′ən): a noble of ancient Rome

peat (pēt): decayed vegetable material which is burnt for heat

per capita (pur kap′i tə): for, from, or by each person

pile (pīl): a strong beam of wood that supports a building

plateau (pla tō′): a flat stretch of high land

platinum (plat′ən əm): a soft, silvery metal

platypus (plat′ə pəs): an egg-laying mammal of Australia with a flat bill like a duck's

plebeian (pli bē′ən): one of the common people of ancient Rome

polder (pōl′dər): low land that has been drained

porcelain (pôr′sə lin): a fine, thin kind of pottery

premier (pri mēr′): the name of the chief officer of government in some countries

prime minister (prīm min′is tər): the head of the majority party in the House of Commons and of the government in Great Britain and some other countries

produce (prō′do͞os): farm products, such as fruit and vegetables

projection (prə jek′shən): in mapmaking, a way of showing the world on a flat surface

prophet (prof′it): one who speaks for God

protectorate (prə tek′tər it): a country that depends upon another nation for its defense

Protestant (prot′is tənt): the name of the followers of Martin Luther who acted in protest against certain practices of the Catholic Church; a Christian who does not belong to the Roman Catholic or the Orthodox Church

puppet government (pup′it guv′ərn mənt): a government in which the officials are controlled, or told what to do, by another government's leaders

Q

quinine (kwī′nīn): a medicine made from the bark of the cinchona tree used to treat certain fevers

R

radioactive (rā′dē ō ak′tiv): a type of mineral that sends out energy in the form of rays

radium (rā′dē əm): a radioactive element

Reformation (ref′ər mā′shən): the religious movement started by Martin Luther

refugee (ref′yo͞o jē′): a person who flees his or her home because of some danger or misfortune

regent (rē′jənt): someone who rules in place of a king

Renaissance (ren′ə säns′): the period of time, beginning about 1350, in which there was a new interest in art, learning, and discovery

republic (ri pub′lik): a nation that elects its leaders

reserve (ri zurv′): something set aside for a special purpose, such as land

rotation (rō tā′shən): the turning of the earth on its axis

S

Sahel (sä hel′): semiarid grassland bordering the desert

samurai (sam′oo rī′): in Japan's Middle Ages, a member of the warrior class

sardine (sär dēn′): a small fish, often canned

satellite (sat′əl īt′): an artificial moon

sauna (sou′nə): a bath similar to a steam bath, but with hot, dry air

savanna (sə van′ə): a broad, grassy plain

scale (skāl): in mapmaking, relative size

serf (surf): in the Middle Ages, a worker who belonged to the land and could not leave it

Shinto (shin′tō): a Japanese religion, in which nature, heroes who died in battle, and ancestors are worshipped

Sinn Fein (shin fān): a party in Ireland that wanted the country to separate from Great Britain and become a republic

smelting (smel′ting): the process of melting ore and extracting the pure metal from it

smorgasbord (smôr′gəs bôrd′): a variety of Swedish foods, such as cheese, seafood, sausage, and pickles

socialist (sō′shə list): a person who thinks that the government should own and operate the factories, farms, railroads, and mines

sorghum (sôr′gəm): a grasslike plant that people can use as food

soviet (sō′vē et′): in the Soviet Union, a council made up of peasants, workers, and soldiers

spinning jenny (spin′ing jen′ē): a machine used for making thread

squire (skwīr): in the Middle Ages, a boy who followed his lord in hunting and in battle

steppe (step): a grassy, treeless plain

swastika (swos′ti kə): a cross with ends bent at right angles: an emblem of the Nazi party

Swedish gymnastics (Swē′dish jim nas′tiks): a type of body-building exercise

Swedish massage (Swē′dish mə säzh′): a way to improve circulation, relax the nerves, and help muscle tone by rubbing the body

symphony (sim′fə nē): a musical work to be played by a large orchestra

---

a bad, ā cake, ä father; e pet, ē me; i it, ī ice; o hot, ō open, ô off; oo wood; o͞o food, oi oil, ou out; u cup, ur turn, yo͞o music; ə ago, taken, pencil, lemon, helpful

---

T

tanker (tang′kər): a ship with large tanks below its decks for carrying oil or other liquids

tapestry (tap′is trē): heavy, embroidered drapery

taro (tär′ō): a tropical plant with a starchy root used for food

Tartar (tär′tər): a member of the tribe of Mongols and Turks who overran parts of Asia and Europe during the Middle Ages

teak (tēk): a hard wood used in building ships and furniture

telescope (tel′ə skōp′): an instrument that magnifies objects seen at a distance

tenant (ten′ənt): in the Middle Ages, a farmer who lived on a manor by the lord's permission; an occupant of a place

textile (teks′tīl): a cloth made by weaving or knitting threads together

tournament (toor′nə mənt): in the Middle Ages, a contest in which knights kept in practice for warfare; a series of contests

tragedy (traj′ə dē): a serious play with an unhappy ending

tribune (trib′yo͞on): in ancient Rome, an official elected to protect the rights of the plebeians

truce (tro͞os): an agreement to stop fighting

tundra (tun′drə): a treeless plain of the Arctic regions

tung oil (tung oil): oil made from nuts and used in paint and varnish

tyrant (tī′rənt): in ancient Greece, a strong ruler who seized power; a cruel and unjust ruler

U

underground resistance (un′der ground′ ri zis′təns): a group that works in secret to overthrow the enemy occupying their country

untouchable (un tuch′ə bəl′): a person outside the caste system in India, who at one time was given the most lowly work

V

vassal (vas′əl): a person or state that owes allegiance to another

veldt (velt): in South Africa and Zimbabwe, an open grassland with scattered bushes and trees

veto (vē′tō): the power of elected officials to prevent decisions that they think are unjust

W

warlord (wôr′lôrd′): a general who controls an area by force

Y

yacht (yot): a trim sailing vessel used for pleasure cruising

---

a bad, ā cake, ä father; e pet, ē me; i it, ī ice; o hot, ō **open**, ô **off**; oo **wood**; o͞o **food**, oi **oil**, ou **out**; u cup, ur **turn**, yo͞o music; ə **ago**, tak**e**n, penc**i**l, lem**o**n, helpf**u**l

---

Index

For pronunciations see guide on page 594.

Acknowledgments

This book was prepared and produced by Edit, Inc., Chicago.

Cover:
Illustration by Robert LoGrippo

Maps:
Chris Ellithorpe, General Cartography, Inc., Yvette Heyden, Liska and Associates, Cathy Meindl, Perspecto Map Co.: Eugene Derdyne, Jay Songero, Lowell Stumpf, John Walter & Associates: Chris Leszcynski
Map skills developed and produced by Educational Challenges, Inc., Alexandria, Va.

Illustrations:
Dev Appleyard, Bob Masheris, Cathy Meindl, Tak Murakami, Alexis Oussenko, Hima Pamoedjo, George Suyeoka

Photographs:
The American Museum of Natural History: 36
Arabian American Oil Co.: 80
Courtesy of The Art Institute of Chicago: *Basket of Apples* by Paul Cézanne, oil on canvas, 1890-94, Helen Birch Bartlett Memorial Collection, 329; *The Big Tree* by Paul Gauguin, oil on canvas, 1891, gift of Kate L. Brewster, 514
Art Resource/Scala: 170, 212, 213, 293, 567
James L. Ballard, 38 center
Roloff Beny, Parthean Prince, Bastian, Teheran, 63 left
Paul Berliner, 261
The Bettmann Archive Inc.: 202, 248, 249, 270, 280, 345
Black Star Publishing Co., Inc.: Harry Black, 108; Victor Englebert, 224 bottom, 226 left; Joe Flowers, 254 bottom, 255 bottom; John Launois, 91; Lawrence Manning, 221; James Pickerell, 86; Fred Ward, 112 bottom right; Nik Wheeler, 58
Lee Boltin 53, a golden goat found in a Sumerian grave at Ur, 87
British Museum: 56
Brown Bros.: 290, 343, 423, 480
Cameramann Int., Inc.: 38 center, 107, 113, 120, 139, 146, 147, 151 top right, 201, 276 left, 417, 456, 465, 466, 503, 513, 515, 516, 519
Colour Library International, Ltd.: 298 top, 307, 324 top, 325 top, 320, 335, 338, 355, 357, 365
Culver Pictures Inc.: 424
J. D. Dallet, 298 bottom
Percival David Foundation of Chinese Art, London: blue and white porcelain temple vase with elephant-head handles, 1351, Yuan Dynasty, height 63.6, 133
The Detroit Institute of Arts: upper half of a figure of an Oni, late 15th–early 16th century, zinc and brass, height 37 cm. (14 9/16 in.), from Wunmonije Compound, Ife, Museum of Ife Antiquities, 13 (79.R.9), photo by Dirk Bakker, courtesy Nigeria National Museums, 231
ET Archive Ltd.: Bodleian Library, 268
Field Museum of Natural History, Chicago: 32
Fotomas Index: detail of the Catalan Map, 1375, 245
French Embassy Press: 316
French Government Tourist Office: 313
Photo *Giraudon:* 312, 376; detail of calendar miniature from the *Très Riches Heures du Duc de Berry,* the castle of Poitiers (July), by the Limbourg brothers, 1413-16, MS 65, fol. 7v, Musée Conde, Chantilly, 263; Musée de Cluny, 267; scene from *The Life of Charlemagne,* detail of the Cartouche, 15th century, Musée Conde, Chantilly, 310; *The Gleaners* by Millet, Louvre, 328
Susan Griggs Agency, London: Ian Yeomans, 471
Madeline Grimoldi, Rome: marble statue carved between 99 B.C. and 1 B.C. by an unknown Roman sculptor, Museo Capitolino, 198
Harvard University: 422
The Image Bank: Joseph Brignolo, 47; Paul Slaughter, 183; Luis Villota, 239
Magnum Photos, Inc.: Bruno Barbey, 60; Rene Burri, 114, 130; Inge Morath, 59
F. G. Mayer, New York, 63 right
The Metropolitan Museum of Art: 88, 89, 169; ceramic foot soldier found in tomb of first emperor, courtesy of the Cultural Relics Bureau, Beijing, 132
NASA: 16
By courtesy of the National Portrait Gallery, London: Elizabeth I, unknown artist, c. 1575, oil on panel, 344
Courtesy of The Newberry Library, Chicago: frontispage of *The History of Don Quixote* by Cervantes, 294
Philadelphia Museum of Art: *Mte. Sainte Victoire* by Paul Cézanne, about 1904-06, oil on canvas, George W. Elkins Collections, 41 left
Photo Researchers, Inc: 454, 455 bottom; Frederick Ayer III, 347; Lee Battaglia, 509; Mark N. Boulton/Camera Press, London, 563 right; Robert Clark, 322; Jerry Cooke, 154; Jack Fields, 398; Thomas D. Friedman, 237; George Gerster, 360; Ralph Gerstle, 494 right; Louis Goldman, 76, 78; Tom Hollyman, 339; George Holton, 494 left; Leslie Holzer, 510, M. P. Kahl, Jr., 563 bottom right; Paolo Koch, 405; Lisl, 119; Fred Marron, 487 top right, 588; Roger Tory Peterson, 563 top left; Porterfield-Chickering, 288; Gianni Tortoli, 192
Photri: 224, 319; Jack Novak, 487 top left
The Pierpont Morgan Library, New York: Illuminations from Houses of the Virgin, from Flanders, ca. 1515, MS 399, p. 265
Camille Saracino-Bozek, 447
Seattle Art Museum: Shubun (ca. 1414-1465) Japanese, Ashikaga (Muromachi) Period, mid-15th century landscape, hanging scroll, ink on paper, Eugene Fuller Memorial Collection, 41 right
Shostal Associates: 289, 521
Donald Smetzer, 75, 92, 93
Smithsonian Institution, Freer Gallery of Art, Washington, D.C.: Pakistani stone sculpture, Gandhara, Kushan Dynasty, A.D. late second–early third century, frieze showing four scenes from the life of Buddha, 106
Snark International: Stele of Hammurabi, Louvre, 55
Sovfoto: Novosti: 497 left; Tass: 490, 497 right; Vladimir Davydov, 483; V. Marikovsky, 492; T. Utkin, 476
Stock, Boston, Inc.: 38 right; Richard Balzer, 142; Daniel Brody, 372; Gabor Demjen, 455 right; Peter Dublin, 152; Owen Franken, 178, 210 top, 233, 236, 254, 256, 296, 406, 434, 435, 436, 437; Jim Holland, 234; Ira Kirschenbaum, 224 top, 226 right; Jean-Claude Lejeune, 99, 177; Mike Malyszko, 427, 449 right; Peter Menzel, 165, 171, 210 bottom right, 210 bottom left, 211, 215; Larry Nelson, 131; Frank Siteman, 299; Rick Smolan, 136; Cary Wolinsky, 104, 112 top, 349 top, 356
Anne Stribling, 252, 255 top right
Taurus Photos: 54, 266, 324 bottom, 388, 393 top, 448, 449 left; Janet Bennett, 387; T. W. Bennett, 451; J. P. Canardy, 382; Henri Gehlen, 11; Vance Henry, 271, 285, 297, 300, 369, 373, 374, 375, 380, 390, 404, 407 top, 410, 455 top, 460, 475, 486, 487 bottom, 488, 489; Jarden, 348 bottom; L. L. T. Rhodes, 243, 276 right, 348 top, 349 bottom; G. R. Richardson, 64, 112 bottom left, 462, 520; R. Wood, 246, 255 top left
The United Nations: 42
United Press Int.: 214, 327, 377, 429
U.S. Department of the Navy, 17
University of Chicago, The Oriental Institute: Egypt, Thebes, Theban Tomb 82/Amenemhet ornamental hieroglyphs, inscription A EP, pl. 18, p. 84
Victoria and Albert Museum: tenth-century bronze, from Madras, 105 bottom
Wide World Photos: 110
Woodfin Camp & Associates: R. Archibald, 127, 151 top left; Craig Aurness, 443; Linda Bartlett, 184 left; Marc Bernheim, 230; Marc and Evelynne Bernheim, 229; Jeff Jay Foxx, 90; Robert Frerck, 522; Lauren Freundman, 137; Cynthia Haas, 395; William Hubbel, 180; Roland Michaud, 68; Albert Moldvay, 207; Thomas Nebbia, 392, 393 bottom, 397; Wally McNamee, 166; Victor Rastelli, 138; Wendy Watriss, 235; Baron Wolman, 184 right; Adam Woolfitt, 181, 189, 200, 209
Katherine Young Photography: 118, 151 bottom, 159, 325 bottom
Photo research by Marilyn Gartman